D0875544

ENGLISH LOCAL GOVERNMENT

ENGLISH POOR LAW HISTORY
PART I. THE OLD POOR LAW

ENGLISH LOCAL GOVERNMENT

A series of eleven volumes on the growth
and structure of English Local Government
by SIDNEY and BEATRICE WEBB

VOLUME 1 The Parish and the County.

VOLUMES 2 and 3 The Manor and the Borough.

VOLUME 4 Statutory Authorities for Special Purposes.
With a new introduction by B. KEITH-LUCAS
which is included in Volume 1. *The Parish and the County.*

VOLUME 5 The Story of the Kings Highway.
With a new introduction by G. J. PONSONBY.

VOLUME 6 English Prisons Under Local Government.
Including a long preface by G. B. Shaw.
With a new introduction by L. RADZINOWICZ.

VOLUME 7 English Poor Law History, Part 1.
The Old Poor Law.

VOLUMES 8 and 9 English Poor Law History. Part 2.
The Last Hundred Years. Volumes 1 and 2.

*VOLUME 10 English Poor Law Policy.
With a new introduction by W. A. ROBSON
which is included in Volume 7, *English Poor Law History, Part 1,
The Old Poor Law.*

*VOLUME 11 The History of Liquor Licensing in England.

*Volumes 10 and 11 were originally published separately, but are now
included to make the scope of the work more comprehensive.

English Poor Law History

PART 1: THE OLD POOR LAW

SIDNEY and BEATRICE
WEBB

With a new Introduction by
W. A. ROBSON

*Professor of Public Administration
in the London School of Economics
and Political Science*

FRANK CASS AND CO. LTD.
1963

First published by Longmans, Green & Co. in 1927.

This edition published by FRANK CASS & Co., 10, Woburn Walk,
London, W.C.1., by the kind permission of the Trustees of the
Passfield Estate.

First published 1927
Reprinted 1963

Printed in Great Britain by
Thomas Nelson and Sons Ltd, Edinburgh

Sidney and Beatrice Webb made a detailed and profound study of the various methods of administering poor relief which had been tried in England through the centuries, and the social or political theories underlying them. The series of monumental works they produced on this subject are of enduring value.

Their *English Poor Law History* extends to three large volumes published in 1927–29. The first covers the old poor law prior to 1834 ; the other two span the century from 1834 to 1929. These form part of the *English Local Government History* series. The volume on *English Poor Law Policy*, published in 1909, was never included by the Webbs in the *English Local Government History*, but forms such a valuable complement to the three volumes mentioned above that it has now been reprinted with them.

These four works constitute the Webbs' contribution as social historians to an understanding of the Poor Law. But they were not only students of history. They were also social reformers ; and in that capacity one must recall two other works of great significance and high quality. These were Sidney Webb's treatise entitled *The Prevention of Destitution ;* and last but far from least the celebrated Minority Report of the Royal Commission on the Poor Law, published in 1909. This was drafted by Sidney Webb and based on investigation and thinking for which Beatrice Webb was mainly responsible. Never had social reformers so massive an armoury of detailed knowledge and understanding at their command as Sidney and Beatrice Webb when they launched their attack on the system of poor relief which had been initiated by the Poor Law Amendment Act of 1834.

In order to appreciate the work of the Webbs in the sphere of the Poor Law, it is necessary to recall the attitude towards poverty which persisted in Britain and in most other countries until the first years of the 20th century. Poverty on a massive scale had been regarded for centuries as inevitable. Individual cases of a deserving kind might be helped by charity, but it was thought that little or nothing could be done to relieve poverty as a whole.

This traditional view came to be questioned in Britain during the closing years of the 19th century ; and it was challenged with growing insistence in the 20th century by many of the leaders of thought and opinion. The Webbs regarded destitution—by which they meant the condition of being without the necessaries of life so that health and strength, and even life itself, would be endangered —as a *disease of society*, and this was the title they gave to the first chapter of their book *The Prevention of Destitution*. This view of poverty was extremely novel forty or fifty years ago ; today it is generally accepted throughout the world.

Poverty is widely regarded nowadays not only as a disease but as a malady which is curable. But when the Webbs began their work on the Poor Law the climate of opinion was entirely different from what it is today. They contributed substantially to the changed outlook.

Before 1834, the old poor law had consisted mainly of a body of laws aimed at repressing the freedom and regulating the conduct of the poor in relation to the rich. They imposed a servile status on the poor which led the Webbs to describe the old poor law as " the relief of destitution within a framework of repression".

The Royal Commission of 1832–4 was not an inquiry into the prevalence and causes of destitution or of pauperism. The Commissioners were asked to concentrate on the abuses in the rural areas arising from the payment of allowances out of the poor rate to agricultural labourers to supplement their wages. This was the famous Speenhamland system. It had led to demoralisation and to an increase of pauperism. The Commissioners believed that pauperism could be reduced and perhaps eventually eliminated by a poor law of sufficient severity.

The three principal recommendations which the Royal Commission made were embodied in the Poor Law Amendment Act, 1834. They were : first that there should be uniformity throughout the country in poor law administration ; second, that the lot of a person receiving poor relief should be *less eligible* than that of the lowest grade of labourer who was self-supporting : third, that an offer of admission to the workhouse should in all cases be substituted for the payment of outdoor relief to able-bodied men. This was the so-called workhouse test.

To achieve uniformity a specialised non-ministerial authority was set up in London named the Poor Law Commission, exercising very extensive powers of supervision and direction over the Boards of Guardians, who were elected to carry out the day-to-day administration of the Poor Law in their respective areas. No machinery of this kind had existed previously and the example has never been followed.

The Royal Commission of 1832 recommended that paupers receiving indoor relief should be divided into four classes : the aged and sick, the children, able-bodied females, and able-bodied men. Each of these classes should be accommodated in separate buildings and dealt with in different ways. The Poor Law authorities did not attempt to carry out this part of the report. Instead, they developed the general mixed workhouse and made it a receptacle for paupers of every kind ; the sick, the aged, orphans and deserted children, vagrants, mental defectives, widows and young girls, hardened ex-prisoners, prostitutes and unmarried mothers, as well as the able-bodied and their families. The general mixed workhouse became a kind of dustbin into which human debris of all kinds was thrown.

In tracing the history of poor law administration throughout the 19th century and the beginning of the 20th century, the Webbs found that the logic of events and the growth of humanitarian feeling had compelled the poor law authorities to depart from the principles which they had been set up to apply.

Thus, a supplementary policy was adopted in respect of children and sick persons which did *not* aim at deterring them from seeking assistance, but endeavoured to supply them with whatever might be needed for adequate training or treatment regardless of the fact that this meant placing them in a better position than the lowest class of independent labourers[1]

The Boards of Guardians were from 1855 permitted, and from 1870 required, to pay for the education of outdoor pauper children ; and the Poor Law Board [2]brought pressure on the Guardians to remove all children from the workhouse. They were to be sent either to Poor Law boarding schools—barrack schools—or to be

[1] *English Poor Law Policy*, pp. 88-89.
[2] The Poor Law Board replaced the Poor Law Commission in 1847. It lasted until 1871 when its functions were taken over by the Local Government Board.

boarded out at public expense with private families.[1]

In the 1860's public criticism was aroused by the condition of the sick poor in the workhouse infirmaries. Almost immediately the Poor Law Board agreed to the provision by the Guardians of expensive institutional treatment. Mr. Gawthorne Hardy, the Board's President, publicly declared that the sick poor were not proper objects of a policy of deterrence. Thenceforward, the central department constantly pressed the Guardians to raise the standard of their outdoor medical service and the workhouse infirmaries to that of the best hospitals and public medical service in any part of the world. Thus, after 1867, there developed in London, for example, the excellent hospitals for infectious disease established by the Metropolitan Asylums Board. Moreover, outdoor relief could be granted in the case of sickness in the family even if the breadwinner was simultaneously earning wages.[2]

Two years later, in 1869, Mr. Goschen issued a minute permitting the Guardians to pay allowances in aid of wages to widows with families in cases when it was manifestly impossible for the mother to earn enough to support her children.[3]

The Lunacy Commissioners had (between 1848 and 1871) come to possess a rival authority over persons of unsound mind, whether or not they were paupers. Their requirements for the accommodation and treatment of pauper lunatics were at first regarded by the Poor Law Board as absurdly extravagant ; but the Board gradually yielded to pressure and instructed the Guardians to provide a higher standard of care and treatment to lunatics in workhouses. Nonetheless mentally unsound paupers remained in the general wards of the workhouse.

As the 19th century wore on, Parliament recognised the blind, the deaf and dumb, the disabled and other handicapped groups as persons for whom the Guardians could, if they wished, provide treatment by paying for their care, maintenance and training in specialized institutions outside the poor law.

For the able-bodied unemployed, in place of the uniformity

[1] Ib., pp. 115-116.
[2] Ib., pp. 119-123.
[3] Ib., pp. 102-104.

which the Royal Commission of 1832 had recommended, three separate systems of relief were introduced. In some parts of the country outdoor relief was forbidden, with certain exceptions, to able-bodied men and women. Other Unions came under an order which permitted outdoor relief to able-bodied men and their families subject to a task of test work being performed by the man. A third variation permitted outdoor relief to be given unconditionally to able-bodied women, while preserving the test work for men. So by the end of the 19th century it had ceased to be the uniform policy of the Local Government Board (which in 1871 became the central authority for Poor Law matters) to insist that the Guardians should maintain at least all the able-bodied unemployed in the workhouse.[1]

The Royal Commission on the Poor Law appointed in 1905 were asked to inquire (1) into the working of the laws relating to the relief of poor persons ; and (2) into the various means which had been adopted outside the Poor Law for meeting distress arising from unemployment, and to consider that modifications were advisable for dealing with distress. Mrs. Webb was a member and undertook, directed or evoked a great deal of investigation more or less on her own initiative.

The Webbs were deeply impressed by the social services which had grown up in the 19th and early 20th centuries to prevent destitution rather than merely to relieve it. This new social structure, embodied in the Factory Acts, in the legislation relating to education, public health, minimum wages, etc., amounted to a framework of prevention which contrasted strongly with the framework of repression represented by the Poor Law.[2] They believed that three new principles of public policy had become embodied in these services : the principle of curative treatment ; the principle of universal provision ; and the principle of compulsion.[3] And they held these principles to be incalculably superior to those of deterrence and less eligibility.

The Royal Commission of 1905–9 found that the old " principles

[1] *English Poor Law Policy*, pp. 87, 90 and 261.
[2] *English Poor Law History, Part II. The Last Hundred Years*, p. vi.
[3] *English Poor Law Policy*, p. 264-5.

of 1834 " had been gradually whittled away in practice by successive governments ; and that the Boards of Guardians were now
faced with a whole series of competing services administered by
other authorities, aiming at the prevention of the various types of
destitution out of which pauperism arose.[1]

The time had come to resolve this conflict of policy in dealing
with those in need of state aid. The Webbs' solution was to deal
with destitute persons according to the particular causes of their
destitution ; to discriminate carefully between them according to
these causes ; to provide for each man, woman or child specialized
care and treatment adapted to his or her individual needs ; and to
abandon the philosophy of deterrence and less eligibility on which
the Poor Law was still officially based. What the Webbs wanted
was to supersede the Poor Law by a new policy based on recognition of the mutual obligations of the individual and the community.[2] They wanted to extend the preventive and curative
outlook over the entire field of dependency and human need.

The philosophy and the programme which the Webbs devised
formed the Minority Report of the Royal Commission on the Poor
Law, published in 1909. No such monumental minority report had
ever appeared either before then or since. It is in two parts and
occupies five hundred pages of print. Part I is entitled *The
Break-up of the Poor Law* ; Part II *The Unemployed.* The
Minority consisted of the Rev. Russell Wakefield, Rector of St.
Mary's, Bryanston Square, and Chairman of the Central (Unem-
ployed) Body for London ; F. Chandler, General Secretary of the
Amalgamated Society of Carpenters ; George Lansbury and
Beatrice Webb.

The Minority Report analysed the causes of unemployment
among those capable of work, and found that the able-bodied fell
into four main classes, each requiring distinct treatment. They
were : the men normally engaged in permanent situations ; the
men engaged in casual or discontinuous employment ; the under-
employed ; and the unemployable.[3] All the members of the Royal

---

[1] *English Poor Law History, Part II. The Last Hundred Years, Vol. II,* p. 470.
[2] *English Poor Law Policy,* p. 270-1.
[3] Minority Report II, p. 338. Edition published by the National Committee
to Promote the Break-up of the Poor Law.

Commission agreed in recommending the setting up of Labour Exchanges (as the Employment Exchanges were then called) on a national basis. But the Minority Report went far beyond this in calling for a national authority to organise the labour market. The Minority were resolutely opposed to any attempt to force back into the Poor Law those sections of the unemployed who were already being relieved by the Distress Committees appointed under the Unemployed Workman Act, 1905. They wished, indeed, to remove the remaining sections of the unemployed from any connection with either the Boards of Guardians or the local authorities dealing with other categories of destitute persons. They wanted a new national body to concentrate exclusively on the causes of unemployment and the best methods of curing it. This, wrote Beatrice Webb many years later, was " the axle round which all our other recommendations turned." [1]

The Labour Exchanges were set up under the Board of Trade in 1909. It was not until 1916, under the stress of the First World War, that the Ministry of Labour was formed to organise the labour market. But the most original and creative of all the recommendations of the Minority Report was ignored, despite the massive unemployment which existed during the inter-war period. This was a scheme, worked out in detail by Professor Sir Arthur Bowley, the eminent statistician, to regularise the aggregate demand for labour as between one year and another by increasing or decreasing public expenditure on works of a capital nature. [2]

---

[1] *Our Partnership*, p. 480.

[2] " In order to meet the periodically recurrent general depressions of Trade, the Government should take advantage of there being at these periods as much Unemployment of capital as there is Unemployment of labour ; that it should definitely undertake, so far as practicable, the Regularisation of the National Demand for Labour ; and that it should, for this purpose, and to the extent of at least £4 million a year, arrange a portion of the ordinary work required by each Department on a Ten Year's Programme ; such £40 million of work for the decade being then put in hand, not by equal annual instalments, but exclusively in the lean years of the trade cycle ; being paid for out of loans for short terms raised as they are required, and being executed with the best available labour, at Standard Rates, engaged in the ordinary way." The Public Organisation of the Labour Market ; Minority Report of the Poor Law Commisison, Part Two Conclusion and Recommendations para 44.

One evening in the early 1930's I was invited to a small evening party given by the Webbs to Sokolnikoff, then Soviet Ambassador. John Maynard Keynes was there. When Keynes came up to greet Mrs. Webb, to whom I was talking, she said, " Ah, Mr. Keynes, we are awaiting with great interest your economic theory to cure unemployment." To which Keynes replied, " Oh, it's all in the Minority Report, Mrs. Webb." It is to be hoped that Keynes's own recognition of the intellectual debt he owed to the Webbs and Bowley will become more widely known than it is at present.

The Webbs organised a national society to promote the break-up of the Poor Law on the lines advocated by the Minority Report. Despite a tremendous propaganda effort the movement did not succeed until many years later—and then not completely. The Webbs were surprised and disappointed at the favourable reception which the Majority Report received. The Majority Report was an extremely able document and it recommended the transfer of public assistance to the county and county borough councils. This proposal took the edge off the opposition to the Poor Law and softened the hatred which the harsher features of the Guardians' administration had aroused. But as we shall see, a more potent factor in defeating the Minority Report was the introduction of National Insurance by Lloyd George in 1911.

In 1929, Neville Chamberlain as Minister of Health abolished the Boards of Guardians and transferred their functions and property to the county and county borough councils, but the Local Government Act of that year did not abolish the Poor Law. It permitted, but did not compel, a local authority to take out of the Poor Law any class of person whom it was authorised to assist or to treat under any other statute, and to declare that it would do so in its administrative scheme. Every county or county borough was enjoined to " have regard to the desirability of securing that, as soon as circumstances permit, all assistance which can lawfully be provided otherwise than by way of poor relief shall be so provided".[1] Thus, a progressive council could remove from the Poor Law the sick, the mentally deficient, the blind, the mothers and infants, the children and adolescents, the handicapped, and

[1] Local Government Act, 1929. Section 5.

other special categories.[1]

The able-bodied unemployed, however, continued to be relieved under the Poor Law until 1934, when the Unemployment Assistance Board was set up to take responsibility for the maintenance and training of all able-bodied persons seeking employment who had exhausted their rights to unemployment benefit. The Board was more or less under the control of the Ministry of Labour. The National Assistance Act, 1948 brought the Poor Law to an end, created the present National Assistance Board, and provided that the Board shall exercise their functions in such manner as shall best promote the welfare of the persons affected.[2] When this Bill was introduced into the Commons, tributes to the work of the Webbs were paid from both sides of the House.

In view of these decisive though belated events the Webbs were unduly pessimistic in writing, in 1928, that the Royal Commission of 1905–9 was a failure from a constructive point of view. They appeared to attribute this to the powerful opposing camps into which the supporters of the Majority and Minority Reports were divided.[3]

The object underlying the Webbs' work in this field was, in Beatrice's words, " to clean up the base of society".[4] The break-up of the Poor Law was only one element in their effort to achieve this immense task. Beatrice Webb, as early as 1888–9, had made an important contribution to the movement against sweated labour by giving evidence she had obtained when working as a trouser hand in the slop clothing trade to a House of Lords Committee.[5] When she gave evidence before the House of Lords Committee, the members were said to become " like clay in the Potter's hand". The campaign to end sweating followed much later and was conducted by other reformers, such as Gertrude Tuckwell, J. J. Mallon, and Mary Macarthur. It resulted in Trade Boards being set up to fix minimum wages in certain industries, and from these the present

[1] *The Local Government Act, 1929. How to make the Best of It* by Sidney Webb. Fabian Tract. No. 231. pp. 7-8.

[2] Sections 1, 2(2).

[3] *English Poor Law History, Part II. The Last Hundred Years*, Vol. II, p. 470.

[4] *Our Partnership*, p. 427.

[5] Beatrice Webb: *My Apprenticeship*. pp. 310-339.

Wages Councils have evolved. Sidney and Beatrice, through their books and lectures, had succeeded in explaining the functions, and justifying the existence, of trade unions, thereby greatly strengthening them in their efforts to raise the standard of living of their members. Sidney Webb had transformed the educational system of London and immensely widened the vocational opportunities open to the underprivileged. He had for many years been one of the leading advocates of non-contributory pensions for the elderly, and the Old Age Pensions Act, 1908, owed much to his efforts to impress on public opinion the need for such a measure.[1]

The attitude of the Webbs towards social insurance was by no means favourable. Their lack of sympathy with this great modern device for helping millions of people to meet the vicissitudes of life was due partly to the fact that the Liberal Government in power in 1910–11 regarded social insurance as a method of defeating the campaign to break-up the Poor Law. George Lansbury told the Webbs that after Lloyd George's triumphant exposition in the House of Commons of his first National Insurance Bill, Charles Masterman, a Liberal M.P. (who was later chairman of the National Insurance Commission), came up to him with ' a pleasant jeering expression ' and said " We have spiked your guns, eh ? ". This showed that he was hostile to the whole conception of the Minority Report and that the Government's insurance schemes were intended to be an alternative method of dealing with the problem of destitution. John Burns, President of the Local Government Board, went about openly saying that social insurance had finally " dished the Webbs".[2] Their close friend and collaborator Haldane was also hostile to the Minority Report.

But the Webbs' dislike of social insurance had deeper reasons. They assumed that the payment of unemployment or sickness benefit and the right to medical treatment, would not necessarily prevent the occurrence of unemployment or sickness. Moreover, they did not approve of unconditional money payments being made to " the average sensual man "—an epithet which was continually

---

[1] *The Break-up of the Poor Law* by Joan Clarke in *The Webbs and Their Work,* edited by Margaret Cole, pp. 101-2.

[2] *Our Partnership,* p. 475.

on their lips, though I never heard them speak of the average
sensual woman. The truth is that the Webbs profoundly distrusted
the good intentions of the common man or his ability to withstand
the slightest temptation. They felt that the state would get
nothing in return for its money in the way either of good conduct
or of the curative treatment of those receiving benefit.[1]

The Webbs were mistaken in seeing social insurance and the
break-up of the Poor Law as alternative policies. Eventually, both
the Minority Report *and* social insurance became cornerstones of
the welfare state.

It must be admitted that the Webbs did not appreciate the great
political, psychological, and administrative advantages of social
insurance. They did not perceive the strong appeal it would make
to the masses just because it gave a right to money payments in
time of need. They feared the demoralising effects of money payments paid as of right to those in distress—indeed, Beatrice felt
that very few people, rich or poor, other than the Webbs themselves,
could be trusted to spend money in the right way. Nor did they
understand the extent to which conditions could be imposed on
those claiming benefit to prevent malingering and to exclude
bogus claims.[2] Yet this very failure resulted from two admirable
qualities of their work : their profound belief in the importance of
dealing with each case of human dependency according to the
needs of the individual ; and their insistence on the importance of

---

[1] *Our Partnership*, p. 430.

[2] " The schemes of insurance are not really helpful to our scheme. Doling
out weekly allowances, and with no kind of treatment attached, is a most
unscientific state aid ; and, if it were not for the advantage of proposing to
transfer the millions from the rich to the poor, we should oppose it root and
branch . . .   The unemployment insurance might bring inadvertently the
compulsory use of the labour exchange, and the standardisation of the conditions
of employment. But the sickness insurance . . . is wholly bad, and I cannot see
how malingering can be staved off except that the amount given is so *wholly
inadequate* that it will be only the very worst workmen who will want to claim
it and remain out of work . . . What the Government shirk is the extension of
treatment and disciplinary supervision—they want merely some mechanical way
of increasing the money income of the wage-earning class in times of unemployment and sickness. No attempt is made to secure an advance in conduct in
return for the increased income." Diary extract, January 1911. *Our Partnership*,
p. 468.

the moral factor in social administration.

They condemned the existing system of poor relief, whether indoor or outdoor, not only because it had no curative or preventive aim, but also because it had a degrading influence on character. On the other hand, they did not deny that moral defects of character can cause destitution in some cases. The Webbs' aim was above all to bring about an improvement in personal character as well as a bettering in the material conditions of life. They were convinced that neglect in infancy, deprivation in childhood, sickness and infirmity, unemployment and under-employment, accounted for nine-tenths of the destitution which occurred year by year. [1]

Sidney and Beatrice Webb were during their lives and perhaps even today, regarded by some people as professional social reformers engaged in a soul-less task, best described by the American term " social engineering". It is true that they disliked sentimentality, and distrusted any attempt to deal with hard cases, or with destitution in general, in an enotional way. But they were never mechanistic in their outlook, and they never forgot the suffering of the individual in the misery reflected in statistical measurements of poverty or human need.

They regarded the moral factor as the ultimate criterion of society. If there were moral and spiritual degradation ; if a large part of the people were reduced to " drinking, begging, cringing and lying" ; if the mass of each generation were submerged in " coarseness and bestiality, apathy and cynical scepticism of every kind", then society was sick. [2] In their eyes the ultimate object of every scheme of reform was the spiritual and moral improvement of human character and an advance in the standard of citizenship. [3]

The plan to break-up the Poor Law was thus not merely a programme of political and administrative reform. It was a plan for ensuring greater welfare, both material and spiritual, for millions of men, women and children, and for raising the level of our

---

[1] *English Poor Law Policy*, p. 304-5.
[2] *The Prevention of Destitution*, p.2.
[3] *Ib.* Chapter 10.

society.

In a presidential address to the Social and Political Education League in May 1908, Sidney Webb presented the idea of what he called " the necessary basis of society". This involved a national minimum standard of life imposed by the Government in four main spheres of state action. These spheres related to (1) The terms and conditions of employment, including a minimum rate of wages ; (2) Leisure and recreation. At least 14–16 hours a day must be assured by law to every wage-earner for sleep, recreation, exercise of body or mind, the duties of citizenship, and family life. (3) Health. This involved on the one hand a sanitary environment, while on the other there must be medical services, hospital accommodation and skilled nursing for the sick. (4) Education. There must be schools and colleges of every grade and an adequate system of scholarships providing maintenance as well as tuition, right up to a post-graduate course for every scholar fitted to receive it. Only by some such policy, declared Sidney Webb, would modern industrial communities escape degeneration and decay.[1]

The concept of the Welfare State undoubtedly involves the idea of a national minimum standard of civilised life for every man, woman and child. This forms a floor below which no-one is permitted to sink ; and an advancing nation will progressively raise its minimum standards as its resources increase.

In all these four spheres we have today achieved a national minimum standard of life, although the state has not always been the only agent involved in attaining it.[2] In regard to education Sidney Webb's utterances were remarkably prophetic of what has come to pass. However, the state has taken a far more active part in supporting or providing recreational services than Sidney Webb envisaged, not only in broadcasting and television, but in assisting opera, drama, music, painting and a wide range of recreational

---

[1] *The Necessary Basis of Society*, p.11.

[2] Thus, minimum wages are imposed by state action only in the case of unorganised or vulnerable groups of workers ; statutory maximum hours are imposed on much larger numbers, including miners, road transport drivers, women and young persons, but the minimum standard in respect of these matters has been achieved for the remaining groups by collective bargaining.

activities aided by local authorities.

The Webbs argued strongly in favour of a comprehensive medical service, carried out by local authorities under a Ministry of Public Health. This health service would offer to everyone medical treatment for all kinds of sickness and disability. But it would not be provided to everyone without payment. The really poor would receive treatment free of charge, but those who could afford to pay would be charged substantial fees. They laid it down, moreover, that in the state medical service the patient should not be free to choose his doctor. Freedom of choice would obtain only in the private sector of medicine. This, thought the Webbs, would lead those who could afford a private doctor to seek treatment outside the health service—a result they apparently wished to achieve. The Webbs, like everyone else, had their blind spots, and some of these are visible in their book *The State and the Doctor*. It was incidental features of this kind which led people to feel that liberty was not a good which came high in the Webbs' scale of values. Despite these defects the Webbs were pioneers in putting forward the first scheme for a comprehensive medical service available to everyone.

Sidney Webb claimed that his conception of the Necessary Basis of Society did not imply an individualist or a collectivist economic order. It was an indispensable foundation for every type of modern society or state, a basis on which any type of superstructure could be placed. "You will notice" he said, in the lecture I have already mentioned, "that to enforce the national minimum will not interfere with the pecuniary profits or the power or the personal development of the exceptional man. The illimitable realm of the upward remains, without restriction, open to him . . . By fencing off the downward way, we divert the forces of competition along the upward way".[1]

Beatrice no less than Sidney believed profoundly in the principle of a national minimum standard. "The sole purpose of the Minority Report" she wrote in *Our Partnership* was to secure a national minimum of civilised life . . . open to all alike . . . by which we meant sufficient nourishment and training when young,

[1] *The Necessary Basis of Society*, pp. 11-12.

a living wage when able-bodied, treatment when sick, and a modest but secure livelihood when disabled or aged".[1]

Nearly 25 years later Beatrice Webb wrote that she *thought* they were sincere in asserting or implying that these conditions could be obtained without fundamentally changing the economic system, without sweeping away the landlords and the capitalists, and penalising the profit-making motive. "How otherwise", she asked "should we have sought the support of Conservative and Liberal leaders and of the majority of the working class who certainly were not at that time convinced Socialists?"[2]

But in the summer of 1912, on returning from the Far East, the Webbs believed that their advocacy of a national minimum of civilised life within the capitalist system was out of date. The reason for this belief was that in the United Kingdom, France, and the United States, the workers were, so the Webbs thought, in open revolt.[3] The outbreak of the First World War two years later, the disastrous Peace of Versailles, followed by the Great Depression, destroyed the Webbs' former belief that a capitalist economy combined with political democracy could secure a satisfactory minimum standard of civilised life for the whole nation. Its realisation, wrote Beatrice, would depend on whether the rulers of the capitalist system would be willing and able to supply the large sums needed for the development of the social services.

In the closing years of her life, she remarked that the resources provided from taxation were quite inadequate to secure proper nutrition of the young, or their training for regular employment and effective citizenship in adult life. She observed that there was a vast amount of preventable disease due to bad housing, a poisoned atmosphere, noise and dirt ; while the maintenance and treatment available under the National Health Insurance scheme was of poor quality and totally inadequate. Pensions for old persons were so low that many were forced to seek extra income from public assistance.[4] Much of this is still true today, despite

[1] *Our Partnership*, pp. 481-2.
[2] Ib., p. 482.
[3] Ib., pp. 490-1.
[4] Ib., pp. 482-3.

the alleged arrival of the Affluent Society.

These observations were written in a mood of deep pessimism which is not hard to understand when we recall that the closing pages of *Our Partnership*, in which they occur, were written when the Second World War was raging and the end not even in sight. Beatrice herself was within a few months of her death at the age of 85.

The great schemes of reform which the Webbs constructed and which arose from their determination to break up the Poor Law went far beyond the relief of destitution or the prevention of pauperism. They went, indeed, far beyond an attempt to clean up only the base of society. They were directed towards ensuring to the workers by hand and by brain "steady progress in health and happiness, honesty and kindliness, culture and sientific knowledge, and the spirit of adventure".[1] This was a noble aim, worthy of two of the finest and most humane individuals I have been privileged to know.

The ideas underlying the Welfare State are derived from several different sources, including the French Revolution, the English Utilitarians, Christian Ethics, Fabian Socialism, Bismarck and Beveridge, Hobhouse, the Webbs, Keynes and Tawney. Both in the realm of ideas and in their concrete application, the Webbs' contribution was one of immense scope, depth and insight.

WILLIAM A. ROBSON.

London School of Economics and Political Science.
30th May, 1962.

[1] Ib., p. 477

PREFACE

THIS volume deals with " The Old Poor Law ", so drastically reformed in 1834 ; and it will be followed by another giving in detail the story of " The Last Hundred Years " of Poor Law Administration, down to 1927.

When, in 1899, we began our historical investigations into English Local Government we found it necessary to limit our own researches in the original sources mainly to the eighteenth century, or, more generally, to the period between 1689 and 1834. It is substantially this period with which we have dealt in the four volumes describing the evolution of the constitutional structure (*The Parish and the County*, 1906 ; *The Manor and the Borough*, 2 vols., 1908 ; and *Statutory Authorities for Special Purposes*, 1922, the last-named ending with a lengthy summary of the old " principles " and the new, upon which our government has been built). In connection with this analysis of structure, we prepared for our own use also an analysis of the development of the principal functions of the organisations with which we were dealing. This work led to the publication of a short study on the regulation of the supply of alcoholic beverages (*The History of Liquor Licensing in England*, 1903) ; and to two further volumes (*The Story of the King's Highway*, 1913 ; and *English Prisons under Local Government*, 1922), in each of which we included a more or less detailed survey of the history before and after the century and a half about which we had consulted the manuscript records. With regard to the Relief of the Poor, which, for a whole century prior to 1834, was more troublesome and more expensive than all the rest of Local Government put together, we have thought it useful to make the history more nearly continuous and complete. We have accordingly put together, along with the results of our own researches, what we have been able to assemble from the available books and pamphlets of the past three or four centuries, so as to present a complete historical study of the development of the English system of Poor Relief.

The " Laws relating to the Poor ", as they used to be called, relate to more than the relief of destitution. They constitute, in fact, a history of the relations between what Disraeli termed " The two nations " over which the kings and queens of England ruled, namely, " the rich and the poor " ; or, at least, a record of the collective and public relations between them. Of these relations, as they were embodied in the law and administration of the past seven or eight centuries, no adequate history has yet been written. We do not offer the present volume as such a history, if only for the reason that we have been unable to push our own researches into the original sources beyond the century and a half between 1689 and 1834. Though, as we gladly recognise, something more has been done than was the case in 1899, there has been, as yet, far too little systematic study of the archives of parish and county, gild and borough, which are still, for the most part, not only unprinted, but also uncalendared, and, indeed, in the majority of places, not even registered or publicly recorded as existing.[1]

---

[1] Only in Shropshire, we believe, has any County Council yet made even an inventory of the parish records existing within the county.

A bibliography of Poor Relief is badly needed, preferably on the lines of Miss Isabel Taylor's useful *Bibliography of Unemployment and the Unemployed* (1909), or Miss Dorothy Ballen's still more exhaustive *Bibliography of Road-making and Roads in the United Kingdom* (1914), both published in the series of studies issued by the London School of Economics and Political Science. In the absence of such a work, and as a help to students who, we hope, will further explore particular periods or subjects, we have endeavoured to give full and exact references to the published matter dealing with each point, including even considerable lists of pamphlet titles.

We have to express our gratitude to the incumbents and officers of hundreds of parishes in all parts of England for allowing us, in past years, access to the

But the Poor Law has once more become, as it was in 1834, a social problem of magnitude and grave import. This volume may find its greatest use in serving as an introduction to its successor, which will give the history of Poor Law Administration from 1834 down to the Report of the Royal Commission of 1905–1909 (of which one of the authors was a member), and from 1909 down to the present day ; and which will include a study of the serious issues now presented, owing to the neglect of timely reform, by an immensely increased aggregate of Poor Relief. It is, indeed, startling to discover how many points of similarity there are—though social relations are now on a different plane— between the problems that were put to the statesman and to the genuine philanthropist a hundred years ago by the swollen volume of Poor Relief in 1827, and those put to their successors of to-day by its still more swollen volume in 1927.

SIDNEY AND BEATRICE WEBB.

PASSFIELD CORNER, LIPHOOK, HANTS,
January 1927.

---

parish archives in their custody ; to the officials of the British Museum and the Public Record Office, and the librarians of various public libraries, for many courtesies ; and to the Right Honourable Neville Chamberlain, M.P., for permission to ransack the library of the Ministry of Health. To Miss Rosetta Piercy we are indebted for much assistance, and for the elaborate index.

CONTENTS

CHAPTER I

Christian Almsgiving—The Parish—The Church Stock—The Church Ale—The Church House—The Church Cess or Rate— The Monastic Institutions—The Gilds—The Municipalities—The Framework of Repression—Continental Reformers—The Growth of a Proletariat—The Tudor Legislation—The City of London — Provincial Town Councils—A Comprehensive Poor Law.

CHAPTER II

The Legislation of 1597–1601—The Action of the Privy Council—How far the Laws were put in Force—The Response of the Parishes—The Privy Council as a Cabinet—The Effect of the Civil War.

CHAPTER III

The New Ideas and Proposals of 1660–1704—The Union of Urban Parishes—The Union of Rural Parishes—Experience and Outcome of the Incorporated Guardians.

CHAPTER IV

General Survey—Doles and Pensions—The Allowance System—Billeting-out the Unemployed—Apprenticeship—The Poorhouse—The Workhouse—The Workhouse as a Device for Profitably Employing Pauper Labour—The Workhouse as an Asylum for the Impotent Poor—The Workhouse as a Means of

CHAPTER I

POOR RELIEF PRIOR TO 1597

THROUGHOUT all Christendom the responsibility for the relief of destitution was, in the Middle Ages, assumed and accepted, individually and collectively, by the Church. To give alms to all who were in need, to feed the hungry, to succour the widow and the fatherless, to visit the sick, were duties incumbent on every Christian, not wholly, and perhaps not even mainly, for the sake of those who were relieved, but for the salvation of the charitable. Almsgiving ranked with prayer and fasting as the outward and visible signs of the inward and spiritual grace, which it was the very purpose of religion to create and spread among all men, as it was its most noticeable effect.[1]

But the relief of the poor by gifts and self-sacrifice was, throughout all Christendom, more than an individual obligation. In addition to the response of the individual Christian to the

---

[1] Much is due to Professor (now Sir William) Ashley, to whose work we are particularly indebted, for introducing to the notice of British students the valuable German studies of the part played by the Church in the relief of the poor. His *Early Economic History and Theory*, 1893, chap. v., pp. 299-376, as supplemented by Miss E. M. Leonard's *Early History of the English Poor Law*, 1900, and *Some Early Tracts on Poor Relief*, by F. R. Salter, 1926, is still the best account in English of the history prior to the seventeenth century. See also *Geschichte der kirchlichen Armenpflege*, by Georg Ratzinger, 1868 and 1884, and *Beiträge zur Geschichte und Reform der Armenpflege*, by Franz Ehrle, 1881. For early Christian charity, see *Die christliche Liebesthätigkeit in der alten Kirche*, by J. G. W. Uhlhorn, 1882, translated as *Christian Charity in the Ancient Church*, 1883 ; and *Bekenntnisbildung und Religionspolitik, 1524-1534*, by Hans Von Schubert, Gotha, 1910. A small volume of 1758 sought to describe the early care for the poor by the Christian Church (*An Account of the Care taken in most Civilised Nations for the Relief of the Poor*, by the Rev. Richard Onely, 1758, 2nd edition, 1772) ; which is better stated in *Charity and Social Life*, by Sir C. S. Loch, 1910. See also *Die Mission und Ausbreitung des Christentums in den drei ersten Jahrhunderten*, by C. G. A. Harnack, 1915, vol. i., and *The Church, the State and the Poor*, by W. E. Chadwick, 1914.

1   B

appeal of any one who was suffering, it was, everywhere and from the first, recognised as a corporate duty of each Christian congregation—the Church in the narrower sense—to gather contributions and offerings, and, presently, to accumulate rent-charges and endowments, to be applied by the Church officers, wholly or in part, for the relief of the poor. There were, indeed, other purposes to which Church revenues had to be devoted. From the sixth century onward, we are told, under the influence of Pope Gregory, it became customary to share such revenues among four main objects, namely, the bishop and the necessary expenses of his office ; the stipends of the parochial clergy ; the maintenance of the fabric of the churches ; and the relief of the poor. Some such allocation became, throughout Western Europe, the basis of the tithe, to which the burden of providing for the poor has always been traditionally attached.

Whether or not, as is alleged, Pope Gregory charged St. Augustine to insist in England on a tripartite division of the tithe, this is what we find in the ordinance ascribed in the eighth century to Egbert, Archbishop of York. " The priests ", he ordained, " are to take tithes of the people, and to make a written list of the names of the givers, and according to the authority of the canons they are to divide them in the presence of men that fear God. The first part they are to take for the adornment of the church ; but the second they are, in all humility, mercifully to distribute with their own hands, for the use of the poor and strangers ; the third part, however, the priests may reserve for themselves." Exactly such a division was confirmed, in the eleventh century, by a law of Ethelred. " The King and the Witan have chosen and said, as right it is, that one-third part of the tithe which belongs to the Church shall go to the reparation of the Church ; and a second part to the servants of God, and a third to God's poor and needy men in thraldom." [1]

---

[1] See for all this, besides the German and French works already cited, the following books concerning the history of the tithe in England. The earlier laws can now be studied, more conveniently than in the great works of Franz Liebermann (*Die Gesetze der Angelsachsen*, 1903–1916) and Reinhold Schmid (*Die Gesetze der Angelsachsen*, 1832 and 1858), in *The Laws of the Earliest English Kings*, by F. L. Attenborough (Cambridge, 1922) and *The Laws of the Kings of England from Edmund to Henry I.*, by A. J. Robertson (Cambridge, 1925). See also *The Historie of Tithes*, by John Selden, 1618 ; *Ancient Laws and Institutes*, by Benjamin Thorpe, 1840 ; *The*

We cannot pretend to trace the rapid disappearance of any universal and compulsory allocation to the relief of the poor of one-third, or any other fraction, of the tithe which every agricultural occupier of land, and some other " producers ", continued to pay ; or to form any estimate of the amount that Christian charity yielded in alms. Already by the twelfth century, it seems, the tithe had ceased to supply any appreciable sum towards the relief of the poor. The high dignitaries of the Church, the alien priories, the various conventual or collegiate bodies in England itself, and lay impropriators gradually got into their hands most of the well-endowed benefices, or the greater part of their tithes ; and, in spite of repeated injunctions, and even statutory provisions, it seems clear that, by the end of the fifteenth century, at any rate, these absentee proprietors made no regular subventions for the poor of the parishes whence their revenues were derived.

The universal acceptance by the Mediaeval Church of the obligation to relieve the suffering of " God's poor " had two noteworthy results in the history of the public relief of the destitute, one of which seems to have been common to the whole of Christendom, and the other peculiar to Great Britain. The relief of destitution afforded by the alms of God-fearing Christians had the unfortunate characteristic that it had no concern for the effect of these alms, either on the individual poverty-stricken person or on the class to which he belonged. " There was as yet ", relates the historian of *Christian Charity in the Ancient Church,* " no reflection as to why alms were given and benevolence exercised. For this was self-evident. Still less was consideration exercised as to whom to give and do good

---

Saxons in England, by J. M. Kemble, 1849 and 1876; *Growth of Church Institutions,* by Edwin Hatch, 1887 ; *A History of Tithes,* by H. W. Clarke, 1891 ; *Ancient Facts and Fictions concerning Churches and Tithes,* by the Earl of Selborne, 1888 ; *English Economic History and Theory,* by Sir William Ashley, 1893, vol. ii. chap. v. ; *Early History of English Poor Relief,* by E. M. Leonard, 1900. In 1599 a Bill " for the relief of the poor out of impropriations and other Church Livings "—thus seeking to put the whole charge upon the tithe and glebe—was actually read a second time in the House of Commons ; but was rejected by 146 to 117 on the motion to go into Committee (*Journals,* Sir Simonds D'Ewes, 1682, p. 561 ; *The State of the Poor,* by Sir F. M. Eden, 1797, vol. i. p. 264 ; *Pauperism and Poor Laws,* by Robert Pashley, 1852, pp. 114-115). As late as 1721, Leslie, the Non-juror, was still proposing to put the whole burden of the relief of the poor upon those who received the tithes (*On the Divine Right of Tithes,* in vol. ii. of Leslie's *Works,* p. 873 ; see *The State of the Poor,* by Sir F. M. Eden, 1797, vol. i. p. 264).

to. Where there was distress, relief was given. ' We communicate to all, and give to every one who is in need ', says
Justin ; and the older Fathers interpret our Lord's saying,
' Give to every one that asketh of thee ', to mean quite simply,
that every suppliant was to receive without distinction. ' Give
simply to all ', it is said in the *Shepherd of Hermas,* ' without
asking doubtfully to whom thou givest, but give to all. For
God desires thee to give to all of that which thou hast. They
who receive will give account to God, why and for what they
receive. They who take anything under an appearance of
pretended need, will have to give account of it to God, but they
who give will be blameless.' Similarly does Clement of Alexandria
warn not to judge who is deserving and who is undeserving.
' For by being fastidious and setting thyself to try who are fit
for thy benevolence, and who not, it is possible that thou mayest
neglect some who are the friends of God.' Still less was it
reflected what the giver of alms and kindnesses would obtain
for himself. The thought, indeed, that almsgiving and beneficence bring a blessing was not absent, this being already stated
in the New Testament. Nay, here and there emerges already
that notion, which goes beyond the New Testament, that this
blessing consists in the expiation of sin. But all these thoughts
are by no means so prominent as they are in Cyprian, and still
more so in later writers. Alms were given, not for the sake
of the giver getting something, but to relieve the poor and
needy, from the direct constraint of sympathising love,
and the consciousness of love experienced in Christ. How
simply does the reference to reward appear in the Epistle
of Barnabas, and how does it still keep within the limits
of apostolic teaching ! ' Hesitate not to give, and give without
grudging, but consider who will be the good Repayer of the
reward.' " [1]

Now and again, it is true, one of the Fathers of the Church
would instruct the faithful that they should not encourage
idleness and fraud by their gifts. The diligent student can
pick out, all down the centuries, from the more statesmanlike
Catholic writers, isolated sentences pointing to the duty of

---

[1] *Christian Charity in the Ancient Church,* by J. G. W. Uhlhorn, translated
by Sophia Taylor, 1883, pp. 121-122 ; *The Shepherd of Hermas,* by C. H. Hoole,
1870.

practical wisdom in almsgiving, the need for some investigation
of cases, and• even the positive demerit of scattering gifts to
importunate beggars like " tossing crusts to a troublesome dog ". [1]
But the overwhelming tendency of regarding alms as an act of
piety, like fasting and prayer, principally from the standpoint
of the state of mind of the giver, was in the direction of dismissing
all considerations with regard to the character of the recipient.
When, in the fourteenth, fifteenth and sixteenth centuries, it
was sought to prohibit gifts to sturdy beggars and able-bodied
vagrants, alike in England and on the continent of Europe, no
attempt was made to prevent, or even to discourage, alms to
the impotent poor. It is needless to remind the reader how
effectively this sense of the moral obligation of almsgiving, as
an emanation of love, far outweighing in social value, by the
mere manifestation and satisfaction of a beneficent emotion,
any possible harm from misdirection, still persists among the
most pious Christians. How hard, it seems, is it to become
convinced that the spirit of love, if it is to be genuinely beneficent
—and therefore really kind—must be disciplined, like the
activities of the physician and the sanitary engineer, by the
knowledge of how things happen, and can be made to happen,
in the world we live in !

The second result of the relief of destitution by the Mediaeval
Church was, we think, peculiar to Britain, outlasting the
Reformation, and only terminated, so far as concerns England
and Wales, by the Poor Law Amendment Act of 1834. Right
down to the universal establishment of Boards of Guardians,
the relief of destitution was inextricably entangled with the
constitution and activities of the ecclesiastical parish. The
parish became, in fact, a " unit of obligation " through which
the King's Government and the Church sought, in close collabora-
tion, to arrange for the due performance of such collective

---

[1] *Beiträge zur Geschichte und Reform der Armenpflege*, by Franz Ehrle, 1881,
pp. 19-34 ; *Economic History and Theory*, by Sir William Ashley, 1893, pp.
315-316 ; *Bekenntnisbildung und Religionspolitik, 1524–1534*, by Hans Von
Schubert, Gotha, 1910. It was in order to keep in conformity with the teaching
of the Church, that when, in later years, there were prohibitions of giving alms
to beggars, these were limited, either expressly or by implication, to giving
alms to able-bodied beggars (as in 23 Edward III. st. 1, c. 7, 1349). So strong
was the feeling that we are told that " it is laid down (in the *Doctor and Student*)
that an Act of Parliament to prohibit the giving of alms is void " ! (*Observations
on the More Ancient Statutes*, by Daines Barrington, 1795, p. 265).

regulation and common services as were deemed essential to the moral and material welfare of the community.[1]

The Parish

How and when the parish was instituted, and became nearly ubiquitous over the whole of England, we do not know. There seems no reason to doubt that it was, in the beginning, merely a " shrift shire ", the district served by a duly commissioned priest ; and that in England, at any rate, it developed out of a sort of geographical delegation of the work of the bishops.[2] How far this development was originally parallel with that on the Continent of Europe we do not pretend to assert ; but any parochial organisation of the Church in France and the Low Countries, Germany and Italy, seems to have been, and to have remained, much less connected with the civil administration. The distinguishing feature of the English parish is its assumption, apparently in or before the fourteenth century, of some of the functions of government, leading everywhere to the unauthorised and apparently spontaneous creation of a local governing body, consisting of the whole of the householders periodically meeting in the parish church, " in vestry assembled ". The presidency of this meeting was everywhere assumed, apparently without question, by the rector or vicar of the parish, whilst its principal officers were the two (or occasionally three or four or even more) householders of the parish, freely chosen, according to varying local custom, to be " keepers of the goods and chattels of the parish ", churchreeves, kirkmasters, or—to use the name which eventually became universal — Churchwardens. Upon this spontaneously arising local governing body in each parish, which soon assumed unchallenged power to levy rates upon the parishioners, the King and Parliament, from the beginning of the sixteenth century onwards, imposed successive civil functions,[3]

---

[1] *The Parish and the County*, by S. and B. Webb, 1906, p. 40.

[2] This is discussed in our volume *The Parish and the County*, 1906 ; see also *Ecclesiastical Cases relative to Duties and Rights of Parochial Clergy*, etc., by Edward Stillingfleet, 1698, part i. p. 348 ; an able pamphlet on *The Rise of the Parochial System in England*, by Rev. Oswald Reichel, 1905 ; *Constitutional History of England*, by W. Stubbs, vol. i. p. 227 of 1880 edition ; *English Dioceses*, by Geoffrey Hill, 1900 ; and other works cited.

[3] Such as the provision of harness and arms for the troops, the succour and passing of maimed soldiers, and the suppression of vagrancy (see the

with corresponding statutory authority, sometimes including
as a parish officer the Constable, who had originally been
appointed in the Lord's Court, and who gradually passed under
the control of the County Justices of the Peace. But the
parish and its incumbent, its Churchwardens and its " inhabitants
in vestry assembled " remained throughout fundamentally part
of the Church organisation, both before and after the Reformation,
under the supervision and direction of the archdeacon and the
bishop. The Churchwardens, in particular, had to be presented
to the archdeacon, at his annual visitation, to be duly sworn in.
They " were directly responsible by custom and common law,
to say nothing of the Canons of the Church, to ' the Ordinary '—
that is, the bishop or his archdeacon—as well as to the ecclesiastical courts, for all the duties of the parish, not merely for
the maintenance and repair of the whole, or at any rate the
greater part, of the church fabric, for the provision of the
materials and utensils necessary for the church services, and,
in conjunction with the incumbent, for the allocation of seats
in the church, the keeping up of ' churchways ', and the administration of the churchyard ; but also, as the records con-
clusively prove, for the duty of relieving the poor." " They
were bound by oath to inquire at all times, and to report annually
to the Ordinary, at the time of his visitation as to the due performance of duty by the incumbent and his curates ; as to the
state of the Church and its furniture, the parsonage and the
churchyard ; and—most far-reaching of all—as to any moral
or religious delinquency of the parishioners ",[1] including,

___

statutes cited in *The Parish and the County*, pp. 37-38). In 1566 the " Act for
preservation of grain ", 8 Elizabeth c. 15, authorising the Churchwardens to
provide for the destruction of vermin, led immediately to the reappearance of
items in parish accounts in payment for mice heads, crows' heads, choughs'
heads, etc. (see, for instance, *Churchwardens' Accounts of the Town of Ludlow*, by
Thomas Wright, Camden Society, 1869, pp. 139-140). A previous statute
(24 Henry VIII. c. 10) had already imposed this duty on the parish (*The
Parish*, by J. Toulmin Smith, 1857, p. 233).
    [1] *The Parish and the County*, 1906, pp. 20-21. A wealth of information as
to the proceedings of the Parish Vestry and Parish Officers prior to the Civil
War is afforded in the " Visitations " of the bishops and archdeacons, and of
the ecclesiastical courts generally ; see the admirable survey in *The Elizabethan
Parish in its Ecclesiastical and Financial Aspects*, by Sedley L. Ware, Baltimore,
1908. Much is to be learnt from the scholarly *Visitation Articles and Injunctions of the Period of the Reformation*, by W. H. Frere and W. P. M. Kennedy,
3 vols. ; and *Elizabethan Episcopal Administration*, by W. P. M. Kennedy, 1924,
3 vols., both published in the *Alcuin Club Collections*. Two valuable works

therefore, into any failure to give the alms required of them.[1]

It was this organisation of the ecclesiastical parish with the clergyman at its head, and with the Churchwardens as its principal officers, which (starting without any statutory direction, and developing its autonomous arrangements for providing a local revenue out of which it not only maintained the parish church but also contrived to give alms and succour to poor travellers or sick folk) became in England, during more than four centuries, the principal Local Authority for the public relief of the destitute. It is, we suggest, very largely to this long-continued entanglement with the ecclesiastical organisation that the English (and, as may here be noticed, also the Scottish[2]) Poor Law system owes some of its most prominent differences from the Continental arrangements for poor relief ; and owes, moreover, some of its most characteristic features during the eighteenth century.

It is interesting to notice some of the expedients by which, usually before there was any regular and systematic levy of a

---

are *Precedents in Causes of Office against Churchwardens and others* (1841) ; and *A Series of Precedents in Criminal Causes from the Act Books of the Ecclesiastical Courts of London, 1475–1640* (1847), both by William Hale Hale, Archdeacon of London.

[1] We may adduce a few examples of this ecclesiastical compulsion to provide for the poor, as an obligation of Christian charity. During the reign of Elizabeth, we are told, the " Act Books " of the Church Courts teem with such presentments as the following : " One Holaway refuses to give to the poor box ' and is found able by the parish '. Thomas Arter will give but a halfpenny to the poor. Arter appears and ' saith that he is not of the wealth that men taketh him to be '. The judge commands him to pay a halfpenny every week, and dismisses him. . . . Here follow the names of such, as being able, refuse notwithstanding to pay to the poor man's box [eight names follow] " (*The Elizabethan Parish in its Ecclesiastical and Financial Aspects*, by Sedley L. Ware, Baltimore, 1908, p. 41 ; quoting from " Visitations of the Archdeaconry of Canterbury " by Arthur Hussey in *Archaeologia Cantiana*, vols. xxv.-xxvii., and *A Series of Precedents in Criminal Causes from the Act Books of the Ecclesiastical Courts of London, 1475–1640*, by Archdeacon W. H. Hale, 1847). When the Churchwardens of Ealing (Middlesex) were reported to the chancellor of the Bishop of London in 1584, for having, among other things, no " poor box ", they replied that there was " no church stock wherewith " to provide these things. Thereupon they were peremptorily ordered to lay an assessment on the parish to put themselves in funds for the purpose (*ibid.*).

[2] This entanglement was still greater in Scotland ; see, for instance, *Poor Relief in Scotland*, by Alexander A. Cormack (Aberdeen, 1923) ; *The Law of Scotland relating to the Poor*, by Alexander C. S. M. Dunlop (Edinburgh, 1825) ; *The Law of Scotland regarding the Poor*, by John Dunlop (Edinburgh, 1854) ; *The Scottish Poor Laws*, by R. P. Lamont (second Scotch edition, Glasgow, 1892) ; *History of the Scotch Poor Law*, by Sir George Nicholls (1856).

compulsory rate or tax on the parishioners, the Parish Vestry
and its officers raised the funds out of which they met the parish
requirements, including the relief of destitute folk. How strictly
they collected the sums arising from the various penalties and
forfeitures that statutes ancient and modern, and church ordinances, directed to be given to the poor we know not.[1] But
the parish had other sources of revenue. In the old accounts,
which have not yet been adequately explored, we read of the
" Church Stock " or the " Parish Stock ", in some cases a flock
of sheep,[2] in others, a herd of cattle, maintained to yield an
annual revenue for the common purposes of the parish. " There
were in some towns [hips] ", we are told in a sermon of 1550,
" some eight and some a dozen kine, given unto a stock for the
relief of the poor, and used in such wise that the poor ' cottingers '
which could make any provision for fodder had the milk for a
very small hire ; and then the number of the stock reserved all
manner of vails beside both the hire of the milk and the prices
of the young veals and old fat wares, was disposed to the relief
of the poor." [3] St. Mary's, Shrewsbury, in 1544, was letting
out 10 cows and 3 sheep for £1 : 1 : 8 per annum for the profit
of the parish ; and in 1595 2 cows were bequeathed to Lapworth
parish (Warwickshire) to be rented out at 20*d.* yearly, one to

---

[1] Thus, by 36 Edward III. c. 8, persons paying more than the statutory rate
of wages to priests were to be fined, and their fines given to the poor ; by
27 Henry VIII. c. 25 persons playing prohibited games, or otherwise infringing
the law then enacted, were to be fined, and their fines similarly disposed of.
A like provision occurs in municipal ordinances. At Norwich, in 1571, the
" Orders for the Poor " provide that those giving alms to " beggars at their
doors " should pay a fine " to go to the use of the poor " (MS. " The Mayor's
Book for the Poor ", in Norwich Town Council archives). Similar provisions
as to this allocation of the fines are common in the statutes of the first half of
the seventeenth century. See on the whole subject, *The Early History of
English Poor Relief*, by E. M. Leonard, 1900.

[2] So, for instance, at Pittington (where it was agreed in 1615 that " a
cessment of sixpence the pound shall be presently levied for the repairing of
the stock of sheep which is much decayed, and other uses of the said Church ")
and at Houghton-le-Spring in the County of Durham (*Churchwardens' Accounts
of Pittington and Other Parishes in the Diocese of Durham from 1580–1700*, Surtees
Society, vol. lxxxiv., 1888, pp. 12, 273 ; " Records of Houghton-le-Spring,"
in *English Historical Review*, October 1895 ; *The Parish and the County*, by
S. and B. Webb, 1906, p. 185). At Pittington, we are told, " for forty years
the parish flock paid all the parish expenses, a cessment being made only for
exceptional expenditure " (*Seventeenth Century Life in the Country Parish*, by
E. Trotter, 1919, p. 27).

[3] *A Sermon preached . . . Before the King's Majesty*, by Thomas Lever,
1550 (in Arber's Reprints).

pay for the mending of a road, and the other for the relief of the poor.[1] The parish of Billericay in Essex in 1599 had a flock of 40 sheep for the relief of the poor.[2] These parish flocks often originated in gifts or bequests, each transferring one or two animals. It became, in fact, customary in an agricultural community for testators to bequeath one or more sheep or cows to the parish to reinforce the " church stock ". Thus, in a single year, 1559, in the small parish of Wootton in Hampshire, no fewer than ten such gifts or bequests of sheep are recorded, making a flock of twelve.[3] Sometimes it was agreed in Vestry, and commanded, that each farmer should find the " eatage " of one member of the flock. In the Pittington records of 1580 we read " Item, it is also agreed and set down by the aforesaid Twelve Men [the Select Vestry] that every £4 rent within this parish, as well as of hamlets as townships, shall graze winter and summer one sheep for the behoof of this church ".[4] The flock, then consisting of " six wethers, ten ewes and five lambs," was sold in 1624. Such parish flocks and herds continued in existence, though we suspect only in a relatively small number of villages, well into the seventeenth century ; and, possibly, in remote and secluded parishes, occasionally, even later. We hear casually in 1631, from a joint report by the Constable, Churchwarden and Overseer, that the tiny parish of Stansted Abbot, in Hertfordshire, has " no stock [for the poor] but 2 cows and xviij[s] iiij[d] yearly rent ".[5]

---

[1] *History of Shrewsbury,* by Hugh Owen and J. B. Blakeway, 1825, vol. ii. p. 342 ; *Memorials of a Warwickshire Parish,* by Sir Robert Hudson, 1904.

[2] *A Series of Precedents in Criminal Causes from the Act Books of the Ecclesiastical Courts of London, 1475–1640,* by Archdeacon W. H. Hale, 1847, p. 221.

[3] *The Manor of Manydown,* by Dean G. W. Kitchen (Hants Record Society), 1895, p. 171.

[4] *Churchwardens' Accounts of Pittington and Other Parishes in the Diocese of Durham from 1580 to 1700,* Surtees Society, vol. lxxxiv., 1888), p. 15.

[5] *Calendar of State Papers (Domestic), Charles I.,* vol. 189, p. 80. For other references to parish stocks of sheep or cattle, their purchase and sale, their grazing, their being rented out, and the disposal of the proceeds, see the parish accounts of Hartland (Devon); Croscombe and Stogursey (Somerset); St. Michael's, Bath ; Littleton (Worcestershire) ; Morton (Derbyshire) ; Rotherfield (Sussex) ; Great Witchingham (Norfolk) ; published (Devon Parishes) in Historical MSS. Commission Reports, vol. v. 1876, vol. vi. pp. 348–349 ; in Somerset Archaeological Society, vol. xli. pp. 26, 46 ; (Worcestershire and Derbyshire Parishes) in *The Midland Antiquary,* vol. i. 1883, pp. 107–108 ; in *Sussex Archaeological Collections,* vol. xli. pp. 26, 46 ; in Norfolk and Norwich Archaeological Society, vol. xiii. p. 207 ; and in *Churchwardens' Accounts of Croscombe,* etc., by Bishop Hobhouse, 1890, pp. xiii, 224.

But the " Church Stock " was often a mere financial fund replenished from time to time by various other expedients, some of which would not at first occur to us. " There were no rates for the poor in my grandfather's days ", records John Aubrey of Wiltshire, " but for Kingston St. Michael (no small parish) the Church Ales of Whitsuntide did the business. In every parish there is (or was) a Church House to which belonged spits, crocks, etc., and utensils for dressing provisions." [1] These " Church Ales " were convivial social gatherings towards which gifts of corn were given to be brewed into ale ; and at which each guest paid for what he consumed, the resulting profit being kept for the Parish Stock. They were sometimes great occasions. " Of all means ever devised for obtaining large sums of money for parish uses, the most popular, as certainly the most efficacious, was the ' Church Ale ', which was, throughout all the Southern Counties, widespread during the first years of Elizabeth's reign." These Church Ales, we are told by the most assiduous student of the Elizabethan Parish, " were usually held at or near Whitsuntide, hence they were also called Whitsun-ales or May-ales in the accounts. If the occasion were an extraordinary one, and it was sought to realize a large sum, notices were sent to the surrounding parishes, say to ten, fifteen, or more, to be read aloud from the pulpits of their respective churches after service, which notices contained invitations to any and all to come and spend their money in feasting and drinking for the benefit of the parish giving the Ale. As the day approached for the opening of the Ale, which, if it were a great one, would be kept for four or five days or more, all was bustle in the parish to prepare for a feasting which often assumed truly Gargantuan proportions. Cuckoo kings and princes were chosen, or lords and ladies of the games ; ale-drawers were appointed. For the brewing of the ale, the wardens bought many quarters of malt out of the Church Stock, but much, too, was donated by the parishioners for the occasion. Breasts of veal, quarters of fat lambs, fowls, eggs, butter, cheese, as well as fruit and spices, were also purchased. Minstrels, drum players and Morris-dancers were engaged or volunteered their services. In

---

[1] *Miscellanies*, by John Aubrey (1659–1670), edition of 1784 ; *Popular Antiquities*, by John Brand, 3rd edition, 1870, vol. i. p. 231 ; *Economic History and Theory*, by Sir W. Ashley, 1893, p. 368 ; *Parochial Antiquities*, by White Kennett, 1818.

the Church House, or church tavern, a general utility building, found in many parishes, the great brewing crocks were furbished and the roasting spits cleaned. Church trenchers and platters, pewter or earthen cups and mugs were brought out for use ; but it was the exception that a parish owned a stock of these sufficient for a great Ale. Many vessels were borrowed or hired from the neighbours or from the wardens of near-by parishes, for, as will presently be seen, provident Churchwardens derived some income from the hiring of the parish pewter as well as money from the loan of parish costumes and stage properties. When the opening day arrived people streamed in from far and wide. If any important personage, or delegation from another village, were expected, the parish went forth in a body with bagpipes to greet them, and (with permission from the ecclesiastical authorities) the church bells were merrily rung out." [1] The form and designation of the festivities varied from place to place. There were at least a dozen kinds of " Ale ", or at any rate, as many names for the festivity. We read of a " Hobby Horse Dance " at Abbot's Bromley in Staffordshire, when " a pot . . . was kept in turn by the reeves of the town, who provided cakes and ale to put into the pot ; all the people who had any kindness to the good intent of the institution of the sport giving pence apiece for themselves and families. . . . The money, after defraying the expenses of the cakes and ale, went to repair the church and support the poor." [2]

The Church Ales of the sixteenth century did not escape the criticism of the Puritan, as they would not in our own day avoid that of the teetotaller. " Well is he ", said Philip Stubbs

---

[1] *The Elizabethan Parish in its Ecclesiastical and Financial Aspects*, by Sedley L. Ware, Baltimore, 1908, pp. 71-72. For other references to Church Ales, see *Churchwardens' Accounts of Croscombe*, etc., by Bishop Hobhouse (Somerset Record Society, 1890–1891) ; *The Anatomie of Abuses*, by Philip Stubbs, 1583 ; *Survey of Cornwall*, by Richard Carew, 1602 ; *Description of England*, by William Harrison, edition of 1899 ; *On Some Star Chamber Proceedings, 34 Eliz. 1592*, by Frederick Brown, 1883 ; *Canterburies' Doom*, by William Prynne, 1646 ; *Manor of Manydown*, by Dean G. W. Kitchen (Hants Record Society, 1895) ; " Social Life in Worcestershire, illustrated by the Quarter Sessions Records ", by J. W. Willis Bund, in *Association of Architectural Societies*, vol. xxiii. part ii. 1897 ; *History of Modern Wiltshire*, by Sir Richard Colt Hoare, 1822, vol. i. p. 22 ; *History of St. Ives*, by J. H. Matthews, 1892 ; *The Parish of Ashburton*, by J. H. Butcher, 1870 ; *Thatcham (Berks) and its Manors*, by Samuel Barfield, 1901, vol. ii. p. 105 ; *Quarter Sessions from Elizabeth to Anne*, by A. H. A. Hamilton, 1878, pp. 28-29.

[2] *The Natural History of Staffordshire*, by Robert Plot, 1686.

in 1583, of the long table on which the beer was served, " that can get the closest to it, and spend the most at it, for he that sittest the closest to it, and spends the most at it, is accounted the godliest man of all the rest . . . because it is spent upon his church forsooth ! " [1] With the change of public opinion, and the growth of Puritanism, the drunkenness and occasional disorder that characterised the Church Ales—if not also the boisterous joviality of the proceedings—became increasingly distasteful ; and they became also, as it seems, less and less profitable ; [2] so that they ceased to be held, in many places. Towards the end of the sixteenth century we see the Justices, instigated by Chief Justice Popham, in Devonshire, Somerset and Berkshire striving, by injunctions and peremptory orders, to suppress them.

Closely associated with the Church Ales was the Church House, one or more cottages which had been given or bequeathed to the parish, and were used for all sorts of public purposes. The Church House at Hackney was described in 1547 as " A tenement builded by the parishioners, called the Church House, that they might meet together and commune of matters, as well for the king's business as for the church and parish ". It might even be used as a common tavern. The Church House at North-leach in Gloucestershire was actually let as a tavern, with a stipulation that the lessee was to " permit the Town to have the use of the same one month at Whitsuntide ", during which

---

[1] *The Anatomie of Abuses*, by Philip Stubbs, 1583, p. 110 (edited by F. J. Furnivall for the New Shakespeare Society). The Churchwardens were even occasionally designated " Alewardens " (*The Elizabethan Parish in its Ecclesiastical and Financial Aspects*, by Sedley L. Ware, Baltimore, 1908, p. 14).

[2] In the parish of Mere (Wilts) where the Church Ales had produced in 1559–1560 six-sevenths of the total revenue of the Churchwardens, they yielded in 1582–1583 only one fourth ; and from that time the parish had to resort to " Collections " according to a " book of rates "—that is, to a duly assessed compulsory tax or rate. (See the " Mere Accounts " by T. H. Baker, in *Wilts Archaeological Magazine*, vol. xxxv. 1907 ; *History of Modern Wiltshire*, by Sir Richard Colt Hoare, 1822, vol. i. p. 21.) But as late as 1600, in the small parish of Wootton (Devon), the Churchwardens note in the accounts, " Received by our King Ale, all things discharged £12 : 14 : 1 ", which seems quite a large sum (*Devon Notes and Queries*, vol. iii., 1905, p. 224). For the attempts at suppression of these Ales, see *Church History of Britain*, by Thomas Fuller, 1655, vol. ii. p. 147, and *Churchwardens' Accounts of Croscombe*, etc., by Bishop Hobhouse, 1890, Appendix B, pp. 245-247 ; which gives also particulars of an attempt in 1633 by Charles I., the Archbishop of Canterbury and the Lord Keeper to bring them again into existence.

the jollifications would be for the profit of the parish.[1] Similarly, in the chapelry or township of Whitwell, part of the parish of Gatcombe, in the Isle of Wight, the Church House was leased in 1574, with the proviso if the " Quarter " [township] " shall need at any time to make a Quarter Ale or Church Ale for the maintenance of the chapel, that it shall be lawful for them to have the use of the said house, with all the rooms, both above and beneath, during their Ale ".[2] In later years, the Church House was often merely let to the highest bidder, when the rent, like other funds, would be lent at interest to tradesmen, and the interest paid into the Church Stock.[3]

One result of the suppression of the Church Ales and similar sources of parish revenue, was the increasing prevalence of the ancient habit of the inhabitants in vestry assembled to impose a " cess " or compulsory rate or tax, in order to enable the parish officers—whether the ancient Churchwardens, the more recently instituted Surveyors of Highways or Overseers of the Poor, or even the Constable who was being insensibly transformed from a manorial to a parochial official—to meet the necessary expenses of the parish. Thus, we read in 1552, in a Nottinghamshire parish of " an assessment that the parishioners were content to pay yearly towards maintenance of the Church Stock,

---

[1] " The Northleach Court Book ", by Rev. D. Royce, in *Transactions of the Gloucestershire and Bristol Archaeological Society*, vol. vii., 1882–1883.

[2] *History of the Isle of Wight*, by Sir Richard Worsley, 1781, p. 210 ; *The Parish*, by Joshua Toulmin Smith, 1857, pp. 496-497.

[3] The " Church House " is often mentioned in local records ; see, for instance, *Ludlow Churchwardens' Accounts*, by Thomas Wright, Camden Society, vol. 29 ; " Gilds of Sodbury " by F. Fox, in *Transactions of the Gloucestershire and Bristol Archaeological Society*, vol. xiii., 1888–1889, parts 1 and 2 ; *The History of Hawstead*, by Sir John Cullom, 1784, p. 73 ; *Wells Wills*, by F. W. Weaver, 1900, p. 52 ; *Somerset Mediaeval Wills, 1383-1558*, by the same (3 vols. Somerset Record Society, 1901–1905) ; *History of the Town and Borough of Calne*, by A. E. W. Marsh, 1904 ; *The Antiquary*, vol. xxvii. p. 169 (for Stanford, Berks) ; *Notes and Queries for Somerset and Dorset*, vol. 94 (for St. John's, Glastonbury) ; *Churchwardens' Accounts for Croscombe*, etc., by Bishop Hobhouse, 1890, pp. xxi, 173 (for Tintinhull) ; *Archaeologia*, vol. 46, p. 198 (for Stratton). In many parishes it became, in the seventeenth and eighteenth centuries, the poorhouse, or the " parish cottage ". At Steeple Ashton (Wilts) the accounts show, in 1558, expenditure for " one dozen of reeds ", and " for mending the Church House with the same reeds " (*The Parish*, by Toulmin Smith, 1857, p. 508). At West Lulworth (Dorset) three centuries later, we find in 1867, " 1½ cwt. of reed sheaves for thatching parish houses " (MS. Vestry Minutes, West Lulworth ; *The Parish and the County*, by S. and B. Webb, 1906, p. 44). Where the premises had been used as poorhouses, they were mostly sold, after 1834, to help pay for the new workhouses.

because other gatherings with hobby horse, and lights, were laid down ".[1] This cess, rate or tax usually bore the name of the Church Rate, perhaps because it was made at the meeting in the church ; but although it provided the expense of repairing the church and conducting the services, there was, it is clear, nothing specially ecclesiastical about the tax or the fund that it replenished, which we find spent on all sorts of secular purposes, from the destruction of vermin to the relief of the poor, according to the discretion of the several officers, the instructions of the Vestry, or the injunctions of the ecclesiastical authorities on the one hand, or those of the County Justices on the other. When it came to a definitely assessed rate or tax, there was for many years every variety of form and method ; the rate might be payable in kind (as in corn or bread or eggs) ; it might be assessed for each yardland or per acre, or per oxgang of 15 acres, or as an arbitrary sum for each named person, or for each farm or house, or according to the " means and substance " of the contributor or the assumed annual value of the premises. In 1586 the parishioners of Elstree (Herts) were contending, some for assessment " by their wealth and goods only, and some others do require that the taxation might be made by the acres of ground only ".[2]

So great was the entanglement in the ecclesiastical parish and

---

[1] " Churchwardens' Accounts of Holme Pierrepont ", by W. H. Stevenson, in *Old Nottinghamshire*, by J. P. Briscoe, second series, 1884. The " lights " were the payments made for the maintenance of a lamp or candle before one of the altars in the church, such sums being sometimes devoted to the general expenses of the church, and thus in aid of the " Church Stock ".

[2] *Precedents in Causes of Office against Churchwardens and Others*, by Archdeacon W. H. Hale, 1841. The rate made by the Parish Vestry, commonly called the Church Rate, which is found as early as the beginning of the fourteenth century (see *Churchwardens' Accounts of Croscombe*, etc., by Bishop Hobhouse, 1890, p. xiii), was never authorised by statute, except during the Commonwealth, by an Ordinance of the Long Parliament of 9th February 1647, and by contemporary Local Ordinances like those for Bristol in 1650 and 1656 (" Ancient Bristol Documents " in *Proceedings of Clifton Antiquarian Club*, vol. i. p. 51-57, 1888). These became void at the Restoration, and although a Bill was introduced in the House of Commons, 18th May 1661, authorising the Churchwardens to make rates for repair of the Church fabric, to be signed (like the Poor Rate) by two Justices, this never became law (*Notebook of Sir John Northcote*, by A. Hamilton, 1877, p. 127). An amendment to enable the Church Rate to be more easily recovered at law was added by the House of Commons in 1692 to a Tithes Bill ; but this eventually passed without it in 1696 (7 and 8 William III. c. 6 ; *House of Lords Manuscripts*, vol. i. N.S., 1900 ; *The Parish and the County*, by S. and B. Webb, 1906, p. 24). Thus, the rate made by the Vestry and Churchwardens for general parish purposes,

the Church organisation of the nascent service of poor relief
that " during the reign of Elizabeth at least ", it can be authoritatively summed up, " the Church Courts took as large a share in
parish government as did the Justices of the Peace. . . . Secular
and ecclesiastical judges had concurrent jurisdiction . . . at
any rate between 1572 and 1597, over the care of the parish
poor." [1]

The Monastic Institutions

But it was not merely in the ecclesiastical parish that the
charity to the poor insisted on by the Christian Church became
more or less elaborately organised. We owe to the Church, in
addition, the establishment throughout all Christendom of a
network of monastic institutions, which made it part of the
religious life to succour the poor and the suffering. With these
thousands of monasteries and nunneries, which by the fifteenth
century had spread over all Europe, we are concerned here only
so far as they contributed to the relief of destitution. In
England alone they came to number, large or small, and including
all the separate " cells " and houses of all the various Orders of
monks, nuns, friars and knights, not very far short of a thousand
establishments—probably not as many as there were Hundreds,
but slightly more than there now are of Petty Sessional Divisions
—averaging, perhaps, one for every sixty square miles of area.
These monastic institutions differed widely among themselves
in nearly every respect ; in constitution and rules, and in the
number of inmates, in wealth, and in the way in which the
corporate income was allocated and consumed. But practically

---

including poor relief, which became invariably known as the Church Rate,
rested, from first to last, on immemorial local custom. When, in the nineteenth
century, it became the subject of intense inter-denominational feeling (which
led to its statutory abolition in 1867), its history and purposes had been largely
forgotten (see *The Principle of Church Rates*, by Robert Swan, 1837 ; *A Few
Remarks upon the Supposed Antiquity of the Church Rates and the Threefold
Division of Tithes*, by John Mitchell Kemble, 1837 ; *Antiquity of the Church
Rate Considered*, by William Hale Hale, 1837 ; *A Brief History of Church Rates*,
by W. Goode, 1838 ; *The Parish*, by Joshua Toulmin Smith, 1857, pp. 597-604 ;
History of English Law, by Sir F. Pollock and F. W. Maitland, 1895, vol. i.
pp. 602-4 ; *The Elizabethan Parish in its Ecclesiastical and Financial Aspects*,
by Sedley L. Ware, Baltimore, 1908).

[1] *The Elizabethan Parish in its Ecclesiastical and Financial Aspects*, by
Sedley L. Ware, Baltimore, 1908, pp. 9-10.

all of them accepted, as an obligation, a more or less extensive
provision for the poor of the neighbourhood ; all of them made
a daily distribution of broken victuals, if not always of money,
at the convent gate ; nearly all of them provided lodging for
poor travellers ; many of them gave some sort of primitive
medical succour to the sick ; whilst, in a relatively small number
of cases, orphans were cared for, and some sort of schooling was
given, if only to a select few children.[1]

As to the extent and efficacy of the relief thus afforded to
the destitute by the monastic institutions, there has been much
controversy. " Many of them ", writes Cardinal Gasquet of
the English monks, " whose revenues were sufficient thereunto,
made hospitals and lodgings within their own houses, wherein
they kept a number of impotent persons with all necessaries for
them, with persons to attend upon them, besides the great alms
they gave daily at their gates to every one that came for it. Yea,
no wayfaring person could depart without a night's lodging,
meat, drink, and money, it not being demanded from whence he
or she came, and whether he would go." [2] On the other hand,
it has been pointed out that, at least at the date of their dissolution, monastic zeal and monastic charity had " grown cold " ;
and that some of the wealthiest of these establishments made " a
very scanty show of almsgiving " in proportion to their income.[3]
Moreover, by the fifteenth century it had already come to be
seriously questioned whether such charity as they dispensed did
not do more harm than good. After the Reformation, at any
rate, blunt Thomas Fuller, the Church's own historian, tells us
in 1655 that " these abbeys did but maintain the poor which
they made. . . . Their hospitality was but charity mistaken,
promiscuously entertaining some who did not need, and more
who did not deserve it. . . . For some vagrants, accounting the
abbey alms their own inheritance, served an apprenticeship, and

[1] But see, on this point, the careful analysis in *The Schools of the Mediaeval
England*, by A. F. Leach, 1915, and *Monastic Schools in the Middle Ages*, by
G. C. Coulton, 1913 (Mediaeval Studies, No. 10).
[2] *Henry VIII. and the English Monasteries*, by (Cardinal) F. A. Gasquet,
1888, vol. ii. p. 500.
[3] *History of the Middle Ages*, by Henry Hallam, vol. iii. p. 302 (specifically
with regard to the accounts of the " opulent monastery " of Bolton Abbey).
The aggregate amount distributed by all the English nunneries seems to have
been very small (*Mediaeval English Nunneries*, by Eileen Power, 1922). See
English Monastic Finances in the Later Middle Ages, by R. H. Snape, 1926.

C

afterwards wrought journey work, to no other trade than begging.
. . . Yea, we may observe that generally such places wherein the
great abbeys were seated . . . swarm most with poor people at
this day, *as if beggary were entailed on them.*" [1]

Whatever may have been, in their best days, the sum total
of the charities of the monastic institutions, it will be obvious
that they cannot have made anything like a systematic provision for what was, necessarily, a national need. In every
country, as G. Ratzinger pointed out in 1868, " the monasteries,
hospitals, etc., were without what is the first requisite for an orderly
relief of the poor—unity, concentration, organisation ". The
several convents were not located where they would have been
most useful as centres of relief ; they had been established,
here and there, with entirely different intentions and from quite
other motives. " It was impossible ", sums up C. H. Pearson,
" that institutions thus scattered should be any efficient substitute
for a Poor Law system." [2]   Nor was the imperfection of the
organisation made good by anything in the administration.
The daily distribution of broken victuals at the convent gate,
like the indiscriminate showering of doles, was not directed
towards any improvement of the condition of the recipients,
but merely to the fulfilment of a duty by the givers. The result
was that every convent inevitably attracted its own swarm of
shameless mendicants. We do not need the testimony of six-
teenth-century observers to be assured that, not merely the
" impotent poor ", but whole troops of " valiant, mighty and idle
beggars . . . commonly use to resort to such places " ; or to be
led confidently to the inference that, far from diminishing the
number of people living in a condition of destitution and vagrancy,
the very existence of such centres of indiscriminate almsgiving
perpetuated and even increased that unsatisfactory section of the

---

[1]   *Church History of Britain until 1648*, by Thomas Fuller, 1655, new edition,
1837 ; *History of Vagrants and Vagrancy*, by C. J. Ribton-Turner, 1887, p. 85.
Fynes Moryson took a similar view : " Neither am I moved with the vulgar
opinion preferring old times to ours, because it is apparent that the cloisters of
monks (who [des-]spoiled all, that they might be beneficial to few), and
gentlemen's houses (who nourished a rabble of servants), lying open to all idle
people for meat and drink, were cause of greater ill than good to the Commonwealth " (*Itinerary*, by Fynes Moryson, 1617, part iii. p. 113 ; *Observations on
the More Ancient Statutes*, by Daines Barrington, 1795, p. 535).

[2]   *Historical Maps of England*, by C. H. Pearson, 1883, p. 50 ; *The Mediaeval
Village*, by G. C. Coulton, 1925, p. 380.

population.[1] On the other hand, whilst it is easy to overstate
the aggregate amount, in the fifteenth century, of all the monastic
charities in England, it is possibly equally easy to exaggerate
the extent of the harm done by their " indiscriminate, inadequate
and unconditional Outdoor Relief ". It would now be thought
absurd to attribute, as was commonly done a hundred years
ago,[2] the organisation of a public system of poor relief in the
second half of the sixteenth century (a development, as we shall
presently mention, not peculiar to England) to the dissolution
by Henry the Eighth and Edward the Sixth of a few hundred
convents of monks and nuns.[3]

The Gilds

There was, however, in the fourteenth and fifteenth centuries,
another growth of social tissue—unconnected with either the
parish or the monastic orders, but nevertheless sharing in the
common entanglement with the religious institutions of the
time—in which the subsequent public organisation for the relief
of destitution found one of its roots. The need with which
neither individual almsgiving nor congregational charity, neither
the ecclesiastical parish nor the monastic institutions, were found
adequately to cope, was met, in England—to a relatively small
extent, it is true, but with significant after-effects—on the one
hand, by the spontaneous democratic organisations of the Craft

[1] See, in confirmation, *The State of the Poor*, by Sir F. M. Eden, 1797, vol. i.
p. 95.
[2] *History of the Protestant Reformation*, by William Cobbett, 1829, of which
Cardinal Gasquet edited a new edition in 1896.
[3] Upon the monastic institutions, their nature, development and effects,
much has been written. On the one side we may consult Cardinal F. A.
Gasquet (*The Eve of the Reformation*, 1900 ; *The Great Pestilence*, 1893 ; *English
Monastic Life*, 1904 ; *The Last Abbot of Glastonbury*, 1895 ; and especially
Henry VIII. and the English Monasteries, editions of 1888, 1893, 1899, etc.) ;
and the more impartial Dr. Augustus Jessopp (*Before the Great Pillage*, 1901 ;
The Coming of the Friars, 1889, and other editions). Very much on the other
side are the various volumes of G. C. Coulton (*Five Centuries of Religion*, 1923 ;
Mediaeval Studies, Nos. 1 to 18 (notably Nos. 1, 6, 10 and 11); *A Mediaeval
Garner*, 1910 ; *The Mediaeval Village*, 1925, especially chaps. 8, 12 and 26).
More restrained is the judgement of such works as Dr. Alexander Savine's
" English Monasteries on the Eve of the Dissolution ", in vol. i. of Dr. Vino-
gradoff's *Studies in Social and Legal History*, 1909 ; F. A. Hibbert's *Dissolution
of the Monasteries as illustrated by the Suppression of the Religious Houses of
Staffordshire*, 1910; Eileen Power's *Mediaeval English Nunneries*, 1922 ; and
R. H. Tawney's *Agrarian Problem in the Sixteenth Century*, 1912 ; as well as
Dr. Liljegren's *The Fall of the Monasteries and Social Changes in England*, 1924.

Gilds in the towns, and the analogous fraternities and religious gilds in the rural villages ; and on the other, by the independent action of the Municipal Corporations ; in both cases often in co-operation with individual founders of endowed hospitals or other institutions. We need do no more than allude briefly to these developments. The extent to which the rural villages of the fourteenth and fifteenth centuries were provided with in-dependent associations, in which nearly every householder was apparently enrolled, has usually been overlooked. These local " gilds, fraternities, mysteries, companies or brotherhoods ", which abounded in the rural parishes of the England of the fourteenth and fifteenth centuries, were always connected with religious observances. They provided and maintained " lights " and paid for masses—occasionally even erecting and endowing a chantry and its priest. On special days their members assembled at the church for collective worship or celebrations. They attended, with simple pomp, each member's funeral. But not the least of the objects for which this social tissue had been developed was that of a primitive mutual insurance. We find these rural fraternities giving alms, and sometimes regular pensions, to members who had fallen into distress. They sometimes found lodgings for strangers and homeless folk, and made urgent provision for widows and orphans. In many cases they seem to have met at least part of the cost of burial. The extent to which they co-operated in the relief of destitution deserves further investigation.[1]

---

[1] For the rural gilds, which should not be confused with the Merchant and Craft Gilds of the towns, see *The Church of our Fathers*, by Dr. Daniel Rock, 1849, vol. ii. pp. 395-453 ; *English Gilds*, by J. Toulmin Smith, 1870 ; *Parish Life in Mediaeval England*, by Cardinal Gasquet ; *The Parish Gilds of Mediaeval England*, by H. F. Westlake, 1919 ; *The Mediaeval Village*, by G. C. Coulton, 1925. " These gilds ", said Blomefield, " also gave an annual charity, stipends to poor persons, found beds and entertainments for poor people that were strangers, and had people to keep and tend the said beds, and did other works of charity " (*Essays towards a Topographical History of Norfolk*, by Francis Blomefield, vol. iii. Norwich, p. 494 ; *The State of the Poor*, by Sir F. M. Eden, 1797, pp. 595-598). When, in a Norfolk village in 1650, the possessions of one of these rural gilds were sold, the following extensive equipment for social entertainment was included : " 30 lbs. of pewter vessels, 92 lbs. of lead ; four spits that weighed 169 lbs., a metal pot that weighed 44 lbs ; two pots of brass of 89 lbs., and a brass pan of 9 lbs." (*ibid.*). A parish gild at South Tawton (Devon) in 1564 records that " We made of our Ale and gathering £40 : 8 : 8 " (*Devon Notes and Queries*, vol. iii., 1905, p. 224). At Chagford, St. Anthony's Gild had a successful Ale in 1599 (*Devon Association for the Advancement of Science*, vol. viii. p. 74).

Better known than that of the rural fraternities, the part played in the towns of the fourteenth and fifteenth centuries by the Merchant and Craft Gilds has also to be mentioned here. Apart from their religious side, we find them making grants to members fallen into distress, sometimes to enable them to start again in business, sometimes merely pensions for the maintenance of aged members or of the widows of members, or of blind, lame or sick persons. Besides such grants from the corporate funds, the members are often found making small contributions, for each other's needs, at each of their periodical meetings, at their pageants, or at their annual celebrations. More important became, in course of time, the administration by the gild of the gifts or bequests of its wealthier members, by means of which these pious founders, partly with the view of securing their own salvation, not only provided funds for gifts for distribution among their fellow-members or to the poor, but also permanently endowed chantries, hospitals, almshouses, and, in a few instances, even schools, many of which were fortunate enough to survive the summary confiscation in the sixteenth century of that part of the endowments that had been devoted to " superstitious uses ".[1]

The Municipalities

Alongside this work of the Merchant and Craft Gilds in the towns must be ranked the participation in the relief of destitution by the Municipal Corporation itself. We see the mayor and

[1] Thus, Gild almshouses seem to have existed at Bristol, Colchester, Hull, Ludlow, Newcastle, Sandwich, Winchester and York (among other places). See for all this, *English Gilds*, by Joshua Toulmin Smith, 1870 ; *Town Life in the Fifteenth Century*, by Mrs. A. S. Green, 1894 ; the histories of the London Companies, especially those by C. M. Clode (Merchant Taylors), A. B. Jupp and W. W. Pocock (carpenters) ; C. Welch (carpenters, gardeners, paviors and pewterers), S. Young (barber-surgeons), William Williams (founders), Sir W. S. Prideaux (goldsmiths), J. B. Heath and J. A. Kingdon (grocers), E. W. Brabrook and W. D. Selby (mercers), R. R. Sharpe (shipwrights), W. H. Black (leather-sellers), J. B. Firth (coopers), J. Nicholl (ironmongers), J. G. Nichols (mercers and stationers), C. R. Rivington (stationers), C. R. B. Barrett (apothecaries), Joseph Daw (butchers), S. E. Atkins and W. H. Overall (clockmakers), C. H. Compton (horners), J. E. Price (needlemakers), J. C. Crace and W. H. Pitman (painters), G. Lambert (pattenmakers), J. W. Sherwell (saddlers), J. Gillespie (salters), J. F. Wadmore (skinners), H. Steward (wiredrawers) and J. Christie (parish clerks) ; *The Twelve Great Livery Companies*, by W. Herbert, 1834 ; *The Livery Companies of the City of London*, by W. C. Hazlitt, 1892 ; *The Gilds and Companies of London*, by George Unwin, 1908 ; Report of the Royal Commission on the City Companies, 1884.

other corporate officers, and frequently the Corporation itself
(as at Bedford and Beverley, Northampton, Winchester and
Wells, among many others) not only administering an ever-
swelling volume of institutional relief, as endowments were
made by gift or bequest, of hospitals, almshouses and schools,
but also making periodical distributions of alms to the poor, out
of the proceeds of land devised for that purpose.[1] But the
Corporation also bore its share of the cost of corporate charity.
The records of most' of the municipalities of the time—we may
instance London and Norwich, Southampton and Lydd, Exeter
and Romney, Chester and Rye, Hereford and Sandwich—reveal
them as establishing a town stock of wheat or rye for sale at
low prices in seasons of scarcity ; importing grain from Danzig
or elsewhere for distribution to the suffering poor ; maintaining
many orphans ; pensioning some of the aged ; even housing a
few of the infirm ; and granting, often " from the town's alms ",
a stream, or at least a rivulet, of doles to favoured widows or
others of " the impotent poor ".[2] Less well known is the fact
that, in not a few towns the Municipal Corporation did not
refrain from levying, before any statutory authorisation, an
obligatory tax, and in some cases (as in London, Ipswich and
Norwich), like the Parish Vestry, a regular direct assessment on all
occupiers, for this among other municipal activities of the time.[3]

[1] For these bequests of money and devises of land, useful materials for study
are now available in such publications as *The Calendar of Wills proved in the
Court of Hustings, 1258–1688* (London), by Reginald R. Sharpe, 1889–1890 ;
Somerset Mediaeval Wills, 1383–1558, by F. W. Weaver, 3 vols. (Somerset
Record Society, 1901–1905); *Lincoln Wills*, by C. W. Foster (Lincoln Record
Society, 1914), and *Testamenta Eboracensia*, by James Raine, 6 vols. (Surtees
Society, 1836–1902); *Durham Wills and Inventories* (Surtees Society, vols. 2, 26,
38). See *The Mediaeval Hospitals of England*, by Rotha M. Clay, 1909.
[2] For instances see *Town Life in the Fifteenth Century*, by Mrs. A. S. Green,
2 vols., 1894; *The Gild Merchant*, by Charles Gross, 2 vols., 1890 ; *Annals of
Ipswich*, by Nathaniel Bacon, 1654 ; *History of Sandwich*, by William Boys,
1792 ; *History of Southampton*, by John S. Davies, 1883 ; *Records of the Corporation of Norwich*, by W. Hudson and J. C. Tingey, 1906–1910 ; *History of
English Philanthropy*, by B. Kirkman Gray, 1905, pp. 25-61 ; and *Early History
of English Poor Relief*, by E. M. Leonard, 1900.
[3] Apart from, and anterior to, the examples of an actual rate or assessment
upon all the burgesses or citizens, which are, before 1572, exceptional and rare,
it must be remembered that instances of compulsory taxation of other kinds
are both much older and more common. There was often a publicly organised
and virtually compulsory " collection " of alms for the support of municipal
institutions, or of food " for the lepers " ; there were leper dues at Ipswich ;
" leper tolls " at Chester (on all foodstuffs brought to market) ; at Southampton
(on all imported wine) ; and at Carlisle (on brewers and Sunday bakers), and

The Framework of Repression

Throughout the whole period surveyed in the foregoing pages, the King, his Council and his Parliament, were enacting and carrying out laws relating to the poor of a character exactly opposite to that of the almsgiving of the mediaeval Church or to that of the benevolent institutions established by pious founders, Craft Gilds and municipal corporations. All these activities were derived from the obligation of the Christian to relieve the suffering of " God's poor ". The King and his nobles were intent upon an altogether different object, namely, maintaining order—that is (as governments always understand it) the maintenance of the then-existing order, based on a social hierarchy of rulers and ruled, of landowners and those who belonged to the land. Thus, for over seven hundred years, from Athelstan and Canute down to Henry the Eighth, the statute book abounds in laws of ever-increasing severity against vagrants, whether as sturdy beggars or rogues addicted to crime and disorder, or as labourers who abstracted themselves from their obligations to the manor or parish to which they belonged, as well as from the service of the " master " to whom it was assumed that they owed their labour. We need not here enumerate either all the statutes, or the persons to whom they were respectively made applicable, whether " landless men " or " beggars able to labour ", " idle persons living suspiciously ", or " outlandish people calling themselves Egyptians " ; or more

---

throughout all Cumberland there was a " leper tithe " on corn. Hospital tolls on farm produce were levied throughout the archbishopric of York for the " hospital " at York, and throughout the bishopric at Durham for the " house " at Kepier. Such instances of indirect taxation for poor relief are multiplied in the sixteenth century. At Cambridge in 1560 a whole series of new town dues or fees, for admission to burgess rights, for the registration of surrenders and conveyances, and for proceedings in the borough courts of justice, were imposed and allocated towards the cost of the Corporation's relief of the poor (*Annals of Cambridge*, by C. H. Cooper, 1842, vol. ii. pp. 60-63, 131-132). Ipswich, in 1571, not only did the same, but also levied for the purpose special tolls on shipping (*Annals of Ipswich*, by Nathaniel Bacon, 1654,). It is pointed out by Lord Ernle that the acts of 1 Edward VI. c. 3 (1547) and 3 and 4 Edward VI. c. 16 (1549) afforded statutory warrant for defraying, from the funds of the parish, and therefore from any " Church " or other rate that it might choose to levy, certain expenses connected with Poor Relief, such as the cost of removal of persons chargeable elsewhere, the provision of " convenient houses " for the impotent poor, and the establishment of Houses of Correction (" The Relief of the Poor from 1601 to 1834 ", in Appendix I. of *English Farming Past and Present*, by R. E. Prothero, afterwards Lord Ernle, 1912, pp. 431-438).

comprehensively, every man " having no land-master, nor using
any lawful merchandise, craft or mystery, able to give no
reckoning how he doth lawfully get his living ". The punishments give the impression of increasing in severity and brutality
with every century ; but in fact they ring the changes continually on temporary imprisonment in the stocks, compulsory
service under a master, whipping " on the bare back until
bloody ", branding with a hot iron, and (even as late as the last
years of the sixteenth century) condemnation to the galleys.[1]
One main object of the Legislature in these Acts was doubtless
the prevention of the disorder, violence and other crime to which
an extensive vagrancy gave rise.   We cannot, however, overlook
the fact that, from the fourteenth century onwards, and especially
after the Black Death (1349)—itself only one of a score of
pestilences in that century—the statutes show a further intention.
The feudal organisation of the Manor, with its basis in serfdom
and customary occupancy of land upon obligations of personal
service, was breaking down.   A new class of freedmen, becoming
free labourers, was thus gradually emerging : " the villein desiring to be quit of customary work and customary dues, in order
that he may become a tenant at a fixed rent, and the landless
labourer determined that at all costs he will get from his employer
something more than the miserable pay allowed him by law ".[2]
The shock which the Great Pestilence itself, and the resulting
scarcity and high wages of labour, gave to the economic organisation of the English village and the ecclesiastical parish was perhaps
unparalleled in severity ; but, as Sir William Ashley suggests, it
may well have done even " more harm to the morality of the people

---

[1] See, for the Act of 1597 hereon, *The State of the Poor*, by Sir F. M. Eden,
1797, vol. i. p. 109.   At the Devon Quarter Sessions in 1598 some felons were
" reprieved for the service of Her Majesty's galleys " (*Quarter Sessions from
Elizabeth to Anne*, by A. H. A. Hamilton, 1878, p. 31) ; see the note upon the
galleys in Daines Barrington's *Observations on the More Ancient Statutes*, 1796,
p. 93.   The Privy Council, on June 19, 1602, directed all Judges of Assize to
let all felons, except those convicted of rape and other grave offences, serve
in the galleys (*Acts of the Privy Council, 1613–1614*, by Sir H. C. Maxwell-Lyte,
1916, p. 489).   " The galleys . . . were at this time being experimented
with in the Queen's navy in rivalry with those of Spain and France " (*History
of England*, by Edward P. Cheyney, vol. ii., 1926, p. 333).   For all these repressive statutes dealing with vagrancy, see *The History of the Poor Laws*, by Rev.
Richard Burn, 1764 ; *The State of the Poor*, by Sir F. M. Eden, vol. i., 1797 ;
History of Vagrants and Vagrancy, by C. J. Ribton-Turner, 1887, pp. 56-99 ;
History of the English Poor Law, by Sir George Nicholls, 1854, vol. i. pp. 34-124.
[2] *The Great Revolt of 1381*, by Sir Charles Oman, 1906, p. 8.

than good to their material prospects. It shook them out of the habits of their lives and the customs of their village; it suggested to them that higher wages could be obtained if they did but refuse to work at the usual rates ; and a few weeks of idleness, with their hands against all the constituted authorities, and the easy object-lesson of lavish almsgiving ever before them, would go far to turn honest men into vagrants." [1] " The world goeth fast from bad to worse ", writes a contemporary author, " when shepherd and cowherd for their part demand more for their labour than the master-bailiff was wont to take in days gone by. Labour is now at so high a price that he who will order his business aright must pay five or six shillings now for what cost two in former times. Labourers of old were not wont to eat of wheaten bread ; their meat was of beans or coarser corn, and their drink of water alone. Cheese and milk were a feast to them, and rarely ate they of other dainties ; their dress was of hodden grey ; then was the world ordered aright for folk of this sort. . . . Three things, all of the same sort, are merciless when they get the upper hand : a water-flood, a wasting fire and the common multitude of small folk. For these will never be checked by reason or discipline ; and therefore, to speak in brief, the present world is so troubled by them that it is well to set a remedy thereunto." [2]

The remedy devised and applied throughout the fourteenth and fifteenth centuries by the government of the country was a determined attempt to bring the labourers back, as nearly as practicable, to the servile conditions of preceding generations. The well-known " Statute of Labourers " of 1350 required " all persons able to labour and without other means of support " to serve any master at the rates customary prior to the pestilence ; they were forbidden to wander out of their respective parishes ; whilst no one was to give anything to able-bodied beggars, because these " do refuse to labour, giving themselves to idleness and vice, and so that they may be, through want, compelled to labour for their necessary living ". [3] A subsequent statute

---

[1] *Economic History and Theory*, by Sir William Ashley, 1893, p. 338.

[2] J. Gower's *Mirour de l'Omme*, written before Wat Tyler's Revolt— probably about 1375—quoted in *Social Life in Britain from the Conquest to the Reformation*, by G. C. Coulton, 1918, p. 353.

[3] 23 Edward III. st. 1, c. 7 (1350), renewed by 25 Edward III. st. 1, c. 7 (1352), see *History of the English Poor Law*, by Sir George Nicholls, 1854, vol. i. p. 37.

dealt—as if in an American slave State—with any man who
had run away from his place of work, who might be claimed
and recovered by his employer, and, at the discretion of the
Justices, "burnt on the forehead with an iron formed to the
letter F in token of his falsity ".[1] In 1388 a further statute
repeated the penalties against absconding labourers in agriculture ; and insisted that children who had been employed in
that occupation before reaching the age of twelve should not
be put to any trade ; whilst providing that the craftsmen not
usually engaged in tillage might be compulsorily conscripted to
help get in the harvest.[2]

Such severe and persistent oppression, spasmodically enforced
by cruel punishments and the exercise of tyranny by landowners
and employers, led naturally to every kind of evasion of the
laws, to sullen resistance, to continual tumult and disorder,
accompanied by no small amount of crimes of violence, and
breaking out repeatedly into organised insurrections on a large
scale. Much more was involved in the contemporary legislation
than is properly covered by such a phrase as the suppression of
vagrancy. We get the impression, as regards the couple of
hundred years that succeeded the Black Death (1348–1349), of a
widespread dislocation of social relations that amounted to an
economic war.[3] The agrarian worker, who was, for the most
part, rapidly becoming an unattached wage-labourer, found
himself both requiring a higher money wage, and able to exact
an increase which the employing and governing class strove
ruthlessly to prohibit and prevent.

What could the labourer do in self-defence ? The time for

We need not refer to the controversies as to the purpose and effect of these
Acts ; but evidence as to their being put into operation is afforded by Miss
Putnam's *Enforcement of the Statutes of Labourers,* 1908.

[1] 34 Edward III. c. 10 (1360).

[2] 12 Richard II. c. 3 (1388). Acts of like import were repeated for more
than a century—see 6 Henry VI. c. 3 (1427) and 11 Henry VII. c. 22 (1495)
and 22 Henry VIII. c. 12 (1530).

[3] It is to be noted that the oppression of the poor in the England of the
fourteenth and fifteenth centuries is paralleled by very similar oppression in
France, and also in Germany, where it had its result in the century of revolt
that culminated in the Peasant Rising of 1525 (*The Mediaeval Village,* by G. C.
Coulton, 1925, chaps. xxiv. and xxv. " The Rebellion of the Poor ", pp. 345-
367). It is interesting to find Lord Acton attributing this long-continued
and widespread revolt to " the demoralising servitude and lawless oppression
which the peasants endured " (*History of Freedom,* by Lord Acton, 1907,
p. 156).

Trade Unionism was not yet come. In the absence of organised combination and collective bargaining, the labourer's best instrument of resistance was mobility—his withdrawal from the village, where he was entangled in the shackles of obsolescent manorial custom and feudal law, in order to gain a freedom of economic bargaining either in a neighbouring borough or the growing urban aggregation of the Metropolis, or merely as an independent stranger on a distant estate where additional labour was required.[1] It looks as if this mobilisation of agrarian labour was, throughout the fifteenth century, sufficiently extensive to defeat, not only the economic strength of the lords of the manor and the growing class of capitalist farmers, but also, in spite of the severest statutes, the effective authority of Parliament. The common impression that the economic position of the agrarian labourer, if not the security and comfort of his life, steadily improved during the century that followed the Black Death may be, in a sense, correct. But it was, perhaps, the labourer who was mobile who usually benefited, and this occurred in so far as the Government failed in suppressing vagrancy. It seems clear that the terrible penal statutes were only partially and spasmodically enforced. Stewards of manors and farmers at fixed rents found it more advantageous to pay the wandering workmen above the rate of statute wages rather than be without the necessary labour force. When the sense of oppression became overwhelming, the popular feeling manifested itself in widespread organised tumults, disturbances and insurrections, from Wat Tyler's rebellion of 1381, and Jack

[1] " On the whole ", states Sir Charles Oman, " it would seem that the landless labourer fared better than the villein during this age of strife. He could easily abscond, since he had no precious acres in the common-field to tether him down. If he was harried, held down to the letter of the statute, and dragged before Justices in his native district, he could always move on to another. He therefore, as it seems, enjoyed a very real if a precarious and spasmodic prosperity. He might at any moment fear the descent of a Justice upon him, if neighbouring landlords grew desperate, but meanwhile he flourished. Langland's *Piers Plowman*, from which so many valuable side-lights on the time can be drawn, describes him as ' waxing fat and kicking '. ' The labourers that have no land and work with their hands deign no longer to dine on the stale vegetables of yesterday; penny-ale will not suit them, nor bacon, but they must have fresh meat or fish, fried or baked, and that hot-and-hotter for the chill of their maw : Unless he be highly paid he will chide, and bewail the time he was made a workman. . . . Then he curses the King and all the King's Justices for making such laws that grieve the labourer ' " (*The Great Revolt of 1381*, by Sir Charles Oman, 1906, pp. 8-9).

Cade's march on London of 1460, to the Pilgrimage of Grace of 1536, and Kett's Norfolk rising of 1549—all of them successfully, but sometimes not without great struggle, put down by the forces which the Government could command. But vagrancy was not actually prevented ; nor, as we shall presently describe, was the habit of making a living by wandering on the roads brought to an end. For generations to come, and even for centuries, the land became more than ever the scene of the goings to and fro of men without settled habitation or assured livelihood ; labourers escaping from their manors or losing their employment by the change from tillage of the soil to sheep-farming ; workers of all sorts attracted to the towns by the demand set up by the growing cloth industry ; retainers dismissed by the impoverished nobles ; discharged soldiers ; perambulating friars, and with them, of course, every kind of demoralised vagrant and fraudulent social parasite. Nor must we forget that throughout this period the urban craftsmen and labourers were no whit less rebellious than the agrarian workers. " There were rife ", Sir Charles Oman reminds us, " in almost every town, old grudges between the rulers and the ruled, the employers and the employed, which were responsible for no small share of the turbulence of the realm, when once the rebellion had broken out. They require no less notice than the feuds of the countryside." [1] The amount of disorder and crime, with a corresponding amount of hardship and suffering to innocent families, can hardly be imagined.

Now, it is clear that the indiscriminate almsgiving of the mediàeval Church, accompanied, as it was, by the savage penalisation, through the civil authorities, not only of vagrancy and

---

[1] *The Great Revolt of 1381*, by Sir Charles Oman, 1906, p. 5. See also, for this period of the revolt, *The Peasants' Rising and the Lollards*, by E. Powell and G. M. Trevelyan, 1899 ; *Studies and Notes Supplementary to Stubbs' Constitutional History*, by C. Petit-Dutaillis (Manchester University Publications, 2 vols., 1914) ; " Studies in the Sources of the Social Revolt in 1381 ", by Kriehn, in *American Historical Review*, vol. vi., 1901 ; *Le Soulèvement des travailleurs d'Angleterre en 1381*, introduction par C. Petit-Dutaillis, 1898 ; *Robert Kett and the Norfolk Rising*, by Joseph Clayton, 1911 ; *Kett's Rebellion in Norfolk*, by F. W. Russell, 1859 ; *The Rising in East Anglia*, by E. Powell, 1896 ; " The Midland Revolt ", by E. F. Gray, in *Transactions Royal Historical Society*, N.S. xviii ; " The Pilgrimage of Grace ", by Mary Bateson, in *English Historical Review*, vol. v. ; " Risings in English Monastic Towns in 1327 ", by N. M. Trenholme, in *American Historical Review*, vol. vi. ; *The Genesis of Lancaster*, by Sir James H. Ramsay, vol. ii., 1913, chaps. x. and xi., pp. 142-177.

mendicancy, but also of all attempts on the part of the manual workers to rise in the social scale, constituted—when regarded as a whole—a monstrous policy, combining, in its treatment of the poor, unmerited indulgence towards the fraudulent and the vicious with an arbitrary ferocity towards the innocent and the energetic : a policy which neither lessened destitution nor maintained order. At last, at the opening of the sixteenth century, we see emerging, not in England alone, a new statecraft relating to destitution, which sought to harmonise, in one and the same public service, provision for the sick and the aged, education for the children, and the setting to work under discipline of the able-bodied unemployed, so that all who could might earn their livelihood.

Continental Reformers

In the first quarter of the sixteenth century we become aware, with regard to the public policy towards the poor, of a new departure in thought, not in one nation only, among those select few, in all the countries of Western Europe, who were giving heed to social problems. It was out of this new intellectual ferment that the systematic public provision for the destitute, so characteristic of the ensuing three or four centuries, actually emerged. What we see ever-increasingly realised, alike in Germany, the Netherlands, Switzerland, England, and, to some extent, France and Scotland, is that no policy of mere repression availed to stop either mendicancy on the one hand, or vagrancy on the other ; that (as distinguished from a fortuitous distribution of voluntary gifts to necessarily selected individuals) a systematic and ubiquitous provision had to be made locally by some organ of government for all those who were actually in need of the means of existence, whatever the cause of their destitution ; that such a provision had no relation to the emotion of pity for the sufferers or the manifestation of Christian charity, but, in view of the failure of the Church and the charitable to cope adequately with the need, was imperatively called for in the public interest as a measure of civil administration ; that the practice of almsgiving, far from being a religious duty, ought, as being socially injurious, to be restrained by law, if not (along with begging and vagrancy) entirely prohibited ; and (as experience quickly proved to be necessary) that the funds required for the proper provision for the poor had necessarily to be raised by some sort of compulsory taxation.

All these ideas, so different from those dominating the Middle Ages, seem to have become suddenly current in Western Europe in the generation that had grown up after the discovery of America in 1492 : to have been widely published, in fact, between 1515 and 1530 ; [1] to have characterised alike the countries in which the Reformation had already prevailed and those in which the Roman Catholic Church was still dominant ; and to have emanated from both Catholic and Protestant theologians and administrators. Thus, we find, about 1516, the distinguished Scottish " Nominalist ", John Major, " that perfect theologian and, beyond all question, most learned master ", then teaching in the University of Paris, declaring that " if the Prince or Community should decree that there should be no beggar in the country, and *should provide for the impotent*, the action would be praiseworthy and lawful ".[2] It is significant that what to-day seems but a commonplace should have reverberated through Western Europe. Within four years of this authoritative Roman Catholic declaration, Martin Luther himself was instructing " the nobility of the German Nation " that " it would be an easy regulation to introduce, if we have sufficient courage and

---

[1] Doubtless forerunners can be traced, whose ideas, " born before their time ", failed to get taken up. Thus Mr. Coulton reminds us of a curious anticipation, by Roger Bacon in the thirteenth century, of the provision by the State of public institutions for boarding and lodging the sick and aged poor, at the expense of State funds, raised partly by taxation. In his *Opus Majus* (Dr. J. H. Bridges' edition of 1897, vol. ii. p. 251) we read " Therefore, as saith Avicenna, it behoves the Prince to forbid idleness and sloth on the part of the people. Those, therefore, who cannot be disciplined by compulsion, should be expelled from the State, unless the cause of their idleness be sickness or old age ; for which cases a house should be founded wherein such may live, and a guardian should be deputed for them. For the State should possess a certain common and public fund composed partly from the law of contracts, partly from pecuniary amercements, partly from the estates or confiscations of rebels, and partly from other sources ; and this fund should be devoted, partly to such as are hindered of their livelihood by sickness or age, partly to doctors of medicine and law, and partly to common uses." (Quoted in *Social Life in Britain*, etc., by G. C. Coulton, 1918, p. 350.)

[2] *Commentary on the Sentences of Peter Lombard*, by John Major, 1516, quoted in *Economic History and Theory*, by Sir William Ashley, 1893, vol. ii. p. 341 ; see for Major and the Nominalists, *History of Philosophy*, by F. Ueberweg (English translation by G. S. Morris), and the life of Major prefixed to the translation of his *History of Greater Britain* (Scottish Historical Society, No. 10, 1892).

earnestness, that every town should provide for its own poor people. Each town could . . . discover which were truly poor. *There must be an administrator or guardian, who shall know all the poor,* and who shall inform the council or the parson of what he has need." [1]

In 1523 Luther promulgated his detailed scheme, prepared in consultation with the leading citizens, of an " Ordinance for a Common Chest ", at Leisneck, now Leisnig, in Saxony, which supplied to the municipal authorities of many a city, not merely of Germany itself, but also of the Netherlands and elsewhere, a model for their dealings with the problem of the relief of destitution. " Begging ", we learn, " is to be rigidly prohibited ; all who are not old and weak shall work ; no beggars are to be permitted to stay who do not belong to the parish. Poor householders who have honourably laboured at their craft or in agriculture, shall, if they can find no other support, be given loans without interest, from the Common Chest ; and this aid shall be given to them without return, if they are really unable to restore it. The income of the Chest shall be composed of the revenues of ecclesiastical estates, of free contributions and—[herein going beyond what any one had so far suggested]— *if necessary, of an assessment upon resident citizens,* and a small poll tax upon servants and journeymen. The administration shall be in the hands of elected citizens." [2] Luther's injunctions seem to have been immediately made the basis of a municipal organisation of poor relief, not only in Protestant but also in Catholic cities. We see them inspiring municipal ordinances at Augsburg, which appointed six " guardians of the poor " (Armenpfleger) in 1522 ; at Altenburg in 1522 ; at Nuremberg (where there had been previous ordinances of 1363 and 1478) in 1522, under the influence of Lazarus Spengler, a measure which Ypres, in the Netherlands, copied in 1525, thereby making itself, as we shall presently describe, famous throughout Western

---

[1] *An den Adel der Deutscher Nation,* 1520, quoted in *Darstellung der in Deutschland zur Zeit der Reformation herrschenden national - ökonomischen Ansichten,* by Heinrich Wiskemann, 1861 , and *Economic History and Theory,* by Sir William Ashley, 1893, vol. ii. p. 342.

[2] For Luther's Ordinance, see *Some Early Tracts on Poor Relief,* by F. R. Salter, 1926, pp. 80-96 ; see also *Zur Geschichte der national - ökonomischen Aussichten in Deutschland während der Reformationsperiode,* by Gustav Schmoller, 1861, p. 71 ; and the article " Armenwesen " by J. Gerhard W. Uhlhorn in *Handwörterbuch der Staatswissenschaften,* 1890, vol. i.

Europe ; at Strassburg, at Regensburg, at Kitzingen in Fran-
conia, and at Breslau (1523) ; at Magdeburg (1524) ; at Baden
Baden (1528) ; and in Wurtemberg in 1536 ; whilst the relief
of the poor by the local ecclesiastical organisation was reorganised on similar lines at Wittenberg (1522) and at Leipzig
(1523).[1]

In 1530, the German Emperor, Charles the Fifth, whom we
know to have been inquiring into the new developments, seems
to have issued an imperial rescript (Reichspolizeiordnung) which
directed that each city and commune should maintain its own
poor, the exact scope and purpose of the document being unknown to us.[2]

A year later (October 7, 1531) the Emperor issued a long
edict for the Netherlands, amounting to a comprehensive scheme
of policy for poor relief. Vagrancy and begging were denounced
and prohibited under pain of imprisonment and severe whipping ;
but friars and pilgrims, and persons who had suffered by war,
fire or floods, were specially excepted. Every city and commune
was commanded to make provision for its own poor, who were
incidentally defined as those who had resided for one year, all
such being ordered to remain where they were settled, and
authorised to share in the provision made. Able-bodied idlers
and rogues were to be put to productive work, and compelled
to earn their own livelihood. Indigent women and orphan
children were to be specially cared for, the latter being put to
school, and, at a proper age, placed out in crafts or service. For
revenue, the Local Authorities were to make collections, once
or twice in every week, not only in the churches and at the
institutions themselves, but also at the citizens' residences, from
door to door.[3] Though wanting in the administrative detail of

----

[1] *Handwörterbuch der Staatswissenschaften*, by Elster, Weber and Wieser,
1923.

[2] *Ibid.*

[3] This edict is referred to in *The History of Commerce*, by Adam Anderson,
vol. ii. p. 55 ; *The State of the Poor*, by Sir F. M. Eden, 1797, vol. i. p. 83, and
in *Poor Relief in Different Parts of Europe*, a German work edited by A. Emming-
haus, of which a greatly abridged translation was issued by E. B. Eastwick,
M.P., in 1873. Similar provisions against beggars and vagabonds seem to have
been included in the Emperor's Code of Criminal Procedure of 1532 ; and
further edicts were issued in 1548 and 1577 ; but apparently only very partially
put in operation ; see *Some Early Tracts on Poor Relief*, by F. R. Salter, 1926,
p. 34. Ghent and Brussels issued ordinances based on the edict in 1534, and
Bruges in 1560, whilst in Spain legislation dates from 1540.

the English Poor Laws of 1597 and 1601, and not yet adopting
the expedient of direct taxation, this imperial edict of 1531,
which perhaps effected no more than to give a stimulus to the
municipal action of the Netherland towns, substantially antici-
pates the first stages of the Elizabethan legislation.

Meanwhile Ulrich Zwingli was moving at Zurich on the same
lines as Luther. In 1524 the monastic institutions were abolished,
a friary being converted into a hospital, an Augustinian monastery
into a kitchen for the supply of cooked food for the destitute,
one nunnery into an orphanage and another into a House of
Correction. In 1525 there were issued the " Ordinance and
Articles touching Almsgiving ", under which all mendicancy
was strictly forbidden. An elaborate organisation, in which
elected laymen predominated, was provided for the supervision
and relief of all the various classes of necessitous folk ; vagrants
(as " poor strangers ") were permitted to pass unmolested
through the town, if they did so without begging ; and, by a
clause of enlightened humanity, soup and bread were even
provided at the public expense for such of these transients as
needed food. Both residential institutions and domiciliary
assistance in the shape of food were freely provided for the sick
and the infirm, but only conditionally on their character and
circumstances being inquired into by the pastor and a trusted
lay member of the Church.[1]

Something of the same kind may be traced in France. At
Rouen, for instance, we hear, only five years after John Major's
declaration of policy, of the Parliament of Normandy issuing
an order of February 17, 1521, organising an elaborate " police
des pauvres " in the city. It is suggested that, because of its
generality, this order failed to get put in operation ; but in
1534 another order actually set up a municipal " bureau des
pauvres ", under a joint board of eight members (four being
lawyers, two Church dignitaries, and two town councillors),
which proceeded gradually to appoint administrative officers,
collect funds, set the unemployed poor to work, distribute relief
to the impotent, and establish institutions for the children, the

---

[1] This " Ordinance and Articles touching Almsgiving " which are set forth
in *Some Early Tracts on Poor Relief*, by F. R. Salter, 1926, pp. 97-103, are
described in *Darstellung der in Deutschland zur Zeit der Reformation herrschenden
national-ökonomischen Aussichten*, by Heinrich Wiskemann, 1861, pp. 73-74.

D

sick and the infirm aged.[1] At Lyons, also, in 1531, when an
extreme dearth caused several thousand persons from the
adjacent country to take refuge in the city, the municipality
established a separate organisation for their relief. This was
developed in 1532 into a permanent department called the
Grande Aumône, which obtained grants from the King; and
in 1535 a local ordinance expressly prohibited all begging.[2]

Nor was centralised action altogether lacking. It is significant
of the common movement of thought that we find Francis I.
in 1536 ordering, in two successive edicts, every commune to
provide for its own poor, under the joint administration of the
priest and the communal officer of the time, the impotent poor
having settled residences to be maintained by doles, and the
able-bodied to be compelled to labour in return for the gifts
made to them. Registers were to be made up and kept in each
parish by the clergy and parish officers ; almsboxes were to be
placed to receive the gifts of the charitable, to which abbeys
and priories, chapters and colleges were specifically required to
contribute, whilst every Sunday the duty of every Christian to
put in his individual gifts was to be emphasised in the sermons.[3]
In Paris, indeed, a special organisation for the relief of the poor,
apparently set up by municipal action as early as 1530, was
established by Royal Ordinance in 1544. The able-bodied were
employed on various public works, whilst the impotent were

---

[1] *Documents concernant les pauvres de Rouen*, by Dr. G. Panel, 3 vols.,
1917, vol. i. p. xvi; see *Some Early Tracts on Poor Relief*, by F. R. Salter,
1926, pp. 104-119.

[2] *Institution de l'aumône générale de Lyon*, cited in *Some Early Tracts on
Poor Relief*, by F. R. Salter, 1926, p. 105. Dr. Panel cites also *Police subsidaire
. . . des poures sumenez à Lyon sur le Rosne*, 1531 ; *La Police de l'almosne de
Lyon*, 1539, two old pamphlets, in his *Documents concernant les pauvres de
Rouen*, vol. i. p. xi.

[3] *Histoire de l'assistance dans les temps anciens et modernes*, by Alexander
Monnier, 1866, p. 307 ; *Du paupérisme*, etc., by C. G. Chamborant, 1842,
pp. 92-95 ; Reitzenstein's article in Schmoller's *Jahrbuch für Gesetzgebung*,
vol. v. ; *Pauperism and Poor Laws*, by R. Pashley, 1852, pp. 192-193 ; *Early
History of English Poor Relief*, by E. M. Leonard, 1900, pp. 290-291 ; *Handwörterbuch der Staatswissenschaften*, by Elster, Weber and Wieser, 1923. A
subsequent ordinance (1566), dated as from Moulins, is said to have given the
right to demand compulsory contributions for the poor to every commune in
France, but it seems seldom to have been made use of before the nineteenth
century. The commune of Bourg-en-Bresse had a poor relief organisation as
early as 1560, and even levied—perhaps under the Royal Ordinance of 1566—
a temporary poor rate in 1573 (*Misère et charité dans une petite ville de France
(Bourg-en-Bresse) de 1560 à 1862*, by E. Ébrard, Bourg, 1866).

cared for in institutions (*hospices*). The governing body of this incorporation was expressly authorised to assess the inhabitants of Paris to meet its expenditure ; but it does not seem to have granted any powers of obtaining the money except from voluntary contributions. There seems to have been another royal ordinance by Henri II., given at Saint Germain-en-Laye on July 9, 1547, which directed that sturdy beggars should be punished by flogging and death ; but also—apparently in view of the inability of the Paris incorporation to get in its rates—required collecting-boxes to be placed in all the churches of Paris, and once more directed the preachers to use their efforts to induce the congregations to give alms, this time specifically towards the cost of the corporate administration of relief for Paris as a whole.[1] The funds still remained short, and as nothing would induce the Parisians to pay, a new Royal Ordinance was invoked on February 13, 1551, with an ingenious device for overcoming the popular reluctance. As we understand it, every householder was, by Commissioners appointed for the purpose, expressly and individually invited to assess himself, by stating what he was prepared to contribute. The replies were to be laid before the Parliament of Paris, which was then to direct payment by all according to their several capacities. We do not know the result of this fiscal device ; but it seems that more or less systematic provision for the poor continued to be made in Paris, under the organisation instituted in 1544, right down to the Revolution.[2]

It was, however, neither to Luther or Zwingli, nor to John Major or his colleagues of the Sorbonne, that England owed its penetration with the new statecraft on the laws relating to the poor ; but, as we imagine, to a brilliant Catholic humanist, Juan Luis Vives (born in 1492 at Valencia in Spain, and appointed, after studying at Paris and Louvain, at the age of

---

[1] *Pauperism and Poor Laws*, by R. Pashley, 1852, pp. 176-177.

[2] *Ibid.* ; see also *La Police des pauvres de Paris*, by G. Montaigne (? 1544), reprinted in *Bulletin de la Société de l'Histoire de Paris*, 1888, p. 105, and 1916, p. 83, and cited in *Some Early Tracts on Poor Relief*, by F. R. Salter, 1926, p. 105 ; *Documents concernant les pauvres de Rouen*, by G. Panel, 1917, p. xi ; and *Handwörterbuch der Staatswissenschaften*, by Elster, Weber and Wieser, 1923. The various "hospices" of France were made the subject of an elaborate ordinance, issued at Fontainebleau in 1561, at the instance of the chancellor, Michel de l'Hospital, who is said to have drafted also the Ordinance of Moulins in 1566 (*Essai sur la vie, les écrits et les lois de Michel de l'Hospital*, by J. E. D. Bernardi, 1807).

twenty-seven, a professor at the latter University), who, like Erasmus, with whom he collaborated, was carrying his talents where he was most befriended. In 1521 Henry the Eighth, accompanied by his Spanish consort Katharine of Arragon, and by Sir Thomas More, visited Bruges, where he made the acquaintance of Vives, whom he seems to have invited to England. In the course of the next six or seven years Vives apparently alternated backwards and forwards between London and Oxford, Bruges and Louvain, at dates about which there is some uncertainty. During this period the municipal authorities of Bruges—probably stirred like those of Ypres by the reforms actually put in operation by so many German cities—applied to him, as a person in whom (as having spent half his adult life among them) they had the fullest confidence, for advice on the knotty problem of how, in the decay of their city, to deal with its swarming poor. In response to this request Vives wrote a long report in Latin (*De subventione pauperum sive de humanis necessitatibus*), which, published at Bruges in 1526, may rank as the earliest treatise exclusively devoted to poor law policy, and may not improbably have been the " best seller " of its time. We are told, at least, that it was translated and published at Strasburg and Lyons in 1532 or 1533, and also in Italy and Spain. We cannot now prove that Vives' book was much read in England, where no English version seems to have been made ; but there is a copy in the Cambridge University Library which belonged to Thomas Knyvett, the tutor of Mary, daughter of James the First ; and it is scarcely to be supposed that so brilliant a controversialist as Vives did not talk over what he was writing, and about the movement that he knew to be taking place on the Continent, with the scholars and Court officials with whom, in Oxford as well as in London, he was actually associating at the time.[1]

Vives' report addressed to the " Consuls and Senate " of the town of Bruges, falls into two parts treating respectively of private and public charity. In the first he deals only with

[1] For the important contribution of Juan Luis Vives (1492–1540) to the history of the Poor Law, the English student could only be referred to Sir William Ashley's *Economic History and Theory*, 1893, vol. ii., and his brief notice of Vives in the second edition (1926, vol. ii. p. 631) of the *Dictionary of Political Economy* ; in supplement of the notices in the *Dictionary of National Biography* and *Encyclopædia Britannica* which do not allude to his work on

individual almsgiving and the generalities of his subject, in a conventional way ; and it is only his second part, which was so widely circulated, that need concern us. He begins—we adopt in the main the excellent summary of Sir William Ashley [1]— with impressing upon the public authorities that it is their duty, in the interest of the community, to see that the destitute are provided for. He points out, possibly under the guidance of Aristotle, that extreme inequality of possessions is likely to lead to rebellion ; he adds—what every great modern city discovers—that the slums are centres of infection and a constant source of moral contamination. He then proceeds to sketch a new poor law, taking as the foundation for it a division of destitute persons into three classes : (1) those sheltered in hospitals and almshouses, (2) homeless beggars, and (3) the honest and shamefaced poor abiding in their own houses. This classification of the destitute suggests to us that which was afterwards made the basis of the measures of Bishop Ridley and his City of London committee under Edward VI. (to be subsequently mentioned). Vives insists on the need for an accurate census of the destitute. For this purpose the magistrates should visit all charitable institutions, and secure an accurate return of their financial position, as well as a list of the inmates and the reason for their reception in each case. Two " senators "

Poor Relief, which Chambers' *Biographical Dictionary* and Chambers' *Encyclopædia* barely mention. But at last in 1926 Mr. F. R. Salter has given us an English translation, with exhaustive annotations, in his *Some Early Tracts on Poor Relief*. A Spanish reprint appeared in 1873, and another as *Tratado del Alma*, in 1916. The authorities for his life, besides the notice in the first volume of *Éloges des hommes Sçavans*, by Teissier (Utrecht, 1696), are *Mémoire sur la vie et les écrits de J. L. Vives*, by A. J. Nameche, in vol. xv. of Mémoires couronnées par l'Académie Royale de Bruxelles, 1841 ; the memoir by Rudolf Heine prefixed to his collection of *Vives ausgewählte pädagogische Schriften* (in Pädagogische Bibliothek, vol. xvi. Leipzig, 1881) ; and *Luis Vives y la filosofía des Renacimento*, by Adolfo Bonilla y Saint Martin (Madrid, 1903). There is a French monograph on him by B. Vadier (Paris, 1892), a Dutch one by W. Francken, and a German one by F. A. Lange, 1907. In England he has been known chiefly as an educationist ; see *Vives and the Renascence Education of Women*, 1912, *The Spanish Element in Vives*, 1913, *The Father of Modern Psychology*, 1915, and *Luis Vives* (in *Hispanic Notes and Monographs*, 1922), with a portrait, all by Dr. Foster Watson ; and *Education during the Renascence*, by W. H. Woodward. An edition of his *Opera*, edited by Nicholas Episcopius, was published at Basel in two great folio volumes as early as 1555 ; but the authoritative edition is that edited by Gregorio Mayans y Siscar in eight volumes, with a biography (Valencia, 1782–1790).

[1] See *English Economic History and Theory*, by Sir William Ashley, 1893, vol. ii. pp. 344-346.

should also be appointed in every parish to visit the poor householders and investigate their condition; and a list should be
drawn up of all homeless beggars, who should be medically
examined to ascertain which of them are really unable to labour.
The treatment of these various classes must be guided by two
principles : all should be made to work who are at all fit for it ;
and begging should be absolutely forbidden. For those who
are unable to work, a refuge must be found in the hospitals and
almshouses. This involves a reformation of these institutions.
All persons capable of work should be turned out ; unless they
have, unfortunately, a legal claim based on relationship to the
founder, in which case some employment must be found for
them within the establishment. In the hospitals, all the sick
should receive medical help ; the insane should be placed in
separate buildings ; the blind should be given some light work.
On the education of the children, Vives lays great stress, as the
one means of securing their moral improvement ; and he urges
the town to be generous in the provision it makes for this purpose.
As to adult beggars strong enough to work, only those should be
permitted to remain who belong to the town ; persons from
elsewhere should be sent home with journey-money ; and for
those who did remain, employment should somehow be provided.
Some could be occupied in public works ; whilst ruined handicraftsmen might be found places as journeymen at wages, or
assisted once more to set up in business. For young people
there should certainly be no difficulty in finding remunerative
employment, as the silk weavers were crying out for additional
labour. If they could be provided for in none of these ways,
it would be better to place them in an almshouse for a time than
allow them to beg in the streets. Poor householders, however,
who were ready and anxious to work, but for whom sufficient
employment could not be obtained, might be given some small
pecuniary assistance in their own homes.

But such measures as these would involve a considerable
expenditure. Vives asserted generally that in most towns the
existing hospitals were so wealthy that their revenues would
suffice for the purpose if wisely administered. The richer
foundations must help those with scantier resources, and they
must allow a part of their income to be spent on the deserving
poor in their own homes. Vives even proposed that when the

foundations in one town had a surplus, this should be shared with other and less fortunate localities. If the endowments did not suffice, they might be supplemented by bequests, by collections in church, and by what the municipality could save from unnecessary expenditure on festivities. Thus, what he proposed was the complete assumption of public responsibility for the relief of all classes of the poor, and its administration by public officers, including the setting to work of the able-bodied, but without suggesting the provision of revenue by compulsory taxation.

The policy advocated by Vives was apparently not adopted at Bruges ; but it is remarkably similar to that put in operation during the same decade at the neighbouring town of Ypres, where regulations (which seem to have been adumbrated as early as 1515, but were, in their later form, to some extent modelled on those which Lazarus Spengler had, in 1522, got adopted at Nuremberg) were successively promulgated in 1525 and 1529. Conditions at Ypres, where the population had dwindled, within a century, from nearly a hundred thousand to less than six thousand, and its cloth factories from many hundreds to a few dozens, were probably even more serious than those at Bruges ; and Vives (as Mr. Salter suggests) may have given earlier advice to the smaller town. By these regulations begging was prohibited, the relief of all the indigent was undertaken as a municipal service, a complete register of those in need was compiled, and able-bodied were provided with employment, the impotent were cared for in institutions duly reorganised for the purpose, four superintendents of the poor were appointed and paid from municipal funds, to be assisted in each parish by four citizens chosen for their local knowledge ; and the necessary revenue was supposed to be obtained in the manner that Vives was suggesting, to which all the ministers of religion were to contribute by their exhortations.

The reforms at Ypres, which were published in England in 1535, were destined to attain throughout all Christendom a temporary notoriety surpassing the work of other cities. In 1530 the four mendicant Orders represented in the town, in conjunction with part of the local clergy, made a formal and public protest against the reforms, largely, as we may infer, because of the completely secular character of the administration.

As is common with regard to all reforms in poor relief, they alleged that the deserving poor were harshly treated by the new administration; and as was natural at the time, that the whole measure was tainted with the Lutheran heresies—in particular, that the prohibition of begging, with the severe discouragement of individual almsgiving, was in contravention of the dictates of the Christian religion. The municipal authorities, which had on their side the local bishop and even the Papal Legate (Campeggio), publicly contradicted all the statements in the protest and elaborately justified their action, quoting the declaration made by John Major fifteen years before. But the religious Orders formally appealed to the Sorbonne, as the highest authority on the philosophy of religion, transmitting for this purpose a complete copy of the town regulations on poor relief. The Sorbonne, on January 16, 1531, pronounced a judgement in favour of the reforms, which, it was declared, were "useful, pious and salutary", and not repugnant to the Gospel or to the example of the Apostles and the Fathers. But the judgement went on to impose certain limitations. Begging could only be rightly prohibited if and when provision was made for all in need; and although it might be forbidden to beg, it could not properly be made penal voluntarily to give alms. In reforming institutions no encroachments must be made on the property of the Church, or of its priesthood. Nor must the townsfolk of Ypres exclude from the advantages of their beneficence the inhabitants of the adjacent rural districts in so far as these might be unable to meet their own needs. This decision of the Sorbonne made the experiment of Ypres known to the whole learned world. The German Emperor, Charles the Fifth, himself sent for a copy of the regulations; and so numerous were the requests for information that, in 1531, these regulations, together with the Sorbonne judgement, had to be published and placed on sale. This volume, unlike that of Vives, was translated into English in 1535 by William Marshall (though without the Sorbonne judgement); and it may well have influenced public opinion towards the legislation that we shall presently describe.[1]

---

[1] *Forma subventionis pauperum quae apud Hyperas Flandrorum urbem viget, universae Reipublicae Christianae longe utilissima* (Antwerp, 1531). Marshall's translation is entitled *The Forme and Maner of Subvention or Helping for pore people devysed and practised in the Cytie of Hypres in Flanders*, etc., 1535. See *Beiträge zur Geschichte und Reform der Armenpflege* by Franz Ehrle

With the subsequent development, on the Continent of Europe, of an organisation—for the most part municipal or, in rural districts, by communes—for the relief of the poor, we are not here concerned. It is, however, plain that the movement for taking the task out of the hands of the Church, and dealing with it as a part of civil government, was common to practically the whole of Western Europe. It prevailed alike in Catholic countries and in those that had adopted the reformed religion ; and in those in which the monastic institutions remained for centuries undisturbed by the law as well as in those in which they were suppressed, or became disused. The English Poor Law, emphatically summed up Sir William Ashley thirty years ago, " was but the English phase of a general European movement of reform ; it was not called for by anything peculiar to England either in its economic development up to the middle of the sixteenth century, or in its ecclesiastical history ".[1] The common impression of its insular peculiarity, which still persists, is due, we think, to a failure to appreciate the extent to which the England of the fourteenth and fifteenth centuries, and at least the earlier part of the sixteenth, was one in thought—first through the Holy Catholic Church, the religious orders and the universities, and then through the Protestant reformers of Germany and Switzerland, the Netherlands and France—with the intellectual development and the current controversies of Western Europe.[2]

(Freiburg in Breisgau, 1881) ; the article " Armenwesen : Geschichte " by J. Gerhard W. Uhlhorn in *Handwörterbuch der Staatswissenschaften* (Jena, 1890), and the corresponding article in the latest edition by Elster, Weber and Wieser, 1923 ; *Das Armenwesen der Reformation*, by Riggenbach, 1883 ; " Die Regelung der Armenpflege im 16ten Jahrhundert ", by Nobbe, in *Zeitschrift für Kirchengeschichte*, vol. x. pp. 569-580.

The incident is well described in *Economic History and Theory*, by Sir William Ashley, 1893, vol. ii. pp. 346-349 ; whilst the English text will be found in *Some Early Tracts on Poor Relief*, by F. R. Salter, 1926.

It is to be noted that the Sorbonne judgement was not universally accepted by the Church. The Spanish Dominican Domingo de Soto vehemently objected to it in his *Commentaries on the Sentences of Peter Lombard*, published in two volumes in 1569-1571 ; and the Council of Trent eventually maintained the older view in favour of individual almsgiving, and of all provision for the poor being administered by the Church (*Handwörterbuch der Staatswissenschaften*, by Elster, Weber and Wieser, 1923).

[1] *Economic History and Theory*, by Sir William Ashley, 1893, vol. i. p. 350.

[2] We may here note that the analogous development in Scotland seems to be closely coincident in date with that, not of Continental Europe, but of England. The statutes of the fifteenth century, notably those of 1425 and

The Growth of a Proletariat

But before passing to an account of the English legislation of the sixteenth century, we have to inquire what it was that started, all in the same generation, the Nominalists of the Sorbonne ; the Protestant leaders of Germany and Switzerland ; the town councillors of Bruges and Ypres, Augsburg and Nuremburg, Rouen and Lyons—even including, as we shall presently describe, in the year 1553, Bishop Ridley, the youthful Edward the Sixth and the Lord Mayor of London himself—on essentially the same project of a systematic and comprehensive provision for all the destitute, by the local municipal authority, at the public expense. We may note first the conviction, voiced by Sir Thomas More in 1516,[1] that the policy of attempting to suppress vagrancy and reduce to a proper proportion the practice of living by mendicancy, by means of penal statutes and brutal punishments, had not proved successful. In all the countries concerned, the result was a constant state of disorder and crime, with recurring tumults that passed spasmodically into organised rebellions. The failure may have seemed to some in great part due to the decay of Christian charity, and the slackening of almsgiving ; or, as others may have thought, merely to the increasing inadequacy of such an unsystematic distribution of doles to cope with the recurrent destitution of an ever-increasing multitude of free wage-labourers no longer protected by manorial custom ; of discharged retainers and disbanded soldiers thrown without resources on a labour market

---

1427, were, like those of England, aimed at vagrancy. The first act recognising local public responsibility for relieving the poor seems to have been that of 1535, which is very like the English Acts of 1531 and 1536. The subsequent Scottish statutes of 1574 and 1579 make much the same advance as the English Acts of 1572 and 1576 ; and the Scottish Act of 1597 closely resembles, in substance though not in phraseology, the English Act of the same year with the significant difference that the expenditors of relief were the (Presbyterian) Church Minister and the Elders—not the Civil officer, the Overseer of the Poor. See *History of the Scotch Poor Law*, by Sir George Nicholls, 1856 ; *The Scottish Poor Laws*, by R. P. Lamont, second Scotch edition, Glasgow, 1892 ; *The Law of Scotland regarding the Poor*, by John Dunlop, 1854 ; *The Law of Scotland relating to the Poor*, by Alexander C. S. M. Dunlop, 1825 ; *Poor Relief in Scotland*, by Alexander A. Cormack, Aberdeen, 1923.

[1] Alluding to the hordes of disorderly vagrants by which Western Europe was plagued, he says, " Neither is there any punishment so horrible that it can keep them from stealing which have no other craft whereby to get their living " (*Utopia*, by Sir Thomas More, published at Louvain in 1516).

becoming increasingly competitive; perhaps also of extruded or apostate monks, and demoralised friars or " pardoners ". We may to-day recognise the opening of the sixteenth century as a period of special economic stress, whether we emphasise the agrarian revolution that was dislocating the manorial organisation, or the growth of manufactures in the towns, involving the production of an urban proletariat; or the rapid increase of commerce, with its unsettlement of one national industry after another. More general causes may be sought in the effect upon current prices in England of the inward flow of the precious metals—to some extent facilitated by the reopening of the German silver mines—in those periods in which the balance of trade led to such an importation, combined with such successive reductions in weight of the current coin of the realm as those carried through under Henry the Eighth and Edward the Sixth.[1] We cannot estimate the relative potency of causes so disparate in their nature. One thing is clear. As was noted by Eden in 1797, the upgrowth of a great body of people continually in a state of destitution, coincided generally with the creation of a numerous class depending for a livelihood entirely on being hired for day-labour at wages. " When the nation ", he observed, " consisted principally of the two classes of landholders and servile cultivators, the latter had, at least in ordinary times, a fund to which they could resort for maintenance ; and although they could not acquire property, they were, in general, certain of food ; because it was the obvious interest of those who could command their services to provide for their support. A West India island is, perhaps, a tolerable picture of the condition of the agricultural class in this country soon after the Conquest.

[1] The years 1519–1521 were years of dearth and terribly high prices in England, as were those of 1527–1531, 1535–1536, 1545–1546 and 1549–1556 (*Records of Seasons, Prices, etc.*, by T. H. Baker, 1885). Between 1511 and 1561 Thorold Rogers estimated that the price of food rose by at least 50 per cent, whereas the rates of wages, always lagging behind and falling short, had risen only 15 per cent by 1550, and only 30 per cent by 1561 (*History of Agriculture and Prices*, by J. E. Thorold Rogers, vol. iv. pp. 292, 355, 524, 545, etc.). Successive " debasements " of the English currency (meaning, rather, reductions in weight of the coins) were made in 1527, 1543, 1545, 1546 and 1551. But when, under Elizabeth, the coins were restored in weight, the rise in prices continued to a higher point than before ; and we may perhaps pray in aid of an explanation the effect of what were, by this time, the growing importations into Europe of the precious metals from the New World, if not also the development of silver mining in Germany, the distribution from country to country being determined by temporary shifting of the balance of trade.

The proprietor of a sugar plantation . . . is bound to feed the negroes belonging to his establishment, whether they are disabled by sickness, accident or old age. . . . The capital stock of Yorkshire [in 1797] is, perhaps, ten times as great as that of the island of Jamaica ; and yet the number of those who, in that part of England, have no visible means of support, and subsist entirely on charity, I doubt not exceeds those in Jamaica of a similar description, in as great a proportion. Rousseau justly inquires, ' Why it is that, in a thriving city the poor are so miserable, whilst such extreme distress is hardly ever experienced in those countries where there are no instances of immense wealth ? ' [1] I should answer that, in cities, people are more poor because they are more independent than in the country. It is one of the natural consequences of freedom that those who are left to shift for themselves must sometimes, from either misconduct or misfortune, be reduced to want. This, however, furnishes no solid argument against the blessings of liberty. A prisoner under the custody of his keeper may perhaps be confident of receiving his bread and his water daily ; yet I believe there are few who would not, even with the contingent possibility of starving, prefer a precarious chance of subsistence from their own industry to the certainty of regular meals in a gaol." [2]

The Tudor Legislation

If we distinguish between merely penal statutes, threatening dire punishment to sturdy beggars or unlicensed vagrants, and those which command and direct that definite provision, of one

---

[1] *La Nouvelle Héloïse*, by J. J. Rousseau, of which a translation had been published (*Julia, or the New Eloisa*) àt Edinburgh in 1794.

[2] *The State of the Poor*, by Sir F. M. Eden, 1797, vol. i. pp. 58-59. The coincidence between the coming of the free wage-labourer and an organised public provision for the destitute cannot, in the nature of things, be exactly proved. The decay of villainage was a gradual process extending over several centuries, but it was pretty complete by 1460 ; see *Villainage in England*, by Paul Vinogradoff, 1892 ; *The End of Villainage in England*, by T. W. Page (New York, 1900) ; *The Great Revolt of 1381*, by Sir Charles Oman, 1906. Villainage is mentioned as a survival in 1529, and Queen Elizabeth emancipated some serfs on the Royal Demesne in 1574 (*Observations on the More Ancient Statutes*, by Daines Barrington, 1795, pp. 307-309 : " Bondmen under the Tudors ", by A. Savine, in *Royal Historical Society's Proceedings*, 1905) ; see *Introduction to Economic History*, by E. Lipson, 1915, pp. 109-112 ; *The Agrarian Problem in the Sixteenth Century*, by R. H. Tawney, 1912.

or other sort, should be made for the destitute,[1] we find the earliest English law that we can recognise as one for the relief of the poor in the statute of Henry the Eighth, in 1531, significantly entitled " How Aged Poor and Impotent Persons compelled to live by alms shall be ordered ". The English Parliament, nearly a decade after action had been taken by various Flemish and German cities—in the very year in which the Emperor Charles the Fifth issued his comprehensive ordinance on the relief of the poor—had got so far as to recognise that the impotent poor needed to be provided for ; but it contented itself in that year with directing the Justices to give them licences to beg, each being assigned to a defined district.[2]

The next step, twenty years after the declaration of John Major, one year after Marshall's translation of the Ypres book, and significantly in accord with the royal ordinances of Charles the Fifth and Francis the First, was to make it a duty of the officials of the Local Authority to look after the poor. In 1536, the Act of 27 Henry VIII. c. 25 (which was enacted before the

---

[1] It has sometimes been said (as by Sir F. M. Eden, *The State of the Poor,* 1797, vol. i. p. 63) " that the English Poor Law dates really not from Elizabeth but from 1391 " (*The Mediaeval Village,* by G. C. Coulton, 1925, p. 380). But the statute referred to, 15 Richard II. c. 6, which was confirmed by 4 Henry IV. c. 12, merely requires impropriators of benefices, as a condition of a licence, to allocate " a convenient sum of money " annually to " the poor parishioners of the said churches, in aid of their living and sustenance for ever, and also that the vicar be well and sufficiently endowed ". As a matter of fact, there is no evidence that this made any provision for the destitute. How little was even expected may be judged from the Royal Articles and Injunctions of 1559 which declared that " non-resident clergy with an income of over £20 must distribute a fortieth of it among the poor, and those with an income over £100 must provide three and a third per cent towards exhibitions for poor scholars at the Universities " (*Elizabethan Episcopal Administration,* by W. P. M. Kennedy, 1924, vol. i. p. xlii).

Begging, too, was regulated and partly forbidden, by statute, in France in 1360, in England repeatedly between 1360 and 1388 (and the latter Act has also been claimed as the earliest Poor Law), as well as in various German cities soon afterwards (*Handwörterbuch der Staatswissenschaften,* by Elster, Weber and Wieser, 1923) ; but this, too, was no provision for the destitute.

[2] 22 Henry VIII. c. 12 ; a temporary Act continued by successive statutes, and not repealed until 1624 by 21 James I. 28 ; see *History of England,* by J. A. Froude, vol. i. (1856), pp. 66-80 ; and *The State of the Poor,* by Sir F. M. Eden, 1797, vol. i. p. 82. " This statute is the first which can be said to make any provision for the relief of poverty ; the previous legislation is wholly directed against vagrancy alone " (*Pauperism and Poor Laws,* by R. Pashley, 1852, pp. 172-174). The statute was novel in its placing the responsibility on the local Justices of the Police ; and in its twofold classification of the poor (*Tudor Constitutional Documents,* by J. R. Tanner, Cambridge, 1922, pp. 467-494).

abolition of the monasteries in the same year), ordered that
the mayor, bailiffs, constables and other head officers of cities,
towns and parishes should " succour, find and keep all and every
the same poor people ", in such wise " as none of them of very
necessity shall be compelled to wander idly and go openly in
begging to ask alms ".   This put the responsibility on the parish
or borough officers.   It is true that these officers were not
authorised to employ for this purpose any of the corporate
funds of their respective places, or to levy the compulsory tax
that Luther had suggested for Leisneck in 1523.   But the head
officers of corporate towns, and the Churchwardens or two others
of every parish, were definitely ordered, as Luther and Zwingli
had advised, and as Vives had expressly recommended, to obtain
money " by gathering and procuring of such charitable and
voluntary alms of the good Christian people within the same,
with boxes every Sunday, holiday and other festival day, or
otherwise among themselves ", so that, in fact, enough might
be got together to enable all " the poor impotent, lame, feeble,
sick and diseased people, being not able to work ", to be fully
provided for.   The clergy were to help by exhortations ;   a
" book of reckoning " was to be kept in each parish ;   and, most
far-reaching of all, the giving of alms, or the making of any
collection, otherwise than to and for " the common boxes and
common gatherings for the purposes of the Act ", was made
illegal and penalised.[1]   Here we find Parliament doing its best
to establish a nation - wide organisation, the public officers of
every parish, township or borough being, for the first time,
definitely charged with the duty of maintaining the impotent
poor ;   the whole of the alms and charitable funds of the place
being concentrated in their hands for this purpose ;   and considerable pressure being brought to bear to make these funds
adequate to the requirements of this new public service.   For

---

[1] This important Act, which assumes, be it noted, the existence of the monastic houses, is cited most fully in *The State of the Poor*, by Sir F. M. Eden,
1797, vol. i. pp. 83-87 ; see also *History of England*, by J. A. Froude, vol. i.
(1856) pp. 66-80 ; *History of the English Poor Law*, by Sir George Nicholls,
1854, vol. i. pp. 121-125 ; *Pauperism and Poor Laws*, by R. Pashley, 1852,
pp. 174-176 ; *Tudor Constitutional Documents*, by J. R. Tanner, Cambridge,
1922, pp. 467-494.   " This statute is the first in which the State not only enacts
that the poor shall be provided for in their own neighbourhood, but also makes
itself responsible for the administration of relief and the raising of funds "
(*Early History of English Poor Relief*, by E. M. Leonard, 1900, pp. 54-56).

a whole generation reliance continued to be placed on voluntary contributions, the pressure exercised on the contributors being steadily increased.[1]

The City of London

The next important step was taken by the Corporation of the City of London, where (as in Paris) the massing of an indigent population, and the plague of vagrancy, had become acutely felt. In 1538 the Corporation was making desperate efforts to save from confiscation and dissolution at least the larger ecclesiastical foundations in the City, which provided beds for the poor and treatment for the sick. The King, in 1544, so far acceded to this request as to refound, with partial endowment, both St. Bartholomew's Hospital (and, as may be added, in 1552 also St. Thomas's Hospital) on condition that the citizens would provide funds for their maintenance. But the attempt to obtain sufficient revenue from voluntary contributions—on which, down to this time, the Poor Law reformers in Germany and the Netherlands, France and Switzerland, as well as those of England had been mainly relying—proved a failure even in the wealthy City of London. The result was the first definitely assessed

[1] By 1 Edward VI. c. 3 (1547) the curate of every parish is specially ordered to preach at them "according to such talent as God has given him". By 5 and 6 Edward VI. c. 2 (1551), two or more special collectors are to be elected in church, who are, from a complete list of householders, to importune every man and woman for promises of weekly contributions, and to inscribe in the book how much each thus promises. Moreover, if any person refuses, the parson and churchwardens are to go at him ; whilst if he still refuses, the bishop is to send for him, " and so take order according to his discretion ". By 1 Mary c. 13 (1553) and 2 and 3 Philip and Mary c. 13 (1555), these provisions are more explicitly renewed, and the bishop is to " take order for the charitable reformation of every such obstinate person " (*Tudor Constitutional Documents* by J. R. Tanner, Cambridge, 1922, pp. 467-494). Unfortunately, we have been unable to investigate the extent to which these Acts were put in operation, or their results (but see *Elizabethan Episcopal Administration*, by W. P. M. Kennedy, 1924, vol. i. p. cxxxvi).

Miss Leonard notes that at Lambeth there is a book made in accordance with the provisions of "the Act 5 and 6 Edward VI. c. 2, entitled ' A Register Book of the Benevolence of ' the Parishioners for the Relief of the Poor ', etc. . . . particularly every man's name and what his devotion is to give weekly towards the sustentation of their poor neighbours according to the King's proceedings ", etc. (*Historical Particulars of Lambeth Palace . . . in addition to the Histories*, etc., by Samuel Denne, in *Miscellaneous Antiquities in continuation of the Bibliotheca Topographica Britannica*, by J. Nichols, 1791, etc. : *Early History of English Poor Relief*, by E. M. Leonard, 1900, pp. 57-58).

compulsory Poor Rate in Great Britain. In 1547 the Common
Council resolved that the Sunday collections in the churches
should be abandoned, and that, instead of these voluntary contributions, " the citizens and inhabitants of the said City shall
further contribute and pay towards the sustentation and maintaining of the said poor personages the moiety or half-deal of one
whole fifteenth ".[1] At this, we are told, the whole City " not
a little grutched and repined " ; but at least some money was
obtained. For the ensuing decade we may trace a succession
of struggles to get the several institutions put on a satisfactory
financial basis ; to extract, from the Corporation, the Livery
Companies and the charitable citizens the necessary revenue
for their maintenance ; and to call into existence an organisation that would be definitely responsible for the whole of the poor
of the City. We see Latimer and Lever and Ridley preaching
eloquent sermons and making appeals to Cecil and the Privy
Council for further help ; the young king (Edward VI.) taking
the matter up in 1551 and 1552 with successive Lord Mayors
(Sir Richard Dobbs and Sir George Barnes) ; and in 1553 a
comprehensive scheme for dealing with all classes of the poor—
a scheme in which we may detect traces of Vives' scheme or
Marshall's book—being drawn up by a committee of twenty-
four leading citizens who were evidently greatly influenced by
Ridley (Bishop of London) and the Lord Mayor. " In the end,"

---

[1] *MS. Journals of the Common Council of the City of London*, vol. 15 (1547),
p. 325.   This order is printed in *Tudor Economic Documents*, by R. H. Tawney
and Eileen Power, 1924, p. 305.   The whole story is well told in *The Early
History of English Poor Relief*, by E. M. Leonard, 1900, pp. 27-40.   For the
subsequent history of the London Bridewell, see *The Order of the Hospitals of
King Henry the VIIIth and King Edward the VIth*, 1557 (in British Museum) ;
*Remembrancia, or Records . . . of the City of London, 1579–1664 ; Memoranda,
References and Documents relating to the Royal Hospitals*, 1836 ; *Extracts from
the Records and Court Books of Bridewell Hospital*, 1798, and *Remarks upon the
Report of a Select Committee on Bridewell Hospital*, 1799, both by the Rev. Thomas
Bowen ; *Bridewell Royal Hospital Past and Present*, by A. J. Copeland, 1888 ;
A Familiar and Friendly Discourse, etc., by John Howe, 1582 ; and a second
Familiar and Friendly Discourse . . . Government of the Poor within this City,
1587, by the same, both privately reprinted by Christ's Hospital, and largely
given in *Tudor Economic Documents*, by R. H. Tawney and Eileen Power, 1924,
vol. iii. pp. 415-443.   For incidental references, see the annals of Stow, Pennant
and Maitland ; *The Autobiography of Thomas Ellwood* ; *The London Spy*, by
Ned Ward, 1703 ; *Solitude in Imprisonment*, by Jonas Hanway, 1776 ; the
fourth plate of Hogarth's " Harlot's Progress " ; *The London Prisons*, by
Hepworth Dixon, 1850 ; and *English Prisons under Local Government*, by S. and
B. Webb, 1922.

Holinshed records,[1] " after sundry meetings (for by means of the good diligence of the Bishop it was well followed) they agreed upon a book that they had devised, wherein they first considered of nine special kinds and sorts of poor people, and those same they brought in these three degrees :—

" Three degrees of poor . . . .
{ The poor by impotency.
Poor by casualty.
Thriftless poor.

" 1. The poor by impotency are also divided into three kinds, that is to say,
{ 1. The fatherless poor man's child.
2. The aged, blind and lame.
3. The diseased person by leprosy, dropsy, etc.

" 2. The poor by casualty are of three kinds, that is to say,
{ 4. The wounded soldier.
5. The decayed householder.
6. The visited by grievous disease.

" 3. The thriftless poor are three kinds in likewise, that is to say,
{ 7. The rioter that consumeth all.
8. The vagabond that will abide in no place.
9. The idle person, as the strumpet, and others."

For the first two " degrees ", in their six kinds of poor, some provision could be made in the three great hospital foundations, together with Christ's Hospital, which had been founded for fatherless children on the land formerly belonging to the Grey Friars. What seemed to be needed to complete the scheme was suitable provision for the third " degree ", the most intractable part of the problem. Bishop Ridley had already applied to Cecil for a grant of the " wide, large, empty house of the King's Majesty called Bridewell " (at Blackfriars). The City Committee proposed to deal, in these or other premises, with the " beggars fallen into misery by lewd and evil service, by wars, by sickness or other adverse fortune ", whom " few or none dare or will receive . . . to work ". For these there had to be some general provision of work " wherewith the willing poor may be exercised, and whereby the froward, strong and sturdy vagabond may be compelled to live profitably to the commonwealth ".[2] For

[1] *Chronicles of England, Scotland and Ireland*, by Raphael Holinshed, 1577 ; repeated in *Historie and Lives of the Kings of England*, by William Martyn, 1615, enlarged by B. R., 1638, cited in Ninth Annual Report of Poor Law Commissioners, 1843, p. 279.

[2] *Chronicles of England, Scotland and Ireland*, by Raphael Holinshed, 3 vols., 1577.

It is, of course, not to be assumed that all this effort by the City of London

this " setting to work ", the committee proposed to induce City traders to supply raw material to be worked up, taking back the manufactured wares, and paying the equivalent of the value that had been added by labour. The trades first suggested were cap-making, feather-bed making and wire-drawing. But though the City Committee desired to have the use of the King's Palace mainly as a place in which to set to work the able-bodied, and perhaps chiefly those of bad character and conduct, it is typical of that generation that this was regarded as but part of the problem, which was to provide for all the various classes of destitute persons.

To quote the Act of the Common Council of February 28, 1555, the institution was to be " partly for the settling of idle and lewd people to work, and partly for the lodging and harbouring of the poor, sick and weak, and sore people of the city, and of poor wayfaring people repairing to the same ". Eventually the scheme received the approval of the Privy Council ; the whole array of " hospitals " was placed under a special committee of the Corporation, consisting of fourteen aldermen and fifty-two Common Councillors ; the King's Palace at Bridewell was granted to the Corporation for the purpose ; and between 1555 and 1557 an entirely new institution seems to have been started, which, during the ensuing century, became the model and supplied the popular name for innumerable " Houses of Correction " all over the country.

Provincial Town Councils

The financial expedient which Luther had suggested in 1523, and to which the City of London had been driven in 1547, was

---

led, in fact, to anything like a complete provision for the destitute. In 1569 the Privy Council felt bound to address an earnest injunction to the City to make more generous provision by the alms of the charitable. " It will be necessary ", runs this injunction, " to provide charitably for such as shall be indeed found unfeignedly impotent by age, sickness or otherwise to get their living by labour ; and for those we earnestly, and in the name of God . . . require and charge you . . . to consider diligently how such of them as dwell within your jurisdiction may be relieved in every parish, by the good order that is devised by a late Act of Parliament ; and that they be not suffered to wander or be abroad, as commonly they do in the streets and highways for lack of sustentation. . . . We think it good that the Bishop . . . be moved by you in our name to direct commandment to the Curates or Ministers in all churches to exhort the parishioners to give their common alms at their churches ", etc. (Common Council Journals, June 1569 ; see *Early History of English Poor Relief*, by E. M. Leonard, 1900, p. 52).

presently adopted in some other English municipalities. In 1557 we find the systematic assessment of the annual value of all but the smallest houses, and the compulsory rating of all the householders for the relief of the poor, definitely ordered by the Town Council of Colchester, payment being summarily enforced by imprisonment and " fine and ransom " at the discretion of the Bailiffs of the Town.[1] At Ipswich, in the same year, the Town Council ordered that " if any inhabitant refuse to pay such money as shall be allotted to him to pay for the use of the poor he shall be punished at the discretion of the Bailiffs ". By 1579, at any rate, these contributions had apparently become, as at Colchester, regular assessments according to the annual value of the premises.[2]

Parliament adopted compulsory measures in 1563. In that year, twenty-seven years after the statutory assumption of the duty of poor relief, the contribution of the householder was, by 5 Elizabeth c. 3, though with much circumlocution, at last made everywhere definitely compulsory on the basis of " ability to pay ". The bishop of each diocese was authorised to bind any person or persons who " of his or their froward wilful mind, shall obstinately refuse to give weekly to the relief of the poor according to his or their abilities ", under penalty of £10, to appear at the next sessions of the Justices, and if any one refused to be so bound, the bishop might commit him to prison. At their next sessions, the Justices were again to " charitably and gently persuade and move the said obstinate persons to extend his or their charity towards the relief of the poor ". If any one

[1] The " Ordinances made by the Bailiffs, Aldermen and Common Council of This Town ", 15 February 1557, in the Mote Hall, " provide that every house, warehouse or shop within the said parishes shall be rated by three or four honest persons of the same parish, and to pay by the year 8d. of the Noble and no person to pay for any house that is rated at 3/4d. and under by the year ". Any one refusing payment of what he is charged " from time to time, and from week to week for and towards the provision for the said poor " is to be reported to the Bailiffs, who " shall commit him or them to prison there to remain till he hath fully paid his said rate, and such other portion of money as shall be by the Bailiffs, thought condign for his fine and ransom " (*History of Essex*, by Philip Morant, 1768, vol. i. p. 180).

[2] *Annals of Ipswich*, by Nathaniel Bacon, 1654, p. 237. At Norwich we see the same process of voluntary contributions passing, in 1570, into regular exactions enforced by punishment, the old voluntary contribution being at first made the basis of assessment, whilst newcomers were individually assessed by the mayor at a proper sum (Orders in the Mayor's Book for the Poor, 1571–1578, etc. in Norwich Corporation MSS. ; *Records of the Corporation of Norwich*, by W. Hudson and J. C. Tingey, 1906–1910 ; *Tudor Economic Documents*, by R. H. Tawney and Eileen Power, 1924).

still refused, the Justices were to impose a tax on him " according
to their good discretions ", in default of payment of which,
" together with the arrearages thereof, if any ", he might be
committed to prison until payment was made.   Here, at length,
we have, in germ, the legally compulsory and universally payable
Poor Rate.[1]   Nine years later, by 14 Elizabeth c. 5 (1572), the
law was codified, and the whole organisation simplified.   The
" aged poor, impotent and decayed persons " who had been
born within each division of the county or had resided there
for three years,[2] were to be actually sought out, registered and
assigned to " meet and convenient places . . . for their habita-
tions and abidings " ; the Justices were straightway to ascertain
what the weekly charge would be for maintaining them, and
immediately to tax and assess the inhabitants, and appoint
collectors of this weekly rate, along with Overseers of the Poor,
an office in which service was made obligatory.   Finally, we
have in this Act what may be considered the first faint beginning,
for the whole country, of that public provision for the able-
bodied which Vives had urged in 1526, and which the City of
London had adopted in 1555.   Whilst once more re-enacting
the severe penal measures against idlers and beggars, rogues
and vagabonds, the statute of 1572 provides (but only if there
are in any place surplus funds after the needs have been met of
the impotent poor) that the Justices may " place and settle to
work the rogues and vagabonds ", either born within the county,
or being three years resident therein, " there to be holden to
work to get their livings and to live and be sustained only upon

---

[1] The passing of 5 Elizabeth c. 3 (for which see *Tudor Constitutional Documents*, by J. R. Tanner, Cambridge, 1922, pp. 467-494) is barely mentioned,
without particulars, in Sir Symonds D'Ewes's *Journals*, 1682, pp. 70-72.   It
may here be noted that the Act of 1563 (though repealed by that of 1572),
in the section enabling the districts for which chapels of ease had been provided
to act as separate authorities for Poor Relief, began the disintegration of the
extensive parishes of the North of England (*Liverpool Vestry Books, 1681-1834*,
by Henry Peet, 1912, vol. i. p. xix), in which, by the Act of 1662, all the separate
townships of parishes outside corporate boroughs were permitted to set up
for themselves in the administration of Poor Relief, as if they were separate
parishes.

[2] It will be seen that the law did not, as yet, provide for the relief, at the
expense of the compulsory Poor Rate, of any but the poor who " belonged "
to the parish.   This was the view which Coke is reported to have held, even a
generation later, when he seems to have said that " he did not know that a
foreigner had a right to be maintained in any place to which he came ; but that
they might let him starve."

their labour and travail ".[1]   This provision was explained and
made more effective by the amending Act of 1576 (18 Elizabeth
c. 3) which directed the Justices to " appoint and order " that
" a competent stock of wool, hemp, flax, iron and other stuff "
should be obtained at the cost of the rates, and given in charge
to the mayor or other head officer or other persons in each place,
as the Justices might decide.   These " collectors and governors
of the poor " were to order and direct the " working of the said
stock ", paying for the work done and selling the commodities
manufactured in order to replenish the capital stock " to the
intent every such poor and needy person, old or young, able to
do any work, standing in necessity of relief, shall not, for want
of work go abroad, either begging, or committing pilferings or
other misdemeanours living in idleness ".   Moreover, recalcitrant
or careless workers might be committed to a House of Correction
to be established in each district by the Justices, evidently on
the model of the City of London " Bridewell " (of which we
have described the establishment, more than a quarter of a
century previously, as a semi-penal institution), there to be
" straitly kept as well in diet as in work, and also punished
from time to time ".[2]

[1] " This statute of the fourteenth of Elizabeth was probably occasioned by
a printed *Petition against the Oppressors of the Poor,* which Ames mentions to
have been dispersed with considerable industry in the year 1567, and repre-
sents to have been written with great spirit " (*Observations on the More Ancient
Statutes,* by Daines Barrington, 1795, p. 536 ; citing *Typographical Antiquities :
Account of Printing in Great Britain and Ireland,* by Joseph Ames, 1785, p. 272 :
and enlarged edition by T. and F. Dibdin, 1810–1819).   We do not know in
what sense Barrington added : " The statute of the fourteenth of Elizabeth,
which relates to the poor, was a very oppressive law ".
  We may note here a curious usage of the House of Lords.   At the close of
each session there seems to have been a " collection for the poor " among the
peers.   In 1572 it is noted that " four lords were appointed to make the usual
collection for the poor " (*Observations on the More Ancient Statutes,* by Daines
Barrington, 1795, p. 537).
  [2] This Act (18 Elizabeth c. 3), barely mentioned in Sir Symonds D'Ewes's
Journals, p. 198, also introduces us to the standing problem of the destitution
of the unmarried mothers of illegitimate children.   This statute directed the
Justices to make an order charging either the mother or the reputed father with
the cost of the keeping of such child, with imprisonment in default of payment.
  The principal sections of the Acts of 1572 and 1576 are conveniently given
in *Tudor Economic Documents,* by R. H. Tawney and Eileen Power, 1924, vol. ii.
pp. 328, 331.   The full text is given in *Tudor Constitutional Documents,* by
J. R. Tanner, Cambridge, 1922, pp. 467-494 ; and in *Some Early Tracts on Poor
Relief,* by F. R. Salter, 1926.
  These two statutes were made temporary in duration, but they were
successively continued in force by 27 Elizabeth c. 2, 29 Elizabeth c. 5 and

A Comprehensive Poor Law

Here, then, in 1572–1576, we have a comprehensive Poor Law, nominally extending to every part of the kingdom, aiming at a complete and systematic maintenance, in the parishes to which they belonged, for all sections of the indigent needing relief, including for the first time (apart from mere penal repression) a definite provision for the unemployed able-bodied, whose labour, presumably usually as home-workers at piecework rates, was to be effectively organised by the public officers, with a penal institution in the background for those only who refused to work, or otherwise misbehaved themselves.

That these statutes were taken seriously, and widely promulgated, we may infer from the learned William Lambard, whose *Eirenarcha*, a treatise on all the duties of a Justice of the Peace, first published in 1581, remained authoritative for a

---

31 Elizabeth c. 10, until they were replaced, first by 39 Elizabeth c. 3 and then by 43 Elizabeth c. 2.

The designations of the officers of the parish varied according to local usage from generation to generation. We may well believe, with Toulmin Smith, that an office analogous to that of Overseer (of a parish) is of some antiquity, the very name having possibly been applied in some places to the person appointed to collect the alms or other contributions of the parishioners, who is mentioned, says Toulmin Smith, in the Year Books (44 Edward III.), and in the old law manual *Doctor and Student* (*The Parish*, by Joshua Toulmin Smith, 1857, p. 178). Such collectors were statutorily authorised by 27 Henry VIII. c. 25 (1536) and 5 and 6 Edward VI. c. 2 (1552). We see in the Vestry Minutes of Steeple Ashton (Wilts) "distributors" appointed by the Vestry in 1573, and again in 1623, in addition to "collectors". The Municipal Ordinance of Colchester, in 1557, already cited, speaks of Surveyors of the Poor (*History of Essex*, by Philip Morant, 1768, vol. i. p. 180), which recalls the Surveyor of Highways which each parish had been directed to appoint by the Act of 1555. The first mention of Overseers in the statute-book is in the Act of 1572 (14 Elizabeth c. 5), where the term is applied to an additional officer to be appointed by the Justices expressly to supervise the labour of the rogues and vagabonds set to work by the Justices' order; whilst "collectors" were also to be appointed by the Justices. It was an innovation of the Act of 1597 (39 Elizabeth c. 3) to unite, in the new office of Overseer of the Poor, the collection of the rates, the setting of the able-bodied poor to work and the relief of the impotent poor; and to require the Justices everywhere to make the appointment. But it seems that the term was not everywhere adopted, or the appointment formally made, for more than a century. At Bishops Stortford (Herts) the collectors went on until 1653, and no Overseer was appointed until 1650 (*Records of St. Michael's Parish Church, Bishops Stortford*, by J. L. Glasscock, 1882, p. 158). At St. John's, Chester, there were no Overseers until 1704, but merely "collectors of the Poor's Rate", who paid the money to the Churchwardens (*Lectures on the History of St. John the Baptist Church and Parish*, by S. Cooper Scott, 1892, p. 124).

century or more. His subsequent manual, *The Duties of Constables*, etc., issued in 1583, includes chapters on the duties of Collectors and Overseers for the Poor, Collectors and Governors of the Poor, and Censors or Wardens and Collectors for the House of Correction. Unfortunately there has been, as yet, little investigation as to the extent to which they were actually put in operation or the way in which they worked. That the Churchwardens were enjoined by the bishops to relieve the poor we may believe.[1] But we imagine that only in an infinitesimal proportion of the 15,000 parishes and townships, or the couple of hundred cities and boroughs, was any compulsory Poor Rate actually levied prior to 1598. It became apparently gradually more usual, though we imagine very far from universal, for the parish officers, especially in the cities, out of any funds at their disposal, to relieve the impotent poor by small money doles, the funds being provided, where there was no compulsory taxation, from charitable endowments, from bequests and donations, from the fines for breaches of particular statutes and from voluntary contributions. It happens to be recorded that the parish officers of Stratton in Cornwall report to the Justices in January 1595 that their parish stock " amounts to the now sum of sixteen pounds " ; and they give the names of ten orphan children " wholly relieved " by the parish, and add that there are more than a hundred poor " which are not able to live of themselves but have relief daily, one thing or another, of the said parish ".[2] More was done in the boroughs than in the rural districts, though probably not in greater proportion to the local needs. We know of such relief being systematically organised, for instance, at Newark, at Colchester and at Norwich. In the borough of Newark in 1570, we find the Alderman and the Assistant for each ward charged to present at each monthly court the names of all poor and sick people, and of such as lack fuel. In the

[1] *Elizabethan Episcopal Administration*, by W. P. M. Kennedy, 1924, vol. i. pp. cxxxvii-cxl.

[2] *Records of the Charity known as Blanchminster's Charity, Stratton*, by R. W. Goulding, 1898, pp. 64-65 ; *The Elizabethan Parish in its Ecclesiastical and Financial Aspects*, by Sedley L. Ware, Baltimore, 1908, pp. 61-62.

Incidentally we hear that " A poorhouse at Waltham Cross was undertaken, and J. S., a chapman, was empowered to collect benevolences for it. His wife got leave to pass through the country at a time the plague was raging in Leicester (1593)" (*Hist. MSS. Com.* VIII. Appendix I. p. 432 ; *Growth of English Industry and Commerce in Modern Times*, by Archdeacon William Cunningham, vol. i. third edition, 1896, pp. 46-47).

accounts of 1585 there are items for clothing distributed.[1] The
" Orders for the Poor " of the Town Council of Norwich in 1571
are exceptionally elaborate ; and with the records of the preceding year, showing poor people living in the " Church " or
" Parish " houses, and others receiving weekly alms, they
indicate a systematic, if not a complete provision for the resident
destitute.[2] We find, in 1580, the mayor of Liverpool, then in
the infancy of its corporate independence, levying £20 in order
to set the poor to work, under the statute of 1576.[3] Systematic
collections continued to be made at church, as at Colchester in
1585, where by warrant of the bailiffs four successive Sundays
were appointed on which the proceeds at all the churches in the
borough (which proved to be very small) were devoted to the fund
for the relief of the poor.[4] Moreover, we know that in various
cities and boroughs at least, notably in Canterbury, Colchester,
King's Lynn, Leicester, Lincoln, Norwich, Rochester, St. Albans,
Windsor and York, there were, at different dates during the last
quarter of the sixteenth century, now and then stocks of raw
material provided, such as flax, wool and hemp, partly out of
specific bequests or donations,[5] but certainly sometimes partly out

---

[1] *Extracts from the Records of the Borough of Newark-upon-Trent*, by R. F. B.
Hodgkinson, 1921, pp. 36-37.
[2] See the extracts given in *Tudor Economic Documents*, by R. H. Tawney
and Eileen Power, 1924, vol. ii. pp. 313-326 ; and *Records of the Corporation of
Norwich*, by W. Hudson and J. C. Tingey, 1906-1910.
[3] *Rise and Progress of Liverpool from 1551 to 1835*, by James Touzeau,
2 vols., 1910; *Liverpool Vestry Books, 1681-1834*, by Henry Peet, 1912, vol. i. p. xx.
[4] *History of Essex*, by Philip Morant, 1768, vol. i. p. 181.
[5] For the next hundred years or so, benevolent testators frequently bequeathed small sums to be used " for setting the poor to work ". Investigation
of charity records, which are notoriously incomplete, revealed forty-six such
bequests between 1572 and 1692 (*History of English Philanthropy*, by B.
Kirkman Gray, 1905, p. 61). A certain proportion of these bequests were made
to the local government authorities.
    Of King's Lynn we read, " This year (1581) a great deal of money was laid
out about St. James's Church, in fitting it up and preparing it for a workhouse
for the employment of the poor in making of bays, etc., which not answering
the charge was in a short time disused. . . . Divers poor people were this
year (1586) set to work at the new building at St. James's in dressing of hemp
and making strings and tows for fishermen ". . . . Continued ill success seems
to have led to a final abandonment of the institution in 1623, when the church
was pulled down (*History and Antiquities of King's Lynn*, by Benjamin
Mackerell, 1738).
    At Leicester we find the Mayor and Corporation in correspondence with the
Earl of Huntingdon between 1584 and 1599 as to an arrangement in the former
year for setting the poor to work on spinning, by means of £100 lent from
Corporation funds to one of their number (Leicester Corporation MSS. in
Hist. MSS. Com. Report, VIII. Appendix I. pp. 430-433).

of public funds ; in some towns in an institution, with primitive machinery and technical instructors, but apparently in other cases given out to be worked up in the people's own homes. Moreover, it is known that the disciplinary institution contemplated in the 1576 Act was set up, not only, as heretofore, in the boroughs but also by the County Justices in certain counties. At their Easter sessions in 1583 the Kent Justices made " ordinances for the House of Correction, Maidstone . . . to be put in execution within the Lathes of Aylesford and Sutton-at-Hone ".[1] There is preserved in the British Museum [2] an elaborate set of orders and rules agreed to, presumably under the authority of the statutes of 1572 and 1576, by the Justices of Suffolk at their Quarter Sessions at Bury St. Edmunds on May 31, 1589, for the " punishing and suppressing of rogues, vagabonds, idle, loitering and lewd persons ", for whose reformation the Justices direct the building, within the town of Bury, of " one convenient house which shall be " called the House of Correction ", for the administration of which, under the authority of the statutes of 1572–1576, including the " setting to work " of able-bodied persons needing relief, a minute and all-embracing code of rules is prescribed. We hear vaguely, in the still very partially explored records of the Municipal Corporations and Quarter Sessions, of similar institutions in the latter part of the sixteenth century at Exeter, Gloucester, King's Lynn, Liverpool, Ipswich, Reading and Winchester ; in the parish of Twyford in Berkshire ; in the county of Somerset ; and in the West Riding of Yorkshire.[3] Between 1572 and 1597 " there are

---

[1] In Lambard's MS. (Additional MSS. 41137 in British Museum) ; see Miss B. H. Putnam's article, entitled " Lambard's *Eirenarcha* and a Kent Wages Assessment of 1563 ", in *English Historical Review*, April 1926.

[2] Harleian MSS. 364 ; *The State of the Poor*, by Sir F. M. Eden, 1797, Appendix VII. pp. cxxxvi-cxlvi ; *History of Vagrants and Vagrancy*, by C. J. Ribton-Turner, 1887, pp. 116-119.

[3] See, for these provincial Houses of Correction, apart from the City of London Bridewell, *Annalls of Ipswich*, by Nathaniel Bacon, 1654 ; *Records of the Borough of Reading*, by Charles Coates, 1802 ; *History of Essex*, by Philip Morant, 1768, vol. i. p. 102 ; " The City of York in the Sixteenth Century ", in *English Historical Review*, April 1888, p. 288 ; *Exeter*, by E. A. Freeman, 1887, p. 177 ; *Bristol*, by Samuel Seyer, 1821–1823, vol. ii. p. 248 ; *History of Gloucestershire*, by Samuel Rudder, 1779, p. 190 ; *The State of the Poor*, by Sir F. M. Eden, 1797 ; *Early History of English Poor Relief*, by E. M. Leonard, 1900 ; *History of English Philanthropy*, by B. Kirkman Gray, 1905 ; *English Prisons under Local Government*, by S. and B. Webb, 1922, pp. 12-17.

innumerable instances in which men and women ' strong and
fit for labour, but having neither masters nor lawful vocations
whereby to get their living ' were adjudged to be vagrants and
ordered to be whipped and then ' burnt through the gristle of
the right ear '. . . . In two months in the early winter of 1591
seventy-one such poor labourers were whipped and burned
through the ear in Middlesex." [1]   It is thus clear that, already by
1590, before the legislation of 1597-1601, all the characteristic
forms of the Poor Law of 1601-1834 were sporadically in operation, with the Overseers of the Poor in close association with the
Churchwardens of the parish ; under the direction simultaneously
of the Parish Vestry and its chairman the rector or vicar, in
some respects also of the archdeacon in his annual visitations,
and at all times of the local Justices of the Peace, who appointed
the Overseers and passed their accounts ; whilst the Quarter
Sessions of the County, or its Sheriff, the Judges on their circuits,
and even the bishop of the diocese would, as we shall presently
describe, be transmitting Orders from the Privy Council of the
King.   This national system of organisation, of what was a not
clearly distinguished combination of penal treatment by hard
labour of the undeserving able-bodied man, the provision of
remunerative employment for the involuntarily unemployed, a
certain amount of indulgent institutional maintenance of orphans
and the " impotent poor ", with a stream of small doles to all
kinds of poor folk, was, we must conclude, very far from amounting to provision for all the indigent even in the relatively few
places in which anything more than voluntary almsgiving was
introduced.[2]   It is loudly complained in 1583, that though there
are hospitals, spittles, lazarhouses and almshouses in some cities,
towns and other places, wherein many poor were relieved, yet

---

[1] *History of England*, by Edward P. Cheyney, vol. ii. 1926, p. 333 ; *Middlesex
Quarter Sessions Records*, by J. C. Jeaffreson, 1887, pp. 43, 101, 109, 190, etc.
   [2] We may note here that, in the last decade of the century, statutory
provision was made, outside the Poor Laws, for the maintenance of " poor,
sick and maimed " soldiers and sailors discharged from the Queen's service.
By successive Acts in 1593, 1597 and 1601 (35 Eliz. c. 4 ; 39 Eliz. c. 21 and
43 Eliz. c. 3) they were to be relieved, not by their parishes but by their counties;
but the county was to be reimbursed by a charge, to be settled by Quarter
Sessions, upon all the parishes, not exceeding sixpence per week on any parish
(*Journals of all Parliaments*, etc., by Sir Symond D'Ewes, 1682, pp. 492-518 ;
Historical MSS. Commission Reports (Hatfield House MSS., vol. iv.) pp. 295-
300 ; *History of England*, by Edward P. Cheyney, vol. ii., 1926, pp. 252-255 ;
History of Vagrants and Vagrancy, by C. J. Ribton-Turner, 1887, p. 130).

those relieved are " not the hundredth part of those that want ". [1] Moreover, there are indications that, in some places where definite provision for the poor had been made after the Acts of 1572 and 1576, the business was presently neglected and the provision abandoned. This brings us to the renewed outburst of legislation of 1597–1601, which is most conveniently dealt with as belonging to the seventeenth century.

[1] *The Anatomie of Abuses*, by Philip Stubbs, 1583, part 2, p. 43 ; see *History of English Philanthropy*, by B. Kirkman Gray, 1905, p. 15. Two pamphlets of this decade, the forerunners of many, are entitled *A Politic Plot for the Honour of the Prince, the Great Profit of the Public State, Relief of the Poor, Preservation of the Rich, Reformation of Rogues and Idle Persons and the Wealth of Thousands who know not how to live*, by Robert Hitchcock, 1580 ; and *Provision for the Poor now in Penurie Out of the Storehouse of God's Plentie*, explained by H. A[rth], 1597.

CHAPTER II

THE ADMINISTRATIVE HIERARCHY OF 1590–1640

DURING the sixteenth century the important stages in the evolution of systematic public provision for the indigent are, as we have seen, in the present state of our knowledge, to be traced mainly in the isolated experiments in the towns and the successive Parliamentary enactments. In the first half of the seventeenth century, or rather from 1590 to 1640, what was of greater importance than the legislation was the attempt, gradually developing out of the orders of the Privy Council, and continued for half a century, at the establishment of an administrative hierarchy, by which it was sought to get the laws relating to the economic condition of the poor systematically put in operation all over the kingdom.[1]

[1] In this chapter we have been much assisted by the extensive collection of facts brought together from many sources in *The Early History of English Poor Relief*, by E. M. Leonard, 1900. The principal contemporary records of national character are the Privy Council Register, and the *State Papers (Domestic)*, for James I. and Charles I. The Privy Council Register does not contain all the documents issued; and the volumes from 1602 to 1612 are missing from the series. Thus Miss Leonard does not mention the important Privy Council Order of June 23, 1605, which is recorded in Quarter Sessions archives, and is given in full in *Three Centuries of Derbyshire Annals*, by J. C. Cox, 1890, vol. i. pp. 4-6; and also in *Quarter Sessions from Elizabeth to Anne*, by A. H. A. Hamilton, 1878, pp. 67-71; nor the serious admonition of the Justices in December 1609 (*ibid*. pp. 77-80).

The absence from the Privy Council records of the two volumes containing the entries from January 1, 1602, to April 30, 1613, has been variously explained. It has been said that Charles I. carried them off in 1641 when he left for the North; and also that they were burnt in the fire at Whitehall in January 1619 (*Tudor Constitutional Documents*, by J. R. Tanner, Cambridge, 1922, p. 213). But three of the volumes noted in the contemporary list as burnt have since turned up. Meanwhile there has lain at the British Museum (Add. MSS. 11402) a volume purchased in 1838, which is evidently a contem-

We may conveniently open with the celebrated legislation of 1597–1601, on which the attention of the later Poor Law annalists has been concentrated, and which certainly gave to the whole system of poor relief the moulding which it has ever since preserved. We have not traced in the local archives, or in contemporary literature, with any particularity, the causes of this new crop of statutes, but it is to be inferred that in the last quarter of the sixteenth century the social condition of the manual working class was changing considerably for the worse. Wheat, barley and rye rose, after 1573, almost continuously in price, the scarcity culminating, in the cold and rainy years 1594–1598, in dearth almost amounting to famine.[1] The changing organisation of the countryside, with the steady increase in sheep-farming and the decline of tillage, the spread of the practice of enclosure and the complete disappearance of the old tie of serfdom, must have been felt most severely in times of scarcity. The years 1596–1597 were specially critical periods " of privation, high prices and threatened internal rebellion. . . . Extreme poverty . . . was so apparent . . . as to become the principal subject of legislation in the Parliament that met in 1597. . . . The main case . . . was the rain. . . . Stow reports that ' this summer, by reason of much rain and great floods, corn waxed scant '. . . . Grain rose to famine prices . . . from five to eight times prices normally prevailing in modern times. . . . ' It maketh the poor to pinch for hunger and the children to cry in the streets not knowing where to have bread.' . . . The effort of the Privy Council and of county and town authorities to secure food for the people . . . sprang partly from fear of popular

porary abstract of the Privy Council Register from 1547 to 1611; and thus covers most of the period for which the Register itself is still missing (*Acts of the Privy Council*, edited by J. R. Dasent, vol. xxv. (1595–1596), 1901, pp. vii-xii ; vol. xxxii. (1601–1604), 1907, pp. vii-viii ; *Acts of the Privy Council*, edited by H. C. Maxwell Lyte (1613–1614), 1921, pp. v-ix). The vain attempts of Charles Greville, as Clerk to the Council, in 1843, to obtain the restitution of this volume to the Privy Council Office, are mentioned in his *Journal of the Reign of Queen Victoria from 1837 to 1852*, 1885, vol. ii. pp. 162-164.

The local records of county, municipal corporation and parish, few of which are yet printed, have still to be searched for traces of local action upon the communication from Whitehall. We have found most useful the records of the Justices' action in the North and West Ridings, Worcestershire, Hertfordshire, Nottinghamshire and Middlesex.

[1] " In 1587 wheat rose to £3 : 4s. the quarter ; in 1594 it was £2 : 16s. and in 1595, £2 : 13 : 4 the quarter " (*The State of the Poor*, by Sir F. M. Eden, 1797, vol. i. p. 134) ; and in 1597 it even reached £5 : 4s.

insurrection. . . . Apprehension of general disturbance was by no means unwarranted. . . . Unemployment was frequent, poverty was everywhere . . . there was . . . constant danger of revolt ".[1] The towns were full of beggars. Men and women " died for want in the streets ".[2]   Here and there the Justices and Municipal Corporations attempted to keep down the price of corn, both by orders fixing, for each local market, a maximum price, and by purchases in bulk—as at Norwich in 1595 of " rye from Danske "[3] (Danzic)—in order to sell to the poor at low rates.   It is clear that much more than the customary amount of destitution and distress forced itself upon public notice.   There were periodical disturbances in London and various other parts of the country which were sometimes scarcely to be distinguished from rebellions. Repeated statutes of great severity, Privy Council proclamations and special Commissions had failed to repress an increase of vagrancy.[4]

The Legislation of 1597–1601

When a new Parliament met in October 1597, after an interval of four years, there was a rush of members to make speeches and to introduce bills connected with the distress and

---

[1] *History of England*, by Edward P. Cheyney, vol. ii., 1926, pp. 1-36 ; see also the same author's *Social Changes in England in the Sixteenth Century*, Boston, 1895.

[2] Here are three entries from the Town Council Minutes, Newcastle-on-Tyne, in 1596-1597 : December 1596, " Paid for the charge of burying 7 poor folk which died in the street " ; September 1597, " Paid for the charges of burying 9 poor folks who died for want in the streets " ; October 1597, " Paid for the charge of burying 16 poor folks who died for want in the streets " (*The Local Historian's Table Book of Remarkable Occurrences*, etc., by Moses A. Richardson, 1841-1846, Historical Division, vol. iii. p. 44).

[3] *Essay towards a Topographical History of Norfolk*, by Francis Blomefield, 1739-1775, vol. ii. Norwich : *Records of the Corporation of Norwich*, by W. Hudson and J. C. Tingey, 1906-1910.

[4] Thus, Stow reports royal proclamations of 1580 and 1583, seeking to put down the " many inconveniences " of vagrancy, mendicity, overcrowding and extreme poverty in the rapidly growing Metropolis (*Survey of London*, by John Stow, vol. ii. pp. 34-35 of Strype's edition of 1755).   Another proclamation of 1593, and a Privy Council Order of the same year, related to the like evils (*History of London*, by W. Maitland, 1775, vol. i. pp. 275-276).   In 1597 a special commission under Privy Seal was issued, appointing Sir Thomas Wyllford to provost-marshal, with large powers for suppressing " unlawful assemblies ", in and about the metropolis, with power summarily to hang offenders on gallows or gibbet (*Pauperism and Poor Laws*, by Robert Pashley, 1852, pp. 211-212).

the discontents.[1] Presently those whom we should nowadays designate the Queen's Ministers got these bills, to the number of a dozen or more, referred to a large and influential committee, including among its members both Francis and Nicholas Bacon, both Thomas and William Cecil, with Coke and most of the lawyers in the House, which was charged to report on the subject generally, and which met almost continuously for weeks in Middle Temple Hall.[2] Meanwhile, the House of Lords was also discussing the subject, and eventually appointed its own committee, including Lord Burleigh and a dozen other lay peers, Archbishop Whitgift and half a dozen bishops, along with the four principal judges, which considered also the bills sent up from the House of Commons. The *Journals* of Sir Symonds D'Ewes give glimpses of much lively debating, and of great interest taken by members, interspersed with a quarrel between the two Houses as to procedure, in which there is visible more concern for the maintenance of their respective privileges and dignities than either knowledge of the subject or senatorial wisdom. In fact, the legislative outcome of these prolonged deliberations upon the social problem, though of apparent bulk and great historic importance, was not remarkable for inventiveness or novelty. The House of Commons Committee recommended, and both Houses in January passed, a set of six statutes dealing respectively with the maintenance of tillage (39 Elizabeth c. 2) and the means of obviating the decay of townships (39 Elizabeth c. 1), in favour of both of which Bacon pleaded with warmth and eloquence;[3] with the punishment of rogues,

---

[1] The proceedings of this session are succinctly reported in Sir Symonds D'Ewes's *Journals*, 1682, pp. 551-592 ; for the best account, see *History of England*, by Edward P. Cheyney, vol. ii., 1926, pp. 259-272.

[2] Among other members were Sandys, who had sat on a similar committee in 1576, and Edward Hext, a Somerset Justice, who had been in communication with Cecil in 1596 as to vagabonds in his neighbourhood, of whom he sent a picturesque account (see *Acts of the Privy Council*, by J. R. Dasent, vol. 25, 1901 ; and *History of Vagrants and Vagrancy*, by C. J. Ribton-Turner, 1887, pp. 125-128, 491-492). The Committee met regularly in Middle Temple Hall for a couple of months. (The reason for meeting in Middle Temple Hall was the lack at Westminster of rooms large enough for committees of fifty or more.) Its proceedings may be followed in the *Journals of all Parliaments*, etc., by Sir Symonds D'Ewes, 1682 ; *Historical Collections of the Last Four Parliaments of Elizabeth*, etc., by Heywood Townshend, 1682 ; *Early History of English Poor Relief*, by E. M. Leonard, 1900, pp. 73-80 ; *Pauperism and Poor Laws*, by Robert Pashley, 1852, pp. 206, 212-215.

[3] See his speech in Sir Symonds D'Ewes's *Journals*, pp. 551-552. Some " Notes on 39 Elizabeth c. 1 and 2 " are given in *Historical MSS. Commission*,

vagabonds and sturdy beggars (39 Elizabeth c. 4), which passed only by 106 to 60 ; with the prevention of deceits and breaches of trust in charitable endowments (39 Elizabeth c. 6) ; with the erection of hospitals, or " abiding and working houses " for the poor (39 Elizabeth c. 5) ; and, finally, with a comprehensive measure for the relief of the indigent (39 Elizabeth c. 3). It is unnecessary to deal here with any of these statutes except the last-named, which appears—to use modern phraseology—to have been drafted by the Government for the House of Commons Committee, in substitution for all the other measures referred to the Committee by the House.   And even this measure (which, as re-enacted with only slight amendments in 1601, is still mainly in force as the basis of the existing legal duty to relieve) did little more than re-enact, in simpler and more systematic form, the legislation of 1572–1576 that we have described. There is, however, a significant shifting of emphasis. The 1597–1598 statute for the first time puts in the forefront the civil power, by requiring the appointment, in every parish, of Overseers of the Poor, and by specifically imposing on them, in conjunction with the Church-wardens, the duty of providing for all the various classes of the destitute, whether able-bodied or impotent, children or aged, lame or blind, or otherwise " without means to maintain them-selves ".   There is no specific restriction to those belonging to the parish.   There is no longer any reliance on voluntary contri-butions. The Overseers are directed to raise whatever funds they require by a direct levy, " weekly or otherwise ", upon every occupier within the parish. The Justices of the Peace,[1] whose part in the levy is reduced to a mere formal allowance of the Overseers' rate, are given the duty of supervising and directing the work of the Parish Officers. Parents having the means to do so are made legally liable to maintain their own children and grandchildren ; and, also if they have the means, children their parents and grandparents, but (a fact often over-looked) only if such parents or grandparents are unable to work

---

part xiv., Addenda, p. 27 ; and reproduced in *Tudor Economic Documents*, by R. H. Tawney and Eileen Power, 1924, vol. i. pp. 88-89.

[1] This Act included a provision in which may be found the germ of the subsequent practice of allowing an appeal to Quarter Sessions against any order of one or more Justices. By Section 5, any person having a grievance against the Poor Rate assessment, or complaining of any act of a Justice, could appeal to Quarter Sessions.

for their own living. The Justices are empowered to commit to the House of Correction (or, as provided in 1601, alternatively to the common gaol) any one refusing to work ; and also to issue a warrant of distress against, and commit to prison, any one failing to pay the Poor Rate. Finally, by an extraordinary provision, which remained in the law, in substance, for nearly three centuries, the Justices are authorised, if any parish is unable to raise enough for the support of its own poor, to levy any other parish or parishes within the same hundred for such sums by way of " Rate in Aid ", as the Justices may think fit.[1] What Bacon, Cecil and Coke are to be credited with, along with their colleagues on the committee, is the redrafting of various halting and confused statutes of past years into one that was (especially as re-enacted in 1601) drastic and direct, explicit in its commands and practically enforceable.[2]

The Action of the Privy Council

The most important step taken in the last decade of the sixteenth century was, however, not the somewhat pretentious

[1] The law was made known in the City of London by a pamphlet entitled : *Certain Articles concerning the Statute lately made for the Reliefe of the Poor, to be executed in London by the Churchwardens and Overseers of every Parish according to the effect of the same Statute,* 1599.

[2] We have not discovered why the 39 Elizabeth c. 3 (1597–1598) was re-enacted in the very next session of Parliament—which gave all its thought, and nearly all its time, to the burning topic of " the monopolies ", and their bearing on " the Queen's Prerogative "—with only slight alterations, as 43 Elizabeth c. 2 (1601). An interesting pamphlet, entitled *A Provision for the Poor now in Penury,* by H[enry] A[rth], 1597 (see *Tudor Economic Documents,* by R. H. Tawney and Eileen Power, 1924, pp. 444-458), throws some light on the extent to which the law was being put in operation, and some of the difficulties of the problem. Moreover, it appears that the judges, on being consulted, had held that the liability to pay the Poor Rate applied to the incumbent and the tithe-owner, and the owner of saleable woods, equally with other inhabitants or occupiers. These decisions were explicitly embodied in the 1601 Act. That statute also (1) made the number of Overseers optional, whether two, three or four, according to the custom of particular parishes ; and enlarged the prescribed date for their annual appointment from Easter week to within a month after Easter ; (2) added gaol to House of Correction, as a place to which offenders might be committed ; (3) made it clear that the apprenticeship of a female child terminated with her marriage before 21 ; (4) removed slight ambiguities as to the powers of Justices of Municipal Corporations and Aldermen of London, and as to parishes lying in two jurisdictions ; (5) prescribed a penalty of £5 on Justices neglecting to appoint Overseers—a penalty that we have never found to be inflicted. The provisions of the Acts of 1597–1598 and 1601 are conveniently contrasted in *The Early History of English Poor Relief,* by E. M. Leonard, 1900, pp. 133-138 ; see also

F

deliverance of Parliament, in its litter of statutes—which effected no great alteration in the substance of the law as laid down in 1572–1576, and might, by themselves, probably have wrought no greater changes in the administration—but the decision apparently made some time between 1586 and 1597, by the principal officers of the Crown, acting as the Privy Council, to establish a centralised administrative hierarchy which should ensure the execution of the law in all the thousands of parishes and townships of England and Wales.

This remarkable episode, which covers practically half a century, deserves more detailed examination than it has yet received. We entertain no doubt that its authorship is to be ascribed to the fertile brain and administrative energy of Lord Burleigh, but its origin is at present unknown to us ; and we can only piece together such scraps of information as have been incidentally afforded. The activities of the Privy Council had been steadily growing during the latter decades of the sixteenth century. In the earlier part of the century these orders seem to have been concerned mainly with the prevention of vagrancy and tumult—in short, with the security of the realm and the maintenance of law and order. Gradually we see them, with increasing frequency, endeavouring to prevent an actual shortage of food, and the high prices occasioned thereby, by compelling farmers to bring to market their hoarded stocks, putting pressure on corn-dealers, causing maximum prices to be fixed in local markets, and promoting both the purchase of corn in bulk from abroad and its distribution to the poor at less than cost price. In the special stress of 1586–1587 this action of the Privy Council was elaborated into a nation-wide policy. We see Burleigh himself drafting a lengthy and detailed proclamation, formally consulting the principal judges (Popham, Mildmay and Manwood) as to its terms, laying it before the Council, and sending it not only to the Lord President of the Council of the North and the Lord President of the Council of Wales, but also to all the sheriffs, and through these, to all the Justices of the Peace ; whilst the Archbishops of Canterbury and York were also writing to all the bishops to direct every clergyman to co-operate by his

---

Eirenarcha, by William Lambard, 1599 ; *The Country Justice*, by Michael Dalton, 1618 ; *History of Local Rates*, by Edwin Cannan, 1896 and 1913 ; and *Tudor Constitutional Documents*, by J. R. Tanner, Cambridge, 1922.

exhortations. This lengthy order, with the accompanying letters, directed the appointment of juries to make a minute and comprehensive survey of all the corn in possession of every citizen, the number of persons in his household, and a rigid rationing of each household, the amount in excess of its own bare requirements until the next harvest (including seed) being peremptorily ordered to be brought to market and sold at a moderate price. But there was a significant addition to the foodstuffs policy. The Justices, with the help of the juries, were commanded to ensure that, not only " the maimed and hurt soldiers " but also " all other impotent persons ", should " be carefully seen unto to be relieved " ; and the Justices were " to do their best to have convenient stock to be provided in every division or other place, according to the statute, for setting the poor to work ".[1]

Here we have an explicit assumption by the Privy Council of the duty of seeing to it that the whole nation is protected from dearth ; [2] and, what specially concerns us here, also of ensuring that the measures for the relief of the poor, both impotent and able-bodied, are actually put in operation. Incidentally we may note the institution of what is to-day an obvious administrative device, namely, the insistence on reports being promptly made by the local agents as to the action taken by them. In this case, as became habitual for the ensuing half-century, the local agents were principally the unpaid Justices of the Peace, then between one and two thousand in number, whose office and functions we have elaborately described,[3] together with the

---

[1] The draft of this remarkable order, extensively corrected in Burleigh's own hand, is among his papers (Lansdowne MSS. in British Museum No. 48) ; and it is printed in *The Early History of English Poor Relief*, by E. M. Leonard, 1900, pp. 318-326. See also *Calendar of State Papers (Domestic)*, vols. 188-189 ; Privy Council Register, vol. xiv. p. 277. For a detailed appreciation of Burleigh's administrative activity, see the remarkable chapter contributed by Miss Lilian Tomn (afterwards Mrs. Knowles, Professor of Economic History at the London School of Economics) to the 3rd edition of *The Growth of English Industry and Commerce in Modern Times*, by Archdeacon W. Cunningham, vol. i., 1896, pp. 53-84; and *The Great Lord Burleigh*, by Martin A. S. Hume, 1898.

[2] With the wisdom and efficacy of the Privy Council policy in respect of the dearth and high price of foodstuffs we are not here concerned. It is interesting to find the Justices of Hertfordshire reporting their opinion, on March 16, 1631, that " this strict looking to the markets is an occasion that the markets are the smaller, the corn dearer, and new shifts and devices found out to prevent doing of good which they cannot meet withal " (*Calendar of State Papers (Domestic)*, vol. 186).

[3] *The Parish and the County*, by S. and B. Webb, 1906.

mayors and other magistrates of the Municipal Corporations. In their reports, which exist for many counties, we see the Justices individually allotted to districts of which they undertake the superintendence ; they make detailed enquiries as to the stocks of corn held in the farmers' households, and the amount required in each for food and seed ; they report how much of the hoards they have required to be sent to market ; in some cases they fix the price at which the grain must be sold ; they personally attend the markets, and persuade the sellers to accept a reasonable price ; in some places a lower price is fixed for poor purchasers, and occasionally benevolent Justices bear the loss of resale to the poor at prices far below market rates.[1]

The Privy Council Order of 1587 was understood as aiming more at ensuring the public food supply than at enforcing the relief of the poor ; and such of the Justices' reports as are extant are usually less specific as to the administration of the Poor Law. But the Gloucestershire Justices declare that they have " seen the poor relieved as we may " ; those of Bedfordshire say they have appointed " Overseers to see in our absence all things duly performed as well for the relief of the poorer sort as otherwise " ; those in charge at Hemlingford specially directed the " collectors " (under the statute of 1572) to see to it that the poor, aged and impotent persons within every township and hamlet be sufficiently relieved as they ought to be ", and to add a weekly supply to the same former relief ", which had become " too slender for them by reason of the dearth ". These Justices also directed the " Overseers " (also under the statute of 1572) to make sure " that all the poor and idle persons in every township and hamlet, which are able to labour and want work, be

---

[1] We may quote an extract from one of these reports. " The Justices of Gloucestershire say that in their several allotments they have ' visited the marketts, seen the poore relieved as we may, searched the barnes, storehouses and grenyers of farmers and others hable to furnishe the marketts with corne, and having consideration to theyr private families have in discretion appointed them a certeyne quantytie of certen kindes of graine to be by them brought weekelie to the markett accordinglie, and of such our appointments have kepte books in writinge and doe finde therapon, that as yet the said farmers and others doe fulfill our appointments in this behalfe without any disobedyence. And further according to the said your lettres we have sett downe several prices upon everie kinde of graine within the severall divisions of this Shire, as in respecte of the distaunce of the places and the present tyme of necessytie we have thought most convenyent, after which rate we will herafter in our several limitts have care to see the same solde as may be beste for the relief of our poore neighbours ' " (*Calendar of State Papers* (*Domestic*), vol. 189, 50).

daily set to work . . . towards the getting of their living ".
More specifically, the Justice in charge of the Blithing Hundred
of Suffolk reported that he had directed that five hundred poor
persons in adjacent townships should be relieved with " bread
and other victual " for the space of twenty-three weeks.[1] But
the particular interest for us of the Order of 1587, and its
execution by the Justices, lies in the fact that it seems to have
been this Order that furnished the model for the centralised
direction of the local administration which marked the following
decades.

In view of the large part assigned to the Justices of the
Peace in the administrative hierarchy that the Privy Council was
establishing, it may be significant that, in 1590, the form of the
Commission of the Peace, which had got into a confused state by
constant additions, was remodelled. Such a revision had been
asked for by the lawyers, notably by William Lambard ; and it
was now undertaken at the instance, apparently, of what we
should now term the Government. A series of conferences of
the judges seem to have been held, under Sir Christopher Wray,
the Chief Justice of the Queen's Bench, Sir Edmund Anderson,
the Chief Justice of Common Pleas and Sir Roger Manwood,
Chief Baron of the Exchequer. These conferences resulted in a
completely redrafted commission, which was approved by the
Lord Keeper, Sir Christopher Hatton, and adopted for the
future.[2] Whether or not this remodelling of the Commission
had any significance in this connection, there soon follows a
stream of communications from the Privy Council to the various
Quarter Sessions, in which it is sought to tighten up the
administration. On October 20, 1592, the Lords of the Council
wrote at length to four trusted " commissioners " in the County
of Devon—and, we imagine, similarly for other counties—insisting on a complete reorganisation of the Justices, their regular
summons to sessions, and their diligent discharge of the important

---

[1] See the reports in *Calendar of State Papers* (*Domestic*), vols. 189-200.

[2] *Eirenarcha*, by William Lambard, who incorporates the new form of the
Commission in the new edition of 1599 ; *History of English Law*, by John
Reeves, vol. v., 1829, p. 228 ; *Select Statutes and Constitutional Documents*, by
G. W. Prothero, 1894, pp. 144-149 ; *The Office of Justice of the Peace in England*,
by Charles Austin Beard (Columbia University Studies), 1904, pp. 141-143,
168-171. The form thus settled in 1590 remained unchanged until 1875
(*Tudor Constitutional Documents*, by J. R. Tanner, Cambridge, 1922,
p. 453).

duties committed to them.[1] The substance of many previous
orders and proclamations for maintaining order and repressing
disturbances is emphasised. In the following years the Justices
were repeatedly incited by orders and proclamations to enforce
the laws for the relief of the poor and the restraint of the multitude of vagrant persons. In July 1595 the Lords of the Council
were again suggesting to the Justices that corn should be obtained
for sale to the poor at lower prices—a step which the Devon
Justices, though admitting that the number of impotent poor is
increasing, report to be unnecessary.[2]

The Queen's Government may be credited with another
device. It had formerly been usual for an oration to be given
at the opening of the session of the law courts at Westminster,
at which many Justices of the Peace attended. This custom
had fallen into disuse, and in 1595 the Lord Keeper Puckering,
who had succeeded Sir Christopher Hatton, seems to have
specially summoned to the Star Chamber the magistrates of
the counties adjacent to London, and others living in its
vicinity, in order to deliver to them an address which he
declared had been specially committed to him and the Lord
Treasurer by the Queen herself. The Justices were to see to it
that the laws regulating corn-dealing were rigorously put in
operation ; they were themselves to attend the markets, and both
to persuade, and to use their authority to compel, the farmers
to bring all their stocks to market ; the Justices were even
to raise money among themselves and other well-to-do persons,
so that they might buy corn in bulk to be retailed without
profit ; they were not to stay in the Metropolis but immediately
to repair to their county seats and enforce all the laws " with a
Herculean courage ". Finally, they were warned what would
happen if they failed in diligence in executing the Orders that
they received. Her Majesty, said Burleigh, " like a good house-
wife looking unto all her household stuff ", had had the list of
names before her, and had with her own hand marked those
who were no longer to remain in the Commission of the Peace ! [3]

[1] Privy Council, October 20, 1592 ; in Devon County archives, printed in
full in *Quarter Sessions from Elizabeth to Anne*, by A. H. A. Hamilton, 1878,
pp. 324-326.
[2] Privy Council, 1595, in Devon County archives, see *ibid.* p. 17.
[3] *Les Reportes des Cases in Camera Stellata, 1593-1609*, by John Hawarde,
edited by W. P. Baildon, 1894, pp. 21 and 50 ; *History of England*, by Edward P.

On Christmas Day, 1596, letters were sent by the Privy Council to the Archbishops of Canterbury and York, and another to the Lord Mayor of London, instructing them to require all the clergy, and all local officers, to press for the observance of the prescribed times of fasting, and for the prevention of waste of victuals, in order to relieve the existing scarcity ; and at the same time to co-operate in the relief of the poor, and in the work of the Collectors for the Poor appointed under the recent statutes.[1]

In 1597 the Devonshire Justices (and probably those of other counties) received an order from their Lord Lieutenant, who had apparently been directed by the Privy Council to stir the Justices to more energetic action to see that the statutes relating to vagrants and the relief of the impotent poor were universally enforced. Quarter Sessions thereupon issued drastic commands to the Constables in all the parishes to " take a view " of all the poor, and also of all the wealthier folk, and report what they found. Every substantial householder was to give free meals, according to his ability, to one, two or more of the poor ; and in default might be called upon to pay eighteenpence per week for each. A special rate was to be levied to provide a stock on which to set the poor to work.[2] At Liverpool, in the same year, we see the Mayor and Corporation induced to institute a list of persons in receipt of poor relief, to set up a poor box for voluntary contributions, and to enter into negotiations for the taking on lease of premises for use as a House of Correction.[3]

We see the new organisation definitely at work in the issue

Cheyney, vol. ii., 1926, pp. 317, 383. An oration to much the same effect was repeated in July 1596 when Egerton had become Lord Keeper after Puckering's death.

[1] Privy Council, December 25, 1596 ; in *Acts of the Privy Council*, edited by J. R. Dasent, vol. xxvi. (1596–1597), 1902, pp. 380-386. Orders were sent on December 19, 1596, and February 10, 1597, that no hindrance was to be put in the way of corn purchased abroad for the relief of scarcity at Shrewsbury and Bristol (*ibid.* pp. 374-375, 479-480). The Mayor of Carmarthen was severely rebuked for excessive consumption of corn for the undue number (80) of local alehouses ; and he was threatened with revocation of charters (*ibid.* p. 390).

[2] Privy Council letter of April 1597 in Devon County archives ; see *Quarter Sessions from Elizabeth to Anne*, by A. H. A. Hamilton, 1878, pp. 15-16.

[3] *Rise and Progress of Liverpool from 1551 to 1835*, by James Touzeau, 1910, vol. i. pp. 133-134 ; *Memorials of Liverpool*, by Sir James Allanson Picton, 1875, vol. i. pp. 114-115 ; *Liverpool Vestry Books, 1681–1834*, by Henry Peet, 1912, p. xx.

by the Privy Council, on April 5, 1598, to all the High Sheriffs and Courts of Quarter Sessions in England and Wales, of a general explanation of the series of new statutes of the preceding session, and a grave injunction as to their enforcement by the Justices in their several neighbourhoods.[1] It can be inferred that Overseers were being appointed in many parishes, and that the statutes of 1597–1598 and 1601 were actually being put in operation, first from the publication in 1601 and 1602 of the earliest batch of separate manuals for Poor Law officials,[2] of which there have since been so many ; and secondly, from the fact that numerous cases of doubt as to the interpretation of the law had, for several years, evidently been coming before the Judges. In 1601, indeed, an " exposition " by the Judges of the statute of 1597–1598, with a series of " resolutions " on particular points, was authoritatively communicated to all Quarter Sessions, so that Justices might know what to do in matters of removal and chargeability, and in respect of the liability to the Poor Rate of incumbents, tithe-owners, colliery proprietors and owners of saleable timber.[3]

How the various Courts of Quarter Sessions were moved to activity is seen from the records of the West Riding, where an important series of " Orders for the Relief of the Poor " was enacted in 1597, directing that no one be allowed to beg outside his own parish, that each parish must relieve its own poor, that no one who has been resident three years shall be removed, and no one at all without a Justice's order, that even persons travelling with a certificate shall be stopped and sent back if they have completed three years' residence in the parish from which they have been dispatched, as none but rogues and wandering beggars ought to be removed, that men able to work shall be compelled

[1] Privy Council Register, April 5, 1598. Of this letter Miss Leonard remarks that " it is the first time in which this interference (of the Privy Council) seems primarily dictated by motives of humanity and not mainly by a desire to maintain order " (*Early History of English Poor Relief*, by E. M. Leonard, 1900, pp. 143-144).

[2] *An Ease for Overseers of the Poor abstracted from the Statutes* (Cambridge, 1601) ; cited in *History of the English Poor Law*, by Sir George Nicholls, 1854, vol. i. p. 218 ; see also *The Effect of the Act of Parliament made (for the Relief of the Poor) in the 43rd year of the Reign of our Sovereign Lady Queen Elizabeth, abbreviated and collected for easier execution, especially of so much thereof as concerneth the Churchwardens and Overseers*, 1602.

[3] *Eirenarcha*, by W. Lambard, 1599 ; *History of Local Rates*, by Edwin Cannan, 1896 and 1913.

to do so, and that this order be proclaimed in every market town.[1]

Even more explicit were the Justices of Essex, whose " Orders for the Relief of the Poor in Essex " for 1598 happen to have been preserved. Quarter Sessions directs that in those parishes in which no Overseers have yet been named, they are now to be named by the Justices of the several Divisions. It is ordered that, with the exception of vagabonds, no persons of three years' residence are to be removed from the parishes in which they are, except in so far as may be ordered by the Justices in lawful cases. Provision is made for one principal House of Correction for the County (at Coxall, now Coggeshall), and for no fewer than twenty-two subsidiary ones in the different Divisions of the County.[2]

The centralised direction does not cease with the demise of the Crown, and was, indeed, specially effective in 1603, just after Elizabeth's death. In September 1603 we see the Privy Council directing the Burgesses of the City of Westminster at once to disburse £100 in relief of the poor, which the Privy Council will repay as soon as practicable. In October 1603 Sir Nicholas Mosley is peremptorily told to inform those persons who were refusing to pay their Poor Rate in Lancashire that they must pay at once, or appear before the Council. In January 1604 all the Justices of the Peace of Lancashire are called upon to express their several opinions as to the projected House of Correction for the county.[3] In 1605 very elaborate " Orders " are sent by the Privy Council, setting forth in detail the administrative duties of the Judges of Assize, of Quarter Sessions, of the several Justices of the Peace, and of the various parish and township officers ; and reminding them of the statutes that they were specially charged to enforce for the relief of the poor, the repression of vagrancy, the regulation of the sale of bread and ale, the

---

[1] *West Riding Sessions Rolls, 1597–1602*, by John Lister (Yorkshire Archaeological Society, 1888), pp. xxx-xxxiv, 84-87. At Wakefield, in 1598, the Churchwardens and Overseers find themselves peremptorily commanded by Quarter Sessions to " take order for the relief of the poor according to the statute lately made in the last Parliament " (*ibid.* p. 118).

[2] Orders by the Justices of the Peace for the Relief of the Poor in Essex, 1598, Harleian MSS., 7020, art. 33, p. 267 ; *Tudor Economic Documents*, by R. H. Tawney and Eileen Power, 1924, vol. ii. pp. 263-364.

[3] *Acts of the Privy Council of England*, edited by J. R. Dasent, vol. xxxii. (1601–1604), 1907, pp. 503, 505, 507-508.

apprenticeship of children, the fixing of wages of labourers and artificers, and the suppression of recusancy and crime.   Every Justice is required to attend every Quarter Sessions—the Clerk is to report to the Assize Judges the names of those in attendance. They are to be assigned to their several Divisional Sessions, for each of which a clerk is to be appointed, and the Parish Constables are to attend their meetings.[1]   But not all counties were efficiently managed.   That much failure of duty continued, among Justices as among parish officers, may perhaps be inferred from the serious admonition made by the Lords of the Council in June 1608, with regard, particularly, to the supervision of alehouses, which was thought to have been neglected by the " inferior and subordinate ministers " of authority.[2]   There were, in fact, disturbances in these years, in various parts of England, which have been ascribed to discontent at the ever-increasing enclosures ; but which coincided, in fact, with bad harvests, high prices and consequent distress.   New proclamations were issued by the Privy Council in 1608, in which they insist, among other things, on the diligent execution of the statutes and orders.[3]   In this connection may be cited the Lord Chancellor's charge in 1608, addressed in the Star Chamber to the Judges and Justices of the kingdom.   He rebukes the crowd of " new and young knights who come in their braveries " to Quarter Sessions, and " stand there like an idol to be gazed upon, and do nothing ".   These new Justices are sharply told that " they are not Justices for their countenance only ".   They are to " remember their oaths, and duties that are for the Justices ".   They are to stop all riotous assemblies at the outset ; and, what is of special significance to us, they are everywhere to see that " the poor be provided for within their parishes ".[4]   A more severe scolding was

[1] See the elaborate Order of June 23, 1605, given in full in *Quarter Sessions from Elizabeth to Anne*, by A. H. A. Hamilton, 1878, pp. 67-71 ; and also in *Three Centuries of Derbyshire Annals*, by J. C. Cox, 1890, vol. 1, pp. 4-6.
We see the North Riding Justices compelling Overseers to attend these monthly meetings : thus, in 1607, " T. H. of Scruton, one of the Overseers of the Poor there, for not keeping his monthly meeting according to the Statute . . . fined 20s. ; also R. G., C. H., and T. O., others of the Overseers for the like, and with like fines " (*North Riding Quarter Sessions Records*, edited by J. C. Atkinson, vol. i. p. 97, October 8, 1607).
[2] *Quarter Sessions from Elizabeth to Anne*, by A. H. A. Hamilton, 1878, p. 73.
[3] Proclamation Book (Privy Council), Nos. 88 and 94 ; *Early History of English Poor Relief*, by E. M. Leonard, 1900, p. 144.
[4] *Les Reportes des Cases in Camera Stellata*, by John Hawarde, edited by W. P. Baildon, 1894. pp. 367-368.

received by the Devon High Sheriff and Justices in December
1609, when a new season of dearth had set in, marked by a
renewal of the exorbitant prices for corn, in which (whether for
this county only, or generally, is not clear) the whole system of
local administration was reviewed, in order to point out the
" want of good correspondence between direction and execution ".
The failure to devolve functions on specific persons who could be
held responsible, was animadverted on, for " the rule seldom
faileth which common experience hath made so certain, that
these duties which concern all men are neglected of every man ".
The remissness of the Justices is calculated to breed " a custom
of disobedience among the vulgar sort of people ". The Lords
of the Council accordingly demand that Quarter Sessions shall
nominate a sort of executive committee of three or four Justices,
who can see to the execution of the orders from the Council,
and— note the insistence on this administrative device—who can
be asked to give an account, from time to time, of what has
actually been done in each matter.[1] In February 1615 it is the
Justices of Surrey who receive specific injunctions, not only to
suppress superfluous alehouses, but at once to take steps to
reduce the number of isolated cottages on the lonely heaths
and commons characteristic of the county, in order to settle
the people in or near villages, where they can conveniently
be " set on work " on the parish stock. In June of the same
year the Justices of all the counties bordering on the Metropolis
are enjoined to take action against vagrants by instituting a
simultaneous " Privy Search ".[2] In 1620 it was apparently the
depression of the cloth manufacture, to be aggravated in 1621–
1622 by bad harvests and high prices, that led to disturbances ;
and this induced the Privy Council to entrust a special commission with the task of getting the Poor Law enforced. Orders
and proclamations followed in 1622 and 1623, addressed to
Quarter Sessions, calling on all the Justices to take up their duties
in their own neighbourhoods.[3] Sometimes the admonition and

---

[1] *Quarter Sessions from Elizabeth to Anne*, by A. H. A. Hamilton, 1878,
pp. 78-80.
[2] *Acts of the Privy Council, 1615–1616*, by Sir H. C. Maxwell-Lyte, 1925,
pp. 64-65.
[3] See for all this, the Privy Council Register and Proclamation Books,
1620–1623 ; the *Calendar of State Papers* (*Domestic*), for these years ; *Early
History of English Poor Relief*, by E. M. Leonard, 1900, p. 144.

incitement comes from the Bishop. Thus the Bishop of Lincoln writes from Westminster in 1622 to the Earl of Salisbury and other Justices for Hertfordshire, saying that the King is much offended at the laxity of the Justices in permitting the county to swarm with rogues and vagrants, and that the Justices are enjoined to put the laws more strictly in force, and also to fix maximum prices for corn, bread and meat, whilst returns are to be obtained from the Constables, and presented by the Custos Rotulorum, as to negligent Justices in order that these may be omitted from the Commission.[1]

In 1625 the Lord Keeper Coventry and other Privy Councillors enjoin and request the Justices of Worcestershire—and, as we learn elsewhere, also all the other Quarter Sessions of the realm—in order to prevent a rise of prices, and alleviate distress, to take steps to restrict any unnecessary consumption of grain, or its transportation to foreign parts ; also, with the same view, to restrict the number of alehouses and moderate the strength of the beer, so as to diminish the consumption of grain.[2] This injunction was repeated in 1630–1631 ; indeed, the incitements of those who were wielding the authority of the Crown culminated in a prolonged endeavour to make what they call " the subordinate government of this realm " use all its statutory powers, and to exercise all possible influence to cope with the renewed distress. Pressure was put on the cloth manufacturers of various counties to maintain employment. Rates in aid of distressed parishes were ordered to be made on the other parishes of the Hundreds. Proclamation after proclamation commanded the execution of the laws. An exceptionally elaborate set of orders and directions was prepared, which were not only addressed to the Justices in Quarter Sessions for every county, and made the subject of injunctions and enquiries by the Judges on their circuits, but were also published by authority in a pamphlet which seems to have enjoyed a wide circulation.[3] A special body of " Com-

[1] *Notes and Extracts from the Hertfordshire Sessions Rolls,* vol. i., 1905, pp. xi, 9, 56-58.

[2] *Calendar of the Worcestershire Quarter Sessions Rolls,* by J. W. Willis Bund, part ii., 1900, pp. cv-cvii, 398-399, 484-485 ; see also *History of Agriculture and Prices,* by J. E. Thorold Rogers, vol. v. p. 195.

[3] The " Book of Orders " was published in 1631 by " the King's Printer " under the following title : *Orders and Directions, together with a Commission, for the Better Administration of Justice, and more perfect information of His Majesty, how and by whom the Laws and Statutes tending to the Relief of the Poor,*

missioners for the Poor " was set up in June 1630, consisting of
ten of the Council. These, the first-recorded Poor Law Commissioners, were Lord Keeper Coventry, Viscount Wentworth
(President of the Council of the North), Sir John Coke (Secretary
of State), Lord Newburgh (Chancellor of the Duchy of Lancaster),
Laud (Bishop of London), the Earls of Manchester, Suffolk,
Bridgewater, Holland and Danby ; and Sir Thomas Edmonds.
This body seems to have been enlarged in January 1631
into a commission including many leading personages of the
moment who were not members of the Council. This commission—a forerunner, *mutatis mutandis*, of the next in time,
exactly two centuries afterwards—appears to have been a
body of exceptional activity and importance. During the
ensuing year it appointed sub-commissions to deal with particular localities, notably Suffolk (Bury St. Edmunds), Devonshire (Exeter), Essex (Colchester), Lincolnshire (Stamford) and
various parishes of the City of London. Moreover, the Commissioners themselves, by committees of their own number, dealt
severally with the correspondence with particular circuits. A
paper in the British Museum shows us the Chancellor of the
Exchequer on the committee dealing with the Western Circuit ;
the Earl of Bridgewater, Viscount Dorchester and Viscount
Falkland on that dealing with Shropshire and the Welsh border ;
Wentworth on that for the Northern Circuit ; Laud and Sir
Edward Coke on that for Lincolnshire ; the Earl of Holland on
that for Norfolk, and the Archbishop of Canterbury (Abbot) and
Viscount Wimbledon on that for Kent.

The Book of Orders issued in January 1631 formed the basis
of Poor Law administration for the remainder of this period of
centralised direction. This volume particularly emphasises the

---

the *well-ordering and training up of Youth in Trades, and the Reformation of
Disorders and Disordered Persons, are executed throughout the Kingdom ; which
his Royal Majesty hath commanded to be published and inquired of by the Body
of his Privy Council, whom he hath made principal Commissioners for this purpose.*
Its contents are largely given in *The State of the Poor*, by Sir F. M. Eden, 1797,
vol. i. pp. 156-160 ; *Report of George Coode . . . on the Law of Settlement and
Removal of the Poor*, 1851, H. C. 675, pp. 226-231 ; *Pauperism and Poor Laws*,
by Robert Pashley, 1852 ; and they are, of course, referred to in *The History
of the English Poor Law*, by Sir George Nicholls, 1854, vol. i. pp. 262-267 ; and
well described in *The Early History of English Poor Relief*, by E. M. Leonard,
1900, pp. 156-159. The reception of the " Book of Orders " by the Liverpool
Corporation in February 1631 is described in *Liverpool Vestry Books, 1681-1834*,
by Henry Peet, 1912, vol. i. pp. xx-xxi.

need for diligence in the execution of their duties by the Justices. These responsible officers are to divide themselves into committees for the several Hundreds, which are to meet monthly, when all the Overseers, Constables and Churchwardens of the parishes within each Hundred are to appear before them. The measures taken in each parish are then to be reported, offenders are to be named, and those in default are to be reprimanded and punished. Every quarter the High Sheriff is to get all the Justices to report to him as to their proceedings in these divisional meetings and otherwise. The Judges are to receive these reports at the six-monthly Assizes ; to take immediate action on them wherever required ; and to report to the " Commissioners for the Poor ", to whom the Council thus delegated the task of central supervision and direction. Nor did the Privy Council rest content with this general injunction. In April 1632 all the High Sheriffs were stirred up to get the negligent Justices to make their reports. A year later there are still many reports lacking ; and on October 16, 1633, the Council writes to all the Judges telling them to find out on their circuits which of the Justices in each county were in default. Eighteen months afterwards the Judges are again reminded that much is still undone, and that they must insist on the Justices making their returns. But enough of instances. There was, in fact, from 1590 to 1640, what is not found in English history before that period, or after it until the establishment of the Poor Law Commission in 1834, an almost continuous series of letters, instructions and orders, emanating from a central government department, in the names of the Privy Council or some members of it, either to the Assize Judges, or to the Lord Lieutenants or High Sheriffs of the various counties, or directly to the Justices of the Peace in Quarter Sessions, insisting that the statutes for the relief of the poor and of maimed soldiers, for the maintenance of tillage and the repression of vagabondage, for the regulation of alehouses and of the sale of ale and bread, and for the suppression of recusancy and crime should be put in operation. Sometimes the Justices are directed to make arrangements for special sessions to consider what needs to be done in their several localities. Sometimes, in years of special distress or disturbance, all the country gentlemen " to whose care a great and principal part of the subordinate government of the realm doth depend ", are called upon to return to their homes, in order to do their duty. Sometimes the Assize Judges or the Justices are directed to intervene in order to prevent employers such as the clothiers of the West Country, or those of Suffolk and Essex, from discharging their workpeople, or paying them wages insufficient for maintenance. It is even more interesting to find the adoption of the modern administrative device of requiring reports to be furnished, not only by Quarter Sessions, but also from each parish, specifying what steps had been taken to carry out the policy imposed from the centre, and with what result. From time to time special commissions were appointed, to give particular consideration to the problem, with separate commissioners deputed to deal with particular districts. We gain a vision, between 1590 and 1640, of a group of vigilant and indefatigable Privy Councillors, wielding unquestioned authority irrespective of which particular monarch sat on the throne, and constantly in receipt of information from all parts of the country ; of these Privy Councillors habitually making use of the Assize Judges on their circuits to inquire and discover how far the Justices of the Peace were performing their duties of supervision and sanction of the action of the parish officers, and to be perpetually exhorting these Justices to greater diligence ; and finally, of Overseers of the Poor actually appointed in at least a fair proportion of the parishes and townships ; perpetually worried by the Justices ; required to make periodical reports of their action or inaction ; and alternately " charged ", exhorted and threatened with penalties, both by the Chairmen of Quarter Sessions and the Assize Judges. What the successive great officers of State between 1590 and 1640 were establishing was, in fact, a highly organised system of Local Government, co-extensive with the kingdom, with a regular official hierarchy, based upon just the amount of centralisation required to ensure that the administrative machinery was everywhere working according to plan. The whole episode demands further investigation from the student of Political Science, in the light of the information to be obtained from the contemporary records.

How far the Laws were put in Force

We have ourselves been unable to investigate, in the parish, municipal and county archives of this period (which, though scanty, exist in greater number and variety than historians appear yet to have realised and are only now beginning to be printed) to what extent this centralised administration succeeded in establishing the ubiquitous system of poor relief at which Parliament had, since 1572–1576, ostensibly aimed. It is clear that there still remained many parishes of England, in which the Poor Laws of 1572–1576, and later, those of 1597–1601, were not put in operation. There is evidence, for instance, that in remote parts of Wales, and also in certain towns and still more isolated rural parishes in England, no Poor Rate was levied until a much later date ; and it may well be that, if there was no complaint that voluntary charity had proved inadequate to local needs, neither Quarter Sessions nor the Assize Judges insisted on a compulsory tax. It seems also that there was a constant tendency among the parishes, with the implicit connivance of the local Justices, to let the Acts and Orders slip into desuetude. In 1622, half a century after the first Act authorising a compulsory levy, it could be said that " though the number of the poor do daily increase, there hath been no collection for them, no not these seven years, in many parishes of this land, especially in country towns [*i.e.* townships] ; but many of those parishes turneth forth their poor, yea and their lusty labourers that will not work, or for any misdemeanour want work, to beg, filch and steal for their maintenance so that the country is pitifully pestered by them ; yea, and the maimed soldiers, that have ventured their lives and lost their limbs in our behalf, are also thus requited ; for when they return home, to live by some labour in their natural country, though they can work well in some kind of labour, every man sayeth, We will not be troubled with their service, but make other shift for our business. So they are turned forth to travel in idleness (the highway to Hell) and seek their meat upon mares (as the proverb goeth), with begging, filching and stealing for their maintenance, until the law bring them unto the fearful end of hanging." [1] A pamphleteer of 1698 could declare that " Though parishes were enabled (by the 43rd of Elizabeth) to make rates, and the owners of estates obliged to the payment, yet in many places no such

---

[1] *Grievous Groans for the Poor, done by a Well-wisher, who wisheth that the Poor of England might be so provided for as none should need to go abegging within this realm*, by M. S., 1622 ; quoted in *The State of the Poor*, by Sir F. M. Eden, 1797, vol. i. pp. 154-155.

rates were made in twenty, thirty or forty years after; and when they were first made, and in many years after, the money, so risen [raised], was inconsiderable to the present charge ".[1] Of the parish of Stow-on-the-Wold (Gloucestershire) it was stated by the Hon. Roger North, sometime in the reign of Charles II. or James II., that no Poor Rate had ever been made there ; and it was subsequently ascertained, by inquiry of the incumbent, that there was no Poor Rate levied there until after 1689, when the first was made at the instance of Lord Chief Baron Atkins, who had a residence in the neighbourhood.[2]   In fact, it was a couple of centuries after the legislation of 1572–1576 before the rate-aided support of the indigent became absolutely universal in all the parishes of England and Wales.   It happens to be recorded that, in the parish of Llanferras in Denbighshire, " it appears from the parish books that no Poor Rate was gathered here before the year 1768 ; but when any of the parishioners were in distress collections were made for them at the church, as is still [1797] the case in Scotland ; and if their case required it, two shillings or three shillings were given to them out of the Church Rate.   Two instances of this are inserted in the books ; the whole expense of the poor in 1719 was five shillings, and in 1740 only two shillings and sixpence.   It does not appear that anything was paid during the intermediate years." [3]   It seems certain that there were, throughout the whole of the seventeenth century, a great many places in which no Overseers were appointed ; and still more in which the provision for the poor amounted to nothing more systematic than casual doles.

It is, however, more profitable to consider the evidence as to what was, in particular parishes, actually being done to put the Poor Laws in operation, rather than what other parishes were leaving undone.   There was, we think, a difference in this respect between the Municipal Corporations in the principal towns, on the one hand, which had most vagrants and beggars and destitute poor, but also most endowments and hospitals and

[1] *Bread for the Poor*, 1698 ; reprinted in *A Collection of Pamphlets concerning the Poor*, 1787 ; see *The State of the Poor*, by Sir F. M. Eden, 1797, vol. i. p. 144.

[2] *Discourse on the Pernicious Tendency of the Laws for the Maintenance and Settlement of the Poor*, by the Hon. Roger North, 1753 (written between 1660 and 1688) ; see *Report on the Law of Settlement and Removal*, by George Coode, 1852, H.C., 675, pp. 277-285, and the footnote at p. 285, giving the comment of North's editor.

[3] *The State of the Poor*, by Sir F. M. Eden. 1797 vol. iii. p. 889.

charitable gifts, and on the other, the vast multitude of tiny rural parishes. We have sufficiently described the work in the cities and boroughs, where compulsory poor rates were levied, though at first not continuously, in the City of London from 1547, at Colchester and Ipswich from 1557, and at Norwich from 1570 ; and where, as might be shown by a hundred examples, both institutional and domiciliary relief, including some rudimentary schooling, primitive medical treatment and regular pensions, were, at the close of the sixteenth century, being given to the impotent poor, whilst the able-bodied were, in various ways, being set to work. In the period ending with the outbreak of the Civil War, this municipal provision for the poor may be taken, in the majority of urban centres, to have increased steadily in extent and in elaboration.

Thus, to cite only a few examples, we see the town of Beverley in 1599, maintaining and educating eighty orphans, and spending £105 a year in employing the poor in knitting, spinning and other work, under the Act of 1597.[1] At Colchester there seems to have been a short-lived attempt at a municipal workhouse in 1594, and in 1612–1613 this was revived, so that the impotent might be relieved and the destitute able-bodied set to work.[2] At Sheffield, then just in the infancy of its industrial development, an interesting municipal census of wealth and poverty was taken in 1615. " By a survaie of the towne of Sheffield made the second daye of Januarie 1615 by twenty foure of the most sufficient inhabitants there, it appearethe that there are in the towne of Sheffelde 2207 people ; of which there are 725 which are not able to live without the charity of their neighbours. These are all begging poore. 100 householders which relieve others. These (though the best sorte) are but poore artificers ; among them is not one which can keepe a teame on his own land, and not above tenn who have grounds of their own that will keepe a cow. 160 householders not able to relieve others. These are such (though they beg not) as are not able to abide the storme of one fortnights sickness but would be thereby

---

[1] *History and Antiquities of Beverley*, by George Oliver, 1829, p. 192.

[2] *History . . . of Essex*, by Philip Morant, 1768, vol. i. p. 182 ; the Appendix gives in full the " Orders and Constitutions for the raising, setting up and maintaining of a Workhouse or Hospital for the setting of such poor to work as are able, and for the relieving of such poor, lame and impotent people as are not able to work ",

driven to beggary. 1222 children and servants of the said householders; the greatest part of which are such as live of small wages, and are constrained to work sore to provide them necessaries." [1]

Outside the City of London and a few score of Municipal Boroughs there may have been less progress. In one direction, however, the County Justices seem almost to have kept pace with the Municipal Corporations. The institution of a House of Correction, in imitation of the Bridewell of the City of London, appears in many of the counties, for use partly as a prison to which sturdy beggars and vagrants might be committed, and partly as a workhouse in which innocent and even meritorious men without employment might be set to work. We have already mentioned the institutions of this sort that the Justices of Essex and Suffolk established in 1589 and 1598. In the following decade the House of Correction was repeatedly pressed on the attention of Quarter Sessions as an indispensable instrument in the struggle against vagrancy. James the First urged the county gentlemen in a Speech from the Throne, to " Look to the Houses of Correction " ; adding " remember that in the time of Chief Justice Popham, there was not a wandering beggar to be found in all Somersetshire, being his native county ".[2] By 7 James I. c. 4 (1607) it was definitely enacted that Houses of Correction were to be provided in every county " with mills, turns, cards and suchlike necessary implements, to set rogues, vagabonds, sturdy beggars or other idle vagrant and disorderly persons on work ". It was under this Act that the Nottingham Justices established a House of Correction at Southwell in 1611, but found some difficulty in discovering an efficient " governor or master " at £20 a year, having to appoint no fewer than four within twenty years ; to issue revised regulations in 1619, and in 1633 to make good the ruinous decay due to " want of opportune repair ".[3] Frequently we find dominant the note of providing employment for the innocent poor. Thus in 1615 the Middlesex Justices were erecting an extensive " Bridewell " in

---

[1] *History of Hallamshire*, by J. Hunter, 1819 and 1869, p. 148 ; *The Growth of English Industry and Commerce in Modern Times*, by W. Cunningham, 1903, p. 347.

[2] King James's *Works*, 1567 ; see *Observations on the More Ancient Statutes*, by Daines Barrington, 1795, p. 537.

[3] *Nottinghamshire County Records*, by H. Hampton Copnall (Nottingham, 1915), pp. 29-30.

Tothill Fields, Westminster (which was repaired and largely rebuilt in 1655) with the following inscription over the gateway : " Here are several sorts of work for the poor of this parish of St. Margaret's, Westminster, and also the County, according to law ; and for such as will beg and live idly in this City of Westminster ".[1] In the North Riding of Yorkshire the intention to find employment for the innocent unemployed is made clear. The North Riding Justices took their House of Correction at Richmond quite seriously as a place for " setting the poor to work " ; in 1620 providing the master or governor, who was a " clothier " of Leeds, with " looms for employing " as well as with " irons . . . for ruling ", and (subject to a deduction from his stipend of fifty pounds a year of ten pounds yearly for each one hundred pounds thus expended) also with " stock ", or materials to be worked up. The master had to find the inmates in " bedding and maintenance of meat and drink ", taking for himself the proceeds of the labour. Later on, the Justices actually pay the statutory wages. In a subsequent bargain with the Master it is expressly stipulated that he is to " allow unto the people to be employed as aforesaid, for their said work and labour, the several salaries hereafter agreed on and set down, that is to say, as shall be set down by Justices of the Peace in pursuance of the statute made for servants' and labourers' wages in the time of " King James ". In 1637 the Justices, observing that " the trade of fishing doth in these parts increase a multitude of poor, who in winter time, when the said trade faileth, are either driven to beg or wander, or else cast upon the charges of the said parishes, which without some means of correcting and setting them to work, are no way able to relieve so great a multitude ", decided to establish another House of Correction at Whitby in which to employ these victims of a seasonal trade.

To what extent any particular House of Correction was of the nature of a penal establishment to which people were compulsorily relegated, and to what extent it was a place where the poor were provided with work under the Poor Law, is not clear.

[1] *Middlesex County Records*, by C. Jeaffreson, 1888–1892, vol. ii. pp. 117-120, 140 ; and vol. iii. ; *The London Prisons*, by Hepworth Dixon, 1850, p. 249 ; *The Criminal Prisons of London*, by H. Mayhew and J. Binny, 1852, p. 362 ; *English Prisons under Local Government*, by S. and B. Webb, 1922, p. 13. We find the Churchwardens of Pittington paying to the County Durham House of Correction from 1623 (*Churchwardens' Accounts of Pittington*, etc., Surtees Society, vol. 84, 1888, p. 82).

In Devonshire, it seems, the poor thought of the institution as one of penal nature. Dunning speaks of " the common workhouse . . . which, though no prison, is in common acceptation near akin to a Bridewell ".[1] It is interesting to note that at Thame (Oxfordshire), at Wrexham (Denbighshire), in the Borough of Warrington (Cheshire) and in the City of Poole (Dorsetshire) we find, at a later date, the House of Correction and the parish poorhouse existing on the same site and sometimes in the same building.[2] But seeing that, in the Richmond House of Correction at least, the inmates received the full current wages at the rates legally prescribed for the ordinary independent labourer, and thus secured continuous paid employment, in shelter and security, there seems no reason why the institution should not have been, in bad seasons, thronged.[3] Bacon, writing at the beginning of the seventeenth century, was certainly of opinion that these institutions, far from being merely prisons, were, in fact, no different from the " General Mixed Workhouse " of the latter part of the nineteenth century. " I commend most ", he said, " houses of relief and correction, which are mixed hospitals, where the impotent person is relieved, and the sturdy beggar buckled to work, and the unable person also not maintained to be idle, which is ever joined with drunkenness and impurity, but is sorted with such work as he can manage and perform." [4] Coke could make a great distinction between the House of Correction and the gaol. " Few or none ", he said, " are committed to the common gaol . . . but they come out worse than they went in. And few are committed to the House of

---

[1] *Bread for the Poor*, by R[ichard] D[unning], Exeter, 1698 ; (not to be confused with either of two other pamphlets with the same title, viz., one by Adam Moore in 1653, and the other by Philo-Anglicus in 1678).

[2] See *The State of the Prisons*, by John Howard, 2nd edition, 1780, pp. 304-305, 343, 399, 414 ; *English Prisons under Local Government*, by S. and B. Webb, 1922, p. 17.

[3] The House of Correction at Richmond, which had been disused since 1607, was ordered in 1615, but not opened until 1620. It was moved to Thirsk about 1670, but the lack of such a place was felt so severely that another had to be established at Richmond in 1676. Meanwhile others had been established at Whitby and Pickering. For all this see *North Riding Quarter Sessions Records*, edited by J. C. Atkinson, vol. i. p. 75, vol. ii. p. 229, vol. iii. p. 134, vol. iv. pp. 55-67, vol. v. pp. 107, 132, vol. vi. p. 249 ; and *Seventeenth Century Life in the Country Parish*, by Eleanor Trotter, 1919.

[4] *Advice to the King touching Mr. Sutton's Estate*, by Francis Bacon [Viscount St. Albans], *Works*, 1837 edition, vol. i. p. 494 ; quoted in Ninth Annual Report of Poor Law Commissioners, 1843, p. 279.

Correction, or Working House, but they come out better." [1]
It looks, however, as if these Houses of Correction underwent a
change.   Whether by reason of the very nature of their administration as " mixed " institutions, or from some other cause, we
see them insensibly becoming, as regards regimen and severity,
and apparently as regards the character of their inmates, practically indistinguishable from the gaols of the time.[2]

The Response of the Parishes

More difficult is it to estimate how much was being done by
the parish officers.   Pending a more systematic exploration of
such parish records as survive, it is hard to say, of the greater
part of rural England, how widespread was the actual administration of Poor Relief by the Churchwardens and Overseers, either
under ancient custom, or under the Poor Laws of 1572–1576, or
1597–1601.   We do not know, for instance, what credence to
give to one Sands, a member for Worcestershire, speaking on a
Bill in 1571 (which sought to increase the punishment of vagrancy,
and which he thereby defeated) when he told the House of

---

[1] Coke's *Institutes*, ii. 729.

[2] Thus the Middlesex Justices are found ordering, for their House of
Correction at Tothill Fields, that " every person committed thither shall be
set to labour, and have no other nurture than he or she shall get with their
labour, except they be sick ".   This was in strict accordance with the provision of the Act 7 James I. c. 4 as regards " rogues, vagabonds and idle
persons ", but can hardly be regarded as very generous " relief " for the
innocently destitute able-bodied.   The master or governor was accorded a
sum of two hundred pounds a year, out of which he was to pay a matron, a
chaplain, a porter and sufficient servants ; to provide " fresh straw every
month and warm pottage thrice a week ", the laundry of the inmates " linen
(if any they have)", and " help " in sickness (*Middlesex County Records*,
vol. ii. pp. 117-120).   We see no specific reference to the innocent destitute ;
but, in 1617, the Justices order that " servants, apprentices and other
unruly and disorderly persons " sent to the House of Correction merely " to
receive correction for the better humbling of them to their duties ", are to
be kept apart from the rogues (*ibid.* p. 130).   The inmates were not always
committed for short terms.   In 1615, one T. T., having already been branded
on the shoulder with the letter R as " a rogue incorrigible ", was sent to the
House of Correction for life (*in perpetuum*).   In 1626 one J. R. was " committed
to the House of Correction to be there flogged and there detained until it
shall appear that the female bastard, begotten by him on the body of Ann M.
is dead " (*ibid.* vol. ii. p. 140, and vol. iii.).

Even the North Riding Justices allowed the inmates of their Houses of
Correction to be charged " discharge fees " of " five shillings as they shall be
able ; otherwise three and fourpence " (*North Riding Quarter Sessions Records*,
vol. i. p. 75, vol. ii. p. 229).

Commons that if the Justices would but take the trouble, there need be no serious vagrancy, as every man might be relieved at his own home ; *and that this was actually done in Worcestershire.*[1] The admonitions of the next quarter of a century can hardly have failed to stir up some of the laggards. In Cornwall, for instance, in April 1597, the Court of Quarter Sessions for this remote county formulated a regular code of orders to parish officers and Justices of the Peace which we cannot suppose to have been entirely inoperative. These orders, as sent by Sir Francis Godolphin to Sir Robert Cecil, required to be made, in each parish, a threefold survey showing those completely indigent, those partly capable of self-support, and those able to contribute respectively. The parish officers were then to report to the Justices whether they would themselves undertake all necessary relief out of such funds and voluntary contributions as they could command, or whether they preferred the Justices, under the 1572 Act, to levy a weekly rate for the purpose. When arrangements for relief had been made, by either expedient, all begging was to be prohibited and severely punished ; the fines for absence from Divine Worship were to be rigorously enforced for the benefit of the poor's fund ; and the whole parish, rich and poor, was to forgo two meals in each week, partly as a religious exercise, and partly as a measure of economy in food. Finally, for the able-bodied, it was provided, in a curious antici- pation of the " Roundsman " system, that " such poor as can- not provide work for themselves are to present themselves in a convenient place in the church on the Sabbath day a little before the ending of morning and evening prayer, and as soon as prayer is ended order shall be taken to send them abroad among such householders as shall maintain them with meat, work and such wages as they can deserve for the week following ". [2]

After the statutes of 1597–1601, and still more after the

---

[1] *Journals of all Parliaments*, etc., by Sir Symonds D'Ewes, 1682, p. 165.

[2] *Report of Historical Manuscripts Commission* (Hatfield MSS.), vol. vii. p. 161. A century later, in the adjacent County of Devon, this " Roundsman " system could be described as an effective device. " For men in husbandry, by giving them lists to work round the parish . . . is very advantageous. . . . The general averseness and abhorrence of the poor to go about with lists and desire work, and work according to such appointments, and to give a constant account thereof, is altogether as effectual as a city workhouse to make such persons to get work for themselves " (*Bread for the Poor*, by R[ichard] D[unning], Exeter, 1698 ; *The State of the Poor*, by Sir F. M. Eden, 1797, vol. i. p. 251).

publication of the Book of Orders of 1631, the evidence already available as to local Poor Law administration increases in volume. Already in 1598, a considerable proportion of the parishes in the West Riding of Yorkshire had Overseers who were perpetually troubling the county authorities with their inquiries, their mistakes, and their experience in levying the Poor Rates. We see the question raised as to whether the Parish or the Wapentake should be the unit of assessment and of charge. Whatever might be the law on the subject, the Court of Quarter Sessions confirms various Poor Rates on Wapentakes. It censures various parish or municipal officers for arbitrary " removals " of " non - settled " poor.[1] In the North Riding of Yorkshire, from 1605 onward, there is frequent mention of Overseers of the Poor, and of the supervision exercised over them by the Justices. In about a score of cases within these years Overseers were presented or bound over to appear at sessions for some neglect of duty, either for failing to meet monthly, or failing to relieve some poor person.[2] Between 1603 and 1641, at least, we find the Nottinghamshire Justices systematically having the parish officers before them, admonishing some of them for neglect, directing Outdoor Relief in particular cases, ordering lodgings to be found for homeless folk, issuing warrants for " setting to work " the able-bodied, requiring sons to contribute towards the maintenance of their parents, and drastically dealing with the mothers of illegitimate children. The obligation of the parish officers to attend the " monthly meetings " of the Justices was, in this county, at least spasmodically

---

[1] *West Riding Sessions Rolls, 1597–1602*, by John Lister (Yorkshire Archaeological Society, 1888), pp. xxvii-xxix ; from which extracts are given in *Tudor Economic Documents*, by R. H. Tawney and Eileen Power, 1924, vol. ii. pp. 365-369.

[2] *Quarter Sessions Records*, by Rev. J. C. Atkinson, North Riding Record Society, vols. i. and ii., 1884, vols. iii. and iv., 1885.

The records for other counties yield similar evidence. Thus, the Overseers for Hemel Hempstead were " presented " to the Hertfordshire Quarter Sessions in 1619 " for not assembling at the Parish Church on Sunday afternoon after Divine service to consider means for the relief of the poor " (*Notes and Extracts from the Hertfordshire Sessions Rolls*, by W. J. Hardy, 1905, vol. i. pp. xxi, 45).

In Worcestershire, in 1634, we find two inhabitants of a parish, presumably the Overseers, bound over to appear at Quarter Sessions " to answer concerning their neglect in not taking care to provide for the relief of the poor of their Parish according to the Statute ". A defaulting Overseer is likewise bound over in 1630 (*Calendar of the Worcestershire Quarter Sessions Rolls*, by J. W. Willis Bund, part ii., 1900, pp. 468, 542).

enforced. In 1615 we see the Churchwardens and Overseers of Scarrington in Nottinghamshire formally " presented " for " not making the monthly meeting ". In 1638 the Parish Constable of Hawton in the same county was presented " for not reminding Churchwardens and Overseers of the Poor of the monthly meeting ".[1] Moreover, in the various counties for which the records of the Justices have been printed—notably those of the West and North Ridings of Yorkshire, Worcestershire and Hertfordshire—we find a constant stream of orders to the Overseers to grant relief in particular cases—orders which may be taken, on the one hand, to indicate that there were many cases that the Churchwardens and Overseers omitted spontaneously to help ; and, on the other hand, as proof that the activity of the Justices, which the Privy Council had stirred up, was resulting in a considerable amount of relief being given. In the West Riding, for instance, it is ordered, as early as April 1598, " that the Churchwardens and Surveyors of the poor within the parish of Brarton shall see and take order that E. C. and her 4 children shall be relieved and provided for as the late statute requireth ".[2] In the North Riding we see the Justices, from the very beginning of their surviving records, constantly ordering the Overseers to give regular allowances to particular poor persons, to provide them with lodging accommodation and even to erect for them houses—of timber, thatched with straw, and costing about £3—on the waste land of the parish.[3] In another direction, too, the commands of the Privy Council were being obeyed, namely, in securing the training in industry of boys and girls. " The Justices ", we are told, were " much occupied in binding out apprentices, a duty which they were required to perform by various statutes and by constant reminders

[1] *Nottinghamshire County Records*, by H. Hampton Copnall, Nottingham, 1915, pp. 12, 118-125.

[2] *West Riding Sessions Rolls*, vol. i. p. 76.

[3] The housing orders are of special interest. On April 29, 1606, there is order that " The Churchwardens and Overseers of the town[ship] of Boltby shall provide a habitation and relief for Ellen Killington according to law, for that she hath dwelt there 20 years last past, and that they likewise put her children prentices according to law " (*ibid.* vol. i. p. 38). On October 8, 1622, we read of " a general assessment to be presently made by the Churchwardens and Overseers of Catterick for the sum of 58/6 disbursed by W. B., Churchwarden there, for erecting of a house for a poor man " (*ibid.* vol. iii. p. 154). And on October 5, 1636, an order is given for " The Parish Officers of Newton to build a house on the waste of the said township as a dwelling for a poor man " (*ibid.* vol. iv. p. 64).

from the Privy Council. The Justices of Norfolk early in the seventeenth century report that they have within the last year put out as apprentices some 500 poor children; those of the West Riding somewhat later that they have apprenticed 200; and those of Somerset 400." [1]

Perhaps the most important evidence yet available, as to the extent to which the continual injunctions and incessant supervision organised by the Privy Council succeeded in their purpose of making the Poor Laws effective, is afforded by the reports from the various parishes (about a thousand in number) which happen to have been preserved among the Privy Council archives. From these parish reports we may infer that the pressure from above, continuous as we have seen, for nearly half a century, had greatly increased the provision for the destitute.

These reports by the Churchwardens, Overseers and Constables of the several parishes, which were summarised and forwarded by the Justices for the Hundred or County, record, in nearly all cases, the disbursement of small sums " to divers poor people according to their necessities ", or to so many " poor people which have weekly relief ", or to impotent and aged people which have weekly pension "—in some cases " monthly pension "—or to " divers young children but too young to place out apprentice which we maintain, and their parents with work " ; or " one old woman is maintained with a monthly pension of five shillings and four pence and a load of coals every year " ; or " for the relief of those that were infected with the plague " ; or, generally, " that the impotent poor within the said Hundreds are relieved ". Very rarely is it reported, from a tiny parish, that " they have in that town[ship] no poor people but such as are able to maintain themselves ".

As regards boys and girls the reports state " that they have four poor children to be placed out apprentice, which are to be bound the next meeting " ; or that " they have placed four poor children apprentices ", or that " they have placed out four apprentices, and with two of them given seven pounds ten shillings " ; or, in another parish, " placed three poor children out apprentice and given with them seven pounds ten shillings ". More usually, it is reported that " they have no poor children fit as yet to be put apprentices ".

[1] *History of England*, by Edward P. Cheyney, vol. ii., 1926, p..335.

With regard to vagrants, this set of reports indicates a great clearance, at least in rural parishes. Sometimes it is said that " we have punished one vagrant ", or " punished three wanderers and sent them into Yorkshire where they were born ". More common is the statement that " wanderers they have none ", or " there have no wanderers come within their town[ship] ".

What is specially interesting is to find that at least a majority of these reports—which may be assumed, however, to come usually from the districts in which most was done—declare that these tiny rural parishes possess small amounts of " town stock ", varying from fifteen shillings to thirty pounds—in one case to £122—which is, in many cases, expressly stated to be " disbursed to poor people for stocks to set them on work ", or to be " bestowed in hemp and employed to set such poor on work as want ", or used " to set such poor on work as need ". In other parishes, where there is no " Town Stock ", it is often explained that " Town Stock they have none because they employ their poor in other work as they want it ", or because " their poor are otherwise set on works ", or " their poor such as want work being set on work otherwise by the town[ship] " ; or that " those that are able are set on work and do not refuse the same ". From a larger place (Bishop's Stortford, Herts) it was reported that they had " stock to set the poor on work to make clothes ; £22 : 10s. of hemp, tow and flax ; 24 children to put to service ; 22 poor spinners set to work ". At Chipping Barnet we hear that " we have in tow and hemp and cloth twenty shillings, and in money to buy more twenty shillings ". From Elstree (Herts) it is reported " we have in stock for the poor remaining forty shillings ", though we set such on work as want upon every occasion ".[1]

---

[1] These reports are all given in *The Early History of the Poor Law*, by E. M. Leonard, 1900. We do not know that Lord Clarendon was thinking of the Relief of the Poor, but it is at least interesting to find him bearing testimony to the social contentment of these years. " I must be so just as to say that, during the whole time that these pressures were exercised, and these new and extraordinary ways were run, that is, from the dissolution of Parlt. in the fourth year to the beginning of this [the long] Parliament, which was above 12 years, this Kingdom and all his Majesty's Dominions . . . enjoyed the greatest calm, and the fullest measure of felicity, that any people in any age, for so long time together, have been blessed with, to the wonder and envy of all the parts of Christendom. . . . England was generally thought secure, with the advantage of its own climate . . . the country rich, and what is more fully enjoying the pleasure of its own wealth. . . . Trade increased to that degree that we were the Exchange of Christendom (the revenue thereof

Taken as a whole, these parish reports of 1631 may fairly be said to indicate, as Miss Leonard observes, not only a widespread system of Poor Relief actually in operation, but also that " the improvement in the administration of poor relief concerned especially the relief of the able-bodied poor ", including " many instances in which taxes were raised for this purpose. . . . The plan of providing work for the unemployed was reported from some district of every county South of the Humber except Cornwall, Northampton, Devon and Wilts ; and in Devon and Wilts also the same plan was tried, although no report of the Justices has been preserved. This form of poor relief thus seems to have been frequently in use in the towns of both east and west, and in the country districts of the Eastern Counties also. It was not quite so general in the country districts of the West, but still was not infrequent even there." The Privy Council failed, indeed, to make the system of relieving the destitute anything like complete. The counties of Northumberland and Durham—perhaps owing to the separate jurisdiction of the County Palatine of Durham—still remained, to a great extent, outside the scheme. Parishes of tiny populations, in remote or isolated parts of Wales and elsewhere, were apparently unaffected. If Parish Vestries or Parish Officers chose obstinately to continue on the old lines, they were seldom interfered with.

The Privy Council as a Cabinet

We are, however, more inclined to wonder that Burleigh and his colleagues and successors accomplished as much as they did, than that they did not wholly succeed in their endeavours. It was, indeed, no small achievement to have constructed what has been styled " a gigantic centralised executive working without haste or rest, making its authority felt in the most minute details of government in the furthest corners of the realm, and occupying itself alike with the most petty and the most important administrative duties ".[1] " As Elizabeth's reign

to the Crown being almost double to what it had been in the best times), and the bullion of all other kingdoms was brought to receive a stamp from the mint of England " (*History of the Rebellion and Civil Wars in England*, etc., by Lord Clarendon, edition of 1888, vol. i. pp. 93-95).

[1] *The Privy Council under the Tudors*, by Lord Eustace Percy, 1907, pp. 18-19.

drew on, her Council became gradually smaller and smaller, and limited almost entirely to office-holders." [1]   This little group of men, " seldom more than nine or ten in number, who sat round the Council table ", came a good deal nearer to forming what would now be termed a Cabinet than is commonly supposed. Nearly all of them held office under the Crown, and most of them were at the head of important departments of State.   Nearly all of them sat in one or other of the two Houses of Parliament. In the House of Commons we know that the Privy Councillors sat together, on a special row of seats near the Speaker.   They are noticed as talking together about the proceedings.   They evidently acted as leaders in the House.   One or other of them took the initiative in bringing matters before the Legislature. They were placed on the important committees, and avowedly acted often as spokesmen for the sovereign, which, in itself, gave to their policy a certain unity and what served as collective responsibility for each other's utterances. [2]

Needless to say, the Privy Council itself was far from being an efficient department.   " Looking backwards from the point of view of the modern highly organised Cabinet system ", it has been lately observed, " one of the things which strikes us most about Elizabeth's Privy Council was its singular lack of organisation.   Up to the year 1590 it seems even to have lacked a presiding officer.   In spite of the multitude of its duties, both in domestic and foreign affairs, we find little or no trace in it of that nice distribution of functions which so eminently characterises the modern English cabinet.   Now and then temporary committees were appointed on particular business, and probably, in a rough sort of way, members of the council were set to the tasks for which they seemed best fitted, but this is as much as can be said.   There was a constant tendency to load down the abler councillors with all sorts of matters, independent of the nominal positions they held." [3]   Moreover, the Privy Council of

---

[1] *The Tudor Privy Council*, by Dorothy M. Gladish, 1915, p. 29.

[2] See the valuable study of Elizabeth's reign in *History of England*, by Edward P. Cheyney, vol. ii., 1926, pp. 185-187 ; also *The Privy Council under the Tudors*, by Lord Eustace Percy, 1907, p. 72 ; and the admirable monograph on all the details by Dorothy M. Gladish, entitled *The Tudor Privy Council*, 1915.

[3] *Mr. Secretary Walsingham and the Policy of Queen Elizabeth*, by Conyers Read, 1926 ; with which should be compared the article " Walsingham and Burleigh in Queen Elizabeth's Privy Council," in *English Historical Review*, January 1913.

1586–1640, unlike a Government Department of the twentieth
century, had not at its command the potent lever of a Grant in
Aid.[1] It had no salaried inspectors to keep it regularly informed
of cases of failure to carry out the law, and to explain verbally to
the local Justices and Overseers what ought to be done. The
one or two thousand country gentlemen who were at that time in
the Commission of the Peace—in 1580 the number was 1738,
including many who were not active—were naturally, for the most
part, not often zealous, and hardly ever continuously diligent, in
the execution of what cannot have been a pleasant duty. They,
too, it must be remembered, had no salaried officers at their
disposal. Bacon himself talks of the " distracted government of
Justices of the Peace ", as being unsatisfactory.[2] We even find
the Justices protesting, here and there, against being so continually harassed and driven, enjoined and instructed, by officials in
London, about what they considered their own business of
maintaining order in their own counties. " Are we Justices or
are we not ", we hear the magistrates protesting at one Court of
Quarter Sessions, when a peremptory instruction from Whitehall
is read to them by the Deputy Clerk of the Peace. It is not to
be imagined that all, or even the greater part of the revulsion of
feeling that produced the Civil War was caused by the manifold
and long-continued encroachments on the local autonomy of
parish and county that we have described. But the suggestion
may be pardoned that, among the crowds of smaller landowners
of Bucks and Devon, Yorkshire and Lincolnshire, as well as
among the farmers who served as Parish Overseers, the resentment of the " personal government " of Charles the First, in
which doubtless religious feelings and objections to " ship

[1] Possibly, as some encouragement to put the law in operation, it became
during the reigns of James I. and Charles I. almost " common form ", in
statutes making new misdemeanour, for the fines to be allocated "to the
poor ". Among such statutes may be instanced those amending the Game
Laws (1 James I. c. 27, 7 James I. c. 11, 21 James I. c. 28); that regulating alehouses and drunkenness (1 James I. c. 9, 4 James I. c. 5, and
21 James I. c. 7); those relating to Sunday observance (3 James I. c. 4,
1 Charles I. c. 1, 3 Charles I. c. 2); that regulating clothmaking (21 James I.
c. 18).

[2] " There is a great difference between that which is done by the distracted government of Justices of the Peace and that which may be done by
a settled ordinance, subject to a regular visitation as this may be " (Advice to
the King touching Mr. Sutton's Estate, by Francis Bacon [Viscount St. Albans],
in Works, edition of 1837, vol. i. p. 494 ; quoted in Ninth Annual Report of
Poor Law Commissioners, 1843, p. 27 a).

money " counted for much, may have perhaps meant also an objection to autocratic injunctions from Whitehall with regard to local affairs.[1]   It looked, indeed, at the Restoration, as if the legislative and administrative efforts of the preceding century and a quarter had been brought to naught.   " At this day ", wrote the wise and experienced Sir Matthew Hale about 1659, " it seems to me that the English nation is more deficient in their prudent provision for the poor than any other cultivated and Christian State." [2]

The Effect of the Civil War

How much the Local Government of parish or borough or county was affected by the Civil War we have not ascertained. The supervision and injunctions of the Privy Council, about such a subject as Poor Relief, were, of course, suspended.   No doubt the demands of the unemployed for work immediately ceased, because both the King and the Parliament started recruiting, at rates of pay for soldiering that far exceeded what had been customary for civilian employment.   In Hertfordshire, for instance, waggoners were hired for the Parliamentary army at half a crown a day, being exactly twice the rate that the local farmers had been paying.   The Grand Jury at Hertford Quarter Sessions is driven to ask, " in regard their harvest is at hand, and their labourers few to gather it ", that " some part of their soldiers . . . may be for a while recalled to assist herein ". The Committee for the Eastern Counties felt compelled to promise to let men return " considering the necessity of their attendance upon their harvest ".[3]   On the other hand, though " setting the

---

[1] It is, at least, interesting to note that one of few protests against the Privy Council's orders in the time of dearth, which interfered with Free Trade in corn, came from Buckinghamshire, John Hampden's own country ; because on a market day at Chipping Wycombe in 1631, when Hampden himself was present, only a quarter of the usual quantity came to market ; the farmers were disgusted at the low prices ; the dealers lost money because the Mayor fixed the price ; and the Justices themselves sold corn to the poor below the current rate (*Calendar of State Papers, Domestic*, vol. 177, 50).

[2] *A Discourse touching provision for the Poor*, by Sir Matthew Hale (written about 1659, but not published until 1683, after his death).

[3] *Hertfordshire during the Civil War and Long Parliament*, by Alfred Kingston, 1894, pp. 182-187.   It was afterwards said that the Roundheads had " been assisted in the Civil Wars by great numbers of the wool workmen who liked much better to rob and plunder for half a crown a day than toil at a melancholy work for sixpence a day " (*Reasons for a Limited Export of Wool*, 1677, p. 8).

poor to work " probably ceased, the local authorities in places undisturbed by the war seem to have continued their relief of the impotent poor. In the Borough of Newark, in 1645-1646, Overseers were not only being duly appointed, but are seen to be active in the distribution, week by week, of money in Outdoor Relief.[1] In the little village of Pittington, in Durham, the levy of a Poor Rate actually began in the year 1648—a year of which it was stated by a contemporary that " there was never more need to make some provision for the poor ".[2] When the armies were disbanded, the whole country—and the Metropolis in particular—swarmed once more with beggars and vagrants with whom the various local authorities strove in vain to cope. A terrible state of things was described in 1646 in a lively pamphlet which made some impression, entitled *Stanley's Remedy, or the Way how to reform Wandering Beggars, Thieves, Highway Robbers and Pickpockets ; or an Abstract of his Discovery, wherein it is shown that Sodom's Sin of Idleness is the Poverty and Misery of this Kingdom.* It was estimated that no fewer than 80,000 sturdy vagrants were wandering up and down the land. In this very year, 1646, the town of Abingdon (Berks) is recorded as taking special authority to levy a Poor Rate—an Ordinance for a Collection for Relief of the Poor of Abingdon—perhaps for the first time. An interesting development was the establishment, in 1647, of a new local body, the Corporation of the Poor of the City of London, to be mentioned in the following chapter. " In

---

[1] Extracts from the *Records of the Borough of Newark-upon-Trent*, by R. F. B. Hodgkinson, 1921, p. 37.

We do not know why the Parish Officers at Stondon, Herts, were neglecting, in October 1644, to pay for the parish children whom they had " boarded out ", but these child farmers or foster parents were then complaining to the Justices of being unable to get their money (*Notes and Extracts from the Hertfordshire Sessions Rolls*, vol. ii. pp. xxxiii and 75).

[2] " In this parish no special Poor Rate [was] ordered or collected till the year 1648, notwithstanding the power of collecting one given in 1573. There were probably few destitute persons in the parish, and such as there were may have been sufficiently aided from the ' stock of the poor ' or from collections. . . . After 1648 poverty seems to have increased in the parish, the cesses for the poor being thenceforth regular and often heavy " (*Churchwardens' Accounts of Pittington*, etc., Surtees Society, vol. 84, 1888, p. 46). The contemporary writer was Sir John Cooke, in his *Unum Necessarium*, etc., 1648, p. 5. In the borough of Liverpool, then in its infancy, a proposal in 1649 for a " weekly assessment " for poor relief was not agreed to ; but in 1656 a " monthly ley " of £3, specifically to put the Overseers of the Poor in funds, was authorised—apparently the earliest Poor Rate to be levied in the town (*Liverpool Vestry Books, 1681-1834*, by Henry Peet, 1912, vol. i. pp. xxii-xxiii).

the beginning of 1652, in consequence of representations from the City of London, it was referred [by Parliament] to a committee to consider and report how the poor might be set to work and relieved, and not suffered to beg ; to review all the Acts touching the poor and to report their defects ; and to receive proposals from the City of London and others touching the poor."[1] In various provincial towns we see the Local Authorities asking help towards building workhouses in which to employ the poor.[2] At Southwell the House of Correction was ordered to be rebuilt in 1653, and equipped with " bolts, shackles, locks and diverse other implements " in 1654 and 1658.[3] In 1653–1657 the Justices of Nottinghamshire are found issuing many orders to the various parish officers directing Outdoor Relief to be given to " a very old man and past ability to work ", " a lame and impotent cripple ", " a poor lame woman ", and so on ; and they issued warrants for " setting to work " men and women unable to maintain themselves.[4] It seems, however, that the system—in 1631 apparently widespread—by which the Parish Officers provided a " Town Stock ", and used it as a means of setting the poor to work, was not again brought into operation. It does not appear to have been urged on the parochial authorities, or spontaneously readopted by them. There was plenty of unemployment in the bad times in which the Commonwealth ended, but " in all England ", wrote Sir Matthew Hale about 1659, " it is rare to see any provision of a stock in any parish for the relief of the [able-bodied] poor ". The pamphleteers of the period called for " Houses of Instruction " or " Houses of Correction ; or for the reclamation of waste land, or for " fishing-busses " to be fitted out to enable the unemployed to gain their own subsistence

[1] *Memorials of the English Affairs,* by Bulstrode Whitelocke, 1709, vol. iii. p. 418 ; *The Interregnum,* by F. C. Inderwick, 1891, pp. 95-96.

[2] So at Great Yarmouth (Norfolk), *Report of the Historical Manuscripts Commission,* vol. ix. p. 320 ; and at Stafford (*Calendar of State Papers* (*Domestic*), February 17, 1654).

[3] *Nottinghamshire County Records,* by H. Hampton Copnall (Nottingham, 1915), p. 30.

[4] *Ibid.* p. 119. In 1653 a farmer in a Nottinghamshire village was presented for refusing to serve in any parish office, and was peremptorily ordered to serve in his turn (*ibid.* p. 57). Nor was severity lacking. In 1655–1666 the same Justices were diligently enforcing the laws against vagrants, ordering men to be " stockt, stript and whipt . . . by the Constable, and sent to their several places of habitation ". In 1659–1660 the Justices ordered the Constables to make " diligent search and set watch and ward " for vagrants, common beggars and robbers (*ibid.* p. 115).

in the North Sea ; [1] they do not so much as mention the " competent stock of flax, hemp, iron, etc.", which the Overseers were supposed to provide in order to set the poor to work, nor was the direction from Whitehall maintained. The social policy of the Commonwealth has not yet received the attention it deserves, but we doubt whether Cromwell gave much attention to the parish administration, or the problems of Poor Relief.[2]

[1] *A Clear and Evident Way for Enriching the Nations of England and Ireland, and for setting very great numbers of poor on work,* by I. D., 1650 ; *Bread for the Poor, and Advancement of the English Nation, promised by enclosure of the wastes and commons of England,* by Adam Moore, 1653 ; see also *The State of the Poor,* by Sir F. M. Eden, 1797, vol. i. pp. 172-173.

[2] Sir George Nicholls notes that " Colonel Ludlow, in his *Memoirs,* says that the changes in the central or supreme government little affected the local administration, which proceeded in its accustomed course under the ordinary authorities " (*History of the English Poor Law,* by Sir George Nicholls, 1854, vol. i. p. 278 ; *Memoirs, 1625–1672,* by Edmund Ludlow, first published in 1698, edition of 1894 by C. H. Firth). It may, however, be pointed out that Cromwell peremptorily removed from office the Select Vestry of Gateshead, replacing them by twenty-four other persons whom he deemed more trustworthy (see the Order of " the Council at Whitehall " of June 22, 1658, in MS. Vestry Minutes, Gateshead, June 1658 ; *Memoirs of the Life of Mr. Ambrose Barnes,* Surtees Society, 1867, vol. i. p. 384 ; *The Parish and the County,* by S. and B. Webb, 1906, pp. 218-219). It must be said that, except for the dislocation caused first by the war, and then by the disbandment of the armies, the economic circumstances of Cromwell's administration seems to have been propitious. " From the commencement of the century to 1642 wages had remained about the same, and from that time they began and continued steadily to rise. . . . Taking a comparison between wages and the price of wheat . . . in 1625 the proportion between the price of a quarter of wheat and the weekly wages of an artisan were as 1 to 9 ; the same proportion in 1650 was as 1 to 7, and in 1655 as 1 to 4. . . . So long as Cromwell lived . . . the high wages remained " (*The Interregnum,* by F. C. Inderwick, 1891, p. 115 ; citing *History of Agriculture and Prices,* by J. E. Thorold Rogers, vol. v. p. 826).

It is to be noted that, during the Commonwealth, the Overseers ceased to be concerned exclusively with Poor Relief. A whole series of new duties were successively placed upon them. They were required to collect money for all sorts of purposes ; by Ordinances of 1643 for the public loan and for the poor clergy of Ireland, by those of 1644 and 1645 for the defence of the Eastern Association and of Surrey, and by that of 1649 for the propagation of the Gospel in New England. They were directed by Ordinance of 1644 to carry into effect the law for the demolition of monuments of idolatry ; and by two of 1650 to execute the laws for the observance of the Lord's Day and for the punishment of swearing. In London, by Ordinance of 1644, they had to distribute fuel to the poor. By Ordinance of 1644 they had to prepare lists of men, horses and arms in their parishes ; and by that of 1654 they were to repair the highways in default of appointment of a Surveyor of Highways. In 1650 an Ordinance required them to receive and distribute the proceeds of forfeitures. Unfortunately no information from the parish records is yet available to indicate to what extent and what result these statutory injunctions were put in operation. They may at least be assumed to have caused some diversion of attention from the earlier duty of relieving the poor.

After the Restoration there was no resumption of the hierarchical national administration.[1] " This elaborate system ", as Archdeacon Cunningham observed, " depended on the cooperation of central and local authorities ; the Civil War and Interregnum gave it a shock from which it could not recover. The machinery which had lain to the hand of Elizabeth's advisers for the regulation of social and industrial conditions was no longer available.   The change in the habits of the landed gentry, against which Elizabeth had striven, as well as the alterations which had been brought about by the war, had rendered a breach in the traditions of local government inevitable.   The political disorder of the times paralysed the central authority.   The vigour of the Elizabethan rule had been due to the power of the Privy Council, backed as it was by the Court of Star Chamber. When these powers were shattered, the supervision which had been exercised over the magistrates by the Council was withdrawn.   Parochial and county officials were left to their own devices till the period of the reformed Parliament, when the Charity Commissioners, the Poor Law Commissioners and the Local Government Board were instituted." [2]   There was, indeed, for more than a century and a half, an almost complete absence of national supervision or centralised administration in poor relief as in other departments of local government.   The eighteenth century in particular was the happy hunting ground of innumerable autonomous local authorities, decaying manors and manorial boroughs, municipal corporations, Vestries, county justices in quarter sessions and special sessions and petty sessions, and an amazing variety of statutory authorities from Courts of Sewers to Turnpike Trusts.   A description of these twenty thousand corporate bodies, with their uncertain constitutions, indefinite boundaries, overlapping jurisdictions and ambiguous powers, will be found in our volumes on *The Parish and the*

[1] " The Restoration gave us back a monarchy, but it did not bring back the governmental machinery . . . such a highly organised and actively administered government as the monarchy of Charles I." (*Growth of English Industry and Commerce in Modern Times*, by Archdeacon W. Cunningham, 3rd edition, 1903, vol. ii. p. 202).   In January 1661 the North Riding Justices seem to have attempted to resume their monthly meetings to supervise the parish administration ; but they presently met with opposition and other difficulties, which caused the attempt to be relinquished (*North Riding Quarter Sessions Records*, vol. iv. p. 31).

[2] *Growth of English Industry and Commerce in Modern Times*, by Archdeacon W. Cunningham, 3rd edition, 1903, vol. ii. p. 203.

County, The Manor and the Borough, and *Statutory Authorities for Special Purposes.* In this account of English Poor Law history we must note, in the seventeenth century, the first appearance of a new kind of specialised " Destitution Authority " in the statutory establishment of Corporations of the Poor, or Incorporated Boards of Guardians, to which we devote the following chapter.

CHAPTER III

THE INCORPORATED GUARDIANS OF THE POOR [1]

THE national administrative hierarchy of the first half of the seventeenth century, ending in the turmoil of civil war, was followed, so far as concerned the Poor Law, by half a century of inaction by the Central Government; and for this period there is at present insufficient evidence available for the kingdom as a whole as to what the County Justices and parish officers did or did not do for the relief of the poor. The latter half of the seventeenth century is characterised, indeed, so far as contemporary publications are concerned, by a remarkable neglect of the parish organisation set up by the Elizabethan legislation—a neglect which may be an indication of the small extent of the parochial Poor Relief of that generation. A series of reformers and

[1] This chapter is largely drawn, with additions, from the detailed account of these Incorporations, dealt with from the standpoint of constitutional structure, in our *Statutory Authorities for Special Purposes*, 1922, pp. 107-151. The voluminous book and pamphlet literature of the period has been summarised, briefly, in *The History of the Poor Laws*, by Rev. Richard Burn, 1764; more adequately, in *The State of the Poor*, by Sir F. M. Eden, 1797, vol. i.; with illustrative facts, in *The Growth of English Industry and Commerce in Modern Times*, by Archdeacon W. Cunningham, vol. ii. part i. (The Mercantile System), sixth edition, 1921; from a different angle, in "The Economics of Employment in England, 1660–1713," by Professor T. E. Gregory, in *Economica* for January 1914, pp. 37-51; and from yet another angle, using additional sources, in *The Position of the Labourer in a System of Nationalism: a Study in the Labour Theories of the later English Nationalists*, by E. S. Furniss, Boston, 1920. But all these useful and painstaking works have been outshone in brilliancy and illumination by *Religion and the Rise of Capitalism*, by R. H. Tawney, 1926, which deals most suggestively with the whole movement of opinion, but which unfortunately appeared too late to afford us guidance for the following chapter, which was already standing in type. A still more recent work, *The English Poor in the Eighteenth Century*, by Dorothy Marshall, 1926, embodies, along with praiseworthy investigation of parish and county archives, yet another selection from the same immense bibliography, nearly the whole of which is accessible at the British Museum.

philanthropists between 1659 and 1704, writing mostly in London, with little reference to the action, or even the existence, of the Churchwardens and Overseers, attacked the problem from the new standpoint of organising a genuinely " profitable employment of the poor ".   This was not a mere revival of the idea of the Elizabethan legislators of 1572–1576 and 1597–1601, which aimed primarily at finding means for the able-bodied to earn their own maintenance ; notwithstanding the large number of parishes in which, as we have described, the " parish stock " was used intermittently between 1601 and 1640 to " set on work " the able-bodied poor, these innumerable small experiments were not even referred to.   What the writers of the latter part of the seventeenth century had in view was largely, and even mainly, making the labour of the poor into a source of actual profit to the nation.   It appeared obviously reasonable that, if capital were provided, and simple manufacturing industries were set up, the labour of the men, women and children thus directed could not fail to add to the nation's wealth.   The various projects and experiments of this generation call for notice, not so much for any economic success that they achieved, as for two other reasons. In the first place they promulgated a view of the profitable employment of the poor that, in spite of repeated failures, for more than a century never ceased to influence both the Poor Law administration itself, and the criticisms by which it was assailed. And in the second place, the efforts of these seventeenth-century philanthropists did, at last, result, as we shall presently describe, if not in adding to the wealth of the nation, at least in the statutory establishment, over a large part of the kingdom, of unions of parishes under new Local Authorities, called Guardians, Trustees, Governors, Directors or Corporations of the Poor, that lasted right down to 1834, and in a few cases lingered even after that date, in supplement of, and often in substitution for, the organisation of Churchwardens and Overseers of the Parish, acting under the supervision and authority of the Justices of the Peace. Before describing these hundred or more new Local Authorities we must give some account of the intellectual ferment from which they arose.

Among the earliest of the philanthropic projectors of this epoch, and the most eminent, were Chief Justice Sir Matthew Hale, whose work (written about 1659, but not published until 1683) we have mentioned in the preceding chapter, and Sir Josiah Child (1630–1699), the Chairman of the East India Company, whose *New Discourse of Trade* (written some time before the Parliament of 1669, but not published until 1670 [1]) contained a remarkable second chapter on the relief of the poor. Both these statesmen, who take rank among the most enlightened of their time, and who certainly wrote with knowledge, ability and insight, convey the impression that the contemporary administration of Poor Relief by the parish authorities amounted to very little even for the impotent poor, and to practically nothing for the able-bodied, and that it completely failed to deal with the social problems of vagrancy and destitution. Both saw the only solution in the creation of a new organisation for employing, at a commercial profit, all the able-bodied poor who presented themselves, and it is interesting that neither of these distinguished authorities saw any economic difficulties in the proposal. Both of them recognised in the conception that led parish officers, even apart from any statutory authority, to refuse relief to those who did not " belong " to the parish, a grave mistake in policy, which went far to create the evil of vagrancy against which the legislators had been struggling for centuries. " The radical error ", wrote Child, " I esteem to be leaving it to the care of every parish to maintain their own poor only ; upon which follows the shifting off, sending or whipping back the poor wanderers to the place of their birth or last abode . . . which is just nothing of good to the Kingdom in general or the poor thereof, though it be sometimes by accident to some of them a punishment without effect." He urged a complete reversal of this policy, and even the abandonment of anything like deterrence. " If a right course be taken for the sustenation of the poor ", he wrote, and setting them on work, you " need invent no stratagems to keep them out, but rather to bring them in. For the conflux of poor to a city or nation well managed, is in effect the conflux of riches to that city or nation ; and therefore the subtle Dutch receive and relieve, or employ, all that come to them, not inquiring what nation, much less what parish, they are of." Sir Josiah Child agreed with Sir Matthew Hale in asking for unions of parishes in order to erect workhouses for the necessary provision

---

[1] An early draft seems to have been published in 1668 as *Brief Observations concerning Trade and Interest of Money.*

of employment; seeing that nothing effective could be done anywhere so long as the parish was the unit of administration and rating. But he made a special point of the formation of one gigantic union of all the parishes in the cities of London and Westminster, the Borough of Southwark and the adjacent urban areas, under a governing body (which he thought might be named " The Fathers of the Poor ") for the specific purpose of employing at manufactures every able-bodied person who was in need.[1] This early appreciation of the need for a single governing authority for the whole metropolitan area found no acceptance.

The reference by Sir Josiah Child to " the subtle Dutch " was characteristic of the time. The close association between the thinkers and writers of England and those of Continental Europe, which we have mentioned as prevailing by the instrumentality of the Holy Catholic Church, the religious orders and the universities, at the opening of the sixteenth century, had been broken during the ensuing century and a half by the combined effects of the Reformation, and the long-continued wars and political troubles of Germany and France and the Netherlands. When, after our own brief Civil War (1642–1646) and the Treaty of Westphalia (1648) there was a revival of English interest in the commercial and social conditions of Western Europe, there seems to have been, without much accurate knowledge, a great deal of intellectual curiosity about what was being done across the Channel. We shall see this influence recurring in most of the publications of this period.[2]

[1] *A Discourse touching Provision for the Poor*, by Sir Matthew Hale, 1683 ; given at length in *History of the Poor Laws*, by Dr. R. Burn, 1764 ; see also *Pauperism and Poor Laws*, by R. Pashley, 1852, pp. 220-222 ; and *The History of the English Poor Law*, by Sir George Nicholls, 1854, vol, i. pp. 302-303 ; *The New Discourse of Trade*, by Sir Josiah Child, 1670, 2nd edition, 1694 ; *The State of the Poor*, by Sir F. M. Eden, 1797, vol. i. pp. 184-188, 214-225. Sir Josiah Child's second chapter, under the title of *Proposals for the Relief and Employment of the Poor*, was reprinted in the *Somers Tracts*, 2nd edition, 1814, vol. ii. pp. 606-613.

[2] Thus, as Kirkman Gray pointed out in connection with the authors whom we are about to quote, " Bellers drew up the rules for the College of Industry from a comparison of all the hospitals of Holland ; Sir Matthew Hale refers to the institutions of Holland, Hamburg and Paris ; the author of *England's Wants* [or *Several Proposals probably beneficial for England, offered to the consideration of both Houses of Parliament*, by Edward Chamberlain, 1667] looks to Brabant, Flanders, and, not only to Rome the capital, but to the whole country of Italy, while Firmin justified his kindly title ' Fathers of the Poor ' [suggested, as we have seen, by Sir Josiah Child] from the usage of the French and Dutch churches " (*A History of English Philanthropy*, by

The " profitable employment " of the poor became the common panacea of the economic writers of the last quarter of the seventeenth century, and it found a place in nearly every pamphlet on the commerce or industry of the nation. Thus the anonymous author of *The Grand Concern of England Displayed* (which was possibly by John Gressot), published in 1673, complained that the sum expended from the Poor Rate went in mere doles, and was " employed only to maintain idle persons ". He urged that, in order to increase the national wealth, all such poor persons, young and old, should be employed in spinning and knitting, or some other useful occupation within their several capacities.[1] This suggestion was worked up into a very definite project by the indefatigable pamphleteer, Richard Haines, who—beginning with the invention of a " spinning engine " on which even children could earn their keep—went on to propose, as the surest way of promoting the linen and woollen industries, the formation of unions of parishes for the purpose of erecting in each district an " almshouse or hospital ", meaning a workhouse in which all the poor (of whom he thought there were at least 200,000 able-

B. Kirkman Gray, 1905, p. 85). We may add that Andrew Yarranton (1616–1685) drew inspiration for *England's Improvement by Land and Sea* (1677) from the industrial schools which he said then existed " in all the towns of Germany for the purpose of training and employing girls, from 6 years onwards, sometimes 200 in a single room, for spinning linen yarn ". For the relief of the poor, the experiments of the cities of Holland and those of Hamburg were thought specially instructive ; and we may trace this feeling also in many of the publications of the eighteenth century ; see, for instance, *Observations on the Defects of the Poor Laws*, etc., by Thomas Alcock, 1752. Pitt's proposals of 1797 were declared by Isaac Wood to have been taken from Count Rumford's experiments at Munich, and those at Hamburg " of which an admirable account has been published by the worthy M. Voght " (*A Letter to Sir William Pulteney . . . containing some Observations on the Bill . . . by the Rt. Hon. William Pitt, etc.*, by Isaac Wood, Shrewsbury, 1797, p. 6).

[1] This is in the *Harleian Miscellany*, vol. viii. p. 524 ; see *The State of the Poor*, by Sir F. M. Eden, 1797, vol. i. pp. 188-191 ; *Early History of English Poor Relief*, by E. M. Leonard, 1900, pp. 275-276. Other industries recommended in this pamphlet were spinning flax, hemp, wool or worsted ; carding, combing, knitting ; working plain work or points ; and making bone lace or thread or silk laces. A similar note was struck by Andrew Yarranton (see above), who thought " there were 100,000 poor now costing 4d. per day who might instead be earning 8d.", the first part of whose *England's Improvement by Sea and Land to Outdo the Dutch without fighting, to Pay Debts without Money, to set to work all the Poor of England*, etc., was published in 1677, and the second part in 1681. He had already published in 1663 *The Improvement . . . of Lands by Clover*. For this author, see *Elements of Political Science*, by P. E. Dove, 1854 ; *Industrial Biographies*, by Samuel Smiles, 1863 ; *Dictionary of Political Economy* and *Dictionary of National Biography*.

bodied unemployed) could be employed at a profit.   The workhouse thus provided would prove to be, Haines thought, not only
the only effective remedy for vagrancy and mendicancy, but also
" the best expedient to perfect the trade and manufactory of
linen cloth ".   " I cannot see ", he wrote in 1678, " how this
[the reforming and employment of beggars, vagrants, etc.] can
be at all effectually accomplished without public workhouses.
. . . In Holland . . . they have public workhouses in every
city for perpetual confinement in cases requiring the same." [1]
But in some ways the most convincing of all these writers was
" that worthy and useful citizen Mr. Thomas Firmin ", a lifelong
philanthropist who had learned to distrust mere almsgiving, and
who, during the plague year (1665), when only twenty-three
years of age, had organised the setting to work, on the making
up of clothing, of both men and women thrown into poverty by
the stoppage of trade.   Later in life, when he had succeeded in
business as a draper, he sunk the greater part of his fortune in
erecting, in Little Britain, a spacious building to be devoted to the
employment of the poor in the linen manufacture.   This experiment, which was continued under his indefatigable personal
superintendence from 1676 until his death twenty-one years later,
was on a scale to employ simultaneously, as we are informed,
though it is hard to credit the assertion, no fewer than 1700
persons as flax dressers, carders, combers, spinners and weavers,
at low wages, it is true, but with earnings near enough to subsistence level for it to be within Firmin's means to eke them out by
gifts of coal and humane conditions of service.   The establishment was at once school and factory, wholesale warehouse and

---

[1] Haines's pamphlets include the following : *The Prevention of Poverty, or
a Discourse of the Causes of the Decay of Trade,* 1674 : *Proposals for building
in every County a Working Almshouse or Hospital, as the best expedient to perfect
the trade and manufactory of Linen Cloth,* 1677 ; *A Postscript to* [the Above],
1677 (?) ; *Provision for the Poor, or reasons for the erecting of a working hospital
in every County,* 1678 ; *A Model of Government for the Good of the Poor and the
Wealth of the Nation, with such a Method and Inspection that Frauds, Corruption
in Officers, Abuses to the Poor, Ill-administration of Materials, etc., therein may
be prevented,* 1678 ; *A Breviat of some Proposals prepared to be offered to the
great wisdom of the Nation . . . for the speedy restoring the Woollen Manufacture,* 1679 ; *A Method of Government for public working Almshouses,* 1679 ;
*England's Weal and Prosperity proposed, or Reasons for erecting Public Work-
houses in every County for the Speedy Promoting of Industry and the Woollen
Manufacture . . . that there may not be a Beggar bred up in the Nation,* 1680 ;
ditto (another edition), 1681.   See *A Complete Memoir of Richard Haines,
1633–1685,* by Charles Reginald Haines, 1899.

retail shop. Children were admitted from three years of age,
and were taught to read as well as to spin. A certain number
of " ancients ", some " nearly blind ", were kept on for such
work as they could perform. Firmin's experiment, in which he
sunk nearly all his capital, and which he described as almost
paying its way (even including the cost of the children's education
and the maintenance of the aged), seemed to demonstrate that
children of tender age could earn at least twopence per day,
whilst adults could be paid sixpence per day, which at that date
was, even in London, almost enough for bare subsistence. Thus,
Firmin's experience served to strengthen the common faith in the
possibility of making actual profit out of the employment of the
poor. Thinking of the populous urban parishes, Firmin was led
confidently to propose " That every parish that abounds in poor
people should set up a school in the nature of a workhouse to
teach the poor children to work in, who for want thereof, now
wander up and down the parish and parts adjacent, and between
begging and stealing get a sorry living, but never bring anything
to their poor parents, nor earn one farthing towards their own
maintenance or the good of the nation ". With this he combined
the suggestions that homework should be provided for mothers
of young children, and that an asylum should be established for
the aged, under " Fathers of the Poor " in every parish.[1] The
strength of the belief in the possibility of getting an actual balance
of profit out of the employment of the poor is shown in the proposal—made, among others, by Richard Dunning in 1686—that
such poor persons should be assigned to undertakers or contractors by whom they should be set to work, whilst such as
refused to be so assigned should be committed to the House of
Correction.[2] The problem was attacked from another side by

---

[1] For Thomas Firmin (1632–1697), whom all men combined to praise, see
the notices in *D.N.B.* and *D.P.E.* ; his own pamphlet, *Some Proposals for the
Employment of the Poor and for the Prevention of Idleness and the Consequences
thereof, Beggary*, first published in 1678, and then in enlarged form in 1681,
and reprinted in Thomas Gilbert's *Collection of Pamphlets*, etc., 1787 ; *The
Charitable Samaritan, or a Short and Impartial Account of* . . . *Mr. T. F.*, by
a Gentleman of his acquaintance, 1698 ; Tillotson's Sermon on the Death of
the Rev. Thomas Gouge, in *Works*, 9th edition, 1728, vol. i. p. 212 ; *Life of
Archbishop Tillotson*, by Dr. T. Birch, 2nd edition, 1753 ; *The State of the Poor*,
by Sir F. M. Eden, 1797, vol. i.

[2] *A Plain and Easy Method showing how the Office of Overseer of the Poor
may be managed whereby it may be £9000 per annum advantage to the County
of Devon*, etc., by Richard Dunning, 1686 ; see also *Bread for the Poor*, by R. D.

the worthy Quaker, John Bellers, who—anticipating in various ways the Communist Utopia-builders of the first half of the nineteenth century—projected a " College of Industry ", which was to be, under the humane administration of the wise, " an epitome of the world ", in which all sorts of useful production and service would be organised, especially to the advantage of the unemployed poor, with capital to be voluntarily provided by the rich, who would, however, draw an annual revenue from the abundance which systematic organisation and the elimination of anarchic rivalry could not fail to produce.[1] " The best materials for building ", he said, " put together without order or method, are little better than rubbish, until they are regularly placed. And the best horses, whilst wild at grass, are but useless and chargeable : and the same are mankind until they are regularly and usefully employed."

In the same year as the " College of Industry ", a more practical examination of the problem was made by John Cary, a merchant of Bristol, in a pamphlet which John Locke declared to be " the best discourse I have ever read on that subject ", and which—alone of all the publications of this half-century—was destined to result in the immediate legislation which we shall presently describe. Cary saw his way, so far as Bristol was concerned, simultaneously to put down mendicancy, save much of the cost of litigation, lessen the cost of, and equalise the rates among, numerous small parishes crowded together in what had become the second commercial centre of the nation, by the establishment of a new and separate Poor Law Authority for the whole city, which could erect a workhouse or hospital, set the

---

(Exeter, 1698). With this we may cite the *Proposals*, etc., of John Appletree, who was Sheriff of Worcestershire in 1696, urging a law to empower unions of parishes to establish workhouses and compel the poor to work (see *The State of the Poor*, by Sir F. M. Eden, 1797, vol. i. pp. 225, 239-243, 248-252).

[1] *Proposals for raising a College of Industry of all Useful Trades and Husbandry, with Profit for the Rich, a Plentiful Living for the Poor, and a Good Education for Youth ; which will be an Advantage to the Government by the Increase of the People and their Riches*, by John Bellers, 1695 and 1714. Bellers, who lived from 1654 to 1725, followed this by *A Supplement to the* [above], 1696 ; *Essays about the Poor, Manufacture, Trade, Plantation and Immorality,* 1699 ; *An Essay for employing the poor to profit,* 1723 ; *An Abstract of George Fox's Advice and Warning to the Magistrates of London . . . concerning the Poor, with some observations thereupon,* 1724 ; *An Epistle to a Friend concerning the Prisoners and Sick in the Prisons and Hospitals of Great Britain,* 1724. See *The State of the Poor,* by Sir F. M. Eden, 1797, vol. i. p. 264. Bellers' suggestions were noticed with approval by Robert Owen and Karl Marx.

able-bodied to work and provide humanely for the aged and the infirm—all of which ends he had the good fortune, in some degree, to see at least temporarily attained.[1]

Meanwhile, though the London projectors and philanthropists seem consistently to have ignored this activity of the Parish Officers, the aggregate amount expended in the relief of the poor went on increasing, and the rising Poor Rates, coupled with the undiminished multitude of vagrants and beggars ever since the disbandment of the armies of the Civil War, led to loud complaints, which found expression in several of the speeches from the Throne made by William the Third. This burden of vagrancy and the Poor Rates was the first subject to be referred by the King for consideration to the Board of Trade, when this department was re-established in 1696 ; and within a year there was produced by the most distinguished of its salaried members, the philosopher John Locke, a reasoned report on the whole policy of the relief of the able-bodied poor.[2]

Locke's report characteristically enough — contained no statistical or other information as to what was the condition of the poor or as to the nature and extent of the evil with which it purported to deal. It said nothing of what was actually being done by the Churchwardens and Overseers or by the Houses of Correction throughout the country, or even what the position was in the City of London, where the Bridewell, which had been in existence for a century and a quarter, had been supplemented by the operations of the new Corporation of the Poor. Locke assumed the correctness of the common impression as to the heavy cost of the poor (though the financial estimate that he

---

[1] Cary's pamphlet was entitled, in the first edition, *An Essay on the State of England in relation to its Trade, its Poor and its Taxes*, by John Cary, 1695. It was republished in several editions, with some alterations, under varying titles (such as *An Essay towards regulating the Trade and employing the Poor in this Kingdom*) in 1717, 1719, 1745, etc. ; and there seem to have been versions in French (1755) and Italian (1764). See *D.N.B.* and *D.P.E.* ; *The State of the Poor*, by Sir F. M. Eden, 1797, vol. i. pp. 248-253 ; Locke's correspondence with Cary (at the British Museum Add. MSS. 5540) ; and the other references given on p. 119.

[2] *A Report of the Board of Trade to the Lords Justices respecting the Relief and Employment of the Poor*, by John Locke, 1697 ; reprinted in his *Works*, vol. x. of 11th edition, 1812 ; and in *An Account of the . . . Society for the Promotion of Industry in . . . Lindsey in the County of Lincoln*, 3rd edition, Louth, 1789. See the biographies of Locke by Lord King (1830 and 1858), and H. R. Fox Bourne (1876) ; and *The State of the Poor*, by Sir F. M. Eden, 1797, vol. i. pp. 243-248.

made came to less than half of the exaggerations then current), but pointed out that the trouble was not new, and that it had " been a growing burden on the Kingdom these many years ; and the last two reigns felt the increase of it as well as the present. . . . The evil has proceeded neither from scarcity of provisions nor from want of employment for the poor, since God has blessed these times with plenty not less than the former." Out of his inner consciousness Locke could suggest no other cause for the increase in poor relief than " the relaxation of discipline and corruption of manners ". He accordingly proposed " as the first step . . . towards the setting the poor on work . . . a restraint of their debauchery . . . more particularly by the suppressing superfluous brandyshops and unnecessary alehouses " ; and " that all men sound of limb and mind, above fourteen and under fifty years of age, begging in maritime counties out of their own parish without a pass, shall be seized on . . . and sent to the next seaport town, there to be kept at hard labour till some of His Majesty's ships coming in or near there give an opportunity of putting them on board, where they shall serve three years under strict discipline ". Other men found begging, over fifty years of age, or maimed, or without passes in inland counties, were to be committed for three years' hard labour at the House of Correction. The Houses of Correction, indeed, he thought too lenient for the poor, " for these Houses are now in most counties complained of to be rather places of ease and preferment to the Masters thereof, than of correction and reformation to those who are sent thither ". Accordingly he proposed that the organisation should be reformed by the device—which reminds us of some of the subsequent proposals of Jeremy Bentham—of compelling the Master " to allow unto every one committed to his charge 4d. per diem for their maintenance in and about London ", or, in cheaper localities, a lesser sum, " to be settled by the Grand Jury and Judge at the Assizes " ; the Master being then left to recoup himself (and make a salary) entirely out of the proceeds of the labour of those who were to be, for this purpose, subjected, as if they were slaves, to his orders, " consideration being had of their age and strength ". The Justices, moreover, were, every quarter, to " make a narrow inquiry " of the House of Correction, so that " if they find any one that is stubborn and not at all mended by the discipline of the place ", he shall be ordered " a longer stay there, and severer

discipline ". For women found begging, somewhat the same
treatment was to be provided ; and also for boys and girls under
fourteen, but in their case varied with being " soundly whipped ".
These proposals, which it is needless to say were seen to be no
more practicable of general application, and no more likely to be
successful against vagrancy and begging, than the repressive
legislation of the preceding centuries, left untouched the case of
the men idle in their own parishes under " the pretence that they
want work ". For these Locke devised what was a century and
a quarter later to be re-invented as the Labour Rate. He proposed that " the Guardian of the Poor "—a new officer to be
chosen by the ratepayers of each parish to serve on a new Board
of Guardians for the Hundred—should assign such men to any
employers willing to take them " at a lower rate than is usually
given ", or failing any such willing employer, parcelled out
compulsorily among all the ratepayers, all of them being bound,
in proportion to their several shares of the Poor Rate, either to
provide their proportion of the employment required, in so many
days, " at such under-rates as the said Guardian of the Poor
shall appoint ", or in default, to pay over the amount of such
wages for the allotted days.

But all these provisions were designed by the philosopher for
those who simply would not work, among whom, it is to be
inferred, that he included all the genuinely able-bodied men who
might be found unemployed. He then turned to those men who
were below par in strength, and those women whom the care of
children kept at home ; and for those especially, together with
all children, he proposed the provision of partial employment,
so as to recoup the community the expense of their relief. He
held it for proved that at least half of those in receipt of parochial
relief would thus be able to earn their own livelihood, and that
they were " neither wholly unable nor unwilling to work, but either
through want of work being provided for them, or their unskilful-
ness in working, do little that turns to public account ". It is
uncertain how far he intended to give support to the idea that
the public employment of these tens of thousands of men, women
and children in spinning and weaving linen or woollen cloth could
be made the means (as Richard Haines supposed) of " perfecting "
these or any other industries, or of making anything in the nature
of a commercial profit. What he argued was that as " every one

must have meat, drink, clothing and firing, so much goes out of the stock of the kingdom whether they work or no.   Supposing, then, there be 100,000 poor in England that live upon the parish . . . if care were taken that every one of those, by some labour in the woollen or other manufacture, should earn but a penny per day (which one with another they might well do, and more), this would gain to England £130,000 per annum." To this end he recommended the setting up, under the supervision of the proposed Board of Guardians for the Hundred, of " working schools " in every parish, in which both children and adults should be set to work upon materials to be supplied from a " common stock " to be provided by the rates of each Hundred.   He would have free meals supplied in these schools to the children, whose attendance would be thus ensured, whilst such a provision for children would, he thought, enable the Parish Officers to bring to an end the relief that they gave to parents overburdened with large families.

Locke's somewhat naïve proposals were quite in line with popular sentiment, but although his report was formally adopted by the Privy Council, its recommendations were never passed into law.[1] They attracted the notice of the capitalist " promoters " of the time, and they were developed into the then fashionable form of a national joint stock company, which was to raise a capital of £300,000, and start little factories all over the country, in which the poor could be set to work with the double object of getting them to earn their keep, and of yielding a dividend to the stock holders.   A Bill for the incorporation of such a body, to be termed " the Governor and Company for maintaining and employing the poor " was actually introduced into Parliament

---

[1] A Bill to carry out Locke's report was introduced, as a private member's measure, into the House of Commons in 1705 (*The Bill intituled an Act for the Relief, Employment and Settlement of the Poor which came from the House of Commons ; and also the Bill intituled an Act for the Better Relief, Employment and Maintenance of the Poor ; and the Scheme of an Act for the Relief of the Poor delivered unto the House of Peers from the Commissioners of Trade and Plantations as drawn by them*, 1705 ; and *The State of the Poor*, by Sir F. M. Eden, 1797, vol. i. p. 248).   The report may possibly have influenced the parishioners of Ealing, then a rural village several miles from the Great Metropolis.   At any rate, the Vestry Minutes record that, on November 21, 1698, the Churchwardens and Overseers were directed to "take and provide one or more houses for workhouses to employ the poor of this parish to work in ; and also to provide a sufficient stock and implements at the charge of the said parish to employ and set the poor to work " (*Annals of Ealing*, by Edith Jackson, 1898, p. 180).

in 1698.[1] That particular measure made no progress, but the subject continued to be referred to in successive speeches from the Throne, in which William the Third repeatedly suggested to the House of Commons that if " you can find proper means of setting the poor at work, you will ease yourselves of a very great burden, and at the same time add so many useful hands to be employed in our manufactures and other public occasions ". In 1704 there were no fewer than four Bills in Parliament designed to put in operation the ideas thus sanctioned, one of which, introduced by the great capitalist *entrepreneur* of the day, Sir Humphrey Mackworth, met with almost universal acceptance, and in the following session actually passed, with great applause, through all its stages in the House of Commons. This measure would have set up in each parish something partaking of the nature of the " Public Workhouse " of Sir Matthew Hale and Sir Josiah Child ; of the " working almshouse or hospital " desired by Richard Haines ; and of the " working school " advocated by Thomas Firmin and John Locke, in which, on materials and working capital raised by the Poor Rate, all the paupers able to work, whatever their age or sex, would have been

[1] See the characteristic chapter entitled " A Scheme for Setting the Poor to Work " in *An Essay on the Probable Means of making the people gainers in the Balance of Trade*, by Dr. Charles Davenant, 1699 ; included in his *Political and Commercial Works*, vol. i. by Sir Charles Whitworth, 1771, vol. ii. pp. 184, 207 ; *The State of the Poor*, by Sir F. M. Eden, 1797, pp. 227-239. Davenant advocated the compulsory employment of every unemployed able-bodied person in manufactures as a method of reducing the cost of production, and thereby increasing the trade of the nation. In a previous work of 1695 he had said that " if public workhouses were set up in every town and county, and if the works and manufactures proper for every place and country were fixed and established in it, the poor would be encouraged and invited to labour and industry, especially if the magistrate made use of his coercive power upon such as are vicious and idle " (*Essay upon Ways and Means*, by Dr. C. Davenant, 1695, Sir C. Whitworth's edition, 1771, vol. i. p. 72 ; *The State of the Poor*, by Sir F. M. Eden, 1797, vol. i. p. 232). The State Papers contain references, about 1690, to various projects for establishing a Corporation of the Poor for the whole kingdom, in order to get established workhouses in which the poor could be set to work (*Calendar of State Papers (Domestic)*, 1690-1691, pp. 369, 422, etc. ; *History of English Law*, by W. S. Houldsworth, vol. vi., 1924, p. 351).

Another writer realised the danger of merely shifting employment from existing factories, but repeated the proposal made under the Commonwealth of organising a sea fishery, for which he urged the establishment of a joint stock company, raising a capital of a million pounds, to be incorporated as the " Fathers of the Poor ", with the management in the hands of a body of " Stewards of the Poor " (*England's Path to Wealth and Honour, in a Dialogue between an Englishman and a Dutchman*, by James Puckle, 1700 ; reprinted in Lord Somers' *Tracts*, second edition, 1814, vol. ii. pp. 371-386).

I

offered, at wages, employment which they could not have refused without foregoing all claim to relief, and probably incurring commitment to a House of Correction.[1]   At the eleventh hour the project was killed dead by Daniel De Foe, who addressed " to the Parliament of England " his telling pamphlet entitled *Giving Alms no Charity, and employing the poor a grievance to the Nation.* In 1705, at a later period of the same session of Parliament, the House of Lords threw out Sir Humphrey Mackworth's Bill ; and no similar measure has afterwards got anything near so close to success.[2]

What Daniel De Foe threw into the discussion was the hardest possible stone of economic disillusionment and worldly cynicism. He struck down at a blow the compassionate efforts of those whom he doubtless regarded as soft-hearted dupes of their sentiments of pity.   But he made no approach to a solution of the real social problem that was presenting itself amid the growing capitalist development of town and country alike.   Whilst he professed to offer a remedy, he failed to propose any.   It was, he said, " a regulation of the poor that is wanted in England, not a setting them to work ".   It was the " regulation " that would put a stop to " poverty, beggary, parish charges, assessments and the like ", but he was unable to formulate any plan even of regulation.   He ignored the prescient observation of Sir Matthew Hale that " some times there are when the honestest tradesman cannot get work ".   He had no sympathy with Firmin's text, " Thanks be to God, there are still amongst us an honest kind of poor people that are content to take any pains for a living . . .

[1] *A Bill for the Better Relief, Employment and Settlement of the Poor, as the same was reported from the Committee of the . . . House of Commons, in order that . . . the same may be farther considered against the next session of Parliament,* by Sir Humphrey Mackworth, 1704 ; see *The State of the Poor,* by Sir F. M. Eden, 1797, vol. i. pp. 243-248; Sir H. M. (1657-1727), who sat in Parliament, with slight intervals, from 1700 to 1713, was engaged, from 1695 to 1711, in coal-mining and copper-smelting near Neath in Glamorganshire as " The Governor and Company of the Mine Adventurers of England ".   He published also *England's Glory, or the Great Improvement of Trade by a Royal Bank or Office of Credit to be opened in London,* 1694 ; *A Vindication of the Rights of the Commons,* etc., 1701 ; and *Sir H. M.'s Proposal, being a New Scheme Offered for the Payment of the Public Debts,* which—a project for paper money inflation—went through half a dozen editions in 1720.

[2] The attempted legislation of 1704—for which see also *The State of the Poor,* by Sir F. M. Eden, 1797, vol. i., and *Pauperism and Poor Laws,* by R. Pashley, 1852, pp. 243-244—excited enough interest to be reprinted sixteen years later as *Three Abstracts of as many Bills, in 1704 depending in Parliament, for the Relief, Employment and Settlement of the Poor,* 1720,

who come least into sight, who fare hard, and work hard to get
bread ". He did not see the grain of truth in Cary's discovery
" that the great cause of begging did proceed from the low wages
for labour, for after about eight months our children [set to work]
could not get [earn] half so much as we expended in their provision ". The most prominent feature in De Foe's diagnosis of
the cause of pauperism, as it has ever since been in that of the
more thoughtless of the rich, is the idleness, intemperance and im-
providence of the manual working wage-earners. " From hence",
he concludes, " come poverty, parish charges and beggary. If
ever one of these wretches falls sick, all they would ask is a pass
to the parish they lived at, and the wife and children to the door
a-begging. . . . As for the craving poor, I am persuaded I do
them no wrong when I say that, if they were incorporated they
would be the richest society in the nation ; and the reason why
so many pretend to want work is that they can live so well with
the pretence of wanting work [that] they would be mad to leave
it and work in earnest. And I affirm of my own knowledge,
when I have wanted a man for labouring work, and offered 9s.
per week to strolling fellows at my door, they have frequently
told me to my face they could get more a-begging, and I once
set a lusty fellow in the stocks for making the experiment." It
was then easy for him to demonstrate how " an alms ill-directed
may be charity to the particular person but becomes an injury
to the public, and no charity to the nation ". But apart from
all misstatement and cynicism it must be admitted that his main
argument is conclusive in its destructive effect, even if it leaves
the problem unsolved. " The erection of parochial manufactures ", he said, " in order to parcel out work to every door,
would be ruinous to the manufacturers themselves ; they would
turn thousands of families out of their employments ; and would
take the bread out of the mouths of diligent and industrious
families to feed vagrants, thieves and beggars, who ought much
rather to be compelled, by legal methods, to seek that work which,
it is plain, is to be had. . . . If they will employ the poor in some
manufacture not made in England before, or not bought with
some manufacture made here before, then they offer at something
extraordinary. But to set poor people at work on the same
thing that other poor people were employed on before, and at the
same time not increase the consumption, is giving to one what

you take from another ; putting a vagabond in an honest man's employment, and putting diligence on the tenters to find some other work to maintain his family." [1]

Although De Foe's pamphlet killed Sir Humphrey Mackworth's Bill, and possibly converted a number of his contemporaries, it was very far from destroying the alluring project of " setting the poor to work ", as a means of increasing the national wealth. We shall find this idea perpetually cropping up all through the eighteenth century. But we have now to deal with the new statutory Poor Law authorities which, in 1696, began to arise out of the intellectual ferment that we have described.

The Union of Urban Parishes

The powerful and convincing pamphlet of John Cary, which we have briefly described, had grown out of the author's experience of the problems of mendicancy and Poor Relief in the City of Bristol, which had become a busy and wealthy seaport and great trade emporium. Cary added agitation to exhortation, and summoned meetings of his fellow-citizens, finally inducing the Mayor and Aldermen of the city and other principal inhabitants to apply to Parliament for a Local Act. The reasons for the application, as is stated in the preamble, were that " it is found

---

[1] De Foe's pamphlet *Giving Alms no Charity and Employing the Poor a Grievance to the Nation*, 1704, was reprinted in the *Collection of Pamphlets concerning the Poor*, by Thomas Gilbert, M.P., 1787 ; and again as a separate pamphlet in 1868, " by a London Physician " ; see *The State of the Poor*, by Sir F. M. Eden, 1797, vol. i. pp. 258-263 ; *Pauperism and Poor Laws*, by R. Pashley, 1852, pp. 243-244 ; *The History of the English Poor Law*, by Sir George Nicholls, 1854, vol. i. p. 387 ; also *D.N.B.* and *D.P.E.* ; and the successive biographies of De Foe, who lived from 1660 to 1731, by W. Wilson (1830), W. Chadwick (1859), W. Lee (1869), W. Minto (1879) and T. Wright (1894). De Foe (under the pseudonym of Andrew Moreton) published another pamphlet bearing on the Poor Law, entitled *Parochial Tyranny*, 1727, forcibly exposing and denouncing the corruption and maladministration of the parochial administration, mainly of the Metropolis (*The Parish and the County*, by S. and B. Webb, 1906, pp. 242, 255).

Mandeville, whose *Fable of the Bees* (1714, enlarged in 1723, and reprinted 1793) was as cynical as De Foe, but allowed for the relief of absolute destitution—" the poor have nothing to stir them up to labour but their wants, which it is wisdom to relieve but folly to cure "—and even advocated employment on public works. " Many rivers ", he said, " are to be made navigable ; canals to be cut in hundreds of places ; some lands are to be drained and secured from inundations for the future ; abundance of soil is to be made fertile ; and thousands of acres rendered more beneficial by being made more accessible."

by experience that the poor in the City of Bristol do daily multiply, and idleness and debauchery amongst the meaner sort doth greatly increase, for want of workhouses to set them to work, and a sufficient authority to compel them thereto, as well to the charge of the inhabitants and grief of the charitable and honest citizens of the said city, as the great distress of the poor themselves for which sufficient redress hath not yet been provided ". An attempt in 1681 to cope with the situation by getting a contractor to employ the poor in spinning yarn at piecework wages had brought no lasting improvement. Cary's proposals, which were destined to be copied up and down the kingdom for a whole century, were summarised as follows :

1. That a spacious workhouse be erected at a general charge, large enough for the poor to be employed therein ; and also for room for such as, being unable to work, are to be relieved by charity.

2. That the rules of the house may force all persons to work that are able, and encourage manufacturers to furnish them with materials to work upon.

3. That persons not able to maintain their children may put them into this workhouse or hospital at what ages they will, so that these children may be bred up to labour, principles of virtue implanted in them at an early age, and laziness be discouraged.

4. That the ancient shall be provided for according to their wants.

5. That the rates of the city being united into one common fund, the magistrates will be freed from the daily trouble which they have about settlement of the poor, the parish officers will be eased, the poor's stock will not be spent in law, but they will be provided for without being sent from parish to parish, and their children will be settled in a way serviceable to the public good, and not be bred up in all manner of vice as they now are.

6. That the governor be empowered to force all poor people to work who do not betake themselves to some lawful employment elsewhere, but spend their time lazily and idly.

7. That the governor have power to settle out the young people at such ages as may be thought fit, the boys to navigation and the maids in service ; and to bind them apprentices for a certain number of years ; that this will prevent children from

being starved by the poverty of their parents and the neglect of parish officers, which is now a great loss to the nation, inasmuch as every person would by his labour add to the wealth of the public.

Parliament passed the Bill on the 18th January 1696,[1] and allowed the City of Bristol to try its experiment. The Act took the whole management and relief of the poor out of the hands of the Overseers of the nineteen crowded city parishes, and estab-

[1] This was not the first " Corporation of the Poor ". Priority must be accorded to " The Corporation of the Poor of the City of London ", established by Ordinance of the Commonwealth of December 17, 1647, which was re-enacted with slight alterations as to constitution and powers in Ordinance of May 7, 1649. Of this body we have been unable to discover the archives ; and little is yet known of its proceedings in detail, though Miss Leonard gives, in her *Early History of English Poor Relief*, 1900, pp. 270, 272-273, some particulars from the Common Council records, the *Calendars of State Papers, King's Pamphlets*, etc. The Ordinance of 1647 was confirmed in 1662 by 13 and 14 Charles II. c. 12 (amended by 22 and 23 Charles II. in 1670, and made perpetual by 12 Anne, st. 1, c. 18, in 1712), which defined the constitution of the Corporation to be the Lord Mayor and Aldermen and fifty-two other citizens chosen by the Common Council ; and which enabled like Corporations of the Poor to be established in the City of Westminster, on the nomination of the Lord Chancellor, and for other parishes within the Bills of Mortality on the nomination of the County Justices (Shaw's *Parish Law*, 1730 ; *A Practical Treatise on the Laws, Customs, Usages and Regulations of the City and Port of London*, by Alexander Pulling, 1st edition, 1842, 3rd edition, 1854, pp. 242-243). We are not aware that any other Corporations were formed, either in Westminster or elsewhere, under this statute. It could even be said officially in 1843 that " no Corporation was formed under this Act of Parliament until the year 1698, and no steps were taken for hiring a workhouse in the City of London until the following year " (Ninth Annual Report of Poor Law Commissioners, 1843, p. 94). This, however, was plainly incorrect, as " reports of the Governors of the Corporation were published in 1655 " (*History of English Philanthropy*, by B. Kirkman Gray, 1905, pp. 72-74), and in the Guildhall library there is *A Short State and Representation of the Proceedings of the President and Governors of the Poor of the City of London*, 1699. The Corporation of the Poor of the City of London continued in existence, and its workhouses to be used, throughout the eighteenth century. In 1723, it was alleged that " the very City workhouse without Bishopsgate is universally complained of by all parts of the City as having not lessened but very much increased their charge to the poor " ; and the Corporation was urged to employ the poor on the land (*To pay all Debts without New Taxes by Charitably Relieving, Politically Reforming and Judiciously Employing the Poor*, 1723 ; a book of over 200 pages in Ministry of Health library). What happened to the administration of the Corporation of the Poor, and what were its relations to the City parishes, we have not ascertained. We gather that it was dissolved, and its workhouse was sold, by authority of the Acts 5 George IV. c. 83, and 10 George IV. c. 43, in the decade preceding the passing of the Poor Law Amendment Act, 1834. On the passing of that Act it was remarked that none of the ninety-six parishes within the City walls possessed a workhouse either singly or in combination (Third and Fourth Annual Reports of Poor Law Commissioners ; Pulling's *Practical Treatise*, etc., 1842, pp. 248-249 ; *Statutory Authorities for Special Purposes*, by S. and B. Webb, 1922, pp. 110-111).

lished a new " Corporation of the Poor " for the whole city, consisting of the Mayor and Aldermen of the city and the Church-wardens of the parishes, together with four persons elected by a public meeting of the inhabitants of each ward. The Corporation of the Poor of the City of Bristol was—if we leave aside the immemorial traditional usages of the Corporations of London, Norwich and a few other ancient municipal bodies, and the early constitution of the Corporation of the Poor of the City of London —the first local governing body directed by Parliamentary statute to be based mainly upon popular election in all the wards of a great city.

The Corporation of the Poor of the City of Bristol was from the outset, as its manuscript minutes show,[1] a dignified and well-organised body, presided over by a " governor " who habitu-ally continued in office for a term of years ; acting under well-framed standing orders ; working through a permanent executive of fifteen members, who were divided into four or five standing committees ; and served by a relatively large staff of salaried officials, including latterly even an " investigator " to detect impostors. " The services of the Guardians ", writes the able governor in 1820, " are gratuitous. No member of the Corpora-tion of the Poor can even supply the Hospital with goods ; nor does the whole body of Guardians put the City to any, the most

---

[1] The principal source for the history of this celebrated " Corporation of the Poor of the City of Bristol " must always be its own well-kept and voluminous MS. Minutes, which we found of great use when describing it in our *Statutory Authorities for Special Purposes*, 1922, pp. 112-114 ; see also the Acts 7 and 8 William III. c. 32 ; 12 Anne, st. 2, c. 15 ; 4 George I. c. 3 ; 18 George II. c. 30 ; 31 George II. c. 56 ; 3 George IV. c. 24 ; 1 William IV. c. 4 ; *An Account of the Proceedings of the Corporation of the Poor of Bristol.* by John Cary, 1700 ; *The State of the Poor*, by Sir F. M. Eden, 1797, vol. ii. pp. 182-203, vol. i. pp. 275-278 ; *Transactions of the Corporation of the Poor in the City of Bristol during a period of 126 years*, by James Johnson (Bristol, 1826) ; *An Address to the Inhabitants of Bristol on the subject of the Poor Rates*, by James Johnson (Bristol, 1820) ; *Observations on the Bill about to be introduced into Parliament by the Corporation of the City and the Poor*, by Thomas Stocking (Bristol, 1822) ; *The Causes of the Present Alarming Amount of the Poor Rates in the City of Bristol explained*, etc., by T J. Manchee (Bristol, 1834) ; *Letters, Essays, etc., illustrative of the Municipal History of Bristol, and of the trade of its port, written and collected by a burgess* (Bristol, 1836) ; Report of Poor Law Inquiry Commissioners, 1834 (Chapman's Report), p. 510 ; Ninth Annual Report of Poor Law Commissioners, 1843, pp. 138-181.

The Bristol Workhouse, which became known as St. Peter's Hospital, was often locally called the Mint, because one of the buildings had been used in recoining the clipped money that was called in under William III. A " sugar house " was hired for additional accommodation, but given up in 1714.

trifling expense ; for when upon Committees, etc., any refreshment is wanted, it is sent for to a neighbouring inn and paid by the respective individuals." [1]

The Bristol Workhouse quickly became widely known as a promising experiment ; and within the next fifteen years thirteen towns—Crediton (1698), Tiverton (1698), Exeter (1698), Hereford (1698), Colchester (1698), Hull (1698), Shaftesbury (1698), King's Lynn (1700), Sudbury (1700), Gloucester (1702), Worcester (1704), Plymouth (1708) and Norwich (1712)—successfully applied to Parliament for Local Acts, which superseded the authority of the Overseers, and incorporated a body of " Guardians of the Poor " to act for the whole city. The idea underlying all these Acts was the desirability of organising the labour of the unemployed, with the double object of maintaining them without disorder and of increasing the national wealth. It was impossible to do this without providing a large and costly workhouse, for which no powers were given by the general law, and which could hardly be established separately in each of the small and densely crowded parishes of an old walled town. Incidentally the union of these parishes brought the great advantage of avoiding much of the complication of the law as to settlement, and of equalising the poor rate throughout the city.

The sanguine projects of so organising the labour of the poor as to produce at least the cost of their maintenance were soon proved to be delusive. At Bristol, for instance, the plan of employing the poor at wages in the workhouse was quickly discovered to involve not less but greater expense per head than their maintenance by doles of outdoor relief. When it was abandoned, the plan of farming out the poor to a contractor was reverted to. " A malt and corn dealer . . . was to bear all the costs and take all the profits of the sack-making business carried on by the city poor. He was to give each worker a small gratuity as he thought fit. . . . Thus the scheme initiated by Cary in the hope of raising wages was used to depress them." [2]

---

[1] *Address to the Inhabitants of Bristol on the subject of the Poor Rates*, by James Johnson, 1820, p. 7.

[2] *History of English Philanthropy*, by B. Kirkman Gray, 1905, p. 212.

The Colchester experiment is described in *The History . . . of Essex*, by Philip Morant, 1768, where its eventual abandonment in 1768 is ascribed to political corruption. " This Workhouse Corporation became, indeed, too much the property of a few, who perhaps made too great an advantage of it.

But the new workhouses were incidentally found of use in providing an alternative to the indiscriminate distribution of money by the Overseers. These early reformers had, in fact, accidentally stumbled on the discovery of the "workhouse test". It became possible to offer maintenance to the able-bodied applicant in a form that he did not like, with the result that the demand for relief immediately fell off, to the great saving of the ratepayers. And so in 1723 Sir Edward Knatchbull induced the House of Commons to pass a general Act (9 George I. c. 7) enabling the officers of separate parishes to hire premises and maintain them as workhouses for the poor. Within a decade, as we shall describe in the following chapter, over a hundred workhouses were set up by parishes under this Act. The demand for Local Acts establishing new bodies of Incorporated Guardians of the Poor was for a time checked. But the general Act of 1723 merely enabled the Churchwardens and Overseers of particular parishes to hire or purchase premises for a workhouse, and gave no power to parishes to combine for the purpose. Accordingly we find presently beginning again the demand for Local Acts incorporating a body of Guardians for a union of parishes. Such new statutory authorities were established at Canterbury (1727), Bury St. Edmunds (1748), Chichester (1753), Chester (1762), Salisbury (1770), Oxford (1771), Southampton (1773) and Maidstone (1780).

We make no attempt to describe in detail the results of the experiments in " setting the poor to work " by the Incorporated Guardians of Bristol and the score of towns which followed its example in the first eighty years of the eighteenth century. Some of them quickly abandoned the experiment. Others discontinued it and resumed it at a later date, when the memory of the earlier failure had been lost. It will be more convenient to see what happened in the subsequent case of Shrewsbury, which was widely and persistently advertised throughout the kingdom.[1]

And it also became a powerful tool in the hands of those odious things, Parties. But it might have been better amended than destroyed " (vol. i. pp. 181-182).

[1] The Shrewsbury House of Industry was greatly " boomed " about 1791–1800 by its enthusiastic promoter, Isaac Wood. We have not seen the MS. Minutes, which possibly still exist : but abundant information is afforded by the Acts 24 George III. c. 15 (1784), and 7 George IV. c. 141 (1826) ; *Directions for the Conduct of the Overseers of the Poor for the Six United Parishes in the Town and Liberties of Shrewsbury*, 1800 ; *Some Account of the Shrewsbury House of Industry*, by Isaac Wood, 1791, which ran through five editions ; *An Introduction to the Fifth Edition of Some Account*, [etc.], by the same, 1800 ;

In 1783 some of the principal inhabitants of what was still the
Metropolis of the Welsh Border, tired of the maladministration
of the Overseers and Vestries of the six little parishes crowded
within the walls and liberties of that ancient city, obtained a
Local Act for the incorporation of a body of Guardians of the
Poor, with power to borrow £10,000 for the erection of a House
of Industry. The Guardians consisted of all owners of freehold
or copyhold property within the city worth £30 a year, and all
inhabitant occupiers rated at £15 a year. This body itself
appointed the Clerk, Treasurer, Governor, Steward, Matron and
Chaplain, but also elected twelve Directors of the Poor in whom
the whole administration was vested. They were fortunate in
finding ready to hand premises admirably suited for their objects,
on a magnificent site at a high cliff in a bend of the Severn,
adjacent to the city. This building had been erected in 1759–
1765 at a cost of £14,000 by the Foundling Hospital of London
for the accommodation of children drafted from its principal
establishment, but had been disused in 1774 on such provincial
homes being discontinued. The Shrewsbury Guardians purchased this building (which had been used by the Government
during the American War for the confinement of prisoners of war)

Observations on the Accounts of the Shrewsbury House of Industry, by the same,
1799; *Letter to Sir William Pulteney, Bart.*, by the same, 1797; *General
Observations on the Year's Account of the Shrewsbury House of Industry*, by the
same, 1800; *An Address to the Parochial Committees at Bath . . . for the
establishment of a House of Industry*, by J. (really Isaac) Wood, 1798; *An
Address to the Poor . . . within the Town of Shrewsbury . . . delivered at the
House of Industry*, by Rev. Thomas Stedman, 1786; *Byelaws, Rules and
Ordinances . . . for the Better Relief and Maintenance of the Poor of Shrewsbury*,
1787; *Appendix to some Account of the Shrewsbury House of Industry, containing
a correspondence with the Rev. J. Howlett*, 1791; *The State of the Poor*, by Sir
F. M. Eden, 1797, vol. ii. pp. 622-643; *Annals of Agriculture*, vol. xxxv.,
1800, pp. 157-163, 608-621; *General View of the Agriculture of Shropshire*, by
Joseph Plymley, 1803, p. 131; *Some Account of . . . Shrewsbury*, by Hugh
Owen, 1808, pp. 333-346; *General View of the Agriculture of North Wales*, by
Walter Davies, 1813, p. 434; *Aris's Birmingham Gazette*, November 15, 1824;
*Report of the Committee appointed to collect information and documents as to the
inexpediency of repealing the . . . Shrewsbury Incorporated House of Industry
Act*, 1824; First Report of Poor Law Inquiry Commissioners, 1834, Appendix
A, Lewis's Report, p. 659; Ninth Annual Report of Poor Law Commissioners,
1843; *Statutory Authorities for Special Purposes*, by S. and B. Webb, 1922,
pp. 117-121.

The example of Shrewsbury was followed in 1791–1792 by five neighbouring
districts of rural character, forming by Local Acts the Incorporations of
Oswestry, Ellesmere, Atcham, Whitchurch and Montgomery and Pool; and
also by two parishes at Bath, whilst an attempt was unsuccessfully made to
form a similar body at Sheffield (*ibid.* p. 118).

for £5500, and rapidly equipped it for its new purpose. The House of Industry which they established, with its farm, its corn-mill and its woollen manufactory, had the good fortune to enlist the devotion of Isaac Wood, an indefatigable local citizen, who evidently lavished upon its administration an incessant personal attention. His enthusiastic descriptions of its success were widely circulated, and did much to revive the faith in the profitable employment of the poor.

The object of the Shrewsbury Directors was, primarily and avowedly, " to furnish employment for the poor and compel them to earn their own support ", which had " been found impracticable in parish workhouses, under the direction and management of those officers who are annually chosen and annually removed. . . . Nor could the still more important object of training up the children of the poor to habits of industry and virtue be here obtained. In these workhouses, as well as in their private dwellings, they are incorporated with the abandoned and depraved." For ten years the experiment had no small measure of success. The erection of a well-planned institution, administered by a standing committee and salaried officers, evidently brought about a great improvement in the condition of the paupers, whilst diminishing the Poor Rates by one-third. Between two and three hundred men, women and children were brought into the House of Industry. Systematic arrangements were made for bathing and medically examining them on admission ; and for the treatment in a separate infirmary of such of them as were sick. Most of them were set to work at preparing, spinning and weaving wool, whilst " at the same time working rooms or shops were set apart for the shoemakers, tailors, carpenters, etc., where those paupers who had been brought up to these occupations were immediately employed, the most intelligent and trusty being appointed to cut out the work and superintend the rest ". But the Shrewsbury Directors never contemplated refusing all outdoor relief. What they believed, as Wood later expressed it, was that " indiscriminate allowances and indiscriminate confinement to a Poor House are equally absurd and injurious. . . . We discriminate. This is the grand hinge upon which every plan of parochial reform ought to turn." " To compel all claimants to come into the House ", he explained, " never made any part of their plan, and is an idea that has never been acted upon in any period of their practice. In cases of real distress the poor are more liberally relieved at their own dwellings than they were before this establishment took place. Nevertheless, by the proper examination of each respective case before a weekly board of respectable Directors, and the regular modes of inquiry instituted by the bye-laws of the House, such a check has been given to fraud and imposition that the amount of the Poor Rate is one third less than when the House was opened in 1784. . . . Such a result could never have been obtained without employment had been provided for the poor in the House of Industry. . . . At the same time our experience has demonstrated, and it is a fact of the utmost moment, that it is not necessary to furnish the employment for the great body of the poor at large ; it is sufficient that you have it to offer to such applicants as allege the want of work in justification of their demands upon the parochial fund. . . . Out of 7000 poor we have never had occasion, at one and the same time, to furnish employment for half seven hundred." At first all was done according to rule, on the policy afterwards adopted as that of the most " enlightened " Poor Law administration. Every case was strictly inquired into. The payment of rent was peremptorily stopped. Those who pleaded sickness were visited and examined by the doctor. Gifts of clothing were discontinued. All constant doles were stopped, relief being only given to tide over temporary emergencies. And where destitution was plainly caused by a large family of young children, the Directors preferred to take some of the children into the House of Industry, rather than relieve the family by a dole. Such a system, it is clear, depended for any success on a strict and continuous policy. After Wood's death—which took place in 1801 from fever caught whilst inspecting the House—the results were less successful. Within a few years we note a complete revulsion of feeling in Shrewsbury itself. The once belauded House of Industry is seen to be a centre of demoralisation rather than of reform. In 1824–1831 we have a successful agitation for the dissolution of the Incorporation, a demand for the sale of the workhouse as a " useless burden ", and a reversion to parish management. " It is curious to find ", reports the Assistant Poor Law Commissioner of 1842, " that the Act . . . which was anxiously watched over in its infancy, and matured into vigour under the eye of its enthusiastic parent; was doomed to live through not half a century ; and that almost before the generation in which it had sprung up had passed away we find it avowed [by the Shrewsbury Committee of 1824] that the objects stated in the preamble had never been attained, and that the mere recital of them in the present day was sufficient to expose their absurdity." [1]

The Union of Rural Parishes

The desirability of combining for the administration of poor relief was even more obvious in the case of thinly inhabited rural parishes, each containing an average of only a few dozen or a few score families, than in that of crowded urban communities. The results of the general Act of 1723, which authorised the establishment of workhouses by one or more parishes, had, after the first flush of apparent success, not been such as to lead to its adoption in rural districts, where the defects of management under parish officers, or the horrors of the farming system, soon outweighed the advantages of the workhouse itself. In the country parishes, at any rate, something more efficient than parochial management was required. Yet not for more than sixty years was the example of Bristol followed in any rural area.

John Cary had pointed out that the only way to get workhouses in the country districts was to incorporate a larger area than the parish. The difficulty was to decide upon this larger area, and upon the constitution of the governing body. Cary's suggestion was that all the Justices of the Peace and all the freeholders of each County should be constituted the Poor Law authority for the entire County. John Locke had proposed the establishment of workhouses in the several Hundreds of each County, with a Guardian of the Poor elected by each parish to form a Board of Guardians for the Hundred. Both these suggestions were, between 1750 and 1755, more than once embodied in general Bills, which failed to become law. The Bill for the establishment of " general County workhouses " struck the

---

[1] *Report of the Committee to the Guardians of the Poor of the Shrewsbury United District*, Shrewsbury, 1831 ; Ninth Annual Report of Poor Law Commissioners, 1843, p. 281. The magnificently placed site of the House of Industry, affording one of the finest views in Europe, together with the substantial building overlooking the Severn, eventually became the property of Shrewsbury School, which was transferred to the premises of the old workhouse, suitably converted for its new uses, in 1882 (*Statutory Authorities for Special Purposes*, by S. and B. Webb, 1922, p. 121).

average country gentleman as " a huge unwieldy scheme, attended with such an amazing certain expense, and liable to so many reasonable objections that the Parliament rejected it. Then it was proposed to have County workhouses to take in children only. But this, though it considerably reduced the other proposal, was subject to very many of the same objections which attended that, and therefore this likewise was rejected." William Hay's project for a workhouse in each Hundred seemed more feasible, but the Hundred varied enormously in size and character in different Counties, and no member succeeded in producing a scheme that commended itself to the County representatives generally.[1] At last, in 1756, the energy and persistence of the gentlemen of two small Hundreds in the south of Suffolk, headed by Admiral Vernon, the victor of Portobello, resulted in the passing of a Local Act, which set up, for these two Hundreds of Carlford and Colneis, a new local governing body, empowered to erect a workhouse, and practically to take over, from the officers of the twenty-eight parishes concerned, the whole administration of the Poor Law.

The objects of the promoters of this Act are well set out in a nearly contemporaneous document. "We propose to incorporate ", says this writer, in order " to administer proper comfort and assistance to the sick, infirm and aged, introduce sobriety and virtue among them, and in an especial manner to render their children useful to society by acquainting them with their duty towards God and man, whence many are saved from untimely end, and all of them enabled to acquire an honest livelihood, and so not remain any longer a burden and reproach to our county. We incorporate too, to ease the respective parishes in their rates, a grievance very loudly and very commonly complained of by all sorts of occupiers ; and also to feed and clothe the objects of their care with that plenty and decency that their wants and situation can reasonably require. . . . Our design, too, is to invite gentlemen to attend to the state and conduct of the

---

[1] The chief advocate in the House of Commons was the zealous William Hay, M.P., who, as early as 1735, actually got passed a series of resolutions for the division of each County into suitable areas, each to have a workhouse, under twelve Guardians. On the revival of interest, Hay published his plan as *Remarks on the Laws relating to the poor, with Proposals for their better Relief and Employment*, 1751. This was commented on in *Observations on the Defects of the Poor Laws*, by Rev. T. Alcock, 1752, and other pamphlets described in the next chapter.

poor—a concern which, however weighty and important in itself, it must be confessed, is not, nor is it likely it ever will be, regarded by them in the separate parishes, seeing that but very few owners of any fashion live where their estates are situated, and whenever it happens that they do reside there, the indelicacy and rudeness of parish meetings oblige them never to come into such assemblies."[1] With such high hopes we see some fifty of the squires and clergy of these Suffolk parishes meeting, in June 1756, at an Ipswich tavern. One of them, the Rev. R. Canning, advances twenty pounds towards the initial expenses. Admiral Vernon, whom they make chairman, gives a site on Nacton Heath on which to build the workhouse, and lends £1000 at 3½ per cent towards its erection. For a couple of years we watch the little group of reformers planning their new institution, carefully ordering the various items of furniture and equipment, and deciding all the details of its organisation. By March 1758 the " Nacton House of Industry " is completed according to the best science of the time ; and we see transferred to it the paupers, male and female, young and old, well and sick, who had previously been lodging in the dilapidated village poorhouses, or eking out by begging and pilfering their weekly doles of out-relief. In the Nacton House of Industry they were apparently well provided for and kindly treated, but set to work at weaving corn-sacks out of hemp ; making cordage of various sorts, especially plough-lines ; and spinning wool for the weavers of Norwich. " This institution ", it was said in 1766, " puts an end to the usual custom of pecuniary payments to the poor, which are generally abused by them, and, as generally, given without discretion. . . . Many children are rendered useful who otherwise would have figured nowhere but in a landscape of Gainsborough's, the spawn of gipsies, lying upon a sunny bank half naked, with their bundles of stolen wood by their sides—a daily task which those who

[1] *A Letter to J. W., Esquire, relating to Mr. G——y's Pamphlet upon the Poor Laws, with some reflections in favour of the House of Industry at Nacton, in the County of Suffolk, and on the Utility of such designs*, 1766, 24 pp. No copy of this is known to us, but voluminous extracts from it are given in a letter signed XX in the *Ipswich Journal*, July 23 and September 10, 1825. The inscription on the House of Industry at Melton was as follows : " Erected in the year 1768 for the Instruction of Youth, the Encouragement of Industry, the Relief of Want, the Support of Age and the comfort of Infirmity and Pain " (MS. Minutes, Incorporated Guardians, Loes and Wilford, 1768 ; *Statutory Authorities for Special Purposes*, by S. and B. Webb, 1922, p. 123).

pretend to have the care of them never fail to exact." " By means of the Act ", wrote Samuel Cooper in 1763, " the poor in these Hundreds are much better maintained, are happier in themselves, and more useful to the public than in any other part of the kingdom ; and by the account which has been published, it appears that this scheme will considerably lessen the present expense, for, from Easter 1758 to Michaelmas 1762, notwithstanding some very extraordinary expenses attending the first institution of it in these Hundreds, a saving has been already made of above £2000 ; and in a few years the debt contracted for its first institution will be cleared, and the rates will not be above half of what they are at present." So successful did the experiment appear, both in the reduction of the Poor Rate and the better maintenance of the poor, that in 1763–1764 no fewer than seven other Hundreds or pairs of Hundreds of Suffolk and Norfolk obtained Local Acts of a similar kind,[1] to be followed, a few years later, by half a dozen more ;[2] so that, by 1785, over the greater part of the area of these two large counties the

[1] These were the Hundreds of Blything (4 George III. c. 56 ; House of Industry at Bulcamp) ; Bosmere and Clayton (4 George III. c. 57 ; House of Industry at Barham) ; Lodden and Clavering (4 George III. c. 90 ; House of Industry at Heckingham) ; Loes and Wilford (5 George III. c. 97 ; House of Industry at Melton) ; Mutford and Lothingland (5 George III. c. 89 ; House of Industry at Oulton) ; Samford (4 George III. c. 59 ; House of Industry at Tattingstone) ; and Wangford (4 George III. c. 91 ; House of Industry at Shipmeadow).

The statistical returns presented to the House of Commons in 1776 include eight of these " Hundred Houses ", which had each cost from £4000 to £12,000 to build, and contained each from 150 to 350 inmates, who were employed in spinning, weaving, and knitting hemp and wool into sacking, twine, cloth and stockings ; making fishing nets, and farming the land. Some of the labour was let out to farmers. Most of the Houses kept a tailor, a shoemaker and a " mantuamaker " at wages (Second Report of House of Commons Committee, May 21, 1776).

[2] East and West Flegg (15 George III. c. 13) ; Mitford and Launditch (15 George III. c. 59 ; House of Industry at Gressinghall) ; Forehoe (16 George III. c. 9 ; House of Industry at Forehoe) ; Cosford and Polsted (19 George III. c. 30 ; House of Industry at Semer) ; Hartismere, Hoxne and Thredling (19 George III. c. 30) ; Stow (18 George III. c. 35 ; House of Industry at One-House) ; and Tunstead and Happing (25 George III. c. 27 ; House of Industry at Smallburgh). There was a belated incorporation of nine Norfolk parishes (Buxton, Everingham, etc.) in 1806, by 46 George III. c. 44 ; and another in 1816, when by 56 George III. c. 66, a number of parishes (Shardlow, Milne, etc.) in Derbyshire, Leicestershire and Nottinghamshire were similarly combined. Neither of these we have explored. More directly imitative may have been the five Unions of Shropshire parishes, arising in 1791–1792 from the early success of the Shrewsbury House of Industry, which we have already described.

administration of the Poor Law had been withdrawn from the parish officers and vested in fourteen new bodies of Incorporated Guardians of the Poor.[1]

These " Incorporations " of Guardians of the Poor were, with insignificant variation, all constituted upon a practically identical plan. All the Justices of the Peace resident within the district, or sometimes within five miles of it ; all the owners of freeholds worth £30 or £60 a year and upwards ; all the Rectors or Vicars of the respective parishes ; sometimes all their curates also ; and all the leaseholders of lands or tenements worth £60, or £100, or £120 a year and upwards, were constituted " Guardians of the Poor ". This indeterminate and unwieldy body, which was

[1] These Suffolk and Norfolk Incorporated Guardians were frequently made the subject of particular references and brief descriptions, though we have found nothing in the nature of a monograph on the subject. For the description in our *Statutory Authorities for Special Purposes*, 1922, pp. 122-144, we had access to the MS. Minutes of those of Colneis and Carlford, Loes and Wilford and Samford. Besides the minutes, the chief sources of information are the various Acts ; the House of Commons Returns as to Poor Laws, 1776 ; the numerous sets of " Rules and Orders " and other printed documents, and the reports of sundry local committees of investigation hereafter cited. Various printed documents of these Incorporations are accidentally preserved in the British Museum, volumes 10351 i. 10 and 10351 i. 24, and others are in the library of the Ministry of Health. Much may be gathered from the files of the *Ipswich Journal*, especially between 1815 and 1830. The chief descriptions of the Houses of Industry at different dates are those in *The Farmer's Tour Through the East of England*, by Arthur Young, 1771, vol. ii. pp. 178-190 ; *Observations on the Poor Laws*, by R. Potter, 1775, pp. 33-49 ; *A Dialogue in two conversations . . . in answer to Observations on the Poor Laws*, by Thomas Mendham, 1775 ; *Considerations on the Poor Laws*, etc., 1775 ; *Thoughts on the Construction and Polity of Prisons*, by Rev. John Jebb, 1786, p. 11 ; *History of the Poor*, by Thomas Ruggles, 1794, vol. ii. (this account was reproduced as appendix to *General View of the Agriculture of Suffolk*, by Arthur Young, 1794) ; *Definitions and Axioms relative to Charity, Charitable Institutions and the Poor Laws*, 1763, by Samuel Cooper, of which the only copy known to us is in the library of the Ministry of Health ; *The Insufficiency of the Causes to which the increase of our Poor and of the Poor's Rates have been commonly ascribed, the True One stated, with an Inquiry into the Mortality of Country Houses of Industry*, etc., by Rev. J. Howlett, 1788 ; *The State of the Poor*, by Sir F. M. Eden, 1797, vol. ii. ; *History of the Poor*, by Thomas Ruggles, 1794 ; *General View of the Agriculture of Norfolk*, by Arthur Young, 1804 ; *Letters on the Kind and Economic Management of the Poor, chiefly as regards Incorporated Poor Houses*, by Edward Moon, 1825. See also the Report of the Poor Law Inquiry Commissioners, 1834, Appendix A, Stuart's Report, p. 355, and pp. 187-198, 203-294 ; and the First and Second Annual Reports of the Poor Law Commissioners, 1835 and 1836, the latter containing a valuable " Report on the administration of the Poor Law Amendment Act in Suffolk and Norfolk ", by James Phillips Kay ; the Ninth Annual Report, 1843, pp. 90-118, 278-315 ; together with *The Christian's Magazine*, 1762-1763, vol. ii. pp. 524, 578 vol. iii. p. 24 ; and *The Annals of Agriculture*, especially about 1800.

K

directed to meet quarterly, became the ultimate governing authority. At its first meeting it was required to appoint twenty-four from among its own number to be "Directors of the Poor ", serving for life, and also to elect a President of the Incorporation. There had also to be chosen, out of the Guardians, sometimes by the whole meeting, sometimes by the Directors only, twenty-four or thirty-six "Acting Guardians ", one-half or one-third of whom retired annually. It was in the hands of these two bodies of Directors and Acting Guardians that the whole executive authority, and practically the entire government, of the Incorporation was legally placed. The exact relation between these two executive bodies, and the precise distribution of duties between them, varied slightly in the different Local Acts. The general principle seems to have been that the Directors were to appoint the Treasurer, the Clerk and other chief officers, and to decide from time to time such large issues of financial policy as borrowing money, acquiring land and erecting work-houses ; whilst the Acting Guardians were to undertake the routine duties of workhouse management. But in many of the Acts it is the Directors and Acting Guardians together who are authorised to perform most of the duties that are recited, and we do not find it easy to make out the line of demarcation. Between them they were always authorised to borrow a substantial capital sum, to erect and maintain a workhouse ; to receive in it such poor persons as the parishes chose to send to them ; to set the inmates to work ; to make bye-laws for their government, and to punish the refractory ; to bind children apprentices to any person legally liable to take them within the district ; apparently to relieve the destitute in any other way they thought fit ; and to levy the cost upon all the parishes within the district, in proportion to the average of the Poor Rates paid by each during the seven years preceding the Act, which was not to be exceeded.

The relation in which these Incorporations stood to the authorities of the County and the Parish was one of some intricacy and obscurity. The Local Acts, under which they were estab-lished, did not professedly relieve the Justices of the Peace from their responsibility for the supervision of the Poor Law adminis-tration ; and did not in any way exempt the new Directors and Guardians of the Poor from magisterial control. They were even expressly required to submit their accounts for allowance at each Quarter Sessions, when an opportunity was afforded for any person to make objection to their proceedings, and for the Court to give such orders as it thought fit. It is, however, easy to see that, as with all the new authorities established under Local Acts, this subjection of the Suffolk and Norfolk Incorporations to the Justices was entirely illusory. Their very creation was taken to imply, and was probably intended to imply, that they were themselves to exercise whatever discretion had previously been exercised in Poor Law administration by the Single or the Double Justice, or in Petty or Special Sessions. We see this supersession of the Justice forcibly described by a fervent admirer of the new system. " When you are incorporated ", he declares to the parishes, " the Directors and Guardians are judges of the measure of relief. When you are disincorporated it will be fixed by the Justices. And do you really believe that these gentlemen are better judges of the real wants of the poor than a committee of the House composed of a mixture of gentlemen and men of business ? Or do you suppose that smaller allowances will be made in the Sessions Hall at Woodbridge than in the committee-room of the House of Industry ? . . . The pauper makes his complaint to the Overseer, and the Overseer takes it to the Committee. If the complaint is unreasonable or experimental . . . the Committee refuses relief, and there is an end of the business ; the pauper grumbles perhaps, but submits, because he knows there is no remedy. Not so in an unincorporated parish. The pauper who is refused relief to-day comes again to-morrow ; frequently with abusive language ; not infrequently with threats. However often repulsed, he returns again to the charge ; drags the Overseer to half the Justices of the County, and at last by importunity and worrying obtains an allowance that he ill-deserves, and which is given rather to purchase quiet and forbearance than because it is wanted."

This quasi-judicial authority of the Directors and Acting Guardians of the new Incorporations comes out in their relations with the parish authorities. The Directors and Acting Guardians took over from the Overseers the whole administration of Poor Law relief ; but the Local Acts did not relieve the parishioners from their statutory obligation to serve as Overseers, and in no way exempted the Overseers from any of their duties or obligations. What happened was that the parish officer acquired, in place of the Justices of the Peace, a new set of masters, from whom he received peremptory orders. He had to attend the meetings of the Directors and Acting Guardians whenever required ; to produce lists of the poor in his parish ; lists of children ; lists of persons liable to take apprentices, and any other information required.[1] Whenever it was desired that outdoor relief should be given in any case, the parish officers had to attend the " Weekly Meeting " of the committee and support the application.[2] The parish officers might even be required to attend regularly at the House of Industry every week as a matter of course, the journey probably sacrificing nearly a whole day of their time.[3] All the outdoor relief that the Directors and Acting Guardians allowed in particular cases was paid weekly under their orders by the Overseers ; [4] and this had to be done, as one order directs, " in specie personally by themselves ".[5] Any failure to discharge these duties, or to obey any of the directions of the Directors and Acting Guardians, might be visited by the penalty of a fine, inflicted not by the Justices but by the Directors and Acting Guardians themselves.[6] In case any parish failed to pay its quota, the Directors and Acting Guardians could themselves inflict a fine on the Overseer.[7]

[1] MS. Minutes, Incorporated Guardians, Colneis and Carlford, March 30, 1778. " That the Churchwardens within the several parishes do make lists of the number of poor with their families . . . and do attend the committee . . . with such lists in order that the committee may judge of the necessitous poor, and give them such relief as their present necessary occasions may require " (MS. Minutes, Incorporated Guardians, Samford, July 14, 1795).

[2] *Ibid.* Loes and Wilford, April 1, 1811. " That no pauper shall be relieved by a weekly committee or quarterly meeting unless accompanied by the Churchwarden or Overseer of the Parish where they live " (*Byelaws, Rules, Orders and Instruction for the Better Government and Support of the Poor in the Hundred of Bosmere and Claydon in Suffolk*, 1813, p. 20).

[3] " Ordered that the Overseers . . . do regularly attend at the Poor House every Wednesday. . . . In case of their non-attendance . . . they will be subject to the penalty under the 44 section of the last Act " (MS. Minutes, Incorporated Guardians, Samford, October 1, 1799).

[4] " Ordered that Mary B. and her son Thomas B. of Bradfield, an idiot, and she old and infirm, be allowed 2/6 a week to be paid by the Overseer until further orders " (*ibid.* Loes and Wilford, July 18, 1768).

[5] *Ibid.* Samford, June 25, 1833.

[6] Two Overseers were summoned to appear before the Directors and Guardians in 1768 and fined a shilling each " for neglect of duty " (*ibid.* Loes and Wilford, December 26, 1768). Two more in 1778 were fined half a guinea each (*ibid.* June 29, 1778).

[7] In 1762 we see an Overseer, who had not paid the contribution due from his parish, after repeated formalities, summarily sentenced by the Directors

The Suffolk and Norfolk Incorporations were thus, in effect, a combination of the Justices and the parish officers, exercising many of the supervising and judicial functions of the one, and most of the administrative duties of the other ; forcibly interpolated between the two, and yet nominally leaving unimpaired the legal powers and obligations of both of them.

Let us now inquire how the elaborate statutory constitutions of these bodies of Incorporated Guardians actually worked in practice. To the first rulers of these Incorporations their organisation seemed devised upon the most perfect principles of administration. " To guard against frauds and jobs ", reports the most enthusiastic of their founders, " all considerable contracts are made at the quarterly meetings in the most public manner. No money is paid by the Treasurer but by order of a quarterly meeting, or by warrant under the hands of the Directors and Acting Guardians, in a quarterly meeting, or in a weekly committee assembled. And at these general quarterly meetings, all the accounts of the preceding quarter are stated and settled, and the vouchers examined and compared with them. And forasmuch as many persons pay to the rates, who are not concerned in the management of the poor, these accounts, so stated and signed by the members of the general quarterly meetings, are referred to His Majesty's Court of Quarter Sessions, there to be finally allowed and confirmed. And here if any man can suggest fraud or mismanagement before such final allowance and confirmation, he may be heard. What better care could be taken to prevent jobs ? " " A committee room," as another enthusiast tells us, " spacious, commodious and pleasantly situated, is set apart for the weekly meetings of the Directors and Guardians. . . . They consist of the principal gentry, clergy and tenantry in the County. They visit in rotation, each taking a month. Two Directors from the gentry, three Acting Guardians from the yeomanry, with the Clerk, form the weekly meeting. The governor of the House attends to answer inquiries and complaints. He brings up his report of the material events of the preceding week. All business respecting the economy of

---

and Acting Guardians themselves, to pay a fine of forty shillings (MS. Minutes, Incorporated Guardians, Colneis and Carlford, December 27, 1762). The penalty on Parish Officers neglecting to raise and pass over the assessments due was raised from £5 to £50 by the Blything Act of 1793 (33 George III. c. 126).

the House and current expenses is then settled. The stores and provisions are inspected, the apothecary who attends for a yearly stipend is examined with respect to the sick. In this whole affair no person complains of the fatigue of attendance, but rather takes pleasure in the discharge of so useful an employment." It was, in fact, assumed that the compulsory incorporation of all the substantial gentry and the leading tenantry of the district as Guardians would ensure the exercise of a constant oversight, by those on whom fell the main burden of the rates, over the administration carried on at their joint expense. When it was objected to the Incorporations that no one would take the trouble to look after them, their sanguine promoters rejoined as a conclusive answer that, " As the attendance is so easy, we may reasonably expect that it will be complied with, especially as it will always be the interest of the persons whose attendance is wanted that this affair should succeed well ". It is needless to say that the great bulk of the squires and clergy neglected, from the outset, to attend even the quarterly meetings, or to pay any attention to the House of Industry. There was indeed nothing for the Guardians—as distinguished from the Directors and Acting Guardians—to do at their meetings, after they had once elected the President, the other officers and the two executive bodies. Even at the first meeting of a new Incorporation only a few score persons would deign to put in an appearance ; and these had perforce to elect themselves as the twenty-four Directors and the twenty-four or thirty-six Acting Guardians that the Act required. The two executive bodies were therefore, in effect, self-elected, renewing themselves on the occurrence of vacancies by simple co-option. Vacancies remained, however, long unfilled, owing to the difficulty of finding persons willing even to promise to serve.

Though no such distinction is expressed in the Acts, both the intention and the practice seems to have been for the Directors to be chosen from among the clergy and gentry, and the Acting Guardians from among such substantial farmers and tradesmen as possessed the statutory qualification. The Directors assumed, as their sphere, the decision of important matters, such as the erection of a building or the borrowing of money, whilst the current administration of relief and the daily management of the House of Industry were left principally to

the Acting Guardians, though Parliament had striven to secure
that some, at least, of the Directors should also be present.
What happened in practice was that the separate meetings of
the two bodies were dropped, as were those of the Guardians at
large. Only one kind of meeting was held, both quarterly and
annually, this being attended indiscriminately by Directors and
Acting Guardians, at which formal resolutions were passed, and
various kinds of relief were administered. For the actual
management of the House of Industry the Directors and Acting
Guardians divided themselves up into small committees of about
five, each being supposed to attend to the management for one
month, and to be absolved from meetings all the rest of the year.
In actual practice we find, in case after case, most of the Directors
and Acting Guardians not attending meetings of any sort, and
hardly any of them ever going to the House of Industry ; the
whole management being left, practically for years together, in
the hands of the paid officials. It was in vain that the Act of
Parliament prescribed penalties for non-attendance, and that
resolutions were passed threatening to put the penalties in force.
In the Loes and Wilford Incorporation, when the grave financial
position had led, in 1791, to a committee of inquiry, it was
reported that within the preceding ten years there had been
forty-five meetings at which there had been no quorum ; that
the prescribed weekly committees had not been held ; and that
in no one case had any Director or Acting Guardian obeyed
the bye-law which required each of them individually to visit
the House at least once in the course of the particular month
assigned to him. Within five years after the reorganisation that
followed this investigation, the system had again broken down.
The Directors and Acting Guardians then tried the experiment
of dividing themselves, not by months in the year, but into
nine continuous subject-committees ; for religion and morality,
industry, maintenance, clothing, medicines, building and repairs,
finance, law and apprenticeship respectively ; each being instructed to meet at least once a quarter as a minimum. We
gather that this proved no more successful than the preceding
arrangement. When the meetings were called at the House of
Industry no members whatever attended. When they were
held in the more comfortable surroundings of the White Hart
Tavern at Wickham Market the record was not much better.

In some Incorporations the device was invented of permitting the Acting Guardians to appoint deputies to attend in their stead ; with the result, as might be imagined, that the privilege was " scandalously " abused ; " the person chosen to discharge " the delegated office being often " so far from equal to its duties that he could not sign his name to the accounts he admitted, nor read even what he allowed ". In despair of securing a better attendance for any length of time, the more active and zealous Directors and Acting Guardians of these Incorporations put their trust in the formulation of elaborate " Rules and Orders ". " When general laws are once established ", fondly remark the compilers of one such code, " the public is in no danger of losing at any future time any of the advantages which a former zeal had promised, or a past vigilance had procured. For should that zeal hereafter abate, or that vigilance relax, the institution, by means of its General Rules, remains like a machine, which, having its springs of motion within itself, will, with but an ordinary attention, and only common application, go on to perform without interruption its accustomed functions, and to produce without variation its usual benefits. Nothing therefore can be more unjust than the common objection to Houses of Industry and similar institutions that, however well they may be administered at first, they will at length fall into neglect. For do but establish General Rules and the objection is at once obviated."

The Suffolk and Norfolk Houses of Industry were thus practically handed over, sooner or later, to the management of the officers, under such " Rules and Orders " as the zeal and wisdom of the squires and clergy had provided. These officers consisted, as a rule, of a Clerk to the Incorporation, usually a local attorney, paid a small salary for the formal business of the Annual Meeting and the preparation of the necessary documents ; a Treasurer, one of the Directors or Acting Guardians, who kept the current balances for his own profit, but sometimes received also a small stipend. More important than these, who seem seldom or never to have visited the institution itself, was the Steward or Master or Governor of the House of Industry, who ran the whole establishment, managed its few acres of land, directed its little manufactures, governed the pauper inmates, and was evidently the mainspring of the administration. For this responsible position the Guardians seem nearly always to have allowed a salary of £40 a year with board and lodging,[1] and sometimes a trifling bonus on the amount of wool spun, or other production of the paupers [2]—a remuneration which did not permit them to find anybody of greater administrative ability than a bankrupt farmer, a village shopkeeper, or a promoted servant or labourer. The Governor was assisted by a Chaplain, at £25 a year, who was for this sum to " read prayers daily and preach one part of the day every Sunday, catechise, visit the sick and bury the dead ".[3] There were also usually several doctors appointed, at from £21 to £40 a year, one to physic the inmates of the House, and the others to look after the outdoor poor in particular districts.[4] Presently the larger Houses have also a Matron, a Schoolmaster and a Schoolmistress.[5] The reader will be prepared to learn that the officers so appointed and left practically uninspected to manage their several institutions were seldom found satisfactory for any length of time. Notwithstanding all the elaborate rules, it was impossible to prevent the Governor of the House from embezzling the material, the stores, or the cash.[6] The quantity of food consumed could not be made to bear any constant relation to the number of inmates, and was always going up.[7]

---

[1] MS. Minutes, Incorporated Guardians, Colneis and Carlford, November 22, 1757 ; *ibid.* Loes and Wilford, June 27, 1768 ; *ibid.* Lodden and Clavering (*An Account of the Proceedings of the Special Committee . . . to enquire into the Expenditure in the House of Industry at Heckingham,* 1793).

[2] At the Tattingstone House of Industry the Guardians presented the Governor annually with a " gratuity " of £50, together with £10 for his daughter, who taught the knitting school, in lieu of salary (MS. Minutes, Incorporated Guardians, Samford, March 26, 1833, April 1, 1834).

[3] *Ibid.* Colneis and Carlford, October 2, 1758 ; elsewhere it was £35 (*ibid.* Loes and Wilford, June 27, 1768) or £30 (*An Account of the Proceedings of the Special Committee . . . to enquire into the Expenditure in the House of Industry at Heckingham,* 1793).

[4] MS. Minutes, Incorporated Guardians, Samford, June 26, 1780. Presently this Incorporation tried the experiment of having one Resident Doctor to do all the work, giving his whole time for a salary of £85 a year, with board and lodging (*ibid.* July 5, 1791). The Lodden and Clavering Guardians gave as much as £105 (*An Account of the Proceedings of the Special Committee . . . to enquire into the Expenditure in the House of Industry at Heckingham,* 1793).

[5] MS. Minutes, Incorporated Guardians, Loes and Wilford, April 11, 1811.

[6] *Ibid.* June 29, 1789.

[7] In one Incorporation it was found that the aggregate weight of food per head had risen by 33 per cent in fifteen years (*An Account of the Proceedings of the Special Committee . . . to enquire into the Expenditure in the House of Industry at Heckingham,* 1793). The Governor's explanation was that " he

There were, however, apart from mere shortcomings of management, two developments in the working of these institutions which, in their unforeseen effects, must, in any case, have gone far to destroy whatever chance they may have had of successful administration. The Directors and Acting Guardians could not refrain, in spite of their rigid theories, from granting practically indiscriminate outdoor relief. Before the first House of Industry had been open a year, we see the grant of weekly doles beginning, at first to " a bedridden man ", then to widows, and presently to families of good character. There was at first some discrimination between those who were forced to enter the House of Industry and those who were not. During the famine years between 1795 and 1800, relief was given indiscriminately to all the labourers, " head money " being often paid for each child where there were more than one in the family. In the final stages of these Incorporations there came to be more outdoor relief than indoor maintenance. For the ten years 1800–1810, the figures in the Loes and Wilford Hundreds were £20,208 outdoor and £32,477 indoor ; in 1810–1820, £51,908 and £37,466 ; and in 1820–1824, £23,917 and £15,037 respectively.

This result was partly caused by the change in the method of apportioning the expenses of the Incorporation among the constituent parishes, which was gradually adopted between 1801 and 1820. The original intention had been to relieve each parish of the administration of its own Poor Law, charging it exactly what it had previously paid as Poor Rate, and undertaking not to exceed that sum.[1] When the new Houses of Industry had paid off their capital debt, it was contemplated that the charge upon the parishes should be rateably reduced. In the Blything Incorporation a reduction of one-eighth was actually made from 1780 onwards, the whole debt of £12,000 having been discharged.

---

was obliged to give the paupers more food than they wanted, or could eat, to preserve order in the House " (*ibid.* p. 2).

[1] This statutory limitation led to a state of insolvency when prices rose steeply in November 1795 ; and a Bill euphemistically entitled " An Act for the Better Relief of the Poor within the several Hundreds and Districts . . . incorporated by divers Acts of Parliament " had to be promptly passed. This measure, which went through all its stages within four weeks (36 George III. c. 10), authorised the Incorporations to increase their precepts on the constituent parishes, for three years without limit, but after 1798 to not more than twice the amount previously authorised (Hansard, vol. 51, pp. 54, 80, 94, 111, 133, 148 and 197).

The Cosford Hundred, too, is reported by 1800 to have reduced its debt of £8000 to £180, and to have reduced its Poor Rate by three-eighths. Generally speaking, however, the parishes continued to pay the same Poor Rates as they had previously done; and sometimes these were even increased. In the course of a few years the numbers of paupers belonging to the several parishes inevitably underwent changes, whilst the parishes continued to contribute in a fixed ratio. This led to complaints from those parishes which found themselves paying in a higher ratio than that of their current pauperism. To satisfy these complaints, and arrange what seemed a fairer basis of contribution, it was provided by various amending Acts, first that the parishes should contribute according to a new triennial or decennial average; and eventually that each parish should bear the cost of the House of Industry in strict proportion to the number of inmates that it sent thither. This change of system had a disastrous consequence. The amending Acts, in fact, unwittingly " offered a direct premium for keeping paupers out of the House ". As the expense per head in the House of Industry was high, each parish saw its way to save money by giving small doles of outdoor relief, rather than augment its numbers in the House. Finally, the quondam "House of Industry " became for the parishes only a sort of co-operative hospital for the sick, an orphan asylum for the deserted children, and a place to which the Overseers could send any able-bodied poor to whom they did not choose to allow the weekly dole.

For a generation, however, it was apparently still possible to believe in the success of these Incorporations. We see them repeatedly belauded by Poor Law reformers; and even imitated in various localities. Of these imitations we have already described the most important, the Shrewsbury House of Industry. Of the others we need describe only that established in the Isle of Wight.

The Isle of Wight, with its few thousand inhabitants scattered among thirty parishes, all within a walk, and none containing any considerable town, formed, it would seem, an obviously convenient unit of administration. The County Justices of the Island, as we have described in our volume on *The Parish and the County*, effected an extra-legal separation between themselves and their colleagues on the mainland of the County; held their own Quarter Sessions, and made their own County Rate, virtually as if the Island were a distinct shire.   Yet so strong was the influence of the immemorial division into parishes that not until 1770 do we find on the Island any common action as to Poor Law;[1] and, as we may add, not for forty years afterwards any common action as to road maintenance.[2]

The thirty Island parishes, having an average population during the first three-quarters of the eighteenth century of a few score families, were plainly incapable of organising separately any sort of Poor Law institution (though Newport had some sort of workhouse in 1732); and their Poor Law administration had evidently remained of the most primitive rural type.   In 1770, when the Suffolk and Norfolk Houses of Industry were still in the first flush of reputed success, the principal gentry and clergy of the Island met and decided to promote a Bill to enable them to follow so promising an example.   Under the Local Act of that session an Incorporation was formed exactly on the model of those of the Suffolk Hundreds.   Eighty acres of Parkhurst Forest were acquired from the Crown, and a spacious House of Industry was erected to accommodate no fewer than 700 paupers, who were employed in agriculture, making corn-sacks, weaving linsey woolsey, knitting stockings, embroidery and lacemaking.   Notwithstanding a lengthy description by Sir F. M. Eden, we know little of the actual working of this constitution.   The House of Industry long continued to enjoy a reputation for moderate success, though the industrial enterprises yielded a very doubtful profit, and the Poor Rates were apparently not reduced.   We hear, at any rate, of no desire to revert to parochial management.

---

[1] For the Incorporated Guardians of the Poor of the Isle of Wight, see the Acts 11 George III. c. 43 (1771), and 16 George III. c. 53 (1776); our *Statutory Authorities for Special Purposes*, 1922, pp. 138-139; *General View of the Agriculture of the County of Hants*, by Abraham and William Driver, 1794 (containing a special section on the Isle of Wight by Rev. R. Warner); a long description in *The State of the Poor*, by Sir F. M. Eden, 1797, vol. ii. pp. 233-266; Report of House of Commons Committee on Poor Laws, 1817 (Sewell's evidence); *Rules . . . for the Management of the Workhouse . . . of the Isle of Wight*, etc., 1832; Report of Poor Law Inquiry Commissioners, 1834, Appendix A, Pringle's Report, p. 305; *The Isle of Wight System of Roads, and System of Guardians of the Poor, not a Model, but a Warning to the Legislature*, 1845.

[2] In 1813 the Isle of Wight Turnpike Trust was formed, by 53 George III. c. 92; and did not come to an end until superseded by the County Council instituted for the Island under the Local Government Act of 1888 (*The Story of the King's Highway*, by S. and B. Webb, 1913, p. 236).

There is something pathetic in the dismal uniformity of the stories of the actual working of the carefully organised administrations of all these bodies of Incorporated Guardians of the Suffolk type. The substitution of the enlightened and public-spirited squires and incumbents for the selfish and ignorant parish officers, and the organisation of the labour of the paupers in a House of Industry, were everywhere going to reduce the Poor Rates, and at the same time to afford a better provision for the children, the sick and the aged. And there is reason to believe that, for a few years in each case, the new bodies not only made better institutional provision for the aged, the sick and the infirm, but also effected some considerable reduction of actual pauperism. As the parishes had to contribute rateably to the common charge, whether or not they made use of the new institution, they promptly disburdened themselves of all their poor, directing them all to go to the House of Industry, and refusing all outdoor relief. So drastically was the reform effected during the first few years that the indignation of the common people was extreme ; and there was, in 1765, even a picturesque little Suffolk rebellion, when a formidable mob, armed with cudgels and scythes, perambulated the County for a week, demolishing the new workhouses and compelling Directors and Acting Guardians to sign written promises to desist from erecting such places in which to imprison the poor—demanding, on the contrary, " that the poor should be maintained as usual ; that they should range at liberty and be their own masters ".[1] When

---

[1] This, the latest " Suffolk rising ", is described in a pamphlet of 1766 entitled *A Letter to J. W., Esquire, relating to Mr. G——y's Pamphlet upon the Poor Laws*, etc., by XX ; see *Statutory Authorities for Special Purposes*, by S. and B. Webb, 1922, p. 140. The establishment of these " Hundred Houses " " stirred up numbers of the common people in appearance to violent measures of redress, under the much-abused pretence of standing up for their liberties, presuming themselves to be judges of the propriety and rectitude of the laws of their country, and as qualified to subvert them with impunity whenever they come in competition with their licentious wills. Their first riotous appearance was made at the White Hart, at Wickham Market. . . . [August 1765] when the Directors of the Hundreds of Loes and Wilford were assembled for the execution of their Poor's Act. A very large body of them, consisting of some hundreds of men, women and children, armed with cudgels and such weapons as they could procure, surrounded the house, threatening destruction to all those who should interest themselves in the building and establishment of a House of Industry within the Hundreds aforesaid." The rioters seem to have made the Directors prisoners, treating them with great " rudeness and indecency " ; they asserted that this " was only the beginning of their work, for they intended that the Nacton house, and all other buildings of that sort

this miniature rebellion had been put down by a troop of dragoons, the erection of the Houses of Industry was continued, and the poor were swept into them. The new buildings were, relatively to anything that had previously existed in the separate parishes, spacious and well planned. The arrangements were carefully considered and humanely designed. In their provision for the education of the children and for the medical attendance and nursing of the sick they seemed to constitute an advance on anything that had hitherto been done for the rural poor. " The poor came to us," says the worthy originator of the first of these Incorporations, " in a most miserable and filthy condition ; they were clothed in rags, and some of them, the children especially, almost literally naked. We expected and were prepared for this ; so that to prevent the introduction of vermin, before they were admitted they were shaved and cleansed thoroughly by washing in warm water, and then all new clothed throughout from head to foot." It was impossible, as a later critic observed, to refuse approval to " institutions that forced cleanliness upon those who are dirty, and wholesome food upon those of depraved appetites ". Yet, within a very few years in each case we see the eulogistic descriptions of the first period succeeded by grave complaints. The cost of maintenance rises ; the industrial enterprises invariably become unprofitable ; the Houses of Industry are decimated by epidemics, and plainly have an excessive death - rate ; they even become places of horrible demoralisation and disorder. A critic of 1813 observes that " In whatever. light these institutions are viewed . . . there is scarcely anything to be perceived but degeneracy and ultimate disappointment. Persons of judgment and deliberate reflection, who once thought favourably of them, now produce reasons for their apostasy . . . both in point of expense, and the morals

---

should be levelled with the ground ". The mob then forced the Directors to sign a paper promising to desist from building the projected workhouse. Five days later they destroyed the Bulcamp House of Industry, and proceeded to Nacton. There, however, the Justices met them with a small force of dragoons, read the Riot Act, and charged the mob, which scattered in all directions. After this tumultuous outburst, the popular opposition seems to have been silenced, if not suppressed. In the abstract of returns to the House of Commons of Poor Law expenditure, 1775, it is noted, under Bulcamp, " in the expenses for building is included £500 for building a part which was pulled down by a mob " (*The Village Labourer, 1760–1832*, by J. L. and Barbara Hammond, 1911, p. 147).

of the poor youth brought up there; as well as the unnatural state the old and infirm are confined to, among strangers who cannot be supposed capable of much sympathy. Experience also teaches us that the children brought up in such places, when grown up are fit only for a manufactory . . . not for outdoor employments, except, indeed, the men become soldiers (such as they be) and the females . . . often have recourse to prostitution." Presently the constituent parishes, not finding their Poor Rates reduced, and gradually discovering both the unprofitableness of the enterprise and the demoralisation of the inmates, themselves revolt against the system; eagerly revert to the grant of doles, and strive to reassume the management of their own poor. In case after case they obtain new Local Acts; sometimes according new powers and removing restrictions found to be inconvenient; sometimes fundamentally changing the constitution, sweeping away the gentry and clergy, and replacing them by a board elected by the parish Vestries; sometimes, again, dissolving the Incorporation, selling or demolishing the workhouse, and reverting to the parochial administration of the Poor Law. Already in 1813 it could be confidently predicted that " These elegant structures will become deserted fabrics ". For this uniform failure, there were, as the student will have seen, abundant causes in the nature of the legal constitutions with which these Incorporated Guardians were equipped, and in the absence alike of any continuous administration by devoted amateurs and of any class of salaried officials competent for such a task. But it would be to miss the most important results of their experience if we did not emphasise that the principal object of all of them—that of so organising the labour of the paupers as to make them a self-supporting community—was, from the outset, a wholly impracticable one. Though this golden dream did not finally fade out of the imagination, even of competent Poor Law experts, until the reign of Victoria—though it still periodically captivates the unwary—it was, we think, the experience of the Incorporated Guardians of the Suffolk and Norfolk Hundreds, even more than with that of the Shrewsbury House of Industry and that of the Bristol Hospital of St. Peter, that actually caused it to be abandoned by all competent Poor Law students. The factors at Norwich, through whom the woollen yarn was disposed of, were, to say the least of it, neither zealous nor scrupulously honest. At House after House the various manufacturing industries that were tried had eventually to be given up, owing to the impossibility of so buying and selling, and so organising the labour, as to make a profit. The Houses of Industry became then mere places to which the sick and impotent poor were driven, and to which resorted such dissolute and worthless persons as found the lax promiscuity not unpleasant. " It has . . . been long a practice," said the Loes and Wilford Committee in 1791, " to receive into your House at the approach of winter a number of lazy, notorious and abandoned prostitutes who, tainted with the foulest of diseases, resort thither for cure ; and when the summer advances then quit their retreat . . . often leaving as a pledge an un-affiliated child : and this, all, with impunity. Nay, instead of being kept apart, and fed on the meanest viands, and compelled to a severe species of toil, the most profligate of them are per-mitted in habits of familiar intercourse, and even to board and to bed, not only with each other, but with others of better character, and especially the young." [1]   Nor did their character improve. " Everybody concerned ", wrote a correspondent of the *Ipswich Journal* in 1825, " knows that this House has been made use of as a kind of second-hand prison for all the incorrigible pilfering rogues and vagabonds among the men, and all the worthless strumpets and vilest among women—in short the very scum of the Hundreds." [2]

Experience and Outcome of the Incorporated Guardians

The long-drawn-out experiments in the establishment of incorporated bodies for Poor Law administration—extending as they do over a century and three-quarters, and relating to both rural and urban conditions in all parts of the country—make up a confused medley which it is difficult to analyse or to classify. With regard to the constitutional structure, we have to note that, whilst invariably including in their membership a strong *ex-officio* element, the new Poor Law bodies introduced what was then a novel feature, in that they nearly always depended, to some extent at least, upon popular choice, either

---

[1] *Report of the Committee appointed to inquire into the Actual State of the House of Industry at Melton*, 1791, p. 10.

[2] *Ipswich Journal*, March 12, 1825.

by nomination by the Vestry, or by actual election by the inhabitants, with or without a definite qualification for the franchise. In this respect they differed essentially in form from the Court of Sewers that we have described in our volume on *Statutory Authorities for Special Purposes*, and even from the Turnpike Trusts and the Improvement Commissions (also described in that volume), which stand, on the whole, subsequently to them in date. The relief of the poor, at that time wholly defrayed from the proceeds of the local rates, was apparently regarded, even by the Parliaments of the period, as rightly involving at any rate some degree of democratic control.

We shall deal in the following chapter with the main results of the various devices of the Poor Law administration between 1660 and 1834. We may, however, give at this point our impressions as to the peculiar advantages and disadvantages of these statutory Poor Law authorities, as compared with the ordinary parish government of the time. The statutory authorities had, in general, the advantage of substituting for annually changing, and often unwilling, individual administrators, a continuously existing and deliberately selected council, acting through salaried officials. Hence we watch, in the Incorporated Guardians, the initiation of something like Poor Law policy ; always crudely empirical and usually ill-adapted to attain its end, but superior, by the mere fact of being a policy, to the variable and haphazard action of individual Overseers. It was, perhaps, an accident that all the Incorporated Guardians made the workhouse an essential part of Poor Law administration. They wanted the workhouse for an impracticable end, namely, to organise profitably the labour of the paupers. Incidentally, however, they introduced what was at the time the only practicable " test " of the genuineness of able-bodied destitution—the " offer of the House ", with the usual result of greatly diminishing pauperism in the earlier years of their existence. This advantage they usually lost after a short time, owing to their failure to recognise the device which they began by unconsciously adopting.

Moreover, although the efficacy of this " test " in reducing the number of paupers was everywhere seen, its drawbacks were not noticed. " This was an important point gained," says a writer of 1813, " but many were unable to maintain themselves, and unhappily were too refractory to accept of their maintenance

L

in the House. These necessarily commenced itinerant beggars, and got a miserable livelihood by wandering through the neighbouring parishes." [1] For most of those who entered the workhouse the method of relief was found to have its own drawbacks. It was the General Mixed Workhouse of the Suffolk Incorporations—not, as is commonly assumed, of the ancient poorhouse of the parish—of which Crabbe gave such a terrible description.[2] It is impossible to-day to realise how bad, under the unscientific administration of the period, was this institutional treatment of the children, the infirm and the aged. Presently it was found that residence in these institutions was equally disastrous to the able-bodied adults. "Their industries," it was remarked, "are worked by the able-bodied inmates in such a feeble and languid manner that the occupation is anything but calculated to preserve, much less generate, habits of industry. . . . With the exception that their dormitories are separate, men, women and children associate as they please. . . . Women of notoriously bad characters are admitted and permitted to communicate freely with the other female inmates. . . . Children of both sexes, from the sad examples of conversation they daily see and hear, are exposed to the pollution of vice at the very dawn of life. . . . Such an indiscriminate mixture of persons of all ages, sexes and characters, it is almost needless to remark, is a system ill calculated to promote the comfort or improvement of paupers who are aggregated together in Houses of Industry." [3]

[1] *General View of the Agriculture of North Wales*, by Walter Davies, 1813, p. 433 ; *Statutory Authorities for Special Purposes*, by S. and B. Webb, 1922, p. 139.

[2] *The Borough*, by George Crabbe, 1808 (Letter XVIII. "The Poor and their Dwellings "). His son made the following comment : " Of one method only I venture to give my sentiments—that of collecting the poor of a Hundred into one building. This admission of a vast number of persons, of all ages and both sexes, of very different inclinations, habits and capacities, into a society, must, at a first view, I conceive, be looked upon as a cause of both vice and misery ; nor does anything which I have heard or read invalidate the opinion ; happily the method is not a prevailing one, as these Houses are I believe still confined to that part of the kingdom where they originated. . . . These odious Houses of Industry seem, thank God, to exist only in Suffolk, near the first founder's residence (one proof they are not very beneficial), in which the poor of a whole Hundred are collected in one building—well fed and clothed I grant—but imprisoned for life " (Note in the edition of the *Works* of Crabbe, by his son, 1834, pp. 234, 242 ; *Statutory Authorities for Special Purposes*, by S. and B. Webb, 1922, p. 134).

[3] Report of Poor Law Inquiry Commissioners, 1834, Appendix A, Lewis's Report, p. 660 ; *Statutory Authorities for Special Purposes*, by S. and B. Webb, p. 120.

It has to be said, however, that many of these statutory Poor Law authorities had the undoubted advantage of combining a number of small or thinly populated parishes into a union large enough to effect a substantial equalisation of rates and to escape the greater part of the difficulties presented by the Law of Settlement, as well as to admit of some sort of classification of paupers, and the employment of permanent salaried officials. On the other hand, it was a grave drawback that these statutory Poor Law authorities escaped all outside control.   Such authoritative criticism, audit and control as were elsewhere given to the Overseers by Petty Sessions, individual Justices of the Peace and the Open Vestry were, to all intents and purposes, non-existent for the statutory body ; and there was, as yet, no central authority to take their place.   This independence was the more dangerous in that the Incorporated Guardians sat always in secret, published no accounts or regular reports and were subject to no outside inspection.   They were moreover endowed, by the careless apathy of Parliament, with extensive powers of apprehending, detaining, controlling and punishing, entirely at their own discretion and without appeal, not only the inmates of their institutions, but also such " idlers and vagrants " as they chose to arrest.[1]   These unpleasant characteristics were seen at their worst in those cases in which the statutory authority was entirely independent of popular election.   The greatest failures of all were the Suffolk and Norfolk Unions where the governing council was nominally composed of the whole body of wealthy residents.

We do not pretend to be able to balance these advantages and disadvantages.   Perhaps more important than any of them was the fact that these statutory bodies made experiments, which, unlike the casual expedients of the annually changing Overseer, were systematically recorded and could be subsequently investigated.   Their experience in workhouse management was

---

[1] The Incorporated Guardians of Colneis and Carlford petition the House of Commons in 1763, " That they conceive it would very much tend to the better government of the said poor if your petitioners were authorised to apprehend any idle, lazy or disorderly persons found within the Hundred begging or refusing to work, and to carry them to some Justice of the Peace ; and if such Justice was authorised to commit such offenders to the House of Industry, there to be dealt with according to law under the direction of the said Justice of the Peace " (MS. Minutes, Incorporated Guardians, Colneis and Carlford, October 3, 1763).   The desired power was given in the Act 4 George III. c. 58 (*Statutory Authorities for Special Purposes*, by S. and B. Webb, 1922, p. 127).

the means by which the idea of obtaining profit, or even maintenance, by " setting the poor " to work, was finally disposed of.
Even more important in the evolution of English Local Government was the fact, to which we have already referred, that it
was the statutory Poor Law authorities that—in contrast with
the County Justices, the Manorial Courts, the Municipal Corporations and the Parish Vestries of the time, and also with the Courts
of Sewers—based their administration on appointed and permanently serving salaried officials, who were merely directed
and supervised by committees of the governing body.   In what
an Assistant Poor Law Commissioner termed their " principle of
combining an elective controlling power with a paid executive ",[1]
or, as we should nowadays say, in their organisation of a permanent Civil Service under administrative committees of elected
representatives, they stood in marked contrast both with the
practice of previous English Local Authorities (and also with
that of the contemporary New England townships) ; and they
may accordingly almost be said to have originated the typical
constitutional machinery of the English Local Government of
to-day.

[1] Report of Poor Law Inquiry Commissioners, 1834, Appendix A, Chapman's Report, pp. 522-523.

CHAPTER IV

METHODS OF POOR RELIEF, 1660–1834

WE now resume the general history of English Poor Law administration in the thousands of parishes throughout the length and
breadth of the land in which the relief of destitution continued
to be carried on by the Churchwardens and Overseers under the
general jurisdiction of the local Justices of the Peace. After the
Civil War, as we have already stated, the King's Government
ceased to interfere with the doings of the Parish Officers and
County Justices in Poor Law as in other departments of local
government. It is just this lack of central control—this very
absence of any authoritative policy of Poor Relief, to be imposed
by government on all Local Authorities alike—that makes any
chronological order in our description impracticable. We could,
of course, follow Sir George Nicholls in describing one after another
of the fourscore or so general statutes, initiated, not by Ministers,
but by private members, in addition to the hundred or more
Local Acts described in the preceding chapter, by which the
Elizabethan Poor Law was successively amended between 1601
and 1834. When such an arid catalogue had been compiled we
might have the Annals of Parliament, but we should be very far
from anything that could be properly described as a history of
the Relief of the Poor in England and Wales. Between the
statute book and the actual administration of the parish officers
there was, in the eighteenth century, normally only a casual
connection. If the trope may be allowed, the two were separated
by the " unplumbed, estranging sea " of ignorance and indifference, amid the assumption of unfettered local autonomy, that
characterises English Local Government between the " Book of
Orders " of Charles the First's Privy Council, and the General and

Special Orders of the Victorian Poor Law Commissioners. The fifteen thousand parishes and townships that were, during these two centuries, separately maintaining, relieving, or neglecting their own poor, habitually did so with the very slightest attention to Parliamentary enactments, and the very smallest knowledge of what was being done elsewhere. Differing greatly from each other in their circumstances—in populations, in industrial conditions, in the kind and degree of their poverty, and in the wisdom and efficiency of their administration—these parishes and townships were at all times at widely different stages of social evolution. Hence we shall set before the reader, not a history of the Poor Law as it was administered in one or other selected area throughout the eighteenth century, but an analysis of the various practices, devices and experiments initiated, elaborated and abandoned in different localities at different dates between the Restoration (1660) and the Poor Law Amendment Act of 1834.[1]

We may, however, usefully be so far chronological as to give, at the outset, a very summary account of the principal changes in the general law, to which the thousands of Local Authorities were at least supposed to make their administration conform. Apart from the so-called Law of Settlement and Removal of 1662, with which we shall deal in a separate chapter,[2] there was, amid many minor changes, no substantial alteration in the Elizabethan Poor Law for more than a century and a half. Provisions of no great importance were made law in 1692 (3 William and Mary, c. 11, sections 11 and 12), by which it was

---

[1] We have, in this chapter, made full use of such works as *The History of the Poor Laws, with Observations*, by Rev. Dr. Richard Burn, 1764 ; *The History of the Poor*, etc., by Thomas Ruggles, 1793 ; *The State of the Poor*, by Sir F. M. Eden, 1797 ; and *The History of the English Poor Law*, by Sir George Nicholls, 1854, with a third volume by Thomas Mackay, 1899. But we have found indispensable the local records of parish and county, as yet mainly unprinted, which the student will have learned to know from our books, *The Parish and the County*, 1906, *The Manor and the Borough*, 1908, and *Statutory Authorities for Special Purposes*, 1922. The statute book and the proceedings of Parliament and of its committees afford, in successive decades, occasionally, much information ; and the voluminous pamphlet literature referred to in the following pages is of special importance.

[2] The Law of Settlement and Removal, which spasmodically and irritatingly oppressed the poor, and greatly perplexed all the officials concerned, was not, strictly speaking, a measure of Poor Relief. With the innumerable proposals and the various statutes by which it was criticised and changed between 1662 and 1832 we shall deal at length in a separate chapter ; and this course we shall adopt also with regard to the equally perplexing side-issue of the Repression of Vagrancy.

sought to compel the enrolment of "all persons who receive collection" in a book which could be periodically scrutinised by the parishioners in vestry assembled ; and to facilitate legal proceedings against parish officers guilty of embezzlement. An Act of 1697 (8 and 9 William III. c. 30) required those in receipt of relief to "openly wear upon the shoulder of the right sleeve a badge or mark with a large Roman P, and the first letter of the name of the parish . . . cut thereon either in red or blue cloth ".

Of greater importance, at least temporarily, was Sir Edward Knatchbull's Act of 1723 (9 George I. c. 7), which gave to single parishes the necessary legal power (already conferred, as described in the preceding chapter, by about a score of Local Acts applicable to various unions of parishes) to build workhouses in which the able-bodied might be employed, and the children, the sick and the aged maintained. Ignoring minor amendments relating to powers of apprenticeship and other details, the first fundamental change in the general statute law relating to poor relief for more than a century and a half was that effected by Thomas Gilbert in 1782 (22 George III. c. 83), when the Act called by his name coupled increased powers to parishes to combine for the provision of institutions for the maintenance of all classes of the destitute except the able-bodied, with explicit directions to the Justices, as well as to the parish officers, within such combinations, to find employment for the able-bodied at wages, or else to give them relief in their own homes. Such a policy of virtually obligatory Outdoor Relief to the able-bodied labourers and their families, in addition to that customary for the sick and aged, developed, in the "double panic of famine and rebellion" that marked the closing years of the eighteenth century, into a regular system of relief in aid of wages. This system, which was sanctioned in effect by Sir William Young's Act of 1796 (36 George III. c. 23), became devastatingly common throughout the countryside of southern England and some parts of the north and midlands, though not in the populous urban centres. An elaborate Parliamentary inquiry into the whole subject of the relief of the poor in 1817 led only to two statutes in 1818–1819 (The Parish Vestry Act, 58 George III. c. 69 ; and The Select Vestry Act, 59 George III. c. 22)—both known indiscriminately as Sturges Bourne's Act—which merely altered the franchise and method of voting in the Open Vestry, and provided for the optional election of a representative body, to be termed the Select Vestry. Finally, after decades of unsuccessful protests and attempts at reform, the Whig Government of 1832 instituted the celebrated Royal Commission of Inquiry, with which we shall deal in the next volume. This led directly to the Poor Law Amendment Act of 1834 (4 and 5 William IV. c. 76), and thus to the drastic centralised administration of the Poor Law Commissioners of 1834–1847.

We may usefully give also some statistical basis to our description. Down to 1776 we are dependent, for any idea of the magnitude of the total expenditure on the relief of the poor, on the casual estimates—little more than guesses—made by successive pamphleteers. The total sum so expended from the Poor Rate was thus estimated at the middle of the seventeenth century at no more than a quarter of a million sterling annually, or about one shilling per head of the population, an amount which, by the end of that century, may be assumed to have doubled. Writers of that generation put the amount at much more. Thus, the author of *The Grand Concern of England Examined*, published in 1673, estimated the Poor Rates at £70,000 per month, or £840,000 per annum. Richard Dunning in 1698, in his *Bread for the Poor*, put the sum at more than £819,000. Indeed, the nameless author of *A Present Proposal for the Poor*, published in 1700, raised the estimate to " a million of money ", among a people which cannot have exceeded five millions ; being four shillings per head of the whole population. This estimate of a million sterling was repeated by other writers of that period.[1]

---

[1] Thus, James Puckle, in his *England's Path to Wealth and Honour, in a Dialogue between an Englishman and a Dutchman*, 1700 (reprinted in the *Somers Tracts*, 2nd edition, 1814, vol. xi. pp. 371-386), states that " the Poor's Rate of England amounts to near a million pounds per annum ". Leslie, in his *Essay on the Divine Right of Tithes* (reprinted in his *Works*, 1721, vol. ii. p. 873) also puts the Poor Rate at one million. The current impression was that the increase was greatest in the manufacturing districts. Thus, an author of 1702 refers to the happy days of Queen Elizabeth, when the Poor Rate was only sixpence, " whereas in our unhappy days, 3s. in the pound throughout the Kingdom is not sufficient to sustain them in a poor and miserable condition more especially in the great cities, and cloathing countries ; for in many places, where there is most of our woollen manufactory made, the Poor Rate is from half a crown to six or seven shillings in the pound, for the trading poor have no way nor shelter but their trade which if that fail once they are downright beggars presently ; whereas the contrary is to be understood of poor husbandmen who have many ways to shelter themselves, as, a common, a cow, a wood, gleaning of corn in harvest, daywork, children to look after cows, hogs, going to plough, etc., besides all provisions 40 per cent cheaper "

There is, however, reason to believe that these estimates (which seem all to have been derived from Dunning's experience of a few parishes in Devonshire, extended by him first to the whole county, and then, still more hypothetically, to the entire kingdom) were considerably exaggerated. Locke's committee at the Board of Trade in 1696 applied for information to the two archbishops, and through them to the bishops and incumbents of parishes. In this way returns of greatly differing value were obtained from 4415 parishes, or nearly one-third of the whole. This gives a better basis for an estimate than any other before his time, or for many years after it ; and the result, as officially declared, was £400,000 for the whole kingdom (of which one-tenth was in the Metropolitan area) ; or less than two shillings per head.[1] Our earliest firm ground is that provided by the energy of Thomas Gilbert in 1776, who, in face of what was universally believed to be a rapidly rising expenditure, induced Parliament to pass an Act, renewed by another in 1786, requiring the Overseers to make returns of the sums raised in Poor Rates and expended in Poor Relief, first for the year 1776, and then for the three years 1783–1785. These returns give, for the poor relief expenditure of 1776, when the population had risen to seven and a half millions, a total of £1,529,780, or about four shillings per head.

(*A Brief History of Trade in England*, 1702 (Brit. Mus. 1138, b. 3), p. 63). We are not inclined to credit the inference that has been drawn from these and subsequent estimates that the total expenditure on Poor Relief was positively smaller in 1750 than in 1700, although the aggregate increase during this period may well have been no greater than during the preceding half-century.

[1] This estimate obtains support from returns obtained from parishes for 1748–1750, the total average expenditure on Poor Relief being given as £689,971 (Supplementary Report by House of Commons Committee on Poor Laws, 1818 ; see *Edinburgh Review*, February 1819).

The first of these Acts (16 George III. c. 40) asked only for the statistics of the preceding year, whilst the second (26 George III. c. 56) ventured to insist on the statistics of the three preceding years. The total raised by the Poor Rate in 1776 proved to be £1,720,316, and the average for 1783–1785 to be £2,167,760. The amount expended in relief of the poor in 1776 was £1,529,780, and the average for 1783–1785 was £2,004,238. The remainder represented both sums paid for County Rates, and sundry expenses which were largely, but not wholly, connected with poor relief. The increase in the cost of poor relief, within this decade, of about 25 per cent was probably at a greater rate than in any previous decade ; and possibly greater than in any subsequent one. See *The State of the Poor*, by Sir F. M. Eden, 1797, vol. i. pp. 362-372 ; *History of the English Poor Law*, by Sir George Nicholls, 1854, vol. ii. pp. 99-103 ; *Abstracts of the Returns*, etc., 1777 ; *ibid.* 1789.

The second return, obtained in 1786, gives an average annual expenditure on poor relief of just over two millions, indicating an increase at the rate of about four per cent per annum, as compared with an increase of population at a rate probably less than a fourth of such a percentage. The next returns were obtained under George Rose's Act of 1803, when the total poor relief expenditure for the year 1802–1803 was found to have risen to £4,267,965, or nearly nine shillings per head of the population. From this figure the total rose, by 1818, to little short of eight millions sterling, or 13s. 3d. per head of the population, the maximum ever attained under the old Poor Law. The total then fell to less than six millions in 1823–1826, but rose again to seven millions in 1832, being about ten shillings per head of the population.

This curve of annual expenditure, rising pretty continuously for more than a century, though possibly at varying rates, but ultimately declining from its highest point, does not lend itself easily to inferences as to the effect of contemporary administrative changes. Indeed, we find it difficult to divide the century and three-quarters between 1660 and 1834 into periods definitely marked by special Poor Law characteristics. The more the details of the local administration all over the country are studied, the less easy does it seem accurately to label particular decades. Thus, even during the general neglect to put the Poor Law effectively in operation, that may be thought to characterise the second half of the seventeenth century, there were many parishes, alike in the Metropolitan area, in provincial boroughs and in rural districts, in which there can be shown to have been active local administration and a substantial amount of relief given. And whilst the second quarter of the eighteenth century witnessed, at least for a time, a considerable development of the workhouse idea, there is every reason to believe that by far the greater part of the country went on as before with its distribution of weekly doles. It has been sometimes claimed in later years that, between 1723 and 1782, Poor Law administration throughout England and Wales was at its best ; and even that, in this half-century, it reached a relatively high point of excellence. Thus, the Whig *doctrinaire* of 1840 could sum the period in the following words : " Under this system of parochial administration, subject to the control of the nearest magistrate, supported by a nearly absolute power of removal, and the total absence of any claim to relief, under any circumstances, if the applicant refused to enter the workhouse, the Poor Laws were administered during nearly the whole of the last century.   There was a great increase of rates, and much local mismanagement, but no general dissatisfaction or alarm.   Agriculture and manufactures improved, our labourers surpassed in diligence and activity those of every other part of Europe, and improved in conduct. . . . The difficult problem, how to afford to the poorer classes adequate relief without material injury to their diligence or their providence, seemed to be solved."[1] But no such conclusion is borne out by the history of local Poor Law administration, which, as we shall see, was, in this halcyon period, marked by most scandalous maladministration of such workhouses as existed, which seem actually to have surpassed in their evil results the primitive parish poorhouses ; by no small amount of tyranny and cruelty towards the impotent poor ; in some places by a mortality among the infants and children which can seldom have been exceeded in any locality at any time ; and, here and there, no little demoralisation of the able-bodied men and women on Outdoor Relief.   We may recognise the calamitous results of the "rate in aid of wages" that was deliberately adopted, as we shall see, in 1795, without ignoring or extenuating the extraordinary muddles and incidental cruelties of the Overseers, the Justices and the Incorporated Guardians of the Poor of the preceding century.

One other warning must be given, and that is the need of remembering the smallness of the population with which the parish authorities had to deal.   There were, between the seventeenth and the nineteenth centuries, from twelve thousand to fifteen thousand separate parishes and townships, the total number of distinct Poor Law authorities steadily increasing, notwithstanding the gradual formation of a couple of hundred statutory Incorporations or Unions, as the numerous townships in the geographically extensive parishes of the northern counties obtained administrative autonomy.   These authorities dealt

---

[1] *Remarks on the Opposition to the Poor Law Amendment Bill*, by a Guardian [Nassau Senior], 1841, pp. 6-7.   This view was adopted officially.   "From 1722 to 1795", report the Poor Law Commissioners, "the parochial administration of Overseers reached the highest point of excellence and power which it ever maintained" (Ninth Annual Report of the Poor Law Commissioners, 1843, p. 98).

with an aggregate population in England and Wales which is estimated to have been, in 1660, no more than five millions ; to have increased by 1714 only to about six millions, by 1760 to about seven millions, and by 1783 to about eight millions ; to have numbered, at the census of 1801, 9,178,980 ; and at the census of 1831 to have risen to no less than 13,897,187. But we shall fail to appreciate at all fairly either the tasks or the achievements of the fifteen thousand Poor Law authorities unless we realise that the vast majority of them were dealing with the pauperism of quite tiny communities, living, for the most part, under conditions of separateness, and even of isolation, from each other. More than two-thirds of all these separate Poor Law administrations were concerned with populations of no more than a couple of hundred families—thousands of them, indeed, with only a few score.[1]

What we have now to attempt is some sort of a picture, in classified detail, of what the public Relief of the Poor actually was over the whole of England in the course of the century and three-quarters prior to the inquiry of 1832–1834. We shall spare the reader any description of the structure of the organisation by which the relief was carried out : we have, indeed, described at great length and in elaborate detail in *The Parish and the County* what the Vestry was, and what were the Churchwardens and Overseers ; and how the Justices of the Peace, on the one hand, and the general body of ratepayers on the other, periodically interfered with the practical autonomy exercised by these parish officers. We have completed this account of the structure by describing in the preceding chapter the various types of " Incorporated Guardians of the Poor ". We have now to recount

---

[1] It is hard to realise how tiny were the populations of all but a small number of the 15,000 separate Poor Law authorities. Even in 1831, when the population of England and Wales was nearing 14,000,000, there were 6681 parishes or townships in which there were fewer than 300 persons (say 70 families) ; and 5353 more in which the population was between 300 and 800. Thus, as late as 1831, four-fifths of all the parishes and townships had fewer than 200 families each. " Even now ", wrote Nassau Senior in 1841, " the average population of an English parish does not exceed 200 families. . . . In . . . the sixteenth century, it did not exceed 50 families " (*Remarks on the Opposition to the Poor Law Amendment Bill*, by a Guardian [Nassau Senior], 1841, p. 5). In 1660, when the total population was not much above one-third of what it was in 1831, the number of parishes and townships among the whole 15,000 in each of which there were resident more than 200 families can hardly have exceeded a few hundred, the majority of them in the Metropolitan area and the provincial cities and boroughs.

what was actually done in the way of relieving the poor. We shall first describe the system of Doles and Pensions, which formed, at all times and in nearly all places, the basis of the Overseer's practice in Poor Relief ; together with its development, in the latter part of our period, into the well-known Allowance System. We shall describe, as an alternative device, the various ways by which the unemployed labourers were, so to speak, occasionally " billeted out " among the ratepayers ; and the corresponding use made of apprenticeship for compulsorily placing out the youths and maidens with whose maintenance the parish found itself saddled. From these devices we shall pass to the whole development that resulted from the persistent belief that there was some way in which the poor could be " set to work ", and could thus be enabled to earn at least their own maintenance. Some of the innumerable projects for the profitable employment of the poor as a public service, notably the Houses of Industry, have already been dealt with in the foregoing chapter on the Incorporated Guardians of the Poor. Thus the section included in this chapter on " The workhouse as a device for profitably employing pauper labour " must be read as a supplement to our account of the similar and more significant activities of the statutory Poor Law Authorities. We shall have, however, especially to describe a more primitive forerunner of the work-house in the " Church House " or parish poorhouse, which characterised, already in the sixteenth and seventeenth centuries, a large proportion of the rural parishes all over England and Wales. We can then deal with the workhouse in the modern sense of the term, distinguishing among the five several objects of its establishment, or purposes that it was made to serve, the heterogeneity and intermingling of which exercised a calamitous influence upon the character and results of the institution. We shall describe how this evil influence was intensified and aggra-vated by the Farming System, which in various places extended, at times, to practically all the functions of parish government. We shall still have to add some account of the perversion of the administration due to the development of the allowance for bastardy ; but the still greater perversions due to the extra-ordinary effects of the Law of Settlement and Removal, and of the administration of the Vagrancy Acts, we relegate to separate chapters.

In this complicated survey we shall make use, not only of the voluminous Parliamentary Papers of the whole period, and various more or less systematic treatises already mentioned, dealing with the law and the history of the statutory Relief of the Poor, but also of the records of the Local Authorities, only a small proportion of which are yet printed, in so far as we have been able to consult them, and of the enormous number of pamphlets, for or against every conceivable project of Poor Law Reform that marked particular decades of the century and a half.[1] The bulk of these pamphlets, of which something like a thousand are still extant, appeared in six successive waves, differing one from the other in general content, and each characterised by the particular note of its time. From 1670 to 1704 we have the rush of specifically philanthropic proposals, such as those of Sir Matthew Hale and Sir Josiah Child, Firmin, Haines, Bellers and Cary, which we have described in the preceding chapter. This movement received a check in 1704 in the deadly effect of the pamphlet by Daniel De Foe, from which we have so freely quoted. The second was connected, in the main, with the desire to restrict the number of recipients of relief by the use of the workhouse, not as a means of employment but as a deterrent ; and it resulted in the establishment of some hundreds of such institutions. Another wave followed about the middle of the eighteenth century emphasising the need for superior administration ; and leading by long-continued and only partially successful attempts, in which William Hay, M.P., was a leading figure, to supersede or subordinate the administration of the parish officials by the establishment of extensive Unions. A later generation, in which Thomas Gilbert, M.P., was a leader, vehemently urged the necessity of maintaining, on the one hand, a well-ordered and humanely administered asylum for the aged and infirm, the sick and the orphan children, whilst absolutely excluding from such an institution the able-bodied men, whose distress from

---

[1] By far the largest mass of Poor Law pamphlets is that in the British Museum, including Sir Edwin Chadwick's collection. Some of those not possessed by the British Museum may be found in the Bodleian Library (principally in the Gough Collection) ; or in the Cambridge University Library (principally in the Pryme Collections) ; or in the Manchester Public Library ; or in the Goldsmiths' Library at the University of London ; whilst others are in the British Library of Economics and Political Science, attached to the London School of Economics, or in the Jones Collection at University College. A few have been preserved only in the library of the Ministry of Health.

unemployment was to be dealt with otherwise. This led to a renewed increase in the amount of Outdoor Relief to this class, and, in the years of severe stress and high prices that marked the close of the eighteenth century, produced upon the acute social problem thus arising a flood of pamphlets, which failed to prevent the general adoption of the Allowance System. The equally severe economic crisis that came after the peace of 1815 caused another great increase in the Poor Rates, and a controversy all along the line which raged, right down to 1834, in pamphlets marked by the note of restriction, and as soon as practicable, of refusal of all public relief, characteristic of these particular decades.

Doles and Pensions

To the annually elected and unpaid Overseer, caring only to get through a disagreeable duty with as little trouble as possible, the easiest and most obvious way of fulfilling his statutory obligation to relieve all destitute persons was to give a small money dole to any one in need. This was all that the Justices insisted on when they chose to intervene. In 1669–1676, in the North Riding, the Overseers of particular parishes were ordered to pay " a very poor infirm woman fourpence weekly " ; in another case to give that sum " to a very poor, aged and impotent man towards the maintenance of himself and family " ; whilst " a poor, impotent, lame, aged man " was to have sixpence weekly, and " a poor woman with six small children tenpence weekly ". A " woman with seven children " was to have " twelvepence weekly until her husband comes out of gaol " ; and two girls, " forsaken by their father and mother, now in York gaol, and not able to maintain themselves by reason of their minority ", were accorded eightpence a week.[1]

The administration was substantially the same in the small towns that were still the typical trading centres. In the borough of Liverpool, for instance, in 1681 beginning to rise as a commercial port, but still inhabited only by seven or eight hundred families, we find the Overseers—with no idea of " setting the poor to work ", no workhouse of any kind, and no " parish stock "—doling out sixpences and shillings in separately entered items to " soldiers'

[1] *North Riding Quarter Sessions Records*, by C. J. Atkinson, vol. vi.; *Seventeenth Century Life in the Country Parish*, by Eleanor Trotter, 1919, pp. 55-56.

wives ", to casually stranded seamen, and to other migrants, as well as to local residents, mostly widowed or infirm women. Orphan children were boarded out with women residents and paid for at the rate of a shilling per week for food, with additional sums occasionally for clothes and boots. About a score of adults, mostly women, seem to have been regular recipients of weekly doles.[1] When the infirmity was chronic, as in old age, or when the illness or lack of employment amounted to what the Overseer chose to consider permanent destitution, or perhaps when the applicant was sufficiently assiduous in his appeals, the name was entered in the " poor's book " ; [2] and the casual dole became what was virtually a pension. In all the considerable parishes, there would presently be a stream of men, women and children calling one evening in the week at the Overseer's farmhouse or shop for their regular " pay ". At Liverpool, for instance, there was soon " an ominous increase in the Poor's Ley. In 1681 it was £40. Ten years later it had increased to £100, and £35 was borrowed to supplement it. The next year it was £160 ; by 1719 it had risen to £520, and then it increased by leaps and bounds, until in 1722 it stood at £1000." [3]

It was to check this tendency of the parish officials to create a pension list that Parliament, as early as 1692, made it definitely a duty of " the inhabitants in vestry assembled " to go through the list every Easter, with a view to striking off those whom they did not " think fit, and allow to receive collection ".[4] This injunction, which was repeated in substance by the Act of 1723, was, we suspect, seldom obeyed. In 1697 a further effort was made at Westminster to check the growth of these local pension lists. This Act, as we have already mentioned, ordered that all persons in receipt of relief should wear badges " openly . . . upon the

---

[1] MS. Minutes, Liverpool Vestry, 1681–1682 ; see *The Poor Law in Liverpool, 1681–1834*, by W. Lyon Blease, 1909 (from *Transactions of the Historic Society of Lancashire and Cheshire*, 1909) ; and the admirably produced printed records entitled *The Liverpool Vestry Books, 1681–1834*, edited by Henry Peet, 2 vols., 1912–1915.

[2] Naturally this gave opportunity for patronage and favouritism ; and also, it may be, for sectarian partiality or persecution. In 1682 we find in Narcissus Luttrell's *Brief Historical Relation of State Affairs, 1678–1714* (1857), vol. i. p. 165, the significant Order by the Justices of Middlesex that " such poor people who go to conventicles, and not to their parish churches shall be put out of the poor's book and have no parish collections ".

[3] *Liverpool Vestry Books, 1681–1834*, by Henry Peet, 1912, vol. i. p. xxviii.

[4] 3 William and Mary, c. 11, sec. 2 (1692).

shoulder of the right sleeve ".[1]   It is, we think, typical that the Liverpool Vestry apparently paid no heed to this statutory requirement for over fifteen years.   At last, in 1713, the Vestry ordered the law to be obeyed, and directed badges marked L.P. to be supplied to all who received weekly allowances.   Any who did not wear these badges publicly on their clothes were " not to be relieved ".   This was evidently soon disregarded, as we find the order repeated in 1718, with the addition that if the Overseers failed in such cases to stop the pensions, the amount was not to be allowed in their accounts.[2]   But it is clear that, although the statute of 1697 remained unrepealed until 1810,[3] nothing could secure compliance with the law on this point.   In 1752 we read that " badges to be worn by the poor are almost universally disused ;   although the officer who relieves any poor person without a badge forfeits twenty shillings for each offence ".[4] The badge had sometimes to be worn also by the children of the person relieved.   The Vestry Minutes of Burton-on-Trent (September 6, 1702) recite that " persons that receive alms out of the poor's levy of this Liberty do often omit the wearing the public badge of this Town ", and order that if they, " *or any of their children* be seen without such badge ", they are to lose their allowance.[5]   On June 6, 1703, it is ordered that four named women " be taken out of constant pay for their stubborn refusal to wear the badge ".   The wearing of a pauper badge may have lasted longer in its application to the inmates of institutions. " The poor in this house ", Sir F. M. Eden found at Hampton (Middlesex) in 1797, " are clothed once a year ;   every person wears a red badge on their shoulder marked P. H. (Parish of Hampton)." [6]

But, while the money dole became the usual form of relief,

---

[1] 8 and 9 William III. c. 30, sec. 2 (1697).

[2] MS. Minutes, Liverpool Vestry, 1712, 1718 ; *The Poor Law in Liverpool, 1681–1834*, by W. Lyon Blease, 1909 ; *The Liverpool Vestry Books, 1681–1834*, by Henry Peet, 1912, vol. i.

[3] 50 George III. c. 52.

[4] *A Letter to the Author of " Considerations on Several Proposals for the Better Maintenance of the Poor* ", 1752, p. 19 ;   also to the same effect, *Observations on the Defects of the Poor Laws*, by Rev. Thomas Alcock, 1752, p. 17.

[5] *Burton on Trent*, by William Molyneux, 1869.

[6] *The State of the Poor*, by Sir F. M. Eden, 1797, vol. ii. p. 436.   See the remarks of Dean Swift, in his " On Giving Badges to the Poor ", and " Considerations about Maintaining the Poor " (*Works*, vol. vii. p. 574).

the use of the " Parish Stock ", as a means of " setting the
poor to work ", in the manner contemplated by the Elizabethan legislation, was still to be found—though, we imagine,
very rarely—during the latter part of the seventeenth century.
Thus, in 1677, the North Riding Quarter Sessions ordered the
Overseers of Tollerton to pay a certain man " sixpence weekly
for his relief and maintenance, *or twenty shillings at one time
payment for enabling him to buy skins to follow his trade of parchment maker* ".[1]   Two years later we find the same Justices ordering
" that the town[ship] of Romanby should not for the future pay
any weekly allowance unto . . . [a widow], or be further chargeable with her *than the providing her a stock* ".[2]

Sometimes it is the " Justices' Poor Law " that is complained
of by parsimonious Vestries or Overseers. Thus, in 1679, we
find the inhabitants of West Tanfield, in the North Riding of
Yorkshire, protesting to Quarter Sessions against an order to
give relief, and alleging, with what we may well believe to be
accuracy, " that there is above 20 lame and blind persons in the
parish that are more necessitous than [the particular woman
who had been ordered relief], and have no allowance but the alms
of the parishioners, and if they had it, would utterly undo the
inhabitants to pay it ".[3]   In 1681 the same Quarter Sessions
issues " a warrant against the Parson of Ainderby Steeple to find
sureties, etc., for reflecting on the Court for easy granting orders
for the relief of the poor of Ainderby Steeple aforesaid ".[4]

But, irrespective of the sporadic interventions of the Justices,
we find, throughout the whole century, parish after parish,
aroused by the continued rise in the Poor Rate or by the advent
of a reformer, now and again trying to check the natural dole-

---

[1] *North Riding Quarter Sessions Records*, by C. J. Atkinson, vol. vi. p. 271 ;
Seventeenth Century Life in the Country Parish, by Eleanor Trotter, 1919, p. 61.
[2] *North Riding Quarter Sessions Records*, by C. J. Atkinson, vol. vii.
[3] *Ibid.* vol. vii. ; *Seventeenth Century Life in the Country Parish*, by Eleanor
Trotter, 1919, p. 79.
[4] N.R.Q.S.R. vol. vii. p. 51 (July 19, 1681) ; Richard Dunning records a
like laxity among the Justices of Devonshire. " Loose idle persons ", he said,
" clamour for relief when they need none ; and if their demands be not
satisfied, complain to the Justices of the Peace, who never do, nor can do less
than order the Overseers to come before them to answer and show cause, etc.,
and such Overseers as live far from the Justice will often give the clamourers
relief merely to save themselves from a journey, especially when they have the
wit to complain in a busy time " (*A Plain and Easy Method of showing how
the Office of Overseer of the Poor may be managed*, etc., by Richard Dunning,
1686, p. 13).

giving and pension-making propensities of the careless Overseer. In the important parish of St. George's, Hanover Square, London, in 1738, the Select Vestry acted through its members who were Justices of the Peace, and we read that the Justices, on allowing the Overseers' accounts, came to the following decision, which is entered as an order of Petty Sessions : " That the present Overseers of the Poor have notice given them by the Clerk that they do not disburse or give away any monies to casual poor except upon extraordinary occasions, or by the consent of some magistrate of this parish signified by writing under his hand ; and that they do not send any poor into the workhouse except upon urgent occasion. It appearing by the butcher's bill in the late Overseers' accounts that a great quantity of mutton is used in the house, which we are of opinion is unnecessary, and occasions a greater number of people to come and continue therein, it is hereby ordered that the Master of the Workhouse have notice to send for less mutton, and that only when the doctor directs it, by thinking it absolutely necessary for sick patients." [1]. And if we turn to the little market town of Minchinhampton, in Gloucestershire, between 1786 and 1802, we see the monthly meetings of the Vestry mainly occupied in " making the calendar " of the Overseers of the separate divisions, striking off some allowances, reducing others, and occasionally entering a new one.[2] In 1811 it is specially resolved that " at every monthly meeting the Overseer for each division shall call over his extra pays for the past month ".[3] In the large and growing parish of St. Pancras, in 1783, the Open Vestry peremptorily orders that " no Overseer do presume to give any such allowances to any person whatsoever but those whose names are inserted in the pension book, not to greater amount than is there specified. Also that all persons requiring relief as out pensioners do attend at a public meeting of the Overseers at the workhouse, to be by them examined as to their merits and pretensions, and that the name of no person whatever be inserted in the pension book as an out pensioner but of those who have previously undergone such examination.[4] Between 1805 and 1835 practically every large parish strove to

[1] *The Parish and the County*, by S. and B. Webb, 1906, pp. 404-405.
[2] MS. Vestry Minutes, Minchinhampton (Gloucestershire), 1786–1802 *passim*.
[3] *Ibid.* April 15, 1811.
[4] MS. Vestry Minutes, St. Pancras (Middlesex), May 29, 1783.

curtail its swollen " calendar ", " pension book ", " weekly table " [1]
or " monthly list ". In some cases a new set of Overseers, or a
newly constituted statutory authority, would take the matter in
hand. Thus, a circular distributed among " the freeholders and
inhabitants " of Nantwich in 1816 recites that " the present
Overseers, taking into consideration the very heavy burden of
the poor rates . . . intend to call a General Vestry before which
the whole of the poor who receive relief shall be summoned to
appear, that the circumstances of each may be investigated. . . .
We are, generally speaking, unfriendly to the system of constant
weekly payment. The poor are placed on a list when sickness
or the badness of trade renders temporary assistance necessary,
and when once their names are entered there, they demand the
same allowance long after the necessity, which first entitled them
to it, has ceased to exist. If an Overseer attempts to stop or
reduce it, they continue, by the concealment or misrepresentation
of their real circumstances, or through the interest and mistaken
kindness of their friends, to counteract his exertions, and seldom
fail to load him with abuse." [2]   It was largely this more methodi-
cal investigation of the parish pension roll that Sturges Bourne
had in view in his legislation of 1818–1819, and the adoption of
his Act by any parish was usually followed, as we have elsewhere
described in the case of Charlton, by a struggle between the new
Select Vestry and the unpaid Overseers. The resulting friction
often led to the appointment of a salaried Overseer, who insensibly
passed from being merely a rate collector and bastardy and
removal officer, into the permanent investigator whom we now
know as the Relieving Officer. " Visiting the Poor "—that is,
investigating the circumstances of the applicants for outdoor
relief—vainly suggested by Jonas Hanway as early as 1780,[3]
begins to be insisted on in the better governed Vestries from the
beginning of the nineteenth century.[4]   When an energetic Vestry

---

[1] So termed in MS. vol. of Churchwardens' Accounts, Holy Cross, Pershore,
Worcestershire, 1750–1780.

[2] Printed Circular, 1816, 4 pp. folio, in British Museum.

[3] *The Citizen's Monitor*, by Jonas Hanway, 1780, pp. 255-256.

[4] Thus, when in 1820 the Greenwich Vestry appointed an Assistant Overseer,
his duties, defined in a lengthy report, were almost identical with those of a
relieving officer of to-day (MS. Vestry Minutes, March 23, 1820). For another
instance, see MS. Vestry Minutes, St. Margaret's, Leicester, December 10,
1832. An earlier case is recorded in 1801. " At Birmingham a person is
constantly employed at a fixed salary to visit the out-poor at their houses,
which prevents much imposition, and saves the town a great deal of money "

or Court of Guardians nerved itself to the duty of going through
the whole list of parish pensioners, the work would occupy the
members for weeks. In 1826 we hear that the new statutory
body of Directors and Guardians of the Poor of Brighton " have
just completed their Herculean task of examining the whole of the
outdoor paupers ".[1] Meanwhile a few parishes, in their new-born
zeal for investigating the claims of the poor, invoked the aid of the
public. For Chesterfield, Wolverhampton and Birmingham, for
instance, printed lists are extant for various years between 1781
and 1796 " of those who receive pay ", and sometimes also of the
inmates of the workhouse. One for Nantwich (Cheshire) for 1816
gives also their ages. In 1833 we learn that " in St. Asaph,
Holywell, Wrexham, and one or two other places in Flintshire
and Denbighshire, a balance sheet of the yearly receipts and
payments, and the names of those who have been relieved, with
the amount granted to each, is printed and distributed amongst
the ratepayers. This practice has been only of recent introduction ; but of such advantage is it considered that the parishes
adjoining those where it exists are beginning to adopt it. The
printing and distributing a list of those receiving relief often
brings to light cases of imposture which otherwise would have
remained undetected ; besides which the paupers seem to dislike
the exposure, as in some instances they have given up a part or
the whole of their relief to prevent it. The printed accounts of
St. Asaph contain the following entry : ' Sundry paupers who
rather than be " classed " (that is, put in the printed list) pay
part of their " rent " '. And in another parish a pauper ceased
to apply for relief on learning that his name had been thus published." [2] The Manchester Churchwardens, in 1814, advertised

---

(*Thoughts on Poor Houses*, etc., by Henry Wansey, 1801, p. 26). Sometimes
the Vestrymen themselves undertook the task of investigation. At Gateshead,
the Select Vestry in 1822, in imitation, as they said, of Dr. Chalmers, resolved
on a great scheme of themselves visiting all the paupers in their own homes,
the parish being divided into four districts, and each district into five sub-
districts ; whilst one vestryman " with a list and a note book " was assigned
to each subdistrict. Much was hoped from this plan ; but the subsequent
half-yearly reports confess that it has not yet been put in operation. Three
years later, we find the duty of visiting assigned to the paid Overseer (MS.
Vestry Minutes, Gateshead, Durham, October 31, 1822, March 31, 1823,
October 28, 1824, April 14, 1825).

[1] *Brighton Herald*, June 10, 1826.

[2] Report of Poor Law Inquiry Commissioners, 1834, Appendix A, Walcott's
Report, p. 185. " In many parishes in Lancashire it is customary to publish
the names of all persons receiving relief, and the public are invited to inform

in the newspapers that "as many families and persons resident in Manchester may be receiving relief from the township who are able to support themselves, the Churchwardens particularly request that all masters and employers, as well as leypayers, will make enquiry into the earnings of all people employed by them, and whether any such are receiving relief undeservedly : such information given to the Churchwardens . . . will be immediately attended to ".[1] At Plymouth, the Guardians resolved " that the list of persons receiving weekly pay be printed and published ".[2] But in practically all the rural parishes of southern England, and in some of the towns, any efforts to keep down the parish pension roll were, as we shall presently see, from about 1795 onwards, rendered nugatory by the systematic policy of the Justices of the Peace.

Outdoor relief did not always take the form of money doles or weekly pensions. In the parish accounts of Steeple Ashton, in Wiltshire, we find an exceptionally early annual reclothing of the poor. Between 1605 and 1622, at any rate, we find the Vestry, with the Vicar and the Churchwarden, repeatedly laying out sums of about fifty shillings in the purchase of linen cloth (or " canvas "), at about thirteen pence per yard, or, " at Bristol Fair ", of " grey frieze ", at fifteen or eighteen pence per yard. It is recorded in the accounts that these stuffs were each time distributed in lengths varying from " one ell and a quarter " to " two ells and a quarter " to about a dozen named women, with a few men and boys. Other entries record gifts of " a pair of shoes ", " frieze to make him a jerkin ", or " for a gown ".[3]

---

the overseers should they know any reason why relief should be withheld " (*Great Britain for the last Forty Years*, by Thomas Hopkins, 1834, p. 288). Publication still (1926) occurs in some rural districts.

[1] *Manchester Gazette*, April 16, 1814.

" In one of the townships in Macclesfield Hundred a plan has been adopted to ascertain the real state of all those who claim relief from the Overseers by annually drawing up a register of various circumstances connected with their situation, on a reference to which the Overseers may be enabled, in every instance, to ascertain what are the real necessities of the claimants " (*General View of the Agriculture of Cheshire*, by Henry Holland, 1808, p. 329).

[2] MS. Minutes, Court of Guardians, Plymouth (Devon), March 21, 1827. More drastic measures followed. Four years later we read that " In order to get rid of many of those at present on the pension list, it is ordered that their weekly pay be gradually lessened every succeeding quarter until they shall be wholly discharged from the pay list " (*Ibid.* September 21, 1831).

[3] From the extracts of Vestry Minutes, Steeple Ashton, Wiltshire, 1603–1628, printed as Appendix B of *The Parish*, by Joshua Toulmin Smith, 1857, pp. 626–644.

In reading the accounts of parish officers or the minutes of
Vestries and Courts of Guardians throughout the seventeenth
and eighteenth centuries, we become aware of a stream of gifts
in kind—shifts or shoes ; half a hundredweight of coal ; a bag of
potatoes ; and even weekly allowances of bread and beer, given
merely as the humanity or caprice of the local authorities
dictated.   In the parish of Holy Cross, Pershore, in Worcestershire,[1] the Open Vestry, between 1750 and 1780, seems to have
met monthly, and every meeting saw about a score of gifts made,
of shifts, petticoats, coats, breeches, waistcoats, shoes, pounds of
wool to be knitted into stockings, " a draft of coals ", and so on,
apparently without stint or restriction.   In some parishes the
substitution of relief in kind for money payments began to be
adopted as a matter of policy.   Thus, at Mitcham, in 1800, " it
is ordered that the poor who are now relieved out of the House
with money shall, after the 1st of January next . . . be relieved
with the following articles, viz., rice, butter, cheese, tea, sugar,
candles and soap ".[2]   And in the same winter of scarcity the
Wiltshire Justices in Quarter Sessions resolved that " one third
of the weekly relief given to any person who shall subsist wholly
on parochial pay be given in some one or more of [seventeen
enumerated articles of food] ".[3]   But by far the most usual form
of relief in kind was the payment of the rent of the applicant's
dwelling-house, so as to ensure him a roof over his head.   In the
records of nearly every parish that we have investigated, the item
of " rent " sooner or later appears, and when it appears it almost
invariably becomes in a very few years one of the principal items
of chargeability.   Many a parish came in this way to pay every
week a substantial sum direct to the landlords of cottage or
tenement property.   At Steeple Ashton (Wilts) in 1609, " there
was paid to R.W. for widow G.'s rent, 8s.".[4]   Two and a quarter
centuries later, in 1833, in the same county, in the parish of Purton,

---

[1] MS. vol. of Churchwardens' Accounts, 1750–1780, Holy Cross, Pershore,
Worcestershire.   The " Request Book " of the parish of Ardingly (Sussex)
shows that " Lucy Holman petitioned for two gowns, an upper and an under
coat, two shimmeys, one pair of pattens, one pair of shoes, one pair of hose,
one bonnet ".   This, however, was " thought unreasonable " (Report of Poor
Law Inquiry Commissioners, Appendix A, Majendie's Report, p. 187).

[2] MS. Vestry Minutes, Mitcham (Surrey), December 4, 1800.

[3] MS. Minutes, Quarter Sessions, Wiltshire, Hilary Term, 1801.

[4] Extracts from Vestry Minutes of Steeple Ashton (Wilts), 1603–1628,
printed as Appendix B to *The Parish*, by Joshua Toulmin Smith, 1857, p. 630.

in the Cricklade district, the Overseer pays £120 per annum to the landowner for cottage rent for the use of the paupers ; and in Castle Eaton, a much smaller parish, about £80 per annum is thus applied.[1] Now and again we find some reformer protesting, as did a committee of the Brighton Vestry, that this was an " objectionable mode of relieving, as it affords encouragement to the building of tenements, and tends to increase the numbers of the poor " thus enabled to reside in the parish.[2] But the influence in the Vestry of cottage owners, coupled with the obvious desirability of " not breaking up the poor man's home ", rendered these protests of no avail. The most that was done in the way of reform was to cease paying the landlord direct, giving the pauper himself a weekly pay of the same amount. From the evidence collected by the Poor Law Inquiry Commissioners of 1832–1834, it is clear that this form of relief was adopted, more or less, in practically all districts. In some parishes it amounted to nearly one-half of the total poor law expenditure.[3]

The Allowance System

One feature common to the doles, pensions and gifts of necessaries, which the importunity of the poor extracted from the Overseer or the Vestry, was the insufficiency of the amount of relief for complete maintenance. Thus, wherever the matter was left to the discretion of the parish, each pauper in receipt of outdoor relief seldom got more than a few pence per week in a country village at the end of the seventeenth century, or more than one or two shillings a week, even in an urban district, at the end of the eighteenth century. It was difficult, in the absence of any other way of preventing starvation, to refuse all assistance to any person without obvious means of subsistence ; and the applicant could, if refused, practically always appeal to the humanity of a Justice of the Peace, who naturally found it easiest to order the Overseer to give relief.[4] Those local records which

---

[1] Report of the Poor Law Inquiry Commissioners, 1834, Appendix A, Okeden's Report, p. 6.

[2] MS. Vestry Minutes, Brighton, June 2, 1824.

[3] See, for instance, Report of the Poor Law Inquiry Commissioners, 1834, Appendix A, p. 174, C. P. Villiers' Report.

[4] Parliament tried to put some check on the liberality of the Justices as early as 1723, when it was provided that the Justice should not order relief " until oath be made of some reasonable cause for having relief, and that

go into detail in the matter indicate, not the grant of anything like adequate maintenance, but a careless disbursement of sixpences and shillings to a series of importunate applicants. The inference cannot be escaped that there was a great amount of sheer inhumanity about the system which individual Justices spasmodically tried to check. In the latter part of the seventeenth century, as we have seen, even the Court of Quarter Sessions made orders for allowances in long strings of individual cases, which the Overseers had apparently neglected. Thus the Derbyshire Quarter Sessions at Easter, 1683, made such orders for " one shilling weekly ", or similar sums, to be paid by the Overseers " for the better relief and maintenance of no fewer than twenty-one separate persons in different parishes ".[1] A peculiar instance of harshness is recorded in 1773 by a competent witness acquainted with the practice of Hertfordshire and North Middlesex. " When allowance out of the workhouse is permitted ", writes the Quaker poet John Scott, " an unkind and indelicate practice frequently obtains. The parish vouchsafes a trifling pittance of a pension , and an industrious son or daughter, from the earnings of their industry, supplies the remainder of the maintenance of the aged or decrepit parent. In such case, an inventory of what little household furniture may be in the pauper's possession is immediately taken, in order that it may revert to the parish at his decease. The poor have sensibility, and it is really cruel to treat as criminals, whose property is confiscated, those who in this respect have no crime but inevitable poverty." [2]

The Overseer making such plainly inadequate allowances as a few pence, or a shilling or two per week, sometimes no more even to man and wife, was easily persuaded that the recipients could and must make up the rest of their subsistence from the proceeds of their labour. Where a poorhouse or workhouse existed, it became a regular practice with the Overseer to bargain

---

application had been made for it to the Overseers of the Poor or the Vestry of the parish and was by them refused ; nor until the Overseers had been summoned to show cause why the relief should not be given " ; and that, if granted, the relief should be entered in the parish book (9 George I. c. 7, 1723 ; *History of the English Poor Law*, by Sir George Nicholls, 1854, vol. ii. pp. 14-15). We do not find that these formalities were observed by the Justices.

[1] *Three Centuries of Derbyshire Annals*, by J. C. Cox, 1890, vol. i. p. 165.

[2] *Observations on the Present State of the Parochial and Vagrant Poor*, 1773, p. 48 [by John Scott].

with the paupers, offering them relief in " the House ", or the alternative of a tiny pittance of weekly pay outside, to enable them to make it up by casual labour.[1] Hence we see that the " rate in aid of wages ", which afterwards became notorious in the scales prescribed by the Justices, had long existed in the spontaneous practice of the Overseers, and was, in fact, the most obvious device for saving themselves trouble and the parish immediate expense. The eighteenth century, even more than the seventeenth or the sixteenth, thought of the poor in the lump, and scarcely ever discriminated in thought, or in the written records, between such categories as the able-bodied, the sick and infirm or the children. But it is clear that from the latter part of the seventeenth century onward, when probably no parish provided any stock of hemp, flax, iron or what not, on which to set the poor to work, there was, in most parishes, a great deal of Outdoor Relief of those able-bodied male adults who found themselves, for longer or shorter periods, unable to live by their labour.

As the century wore on, the total amount annually distributed in this way among the poor, and especially the amount given to able-bodied men out of employment, steadily increased. There is reason to infer that the decade immediately following the peace of 1763—when a great expansion of trade and an apparent growth of national prosperity was taking place—was marked also by an unusually great increase in pauperism, especially in the form of Outdoor Relief—an increase that was statistically demonstrated, as we have already mentioned, by the returns obtained in 1776 and 1786. In 1782 Thomas Gilbert, M.P. for Lichfield, who had for years been pressing for Poor Law reform (and had even carried a Bill through the House of Commons in 1765, only to have it rejected by the House of Lords by 66 to 59), at last succeeded in carrying through Parliament a statute (universally known as " Gilbert's Act "), which had for its main object the establishment by unions of parishes of reformed workhouses in which the aged, the sick and the infirm together with their dependent children, and all the orphans, might be humanely provided for. In order to secure their comfort, and the proper conduct of the institution, the statute provided, and, as we should nowadays say, wisely

---

[1] Report of Poor Law Inquiry Commissioners, 1834, Appendix A, Villiers' Report, pp. 3-10.

provided, that able-bodied persons should not be admitted to the asylum and hospital that was intended. This decision involved, however, some other provision for the able-bodied, and this was found in a direction that any applicant who could not get employment in the ordinary way should by the Poor Law Guardians—without explaining how—be provided with it, and be fed and lodged until it could be given. Failing such relief, any Justice of the Peace was expressly empowered, after inquiry upon oath, to order " some weekly or other relief ". In the sixty-seven Unions that were established under Gilbert's Act during the ensuing decades, comprising 924 parishes, we do not find that the able-bodied men in want of employment were, otherwise than exceptionally, actually provided with such employment, which the Guardians naturally found difficult, if not impossible, to procure. What did happen was that the statutory exclusion of the able-bodied from the sixty-seven new Gilbert Union Workhouses, which was doubtless an unmixed advantage to these institutions and their inmates, almost necessarily involved the free use by the Justices of their power of ordering Outdoor Relief.[1]

[1] " Gilbert's Act "—the most carefully devised, the most elaborate and perhaps the most influential, for both good and evil, of all the scores of Poor Law Statutes between 1601 and 1834—was the subject of much pamphlet and other controversy. It was explained and amended by 33 George III. c. 35, 1793 ; 41 George III. c. 9, 1801 ; 42 and 43 George III. c. 74 and c. 110, 1802 ; 1 and 2 George IV. c. 56, 1821 ; and was not repealed until the Statute Law Revision Act of 1871.

For its results, see *The History of the English Poor Law*, by Sir George Nicholls, 1854, vol. ii. pp. 89-98 ; *The State of the Poor*, by Sir F. M. Eden, 1797, vol. i. pp. 270-279 ; *History of the Poor*, by Thomas Ruggles, 1793. Among the scores of pamphlets dating from 1776 to 1788 that are still extant, we may cite, as most informative, the score or so indexed as either by Thomas Gilbert himself or as addressed to him ; the *Observations on the Bill*, etc., by Rev. Richard Burn, 1776 ; *A Dissertation on the Poor Laws*, by a wellwisher to mankind, the Rev. Joseph Townsend, 1785, and several other editions ; and the *Collection of Pamphlets concerning the Poor . . . with Observations by the Editor*, which Gilbert published in 1787.

Others which may be mentioned are : *Thoughts on the Present State of the Poor, and the intended Bill for their Better Relief and Employment*, by a Kentishman, 1776 ; *Remarks upon the late Resolutions of the H. of C. respecting the proposed change of the Poor Laws*, etc., by Rev. Henry Zouch, 1776 ; *The Outlines of a Scheme for the General Relief, Instruction, Employment and Maintenance of the Poor*, etc., by James Peacock, 1777 ; also, by the same, *Proposals for a Magnificent and Interesting Establishment for the Employment of the Poor*, 1790 ; *Reasons for the late Increase of the Poor Rates, or a Comparative View of the Price of Labour and Provisions*, 1777 ; *An Address to the People of England on the Increase of their Poor Rates*, by John Burnby, 1780 (in library of Ministry of Health) ; *A View of Real Grievances, with Remedies*, 1782 and 1786 ; *Hints relative to the Management of the Poor*, etc., by Philip Lebrocq, 1784 ; *An*

The worst effects of this indiscriminate and widespread
Outdoor Relief to the able-bodied labourers were seen, however,
not when the relief was given at the time when they were wholly
unemployed, but when it took the form of small regular sums
insufficient for maintenance, and intended to be eked out by
casual or underpaid labour. This " rate in aid of wages ", as it
came to be called, was not altogether a new thing. Apart from
its occasional accompaniment of any system of Outdoor Relief,
we hear of its existence in the clothing centres immediately after
the enactment of the statute of 1601. Thus, of Colchester, it
was said, relating to the reign of James I., that " the bay-makers,
or rather the bay-merchants, are the chiefs in the town, and at
all assessments they rule the roast ; and they give the poor
starving wages for their work, as fourpence per day, and make
them amends in collections, out of which they allow sixpence
per day. And so the charge of the bay-making falls upon the
owners and general inhabitants, whereof the gains fall in their
purses, which secret they were content to discover even to
strangers complaining that they had no redress, because their
Justices were of the same faction." [1] When this practice
became, in any locality, systematised and general, the economic
results were calamitous. This came about in what has been
aptly termed the " double panic of famine and revolution ",[2]
caused by the rise in the price of food which resulted from
the bad harvests of the closing decade of the eighteenth century, and the consequent distress of practically the whole of
the rural labourers. The distress might have been met by a
corresponding rise in the labourer's remuneration ; but the

Essay on Parish Workhouses, etc., by Edmund Gillingwater, 1786 ; *Inferior
Politics, or Considerations on the Wickedness and Profligacy of the Poor*, etc., by
Hewling Luson, 1787 ; *A Plan for Rendering the Poor Independent*, by Dr.
Richard Price, 1786 ; *An Account of a Society for encouraging the Industrious
Poor*, by Joseph Priestley, 1787 ; *A General Plan of Parochial and Provincial
Police*, by William Godschall, 1787 ; *Hints respecting the Poor*, etc., by Rev. T.
Haweis, 1788 ; and *A Defence of the Statute passed in the Forty-Third year of
Elizabeth, concerning the Employment and Relief of the Poor, with Proposals for
Enforcing it* [by Thomas Ruggles], Bury St. Edmunds, 1788 ; and — perhaps
the most informative and suggestive of all these publications—*The Insufficiency
of the Causes to which the increase of our Poor and of the Poor Rates have been
ascribed*, etc., by Rev. J. Howlett, 1788.

[1] *Discourse on the Pernicious Tendency of the Laws for the Maintenance
and Settlement of the Poor*, by the Hon. Roger North, 1753 (but written,
apparently, in the first decade of the century). Bay or bays = baize.

[2] *Dispauperization*, by J. R. Pretyman, 1878, p. 27.

farmers and landowners stoutly resisted any increase of wages, on the ground that " it would be difficult to reduce them when the cause for it had ceased ".[1]   On the other hand, it was feared by many that if the distress of the labourers became too acute, it would lead to an outbreak of the revolutionary spirit then upsetting France.   In the spring of 1795, when the price of food rose all over the country, a whole series of petty disturbances took place from Carlisle to Seaford, and from Devonshire to Suffolk, sometimes only suppressed by calling out the troops. These were largely in the nature of food riots, by women in their marketing, who tumultuously seized the flour, butter or meat, for which outrageously high prices were being demanded, and distributed it among the crowd at the rates they thought fair.[2]

In this predicament the public-spirited members of the governing class turned from one expedient to another.   It was urged by some that a remedy for the high prices might be found in a voluntary diminution in the consumption, and consequently in the demand, for wheaten flour.   The rich were to abstain from pastry on their tables, and from the use of hair powder on their footmen's heads ; whilst the poor were to eat barley bread and oatmeal, or at least be content with wheaten flour of less whiteness.   Other persons, realising more adequately the futility of such proposals, suggested that pressure should be put on the farmers to pay wages at least sufficient to maintain their labourers.[3]

[1] Report of Poor Law Inquiry Commissioners, 1834, Appendix A, Villiers' Report, p. 14.   This desire to stave off a rise of wages is expressly assigned as the motive for the Justices' scales of Speenhamland (1795) and Warwickshire (1797) ; for those fixed in Sussex and Essex in 1800 and 1810 (*ibid.* Majendie's Report, p. 167) ; and for that in Suffolk, after the peace of 1815 (*ibid.* Henry Stuart's Report, p. 349).   In the latter case, as in 1795–1797, it appeared to the magistrates as the only practicable alternative to enforcing by law a definite minimum wage.   " When that state of affairs arose," writes even one of the Assistant Poor Law Commissioners in 1833, " which drove nearly the whole of the labouring population to seek food and protection from them [the magistrates], being without the power of prescribing the rate of wages, there was no alternative left to them but to save the people from starvation " (*ibid.* Henry Stuart's Report, p. 351).

[2] *Ipswich Journal*, March 28 and April 18, 1795 ; *Reading Mercury*, April 20 and 27, 1795 ; *The State of the Poor*, by Sir F. M. Eden, 1797, vol. ii. p. 591 ; *The Village Labourer, 1760–1832*, by J. L. and B. Hammond, 1912, pp. 120-122.

[3] The best account of this whole controversy, and of the contemporary proposals, has been given by Mr. and Mrs. Hammond in *The Village Labourer, 1760–1832*, 1912, pp. 106-165.   The principal publications were the following : *A Plan for the Better Maintenance and Regulation of the Parochial Poor*, by Thomas Hall (in *Letters and Papers of Bath and West of England Agricultural Society*, vol. vi. art. 23), 1792; *On the Best Means of Providing for the Poor*, by

A widespread movement arose among philanthropic landlords in favour of reviving the old practice of fixing wages by law, in proportion to the current price of wheat. This policy was supported in several counties by resolution of the Justices. Thus, at Bury St. Edmunds, we find Quarter Sessions resolving " that the members for this county be requested by the chairman to bring a bill into Parliament so to regulate the price of labour that it may fluctuate with the average price of corn ".[1]   In the same month Arthur Young, who had attended this Suffolk meeting,

---

W[illiam] M[atthews] (in the same), 1792 ; *The Benefit of Starving : or the Advantages of Hunger and Nakedness, intended as a cordial to the poor and an apology for the rich : addressed to the Rev. Rowland Hill*, 1792 ; *The Duty of the Overseers of the Poor to be delivered to them at their appointment*, by a County Magistrate, 1792 ; *An Essay on the Best Means of Providing Employment for the People*, by Samuel Crumpe, 1793 ; *The Complaints of the Poor People of England*, by George Dyer, 1793 (chapters on Poor Rates, Poorhouses, Work-houses, etc.) ; *Some Hints to the Legislature for the Formation of a Plan for the Immediate Employment of the Destitute Poor*, 1793 ; *An Address to the Public on the Propriety of Establishing Schools for Spinning . . . with a view to the Better Relief and Employment of the Poor*, by Rev. Mr. Bowyer, 1795 ; *Address to the Landholders of the Kingdom for the Habitation of Labourers in the Country*, by Thomas Davis (in *Bath Papers*, vol. vii. art. 14, 1795) ; *On the Poor's Rates, and Outlines of a Scheme to Alleviate the very Unequal Burden*, by Sir Mordant Martin (in *Letters and Papers of Bath and West of England Agricultural Society*, vol. vii. art. 8), 1795 ; *Observations on the Present State of the Poor, and Measures proposed for its Improvement*, by Edward Wilson, Reading, 1795 ; *An Enquiry . . . on the Cause of Poverty and of the extremely miserable state of the Poor*, 1795 ; *Hints for the Relief of the Poor*, 1795 ; *A Letter to Sir T. C. Bunbury, Bart., on the Poor Rate and the High Prices of Provisions, with some proposals for reducing both*, by a Suffolk Gentleman, Ipswich, 1795 ; *The Case of Labourers in Husbandry stated and considered, with an Appendix shewing earnings and expenses of Labouring Families*, by Rev. David Davies, 1795 ; *A Proposal for a Perpetual Equalisation of the Pay of the Labouring Poor*, 1795 ; *Thoughts on the most Effectual Mode of Relieving the Poor during the Present Scarcity*, 1795 ; *The Prevention of Poverty by Beneficial Clubs, with Preliminary Observations upon Houses of Industry and the Poor Laws*, by Edward Jones, 1796 ; *Remarks upon the Present State of the Poor*, by Joseph Godfrey Sherer, Southampton, 1796 ; *An Inquiry into the Causes and Production of Poverty and the State of the Poor, together with the Proposed Means for their . . . Relief*, by John Vancouver, 1796 ; *An Account of a new Poorhouse in the Parish of Boldre . . . near Lymington*, by John Walter, T. Robbins and W. Gilpin, 1796 ; *Provision for the Poor by the Union of Houses of Industry with Country Parishes* : a Letter addressed to an M.P., 1797 ; *The Duties of Overseers of the Poor, and the Sufficiency of the Present System of Poor Laws considered in a Charge to the Grand Jury . . . Isle of Ely . . .* 1799, by James Nasmyth, Wisbech, 1799 ; *Observations on the Present State and Influence of the Poor Laws*, etc., by Robert Saunders, 1799.

[1] MS. Minutes, Quarter Sessions, West Suffolk, October 12, 1795 ; *Annals of Agriculture*, vol. xxv. pp. 345 and 316, with Arthur Young's comments. The same proposal was made in 1805 in the *General View of the Agriculture of the County of Hereford*, by John Duncan, 1805, p. 155.

with not a little sympathy with the proposal, issued a circular-letter to the correspondents of the Board of Agriculture inviting their comments upon the proposal of the West Suffolk and other Quarter Sessions. Most of the replies were critical, and even adverse, but there was some influential support, including a powerful argument from the Rev. J. Howlett, Vicar of Dunmow, and also by David Davies, two of the ablest and best-informed of the pamphleteers of that generation. It is interesting to find the proposal supported also by " a numerous meeting of the day labourers of the little parishes of Heacham, Snettisham and Sedgford, in the county of Norfolk, this day, 5th of November [1795], in the parish church of Heacham ", of which " Adam Moore, labourer at Heacham, clerk of the meeting" inserted as an advertisement in the local newspaper a lengthy report of the conclusions. These labourers indignantly repudiated as an insult the charitable practice of selling them flour below the market price ; they demanded that " the price of labour should at all times be proportioned to the price of wheat " ; they arranged for a petition to Parliament to regulate wages on this plan to be immediately signed throughout the county, each person sub-scribing a shilling towards the expenses ; and they resolved that a delegate meeting should be subsequently held in some central town to carry out this project. Unfortunately we hear no more of this incipient combination, which was probably immediately suppressed under the repressive legislation which Pitt was, in this very month, carrying through Parliament.

A Minimum Wage Bill was, however, introduced into the House of Commons by Samuel Whitbread, backed by Charles (afterwards Earl) Grey and, as desired by Quarter Sessions, by the Members for Suffolk. It proposed to revive and amend the Act of Elizabeth by providing that Quarter Sessions might fix and declare the wages and working hours of all labourers in husbandry (other than those at piecework and those employed by the parish), with or without beer or cider, " respect being had to the value of money and the plenty or scarcity of the time ". Appropriate provision was made for youths under age, and for those unable from infirmity to do a full day's work. Subject to these exceptions, no labourer was to be hired below the fixed rate ; and any employer breaking the law was subjected to a fine, and, in default of payment, to imprisonment. This Bill received at first no

small measure of support; but it was eventually fiercely denounced
by Pitt, who promised instead a general reform of the Poor Law,
restoring it to its Elizabethan benevolence and humanity. Notwithstanding the support of Fox, and a sturdy defence of the
Bill by Whitbread himself, the House of Commons was too much
under the spell of Pitt's dazzling speech to do other than negative
the second reading without a division.[1]

Meanwhile the obvious insufficiency of the agricultural
labourer's wage had been discussed at every Justices' meeting.
In Hampshire the Justices referred the " state of the poor " to
a committee, the members of which unanimously agreed upon
an able and elaborate report to the following Quarter Sessions.
They pointed out that the labourer must be supplied with the
necessaries of life, defined as everything that is " requisite to
support his frame for its longest continuance and its best use ".
They argued with remarkable foresight, that if the farmers
would only put the labourers in a position to get such full
subsistence, " they would be gaining, not losing by the change ;
in short, that the better support of their labourers is recommended
for their own advantage ; immediately, on a balance of work
done, and mediately, by length of life, sickness prevented,
spirit contented, honesty retained, quiet established, order
confirmed and security gained ". But they hesitated to recom-

---

[1] *Parliamentary Register*, 1795–1796. We shall deal with Pitt's scheme
of Poor Law in our next volume. In 1800, when things had got worse, and
Pitt had abandoned all idea of Poor Law reform, Whitbread tried again. His
Bill this time got hardly any support, and was summarily rejected, February 25,
1800. Whitbread tried again in 1807, with a Bill reforming the Poor Law
generally, but could make no progress in a specially reactionary Parliament
(see *A Letter to Samuel Whitbread, M.P., on his Proposed Bill for the Amendment of the Poor Laws*, by T. R. Malthus, 1807 ; *Substance of a Bill for Promoting
and Encouraging Industry amongst the Labouring Classes . . . and for the
Relief and Regulation of the Necessitous and Criminal Poor*, 1807 ; *Observations
on Mr. Whitbread's Poor Bill . . . intended as a Supplement to a Short Inquiry
into the Policy, Humanity and Past Effects of the Poor Laws*, by John Weyland,
1807 ; also, by the same, *The Principle of the English Poor Laws illustrated
from evidence given by Scottish proprietors*, 1815 ; *A Letter to the Bishop of
Durham on the principle and detail of the measures now under the consideration
of Parliament for promoting . . . industry and for the relief and regulation of
the poor*, by Thomas Bernard, 1807 ; and *Political Register*, by William
Cobbett, August 29, 1807). The project of a Legal Minimum Wage was
revived in 1827, when it was urged on the House of Commons Committee
on Emigration, only to be rejected in the Report as " absurd " and " extravagant " (Report of Select Committee on Emigration, 1827). See *The Village
Labourer, 1760–1832*, by J. L. and B. Hammond, 1912, pp. 139-145, 118; and
The Rise of Modern Industry, by the same, 1925, pp. 91-92.

mend the fixing of a minimum wage by law. They admonished the farmers to give better wages ; and they recommended their brother-Justices, when the farmers were obdurate, to order the Overseers to make up the deficiency.[1] The Bucks Justices went a step further, and definitely ordered the wages of married men to be made up to a minimum of six shillings a week, with a shilling extra for each child.[2] But what proved to be the decisive action was taken by the Berkshire Justices, in a district in which, because of a recent failure in the cloth trade there, the distress happened to be exceptionally severe. In May 1795 the Justices of the County " and other discreet persons " met at Speen, the centre of the district known as Speenhamland, near Newbury, to consider the proposal referred to them at the last Quarter

[1] MS. Minutes, Hampshire Quarter Sessions, July 14, 1795; printed in full in *Annals of Agriculture*, vol. xxv., pp. 349-398. The draftsman, and substantially the author of the report, was the Rev. Edmund Poulter, J.P., a Prebendary of Winchester—see his *Enquiry into the State of the Poor*, 1795. The policy of making up wages out of the Poor Rate had, we find, been expressly adopted by the Dorsetshire Justices two years before, apparently on the occasion of some local rebellion, actual or apprehended—see the lengthy Order of Quarter Sessions in its MS. Minutes, October 27 and December 1, 1792, cited in *The Parish and the County*, by S. and B. Webb, 1906, p. 356.

[2] Their order runs as follows : " The Court took into their consideration the situation of the poor industrious labourers and their families ; and it having appeared to the magistrates now assembled that the mode adopted of employing all poor labourers indiscriminately as roundsmen at an under price hath been attended with great inconvenience and abuse, and requires a speedy and effectual remedy ; and it appearing to this Court that the following incomes are at this time absolutely necessary for the support of the industrious labourer and his family, and that where it happens that the labourer and his wife and such of his children as may be able duly and honestly to perform the several labours on which they may be employed and yet do not earn the weekly sums after mentioned, the same ought to be made up to them by the parish officers, viz. : For a single man according to his labour. For a man and his wife not less than 6s. per week. For a man and his wife with one or two small children, 7s. per week. For every additional child under the age of ten years, 1s. per week. That allowance at the discretion of the magistrates, but not less than the above allowance, be made to the families of poor labourers from this time till further order by this Court, and that it be recommended to the magistrates of the county at large to adopt the same plan as relief to such families.

" And it is ordered that the Clerk of the Peace for the said county do write to all the acting Justices of this county to inform them of the above resolution and recommendation of this Court and also transmit a copy of this order to the Churchwardens and Overseers of the Poor of every parish and township within the county in order to their regulating their allowance of relief to poor families accordingly.

" Ordered that the order of this Court be printed in such manner that it may be pasted in the books of the Overseers of the respective parishes in this county, respecting the allowance to the industrious poor for labour " (MS. Minutes, Quarter Sessions, Buckinghamshire, January 1795).

N

Sessions, to fix agricultural wages by law. At this meeting held " at the Pelican Inn, Speenhamland," the seven clergymen and thirteen squires who attended decided unanimously that the labouring poor needed further assistance in their distress, but that it was inexpedient to revive the fixing of wages by law. As in Hampshire, they " earnestly recommended " the farmers to raise wages. And they concluded with the decision that was destined to exercise so widespread an influence, in favour of the systematic " rate in aid of wages ". The magistrates present resolved " that they will in their several divisions make the following calculations and allowances for the relief of all poor and industrious men and their families who, to the satisfaction of the Justices of their parish, shall endeavour (as far as they can) for their own support and maintenance, that is to say :

" When the gallon loaf of second flour weighing 8 lb. 11 oz. shall cost 1s., then every poor and industrious man shall have for his own support 3s. weekly, either produced by his own or his family's labour or an allowance from the poor rates, and for the support of his wife and every other of his family 1s. 6d.

" When the gallon loaf shall cost 1s. 4d., then every poor and industrious man shall have 4s. weekly for his own, and 1s. 10d. for the support of every other of his family.

" And so in proportion as the price of bread rises or falls (that is to say) 3d. to the man and 1d. to every other of the family on every penny which the loaf rises above a shilling." [1]

This " Berkshire Bread Act ", as it was afterwards called, which was then and there entered by the Deputy Clerk of the Peace in the Minute Book of the Berkshire Quarter Sessions as an Order of the Court, seemed, to the average Overseer and Justice of the Peace of the time, to supply exactly what the circumstances required. Its doubly graduated scale, varying according to the price of bread, and also to the size of the family, was widely adopted in rural parishes. The arithmetical precision with which it seemed to regulate the relief gave almost

---

[1] *Reading Mercury*, May 11, 1795 ; Sir F. M. Eden's *State of the Poor*, 1797, vol. i. pp. 575-577 ; Sir George Nicholl's *History of the English Poor Law*, 1854, vol. ii. p. 131 ; *Pauperism and Poor Laws*, by Robert Pashley, 1852, p. 258 ; Report of the Poor Law Inquiry Commissioners, 1834, General Report, pp. 161-163 of reprint. It is to be noted that the poor rates of Newbury had risen to an exceptional height, four times the average for the county, owing to the failure of the local manufacture of broadcloth ; see *General View of the Agriculture in Berkshire*, by William Pearce, 1794, p. 41.

the glamour of science to its policy of making up wages out of the rates.[1]   And the Justices of the Peace themselves may claim that the grant of partial support to persons at work was supported by good contemporary authority.   Malthus himself could not " see what else could have been done ".   Dr. Patrick Colquhoun, the great police reformer, fully approved of the system of a " rate in aid of wages ".   In dealing with " the useful poor, who are able and willing to work ", he declared that " the great art . . . is to establish systems whereby the poor man, verging upon indigence, may be propped up and kept in his

---

[1] The Gloucestershire Justices adopted a slightly lower scale, on the same lines, which was printed as the " Table of Allowances for the Poor as settled by the Magistrates ", with the standard income worked out in tabular form for families of ten different sizes, and for bread at fifteen different prices (= 150 standard incomes), varying from 1s. 8d. for a single woman, with the 8 lb. loaf at 1s. up to 21s. 2d. for a man, wife and seven children, with the 8 lb. loaf at 2s. 2d. The printed table concludes with the direction, " Upon bringing to account the amount of the earnings of every individual, the deficiency [is] made good by the parish " (MS. Minutes, Quarter Sessions, Gloucestershire, Michaelmas, 1795). At Chertsey in Surrey, we have it in evidence that the Justices sent their " scale " to the Overseers, and insisted on relief being given according to it. (See evidence of Lacoast before House of Commons Committee of 1817 ; *A Summary View of the Report and Evidence relative to the Poor Law*, by S. W. Nicholl (York, 1818), p. 43.)

Comparison of the scales is not without interest.   The following are among those accessible in print :

Arundel (Sussex), 1832, Poor Law Inquiry Commissioners, General Report, pp. 18-21 and Appendix A, 547.
Cambridge (Cambs), 1829, Poor Law Inquiry Commissioners, General Report, p. 241.
Cambridgeshire, 1821, Poor Law Inquiry Commissioners, General Report, p. 584 ; and *The Strength of the People*, by Helen Bosanquet, 1902, p. 147.
Chelmsford (Essex), 1821, Poor Law Inquiry Commissioners, General Report, Appendix A, p. 223.
Chichester (Sussex), 1804-1805, Poor Law Inquiry Commissioners, General Report, p. 103 and Appendix A, p. 546.
Hindon (Wilts), 1817 (a specially elaborate one), House of Commons Committee of 1817 (Bennett's evidence).
Huntingdonshire, Poor Law Inquiry Commissioners, Appendix A, p. 680.
Ongar and Harlow (Essex), 1801, Poor Law Inquiry Commissioners, Appendix A, p. 222.
Speenhamland (Berks), 1795, Poor Law Inquiry Commissioners, General Report, pp. 101-102.   (For other references, see preceding page.)
Stourbridge (Dorset), Molesworth's *History of England*, vol. i. p. 51.
Sturminster (Wilts), *A Letter to the Rev. H. F. Yeatman from Henry Walter*, 1833.
Uttlesford, etc. (Essex), 1826, Poor Law Inquiry Commissioners, General Report, p. 21, and Appendix A, p. 227.
Warminster (Wilts), Poor Law Inquiry Commissioners, General Report, Appendix A, p. 438.
Weyhill, 1830, Poor Law Inquiry Commissioners, General Report, Appendix A, p. 344.

station. Whenever this can be effected, it is done upon an average at one-tenth of the expense at most that must be incurred by permitting a family to retrograde into a state of indigence, where they must be wholly maintained by the public." [1] Moreover, there seemed something to be said for a definite scale, nicely adjusted to needs, and independent alike of the caprice of particular Justices and of the favour of the Overseer. "In a town divided by religious sects", said one authority, "partialities would be shown, or at least would be sure to be suspected in the distribution of parish relief . . . were it not for the establishment of an invariable standard, notorious and applicable to all." [2]

The view taken by the Justices was promptly ratified, in effect, by Parliament itself. In the very session after the Speenhamland Act, which was fully in the minds of Members, it was expressly enacted that the Overseers might, with the approval of the Vestry, or with the consent of a local magistrate, give Outdoor Relief to persons in distress ; and that a single local magistrate might "at his just discretion order relief to any industrious poor person ".[3]

Between 1795 and 1833 the principle of making up wages

[1] *A Treatise on the Police of the Metropolis*, by P. Colquhoun, 1800, pp. 366-367. The account given by Malthus in 1800 is as follows : "The poor complained to the Justices that their wages would not enable them to supply their families in the single article of bread. The Justices, very humanely, and I am far from saying improperly, listened to their complaints, inquired what was the smallest sum on which they could support their families at the then price of bread, and gave an order of relief on the parish accordingly. . . . To say the truth, I hardly see what else could have been done " (*An Investigation into the Cause of the Present High Price of Provisions*, by the Author of the Essay on the Principle of Population, 1800, pp. 9, 11).

[2] Report of Poor Law Inquiry Commissioners, 1834, Appendix A, Wilson's Report, p. 144. "The publication of these scales has been much complained of, but we think rather unreasonably. . . . The evil resides in the practice, not in the scale, which is its almost inevitable consequence. When a magistrate takes on himself ' to regulate the incomes of the industrious poor ' within his jurisdiction, he of course frames for himself some standard by which to regulate them : if he does not, all must be favour or caprice ; of course, also, the magistrates must be anxious to make their individual standards correspond, or in other words to agree on a scale " (General Report of the Poor Law Inquiry Commissioners, 1834, pp. 130-131).

[3] One Justice could give an order for relief for one month ; two Justices could renew this month by month indefinitely (36 George III. c. 23) ; in 1815, by East's Act, it was added that two Justices might order relief for six months at a time, and renew the order indefinitely ; but the amount so ordered, after the first month, was limited either to three shillings per week per person, or to three-fourths of the average cost of maintenance in the local workhouse (55 George III. c. 137).

by Outdoor Relief, according to a definite scale depending on the price of bread and the number of children in the family, spread to nearly every county of England and Wales, being adopted, in principle, at one time or another, by practically every rural parish outside Northumberland of which we happen to have examined the records.[1] Nor was it altogether confined to the agricultural labourers. In the weaving districts of Lancashire and Cheshire, in the districts where the hosiery trade was carried on, and in various industrial areas of the Midland Counties many instances were reported of money doles being regularly allowed to operatives in full work at wages, especially where there were several children.[2] The scales of the different counties or divisions of counties were usually fixed at meetings of Justices, and they were distributed by the Clerk of the Peace or the clerk of the petty sessional division to all the Overseers of the district. In 1833 these scales, printed and framed, were often found hanging up in a conspicuous position in the meeting rooms of Select Vestries or Incorporated Guardians, and occasionally in the " Justice Room " of Quarter Sessions itself.[3] At Bocking, in Essex, in 1833, the printed copy in use by the Overseer even bore the magic heading " according to Act of Parliament ".[4] To this authoritative issue and official publica-

---

[1] It is sometimes assumed that these scales prevailed only in the southern part of England ; and Poulett Scrope expressly stated in 1831 that the practice " has not yet been introduced in the counties in the North of England and in Wales " (*A Second Letter to the Magistrates of the South of England*, by G. Poulett Scrope, 1831, p. 2). But the Assistant Poor Law Commissioners in 1833 found definite scales in use, to a greater or smaller extent, in North Wales, Lancashire, Yorkshire and Durham, as well as throughout the Midlands and in all the southern counties. " In the weaving districts of South Lancashire, for example, it was the practice to make allowances in aid of wages to able-bodied weavers who had more than two children under ten years of age " (*The Town Labourer, 1760–1832*, by J. L. and B. Hammond, citing *Extracts from information received by the Poor Law Commission*, 1833, p. 340). We have not come across any instance in Northumberland. Their introduction to the northern counties was, however, later than in the south ; thus, the regular allowance system is said to have only begun in the West Riding in the bad times of 1826 (Report of Poor Law Inquiry Commissioners, 1834, Appendix A, p. 732). It was only in particular parishes that the principle had been definitely repudiated. The Allowance System was fully described and condemned in the Report of the House of Commons Committee on Labourers' Wages, 1825 ; see also the elaborate reports on the system by G. Taylor in Appendix C to Report of Poor Law Inquiry Commissioners, 1834, pp. 51-76.

[2] Poor Law Commission : Extracts from Information Received, etc., 1833.

[3] Report of P. L. Com., 1834, Appendix A, Majendie's Report, p. 234.

[4] *Ibid.* p. 229. The sum fixed by the scale (in Suffolk and Norfolk called

tion of the scales may be attributed the widespread conviction, on the part of the labouring poor, that they had a " legal right ", not merely to relief from immediate destitution, but also to a regular minimum of maintenance for themselves and their children, whatever their capacity or industry.[1]

It is interesting to note that the policy of the Allowance System, embodied in the Speenhamland Scale, met with little criticism so long as the war lasted. We find little denunciation of its effects until after 1815, when many causes united to create social difficulties. When the Allowance System came to be resented, and was felt to be irksome and injurious, one reaction was for the Justices and the Vestries simply to reduce the amount which the scales allowed to the labourers. What the Berkshire magistrates had thought, in 1795, to be the indispensable minimum for life was a sum that would provide each man with three gallon loaves per week (each loaf weighing 8 lb. 11 oz.) and one and a half gallon loaves for each other member of the household, whether wife or child. For man and wife and three children this was equivalent to 19¼ quartern loaves weekly. To give an idea of what would be in 1926 a corresponding income for the household of five, we might take the quartern loaf at ninepence, and the total weekly income accordingly at fourteen shillings and sevenpence—about one-half of what a parsimonious Board of Guardians would to-day (1926) regard as a bare subsistence ! The scales fixed for Northamptonshire in 1816, and those for Cambridgeshire and Essex in 1821, were roughly

---

" walking pay ") was known as the " county allowance ", the " Government allowance ", and even the " Act of Parliament allowance ". " When, in 1833, the Assistant Commissioner inquiring into the Poor Law entered the office of the Overseer at Bocking in Essex, he found himself confronted with a printed copy of the scale there in force, bearing the magic heading " According to Act of Parliament " ! (*The Parish and the County*, by S. and B. Webb, 1906, p. 548).

[1] The assertion of this supposed right occasionally took an amusing form. Thus, " the paupers of Potterne (Wilts) raised a subscription amongst themselves, and bought a Burn's *Justice*, for the avowed purpose of puzzling the Overseers and magistrates " (Report of Poor Law Inquiry Commissioners, 1834, Appendix A, Okeden's Report, p. 7). " Great indignation was expressed ", writes a well-informed witness, " and gross ignorance attributed to the labouring classes because they demanded a minimum of wages, while in real life they did but imitate an example which had been set to them by persons in much higher stations. The whole allowance system depends upon the existence of a minimum of wages ; it gives a man not the sum which he earns, but that on which it is supposed that he ought to live " (Appendix C to Report of Poor Law Inquiry Commissioners, p. 493, Letter from Fred. Calvert).

equivalent to less than four gallon loaves for the man and wife, who would have received four and a half gallon loaves by the Speenhamland scale of 1795. The complicated scale of Hindon, in Wiltshire, in 1817 allowed actually less than three gallon loaves for man and wife. So far were the reductions pushed that, in 1826, the scale fixed by the Dorsetshire Justices gave, for the man, only one and a half gallon loaves plus one penny, whilst each additional member of the household who was over fourteen, whether wife or child, got only one and one-sixth gallon loaves. The Hampshire Justices went even lower in their conception of a subsistence wage. In 1822 their scale provided only one gallon loaf per head for the entire household, plus fourpence per head when there were four in family, threepence per head where there were six in family, and twopence per head where there were more than six. In 1830 it could be stated on the authority of J. R. M'Culloch that " the Allowance Scales now issued from time to time by the magistrates are usually framed on the principle that every labourer should have a gallon loaf for every member of his family, and one over ; that is, four loaves for three persons, five loaves for four, six for five, and so on ". Thus, a man with wife and three young children, who would have received what would have brought him nine gallon loaves a week in 1795, was allowed in 1830 only six gallon loaves. or what in 1926 would be equivalent to a total family income of no more than nine shillings and ninepence per week for five persons. " In thirty-five years ", observe Mr. and Mrs. Hammond, " the standard had dropped, according to M'Culloch's statement, as much as one-third ; and this not because of war or famine, for in 1826 England had had eleven years of peace [and in 1830, fifteen years], but in the ordinary course of the life of the nation. Is such a decline in the standard of life recorded anywhere else in history ? " [1] The labourers' revolt in and around Hampshire in the autumn of 1830 takes on a new aspect when this fact (of which the histories had failed to inform us) is borne in mind.

The reports of the House of Commons Committees of 1817,

[1] See *The Village Labourer, 1760–1832*, by J. L. and B. Hammond, 1912, p. 185 ; Board of Agriculture Report on the Agricultural State of the Kingdom, 1816 ; *Political Register*, by William Cobbett, October 5, 1816, September 21, 1822, and September 9, 1826 ; *Principles of Political Economy*, by J. R. M'Culloch, 1825 ; *Edinburgh Review*, January 1831, p. 353.

1822, 1825 and 1828, aided by strong articles in the *Edinburgh Review* and a cloud of pamphlets,[1] gradually began to shake the confidence of the Justices in the simple remedy of the Speenhamland scale, but without putting any new idea in its place. The Suffolk Justices sent an able and eloquent memorial to the House of Commons Committee in 1817, protesting forcibly against the system.[2] The Staffordshire Quarter Sessions denounced it in the following year.[3] From 1818 onward petty sessional meetings of magistrates occasionally protested against any payment from the rates to labourers in private employment. Such payments were more than once declared to be illegal. In a few cases energetic ratepayers successfully appealed to Quarter Sessions against the allowance of Overseers' accounts containing payments of this nature.[4] In 1829 the question was elaborately

[1] Among the pamphlets, the four by G. Poulett Scrope, 1829–1831, were perhaps the most weighty and influential; see also those by Rev. C. D. Brereton, 1822–1831, and that by D. O. Parry Okeden, 1830; *A Letter to the Proprietors and Occupiers of Land at Bledlow on their system of giving bread money in aid of wages,* by Sir George Stephen, 1833; *The Necessity of the Anti-Pauper System Shewn by an example of the Misery and Oppression produced by the Allowance System,* by Rev. J. Bosworth, 1829; *The Causes and Remedies of Pauperism in the United Kingdom considered,* by Sir R. J. Wilmot Horton, 1829; *A Letter to the Magistrates of the South and West of England on the expediency and facility of correcting certain abuses of the Poor Laws,* by One of their Number, 1828.

[2] *Ipswich Journal,* November 15, 1817; the memorial was reprinted in the *Edinburgh Review.*

[3] " That the practice of paying parish labourers a certain portion of their wages out of the poor's rate is highly detrimental to the public welfare, as well as illegal; and it is recommended to the several magistrates of this county, collectively and individually, to discountenance the same as much as possible, by disallowing in future all sums so paid in the Overseers' accounts " (Staffordshire Quarter Sessions, October 21, 1818; Report of Poor Law Inquiry Commissioners, Appendix A, Moylan's Report, p. 267).

[4] At Easter Quarter Sessions for Hampshire, 1819, the rector of Over Wallop so appealed. The chairman (Earl of Carnarvon), in announcing the decision of the Bench to disallow £25, being the amount of the items of allowances to men in employment, said that the practice of making up wages was illegal, and ordered the Overseers to discontinue the practice. A full report of this case is given in Report of the Poor Law Inquiry Commissioners, 1834, Appendix A, Chadwick's Report, pp. 56-57; see also *Gentleman's Magazine,* May 1819, p. 475; also *Derby Mercury,* May 13, 1819. That this decision had some effect in stopping the practice for a time we learn from *An Inquiry into the Causes of the Progressive Depreciation of Agricultural Labour in Modern Times, with Suggestions for its Remedy,* by John Barton, 1820, where it is stated (p. 81) that the Justices in some counties have stopped the allowances to labourers—a remedy denounced as " crude and oppressive ". A similar legal decision was subsequently given by the Dorset Quarter Sessions; see *A Letter to the Magistrates of the South of England on the urgent necessity of putting a stop to the illegal practice of making up wages out of rates, to which alone is owing*

discussed in Parliament on Slaney's "Labourers' Wages Bill", by which it was sought to prohibit these allowances out of the rates. Everybody agreed about the evil results of the practice, and no one dared to vote against the Bill, which, however, failed to become law.[1] In the years 1828 to 1831 Poulett Scrope, M.P., a well-known magistrate, appealed again and again to his brother magistrates in the southern counties, "exercising as by law you do, the office of auditors of the parish accounts" to "refuse to sanction any payments from parish rates to able-bodied men while working for a farmer". He urged them to get resolutions passed at Quarter Sessions declaring any such rate in aid of wages to be illegal, and refusing to pass the items in the parish accounts. But, notwithstanding all these appeals, the practice continued to be almost universal in the rural districts south of the line from the Severn to the Wash, spreading in less systematic form to the rural parts of nearly all the other counties, owing, as Poulett Scrope declared, to the fear of the landlords that a stoppage of the parish allowance, by causing an increase in wages, would throw such a burden on the farmer as would compel rents to be reduced.[2] At last even the magistrates of Buckinghamshire were spurred

---

the misery and revolt of the agricultural peasantry, by G. Poulett Scrope, 1831, p. 4, and *A Letter to the Rev. H. F. Yeatman from Henry Walter*, 1833, p. 36. A stand against it was also made by the bench at Leckhampstead, Berks ; see *A Second Letter to the Magistrates of the South of England*, etc., by the same author, 1831. The Buckinghamshire Quarter Sessions had obtained counsel's opinion to the same effect as early as 1809, but did not act upon it (MS. Minutes, Quarter Sessions, Buckinghamshire, Epiphany, 1809). It is strange that no case on the point seems ever to have been taken to the superior Courts.

[1] The second reading was passed without a division. But there was no enthusiasm for the Bill. Peel "doubted whether a system which had so long existed, and which had been so uniformly acted on for so many years, could safely be removed otherwise than gradually". Joseph Cripps, M.P. for Cirencester, spoke for his fellow-Justices when he declared, that the Bill "prescribed actual starvation, and neither magistrates nor parish officers could enforce it" (see Hansard, February 24, May 4 and 9, 1829; *Bucks Gazette*, May 9, 1829).

[2] That there was some ground for this apprehension on the part of the landlords is shown by the fact that in 1830 we find the Vestries of Petheram and Callington (Cornwall) collectively petitioning their landlords for a reduction of rent, in order that they may be in a position to pay higher wages. They explain that "The immediate cause of our thus addressing you is a recent decision of the magistrates of our district that a general advance of the wages of agricultural labourers must be acceded to, and having signified their determination that, in every instance when a married man does not receive the full amount of the advanced rate of wages, to make an order on the Overseers for the deficiency to be paid out of the poor's rate as relief" (*The West Briton*, December 24, 1830).

into taking action. The Lord Lieutenant, the Duke of Buckingham, lays the matter before the Quarter Sessions in a long and able letter, in which he complains of the practical failure of the magistrates to enforce their own views of poor law policy. " We have long refused in our respective parishes to sign the books or authorise the levy of rates where the labour has been paid in the manner which I have stated. The farmers have set us at defiance, and, notwithstanding the absence of magistrates' signature, the books are handed down from Overseer to Overseer, and rates are thus illegally levied upon the parishes. My advice to the magistrates is to take legal opinion whether they cannot punish, by some legal process, the parish officers." He urges public-spirited occupiers and owners to appeal against such unauthorised rates. He advocates the provision of workhouses, and earnestly advises the magistrates " to take the superintendence of the levies and expenditure of the Poor Rates into their own hands ".[1] The magistrates, apparently convinced of the necessity for some action, adjourned the sessions to allow definite resolutions and a printed circular to the Churchwardens and Overseers to be drawn up. At the adjourned meeting resolutions were adopted in the following terms, from which we see that the Bucks Justices, like so many other people, were still dominated by the idea, persistent for a couple of centuries, of setting the poor profitably to work. It was resolved " that it is the opinion of this court that they cannot do better than recommend to the attention of the landed interest of this county the terms and provisions of the several Acts of Parliament now in force for the erection and maintenance of workhouses, and especially of the Act of 22 George III. c. 83 whereby parishes are empowered to borrow money upon security of their rates for the erection, providing or hiring of workhouses within their respective parishes or districts of united parishes, and whereby the Guardians of the Poor appointed in obedience to the provisions of the said Acts, are directed to lodge, maintain and provide for such able-bodied poor as are willing to work, but cannot obtain work, and who may apply for relief, and are directed to employ them, receiving the money to be earned by such work, applying it in such maintenance as

---

[1] *Bucks Gazette*, February 6, 1830. The Berks Quarter Sessions published a lengthy proclamation against the system in 1828 ; see Report of Poor Law Inquiry Commissioners, Appendix A, Chadwick's Report, p. 55.

far as the same will go, and paying the surplus, if any, to the pauper, and whereby the pauper who shall refuse or run away from such work is liable on conviction before any Justice or Justices of the Peace in or near the place where the workhouse is situated to hard labour in the House of Correction not exceeding three calendar months nor less than one ; and this court in the strongest manner recommend the adoption of such workhouses as the best mode of setting to work those able-bodied poor, who are really unable to find other employment, and of deterring those, who wilfully throw themselves out of work, from becoming a burthen on their respective parishes." " It was also resolved that the practice now almost universally prevalent throughout this county of paying part of the price of labour for work done for the benefit of any private individual, out of the monies raised by rate for the relief of the poor, is illegal, and the Justices present are determined to resist by all lawful means the continuance of such practice. They also declare their opinion of the illegality of the practice prevalent in many parishes of farming the labour of the poor for the private profit of a contractor. They also recommend that strict attention be paid to the keeping of the book in each parish required by the Acts of 3 William and Mary, c. 11, sec. 2., and 9 George I. c. 7, sec. 4, wherein it is directed that a list shall be kept of all persons who ought to receive parochial relief under the 43rd of Elizabeth, and that such book shall be produced to the magistrates when called upon to allow the rates for parochial relief." " It was also resolved that it appearing in many cases much evil has arisen from young men marrying not having means of supporting themselves and immediately throwing themselves on their respective parishes for relief. The Justices present express their determination to discountenance the said practice and to avoid in every practicable manner the giving orders for the relief of any person in respect of his family who shall have married without having at the time of such marriage probable or apparent means of maintaining a family." " The Justices present also recommend in the strongest manner the adoption of the system (where practicable and which is provided by the law) of taking on lease lands whereon to employ their superabundant population on piecework ; and also letting lands in small quantities to the labourers for their individual occupation in order to give additional facility for the employment

of infant labour, and generally to decrease the burthen of the
Poor Rate." "It was also resolved that the Justices present
also pledge themselves to disallow and strike out all items which
shall appear in Overseers' accounts not in accordance with the
spirit of the foregoing resolutions." "It was also resolved that
this Court is of opinion that it is become highly expedient and
necessary that the accounts of the Overseers of all parishes and
places in this county shall be kept on one uniform plan ", which
a committee was thereupon appointed to prepare and submit to
the next sessions.[1]

The chief result of this tardy conversion of the Justices
against their own expedient of " the scale " was, not the giving
up of the " rate in aid of wages ", but the abandonment of any
rule as to affording complete maintenance thereby. The Overseers
or Vestries became again free to give what allowances they
pleased, with an endless diversity of practice from parish to
parish. In some districts it was found, in 1833, that the " allowance " was refused to able-bodied men until the appearance of
a second, a third, or a fourth child. On the other hand, we
learn that " Some Vestries have adopted allowance according to

[1] MS. Minutes, Quarter Sessions, Buckinghamshire, February 2, 1830.
During the years 1829–1831 it would appear that practically every Quarter
Sessions was discussing " the state of the poor ", we infer, to no more advantage
than Buckinghamshire. The Cambridgeshire Justices in 1829 issued to all
the Overseers in the county a circular which occupies three-quarters of a column
in the local newspapers, insisting on more strict observation of the law relating
to poor relief, greater discrimination as to the character of the recipients,
and the abandonment of the allowance system. They required also more
formal accounts from the Overseers, and announced that the Minute books of
the Vestries must also be produced. See the circular in *Bucks Gazette*, May 9,
1829.

We find the Chairman of the Norfolk Quarter Sessions, at Norwich in
1829, earnestly exhorting the magistrates to resist the allowance system as
most pernicious and unfair (*Norwich Mercury*, May 22, 1829). In the course
of a discussion among the West Suffolk Justices, at Bury Quarter Sessions,
Easter 1831, it was said that the allowance system had been entirely stopped
by the magistrates at Mundesley (Norfolk) ; but that in the Oswaldlaw
Division of Worcestershire Lord Calthorpe had refused to act on the decision
to disallow such items, on the ground that they had been customary since
1774 (*Colchester Gazette*, April 25, 1831).

It was in view of the fact that " the state of the poor . . . would probably
be discussed at the next Quarter Sessions ", that Lloyd Baker wrote the pamphlet
in which he described the successful introduction of the workhouse test in
his own parish of Uley, where fifteen successive poor rates of 20d. in the pound
had not sufficed to meet the expenditure in the year 1829–1830 (see *A Letter
to the Rev. George Cooke, D.D., Chairman of the Quarter Sessions for the County
of Gloucester*, by T. J. L. Baker, Gloucester, 1830) ; see p. 258.

families, without enquiry into earnings, as the lesser evil, and the only mode of protecting the industrious man, who, in the other case [of making up any earnings to a fixed sum] would be exerting himself merely to save the parish ".[1]

Billeting out the Unemployed

The general adoption of the Justices' scales of Out Relief had, so to speak, submerged an older device for ensuring maintenance for all the labourers, which the abandonment of the scale between 1820 and 1835 brought prominently before the public. This was the sharing among all the ratepayers of an assumed obligation to find employment at wages for all the labourers belonging to the parish. We imagine that this may have been a survival from the mediæval assumption of there being some customary obligation on those who employed labourers at wages to provide them with continuous livelihood. In 1528 we even find the Privy Council admonishing the cloth manufacturers of various counties that it was their individual duty, even in times of trade depression, to provide employment for the wage-earners whom they had severally engaged in their service.[2] In the small rural parishes, where the half a dozen farmers were practically the only employers, it may easily have become usual to regard their individual duty to provide a continuous livelihood for the labourers as a common obligation, to be most conveniently discharged by the whole body of householders or ratepayers in turn. In Cornwall the Justices seem very early to have regularised the system by express order. In 1597 we read that " Such poor as cannot provide work for themselves are to present themselves in a convenient place in the church on the Sabbath Day a little before the ending of morning and evening prayer, and as soon as prayer is ended, order shall be taken to send them abroad among such householders as shall maintain them in meat, work and such wages as they can deserve for the week following ".[3] Similarly, two centuries

---

[1] Report of the Poor Law Inquiry Commissioners, 1834, Appendix A, Majendie's Report, p. 167.

[2] See, for this and other cases, Miss Leonard's *Early History of English Poor Relief*, 1900, pp. 48, 85, 115, 147, 152, 223, 230, 232.

[3] Hatfield MSS. vii. p. 161, quoted by Miss E. M. Leonard's *Early History of English Poor Relief*, 1900, p. 131 ; see also *Tudor Economic Documents*, by

later, Sir F. M. Eden reported of Winslow, Bucks, that "Most labourers are (as it is termed) on the rounds ; that is they go to work from one house to another round the parish. In winter, sometimes, 40 persons are on the rounds. They are wholly paid by the parish unless the householders choose to employ them ; and from these circumstances labourers often become very lazy and imperious. Children, about ten years old, are put on the rounds, and receive from the parish from 1s. 6d. to 3s. a week." Throughout the eighteenth century we find the custom existing under various names, and differing slightly in form, in a certain proportion of parishes in all parts of England and Wales.[1] The two varieties of which we find most mention were the "Roundsman" or "House Row" system,[2] and the "Labour Rate". In many places the practice was for parishioners without employment to be assigned by the Overseer to particular farmers who accepted, in turn, the obligation of finding work at such wages as they chose. It was, in fact, a sort of billeting of the unemployed labourer upon the parishioners in rotation, each in turn having to provide maintenance and being free to exact service. Thus, it was economically analogous to the parish apprenticeship system to be presently described. The relation of master and servant was maintained, and the employer, having anyhow to maintain the labourer, had every motive to make him work. On the other hand, though the labourer, like a slave, was sure of some sort

---

R. H. Tawney and Eileen Power, 1924, vol. ii. pp. 660-661. For similar practices in the towns, see *ibid.* p. 232. Some such system is perhaps indicated, as Sir F. M. Eden observes (*State of the Poor*, 1797, vol. i. p. 103) by the terms of the statute 1 Edward VI. c. 3, 1547.

[1] Sir F. M. Eden, in *The State of the Poor*, 1797, describes various parishes in which the Roundsman system then prevailed ; he says it was usual in winter time in the Midlands (vol. i. p. 103), and well known in Buckinghamshire (vol. ii. pp. 27, 29, 384). See also the reference in *General View of the Agriculture of Bedfordshire*, by Thomas Batchelor, 1808, pp. 608-690.

[2] Other synonyms were the "billet system", the "ticket system", "stem-men", "going the rounds", the "stem system" or "relief in lieu of labour". See *A Plan to Regulate the employment of Labouring Poor as acted on in the Parish of Oundle*, 1823. "In the winter" [at Kibworth-Beauchamp, Leicestershire], "and at other times, when a man is out of work, he applies to the Overseer, who sends him from house to house to get employ : the housekeeper who employs him is obliged to give him victuals and sixpence a day ; the parish adds fourpence (total tenpence a day) for the support of his family ; persons working in this manner are called roundsmen, from their going round the village or township for employ" (*The State of the Poor*, by Sir F. M. Eden, 1797, vol. ii. p. 384).

of a living, his comfort depended on his gaining his master's approval.[1] Like the parish apprenticeship system, this un-regulated servitude led to "sweating", especially in the form of under-feeding. If we remember how low were the wages earned by even the best agricultural labourers, whom farmers were glad to employ, we may imagine what sort of a pittance they would give to labourers compulsorily forced upon them. Such starvation wages of the "Roundsmen" disturbed, in 1795, the humane minds of the Buckinghamshire Justices. At the Epiphany Quarter Sessions, when four clergymen and three laymen were present, we learn that "The Court took into their consideration the situation of the poor industrious labourers and their families, and it having appeared to the magistrates now assembled, that the mode adopted of employing all poor labourers indiscriminately as Roundsmen, at an under price, hath been attended with great inconvenience and abuse, and requires a speedy and effectual remedy, and it appearing to this Court that the following incomes are at this time absolutely necessary for the support of the industrious labourer and his family, and that, where it happens the labourer and his wife and such of his children as may be able duly and honestly perform the several labours on which they may be employed, and yet do not earn the weekly sums aftermentioned, the same ought to be made up to them by the parish officers ".[2] This humane con-sideration of the Buckinghamshire Justices proved to be calamit-ous. The combination of the "scale" with the "Roundsman" system resulted in the complete perversion of the latter device. Instead of the farmer having to maintain the "Roundsmen" allotted to him, he could pay them as little as he liked, knowing that the balance would be made up by the parish. The farmers soon made this a regular system. "At Deddington", we are told, "during the seven winter months, about sixty men apply every morning to the Overseer for work or pay. He ranges them under a shed in a yard. If a farmer or any one else wants

---

[1] The voluntary sharing-out of the unemployed labourers among the local farmers survived in country villages down to the second half of the nineteenth century. In 1854 we read in a description of contemporary agriculture, that "The surplus labourers are employed in turns by the farmers . . . these odd men were called roundsmen " (*Journal of Royal Agricultural Society*, vol. xv. ii. 262).

[2] MS. Minutes, Quarter Sessions, Buckinghamshire, Epiphany 1795.

a man, he sends to the yard for one, and pays half the day's wages ; the rest is paid by the parish. At the close of the day the unemployed are paid the wages of the day, minus two pence."[1] "At the parish of Bodicott . . . a printed form is delivered to those who apply for work. The labourer takes this to the farmers in succession, who, if they do not want his labour, sign their names. The man on his return receives from the Overseer the day's pay of an industrious labourer, with the reduction of two pence."[2] By 1833, at any rate, when the system was described by the Assistant Poor Law Commissioners, the payment by the farmer had in many places sunk to a merely nominal sum, which the Roundsman regarded as pocket money, over and above the maintenance which he got from the Overseer. The farmer thus obtained the Roundsman's labour practically gratuitously, and came to regard it positively as a perquisite ; justified, as one Worcestershire farmer put it, " by the obvious injustice to the agriculturist of the poor rate assessment itself, which fixed upon land, merely from its visible quality, a far greater share of the burden of maintaining the poor ".[3] At Burwash

---

[1] Report of the Poor Law Inquiry Commissioners, 1834, Appendix A, Okeden's Report, p. 2.

[2] *Ibid.* An intermediate stage is described in 1808. " When a labourer can obtain no employment, he applies to the acting Overseer, from whom he passes on to the different farmers all round the parish, being employed by each of them after the rate of one day for every £20 rent. The allowance to a labourer on the rounds is commonly 2d. per day below the pay of other labourers. . . . Boys receive from 4d. to 6d. per day on the rounds, the whole of which is often repaid to the farmers by the Overseer. About half the pay of the men is returned in the same manner. . . . The practice in question has a very bad effect on the industry of the poor. They are often employed in trivial business, the boys in particular are of little use in the winter season. The men are careful not to earn more than they receive and seem to think it the safer extreme to perform too little rather than too much " (*General View of the Agriculture of the County of Bedford*, by Batchelor, 1808, p. 608).

In the *General Report on the Agriculture and Minerals of Derbyshire*, by John Farey, 1817, vol. iii. p. 529, we read that " Going the rounds " or " House Row ", as the system was here called, by order of " the Overseer, and receiving from him a part of their wages, by those who could not otherwise obtain work, was formerly pretty much practised ", but was at that date almost discontinued.

[3] Report of the Poor Law Inquiry Commissioners, Appendix A, Villiers' Report, p. 12.   " The combination of the Speenhamland system with the Roundsman system produced universal pauperism. A man could not get any help from the rates unless he was destitute, and unless he got help from the rates he could not obtain employment, for a farmer would not pay a man 10s. a week when he could employ the roundsman at half that sum. Free movement from village to village was checked by the settlement laws. Nor were the labourers the only victims ; the yeoman and small farmer who spent little on wages had to pay part of the wages bill of their richer neighbours "

in Sussex, instead of sharing the labourers according to assess-ment, " in the year 1822 the surplus labourers were put up to auction, and hired as low as two pence and three pence per day, the rest of their maintenance being made up by the parish. The consequence was that the farmers turned off their regular hands, in order to hire them by auction when they wanted them."[1] In this final form the Roundsman system was wholly disastrous. The farmer, not paying the Roundsmen any wages, and feeling that he got their labour gratuitously, was contented with the lowest possible standard of effort and conduct. The Roundsman, getting little or nothing from the farmer, and being assured of the same maintenance in any event, dawdled about his work, or neglected it altogether.[2] The whole system came to be recognised as " a wasteful and unequal tax ".[3]

In some parishes a peculiar modification of the Roundsman system was introduced by common consent. Each occupier of land undertook to employ, at wages fixed by the parish, his quota of the unemployed labourers. This avoided the evils attendant on the allowance system, and left the farmer every inducement to exact a good day's work, whilst it protected the labourers from extreme degradation of wages. It had, however, the unexpected result of causing the dismissal from service of the unpauperised labourers, as each farmer preferred to restrict the employment to those for whom he was obliged to find wages. To meet this objection some unknown parish reformer,[4] anxious to re-establish the normal relationship between master and servant, invented the device of a Labour Rate, alongside the normal assessment for the relief of the impotent poor. In its

(*The Rise of Modern Industry*, by J. L. and Barbara Hammond, 2nd edition, 1926, pp. 94-95).

[1] Report of the Poor Law Inquiry Commissioners, 1834, Appendix A, Majendie's Report, p. 177.

[2] Recalcitrant workmen could apparently be punished, but the cases reported are extremely rare. The following is our only example. " The magistrates of the Isle of Ely have lately committed fifteen labourers in husbandry to prison for not performing a reasonable day's work for their masters, who found them employment to alleviate the pressure of the poor rate " (*Ipswich Journal*, February 7, 1818).

[3] *Tait's Magazine*, 1834, p. 37.

[4] C. P. Villiers observes that the plan of the Labour Rate is said to have been devised by a Mr. Chamberlayne, of Cropredy, Oxfordshire (Report of Poor Law Inquiry Commissioners, Appendix A, p. 12). But, as we have mentioned, much the same plan was proposed by John Locke in 1696 ; and it had probably been adopted informally from time to time in various districts.

most perfect form this device had a certain plausible completeness. What the parish had to ensure was that none of its settled labourers should be without employment. Therefore the total amount of the wages for the year of all the wage-earners belonging to the parish was computed, each mechanic or labourer being priced for this purpose according to what was assumed to be his market value, less a small discount. The total thus estimated was divided among all the ratepayers, with or without the exemption of special classes, sometimes according to rateable value, sometimes according to acreage. Each ratepayer undertook to pay in wages to " settled labourers " during the year—credit being given only for the prices adopted in computing the Labour Rate—an amount at least equal to that at which he had been assessed to this " Labour Rate ". Any deficiency in his labour bill had to be compensated for by an equivalent payment to the Overseer, in order to enable the parish to find maintenance for the surplus labourers. The employer thus retained his full authority over his labourers, and they their full inducement to keep in private employment in preference to being thrown on the parish for a pittance of outdoor relief. The system was so plausible, and had really so beneficial an effect on the labourers demoralised by the allowance and Roundsman systems, that it was adopted about 1829–1830 by many rural parishes. To the average farmer, it seemed merely a systematic sharing of the labourers. The cottager, the shopkeeper, the innkeeper and the clergyman—and to a lesser extent the occupier of pasture land, as well as the private residents—having no occasion for so large a labour bill as was expected from them, felt it an irksome and intolerable burden, and were sometimes excused from participation. The details of the Labour Rate varied from parish to parish. It had, in fact, at first no legal authority. Any ratepayer could refuse to pay the sum due from him as compensation for deficiency in his wages bill, or could dispute the correctness of the somewhat complicated assessment.[1] To

[1] Thus, at Hasilbury Bryan, a small Dorsetshire parish, " the Overseers . . . had been in the habit of sharing out the pauper labourers among the farmers (including themselves) and then paid for the work done by such labourers wholly out of the poor's rates ". The local Justices refused to interfere, but in July 1823 the incumbent appealed to Quarter Sessions and got a decision forbidding it (*A Letter to the Rev. H. F. Yeatman* from Henry Walter, B.D., F.R.S., 1833, p. 18); compare the Report of Poor Law Inquiry Commissioners, 1834, Appendix A, Okeden's Report, p. 20. To obviate such individual

remedy this defect, Parliament in 1831, at the instance of Sir Charles Burrell, M.P., a Sussex magnate, authorised, by a temporary Act for three years (2 and 3 William IV. c. 96), a three-fourths majority of the ratepayers of any rural parish in which the rate exceeded 5s. in the £ on the rack rent, to agree, with the approval of the Justices in Petty Sessions, to any plan for relieving or employing the poor, except the rate in aid of wages. Under this provision numerous parishes adopted a compulsory Labour Rate in some such form as we have described. Beyond the difficulty of an equitable assessment, it had the serious disadvantage of practically compelling each farmer to confine his employment to the " settled poor " of his own parish. It was argued that the plan must, in the end, tend to create a sort of " general post ", the " unsettled " labourers of each parish being summarily dismissed, and having to return to the parishes in which they had a settlement, quite irrespective of whether there was any local opportunity for the profitable use of their labour. The result might have been a hindrance to the expansion of growing industrial areas, and a stereotyping of the stationary villages into what one Assistant Commissioner happily termed " stagnant centres of unproductive labour ".[1] The

---

objections, " In the parish of Winterbourne Basset, in the Marlborough district (Wilts), Lord Holland, who owns the whole of the parish, has made the consent of the farmers to a Labour Rate a condition of their leases " (*ibid.* p. 6). See the published *Resolutions of the Vestry of Campsey Ash on the Suggestions of the . . . Duke of Grafton and the Magistrates of the County of Suffolk, respecting a Labour Rate*, Woodbridge, 1830 ; also *A Letter to . . . Lord Nugent, Chairman of a Committee of the H. of C. upon a Bill . . . for the Regulation of Labourers' Wages, with reference to its operation on the Poor's Rate*, etc., by a Parochial Vestryman, 1830.

[1] See Power's Report and Cowell's Report in Appendix A, and also Appendix D, of Report of Poor Law Inquiry Commissioners, giving a good summary of the pros and cons and elaborate particulars of local agreements. The Act of 1831, 2 and 3 William IV. c. 96, was temporary only, expiring in 1834. In 1833 a Bill was introduced for its renewal. Francis Place tells us the sequel. " Early in March 1833 Lord Althorp wrote to the Commissioners of the Poor Law Inquiry and requested them to inform him whether the adoption of the Labour Rate Bill (the renewal) as a temporary and palliative measure would have the tendency to increase the evil of the Poor Laws. The answer of the Commissioners seemed to me so very likely to do good service if it were put into the proper hands that I applied for money to enable me to print 10,000 copies, and also for the names of all persons who had either been examined or corresponded with or were to interfere in the matter. The money and the names were furnished. I wrote an appropriate head, printed and sent copies in franks and by coach parcels free of expense to every person indicated. The consequence was that all proceedings were at once stopped, and nothing more was heard of the mischievous Bill either within or without the House "

House of Commons, in 1833, was accordingly persuaded not to renew the Act by which the plan had been sanctioned.

Apprenticeship

The foregoing devices of finding work or wages for the destitute concerned, in the main, adult able-bodied men or women. For the pauper boy or girl between twelve and twenty-one subsistence with work was often found by the system of apprenticeship. By the Act of 1601,[1] the Churchwardens and Overseers were empowered to bind any children " whose parents they judge not able to maintain them, to be apprenticed where they think fit, till such man child come to the age of twenty-four,[2] and such woman child to the age of twenty-one or marriage ". It has been suggested that this provision was designed to effect a general compulsory education of the children of the whole labouring population, without reference to any application by their parents for poor relief. But whatever may have been the intention and early practice of the law, parochial administrators of the eighteenth and early nineteenth centuries certainly assumed their powers to be limited to children actually chargeable to the parish funds.[3]

Parish apprenticeship, as practised during the eighteenth and early nineteenth centuries, may be roughly divided into three kinds : the binding of an individual child to a master who,

---

(Add. MSS. 35150, p. 45 ; Place to Parkes, May 11, 1835). The reply of the Poor Law Commissioners, signed by six of them, condemned the whole system. Sturges Bourne refused to concur in this report, which was vigorously answered in *Strictures on the Reply of the Poor Law Commissioners to the Inquiry of . . . Viscount Althorp . . . on the subject of Labour Rates*, by John M. Paine, 1834. Place's reprint is entitled *Poor Law Inquiry : Labour Rate*, 1833. A contemporary MS. diary by Richard Potter, M.P., states that the reason that the Bill failed to pass was because it was felt that a wider measure of Poor Law Reform was pending.

[1] 43 Elizabeth, c. 2, sec. 5 (1601), continued by 1 James I. c. 25 (1604). Another Act (3 Charles I. c. 5, 1628) expressly empowers persons to whom apprentices have been bound by the Overseer to receive and keep such apprentices notwithstanding the various statutory restrictions on apprenticeship.

[2] This long servitude continued to be legally possible, as regards the rest of England, down to 1778 (18 George III. c. 47), but the limit was reduced, as regards London parishes, to seven years, or until 21, by the Act of 7 George III. c. 39 (1767) ; see Jonas Hanway's *The Citizen's Monitor*, 1780, p. 208.

[3] The Leeds Vestry even decided in 1772 that they would restrict apprenticeship to children whose parents were in the workhouse, to the exclusion of the children of persons " occasionally chargeable to the town " (MS. Vestry Minutes, Leeds, November 22, 1772).

in consideration of a money premium, voluntarily undertook its maintenance and education ; the ceding of children in batches to manufacturers requiring child-labour in the new factories ; and the allotment of the parish children among the ratepayers of the parish, who were compelled either to accept them as employees or pay a fine.

What we may term voluntary individual apprenticeship did not, as practised by parish authorities, differ in form from the action of a careful parent willing to make a pecuniary sacrifice at the outset in order to get his child provided with a permanent means of livelihood. In the typical contract of apprenticeship there may be supposed to be two distinct objects, first, the equipment of the child with a life-supporting occupation, and second, his maintenance during adolescence. In form the contract entered into by the Churchwardens and Overseers secured both these objects.[1] Vestry minutes show that it was usual to pay a premium ranging from two to ten pounds.[2] The difference to the future welfare of the apprentice lay in the choice of a master and the real intentions of both parties to the bargain. The Overseer seldom took the trouble to discover a master craftsman in a skilled trade who could be induced, by a substantial premium, to take a parish boy. What the Poor Law administrators were thinking about was merely how to get the boy off their hands. Throughout the whole of the eighteenth century we find constant complaints of the indifference of

---

[1] The indentures of apprenticeship were drawn up according to a common form printed in Burn's *Justice*, and other usual textbooks. An actual document of 1739 is quoted by Dr. Cox. The apprentice " shall his said master faithfully and obediently serve, and in all things dutifully behave himself to him and his family as doth become such a servant ". And the master is to " instruct him in some honest calling, trade and employment, and shall at all times during the term of apprenticeship find and provide for him sufficient meat, drink, washing and lodging, and all sorts of apparel, and all other things meet and necessary " in consideration of which the Churchwardens and Overseers pay a premium of £3 (*Three Centuries of Derbyshire Annals*, by J. C. Cox, vol. ii., 1890, p. 179).

[2] We give one out of many examples. " That any person in future who shall, with the approbation of the officers for the time being, take any girl as a servant from the said poor house, shall together with the clothes she may then have, receive one pound, and at the expiration of the first year's service shall receive two pounds ; at the second two pounds ; and at the expiration of the third year, should she continue so long in the same place, shall receive one pound more : the above sums to be applied towards clothing the said girls. Also that an agreement be made . . . that the girls be released at the expiration of five years " (MS. Vestry Minutes, Woolwich (Kent), July 6, 1785).

Churchwardens and Overseers to anything beyond saving the parish the keep of the boy or girl. In 1732 a writer denounces the "very bad practice in parish officers who, to save expense, are apt to ruin children, by putting them out as early as they can, to any sorry masters that will take them, without any concern for their education or welfare, on account of the little money that is given with them ".[1] "The chief view of the Overseer ", wrote Sir John Fielding in 1768, was "to get rid of the object and fix his settlement in another parish." [2] "The immediate interest of the parishes ", says an observer half a century later, "is to relieve themselves of their charge . . . they care little therefore for their prospects in after life." [3]

"There is no doubt ", says another, "that they are often taken by needy persons on account of the bribe offered in the premium." [4] From 1692 onward Overseers were, in fact, under a special temptation in this matter, because, by the statute of

---

[1] *An Account of the Workhouses in Great Britain in the Year 1732.*

[2] *Extracts from such of the Penal Laws as particularly relate to the Peace and Good Order of the Metropolis*, by Sir John Fielding, 1768, p. 414.

[3] Report of the Poor Law Inquiry Commissioners, Appendix A, Villiers' Report, p. 6.

[4] Report of Poor Law Inquiry Commissioners, Appendix A, Pringle's Report, p. 330.

There were, of course, exceptional parishes which had adopted, by 1833, a more enlightened policy. At Brighton in Sussex apprenticeship was managed by a special committee of the Directors and Guardians of the Poor, who made careful inquiry into the character of the proposed masters, and paid as much as £10 premium (see, for instance, MS. Minutes, Incorporated Guardians, Brighton, September 20, 1824, and April 18, 1825). In 1833, the Assistant Poor Law Commissioner was able to report that the pauper boys of Brighton were apprenticed to respectable tradesmen, every attention being paid to the character and circumstances of the Master (Report of Poor Law Inquiry Commissioners, Appendix A; Report, p. 543). At Birmingham, too, it was reported of the children that "at the proper age they are apprenticed to masters in different trades, to whose character the greatest attention is paid ; and the governor is required to visit and examine the masters and apprentices periodically, as a means of ascertaining the conduct of each " (*ibid.* Villiers' Report, p. 7). In the *Hints for the Information of the Overseers of the Poor of the Parishes of St. Giles and St. George's, Bloomsbury*, 1781, it is enjoined that when children are apprenticed, "the boys to handicraft trades, or to the sea service, the girls to trades proper for them or as household servants, the officers . . . should first cause strict enquiry to be made respecting the characters of the persons who may from time to time apply to have them as apprentices. And as a register is kept by the Vestry Clerk of the names and places of abode of all persons to whom apprentices are bound, the messenger should be frequently directed to take opportunities of visiting the children who may be placed out apprentice, and enquire how they are treated by their masters or mistresses, and report the result of his enquiries from time to time to the officers at their meetings."

that year, 3 William III. c. 2. sec. 8, duly indentured apprentices acquired a settlement in the parish in which they served. Thus, if parish authorities could find a master living in another parish willing to take their apprentice, their parish was relieved, not only of the boy's keep, but also of any future liability for the maintenance of himself and of the woman he would presently marry, and of the family of young children whom he would soon bring into the world. Hence the worst possible master in another parish was preferred to the best residing in the parish having the boy to apprentice. Such a seeking of new settlements for parish apprentices became a standing policy. Dr. Burn, in 1764, described it as one of the chief duties of an Overseer as commonly understood, " to bind out poor children apprentice, no matter to whom or to what trade, but to take special care that the master live in another parish ".[1] Sixty years later the policy was still unchanged. " The practice in some towns," it was reported in 1833, " pursued systematically, is to bind the parish apprentices into out townships, in order to shift the settlement, so that the binding parish may be rid of them. When I inquired of the Assistant Overseer of the borough . . . how the apprentices turned out after they were bound, his answer was ' We have nothing to do with them afterwards '."[2] "The object of Overseers ", said a Mile End parish reformer, " is to get rid of the boy, to find a master in another parish. They seldom take any trouble to enquire into the character of the master who applies for one, nor ever after make any enquiry about the lad . . . they have got him off the parish and they think they have gained something ; but as other parishes do the same, nothing is gained : we have only placed ours on some other parish, and in return have got another one placed on ours."[3] But though the parishes gained nothing by this " general post ", the result was practically to destroy even such little supervision over the parish apprentices as Churchwardens and Overseers would have exercised had the

---

[1] *History of the Poor Laws,* by Rev. Dr. Burn, 1764, p. 121.

[2] Report of Poor Law Inquiry Commissioners, Appendix A, Henderson's Report, p. 923. In 1822 the Vestry of Stoke Damarel (Devonport) agreed to pay " a premium not exceeding nine pounds . . . with the girls and seven pounds with the boys, provided they are taken from the workhouse, and *bound without the limits of the parish* " (MS. Vestry Minutes, Stoke Damarel, Devonshire, December 6, 1822).

[3] Report of Poor Law Inquiry Commissioners, Appendix A, Chadwick's Report, p. 145.

binding been in their own parish. Hence there were "many instances where the masters having obtained the first part of the premium then turned them adrift ".[1] " Few of these poor children ", had said an old writer, " now serve out their time, and many of them are driven by neglect or cruelty into such immoralities as too frequently render them the objects of public justice. Many of those who take parish apprentices are so inhuman as to regard only the pecuniary consideration ; and having once received that, they, by ill-usage and undue severity, often drive the poor creatures from them, and so leave them in a more destitute condition at a riper age for mischief than they were in when first they became the care of the parish officers." [2]

With parish officers so oblivious of anything beyond getting the children off their hands, we may imagine with what eagerness they welcomed the applications of manufacturers requiring child labour. This wholesale disposal of parish children to capitalist employers was resorted to quite early in the eighteenth century. Felkin, the historian of the hosiery and lace manufacture, records that about 1730 parishes offered £5 for each boy or girl taken off their hands, and that one manufacturer at Nottingham ran his shop of frames entirely by parish apprentices, having usually twenty-five at work, and never having had an adult journeyman for thirty years.[3] Yet no trade at that period offered worse prospects. " At this epoch, 1740 to 1750, the wages for making the common kinds of worsted hose were reduced very low ; and many of the parish apprentices, ill-managed, ill-taught, and little cared for, were reduced almost to starvation." [4] In 1774 the

[1] Report of Poor Law Inquiry Commissioners, Appendix A, Chadwick's Report, p. 145.

[2] *Treatise on the Better Employment and more comfortable support of the Poor in Workhouses*, by William Bailey, 1758, p. 5. *The Times* of June 27, 1801, in reporting the conviction of a master for grossly ill-treating his parish apprentices, described these as " the most helpless and miserable part of the human creation ", and suggested that masters should be compelled to produce their apprentices publicly every Sunday in Church, " where by the inspection of the parishioners they would be guarded against that degree at least of cruelty or neglect which would be evident in their persons and reflect infamy upon their masters ".

[3] *History of the Machine-wrought Hosiery and Lace Manufactures*, by William Felkin, Cambridge, 1867, p. 75.

[4] *Ibid.* p. 82. In framework knitting, " small worsted stockings " were deemed the worst work, and this in general was done by apprentices. " Some, boys who are paupers, are put to this work at the age of 10 or 11. . . . The work affects the nerves very much " (Report of the Committee on the Framework Knitters' Petition, 1778 ; House of Commons Journals, vol. xxxvi. p. 740).

aristocratic "Directors and Governors of the Poor", of St. George's, Hanover Square, were supplying young children to a London silk manufacturer, apparently without any formal apprenticeship. The death of one of them led to inquiry, which revealed such systematic underfeeding and cruelty as to lead the "Directors and Governors" to "order that all the children which are not bound to the said Mr. P. be immediately fetched and brought away by the messenger ".[1] The progress of the industrial revolution led to a demand for child labour in one manufacture after another. High up in the lonely valleys of Lancashire and Yorkshire mills were built by the side of rushing streams, where the new machines could be driven by water power, and needed only " tending " by docile fingers, and bodies small enough to creep under the frames. The necessary operatives had to be brought from somewhere, and the cheapest source was the workhouse of the south of England. Parish officers accordingly found themselves importuned by the agents sent by manufacturers to recruit their staffs, who, without asking any premium, carried off the children literally by cartloads, taking even infants of three or four years old. The large numbers of children required by the new mills were, in fact, " chiefly collected from parish workhouses ",[2] the largest supply coming from those of London and Westminster,[3] whence they were taken, as Sir Samuel Romilly put it, "in carts like so many negro slaves ",[4] in batches of five to fifty on the same day.[5] " Horner could tell

---

[1] MS. Minutes, Incorporated Guardians, St. George's, Hanover Square, June 1, 1774.

[2] *Treatise on Poverty ; its Consequences and its Remedy*, by William Sabatier, 1797, p. 103 ; see also the *Letter to the Bishop of Gloucester on the Removal of poor children from their Settlements to cotton and other manufactories at Manchester*, by a Friend to the Poor, 1792 (Bodleian Library).

[3] *Description of the Country from Thirty to Forty Miles round Manchester*, by J. Aiken, 1795, p. 219 : Sir F. M. Eden's *State of the Poor*, 1797, vol. i. p. 421. We are reminded of the existence at this period of textile manufactures in Surrey by the following case from the Mitcham records : " It is further ordered that the Churchwardens and Overseers do agree with Messrs. Betts & Co. stocking manufacturers at Cheam, to apprentice so many of the boys of the workhouse to them as the Justices shall think proper, at five guineas per boy, and that the said Messrs. Betts & Co. do find the said boys in proper clothing during the said apprenticeships " (MS. Vestry Minutes, Mitcham, Surrey, Sunday December 13, 1795).

[4] Hansard, 1807, p. 800, vol. ix. ; see *The Rise of Modern Industry*, by J. L. and B. Hammond, 1925, p. 201.

[5] Report of Select Committee on Parish Apprentices, Hansard, April 11, 1815, pp. 533-541.

the House of Commons of a contract between a London parish and a Lancashire manufacturer in which the manufacturer undertook to receive one idiot with every twenty sound children." So systematic and widespread had this infantile recruiting become by 1802, and so gross were the evils which arose, that even the best of the manufacturers themselves called for legal regulation. The Act of 1802, introduced by Sir Robert Peel (the elder), himself the greatest employer of child labour, made some attempt to protect the "health and morals" of these parish apprentices in cotton and woollen mills.[1] How far this Act was made effective is a matter of doubt. It is interesting to note that even this very moderate amount of protection of children against ill-usage was opposed by millowners—at Burley, near Otley, in Yorkshire, for instance—on the ground that " free labourers cannot be obtained to perform the nightwork but upon very disadvantageous terms to the manufacturers ".[2] But attention had now been called to the horrors of the unregulated mills, and, here and there, a well-managed parish would make its own inspection. Thus the Brighton Directors and Guardians of the Poor sent two of their members in 1805 to visit the parish children apprenticed at Backbarrow in Lancashire. They saw the children at their work, which they thought " far from laborious " ; they found them, as they considered, well clothed, comfortably lodged and sufficiently well fed ; but they add " respecting their education, it is more limited than we had reason to expect, as the clergyman that has charge of them attends only for two hours every Sunday evening ; consequently their improvement cannot be much, as there are 140 children ; nor had any one of ours been instructed to write ". Some light is thrown on the standard which these optimistic visitors applied when we find them reporting, without any disapproval, that the children were employed fourteen hours a day (being, we may note, two hours in excess of the legal limit under 42 George III. c. 73, sec. 4), except " during a short time in the height of the summer, when from want of water they occasionally worked longer "—a practice at that time quite illegal.[3] But this wholesale apprenticeship to

---

[1] See the full report of his speech in *Lancaster Gazetteer*, April 10, 1802.

[2] *The Town Labourer, 1760–1832*, 1917, p. 152; *The Rise of Modern Industry*, 1925, p. 197, both by J. L. and B. Hammond.

[3] MS. Minutes, Incorporated Guardians, Brighton, Sussex, June 3 and 18, 1805. Evidence was given in 1815 that the apprentices at Backbarrow had

manufacturers lent itself too obviously to the designs of the Overseers to be easily relinquished, so long as it was profitable to the employers. As late as 1815 it was found that no fewer than 2026 children, from eleven London parishes alone, had been, within ten years, bound to manufacturers at a distance.[1] Nor was the practice confined to the northern counties, nor to cotton and woollen mills. "The system of apprenticing children from the neighbouring parishes for the purpose of changing their settlement" was stated to be one principal cause of the hosiery trade being overstocked with hands.[2] A bookseller at Tewkesbury remembered, in 1833, having seen the parish apprentices from other districts "coming into the town by cartloads".[3] Many parishes in the neighbourhood, like the Gloucester Incorporated Guardians, sent their workhouse master to Kidderminster to place out boys among the carpet manufacturers, with the result that as many as one-fifth of the inhabitants of that town were estimated, in 1833, to be non-parishioners.[4] At Tamworth, in Staffordshire, it appears to " have been formerly the practice for the great manufacturers of this neighbourhood to take apprentices for seven years, securing them thereby a settlement in the parish. When the period of apprenticeship expired, these were replaced by more youthful hands, who in their turn made room for others, and thus multitudes of children from London and other places were brought and settled in Tamworth," to the great burden of its poor rates when, as constantly happened, these persons subsequently became chargeable.[5]

---

never heard of the Act of 1802 prohibiting their employment for more than twelve hours a day (Report of Peel's Committee, 1816, p. 421).

[1] Report of H. of C. Select Committee on Parish Apprentices, Hansard, April 11, 1815, pp. 533-541.

[2] *Ibid.*

[3] Report of Poor Law Inquiry Commissioners, Appendix A, Villiers' Report, pp. 8, 40.

[4] MS. Minutes, Incorporated Guardians, Gloucester, September 7, 1809; Report of the Poor Law Inquiry Commissioners, 1834, Appendix A, Villiers' Report, p. 38.

[5] *Ibid.* Moylan's Report, p. 271. It was one injurious result of the unrestricted recruiting of children by the textile industry, as noticed by John Fielden, that the millowners were "independent " of the adult male operatives, and could fix what hours of work they chose. "It is evident, in short, that the long hours of work were brought about by the circumstance of so great a number of destitute children being supplied from the different parts of the country that the masters were independent of the hands " (*The Curse of the Factory System*, by John Fielden, 1836, p. 12).

Meanwhile attempts were being made to introduce some control over the action of the Overseers themselves. The Elizabethan statute required the consent of two Justices to any contract of apprenticeship of a pauper child, but this consent seems, at the beginning of the eighteenth century, to have been given as a matter of course. It was presently decided that their action in the matter was not merely ministerial, but judicial, involving a genuine inquiry into the circumstances of each case. The duty of the Justices to exercise a careful judgement as to " the fitness of the persons to whom the poor children are thus to be apprenticed ", was feelingly expressed by Chief Justice Kenyon, who observed that Overseers " were frequently obscure people . . . not always attentive to the feelings of parents ", and that the Justices " are guardians of the morals of the people and ought to take care that the apprentices are not placed with masters who may corrupt their morals ".[1]   In 1800 we find the Middlesex Quarter Sessions concerned about the laxity with which individual Justices signed apprenticeship indentures. " It being represented to this Court that several poor children bound out by different parishes to persons who carry on the business of tambour working and other trades in and about the Metropolis, more especially those of a sedentary nature, are kept and employed in such trades in a manner extremely prejudicial to their health, and that frequently the necessaries of life given to them . . . were not sufficient for their support ; and it being stated that several cases of this sort had come before the Magistrates . . . and that complaints had been frequently made of the improper conduct . . . of the masters and mistresses towards such poor apprentices, it is ordered that it be recommended that

---

[1] R. v. Hamstall Ridware, 3 T.R. 381 ; 1 Bott, 620 ; Burn's *Justice*, iv. 116.   A contemporary moralist lays stress on the duties of Justices towards apprentices.   " In placing out parish apprentices, let him not, through fear of giving offence to the principal inhabitants by refusing to ratify their bargain, consign the friendless child to an unfeeling and profligate master ; nor doom him to a trade which will manifestly be ruinous to his health.   In the case of some particular trades and manufactures which, under common management, prove injurious to the health and morals of the persons employed in them, Justices of the Peace may sometimes do great service to the community by strongly recommending the adoption of proper rules and precautions, even when the law does not give them the power of enforcing it " (*Enquiry into the Duties of Men*, by T. Gisborne, 1794, p. 292).   See, to like effect, *The Superintending Power of the Magistrate and the Discretionary Power of Parish Officers in the Apprenticing of Parish Children considered*, 1787.

in every case where the assent of two Justices is necessary to the binding out any child as an apprentice, that the two magistrates be present . . . and that they require the attendance of the master and apprentice before them at the same time, and that the Magistrates do make a strict enquiry . . . into the situation in life and circumstances of the person proposing to take such apprentice, and that they satisfy themselves . . . of the fitness of such person to . . . maintain such apprentice in a suitable manner with sufficient and proper meat, drink and clothing and to teach such apprentice in his business." [1] Two years later Parliament enacted that a detailed register should be kept by Overseers recording the placing out of all apprenticed children, each entry having to be approved and authenticated by a Justice ; the book being open to public inspection without charge ; and heavy penalties were imposed on Overseers neglecting this duty.[2] But it is clear that the evils still continued. In 1811 the House of Commons appointed a committee to inquire into the fate of the boys and girls bound apprentice by Metropolitan parishes.[3] This committee, which did not report until 1815, revealed an almost complete absence of any care of or supervision over parish apprentices by the parochial authorities.[4]

[1] MS. Minutes, Quarter Sessions, Middlesex, May 29, 1800.

[2] 42 George III. c. 46 (1802).

[3] Hansard, June 7, 1811. It was probably in reference to this action that the Vestry of St. George's, Hanover Square, in 1811, asked all its members who were in Parliament to oppose a projected Bill which would hamper the binding out of parish apprentices (MS. Vestry Minutes, St. George's, Hanover Square, Middlesex, May 1, 1811). Possibly it was for this aristocratic Select Vestry that Mr. Wortley strongly opposed the motion, insisting that " although in the higher ranks of society it was true that to cultivate the affections of children for their family was the source of every virtue, yet that it was not so among the lower orders, and that it was a benefit to the children to take them away from their miserable and depraved parents. He said too that it would be highly injurious to the public to put a stop to the binding so many apprentices to the cotton manufacturers, as it must necessarily raise the price of labour and enhance the price of cotton manufactured goods " (*Life of Sir Samuel Romilly*, by himself, edition of 1842, vol. ii. p. 204).

[4] Hansard, April 11, 1815. Great help was given to the movement for reform by Sir Samuel Romilly. We may cite his own description of the evils. " It is a very common practice with the great populous parishes in London to bind children in large numbers to the proprietors of cotton mills in Lancashire and Yorkshire, at a distance of 200 miles. The children, who are sent off by waggonloads at a time, are as much lost for ever to their parents as if they were shipped to the West Indies. The parishes that bind them, by procuring a settlement for the children at the end of forty days, get rid of them for ever ; and the poor children have not a human being in the world to whom they can look for redress against the wrongs they may be exposed to from these

The following year, in view of the fact that " many grievances
have arisen from the binding of poor children as apprentices by
parish officers to improper persons, and to persons residing at
a distance from the parishes to which such poor children belong,
whereby the said parish officers and the parents of the children
are deprived of the opportunity of knowing the manner in which
such children are treated, and the parents and children have in
many instances become estranged from each other ", a long code
of regulations on parish apprenticeship was, at the instance of
Wilbraham Bootle, M.P., passed into law.   The minimum age
of apprenticeship was fixed at nine, and it was forbidden to send
London children to any greater distance than forty miles.
Every step was taken to make the inquiry and consent of the
Justices a reality, and, what was even more efficacious, no
apprentice could be bound in another parish without the express
concurrence of two Justices of the other parish, as well as that
of two Justices of the home parish.   And, to make the law
automatically effective, it was provided that no settlement should
be gained by apprenticeship unless all its elaborate requirements
had been duly complied with.[1]

But by this time many circumstances were co-operating to
bring to an end the wholesale recruiting of workhouse children
by manufacturers.   In the cotton and woollen mills parish
apprentices were, by 1815, no longer in demand.   " The plan
of employing apprentices was always troublesome to the master.
He had to feed them, clothe them, lodge them and supply them
with medical advice and religious instruction ; and though the
latter duty was for the most part neglected, the former could
not be.   He was at length relieved from this weight of responsibility " by the improvement of the steam engine enabling him
to transfer his mills from the neighbourhood of water power to

wholesale dealers in them, whose object is to get everything that they can
possibly wring from their excessive labour and fatigue.   Instances have come
to my knowledge of the anguish sustained by poor persons, on having their
children torn from them, which could not fail to excite a strong interest in
their favour, if they were more generally known.   Instances have recently
occurred of masters who, with 200 such apprentices, have become bankrupts,
and been obliged to send all their apprentices to the poorhouse of the parish
in which their manufactory happened to be established, to be supported by
strangers, and by strangers who consider them as fraudulently thrown upon
them for relief " (*Life of Sir Samuel Romilly*, by himself, edition of 1842,
vol. ii. p. 188).

[1] 56 George III. c. 139.

large urban centres where " the children of the neighbourhood were, on almost every account, preferable to apprentices from distant quarters, and particularly because they were (between 1802 and 1819) exempt from the restrictions of Sir Robert Peel's Act ".[1] The stringency of the 1816 Act greatly hampered the parish authorities, whilst Justices, in some cases (as in Warwickshire) flatly refused to allow pauper children to be sent to the cotton mills at all.[2] The new Factory Act of 1819 put additional restrictions on the employment in textile mills of any persons under sixteen, whether parish apprentices or not. Finally, the parishes into which the apprentices came, keenly aware of the growth of their own pauperism, began strongly to object to being made the dumping-ground for parish apprentices from other parts.

The practical discontinuance, in nearly all counties, of the wholesale apprenticeship to manufacturers, and a contemporary increase of difficulty in finding masters willing to take individual apprentices, forced the Overseers to rely on their powers of compelling parishioners to take the parish children off their hands.[3] These compulsory powers had, here and there, at all

---

[1] *Evils of the Factory System demonstrated by Parliamentary Evidence*, by Charles Wing, 1837.

[2] Price's evidence, see Report of Select Committee on Parish Apprentices, Hansard, April 11, 1815, pp. 533-541.

Already in 1784 we read, the Lancashire magistrates in Quarter Sessions had decided that they would refuse to approve the apprenticing of local children to the new cotton mills (*Enquiry into the Duties of Man*, by T. Gisborne, 1794, p. 293).

[3] Most information as to this compulsory apprenticeship is to be found in Capt. Chapman's Report (pp. 432-435 of Appendix A of Report of Poor Law Inquiry Commissioners).

The statute (43 Eliz. c. 2, sec. 5) merely empowered the Churchwardens and Overseers with the assent of two Justices, to bind the children apprentice " where they shall see convenient " ; so that, as was rightly observed in 1801, " this oppressive burden on small estates arises not from that Act itself, but from the rule that it seems certain was at that time established " (*Means of Reforming the Morals of the Poor*, by John Hill, London, 1801, sec. xi.). It seems, in fact, to have been understood from the first that " the Justices may force " any person assessed at £10 " to take a parish apprentice, for the power to compel is consequent to their authority to put him out " ; (1 Bott, 604 ; see the *Resolutions of the Judges of Assize*, 1633). In 1696, there being doubt whether the persons to whom such " children are to be bound are compellable to receive such children as apprentices ", it was enacted (8 and 9 William III., c. 30) that they should then be so compellable, under penalty of £10. Not until 1789 was it settled, by Lord Kenyon's judgement in R. v. Clapp (3 T.R. 107 and 1 Bott, 619) that the persons so compellable were all occupiers of land, etc., within the parish, whether residents or not, and that the burden of

times been resorted to.[1]　But we gather that, during the manufacturers' demand for child labour, they had remained generally
in abeyance.　Towards the end of the eighteenth century the
authorities of the Norfolk and Suffolk Unions were sparing themselves all trouble with their boys and girls by the simple expedient
of drafting them out by lot, at the age of fourteen, among the
parishioners, each occupier being compelled to maintain the
child for one year, or pay a fine of a pound.[2]　In 1833 we find
this power of compulsion systematically employed, from Cornwall
to Yorkshire, as a means of relieving the parish of its pauper
boys and girls.　The details as to the allotment varied from parish
to parish.　The assumption was that the burden of maintaining
these children, after the age of fourteen (or even as early as nine
or ten), should be shared among the individual parishioners.
Usually all the occupiers rated at ten pounds a year or upwards
would be made liable to this charge ; occasionally ministers of
religion would be passed over ; whilst in the West Riding of
Yorkshire the practice was to exempt all persons rated at less
than thirty pounds a year.　Often the boys and girls would be
allotted to the parishioners in rotation as their names appeared
on the rate book ; sometimes the rotation would be by properties,

---

so providing for the children was to be shared among them in proportion to
their assessments.　Other statutes of 1792, 1802 and 1816 (32 George III.
c. 45, 42 George III. c. 119, and 56 George III. c. 139), provided for the
registration, transfer, etc., of parish apprentices.　By 2 and 3 Anne, c. 6, sec. 1.
(1704) and 4 Anne, c. 19, sec. 16 (1706), every master of a ship could be compelled
to take as a parish apprentice one boy over thirteen for every fifty tons burden
of his ship, and, on payment merely of £2 : 10s. by the parish for his outfit,
maintain him until the age of twenty-one.

[1] In 1758 we hear complaints of the " incumbrance " laid on " estates and
families " by the method of putting out poor children apprentices " (*Treatise
on the Better Employment and more complete support of the Poor in Workhouse,*
by William Bailey, 1758, p. 5).

[2] " The boys and girls at 14 are ' drafted out to the parishes to which
they belong.　If a person to whose lot a child falls should refuse to take him
or her for a year (which is the stated term) he forfeits 20s., which goes to the
master who accepts his allotment : if he should likewise refuse, he also forfeits
the same sum, which is then paid to the third person on his accepting the child ,
when the year is expired, the child is again put by lot to another master, in
case his old master does not wish to keep him, and he is not able to provide
for himself ' " (*The State of the Poor,* by Sir F. M. Eden, 1797, vol. ii. pp. 453-
471, as to the Hundreds of Mitford and Launditch, incorporated under Local
Act of 1775).　Lord Ellenborough, in 1808, " reprobated this practice of the
directors allotting children out " instead of apprenticing them, in a case
relating to the Stowmarket Hundred of Suffolk (R. v. Stowmarket, 9 East,
211 ; Burn's *Justice,* vol. i. p. 123 of 1820 edition).

sometimes by persons ; frequently the children would be placed out simply by casting lots ; or their masters might be arbitrarily selected. The local Justices sometimes chose such parishioners as they thought fit. At Leeds there was " a book in which any member [of the workhouse board] enters the name of any individual occupier . . . whom he thinks able and proper to bear an apprentice ".[1] In the neighbouring parish of Knaresborough " the practice is to have a meeting of the ratepayers once a year, who select thirty persons who are considered suitable to receive apprentices ; then the meeting select twelve out of the thirty as the most suitable ".[2] The unfortunate parishioner on whom the lot fell was bound to maintain the apprentice until the age of twenty-one, a period which might be as much as eleven years, even if he had no trade which he could teach him, and no opportunity for employing his services. The only alternative was to pay the statutory penalty of £10. In agricultural parishes the occupiers, being nearly always farmers, preferred to accept their share of apprentices, out of whose labour they made what they could.[3] In urban parishes, on the other hand, many of the parishioners elected rather to pay the fine, in which case the boy or girl would be tendered to another occupier. We hear of cases in which a boy would in this way " earn " for the parish £30, or even £50, before a master could be found to accept him. The Vestry of Leeds had a revenue from these fines amounting to more than £1000 a year.[4] In some cases the fund thus raised by fines would be spent by the parish authorities as premiums to induce masters in other parishes to take the children off their hands altogether.

The system of compulsory apprenticeship was somewhat analogous to the " Roundsman " and " Labour Rate " devices for sharing the burden of the adults. It differed from these for the worse by the binding of the apprentice, and his consequent

---

[1] Report of Poor Law Inquiry Commissioners, Appendix A, Tweedy's Report, p. 783.

[2] *Ibid.* Tweedy's Report, p. 779.

[3] Sometimes there would be a combination of voluntary selection (with compulsion in the background) and actually compulsory allotment. Thus in South Devon in 1833, " Farmers in general choose their own apprentices, but if any extra children, probably weak or idle ones remain, and they refuse to take them, the children are then bound by lot " (*ibid.* Chapman's Report, p. 433).

[4] *Ibid.* Tweedy's Report, p. 783.

P

involuntary servitude for a long term of years. Its results on the children themselves were almost universally bad. " The parish apprentice ", wrote an observer of 1833, " may be said to be a slave, attached to the soil for seven and in some cases eleven years, during which, in some instances, they are treated worse than slaves. They almost universally prove worthless, depraved and abandoned characters." These unhappy conscripts " are represented as growing up careless and improvident, because they are kept so long without dependence on their own resources. They are said to become extremely impatient of control at about 18, and frequently to commit petty thefts, so as to cause their indentures to be broken ; and the females are represented as taking means to get themselves with child for the same purpose." [1] So obviously bad was the system that magistrates became more and more reluctant to give their consent to the indentures, and parishes abandoned it. But the Overseers usually felt that they had no alternative. The children at ten or twelve, or even at fourteen, were not worth their keep to any employer, and he could only recoup himself by getting their labour in the later years for bare subsistence. In fact, the only other way seemed to be to place the children out at temporary hirings, paying an allowance towards their maintenance, and this expedient was actually adopted in a few parishes in Cornwall and Devonshire. Thus, we read that, in 1833, " in the parish of South Petherwin . . . the children are collected annually at a public Vestry, and are let out at yearly hiring, the parish giving small premiums, which vary according to the character and capabilities of the child, from 11½d. to ½d. per week, with a small allowance for clothing ".[2]

Surveying the evidence, we may summarise the position of parish apprenticeship in 1833 by the following conclusions. Changes in the distribution of the textile manufactures, and in the character of machinery, together with increasing legal restrictions, had practically killed out (except in a few districts, such as Worcestershire and Staffordshire) [3] the device of the wholesale apprenticeship of pauper children to capitalist manufacturers. The regular binding of individual children, to masters voluntarily taking them in consideration of a premium, was

---

[1] Report of Poor Law Inquiry Commissioners, Appendix A, Chapman's Report, 432-433.
[2] *Ibid.* Chapman's Report, p. 432.   [3] *Ibid.* Villiers' Report, p. 8.

going on in every urban parish, and occasionally elsewhere. But this expedient was becoming every day more troublesome and expensive, and less adequate to the need. The law and the practice of the Justices now made many formalities before a boy could be legally bound. The increasing alertness to prevent new settlements interfered with the choice of any master who was not a parishioner. Changes in industry diminished the number of persons willing to take apprentices at all, whilst the bad reputation of workhouse children made it increasingly difficult to get them accepted. Meanwhile, the great increase in pauperism involved a corresponding increase in the number of children for whom the Overseers were compelled to find places. In despair, the parish authorities resorted to one of two alternatives. In many counties, notably Cornwall, Devon, Somerset, Suffolk, Norfolk and Yorkshire, they fell back on their powers of compulsion. The allotting among the parishioners of all the parish children of a certain age, according to one scheme or another, became as normal as the Roundsman system or the Labour Rate. Elsewhere, notably in the counties of Sussex, Surrey, Kent and Berkshire, where the Allowance System under the Justices' scale was most completely adopted, the orphans and other children were simply kept in the poorhouse or workhouse up to a certain age, and then turned out to find employment, with the regular weekly allowance in the same way as adults. In the Metropolitan parishes there was great difficulty in getting the children off. Overseer would bid against Overseer in premiums to tradesmen, unless the ratepayers revolted at such sums being paid, but, nevertheless, enough masters could not be found. The despairing officials in 1833 could see no solution but a wholesale emigration of the big boys and girls who were accumulating in the workhouses.[1] A well-informed observer suggested to the Poor Law Inquiry Commissioners that the best course would be entirely to withdraw from the Overseers any power of apprenticeship, which proved, in practice, to be disastrous to the interests of the parish and a curse to both apprentice and master alike.[2]

[1] Report of Poor Law Inquiry Commissioners, Appendix A, Chadwick's Report, p. 141.

[2] " It may seem rash to recommend a repeal of the power to bind out parish apprentices, but I am well convinced that such an alternative would be highly favourable. Parish binding degrades the character, and often ruins the apprentice for after life. He has no sufficient motive for good conduct.

The Poorhouse

In describing the doles and pensions disbursed by the
Churchwardens and Overseers, with their development at the
hands of the Justices of the Peace into the calamitous Allowance
System ; and, again, in our account of the various forms of
" billeting out the able-bodied labourers " and (under the name
of apprenticeship) also the youths and maidens, we have so far
left out of sight the existence, in many parishes, of the primitive
institution of the poorhouse.   The attempt to put effectively
in operation the idea of profitably employing the labour of the
applicants for relief led, as we have seen, to the establishment,
from 1696 onward, of Houses of Industry for Unions of parishes.
The parish poorhouse and the Union House of Industry often
differed widely in character and were distinct in origin and
purpose, but it is from the pair of them that has sprung the
ubiquitous modern workhouse, destined to become, after 1834,
the central feature of English Poor Law administration.

The parish poorhouse, as it existed from the sixteenth to
the nineteenth century, was at the outset nothing that could
be termed an institution.   It consisted usually of a cottage, or
several cottages, used indiscriminately as free lodgings for some
of the parish pensioners, as an occasional receptacle for the
disabled and sick, and as a temporary shelter for tramps and for
paupers awaiting removal to other parishes.   We are told that
" No regular provision for the diet is made, and little order or
discipline is maintained in them.   Some of the paupers who are
placed there work for private employers and maintain themselves ; others receive pay from the parish and also provide their
own food.   Houses of this description appeared in general to

---

He has a settled conviction that he must be a domestic slave till twenty-one,
while he sees other lads, no stronger or cleverer than himself, earning wages,
and at their own or their parents' disposal.   He is at the same time well aware
that he must be maintained till the apprenticeship expires, let his conduct be
good or bad, and provided he can escape the master's lash and the magistrate's
committal he cares for little else ; he is often ill-treated and his complaints
[are] with great difficulty heard. . . . Masters on the other hand, considering
parish apprentices as a burden, take little or no care to instruct them but confine
them as much as possible to drudgery. . . . Much tyranny, too, is exercised
towards masters in unfair bindings. . . . Both are dissatisfied, both corrupted
and it may be safely asserted that in very many cases parish binding is a curse to
both " (Report of Poor Law Inquiry Commissioners, 1834, Appendix C, p. 377).

be dirty and disorderly." [1] "They generally consist", says another account, "of several small adjoining tenements, in which the pauper occupies one or two rooms according to the size of his family." Where the parish contained only a few score families (and such parishes, as we are apt to forget, constituted during the eighteenth century the great majority of all the 15,000 separate Poor Law Authorities) the "parish house", or poorhouse, was simply a place of free lodging, admission to which went by favour of the Churchwardens and Overseers. [2] In more populous places, and with larger premises, such poorhouses might be occupied by sixty or eighty residents, "made up of a dozen or more neglected children, twenty or thirty ablebodied adult paupers of both sexes and probably an equal number of aged and impotent persons who are proper objects of relief. Among these the mothers of bastard children and prostitutes live without shame, and associate freely with the youth, who have also the example and conversation of the frequent inmates of the county gaol, the poacher, the vagrant, the decayed beggar and other characters of the worst description. To these may often be added a solitary blind person, one or two idiots, and not infrequently are heard, from among the rest, the incessant ravings of some neglected lunatic. In such receptacles the sick poor are often immured." [3] The result was frequently a pandemonium. "Where", reports an observer, "a number of paupers of all ages, sexes, characters and dispositions are herded together, and subject to no superintendence, little else is to be expected than a mass of poverty, misery and vice. . . . To the aged they are places of punishment, from the occurrence, at all hours, of disturbances and brawls; and to the young, schools of idleness and profligacy, where example quickly corrupts the better inclined to the level of the worst. These establishments may indeed save parishes a few pounds annually in rents, but the sacrifice

[1] Report of Poor Law Inquiry Commissioners, Appendix A, Villiers' Report, p. 1.

[2] "Parish houses are [in 1832] very common in Hants. In these, widows or persons with families that are large, are allowed to live rent free; but there is a great deal of partiality shown in granting these houses" (Rev. Peyton Blakiston, in an able report to the Poor Law Inquiry Commissioners, Appendix C, p. 4; he was the author of *Hints for the Improvement of the Condition of the Labouring Classes*, 1831).

[3] General Report of Poor Law Inquiry Commissioners, 1833.

of morality and spread of vicious habits which they occasion is incalculable." [1]

In many, perhaps in the majority, of cases the poorhouse had belonged to the parish for several centuries. In many parishes the building was formerly known as the Church House, and had been used, as we have described, for " Church Ales " and as a centre of popular recreation. In other parishes the Elizabethan statutes led to the gift or devise of cottages for the poor ; and we find them also occasionally built on the village green, or on a neighbouring common, often by permission of the lord of the manor, by the parish officers and the Vestry, at the expense of the Poor Rate.[2]

We cannot omit from the picture of English Poor Law administration the characteristic parish poorhouse, of which thousands must have continued in existence during the eighteenth century. But though they were perhaps the commonest form of what was subsequently known as the workhouse, they can hardly be said to have represented anything that can be called a poor law policy. The accidental ownership, by the parish, of a cottage or two seemed, to the average Overseer, happily to solve the constantly recurring problem of how he was, especially in parishes in which house-room was scarce, to provide a roof for the homeless widow or pauper family, or for the destitute wanderer. This sort of poorhouse was nothing more than a gratuitous shelter. It had none of the characteristics that we now ascribe to " indoor relief " ; it was in fact merely one form of relief in kind.[3]

[1] Report of Poor Law Inquiry Commissioners, Appendix A, Walcott's Report, p. 173.

[2] Thus, at Stoke Newington (Middlesex) in 1709 the Vestry contracted for the erection of four houses on " the parish field ", in which to accommodate poor refugees from the Palatinate (MS. Vestry Minutes, Stoke Newington, August 15 and September 16, 1709 ; see Lysons' *Environs of London*, vol. i. p. 582). We have already described the erection of such cottages in the North Riding of Yorkshire by the parish officers (*Seventeenth Century Life in the Country Parish*, by Eleanor Trotter, 1919).

[3] Thus, apparently, no furniture—not a bed—was supplied ; and even the aged lay on the wooden floor (*A Brief Statement of Facts wherein several instances of unparalleled Inhumanity, Cruelty and Neglect in the Treatment of the Poor in the Parish of Damerham South* [Wilts], by Philip Henvill, Salisbury, 1796, p. 16).

The Workhouse

By the beginning of the nineteenth century nearly all the urban parishes and many of those in rural districts had, either separately or in combination, superseded the " poorhouse " or free shelter, by a definitely organised " workhouse," having in command a " master " or " governor ", a " matron " or a " governess ", conducted under a regular discipline, and providing maintenance in common on a systematic dietary.[1] Of such workhouses and poorhouses, there were, in 1815, over four thousand, apparently containing something like one hundred thousand resident paupers.[2]

It is impossible to say when the first workhouse in the modern sense—as distinguished, on the one hand, from the mere poorhouse, and on the other from the Bridewell, or House of Correction —was established in England. The Act of 1601 (43 Elizabeth c. 2), whilst ordering the Overseers to set the able-bodied poor to work, and to provide " convenient houses of dwelling " for the impotent poor, had made no express provision for purchasing or erecting a building, and had not authorised any borrowing of money for the purpose. But the earlier Act of 1597 (39 Elizabeth c. 5), made perpetual in 1623 (21 James I. c. 1), had incidentally authorised the erecting by private donors of " hospitals or abiding and working houses for the poor " ; and if the parish chose to pay for it out of the current rates, there was, we imagine, nothing

---

[1] " A workhouse ", writes C. P. Villiers in 1833, " is known by having a master or a matron, a regular dietary and the inmates being subject to some control " (Report of Poor Law Inquiry Commissioners, Appendix A, Villiers' Report, p. 1). Usually the three attributes are found together. A few exceptional cases are referred to in which paupers in poorhouses, without any master, were supplied with food by contract at the expense of the Poor Rate (*Ibid.* Chapman's Report, p. 425).

[2] Second Report from the House of Commons Committee on Poor Laws, 1818. In Devonshire, in 1808, it is incidentally recorded that, out of 473 parishes, 103 have workhouses, the proportion being lowest in the moorland districts (*General View of the Agriculture of Devon*, by Charles Vancouver, 1808). The City of London seems to have been exceptionally unprovided for. The hundred and odd minute parishes of the old City, after having a joint workhouse in 1647, and again in 1698, reverted to individual poorhouses or workhouses, which were, during the eighteenth century, repeatedly instituted, abandoned and reinstituted in particular parishes. In 1803 the City parishes were nearly all without workhouses (*The State of the Population, the Poor and Poor Rates of every separate Parish within the Bills of Mortality, 1805*). In 1834 we find it expressly recorded that there was no workhouse in ninety-six of the City parishes ; see *The Laws, Customs, Usages and Regulations of the City and Port of London*, by Alex. Pulling, 1842, p. 248.

to prevent the Vestry, acting through the Churchwardens and Overseers, from purchasing or building the necessary premises, and starting what we should now term a General Mixed Workhouse. It is, however, probable that the need seemed, at first, to be fully met by the provision by the Justices, at the expense of the county or municipal corporation, of the Houses of Correction that we have described. The first of these, the Bridewell of the City of London, was, as we have seen, designed in 1555, not exclusively for " the froward, strong and sturdy vagabond ", but also " for the lodging and harbouring of the poor, sick and weak . . . and of poor wayfaring people ". And when we find the Justices of Essex, in 1598, as we have described, providing not only one principal House of Correction at Coxall (now Coggeshall), but also twenty-two subsidiary establishments in as many different towns and villages within this single county, it is easy to understand that such a network of county institutions made provision at parish expense unnecessary. The earliest parish workhouse that we have noted is that of St. Giles in the Fields, London, a suburb which had become very populous at the beginning of the seventeenth century. During the outbreak of plague in 1640–1641, the Vestry had acquired a " pest house " ; and after the abatement of the sickness, this building, we are told, was, under the Commonwealth, converted into a workhouse for the reception of both impotent and able-bodied poor.[1] It was, however, not for another half-century, and not until the idea of profitably employing the poor in institutions, had led, as we have described, to the establishment of municipal " Houses of Industry " at Bristol and elsewhere, that Parish Vestries took to starting workhouses of their own. In 1698, the parish officers of Ealing (Middlesex) were directed by the Open Vestry to " take and provide one or more houses for workhouses to employ the poor of this parish to work in ". A workhouse with an adjoining spinning-house was accordingly built.[2] The first of Matthew Marryott's workhouses, to be presently described, was opened at Olney in Buckinghamshire in 1714 ; [3] and the Churchwardens' accounts of St. Martin's, Leicester, show them to be building a

---

[1] *Account of the Hospital and Parish of St. Giles's in the Fields*, by John Parton, 1822 : *The Great Plague of London*, by W. G. Bell, 1924, pp. 37-38.

[2] *Annals of Ealing*, by Edith Jackson, 1898, p. 150.

[3] *An Account of Several Workhouses for Employing and Maintaining the Poor*, 1725 and 1732.

workhouse in the same year.[1] At Kettering (Northants), in 1717, it was formally decided by the Open Vestry that a work-house should be erected, a committee of seven persons being appointed to be " the chief managers of the said business ", subject to ratification of their proceedings by the Vestry.[2]

Frequently the establishment of an " institution " met with hot and sometimes long-continued opposition from one or another section of the inhabitants. Thus, at Leeds, the little group of principal inhabitants, the Mayor and Aldermen, the Vicar, Churchwardens and Overseers, together with fifteen others, set up a workhouse as early as 1726 in order to set the poor to work. Two years later the Open Vestry peremptorily orders " that the workhouse be discontinued, and that the poor children and other poor persons there be with all convenient speed taken care of and provided for by the respective Overseers of the Poor to whose divisions they belong, and that the stock and materials belonging to the workhouse be scheduled and apprised and sold at the discretion of the present committee ". And though there is, in 1738, a resolution passed by the Vestry in favour of the re-establishment of the workhouse, and a Board of Directors and Managers are actually elected, we gather that it was twenty years more before the Board could persuade the Vestry to appoint a salaried master and mistress, and adopt a definite code of rules " for the government of the poor ".[3] At Manchester, political and religious animosity stood in the way of the establishment of a workhouse for half a century. In 1731 the principal inhabitants agreed among themselves to promote a Bill to incorporate a body of twenty-four Guardians of the Poor, eight to be nominated by the Tories, eight by the Whigs and eight by the Presbyterians, with the express object of erecting a workhouse. But we are told that this promising attempt at conciliation and compromise was thwarted by the " High Church " party, backed up by the lord of the manor, a like fate overtaking a similar proposal in 1763.[4]

---

[1] *Accounts of the Churchwardens of St. Martin's, Leicester, 1489-1844*, by Thomas North, Leicester, 1844.

[2] Vestry Minutes, Kettering, 1717, in *Sketch of the History of Kettering*, by F. W. Bull, 1891 : *The Parish and the County*, by S. and B. Webb, 1906, p. 131.

[3] MS. Vestry Minutes, Leeds, March 6, 1725 ; May 26, 1726 ; January 12, 1728 ; September 22, 1738 ; June 8, 1758; and May 9, 1771. *The Parish and the County*, by S. and B. Webb, 1906, pp. 50-51.

[4] *Case in relation to an Act of Parliament . . . devised for the erecting a Workhouse in the Parish of Manchester*, 1730 ; *The Case of the Petitioners against*

It was not until 1790 that the Churchwardens and Overseers, urging that "the township of Manchester . . . is very
populous; and the poor thereof are becoming exceedingly
numerous", obtained Parliamentary powers to have "a proper
and commodious poor house . . . and proper powers given for
governing and regulating the poor of the said township ".[1]

One interesting feature of the workhouse as an institution
for the poor, as we find it throughout three centuries, is that
although (as will be described in the following pages) it was
frequently started with a special design, or for a particular
purpose—such as profitably employing the able-bodied, providing
an asylum for the impotent, or supplying a deterrent to applicants
for relief—it was always crumbling back into what the twentieth
century terms the General Mixed Workhouse, in which all
destitute persons, irrespective of age, sex and condition, are
indiscriminately housed and maintained.　Such an institution,
admitting all sections of the poor—whether the widely distributed village poorhouse or the Bridewell of the City of London—
was, as we have seen, the original, out of which all the varieties of
workhouse of the seventeenth and eighteenth centuries emerged,
and to which they were always reverting—just (as the world
learned from Darwin) as all the varieties of pigeons tend to revert
to the original " blue rock " !　Such a reversion came inevitably
from the fact that the institution had always been started, and
was always maintained, not by an authority having any special
duty to provide education for the children, or medical treatment
for the sick, or comfortable superannuation for the aged, or
employment for the able-bodied, but by a " Mixed Authority ",
responsible for the poor as a whole, and almost necessarily
administering through " mixed officials ", dealing out treatment
to the inmates as an aggregate.　But, at the beginning of the
seventeenth century, even so wise a man as Bacon positively
preferred the " blue rock " to the differentiated varieties !　" I
commend most ", he officially advised King James the First,
" Houses of Relief and Correction, which are mixed hospitals,

---

*bringing in a Bill for erecting a new workhouse in the Town of Manchester and
establishing a perpetual succession of guardians for ordering the relief and employment of the poor,* 1731 ; *History of the County Palatine of Lancaster,* by
Edward Baines, 1836, vol. ii. pp. 293, 306 ; *The Parish and the County,* by
S. and B. Webb, 1906, pp. 98-105, 150-169.

[1] Preamble to 30 George III. c. 81 (Manchester Local Act).

where the impotent person is relieved, and the sturdy beggar buckled to work, and the unable person also not maintained to be idle, which is ever joined with drunkenness and impurity, but is sorted with such works as he can manage and perform ; and where the uses are not distinguished as in other hospitals, whereof some are for aged and impotent, and some for children, and some for correction of vagabonds ; but are general and promiscuous, so that they may take off poor of every sort from the country as the country breeds them ; and thus the poor themselves shall find the provision, and other people the sweetness of the abatement of the tax. Now, if it be objected, that Houses of Correction in all places have not done the good expected (as it cannot be denied, but in most places they have done much good), it must be remembered that there is a great difference between that which is done by the distracted government of Justices of the Peace and that which may be done by a settled Ordinance, subject to a regular visitation, as this may be. And, besides, the want hath been commonly in Houses of Correction of a common stock, for the materials of the labour, which in this case may be likewise supplied." [1]

Except for the common attributes of providing lodging and complete maintenance, under some kind of control, and according to some sort of common rule, the workhouses of the eighteenth century differed, in their conception and in their administration, indefinitely one from another. This extreme diversity arose largely from the fact that their promoters and administrators aimed at no fewer than six distinct objects and uses—these uses being, indeed, often mutually inconsistent devices, adopted, in varying sequence between 1660 and 1830, for dealing with the settled poor.

We classify under the following heads the six distinct uses for which workhouses were established in the two centuries preceding the Poor Law Amendment Act of 1834, placing them, as far as practicable, in chronological order as each became the typical, if not the dominant, aim of the Poor Law Authorities of successive decades.

---

[1] *Advice to the King, touching Mr. Sutton's Estate* (Charterhouse), by Sir Francis Bacon (Viscount St. Albans), in *The Works of Lord Bacon*, 1837 edition, vol i. p. 495 ; cited in Ninth Annual Report of Poor Law Commissioners, 1843, pp. 279-280.

1. The workhouse as a means of profitably employing the poor ;
2. The workhouse as a penal establishment for the idle ;
3. The workhouse as a deterrent ;
4. The workhouse as an asylum for the impotent poor ;
5. The workhouse as a means of applying the test by regimen ;
6. The workhouse as an institution for specialised treatment.

The student must, however, bear always in mind that the contemporary Poor Law Authorities, whether Churchwardens and Overseers, Incorporated Governors or Guardians of the Poor, Open Vestries or Vestry Committees, rarely distinguished in their own minds between these several uses of the workhouse, and invariably attempted to combine some or all of them. Moreover, the same policy was seldom carried out consistently in any place or for any length of time. Every parish modified its particular combination of all these uses of the workhouse according to the character and ideas of the particular set of Governors or Overseers who reigned over it for the moment.[1] Hence it is not possible to present to the reader typical instances in which the workhouse was used only as a place of employment,

---

[1] Hence we find all the various names given to this parish institution used indiscriminately for all varieties of it. Whether it was called " hospital ", " abiding house ", " poor house ", " workhouse ", " house of industry ", " house of maintenance " ; or, as Sir F. M. Eden records (vol. ii. p. 692) of Empingham (Rutlandshire), " both to obviate prejudice against the name of Poor or Workhouse, and because it is a protection to the aged, sick and infirm ", " house of protection " ; or (by the Quakers at Philadelphia, U.S.A.) " bettering house ", no inference can be drawn from the name used in a particular instance as to the kind of institution that it denoted.

It was often supposed that unfortunate associations with particular names given to the institution accounted for the reluctance of the poor to partake of its advantages. " It's true ", wrote a legal commentator of 1710, " some other names than those of Bridewell, House of Correction and Workhouse—and good management—would invite the young ones into a working society with credit and delight . . . and then industry and emulation would be fashionable " (*Legal Provisions for the Poor*, by S[amuel] C[arter], 1710).

It is significant that the Poor Law Inquiry Commissioners of 1832–1834 do not attempt, in their General Report, to discriminate among these half a dozen different uses of the workhouse. After devoting thirty-three pages of scathing denunciation to the various kinds of " Outdoor Relief " of the able-bodied, they dismiss the four thousand existing institutions, with their hundred thousand inmates, in three pages on " Indoor Relief ", which certainly fail to give any adequate idea of the extent or diversity of this form of provision, or of the difficulties to which it led. But to have dealt adequately or equally with the workhouses would have weakened the force of the Commissioners' indictment of Outdoor Relief to the able-bodied.

a penal establishment, a mere instrument of deterrence or an asylum for the impotent. All that we can do is, by a selection of instances and contemporary descriptions, to give some idea of the use of the workhouse between the close of the seventeenth and the beginning of the nineteenth centuries as a device for organising employment, correcting idleness and disorder, deterring applicants for relief, maintaining the orphans, the sick and the aged, or treating, with a view to their improvement, special classes of the community.

The Workhouse as a Device for profitably employing Pauper Labour

We have described in the preceding chapter the energy and persistence with which the philanthropists and statesmen of the latter part of the seventeenth century pushed the idea of organising the labour of the poor in such a way as to add to the wealth of the nation. Every able-bodied adult without visible means of subsistence was, to quote the words of Sir Matthew Hale, " to be put into a capacity of eating his own bread ", with the double object of relieving the rates from the cost of his maintenance, and increasing the manufactures of the nation. In the case of young children, the productivity of their labour was regarded as of secondary importance, the chief object being that " they may be bred up to labour, principles of virtue being implanted in them at an early age, and laziness discouraged ". Hence we have the " workhouse " in its primary or literal intention of a " House of Industry "—as a device for organising the unemployed and training the young to work. Notwithstanding the cold water thrown upon the proposal by De Foe in 1704, as we have described, the idea of profitably employing the poor continued to recur, in combination with all sorts of Poor Relief methods, for the whole of the eighteenth century.[1] In the year of the

---

[1] In addition to other publications of the first half of the century elsewhere referred to, we may cite the following : *A Present Remedy for the Poor : or the most probable means to provide well for the Poor of the Nation*, etc., by M. D., 1700 ; *Exporting Unmanufactured Goods the only Cause of the Want of Employ for our Poor*, 1700 ; *Some Thoughts concerning the Maintenance of the Poor*, 1700 ; *Workhouses the Best Charity*, by Thomas Cooke, 1702 ; *Queries relating to the Poor of England*, 1716 ; *The Miseries of the Poor are a National Sin . . . we shall remove that guilt . . . by the . . . employment of the poor under one general law*, 1717, and *Particular Answers to the most material objections . . .*

South Sea Bubble—to quote the title of a pamphlet of 1720—
" *The Regular Government and Judicious Employment of the Poor* "
could even be recommended as " *the most Probable Means of
Raising and Securing Public Credit* " !

The experiment was perhaps tried under the most promising
auspices in 1696 at the spacious workhouse of the Bristol Corporation of the Poor, the establishment of which we have described.
At first Bristol was delighted with the success of " St. Peter's
Hospital ". " The poor of both sexes and all ages " were, we
are told, " employed in beating hemp, dressing and spinning flax,
or in carding and spinning wool and cotton." The Overseers of
the several parishes referred to this employment most of the
applicants for doles ; and these were encouraged to labour by
wages at rates supposed to be proportionate to the value of their
work. Within a very few years, however, Cary himself, the enthusiastic promoter, had to confess that the whole scheme of
employment was a financial failure, as neither the children nor
the adults could, at the current price of their wares, produce as
much in gross profit as it cost to organise and direct their labour,
let alone supply them with food and clothing.

A similar result had to be reported, a century later, about
the Shrewsbury " House of Industry ", which was established in
1783, and managed under the best possible auspices for a whole
decade. The plan " to furnish employment for the poor and com-

---

to the proposal . . . *relieving, reforming and employing all the poor of Great
Britain*, 1722, both by Lawrence Braddon ; *A Corporation humbly proposed
for Relieving, Reforming and Employing the Poor*, in a Letter to a Justice of the
Peace of Middlesex, 1720 ; *An Account of the Charge for Supporting the Poor in
the City of Norwich*, by J. F., 1720 ; *Proposed preventions of all stockjobbing and
bubbling in relation to the desired Charter and Commission for relieving, reforming
and employing the Poor, in a letter to an eminent lawyer*, 1722 ; *Letter to a
Member of Parliament concerning the employing and providing for the poor*,
Dublin, 1723 ; *Ways and Means for Suppressing Beggary by erecting General
Hospitals and Charitable Corporations with an account of that at Jurus*, by
Abraham Castries, 1726 ; *A Devonshire Hospital, being a Treatise showing how
the poor of the County of Devon may be provided for*, by a Philo-Devonian,
Exeter, 1727 ; *Proposals to the Mayor, Justices &c. of Boston for Maintaining
the Poor*, 1732 ; *Some Considerations for employing the Poor of this Kingdom*,
etc., by an M.P., 1737 ; *A New Scheme for reducing the Laws relating to the Poor
into one Act of Parliament*, 1737 ; *An Inquiry into the Causes of the Increase
and Miseries of the Poor of England*, 1738 ; *Directions for High and Petty
Constables, Churchwardens, Overseers of the Poor &c. that they may not err in
the execution of their Several Offices, Settlements of the Poor &c.*, by J. H., 1741 ;
*A Short View of the Frauds, Abuses and Impositions of Parish Officers with some
Considerations on the Laws relating to the Poor*, 1744.

pel them to earn their own support " seemed at first successful.
They were put to preparing, spinning and weaving wool, whilst
" at the same time working rooms or shops were set apart for the
shoemakers, etc., where those paupers who had been brought up
to these occupations were immediately employed, the most intelligent and trusty being appointed to cut out the work, and
superintend the rest ". The usual result ensued in a great
diminution of pauperism, and the experiment was copied in
half a dozen other places. But within a few years it was recognised that the industrial work in such institutions was being
carried on at a pecuniary loss. The industries, we are told by a
later observer, are " worked by the able-bodied inmates in such a
feeble and languid manner that the occupation is anything but
calculated to preserve, much less generate, habits of industry ".[1]

An equally striking experiment was put in operation in the
dozen or more unions of parishes in Suffolk and Norfolk, in which,
as we have described, new Poor Law Authorities were incorporated by Acts of Parliament from 1756 onward and workhouses built for the employment of the poor. Here they were
put to weaving corn-sacks out of hemp : making ploughlines and
various other sorts of twine and cordage ; spinning, weaving,
and knitting wool and hemp into sacking, cloth and stockings ;
making fishing-nets and cultivating the land. The result was,
so far as industrial profit was concerned, the most uniform and
dismal failure. At workhouse after workhouse the various manufactures that were tried had eventually to be given up, owing to
the impossibility of so securing either honest management or
continuous industry, either economical purchase of the raw
materials or the full market price for the commodities produced.
Nor was any greater financial success achieved when the workers
were employed at piecework rates away from the workhouse
atmosphere. In the Samford Hundred Union, one of the

---

[1] *Some Account of the Shrewsbury House of Industry*, by Isaac Wood, 1791 ;
a work which went through five editions ; *Report of the Committee appointed to
collect information and documents as to the inexpediency of repealing the . . .
Shrewsbury Incorporated House of Industry Act*, 1824 ; Report of Poor Law
Inquiry Commissioners, 1834, Appendix A, Lewis's Report, p. 659 ; *Statutory
Authorities for Special Purposes*, by S. and B. Webb, 1922, pp. 116-121. Of
the neighbouring Ellesmere House of Industry, established in imitation of
Shrewsbury in 1791, Sir F. M. Eden could report in 1797 that " notwithstanding
the promised advantages of this institution, it is said that the incorporated
parishes are, in general, heartily sorry that they ever engaged in the erection "
(*State of the Poor*, by Sir F. M. Eden, 1797, vol. ii. pp. 619-620).

Suffolk incorporations under Local Acts, where arrangements for the employment of the indoor poor had long existed, the system was extended in 1831 to women and children living in their own homes. Twenty knitting schools were established in different villages where knitting was taught and the work carried on. The worsted yarn spun in the workhouse was given out to these schools and, through the agency of the schoolmistress, also to women and children working at home. The stockings and vests so knitted were paid for at fixed rates for each article ; and they had then to be sold for the profit of the institution. The result was calamitous, the small sums obtained being often no more than the price at which the yarn could have been bought at Norwich.

Apart, however, from the Houses of Industry, established under the Incorporated Guardians of the Poor, it is of interest to see, in " the Articles and Orders to be observed " in the hundreds of little workhouses that were, during the eighteenth century, developing out of parish poorhouses, or which were, here and there, established under the general statute of 1723, the same vision of profitable manufactures to be carried on in relief of the rates. We find detailed instructions as to the character of the employment to be given, the trades to be undertaken and the hours to be worked ; where the raw material was to be bought, what processes were to be used, and how the finished product was to be disposed of.[1] Most frequently, as will already have been noticed, the work chosen was the production of coarse textile fabrics from hemp, flax or wool. Thus at Minchinhampton in 1796, the Vestry orders half a hundredweight of flax or hemp to be bought, at tenpence or a shilling per pound, to be spun and worked up in the workhouse.[2] Notwithstanding the failure on this occasion to make any profit, we see, a generation later, the same Vestry making a more ambitious attempt. " It is unanimously agreed that an institution should be formed for employing the poor in wool-spinning " ; and a committee, including local

---

[1] The Greenwich " Articles and Orders " contain a separate section headed " Rules for Management of Trade ", including provisions that the mops are to be made in strict conformity with the specification approved by the committee, and they are to be sold only for ready money and in batches of not less than six (MS. Vestry Minutes, Greenwich, July 1, 1808 ; also printed in the volume entitled *Account of the Legacies, Gifts, Rents, Fees, etc., appertaining to the Church and Poor . . . of St. Alphege, Greenwich*, by John Kimbell, 1816).

[2] MS. Vestry Minutes, Minchinhampton (Glos.), January 19, 1796.

millowners, is authorised to lay out £150 from the parish funds
in this manufacturing enterprise, for which the local squire, " Mr.
Ricardo ", a son of the economist, agrees to lend a house.[1] The
result, we learn, was financially quite unsatisfactory. The Isle
of Wight workhouse carried on for some time a manufacture of
linsey-woolsey and drill ; but subsequently turned to embroidery
and lace-making by the girls.[2] In the workhouse of the Bosmere
and Clayton Union (Suffolk) the inmates were, in 1833, found
spinning wool, weaving cloth, making bedding and knitting
stockings.[3] In the Mutford and Lothingland workhouse there
was a fishing-net manufactory, the twine being brought in by
the smack-owners, the children " braiding " the twine and the
men filling the needles for the children.[4] At Kendal, in 1800,
the workhouse begins the manufacture of " hardens ", a kind of
coarse sacking, the children teasing the wool by hand and the
adults weaving the yarn on the hand-loom, which was continued
for nearly fifty years.[5] The extensive workhouse at Liverpool
included a cotton-cloth manufactory, which turned out, in 1825,
no less than 5785 pieces, containing 173,550 yards.[6] Chelsea
in 1792 had even tried silk manufacture, with what success we
are not informed.[7] This industry was carried on, too, in the
Sudbury workhouse, to the extent of keeping a few hand-looms,
on which paupers who knew how to weave were employed on

[1] M.S. Vestry Minutes, Minchinhampton (Glos.), October 31, 1828. The
Norwich Guardians employed the inmates of their workhouse in the local
industry of spinning and weaving worsted (MS. Minutes, Incorporated Guardians,
Norwich, June 7, 1803).

[2] Report of Poor Law Inquiry Commissioners, 1834, Appendix A, Pringle's
Report, p. 305 ; *General View of the Agriculture of Hampshire*, by A. and W.
Driver, p. 64.

[3] Report of Poor Law Inquiry Commissioners, Appendix A, Stuart's Report,
p. 360. The knitting by hand of stockings and other garments seems to have
been carried on in practically all the Suffolk and Norfolk workhouses. Framework
knitting was for some time done in the workhouse at Basford (Notts), but the
frames were standing idle in 1833 (*ibid.* Appendix A, Wylde's Report, p. 151).

[4] *Ibid.* Appendix A, Stuart's Report, p. 363, and Appendix C, p. 195.

[5] *Ibid.* p. 312 ; also *Annals of Kendal*, by Cornelius Nicholson, 1861 ; Sir
F. M. Eden's *State of the Poor*, 1797, vol. iii. pp. 750, 771. Similar work seems
to have been done in 1832 in the workhouse at Wangford (Suffolk) (Report of
Poor Law Inquiry Commissioners, Appendix C, p. 192). In the Blything
Hundred workhouse at Sudbury (Suffolk), a quantity of hempen cloth was
woven in 1833, the yarn being spun by the children (*ibid.* Appendix C, pp.
187-190). Common sack-making was done at Winchester, Rugby, the Isle of
Wight and other places.

[6] MS. Vestry Minutes, Liverpool, April 5, 1825.

[7] MS. Vestry Minutes, Chelsea, June 7, 1792.

Q

materials sent in by the master-manufacturers of the district.[1] The same industry was pursued on a more extensive scale in the Coventry workhouse.[2]   Christchurch, Spitalfields, had thirty-five looms in the workhouse, on which the paupers made bunting, from material supplied by a contractor, who paid for the work done.   The paupers were allowed twopence in the shilling.[3]   In the workhouse of St. Anne, Soho, the women were employed in needlework for ready-made linen garments, and the men in picking hair and carding wool for the upholsterers ; both receiving one-sixth of their earnings.[4]   St. Paul's, Covent Garden, carried on needlework, picking and sorting hair and making sacking, but its speciality was carpet-beating, which it performed for many of the nobility and gentry of the West End.[5]   Other businesses carried on in Metropolitan workhouses were picking and winding cotton, cutting wood, stripping feathers, making paper bags, polishing horn and heading pins.[6]   The inmates of the workhouses at Shardlow (Derbyshire) were employed in 1833 in " manufacturing hemp, grinding corn, [making] framework stockings, list shoes, whipcord, winding cotton, [making] list and carpeting, running lace, seaming and sewing, working in the house and kitchen ".[7]   At Hackney, a special committee reported that " the most useful means of employing the poor within the house " were, for boys, spinning "shule" for floorcloth manufacturers, picking oakum and winding twills for weavers ; for girls, spinning flax, wool and hemp, knitting woollen garments, picking feathers, making sacks for the army, twisting yarn for the fringe manufacturers and common needlework ; for men,

---

[1] Report of Poor Law Inquiry Commissioners, Appendix A, Stuart's Report, p. 375.

[2] *Ibid.* Appendix A, Villiers' Report, p. 22.

[3] Report from the House of Commons Committee on the Poor Law, 1817 (Heaver's evidence).

[4] Report of Poor Law Inquiry Commissioners, Appendix A, Codd's Report, p. 55.

[5] *Ibid.* p. 58.   [6] *Ibid.* p. 60.

[7] *Ibid.* Pilkington's Report, p. 395.   An earlier pleasing vision of a London workhouse—a newly erected large building, then considered a model establishment—may be cited.   " I had ", wrote Jonas Hanway in 1780, " great pleasure lately on occasion of visiting the workhouse of St. Martin's in the Fields, in seeing one apartment filled with very decent women who I presume were come to decay, working with their needle on fine linen, taken in as work to be paid for, towards the support of the workhouse.   In another room was a number of little girls making cauls for wigs : their appearance also did honour to humanity " (*The Citizen's Monitor*, by Jonas Hanway, 1780, p. 141).

picking oakum, knotting rope, making cordage, twine and chains for bricklayers' scaffolds.[1] At Devonport, the account for junk and oakum was considerable, and represented a great deal of oakum picking, which was nearly everywhere a task set to men.[2] In Buckinghamshire, in 1812, " the making of lace and the plaiting of straw employ all the women, boys, girls and children throughout the county ; it is impossible to pass a poorhouse without seeing some persons so employed ".[3]

Here we digress to describe ways of employing the poor which neither depended on an organised House of Industry, nor involved the making of pecuniary profit, but which seemed, at least, to be productive of public advantage, and to effect a saving of public expense. Thus at Liverpool, in the severe winter of 1767–1768, the Town Council employed a great number of destitute labourers to clear an abandoned stone quarry, and erect an artificial mound, which became one of the earliest municipal recreation grounds.[4] At Mitcham in 1812, we find a Vestry meeting called "to consider the most effectual means of employing the several families now depending on the parish for subsistence ". It was unanimously " agreed to and ordered that several men should forthwith be employed on the highways in scraping the roads, others in digging and sifting gravel (for store) for the use of the several roads of this parish ".[5]

In the bad times of 1816 such parish employment of the poor became, for the moment, a common panacea. The funds for the purpose were taken indiscriminately from the poor rate or the highway rate, or obtained by voluntary subscriptions. Vestries, as at Greenwich, were " impressed with a serious sense of the Eventful Nature of the Times ", and conceived themselves each to be " standing forward to take its part in a great work of national importance, namely that each parish in the nation should devise as far as possible speedy and lasting means of finding within its

---

[1] MS. Minutes, Incorporated Guardians, Hackney, February 5, 1811. Mop making was done at Greenwich, Lymington and elsewhere, and plaiting straw for sailors' hats employed the inmates of the Portsea workhouse (Report of Poor Law Inquiry Commissioners, Appendix A, Pringle's Report, p. 291).

[2] MS. Minutes, Improvement Commissioners, Devonport, November 13, 1818 ; MS. Minutes, Incorporated Guardians, Devonport, June 25, 1828.

[3] *General View of the Agriculture of Buckinghamshire*, by Rev. St. John Priest, 1813, p. 81.

[4] *Annals of Liverpool*, by Sir James Allanson Picton, 1875, vol. i. p. 205.

[5] MS. Vestry Minutes, Mitcham (Surrey), December 9, 1812.

own district employment for its own poor ". With this object
the Greenwich Vestry improved the roads, lowered the hills,
and established an " extensive night watch ", thereby, as we
learn, preventing " fearful moral depravity . . . by keeping
from the minds of the labouring poor that worst of all evils,
idleness " [1] It was with this view of devising a " lasting means "
of " finding within its own district employment for its own
poor ", that the Overseers of a parish so often entered into
contracts with the local Town Council or Improvement Commissioners for cleansing the streets and removing the refuse.
Thus, both at Plymouth and at Brighton we find the statutory
body of Poor Law Guardians bargaining with the statutory
body of Improvement Commissioners as to the terms on which
the paupers shall be employed to " remove the dung and soil of
the town ".[2] In the rural parishes it was common for the
Surveyor of Highways to oblige the Overseer by engaging the
able-bodied paupers to work on the roads, and in some cases
the two offices would be held in combination by a single paid
assistant, with the express object of avoiding the triangular
wrangle that otherwise arose between Surveyor, Overseer and
paupers, as to the date, speed and pay at which the work should
be done.

In a few cases there were " parish farms " on which the
paupers were employed. Usually this was merely a development of putting the poor to work on the roads. When the " idle
and unprofitable " character of road work became apparent, a
few acres of land would be hired, and applicants for relief would
be put to digging. How much the small and costly crops of
potatoes thus raised contributed towards the wages paid to the
labourers is extremely doubtful. In one instance, at any rate,

[1] MS. Vestry Minutes, Greenwich (Kent), June 6, 1817.

[2] MS. Minutes, Incorporated Guardians, Plymouth (Devon), December 26,
1827, April 9 and June 25, 1828 ; MS. Minutes, Incorporated Guardians,
Brighton (Sussex), April 12, 1824. In 1832 an interesting report was obtained
by the Select Vestry of St. George's, Hanover Square, as to the numbers,
wages and work of the paupers employed by ten other important parishes of
London. From six to seventy-two men were employed in each parish, at from
8s. to 12s. per week, in sweeping, cleansing and watering the streets. In the
end the Paving Committee of the Vestry agreed with the Directors of the Poor
that experience showed " that it is not advisable to recommend the system of
watering the streets by paupers ", but " that the Surveyor be directed to turn
his mind to the subject of increasing the number of paupers employed in
sweeping the streets " (MS. Vestry Minutes, St. George's, Hanover Square
(London), July 26, 1832).

we find a parish conducting a regular farm for over eighty years. At Cranbrook in Kent, a farm of 499 acres was, about 1774, taken by the parish trustees (a committee of the local gentry) at a rental of £302 a year, and conducted with borrowed capital. In 1816 they were farming 429 acres at a rent of £448 a year. In addition to about twenty labourers who were permanently employed, the farm found employment, without other wages than " pence money ", for an average of thirty men and boys living in the poorhouse, and it is stated to have been extremely useful in training the boys for agricultural work. In times of high prices the farm seems to have yielded a substantial income to the parish, and in 1830 its continuance was deliberately decided on. This enterprise, which continued to be managed by a body of six trustees, in consultation with a parish committee, seems to have lasted altogether over eighty years. In 1855 the Poor Law Board, notwithstanding its financial success, required the parish to give it up ; " and after discharging all their liabilities they (the trustees) were left with a handsome balance of between £3000 and £4000 ", which it is said that they paid over to the Poor Law Board.[1] We state the facts as we find them recorded, but we must own to some curiosity about this unique example.[2]

The report of the House of Commons Committee on the Poor Laws in 1817, for which Sturges Bourne and Frankland Lewis were mainly responsible, was so far favourable to the parish farm as to lead to the grant by Parliament in 1819 of express powers to Churchwardens and Overseers, with the consent of the Vestry, to utilise any parish land, or to buy or hire land up to twenty acres, in order to set to work, in the cultivation of such land, any able-bodied men needing relief. These were to be paid " reasonable wages " and to have the status of independent wage-earners. Moreover, the parish officers and Vestry might

---

[1] *The Weald of Kent*, by Robert Furley, 1871, vol. ii. part ii. p. 668 ; compare the detailed account by Sir John Sinclair, printed as Appendix D to Report of House of Commons Committee on Poor Laws, 1817 ; the Report of the Poor Law Inquiry Commissioners, 1834, Appendix, p. 210, Majendie's Report.

[2] It should be added that at Benenden, also in Kent, and not far from Cranbrook, it was stated in 1816 that the parish had for ten years farmed a hundred acres by pauper labour, and that it claimed to have made a profit of £200 a year (Sir John Sinclair's Report, Appendix D to Report of House of Commons Committee on Poor Laws, 1817).

let any of its land at a reasonable rent for cultivation by independent smallholders.[1]

Whatever may have been done in particular cases, the scanty information about parish farms seems nearly always to relate to brief experiments, quickly abandoned as unsuccessful, with unsatisfactory financial results.[2]　An able critic reported in 1832 as follows : " I have never found parochial farms, upon any considerable extent, to succeed.　The Parish Officer will not overlook them in the same manner as if his own immediate interests were at stake, nor could he (if he were so disposed) keep a diligent eye upon so many men as spade husbandry would employ.　The parish, too, would be much at his mercy, and the men at day work would not do half a day's work, and those at task work would endeavour to do it imperfectly.　But on the other hand, it must not be supposed that a parish could get on with no land, as in that case the payments to applicants would soon increase immensely.　The proper quantity of land to be kept in the hands of the parish is that which will furnish the applicants for employment with task work." [3]　On this view many rural parishes, without really contemplating farming, would take care to have at their disposal a small plot of land on which able-bodied men applying for relief could be set to work.　We read that in 1832 " The parish of Boldre (Hants) has lately taken a farm upon which they employ their applicants for

---

[1] 59 George III. c. 12, sec. 12-14, 1819.　These powers were subject to the limitation that not more than a shilling rate could be so expended in any year without the consent of a majority of the ratepayers in Vestry assembled, together with the written assent of two-thirds in value of them ; or by way of annuity for a term of years, with the like consent, not exceeding in total value five shillings in the pound.　The maximum of land was raised to fifty acres by 1 and 2 William IV. c. 42, 1831.　We believe that few, if any, parishes ever put these powers in force from 1819 to 1834 ; and none were subsequently permitted to do so.　(*History of the English Poor Law*, by Sir George Nicholls, 1854, vol. ii. pp. 196-197, 214-217.)

[2] Three minor projects connected with land tenure may here be mentioned. By 1 and 2 William IV. c. 42, 1831, the Churchwardens and Overseers were empowered (if they could get the consent of the lord of the manor and all other persons owning rights) to enclose not exceeding fifty acres of waste or common, and to cultivate or let any portion of it for the benefit of the parish. By 1 and 2 William IV. c. 59, 1831, the Churchwardens and Overseers were empowered with the consent of the Treasury, to enclose not exceeding fifty acres of Crown lands with similar objects.　And by 2 William IV. c. 42, 1831, the parish authorities were authorised to let any land they owned for allotments to " industrious cottagers of good character ", the rent to be used to purchase fuel to be distributed in the winter among the " poor parishioners ".

[3] Report of Poor Law Inquiry Commissioners, 1834, Appendix C, p. 2.

relief . . . and have thus succeeded in driving away the majority of applicants ".[1] In some of the Metropolitan parishes, where the Surveyors of Highways cordially co-operated with the Overseers, the severe work of breaking the stone for macadamising the roads, done under supervision at piecework rates, was used with success as a test of destitution for able-bodied men. An average workman could earn ten shillings a week at this work, but " not more than one in ten of those who apply for relief, and are sent to work, come to or remain " at the stone-yard. So at Putney, in 1818–1819, when the Overseer "organised a plan for employing the able-bodied in digging and wheeling gravel " at piecework rates, the number in receipt of this substitute for relief gradually fell away to two, and the total rates were reduced by one-half. Unfortunately, the cases in which employment of this sort could be found were, owing to the absence of any sort of unity in the London local administration of the time, with its multiplicity of paving boards and estate trusts, far below the requirements of the able-bodied pauperism of the whole Metropolis.[2] In the celebrated instance of the parish of Cookham, in Berkshire, where Whately was the incumbent, the plan was adopted, whenever able-bodied men applied for relief, of " giving them hard work at low wages by the piece, and exacting more work at a lower price than is paid for any other labour in the parish. . . . The work provided was trenching ; an acre of hard gravelly ground was hired for the purpose. . . . About sixty-three heads of families, which were formerly constantly on the parish, now at once disappeared." [3]

At Norwich in 1826, when many mechanics and weavers were out of employment, and a large fund was raised in London in relief of the general distress of the manufacturing population, the Paving Commissioners agreed to macadamise one of the streets, half the wages of the men at the rate of 1s. per day being

---

[1] Report of Poor Law Inquiry Commissioners, 1834, Appendix C, p. 2.

[2] *Ibid.* Appendix A, Codd's Report, pp. 54–59.

[3] *Ibid.* Chadwick's Report, p. 25. Other parishes that were reputed to have been similarly " reformed " by the exaction of spade labour from every able-bodied male applicant for relief were Hatfield, Welwyn, St. Mary's, Nottingham, White Waltham, Swallowfield and Downham (*The Rights of Industry*, part iii., " On the Best Form of Relief to the Able-bodied Poor ", by G. Poulett Scrope, 1848, p. 18). These experiences did not make for the panacea of a " well-regulated workhouse " that was preferred by the Poor Law Inquiry Commissioners ; and they were accordingly given no prominence in their General Report of 1834.

paid by the Incorporated Guardians and half from the charitable funds. Later on it was found preferable, taking a hint from the experience of Nottingham and other towns, to pay for the work by the piece instead of by day wages, with the result that far more work was done per head per day, and three-fourths of the able-bodied and unmarried applicants for relief, being refused anything except this employment, declined to accept it. So successful seemed the experiment that, when the Paving Commissioners would undertake no more paving work, the voluntary committee which had been formed for the relief of the poor decided to expend the grant received from London on cultivating seven acres of Mousehold Heath by spade labour. The Incorporated Guardians also took twenty-five acres of land, on which they set to work the able-bodied paupers in digging potatoes.[1] But it was at Bristol that the provision of employment, at low rates of pay, for persons residing in their own homes, was most systematically applied and most persistently continued. The Bristol Corporation of the Poor, after many vacillations of policy since its establishment in 1696, definitely adopted in 1822 the plan of refusing any other relief to able-bodied male applicants than employment in its own stone yard at Clifton, under strict supervision by a paid ganger having the authority of a police constable. " The general principle ", it was said, was " to insist upon early hours and attendance during the full working hours, so that the pauper may not only earn little pay, but go home fatigued and tired. . . . Under these circumstances it seems to have proved possible to dispense with piece work, the men being paid from eightpence to one and eightpence per day, according to the size of their families. When persons stand the test of such work during a month, or sometimes a fortnight, and thus give proof of their readiness to work, they are furnished . . . with a ticket for a fortnight's pay to enable them to seek employment elsewhere ; if they do not succeed they have only to return." For the women and infirm men, workshops were taken in the town, and employment was there provided in making lace, plaiting straw, winding worsted and knitting. Here, too, there was no payment by the piece, the workers being paid for twelve hours' employment from sevenpence to one and sevenpence per day, according to the size of their families. One day in every

[1] *Norfolk Chronicle*, January 28, February 4, May 13 and June 3, 1826.

week was not paid for, the pauper being required to spend it at whatever part of the week he chose, in looking for other employment. On these forms of relief with task work, the Bristol Corporation of the Poor spent, between 1822 and 1833, £250 to £350 per week, without pecuniary profit, but, as they believed, with great success in relieving the worthy, whilst discouraging the merely idle and profligate.[1]

It is, however, plain that we have, in these later instances, got far away from the " profitable employment of the poor ", in the sense in which this phrase was used by the philanthropists and legislators of the seventeenth century, or in which it awakened the hopes of successive generations of reformers in the course of the eighteenth and nineteenth centuries. Such success as was achieved in any of these experiments was not in the pecuniary result of " setting the poor to work ", but in its deterrent effect, with which we shall deal hereafter.

Why the Workhouse as a Means of profitably employing the Poor was always a Financial Failure

By the end of the eighteenth century it had become everywhere apparent that the panacea of so organising the labour of the poor as to make it yield a profit, whether in " Houses of Industry " or parish workhouses, was an utter failure. If we may believe the returns presented to Parliament by the industry of John Rickman and Thomas Poole in 1805,[2] the total value of

---

[1] Report of Poor Law Inquiry Commissioners, Appendix A, Chapman's Report, pp. 512-513.

[2] The Act 43 George III. c. 144 (1803), passed at the instance of George Rose, the ablest of Pitt's lieutenants, required elaborate returns to be made by the Overseers of all parishes, through the High Constables and Clerks of the Peace, to the Secretary of State at the Home Office. As fees were allowed to all the local officers, and made payable by Quarter Sessions, voluminous returns were made, and John Rickman and Thomas Poole were specially engaged to tabulate them. See the charming *Thomas Poole and his Friends*, by Mrs. Henry Sandford, 1888, vol ii. chap. v. The subsequent annual returns were arranged for the printer by the clerks at the House of Commons, who were paid extra for this labour ; but Rickman's life, from 1816 to 1839, was largely devoted to the tabulation of these and other returns by Local Authorities (*Life of John Rickman*, by Orlo Williams, 1912, p. 134).

For the year ended March 25, 1832, " Out of £7,036,968 expended in that year for the relief of the poor, less than £354,000, or scarcely more than one-twentieth part, was paid for work, including work on the roads and in the workhouses " (General Report of the Poor Law Inquiry Commissioners, 1834, p. 36).

the manufactures produced in all the English workhouses was £70,970, as against £39,558 spent in materials alone, showing for the year a surplus available for maintenance or wages, and all other expenses, of no more than £31,412, or just over £600 per week—perhaps amounting on an average to no more than a few shillings per day for each workhouse. In many workhouses the produce of sales did not even repay the outlay on materials. Where a so-called profit was shown, this invariably took no account either of establishment charges or of the food and clothing of the paupers employed ; and was nevertheless, at best, insignificant in amount per person. From the standpoint of making each pauper earn his own bread the failure of the workhouse manufactories was ludicrous in its completeness. Instead of the average earnings of half a crown a week each hoped for by Sir Matthew Hale, or of four shillings expected by Henry Fielding, the most successful workhouses only showed gross " profits " of less than a penny a day for each person employed.[1]

The reasons for this uniform failure to make the pauper maintain himself, let alone yield profit to his employer, are many

---

[1] Towards the end of the eighteenth century the whole subject was ably examined and fiercely argued ; see, for instance, *The True Alarm, or an Essay showing the Pernicious Influence of Houses of Industry*, 1787 ; and especially the valuable *Observations on Various Plans offered to the Public for the Relief of the Poor*, by Joseph Townsend, 1788.

We give some figures of the actual " profits " (being surplus of sales over cost of materials) made by typical workhouses, drawn from various sources, extending over more than a century. At Chatham, in 1725, the 73 inmates earned only £25 in the year ; and at Peterborough in 1724, 219 inmates produced only £21. In 1816–1817 seven workhouses in Kent showed " net earnings " varying from £22 to £172, giving the unusually high average of £1 : 8 : 6 per head per annum, or about one penny per day (Report of House of Commons Committee on Poor Laws, 1817). The Bosmere and Clayton workhouse in 1832 made £69 " after charging the price of the raw material and the wages of the mechanics who are hired to conduct the manufacture, together with small rewards to the inmates who are engaged in it, and taking credit for the sales and house consumption " (Report of Poor Law Inquiry Commissioners, 1834, Appendix A, p. 361). The Mutford and Lothingland workhouse made, with its 230 inmates, " upwards of £200 " (p. 365). At Frome the " profit " was £108 (p. 425). The Isle of Wight workhouse, with 667 inmates, only made £58 in 1832 (p. 305), though it was said, in 1817, to be making from £150 to £200 a year (Report of House of Commons Committee on Poor Laws, 1817, Sewell's evidence). The most profitable that we have discovered was the workhouse at Liverpool, which was universally regarded as a great success, and which, with its thousand inmates, made in 1824 as much as £450, or no more than a few pence per person per week ; followed, moreover, in 1826, by no profit whatever (MS. Vestry Minutes, Liverpool, April 5, 1825).

and complicated. It was not merely that it was never possible, in the infantile condition of public administration in the eighteenth century, to secure, for long, even honest management, still less skilful and zealous industrial organisation. There was no idea of a systematic and regular audit : hardly anywhere, indeed, were detailed accounts kept with any system or regularity. The choice of the industry to be carried on was necessarily made with scanty information and without experience. The management had to be entrusted to persons without special training, who had little or no interest, pecuniary or otherwise, in making a profit. The provision of the necessary plant, the purchases of raw material and the sales of the product were all inevitably con-ducted less advantageously than by the individual manufacturer. Nor is the invariable financial failure to be explained only by the inferiority of the labour in intensity or speed, though this goes a long way. There was practically no choice of operatives —indeed, there was automatically a constant adverse selection of those who, from age, state of health, weakness of character or positive vice, were least fit to earn their living—and such as were employed had practically no incentive to exert themselves. " No man ", sums up one Assistant Poor Law Commissioner, " will give his heart to the work when he knows that the only object in his employment is to keep him from idleness, or from plotting mischief, and no vigilance on the part of the taskmaster can enforce it." [1] No less apparent was the failure from the standpoint of securing good conduct, order and discipline among the paupers themselves. The inmates of a workhouse had neces-sarily to be provided with complete maintenance, whether they did much work or little ; and the mere cost of food and clothing was found to come to much more than the pittance elsewhere given by way of Outdoor Relief. The workhouse inmate, secure of his living, could naturally not be induced to give any very strenuous labour. In the eighteenth century every sort of punishment was tried, without effectually increasing the output over any length of time. With the growth of humanitarian feel-ings, and the withdrawal by Parliament in 1814–1816 of the special penal powers accorded in Local Acts, governors of workhouses found it hopeless to exact labour from men who chose to be

---

[1] Report of Poor Law Inquiry Commissioners, Appendix A, Stuart's Report, p. 346.

obstinate in their idleness. A system of rewards was often tried ; but out of gross earnings so small as seldom to amount to a penny a day, no appreciable inducement could be offered, and any such promise to the paupers usually ate up all the profit.[1] All these disadvantages were accentuated, after 1770, by the Industrial Revolution which, in trade after trade, was making inevitable an incessant change in machinery, the redivision of labour and, most important of all, the use of water or steam power—transformations which were impracticable under the conditions of workhouse industry.[2] We shall, however, miss the most pregnant lesson unless we realise that the financial failure is rooted in the fallacy that the mere application of labour in itself ensures the production of commodities of exchange value. Profitable production, as the Consumers' Co-operative Movement has discovered, must start from an actual demand by consumers, ascertained or correctly foreseen ; and, if pecuniary loss is to be avoided, it is this demand that must govern the kind, the amount, the place and the date of the production. To employ the unemployed, wherever they happen to be, just because they are unemployed and when they are unemployed—still more, to set them to work on what they can do rather than on what is re-

---

[1] At Wangford (Suffolk), where a sack and coarse cloth manufactory was started in the House of Industry, it was reported in 1832 that "several of the inmates have been committed to prison for disorderly conduct and refusing to work, in spite of the fact that the gratuities and rewards to paupers residing in the House amount in late years to £120 per annum ", and no profit could be reported (Report of Poor Law Inquiry Commissioners, Appendix C, Clarke's Report, p. 192). In the neighbouring Hundred of Bosmere and Clayton " the inmates were set to work on spinning wool, but the employment was so intricate and perplexing to these rough fellows, that there was a constant succession of mutinies, and outdoor relief to this description of pauper was at last admitted " (*ibid.* Appendix A, Stuart's Report, p. 360).

[2] The economic deficiencies of workhouses as manufacturing establishments were well described by an able contractor in 1832. " I found manufacturing in the workhouse objectionable on several grounds. . . . You can rarely get anything to pay the expenses because with paupers you cannot enforce . . . that regularity . . . and attention to small savings which a manufacturer can enforce from paid workmen. These small savings make the profit of the manufacturer. Then machinery has made such progress that, unless the workhouse was formed into one immense manufactory, I do not believe that, if the raw material were given to the parish, any return could be obtained for pauper labour. Both with the adults and the children there is great loss in teaching them the trade. Besides this you must get a paid superintendent, for I never knew a pauper who, even if he were well acquainted with any branch of manufacture, could be depended on as superintendent of a department " (Report of Poor Law Inquiry Commissioners, Chadwick's Report, p. 197, Mott's evidence).

quired, or even at their own trades just because their own trades are slack—is to ignore the requirement that exchange value can be produced, not by labour as such, but only by laboriously satisfying in some way a spontaneous demand, which has therefore to be ascertained and conformed to.

From the standpoint of institutional administration, what was even more important than the commercial failure was the demoralisation caused by the relaxation of discipline incident upon the introduction of manufacturing processes into an establishment containing men, women and children of all ages and the most diverse conditions. All classification of the paupers according to age, sex or previous conduct had to give way to the division of labour required by the processes of the industry; with the result that old and young, male and female, innocent and depraved, worked side by side, in the workroom or weaving shed, where the standard of zeal in work, order in conduct and decency in conversation tended inevitably to be set by the worst and wickedest.

It is clear that, whether from the standpoint of pecuniary result or from that of effect on character, the use of the workhouse as a manufacturing establishment was, as regards the able-bodied men, far inferior to the provision of tasks of employment for men residing in their own homes. The man living in the workhouse had to be completely maintained, however little work was got out of him. The man living at home could be offered a task at a definite rate of piecework pay, which was, in practice, much less than the cost of maintaining him in an establishment with a fixed dietary and a salaried staff. What was still more effective in securing industry, regularity and order, the man living at home found his maintenance absolutely dependent on his conduct—if his task was not done, he did not get the money to take home to buy his food with. Hence we find the Corporation of the Poor of the City of Bristol, established for the express purpose of creating a House of Industry, had very soon transformed their St. Peter's Hospital into quite another kind of institution. When inspected in 1833 their carefully classified workhouse was " an infirmary or hospital ", used for the aged, the sick, the lunatic and the children. Able-bodied applicants for relief were not admitted, but were given relief, under strict discipline, in the form of task work in a stone-yard.

In the case of the tens of thousands of orphan or neglected children in the workhouses the failure was of another character. The docility and complete dependence of these little workers— their inability to abscond and the facility with which they could be punished—seemed to make their compulsory labour almost as profitable as if it had been freely tendered for wages to an employer, whilst the superior authority exercised by the workhouse master appeared to give him, in this exceptional case, a positive advantage over private enterprise. At a certain stage in the evolution of industrial processes, when machinery has superseded physical strength and has not itself yet become rapid or complicated—a stage which various textile industries passed at different dates in the eighteenth century—the labour of little children is particularly applicable. This explains the oft-repeated and now scarcely credible statement that " at four years of age there are sundry employments in which children can earn their living ".[1]

But with regard to children other considerations came more and more into view. From the first the profit to be obtained from the children's labour had been regarded, by enlightened enthusiasts like John Cary, as of secondary importance. There seemed no alternative to their passing their childhood in a Poor Law institution ; and what had really to be aimed at was their training for self - support in adult life. It became, however, more and more recognised that in this respect, no less than in the matter of pecuniary profit, the employment of children in workhouse industries, conducted with commercial objects, was a complete failure. The industry which offered the best chance of immediately relieving the rates by the children's earnings was not that which would best enable them to earn an independent livelihood as adults. " The immediate interest of the parishes ", with regard to the children, reported C. P. Villiers in 1833, " is to relieve themselves of their charge, or to turn their work to some present advantage ; they care little therefore for their prospects in after life, and, what is of great importance, they are indifferent to the general consequences of bringing up to trades already overstocked. . . . In the workhouse at Worcester they

---

[1] See Edward Chamberlayne's *Angliae Notitia, or the Present State of England*, 1687, as to the profitableness of child labour at Norwich, which Macaulay refers to in a well-known passage (*History of England*, vol. i. p. 419).

are brought up to glove-making, though the grievance in the town is that the trade is leaving it. In the house at Bromsgrove in Worcestershire, the employment is making nails, at which the children all work ; this business is also overstocked, and there is a general complaint among the farmers in the neighbourhood that they cannot get domestic servants because they are all brought up to nailing. At Tewkesbury in Gloucestershire . . . it is much the practice to teach them stocking-weaving, while hundreds in that trade are unemployed." [1] The failure was even more obvious when no genuine attempt was made to teach any trade which was carried on in the neighbourhood. At Alverstoke (Hants) we learn that " spinning the thread and weaving sacking is the chief employment. This, however, is of no use to the boys as a trade, and there is great difficulty in finding them places when they leave the house." [2] At the Isle of Wight it was decided to give up weaving, because, " without being useful to the boys as a trade, it unfits them for husbandry labour ", to which most of them had to turn.[3] The Chelsea Vestry discovered that girls were returned from places found for them in domestic service because they knew nothing of household work, having been engaged exclusively in silk manufacture.[4] " Experience proves to me ", writes an able critic in 1832, " that the truest and best policy is that a workhouse education should be directed to future usefulness rather than present profit. At this moment the generality of parochial workhouses in Hampshire do not supply any effective religious and moral instruction ; the children cannot do even the coarsest needlework in a creditable manner ; nor are they practised in that kind of work which, as domestic servants, they would be required to perform." [5] Here and there an attempt began to be made at a new policy. The same critic

---

[1] Report of Poor Law Inquiry Commissioners, Appendix A, Villiers' Report, p. 6. " The great aim . . . seems to be to reduce the expense to the several parishes, on which account they endeavour to realise as much as possible by labour in manufacturing. Thus, at Winchester, and also at Rugby in Warwickshire the manufacture of sacks is carried on. This were well, provided the aged and infirm were alone employed in it ; but the boys and girls are also thus employed, and by this means are educated for sack manufacturers, but not for those purposes of life for which they are likely to be wanted, such as farming and domestic service " (*ibid.* Appendix C, p. 3).

[2] *Ibid.* Appendix A, Pringle's Report, p. 292.

[3] *Ibid.* p. 305.

[4] MS. Vestry Minutes, Chelsea, June 7, 1792.

[5] Report of Poor Law Inquiry Commissioners, Appendix C, p. 1.

describes its initiation in a small Hampshire port. " Lymington once had a mop manufactory in the house. . . . At Christmas 1830, the house was remodelled as to its discipline. All the bad female characters were turned out, and allowed so much per week (the workhouse not affording the means of a separate classifica- tion). A schoolmistress was introduced to teach needlework and reading ; the girls were taught housework, etc. ; and during the past year several have got places, others are in demand, and not one has turned out badly. Before that no one would take a girl out of the workhouse." [1]

The Workhouse as House of Correction

We need not dwell at any length upon the use of the work- house as a place of penal discipline : a kind of minor House of Correction, entered not through the portal of crime and con- viction in a court of justice, but through that of destitution or application for relief. There has been, indeed, in Tudor times, no very clear distinction between the two. A " sturdy beggar " ran a great risk of being whipped, or set in the stocks, or put in the local gaol, for no other crime than that of being destitute. In the eighteenth century, when a Local Act was sought to in- corporate a body of Governors and Directors of the Poor, or to facilitate the establishment of a House of Industry, it usually seems to have occurred to the promoters, not only to take powers to punish those who would not work, but also to give the work- house authorities large disciplinary powers over all the poor of the neighbourhood. It was common form to give the Guardians power to sentence " rogues, vagabonds, sturdy beggars or idle or disorderly persons " to one year's confinement with hard labour, for no other offence than that of being deemed to belong to one or other of the classes so designated.[2] Many Acts em- powered the Guardians, not merely to deal with such persons who voluntarily entered the workhouse, but also to " seize vagabonds ",[3] " apprehend idlers ",[4] pursue and bring back

---

[1] Report of Poor Law Inquiry Commissioners, Appendix C, p. 3.
[2] See, for instance, the Exeter Act of 1774. At Canterbury the House of Correction, or Bridewell, formed part of the workhouse ; and the paupers were incarcerated there whenever the master chose to order it.
[3] Southampton Act of 1773.
[4] Colneis and Carlford Act of 1764.

" runaway poor ", [1] or arrest and detain any child found begging
in the street. [2] The poor might be compulsorily hired out to
farmers needing hands at harvest time, [3] or to any one willing to
pay for their labour, [4] or might be simply farmed out into the
hands of a contractor to maintain and employ at a fixed price. [5]
The Plymouth Guardians obtained power in 1759 compulsorily
to ship vagrants on board any vessel that could be induced to
take them, the destination and treatment whilst on board being
apparently immaterial. The Chester Guardians even obtained a
clause in their Act of 1762 giving them power to punish the
mothers of bastard children, whether or not they became chargeable, not only by hard labour and the wearing of a special badge,
but also by public whipping.

We have no record of the justice and mercy with which these
enormous powers were exercised. The MS. minutes of the Incorporated Guardians of such towns as Gloucester and Plymouth,
Norwich and Bristol afford such glimpses as the following.
" Ordered that Ann Wheeler, mother of a base-born child now
chargeable to this house, shall receive fifty lashes according to
an advertisement sometime since inserted in the *Gloucester
Journal* for ye discouragement of bastardy, and that she be
carried to-morrow before two of the Justices of the Peace for
this city in order to swear her child " (*i.e.* declare upon oath
the name of the father). " Ordered that Sarah Davis be tasked
two shillings per week, and, if not regularly performed, be flogged
by the beadle." " Ordered that Ann Wells, who has been guilty
of embezzling sundry things in this house be punished by flogging
publicly in the Courtyard on the 6th inst., as an example for other
paupers not to be guilty of the like offences, and that Beadle
Powell be ordered to punish her." [6] Even without any special
statutory authority, the managers of workhouses seem always to
have assumed the power to inflict corporal punishment on children,
and to punish adults by solitary confinement, reduction of diet
and the stoppage of leave to go out. The " Orders to be observed "
in the Woolwich workhouse in 1732 are most explicit about the

---

[1] Montgomery and Pool Act of 1796.
[2] St. Sepulchre, London, Act of 1772.
[3] Loes and Wilford Act of 1765.
[4] Isle of Wight Act of 1771.   [5] Bermondsey (Surrey) Act of 1758.
[6] MS. Minutes, Incorporated Guardians, Gloucester, May 1, 1766, May 30,
1776 and March 3, 1785.

children. " That the children and other fit persons pick oakum and other light work, and be moderately tasked, and if they are idle and do not their tasks, or make too great waste, that they go sometimes without their meals, and sometimes have moderate corporal punishment at the discretion of the Master and Mistress." [1] At Greenwich in 1808 adult paupers who refused to work were ordered to be put in solitary confinement, and fed on bread and water ; and those who " smoke in bed ", or in any room of the house except the hall and kitchen, are to be " severely punished ".[2] The Hackney Trustees of the Poor in 1811 appointed a committee to consider how they could punish the refractory poor ; and this committee, after inspecting the place of confinement that was used, significantly report that they " do not perceive that the punishment can be increased " ; but they add a recommendation that " females with bastard children " should wear a special dress.[3] In 1816 it was stated to the House of Commons that in one workhouse there was " a young girl who had been chained to the wall with a chain that weighed 28 lbs. with which she escaped and fled to a humane person, who took the chain off and weighed it. The reason assigned for her confinement was that she was infected with a disorder which it was feared she might communicate to others." [4] The existence down to 1814 and, as we infer, the frequent use of such drastic powers, fully account for the objection to the workhouse universally entertained by the poor, and cannot have failed, we think, to strengthen the reluctance of the Justices of the Peace in most parishes to allow the deserving poor to be forced to enter these institutions. When in 1814 and 1816 the House of Commons, at the instance of Sir Samuel Romilly and Sir R. Heron, summarily withdrew all this punitive authority from the managers or masters of workhouses [5] their uses as Houses of Correction may be said to have come to an end.

[1] MS. Vestry Minutes, Woolwich, July 11, 1732.

[2] MS. Vestry Minutes, Greenwich, July 1, 1808.

[3] MS. Minutes, Hackney Trustees of the Poor, February 5, 1811.

[4] Hansard, 1816, p. 851 ; Ninth Annual Report of Poor Law Commissioners, 1843, p. 24 ; *History of the English Poor Law*, vol. iii., by Thomas Mackay, 1899, p. 337.

[5] *Life of Sir Samuel Romilly*, by himself, edition of 1842. The Act 54 George III. c. 170, besides repealing all the provisions by which Local Acts since 1714 had varied the general Law of Settlement, also repealed all the provisions enabling Poor Law Authorities to inflict corporal punishment on any adult, or to confine him as a punishment for more than twenty-four hours.

The Workhouse as a Deterrent

The workhouse as a means of employing the poor, and the workhouse as a place of discipline and correction, assumed, like the earlier poorhouse, the reception, the lasting maintenance and the continuous treatment of paupers in one way or another. The utility of the device subsequently termed the " workhouse test " lay in the success with which, even without requiring hard labour, the mere restraint of an institution was found, except in the very direst necessity, to prevent persons from applying for relief when this involved admission.

We trace the first systematic use of the " offer of the House ", as a deterrent, to the Act 9 George I. c. 7, 1723.[1] Of the promoters of this Act, and their motives, little is known to us. If we may believe a contemporary pamphlet, which was, two generations later, embodied in Sir F. M. Eden's well-known work, the statute took its origin, not from the score of Houses of Industry already then established, as we have described, under Local Acts in ancient corporate towns, where the profitable employment of the poor had proved delusive ; nor yet from the revival of an analogous project in John Bellers' *College of Industry* (1695), but from certain successful experiments in reducing pauperism carried on between 1714 and 1722 in the Home Counties by one Matthew Marryott, of Olney, Buckinghamshire.[2]

An Act of 1816, 56 George III. c. 129, forbade any compulsory removal to a workhouse and any chaining or manacling of any inmate ; any apprenticeship of a child to an officer of a workhouse, and any hiring out of paupers (*History of the English Poor Law*, by Sir George Nicholls, 1854, pp. 158, 164-165 ; Ninth Annual Report of Poor Law Commissioners, 1843, pp. 22-24).

[1] House of Commons Journals, vol. xx., November 17, December 6 and 13, January 16, 21 and 25, March 20 and 22, 1723. The Bill, as brought in by Sir Edmund Knatchbull, did not contain the workhouse clause, which was introduced in committee upon an instruction from the House.

This statute was subsequently denounced as the first breach in the " rights " of the poor under the Elizabethan Poor Law ; see, for instance, the *Financial, Monetary and Statistical History of England*, by Thomas Doubleday, 1847, p. 108. The conception of deterrence of applicants and thereby discouraging pauperism —not by the restraint of an institution, but by the exaction of hard manual labour—had been suggested in 1646 in the pamphlet entitled *Stanley's Remedy* (copiously quoted in Sir F. M. Eden's *State of the Poor*, 1797, vol. i. pp. 165-170), in which it was stated that one Harman, of Sutton Coleshill, had staved off the importunities of vagrants by putting them to work at gathering stones.

[2] The only account of this reformer, and of his experiments in workhouse management, is derived from two anonymous pamphlets, *An Account of several workhouses for employing and maintaining the poor* (of which editions were

Marryott's policy was to use the new house solely as a means of reducing pauperism. In his view " the advantage of the work-house to the parish does not arise from what the poor people can do towards their own subsistence, but from the apprehensions the poor have of it. These prompt them to exert and do their utmost to keep themselves off the parish and render them exceedingly averse to submit to come into the house until extreme necessity compels them ".[1] If Parliament acted on this view, we must credit it with having momentarily turned its back on the policy of finding profitable employment for the poor, and with having deliberately and consciously adopted what was, more than a century later, to become celebrated as the " work-house test". At any rate, one section of the Act explicitly authorised the withholding of relief from any person who refused to come into the workhouse ; and it seems to have been assumed, though this was not explicitly enacted, that under such circumstances no Justice of the Peace could order Outdoor Relief to be given. Overseers and Vestries were thus put in a position to " offer the House " to any persons whom they did not think deserving of a dole or parish pension. This evidently brought about a marked reduction of the doles and pensions. Within a

---

published in 1725 and 1732, and from which Sir F. M. Eden quotes) ; and *A Representation of some mismanagements by Parish Officers*, etc., 1726, which escaped Eden's attention. Both of these seem to have been written by Marryott himself, or by some relative of his who is said to have been governor of the workhouse at St. Giles in the Fields, London. Their object was apparently to obtain further employment for him, or even a " national testimonial " for his services in initiating a hundred and fifty workhouses, and acting as paid master or manager of nearly thirty of them. " He was ", we are told in the second pamphlet, dated 1726, " born at Olney, a market town in Buckinghamshire ; and it is now about twenty years ago since that parish was so much oppressed and overburdened with the Poor Rate that the most substantial inhabitants were in danger of being ruined by the growing charge. In these perplexing circumstances they knew not what to do ; they proposed several expedients for their preservation, but none would take, till this man, a parishioner of the place, started the design of a House of Maintenance, and though some of the inhabitants approved the hint, yet others rejected it as an impracticable novelty, so that full seven years were spent from the first motion of it, before he could bring the whole parish to begin the undertaking, which at length under his management they did, and with so much success that in two or three years time he reduced the rates to the one third part of what they amounted to before " (p. 14). He was then sent for from " far and near " to do the same service to other parishes ; and from this sprang the Act of 9 George I. c. 7 ; see *The State of the Poor*, by Sir F. M. Eden, 1797, vol. i. pp. 267-285.

[1] *An Account of several workhouses for employing and maintaining the poor*, 1732.

few years no fewer than a hundred and fifty workhouses had been built, with the result of everywhere reducing the rates. " Very great numbers of lazy people," we are told, "rather than submit to the confinement and labour of the workhouse, are content to throw off the mask and maintain themselves by their own industry " ; and this was so remarkable " at Maidstone that, when the workhouse started there in 1720 was finished, and public notice given that all who came to demand their weekly pay should immediately be sent thither, little more than half the poor upon the list came to the Overseers to receive their allowance ".[1] During the next fifty years parish after parish repeated the experiment, with the same apparent success. Thus, at Chester, when the parishes united to establish a work-house in 1750, " the Overseers were directed to stop all outdoor relief (except to casual poor) ; and no rents are, for the future, to be paid out of the Poor Rates ".[2] " The terror of a workhouse", we read in 1762, " has been everywhere found so great as to drive all idle poor out, instead of inviting others to come in to any place where they are sure to be put to hard labour." [3] In 1776 a committee of the Kensington Vestry, presided over by the Earl of Rosebery, reported that they could greatly re-duce " the weekly lists " if a workhouse were provided, as many " who are now constantly relieved . . . would not become burden-some to the parish, by entering such an establishment ".[4]

[1] *An Account of several workhouses for employing and maintaining the poor*, 1732. It will be noted that parishes had not waited for a new Act of Parliament, but had built workhouses at the expense of the poor rate, under their general powers, relying, perhaps, on the Acts of 1597 and 1623. Thus, Marryott's original workhouse at Olney seems to have been opened about 1714, and St. Martin's, Leicester, built its workhouse in the same year (see Thomas North's *Accounts of the Churchwardens of St. Martin's, Leicester, 1489-1844*, Leicester, 1844). Those of Hemel Hempstead, Maidstone, Bedford and others date from 1720, and those of Tunbridge and others from 1721 (Sir F. M. Eden's *State of the Poor*, vol. ii. pp. 266-272). Reference may be made also to *Proposals made in the year 1720 . . . to the parishioners of Stroud, near Rochester . . . for building a workhouse there ; with an account of the good success thereof, and likewise of several workhouses in Essex*, etc., by Caleb Parfect, 1725.

[2] *Lectures on the History of S. John Baptist Church and Parish*, by S. Cooper Scott, Chester, 1892, p. 148. So in the City of London parish of St. Helen's, Bishopsgate, when a workhouse was started the Vestry gave definite orders that no relief should be given except in the workhouse (MS. Vestry Minutes, April 22, 1762 ; *Annals of St. Helen's, Bishopsgate*, by J. E. Cox, 1876, p. 155).

[3] *The Case of the Parish of St. James's, Westminster, as to their Poor, and a workhouse*, 1762.

[4] MS. Vestry Minutes, Kensington, December 10, 1776.

The Workhouse as Asylum for the Impotent Poor

Throughout all these experiments the workhouse continued to be, like the rudimentary poorhouse, a refuge for the homeless poor, and all those who imperatively needed looking after. With the failure of the " profitable employment of the poor ", and the abandonment of the " offer of the House " as a deterrent, the institution became, in the last quarter of the eighteenth century, almost exclusively an asylum for the impotent.[1] The orphan and deserted children sometimes made up half the inmates. Along with these would be found the friendless old men and women, the chronically infirm and the bedridden, with a few lunatics and idiots. With them would be indiscriminately mingled the man or woman stricken with " fever " (a term which then included nearly all acute illness), persons at the point of death from phthisis, the unmarried woman in childbirth, and even the prostitute suffering from venereal disease.[2] In the well-known words of Crabbe :

> There children dwell who know no parents' care ;
> Parents, who know no children's love, dwell there !
> Heart-broken matrons on their joyless bed,
> Forsaken wives, and mothers never wed ;
> Dejected widows with unheeded tears,
> And crippled age with more than childhood's fears ;
> The lame, the blind, and, far the happiest they !
> The moping idiot and the madman gay,
> Here too the sick their final doom receive,
> Here brought, amid the scenes of grief, to grieve.[3]

To these some parish authorities added the incorrigibly idle or dissolute youth or adult man, to whose presence at large on " parish pay " the respectable inhabitants objected. Classification there was, for the most part, none ; even the separation of the sexes was little attended to. The average farmer or shopkeeper who acted as Overseer, or served on the workhouse committee, had, in fact, no other idea—when he had given up

---

[1] Gisborne, in 1794, refers to the workhouses as " those receptacles of the old and the infirm, of widows and orphans " (*Enquiry into the Duties of Man*, by T. Gisborne, 1794, p. 292).

[2] The last-named unfortunate class seems to have formed a specially large element in the London workhouses (Report of Poor Law Inquiry Commissioners, Appendix A, Codd's Report, pp. 75-79).

[3] *The Village*, by George Crabbe, 1783, book i. pp. 16-17.

the chimera of profitable employment—than that of keeping the paupers alive. If those in charge were benevolently inclined, or anxious for the custom or good opinion of their poorer neighbours, the result was an extraordinarily liberal dietary,[1] the provision of beer at every meal—sometimes even gin—permission to smoke, and freedom to come and go at will. In the West Riding of Yorkshire, we are told, " the Overseers rather

---

[1] The dietaries of the workhouses of 1780–1833 are amazing to modern notions either of health or discipline. Thus, the Brighton workhouse, typical of many others, gave all its inmates three meals a day without limit of quantity ; meat six days in the week (and the seventh, pease soup) ; the men having a quart of beer daily, the children a pint, and the women a pint of beer and a pint of tea (Report of Poor Law Inquiry Commissioners, Appendix A, Maclean's Report, p. 532). The Chester workhouse gave a hot dinner every day, of six ounces of beef (weight when boiled) and mashed potatoes, or the equivalent in Irish stew, five days a week, the other two days being devoted to oatmeal " sturrow " with treacle or buttermilk ; unlimited milk gruel or broth and seven ounces of bread at breakfast and supper ; the ration of beer is only half a pint but some are allowed gin ; whilst the men over fifty years of age are allowed half an ounce of tobacco or snuff weekly, and the women half an ounce of tea and a quarter of a pound of sugar (*ibid.* Moylan's Report, p. 275). The Gloucester Guardians decided in 1825 on a drastic cutting down of the workhouse dietary, resolving " that the allowance of beer to the women be reduced to two pints each day ; that of bread to women to seven pounds per week ; that of meat to each individual to ten ounces per day ; that of bread to children to six pounds per week, and for those under eight, to five pounds " (MS. Minutes, May 23, 1825). An allowance of beer, at two meals daily, to all adults was almost invariable ; and sometimes children had it also. The food was often served in the dormitories and eaten " on the beds " (So at Norwich ; see Sir F. M. Eden's *State of the Poor*, vol. ii. pp. 477-524) ; and notices would be put up stating that " any person in this House taking more food than they can consume, and wasting, selling or otherwise disposing of it, will be proceeded against according to law " (Report of Poor Law Inquiry Commissioners, Appendix A, Cowell's Report, p. 601). Even the newly built workhouse of St. Martin's in the Fields, regarded in 1780 as the finest and most perfectly equipped in London, had, as Jonas Hanway noted with regret, " no halls for their regular dieting. . . . A few of the paupers mess together, but all are left to eat in their chambers or dormitories " (*The Citizen's Monitor*, by Jonas Hanway, 1780, p. 174). Naturally, the waste was enormous. The amount of meat and bacon consumed in the workhouse at St. Giles, Reading, was found to be nearly twice as much per head as that consumed in the workhouse at Lambeth (Report of Poor Law Inquiry Commissioners, Appendix A, Chadwick's Report, p. 8). At Norwich, in 1784, it was found that the average amount of meat consumed in the workhouse amounted to 18¾ or 19½ ounces of cooked beef, without bone, for each man, woman and child daily (Sir F. M. Eden's *State of the Poor*, 1797, vol. ii. pp. 477-524 ; see also *Reports of the Special Provisions Committee appointed by the Court of Guardians in the City of Norwich, with an account of the savings . . . produced . . in the diet of the workhouse*, by E. Rigby, 1788 ; and *Further Facts relating to the care of the Poor and the Management of the Workhouse in the City of Norwich*, by the same, Norwich, 1812). For the Greenwich dietary, see MS. Vestry Minutes, July 1, 1808 ; for that at Minchinhampton, see MS. Vestry Minutes, July 21, 1791.

take a pride in supplying them with the best of everything, and plenty of it ".[1]   When it was proposed to give the Southampton paupers brown bread instead of white, the Guardians indignantly declared that " they would never consent to reduce the comforts of the poor ".   This generous treatment of the workhouse inmates went only to giving them the indulgences that they craved : it never occurred to the Poor Law Authorities to insist on adequate cubic space, ventilation, cleanliness, quiet or even decency.   The overcrowding, insanitation, filth and gross indecency of workhouse life during the whole of the eighteenth, and even for the first thirty or forty years of the nineteenth, century are simply indescribable.

The evil promiscuity in squalor and filth of the workhouse was at once complained of and resented.   " These workhouses," wrote Daniel De Foe in 1729, " though in appearance beneficial, yet have in some respects an evil tendency, for they mix the good and the bad, and often make reprobates of all alike.   We all, alas, are subject to misfortune.   And if an honest gentleman or trader should leave a wife or children unprovided for, what a shocking thing it is to think they must be mixed with vagrants, beggars, thieves and night-walkers ; to receive their insults, to bear their blasphemous and obscene discourse, to be suffocated with their nastiness, and eat[en] up with their vermin." [2] " These wretched receptacles of misery, or rather, parish prisons, called workhouses," said John Scott in 1773, " are scenes of filthiness and confusion ; that old and young, sick and healthy, are promiscuously crowded into ill-contrived apartments, not of sufficient capacity to contain with convenience half the number of miserable beings condemned to such deplorable inhabitation." [3] " Crowded workhouses ", wrote a cool observer in 1807, " are the sinks of vice, for in them the old and the young, the healthy and those afflicted with loathsome diseases, the necessitous and the abandoned, are all mixed in one house, or perhaps in one

---

[1] Report of Poor Law Inquiry Commissioners, Appendix A, Tweedy's Report, p. 726.   At Nottingham a proposal to introduce, for the sake of economy, shoes with wooden soles, had to be abandoned, after the shoes had been actually bought, because " the paupers complained of the hardship " of having to wear what was the usual footgear of Lancashire, Yorkshire and Cheshire (ibid. Cowell's Report, p. 601).

[2] Parochial Tyranny, by Andrew Moreton [Daniel De Foe], 1729.

[3] On the Present State of the Parochial and Vagrant Poor [by John Scott, the Quaker poet], 1773.

room. Here the young, the unfortunate, and persons of weak yet honest minds, repeatedly have their ears assailed with infamous oaths, and descriptions of every species of vice, deception and theft. The scene is in the highest degree horrid, and infinitely surpasses any powers of description." [1] This writer therefore recommended their abolition in favour of Outdoor Relief, with the provision of parish cottages for the aged. " Workhouses ", said an able witness before the House of Commons Committee of 1817, " act two ways. One a little good, and [the other] a very great evil ; the little good is that they act as gaols to terrify the people from coming to the parish ; the evil is that when they are [there], however loth they were to get there, they soon become used to it, and never get out again." [2]

At Norwich, we read, " In 1826, and for some years previous, the workhouse was in every part of it, a scene of filth, wretchedness and indecency which baffles all description, without regulations of any kind. Imagine, too, paupers who, for weeks, months and years together, breakfasted, dined and supped, without any order or regularity ; who had neither knife, fork or plate ; they were to be seen in groups with their hot puddings and meat in their hands, literally gnawing it. Imagine 600 persons indiscriminately lodged, crowded into rooms seldom or never ventilated, the beds and bedding swarming with vermin ; single and married, old and young, all mixed without regard to decency—I say, imagine this, and you will have a tolerable idea of the workhouse as it was." [3] Such a state of things

---

[1] *View of the Agriculture of Middlesex*, by John Middleton, 1807, p. 7.

[2] Report of House of Commons Select Committee on the Poor Laws, 1817 (Vivian's evidence).

[3] Isaac Wiseman, in *Norwich Mercury*, March 7, 1829. The small workhouses were as bad as the larger ones. In 1815 an intelligent critic reported that " the state of some of the workhouses was dreadful, particularly one at Modbury, in Devonshire ; there were sixty old persons, thirteen of whom were in one room, with a small casement at the end of it ; some of the provisions were kept in the same room, which consisted of sour bad barley bread ; we tasted some of that bread, which was most unpalatable. The passage to the room was open to the weather in many places. The poor complained heavily of the situation in which they were placed ; and some of them expressed a wish for death ; it was a sleeping room as well as a general keeping room ; they were in this room day and night. . . . They were not farmed, it was under the management of the Overseers " (Minutes of Evidence taken before House of Commons Committee on the State of Madhouses, 1815, Alexander's evidence, p. 55).

naturally increased the reluctance of the Justices to allow
Overseers to compel the respectable poor to enter the workhouse.
The result was that it became in many counties a place of refuge
for the lowest and worst of the population. " Everybody concerned knows ", wrote a critic of 1825, " that this House [Loes
and Wilford Hundreds of Suffolk] has been made use of as a
kind of secondhand prison for all the incorrigible pilfering rogues
and vagabonds among the men, and all the worthless strumpets
and vilest among women—in short, the very scum of the Hundreds
—and it is always admitted that such characters are the worse
for associating together in great numbers—yet the good are to be
crammed into this grand emporium of vice and compelled to
associate with the bad ; and who can believe the classifying and
separating the sexes is done to the extent represented, when
there are so many living proofs to the contrary ? " [1]   Of effective
discipline there was next to none.   The master, or other officers,
could be flouted with impunity.   The nominal power to put a
pauper in confinement for twenty-four hours, or to reduce his
diet, went for nothing in the somewhat weak hands of the
workhouse governors of the period, among the turbulent and
profligate crowd which filled some of the workhouses.   Indeed,
so far had gone the relaxation of discipline that by 1833 the able-
bodied paupers were able, in many workhouses, to do practically
as they liked.   The testimony of the Masters of Workhouses and
salaried Overseers of the Metropolitan parishes discloses an almost
inconceivable state of official helplessness in face of pauper turbulence.   " We first received them into the house," pathetically
recites the Assistant Overseer of St. Botolph Without, Bishopsgate, in describing the conduct of a score of able-bodied paupers,
" but they were so refractory and behaved so ill, that the old
people petitioned to be relieved of them ; they would beat them
and steal their victuals . . . and would annoy them in every
way, besides doing everything they could to plague the master
and mistress of the House, until we were obliged, in justice to the
other inmates to send them to farmed houses. . . . At such
houses . . . they were so disorderly and irregular that the
owners refused to keep them, and sent them back to us." [2]

[1] *Ipswich Journal*, March 12, 1825.
[2] Report of Poor Law Inquiry Commissioners, Appendix A, Codd's Report,
p. 89.

" When it is attempted to restrict them," states the Master of St. Pancras workhouse, " however little, or to control them, however lightly . . . they revenge themselves by breaking our windows or destroying other property . . . in fact, with the want of power which Managers of Workhouses now have, there is nothing which does not lead the violent and worthless to act worse than they did before." [1] " It is not uncommon ", testifies the Assistant Overseer of St. Andrew's, Holborn, "for the paupers to break the windows of the wards in which they are kept, to assault the subordinate officers of the parish, and to commit other acts of violence." [2] What it came to in the end was that the specially turbulent and refractory paupers were able to exact, from Overseer or magistrate, unconditional Outdoor Relief, as the price of being rid of them.

The worst aspect of the workhouse, as an asylum for the destitute, was, however, its provision for the children, who made up a large proportion of its inmates ; by 1834 apparently numbering in the aggregate forty or fifty thousand. When once the idea of profitably employing the poor was given up, nothing whatever was done, in the vast majority of cases, for the children's education. In some corner of the workhouse yard, or in a shed, an old pauper, reputed to be able to read, might be found in charge of a dozen or a score of children of all ages, whose turbulent idleness would be varied by errands to buy spirits or tobacco for the other paupers, with whom they freely mixed. It is needless to describe, after such a training, the propensities, the habits and the fate of the workhouse child of 1820 or 1830. We do not need to be told that increasing difficulty was found in placing out the girls in domestic service or apprenticing the boys to handicrafts. The evil was not mended by bribing, as we have already described, needy and unscrupulous persons (in other parishes) to accept a workhouse boy as an apprentice, or by compelling every ratepayer to take one in turn. The age up to which the children remained in the workhouses steadily rose, the depravity increasing accordingly. The Poor Law administrators of this period were, in fact, in this way actually recruiting not only the pauper but also the criminal class. " In by far the greater number of cases ", truthfully say

[1] Report of Poor Law Inquiry Commissioners, Appendix A, Codd s Report, p. 74.   [2] *Ibid.* p. 79.

the Poor Law Inquiry Commissioners, the workhouse of 1833—
which was, be it remembered, the home of possibly a hundred
thousand people in some four thousand Unions or parishes—was
a place " in which the young are trained in idleness, ignorance and
vice ; the able-bodied maintained in sluggish, sensual indolence ;
the aged and more respectable exposed to all the misery that is
incident to dwelling in such a society, without government or
classification ; and the whole body of inmates subsisted on food
far exceeding both in kind and in amount, not merely the diet
of the independent labourer, but that of the majority of the
persons who contribute to their support ".[1]

Such being the state of the workhouses, it is not surprising
that, by 1815, there had sprung up a movement for their total
abolition. In many parishes, the able-bodied paupers, however
turbulent or undeserving their conduct, ceased to be sent to the
workhouse, and were put, as a matter of course, on the list for
regular Outdoor Relief. In the Suffolk Hundreds, where the

---

[1] Report of Poor Law Inquiry Commissioners, 1834, " Indoors Relief ",
p. 45 of reprint. Between 1800 and 1812 the pamphlet literature, which in
these years of war became less prolific, dealt largely with criticisms of the
workhouse. See, among others, *Considerations on the Increase of the Poor
Rate, and on the State of the Workhouse in Kingston upon Hull*, etc., 1800 ;
Parochial Regulations relative to the Management of the Poor of Bradford [Wilts],
etc., edited by T. Bush and others, Bristol, 1801 ; *The Means of Reforming the
Morals of the Poor by the Prevention of Poverty, and a Plan for Ameliorating the
Condition of Parish Paupers*, by John Hill, 1801 ; *Thoughts on Poorhouses,
with a View to their General Reform, particularly that of Salisbury*, etc., by
Henry Wansey, 1801 ; *An Inquiry into the Propriety of applying Wastes to
the better maintenance and support of the Poor ; with instances of the great effects
which have attended their acquisition of Property in keeping them from the Parish*,
by Arthur Young, Bury St. Edmunds, 1801 ; *Democracy the Cause of the Present
Dearth and Sufferings of the Poor*, by J. W., 1801 ; *A Proposal on Behalf of the
Married Poor*, 1801 ; *Remarks on the Poor Laws and on the State of the Poor*,
by Charles Weston, 1802 ; *Mr. Adam's Speech at the Bar of the H. of C. 21 June
1803 against the . . . S. James's Poor Bill*, 1804 ; *A Plan of a House of Industry
established at Heddon on the Wall, with rules and regulations for conducting the
same*, etc., by Thomas Allason, Newcastle, 1805 ; *On Employing the Poor in
Parish Workhouses*, by Benjamin Pryor, in *Letters and Papers of Bath and
West of England Agricultural Society*, vol. x. art. 10, 1805 ; *The State of the
Population, the Poor and Poor Rates in the . . . County of Middlesex*, 1805 ;
*Outline of a Plan for Reducing the Poor's Rate and amending the condition of the
Aged and unfortunate*, 1805 ; *The Principles and Regulations of Tranquillity*,
etc., 1806 ; and *The Wants of the People and the Means of Government, or
Objections to the Interference of the Legislature in the Affairs of the Poor*, 1807,
these by John Bone, who had some connection with a " Society for the Gradual
Abolition of the Poor's Rate." Southey, in *The Doctor* (1813) incidentally
refers to the workhouses as " those moral lazarhouses in which age and infancy,
the harlot and the idiot, the profligate and the unfortunate are herded
together " (p. 28 of 1848 edition).

Unions had been incorporated with such glowing hopes, and with so marked an immediate success, a strong movement set in about 1825 in favour of their complete dissolution and of a reversion to the former plan of Outdoor Relief under parish management. Ceasing to make full use of the Union workhouse, the parishes objected to having to contribute at a rate fixed according to the average number of their paupers in the institution during the preceding ten years. Humane clergymen protested against "withdrawing the poor from the influence and protection of those amongst whom they live, and to give strangers power and authority over their concerns ".[1] Similar movements for abolishing the workhouses, and retransforming them into the older " parish house ", or mere place of shelter, are reported from Derbyshire,[2] Wiltshire,[2] Dorset,[2] Herefordshire,[2] Oxfordshire,[2] Shropshire,[3] and other counties ; and thousands of parishes had, by 1833, reverted to the more elementary device of giving doles and pensions to all their poor. In 1833 the Assistant Poor Law Commissioners found the workhouse, in many parishes, used by the Overseers merely as a means of bargaining with the poor. By threatening to confine their relief to the workhouse, the Overseers induced them to accept lower rates of Outdoor Relief than they demanded. On the other hand, the paupers already in the workhouse would be induced to go out on the promise of a weekly allowance. " The practice of our Overseers ", said one witness in 1833, " is to bribe paupers by a small weekly stipend to keep out of the House, rather than invite them or require them to come into it." [4] " Many other parishes ", it was said, " which, though complaining of the number, imposition, and the idleness of their paupers, keep their parish houses for no other purpose, or very little, but as scarecrows to frighten those whom nothing else will frighten. . . . The Overseer may say to the pauper (who looking at the scale sees himself ' entitled ' to a much higher allowance) ' Be content with five shillings and I will not send you into the House '." [5]

The officials of the London workhouses, which continued to

---

[1] *Ipswich Journal*, March 12, 1825.
[2] Report of Poor Law Inquiry Commissioners, Appendix A.
[3] *Birmingham Gazette*, November 15, 1824.
[4] Report of Poor Law Inquiry Commissioners, Appendix A, Codd's Report, p. 80.
[5] *Ibid.* Pilkington's Report, p. 83.

be filled, to a considerable extent, with a semi-criminal population, would have preferred to convert them into Houses of
Correction, governed under the plenary powers of summary
punishment which Parliament had withdrawn. But realising
that public opinion made effective punishment impossible, they
advocated the reorganisation of the workhouse on Marryott's
plan of using it merely as a deterrent. " I am decidedly of
opinion ", said the Assistant Overseer of St. Andrew's, Holborn,
" that if we had an establishment into which we could receive all
parties who apply to us, diet them according to their merits,
work them hard, and restrict them from too easy egress, we
should get rid of at least a third of those who are now a burthen
to us." [1] The Vestry Clerk of St. George's, Hanover Square, took
the same view. " If ", he said, " we had a house in which we
could set all who apply to work and keep them under a strong
system of discipline, I have not the least doubt that nearly all
the idle and dissolute would be deterred from applying for relief
at all." [2] But any such penal institution was incompatible with
the use of the workhouse as an asylum for the children, the aged,
the sick and the mentally defective.

The Workhouse as a Means of applying the Test by Regimen

The Poor Law administrators at the beginning of the nineteenth century were, as we now see, on the horns of a dilemma.
The Justices of the Peace had, by 1820, become theoretically
convinced that Outdoor Relief to the able-bodied enormously
increased the volume of pauperism. Yet it was impossible for
individual magistrates to allow the deserving poor to be driven
into the sort of workhouse that was provided. What seemed a
way out was discovered in the form of what we may call the Test
by Regimen.

So far as we can ascertain, the first person deliberately and
consciously to put in practice the new system of the test by
regimen was Robert Lowe, the rector of ·Bingham and Prebendary
of Southwell.[3] " In this neighbourhood ", writes the Assistant

---

[1] Report of Poor Law Inquiry Commissioners, Appendix A, Codd's Report,
p. 79.   [2] *Ibid.* p. 77.
   [3] The rector of Bingham was a cousin of the Rev. J. T. Becher of Southwell,
who was also distinguished as a social reformer (see p. 257) ; and the father
of Robert Lowe, who was successively a member of the Legislative Council

Poor Law Commissioner in 1833, " the merit of being the first to employ the workhouse as an agent for a moral regeneration of the labouring classes, is due to the Rev. Mr. Lowe ", who became incumbent of Bingham, near Nottingham, a parish containing in 1821 a population of 1574, " completely pauperised " by indiscriminate outdoor relief and general laxity at the workhouse. " The state of morals was such as invariably accompanies this manner of administering the Poor Laws. The labourers were turbulent, idle, dissolute and profuse. The poor . . . were completely masters ; scarcely a night passed without mischief, and in the two years preceding 1818 seven men of the parish were transported for felonies." In 1818 Lowe started to reform the Poor Law administration. " Knowing that it was impossible to refuse relief, according to the practice and custom of the country, he devised means for rendering relief so irksome and disagreeable that none would consent to receive it who could possibly do without it, *while at the same time it should come in the shape of comfort and consolation to those whom every benevolent man would wish to succour the old, infirm, idiots and cripples.*" The potent instrument for effecting this reform was found, as is well known, in the strict application of a deliberate regimen so framed as to deter the able-bodied and the vicious whilst at the same time providing them with the necessaries of life if they chose to submit to it. Outdoor Relief was absolutely refused to able-bodied men and their families, who were at once ordered into the workhouse. There they found a clean dwelling, a good bed and three meals a day, including meat three times a week. But they also found an appalling strictness of classification, order, regularity, cleanliness, confinement and discipline. " The man goes to one part of the house, the wife to the other, and the children into the schoolroom. Separation is strictly enforced. Their own clothes are taken off, and the uniform of the workhouse put on. No beer, tobacco or snuff is allowed. Regular hours [must be] kept, or meals forfeited. Every one must appear in a state of cleanliness. No access to bedrooms during the day. No communication with friends out of doors."

---

and the Legislative Assembly of New South Wales ; of the House of Commons ; of the British Cabinet (Chancellor of the Exchequer, 1868–1873, Home Secretary, 1873–1874) ; and, as Viscount Sherbrooke, of the House of Lords (*Life and Letters of . . . Robert Lowe, Viscount Sherbrooke*, by A. Patchett Martin, 1893, vol. i. pp. 46-50).

What the incumbent of Bingham instituted was (to use his own words in a letter to his friend and neighbour, the Rev. J. T. Becher of Southwell) " the system of forcing able-bodied paupers to provide for themselves through the terror of a well-disciplined workhouse ". This effect of a workhouse had, as we have seen, been discovered by Matthew Marriot or Marryott a century before. What was new in Lowe's experiment was his reliance, not on bad treatment by underfeeding, overcrowding and squalor, but on hygienic treatment under conditions that were unpleasant.

The effect of this regimen, though introduced in a tiny work-house with only one small yard, seems to have been magical. Though the diet was liberal, and the workhouse accommodation sanitary, no able-bodied labourer would endure the enforced quiet, regularity, cleanliness, monotony, confinement and de-privation of alcohol and tobacco. The 103 " roundsmen ", and the 78 persons previously in receipt of Outdoor Relief, dropped to 27 pensioners, all old, blind or crippled. These were permitted to live with relations, " as such examples of giving relief out of the workhouse ", emphatically reports the Assistant Poor Law Commissioner, " produce no mischief ". At the same time the number of inmates of the workhouse fell from 45 to 12, all of them old, infirm or idiots, " to whom ", it was optimistically reported, " a workhouse is really a place of comfort ". The total cost of poor relief in Bingham, which had, in 1816–1818, exceeded £1200, fell in 1818–1819 to £984, in the following year to £711, and then dropped permanently to a steady average, for the twelve years 1820–1832, of £373 per annum. Meanwhile the total popula-tion of the parish had risen from 1574, in 1821, to 1738, in 1831 ; wages had advanced to 12s. a week, and were paid regularly all the year round ; and the general conduct of the parishioners had greatly improved.[1]

Three years later a similar regimen was introduced at South-well, a parish only a few miles from Bingham, the two incumbents being in friendly communication with each other. The in-

[1] For the Bingham experiment, see the Report of the Poor Law Inquiry Commissioners, 1834, Appendix A, Cowell's Report, pp. 611-613, and Wylde's Report, p. 124 ; Lowe to Becher, April 4, 1834, in *Life and Letters of . . . Robert Lowe, Viscount Sherbrooke*, by A. Patchett Martin, 1893, vol. i. pp. 46-50 ; Sir George Nicholls' *History of the English Poor Law*, 1854, vol. ii. pp. 240-251 ; and his earlier *Eight Letters on the Management of the Poor*, by an Overseer (Nottingham, 1822), p. 45—republished from the *Nottingham Journal*, where they appeared in 1821.

habitants of Southwell had been, since 1795, grossly pauperised ; and in 1806 the incumbent, the Rev. J. T. Becher, began what proved to be a long series of experiments in reform of Poor Law administration. A workhouse was built ; a paid Assistant Over-seer was appointed ; relief was given in kind ; cottage rents were paid instead of granting pensions ; then the payment of rents was practically given up and a sort of Allowance System according to scale was adopted ; various plans of employing the poor were tried, abandoned and tried again, but without success ; and in 1821 the total outlay on relief amounted to £1628, a figure which, in the whole history of the parish, had only once before been exceeded. Thus, three years after the reform at Bingham, things at Southwell were, we may infer, almost at their worst. In that year Becher induced Captain Nicholls, a retired officer of the East India Company's mercantile marine service, to undertake the office of Overseer and Surveyor of Highways. Nicholls, who went to see the workhouse at Bingham, when he discussed its " Test by Regimen " with the incumbent, refused all Outdoor Relief or payment of cottage rents to the able-bodied and their families , and introduced a strict regimen at the workhouse.[1] Able-bodied men of good character who really needed work in the winter were found temporary employment on the roads—this had apparently not been done at Bingham—but any who entered the workhouse were put to crush bones, break stones, or dig holes ; and they quickly took their departure. The result was that the Outdoor Relief, which had between 1813 and 1821 averaged £820 a year, fell to a steady average, between 1823 and 1832, of £252 a year ; the payments for rents and parish employment altogether ceased ; the inmates of the workhouse dropped from 80 to 11 ; and the total cost of poor relief fell from £1628 in 1821 to a steady average, between 1823 and 1832, of £400 a year.[2]

[1] The rules were (1) to separate the men and women, (2) to prevent any from going out or seeing visitors, and to make them keep regular hours, (3) to prevent smoking, (4) to disallow beer, (5) to find them work, and (6) to treat and feed them well.

[2] The Southwell experiment became more widely known than others, partly because Nicholls wrote about it in the local newspaper, the *Nottingham Journal*, in 1821, and republished these articles as *Eight Letters on the Management of the Poor, Etc.*, by an Overseer (1822). This contemporary account by the author of the experiment differs somewhat from his later recollections in his *History of the English Poor Law*, vol. ii. pp. 240-251 : see also his biography by H. G. Willink in the preface to vol. i. of the new edition of 1899 ; also Report of Poor Law Inquiry Commissioners, 1834, Appendix A, Cowell's Report,

The third experiment, which was directly derived from the experience of Bingham, was that of Uley in Gloucestershire, where the Test by Regimen was introduced in 1830 by J. H. Lloyd Baker, a local landowner and Justice of the Peace, honourably known for his philanthropic work in various fields. The parish of Uley, which had, in 1831, 2641 inhabitants, contained a turbulent and demoralised industrial population, seriously suffering at that date from the decay of the local woollen manufacture. The Allowance System was in full operation, and practically all the labourers were pauperised ; the poor rate amounted in 1829–1830 to no less than £3185 ; factories were being closed and farms were beginning to lie vacant. At the urgent instance of Lowe of Bingham, Baker took the workhouse in 1830 practically into his own management, drew up strict rules as to regimen, and refused Outdoor Relief to any able-bodied labourer. The pivot of the system was the rigorous application of a strict regimen at the workhouse. " Make the House so disagreeable ", writes Baker in 1832, " that no one will stay to work who can work elsewhere." Two years of this treatment at Uley reduced the numbers receiving Outdoor Relief from 977 to 125, whilst the inmates of the workhouse fell to 14 only, none of whom were able to work.[1]

---

pp. 613-618, and Wylde's Report, pp. 103-106, 129-130 ; *The Anti-Pauper System and the Administration of the Poor Laws at Southwell*, by Rev. J. T. Becher, 1828, 2nd edition, 1834 ; *A Report concerning the House of Correction at Southwell, etc.*, 1806 ; *A Letter to the Rev. J. T. Becher of Southwell in reply to certain charges, etc.*, by John W. Cowell, 1834 ; Lowe to Bingham, April 4, 1834, in *Life and Letters of . . . Robert Lowe, Viscount Sherbrooke*, by A. Patchett Martin, 1893, vol. i. pp. 46-50 ; and Becher's evidence before the House of Lords Select Committee on Poor Laws, 1831. Becher (1770-1848) was an innovator in various fields ; see his pamphlets, *The Constitution of Friendly Societies upon Legal and Scientific Principles*, 1824 ; *Tables showing the . . . contributions to be paid . . . by members of Friendly Societies*, 1825 ; *Observations upon the Report of the Select Committee . . . on the Laws respecting Friendly Societies*, 1826 ; *Rules of the Northampton Equitable Friendly Society*, by J. T. B. and J. Finlaison, 1837. An Account of " the Becher Clubs " and " the Southwell Tables " is given in *Mutual Thrift*, by J. Frome Wilkinson.

He was a friend of Lord Byron, who addressed to him the verses beginning " Dear Becher, you tell me to mix with mankind ".

[1] For the Uley experiment, see *A Letter to the Rev. George Cooke, D.D., Chairman of the Quarter Session for the County of Gloucester*, by J. H. L. Baker, Gloucester, 1830 ; Report of Poor Law Inquiry Commissioners, Appendix A, Cowell's Report, pp. 619-634, the full " rules and orders " at pp. 650-652, and Bishop's Report, pp. 885-886. For J. H. L. Baker's life and home, reference may be made to the account of his son and successor by F. von Holtzendorf, *Ein englischer Landsquire*, 1877, translated as *An English Country Squire at Hardwicke Court*, 1878.

Between 1825 and 1835 a few other parishes up and down the country followed the examples of Bingham, Southwell and Uley, with like results. At Penzance in Cornwall the strict regimen was introduced into the workhouse in 1825–1826, with the usual reduction in pauperism.[1] The parish of St. Werburgh, Derby, was reformed by the incumbent (Mozley) in 1826, on the lines adopted at Uley.[2] At Redruth in Cornwall a strictly disciplined workhouse system, and refusal of Outdoor Relief to the able-bodied, adopted in 1831, got rid of four-fifths of the paupers.[3] An exceptional experiment of this decade was that of the Hundred of Thurgarton, in Nottinghamshire, where, under the direct inspiration of Becher, 49 small parishes, having a total population of about 10,000, formed themselves into a Union under Gilbert's Act, and built themselves a Union workhouse at Upton. Here the same strict regimen was applied to the workhouse inmates ; and we are told that the number of able-bodied applicants for relief was at once reduced ;[4] although it is to be observed that an exact compliance with Gilbert's Act would have prevented the admission of able-bodied men to the Union workhouse built under its provisions, if any man had been so misguided as to demand it.

We shall discuss at a later stage the shortcomings and difficulties of this "Test by Regimen". We need here note only how easily and almost imperceptibly it becomes confused (as we suspect it was at Uley) with the use of the " properly regulated workhouse " as a mere expedient for the deterrence of all applicants for relief. If the deterrence is sufficiently great, there will, of course, be no applicants whatever. The very word "test" ought to have suggested that those applicants who passed the test, and who demonstrated, by remaining in the institution, that their destitution was genuine and irremediable, could not justly be continuously subjected to the semi-penal treatment on which the efficacy of the test depended. Moreover, apart from any question of severity, the particular regimen imposed on new-comers

---

[1] Report of Poor Law Inquiry Commissioners, Appendix A, Chapman's Report, p. 428.

[2] *Ibid.* Pilkington's Report, pp. 384-386.

[3] *Ibid.* Chapman's Report, pp. 426, 506-507.

[4] *Ibid.* Cowell's Report, p. 618. This Union was voluntarily dissolved, and a new one formed under the Act of 1834, some time before 1843 (Ninth Annual Report of Poor Law Commissioners, 1843, p. 112).

in order to make the test effective was not necessarily that appropriate or beneficent to permanent residents. In fact, the most obvious justification, to that generation, of the " Test by Regimen " was found in the expectation and belief that no one would long endure it ; and that (as Harriet Martineau described in her *Paupers and Poor Law Illustrated*) the workhouse would be promptly emptied, and would remain empty, in a parish that had been, by use of this device, completely " dispauperised ". But this conception of the workhouse provided no asylum for the aged, no place of treatment for the sick or the nursing mothers, no refuge for the infirm or the mentally defective, and no educational institution for the orphan or deserted children—and these, in fact, habitually made up seven-eighths of " the destitute " for whom the law directed relief to be given !

The Workhouse as a Place of Specialised Institutional Treatment

It is a leading feature of the relief of the poor in France and Germany, as it is of that of Great Britain to-day, to provide, in highly organised institutions, the specific treatment appropriate to particular classes of persons needing relief. Experience has proved that the children, the insane and the sick—to name only some of the most obvious classes—can be best provided for separately from the general body of paupers, and apart from each other. Of such specialised institutional treatment of particular classes, the English Poor Law of the sixteenth and seventeenth and eighteenth centuries knew practically nothing. Right down to 1834 it was usual to find, even in the best-regulated workhouse, an almost unrestricted intermingling of the young and the old, the healthy and the sick, the sane and the insane, all being subjected to practically the same treatment, provided with exactly the same food and—with some variation as to the task of work exacted—put under a common regimen.

We may, however, trace, here and there, a few quite exceptional beginnings of that specialised institutional treatment, which forms the most conspicuous feature of the twentieth century collective provision for those requiring it. The earliest and as we may imagine, quite unique experiment of this kind with regard to children, appears to have been made, on behalf of a dozen populous parishes in Westminster and Clerkenwell, by the Middlesex Justices in Quarter Sessions, in 1686. They acquired, we are told, " a large house at Clerkenwell . . . which cost the several parishes . . . at least £5000 building, which house is by the Justices of the County . . . set apart for the reception and breeding up of poor fatherless and motherless infants left to the parish care, and for the instructing of them in religion and virtue, and making them capable of getting an honest livelihood by their labour ". We gather that the Justices appointed one of their own number to be the governor of this institution ; that fifty children were first admitted, the several parishes being each invited to nominate from two to five, according to the relative populations ; and that the number was presently increased. Of what happened to this experiment we know nothing ; but we infer that it was shortlived. Apparently no definite provision had been made for a revenue, and charitable donations were invited. The parishes (and any one else who chose to send in a child) were expected to contribute something like three shillings per week for its maintenance ; a sum that they were unlikely to pay. Private benefactors were invited to endow particular children, by gifts of fifty pounds, which would cover maintenance and apprenticeship, with ten pounds present when " out of his time " ; or of a hundred and twenty pounds, to secure a superior apprenticeship, with a present of no less than a hundred pounds when " out of his time ". With such amateur financing the experiment doubtless came almost immediately to an end.[1] Not for nearly a century do we find anything of the sort attempted by the parishes themselves. St. James's, Westminster, set up a separate " workhouse school " in 1781, in King Street, St. James's Square, where several hundreds of its older children were boarded, lodged and employed, with some modicum of technical instruction.[2] But these cases continued to be rare. The parish of Birmingham, we read in 1833, " alone affords an instance of superior and

[1] Order of Middlesex Quarter Sessions, February 22, 1686 ; *An Account of the General Nursery or College of Infants set up by the Justices of the Peace for the County of Middlesex, with the Constitution and Ends thereof*, 1686 (B.M. 1027, i. 30).

[2] *Sketch of the State of the Children of the Poor in the year 1756, and of the present state and management of all the poor in the Parish of St. James, Westminster, in January, 1797* (1797).

intelligent management with regard to the infant poor. . . . An asylum is established for this purpose which is able to hold upwards of 400 children ; these are chiefly such as are without parents at all, or whose parents profess their inability to support them. The children are instructed in sundry trades to which they may be afterwards bound ; and a certain number of hours is set apart in each day for attending a school in the house, where they are taught to read and write. . . . The children are thus maintained, while in the asylum, at the rate of two and sixpence a head, including all expenses. The result has been proved by experience to be extremely favourable to them in after life." [1]

Almost equally exceptional was the provision of any specialised treatment in the workhouse for the insane. These were, between 1807 and 1830, increasingly put out by contract to keepers of private madhouses, but nearly every workhouse had its imbeciles and idiots, and generally also a few harmless lunatics, mixing without discrimination among its general mass of paupers.

---

[1] Report of Poor Law Inquiry Commissioners, Appendix A, Villiers' Report, p. 7. Other parishes, as at Greenwich, contented themselves with paying a clergyman £30 a year " to visit the sick and catechise the children in the workhouse " (MS. Vestry Minutes, Greenwich (Kent), June 26, 1812).

Villiers was apparently so much impressed at finding at Birmingham any sort of separate Poor Law Institution for the children that he was contented with a low educational standard. In 1842, when a special report was made to the Poor Law Commissioners, it was said that " the Asylum is under the distinct management of a separate set of officers, including a governor, matron and schoolmistress—the persons holding these situations being in the relation of husband, wife and daughter. The governor acts as schoolmaster to the boys. The education imparted is about equal to that usually given in most of the adjoining Unions. Some of the elder boys are employed in tailoring and shoe-making, and the elder girls in domestic occupations. . . . No undue severity is practised towards them " (Ninth Annual Report of Poor Law Commissioners, 1843, p. 250).

It may be added that, in 1831, the Incorporated Guardians of the Poor of Birmingham had got as far as to obtain statutory power (never actually put in operation) to maintain a public crèche, or day nursery, for the convenience of mothers having to go to work (or shall we say, for that of the employers who wished to have more of such labour at their disposal ?). The preamble of the Birmingham Local Act (1 and 2 William IV. c. 67) recites : " And whereas many persons in the said town of Birmingham, who receive parochial relief, would be enabled to provide for their families by their industry if their children under seven years of age could be taken care of during the hours of labour, and it would greatly tend to diminish crime and the number of juvenile offenders and pauperism if such children were placed during such period in some room or place for their protection ; and whereas it would be beneficial if the Guardians had authority to apply for the purposes aforesaid a portion of the relief which such persons would otherwise receive for their children " (Statutory Authorities for Special Purposes, by S. and B. Webb, 1922, p. 145).

Right down to 1834, it was almost unknown for any separate provision to be made for them. It was quite exceptional that the Bristol Corporation of the Poor, having a large number of insane paupers, made, by 1813, an attempt to provide for their specific treatment inside the St. Peter's Hospital, as their general workhouse was called. A separate ward was set aside for the female lunatics, with a special attendant ; and there was a range of underground cells, in which incurable lunatics were allowed to linger out a solitary existence on " plenty of clean straw ".[1]

A few workhouses began, at the end of the eighteenth century, to provide separate accommodation for the sick, or at any rate for those suffering from " fever ", though this was more for the sake of protecting the healthy than from any sense of the importance of specific treatment for the cure of disease. How badly this was needed may be inferred from the following example which was quoted on the second reading of Sir William Young's Bill in 1795, by Mr. (afterwards Sir Edward Hyde) East. He stated " that within his own knowledge, a fever had broken out in a parish workhouse where there were thirty persons, and that of these only three survived, the Overseers being afraid to go near them, and therefore giving them no relief ".[2] It is noted as a remarkable feature of the new workhouse of St. Martin's in the Fields in 1780, that it included separate rooms or " infirmaries for different kinds of diseases ".[3] At Liverpool, as we have described in *The Parish and the County*, the Vestry, which had been thoughtfully providing for the sick poor for a whole generation, in 1801 bought a site near the workhouse, and built a " House of Recovery " or fever hospital, at a cost of £5000.[4] This building

[1] Report of the House of Commons Committee on the State of Madhouses, 1815, p. 54.
[2] Ninth Annual Report of Poor Law Commissioners, 1843, p. 102.
[3] *The Citizen's Monitor*, by Jonas Hanway, 1780, p. 174.
[4] The Liverpool Vestry had appointed a salaried medical officer " to take care of the poor " as early as 1768. In 1778 it had subscribed largely to the establishment of a public dispensary, which was enlarged into a hospital, to which a considerable annual subscription was afterwards given. In 1786 four houses were made into hospitals for casual paupers. In 1787 the Vestry began to send its pauper lunatics to the asylum then established by voluntary subscriptions. All this still left unprovided for those suffering from infectious diseases, for which Dr. James Currie began a ten years' agitation soon after 1790 (MS. Vestry Minutes, Liverpool, 1778–1788, and April 20, 1802 ; *Liverpool Vestry Books 1681–1834*, by Henry Peet, vol. ii., 1915, pp. lv-lvi, 11-12 ; *Life, Writings and Correspondence of James Currie of Liverpool*, by W. W. Currie, 1831, vol. i. p. 338 ; *The Parish and the County*, by S. and B. Webb, 1906, pp. 137-140).

was wholly detached from the workhouse, though administered as a part of that institution. Its 140 patients were tended, of course, only by pauper nurses ; but it had the best medical services that the town could supply, and, as late as 1833, it seems to have stood far in advance of any other poor law institution for the sick.[1] The Brighton Directors and Guardians of the Poor had decided in 1825 to spend £1000 in " erecting an additional building separate from the present workhouse, for the reception of paupers afflicted with contagious and other diseases " ;[2] but, unlike the Liverpool Vestry, they seem to have dallied over the work. When, in 1830, " fever " again broke out in the Brighton workhouse, the new infirmary was not yet begun ; and three paupers had to be removed to the fever wards of the Sussex County Hospital, a voluntary institution ; and the workhouse committee reports that it " cannot but regret [that] in such an establishment as the Poor House of this parish, no better provision is made for the sick poor, and particularly for such cases as the above ".[3] On its strong recommendation the Guardians again decided to erect a building for use as an infirmary for the sick poor.

These few and exceptional instances of the development of the workhouse into a place of specialised institutional treatment were, it will easily be understood, in no way typical of the Poor Law administration even of 1820–1835 ; and they are cited merely as the earliest experiments in a phase of relief which was characteristic of a much later period.

The Problem of the Area of Administration

Underlying all the difficulties and shortcomings of the workhouse in all its manifold uses, and the administration of the Overseers under the Parish Vestries and the Justices of the Peace, was, as is now apparent, the ever-recurring problem of what should be

---

[1] Report of Poor Law Inquiry Commissioners, Appendix A, Henderson's Report, p. 916.

[2] MS. Minutes, Incorporated Guardians, Brighton (Sussex), February 7, 1825.

[3] *Ibid.* October 21, 1830 ; a similar proposal was made for the Metropolis— half a century too soon !—see *Remarks on the Situation of the Poor in the Metropolis, as contributing to the progress of contagious diseases, with a plan for the institution of Houses of Recovery for persons affected by fever*, etc., by Thomas Archibald Murray, 1801.

the area of local government. It was this problem that led, as we have seen, to the formation of " Corporations of the Poor ", and bodies of Incorporated Guardians or Governors and Directors of the Poor in the municipal boroughs and in rural Hundreds, as well as to the establishment of Unions of parishes under the Act of 1723. In the middle of the eighteenth century the steady rise in the aggregate cost of Poor Relief, of the amount of which exaggerated ideas seem to have been prevalent, again disquieted the nation ; and there was a new rush of proposals for a reform of the whole system of Poor Relief.[1] There is, in this pamphlet literature, no consideration of the success or failure of the different kinds of workhouses, and indeed, no evidence of knowledge of the past experiments, or of their results either upon the character of the able-bodied unemployed, or upon the condition of the " impotent poor ". Once more we see how wasteful, from the standpoint of social progress, is the failure to observe, record and publish the actual outcome of social experiments. In the absence of any action by the successive Ministries of George II. and George III., the rush of proposals by squires and magistrates, clergymen and philanthropists between 1750 and 1776 (when the American War broke out) failed at first to find embodiment in legislative enactments. But they led, in 1782, to an optional statute which was afterwards stigmatised by J. R. M'Culloch as " the first great inroad on the old system of Poor Law ", and as having in the end " the worst possible effects ".[2]

We begin with the forerunners of these proposals. It is difficult to estimate how far the idea of profitably employing the poor and the idea of deterrence by institutional restraint were mingled with the prospect of obtaining a larger unit of administration than the parish and the hope of securing management superior to that of the unpaid Overseer, in the lifelong efforts of William Hay, M.P., to obtain Poor Law reform. But the central feature of his proposals, as it was of those of the ensuing generation, was to get the county, the Hundred, or some other division substituted for the parish as the Local Authority for Poor Relief.[3]

---

[1] These were summarised in *The History of the Poor Laws, with Observations*, by Richard Burn, 1764 ; and again, more fully, in *The State of the Poor*, by Sir F. M. Eden, 1797, vol. i.

[2] *The English Poor Law System*, by Dr. P. F. Aschrott, 1888, p. 20.

[3] William Hay, M.P. (1695–1755), published first in 1735 his *Remarks on the Laws relating to the Poor, etc., with Proposals for their Better Relief and*

Hay actually got a series of resolutions passed by the House of Commons as early as 1735, in favour of Unions of parishes, which should build workhouses, in which the orphans and the impotent or infirm poor should be housed, but which should also become centres at which every kind of trade or business might be carried on for the profit of the Union, in which all poor persons able to labour should be set to work, whether they voluntarily presented themselves for employment or were sent thither by a Justice of the Peace. Hay brought in a Bill in the following session ; but he found the House apathetic, and unwilling to face so large a project, so that the Bill dropped after it had passed both its Second Reading and its Committee stages. For another fifteen years the question slept. The idea of substituting for the parish or township the county, or some division of it, was commonly accepted by the pamphleteers of 1750–1776, but hardly any two of them could agree either upon the area or upon the policy to be followed. Henry Fielding in 1751, in his *Enquiry into the Causes of the Late Increase of Robberies, with some Proposals for remedying the growing Evil*—believing that no division less than a county would prove suitable—advocated the establishment of one gigantic workhouse, with a threefold classification of its inmates into the able-bodied, the sick and those impotent from age, infirmity or childhood, which should serve for the entire county of Middlesex.[1] On the other hand, Samuel Cooper, in his *Definitions*

Employment, by a Member of Parliament, with an Appendix containing the Resolutions of the House of Commons on the same subject. In 1751 he republished this pamphlet under the same title, with a new preface. This was included in his collected *Works*, 1794. He was M.P. for Seaford, 1734–1755 ; a Commissioner for Victualling the Navy, 1738 ; and Keeper of the Records of the Tower, 1753.

Hay's efforts to induce the House of Commons to take action, which seemed in 1735 and 1751 to produce no result, led perhaps to its appointment, in March 1759, of a committee to consider the state of the poor, and the laws enacted for their maintenance (*History of England*, by Tobias Smollett, vol. iv. of 1848 edition, pp. 143-144). The committee reported in May of the same year, presenting a long series of resolutions, generally in favour of properly organised workhouses; against Outdoor Relief for the able-bodied, in favour of the provision of employment in works and manufactures, and in the cultivation of waste land by incorporated bodies of Governors and Trustees, for counties and ridings, and (on these reforms being accomplished) in favour of the total abolition both of Settlement and Removal and of the Passing of Vagrants. No legislation followed.

[1] This was repeated, in substance, in *A Proposal for Making an Effectual Provision for the Poor*, etc., by Henry Fielding, 1753 ; see *Observations upon Mr. Fielding's Plan for a Preservatory and Reformatory*, 1758 ; and compare

and Axioms relative to Charity, Charitable Institutions and the Poor Laws, in 1763,[1] pointed to the initial success of the incorporation of the Hundreds of Colneis and Carlford (Suffolk) ; and advocated the establishment, all over the kingdom, of " Hundred Houses ". Dean Tucker, in 1760, in his *Manifold Causes of the Increase of the Poor distinctly set forth, together with . . . Proposals for removing . . . some of the Principal Evils,* etc.,[2] whilst equally objecting to the parish, and its annually elected officers, preferred (in interesting anticipation of the Poor Law Commissioners of 1834–1847) the incorporation into Unions of all the parishes within a radius of about six miles from each market town. Another writer, William Bailey, in his *Treatise on the Better Employment and More Comfortable Support of the Poor in Workhouses,* etc., 1758, thought less of how many separate workhouses there ought to be or what should be the unit of administration, than of the advantage which their universal establishment would afford to the unemployed labourers, whom he thought it would be quite easy to set to work. Thomas Alcock in 1752 argued along the same lines as William Hay, with interesting examples from the institutions of the Dutch, which were, he said, found to be both usefully deterrent, and profitable to their managers.[3] Though he wished to provide separately for the sick and the impotent poor, he made no distinction between the innocent unemployed and the able-bodied vagrant, but would set them all to productive labour of various kinds. " Materials ", he proposed, " should be provided for the employment of all those that should be able

---

A Plan for the Relief of the Poor, etc., by Saunders Welch, 1758. A vision of the effect of Poor Relief on morals and order is afforded by *Friendly Advice to the Poor, written at the request of the Officers of the Township of Manchester,* by John Clayton, 1755. This was answered by *A Sequel to the Friendly Advice to the Poor of the Town of Manchester,* by Joseph Stot, cobbler, 1756.

[1] We have found a copy of this pamphlet only in the library of the Ministry of Health ; it was an answer to *Considerations on the Fatal Effects of the Present Excess of Public Charity to a Trading Nation.*

[2] See also his *Letter from Dean Tucker to Dr. Stonehouse on Mr. Pew's Pamphlet,* 1792 ; in answer to *Twenty Minutes Observations on a Better Mode of Providing for the Poor,* by Richard Pew, 1783. The latter wrote also *Letter from Richard Pew respecting his Pamphlet,* 1792 ; and *A Plan for the General Prevention of Poverty,* by Richard Pew, 1795. All these were reprinted in the *Letters and Papers of the Bath and West of England Agricultural Society,* vols. vi. and vii.

[3] *Observations on the Effect of the Poor Laws,* by Thomas Alcock, 1752. He also published *Remarks on Two Bills for the Better Maintenance of the Poor,* etc., 1753.

to work, as hemp, flax, wool, leather, yarn both linen and woollen ;
iron, wood, etc. ; and likewise proper implements and working
tools as spinning wheels, cards, turns, knitting and other needles,
looms, shovels, axes, hammers, saws for stone and timber, and
perhaps some sort of mills where a stream could be had, as corn,
fulling, paper mills, etc.   Here several sorts of business, and some
small manufactures might be carried on, as spinning, weaving,
stocking and net knitting, sawing, ropemaking, woolcombing,
particularly in the West of England where the woollen trade is
considerable." Only in this way, he suggested, could the
terrible cost of Poor Relief—which he seems to have grossly
exaggerated by estimating it at three million pounds a year, or
twice as much as is likely to have been spent at that date—be
appreciably reduced.   He appears to have looked forward to an
eventual cessation of all relief to the able-bodied other than the
provision of profitable employment.   The anonymous author of
*Considerations on Several Proposals lately made for the Better
Maintenance of the Poor* [1] had much to object to in the schemes of
Hay and Fielding, as involving far too great a charge on the
County Rate : he preferred to rely on voluntary contributions,
but he, too, wanted the complete disestablishment of the parish,
and the substitution of areas of administration, which, he thought,
should be " Constabularies ", the Parish Constables sending up
lists of indigent people to the High Constable every month, and
the High Constables reporting them monthly to Special Sessions
of the Justices.   Much the same line was taken by James Massie
in his *Plan for the Establishment of Charity Houses . . . considerations relating to the Poor and the Poor's Laws*, 1758, though
he was less troubled about replacing the numerous existing poorhouses by larger new workhouses, than about the establishment
of institutions for " fallen " women, and the wasteful and troublesome results of the Law of Settlement and Removal, which he
wished wholly to abolish, relieving wherever destitution occurred,
and placing the cost upon a National Poor Rate.   This National

---

[1] The author of this pamphlet of 1751 (a second edition in 1752) ; and
also of two others, *Considerations on the Laws relating to the Poor*, 1759, and
Further Considerations on the Laws relating to the Poor, 1760, was Charles Gray,
M.P. for Colchester.   His first work was answered anonymously by *A Letter
to the Author of Considerations on Several Proposals for the Better Maintenance
of the Poor*, 1752 ; and also by *An Impartial Examination of a Pamphlet
entitled " Considerations on Several Proposals lately made for the Better Maintenance of the Poor "*, 1752.

Rate (to the extent of one-half the cost, the balance being raised by voluntary contributions) was advocated also by Lord Kames, who deprecated both almsgiving and the Poor Law, at any rate as regards the able-bodied male adults ; but who wished to see, under the Justices of the Peace, a complete series of Hospitals for the Impotent Poor and Houses of Correction for the able-bodied and the vagrants.[1] Another conception of administration had been propounded in 1753 by Willes Hill (1718–1793), M.P. for Warwick, 1714–1756, who had succeeded in 1742 to the Irish earldom of Hillsborough, and was subsequently to become a Cabinet Minister, 1763–1782, and Marquis of Downshire in 1789. He drafted a codifying statute re-enacting the then existing Poor Laws with suitable amendments, and, in particular, abolishing the whole notion of Settlement and Removal, but adding provisions for the establishment in each county of a new " Corporation of the Poor ", consisting of governors subscribing not less than £5 a year, in supplement of church collections, a national Grant in Aid, and a rate to be levied on all the parishes, limited to threepence in the pound for capital outlay, and sixpence in the pound for maintenance charges. This august body was to be empowered to erect and maintain one or more " working hospitals " for the county as a whole, having each three distinct departments for the children, the aged and the sick respectively. Admission was to be by recommendation of one of the governors of the Corporation. Room was to be found for the blind and the crippled, the idiots and the lunatics. How far the deserving able-bodied unemployed were to be eligible for such a recommendation is not clear, but " idle and disorderly persons ", vagrants and recalcitrants were to be committed to the House of Correction. Another draft Bill was published in 1753 by Sir Richard Lloyd, agreeing with the Earl of Hillsborough in superimposing, on the parochial Poor Law machinery, a semi-philanthropic organisation for maintaining non-parochial institutions, partly at the expense of the subscribers, and partly supported by charges on the parish rates. But Sir Richard Lloyd demurred to one organisation for the whole county, and proposed that the Justices in Quarter Sessions should divide the county into districts, for each of which a body of " Guardians of the Poor " should be appointed, taken from among the Justices and other

[1] *Sketches of the History of Man,* by Lord Kames, 1774.

persons of considerable estate. Each of these District Boards of Guardians—raising capital by a lottery, and by special donations—was to establish and maintain a House of Industry, in which the poor could be set to work for their own maintenance. It was to be left free to the parish Vestries and Overseers to send to the District House of Industry such persons in need of relief as they thought fit, paying out of the parochial Poor Rate their proportionate share of maintenance according to the number thus maintained.[1] More substantial and more widely influential seems to have been Dr. Richard Burn's *History of the Poor Laws*, in 1764, in which he pointed out that all the schemes of the contemporary pamphleteers were too ambitious in their scope to be anywhere within reach of enactment and execution. The Bill for the establishment of " general county workhouses " struck the average country gentleman as " a huge unwieldy scheme, attended with such an amazing certain expense, and liable to so many reasonable objections that the Parliament rejected it ". He very sensibly demurred to those suggested classifications of the persons to be relieved which lumped together all the able-bodied unemployed with the rogues and vagabonds. His own threefold classification was, on the one hand, all those incapable of labour, whether through age, sickness or infirmity, and on the other, two distinct sections of the able-bodied, the one innocent, for whom employment must be found, and the other guilty of vagrancy or crime, who ought to be relegated to the House of Correction. He would peremptorily forbid all gifts to beggars. But even he so far agreed with his contemporaries as to propose to reduce the Parish Officers to mere collectors of the names of persons in need of relief ; and to supersede them in their function of " setting the poor to work " by a salaried General Overseer to be appointed by the Justices for each Hundred.[2]

---

[1] *The History of the Poor Laws, with Observations*, by Richard Burn, 1764, pp. 192-196 ; *The State of the Poor*, by Sir F. M. Eden, 1797, vol. i. p. 318. The idea of the profitable employment of the poor was crudely revived in *A Proposal for Raising Timber, and for effectually supporting the Poor in Great Britain*, by Nicholas Turner, 1757 ; and, even more universally in *A General Plan for the Poor and rendering the useless hands in England . . . of Public Benefit by employing them in Manufactures and Husbandry*, by a Gentleman, 1764.

[2] This, the first history of the English Poor Laws, was by the learned Westmorland rector who had already compiled the legal manual for Magistrates entitled *The Justice of the Peace and Parish Officer*, 1755, which went through no fewer than thirty editions in the ensuing century, the last being published

Apart from the Local Acts obtained, as we have already described, for various Suffolk and Norfolk Hundreds, the only immediate outcome of this cloud of witnesses to the defects of the parish administration were the two Acts (2 George III. c. 22 and 7 George III. c. 39) to be subsequently referred to, which that indefatigable practical reformer Jonas Hanway, who had been horrified at the infant mortality in the London workhouses, got passed in 1761 and 1767, requiring London parishes to send all their infants under six years of age away from the workhouses into the adjacent country, not less than three miles away from any part of the Cities of London and Westminster.

The dominant note of all these proposals, from William Hay to Lord Kames, was the imperative necessity of relieving the parish, with its annually chosen unpaid officers, of the burden of making the indispensable institutional provision for the various classes of the impotent poor.[1] Everybody wanted better

---

in 1869. His proposals in the *History of the Poor Laws* evoked an anonymous answer entitled *An Examination of the Alterations in the Poor's Laws proposed by Dr. Burn, and a Refutation of his Objections to Workhouses so far as they relate to Hundred Houses*, 1766. He subsequently published *Observations on the Bill intended to be offered to Parliament for the Better Relief and Employment of the Poor*, 1776.

A more conveniently arranged law book, *A Digest of the Poor Laws in order to their being reduced into one Act*, by Owen Ruffhead, appeared in 1768 ; see also *An Analysis of the Law concerning Parochial Provision for the Poor*, by Edward Wynne, 1767.

[1] Among the other pamphlets of these years, not differing essentially from the views of those already mentioned, may be cited, *Proposals for a Scheme for the Better Maintenance and Employment of the Poor*, 1757 ; *The Old Englishman's Letters for the Poor of Old England*, by William Homer, 1758 ; *Populousness with Economy the Wealth and Strength of a Kingdom : humbly submitted to both Houses of Parliament on behalf of the Poor*, 1759 ; *Considerations humbly offered to Parliament relative to the heads of a Bill for Promoting Industry, Suppressing Idleness and Begging, and Saving above One Million Sterling yearly of the money now actually paid by the Nation to the Poor*, 1758 ; *A Plea for the Poor*, etc., by a Merchant of the City of London, 1759 ; *A Scheme for the Better Relief and Employment of the Poor*, by an M.P., 1764 ; *Observations on the Number and Misery of the Poor, on the Heavy Rates levied for their Maintenance, and on the Causes of Poverty*, by —— Becket, 1765 ; *An Inquiry into the Management of the Poor and our usual Polity respecting the Common People*, etc., 1767 ; *Five Letters on the State of the Poor in Kent*, etc., by —— Bowyer, 1770 ; *Observations on the Present State of the Parochial and Vagrant Poor*, an able work by John Scott, " The Quaker poet ", 1773 ; *Considerations on the Poor Laws*, etc., 1775 ; *Observations on the Poor Laws, on the Present State of the Poor, and on Houses of Industry*, by Rev. R. Potter, 1775 ; *A Dialogue . . . between a Gentleman, a Pauper and his Friend intended as an answer to a Pamphlet . . . by the Rev. Mr. Potter* (as above) ; by Thomas Mendham, Norwich, 1775 ; *Considerations on the Present State of the Poor in Great Britain*, by Humanus, 1773 and 1775 ; *Remarks on the Resolutions of the H. of C. with*

administration than could be got from the Overseer, and a larger unit than the parish.   But the country gentlemen were afraid of the elaborate and costly organisation that would have to be set up for the county as a whole ; and they could not agree among themselves on any lesser unit, whether the Hundred, the " Constabulary," or district of a High Constable, or (as we should now say) the Petty Sessional Division.   They shrank from the capital cost of the extensive institutions required ; and they could not bring themselves to lay any new charge on the County Rate.   What is remarkable is their complete ignorance of all the previous experiments, and their lack of any idea of applying the device of " deterrence ".   The parish poorhouse or workhouse, as they knew it, and even such similar institutions as continued to be maintained under Local Acts in a few municipal boroughs, were, in the eighteenth century, always " general mixed work-houses," in which were herded together the young and the old, the healthy and the sick, the blind and the crippled, and even the idiot and the lunatic.   The idea of a series of specialised institutions was not yet born.   The maladministration of the mixed institutions was made worse by the system of " farming " the poor that we shall presently describe.   But apart from this administrative perversion, the mere fact that considerably more than half the workhouse inmates were (as is always found to be the case) not able-bodied adults, who might possibly be expected to get their own living, but children, women with babies, the sick or infirm, the aged or the mentally defective, whose self-support was often quite impossible, made the expedient of deterrence seem, to the humane man of property, inept and cruel.

The Gilbert Act Unions

The eventual outcome of a whole generation of proposals of reform was the well-known " Act for the Better Relief and Employment of the Poor " (22 George III. c. 83)—already mentioned by us in respect of its encouragement of Outdoor Relief to the able-bodied—which was passed into law in 1782 by the strenuous

---

respect to the Poor, Vagrants and Houses of Correction, by a Justice of the Peace in the County of York, 1775 ; and *An Address on the Expediency of a Regular Plan for the Maintenance and Government of the Poor*, by Richard Woodward, 1775 ; also, by the same, *An Argument in Support of the Right of the Poor in the Kingdom of Ireland to a National Provision*, 1775.

and long-continued efforts of Thomas Gilbert (1720–1798), M.P.,
who had been for years occupied with the subject.[1] He had been
in the House of Commons since 1763, first for Newcastle-under-
Lyme, and from 1768 for Lichfield, and had become one of the
most influential of the " country gentlemen " legislators. He
was rewarded by government sinecures, and from 1784 until his
retirement in 1795 he held the important office of Chairman of
the Committee on Ways and Means, exercising no small influence
on the action of the House in respect of highways, canals and
Local Acts generally.

" Gilbert's Act ", as the statute of 1782 has always been
called (which was accompanied the same session by another
measure promoted by Gilbert relating to Houses of Correction,
22 George III. c. 64), was a long, detailed and well-drafted measure,
with elaborate schedules of minute prescriptions, the outcome of
great thought and full consideration of the suggestions of others.
Its leading idea was to get the administration of the Poor Law
out of the hands of the annually elected unpaid Overseers, whom
that generation was disposed to blame for all the maladministration,[2] and to secure establishment and maintenance of a well-

---

[1] Gilbert's Act is fully summarised in *History of the English Poor Law*, by
Sir George Nicholls, 1854, vol. ii. pp. 89-98 ; and its enactment is described in
The State of the Poor, by Sir F. M. Eden, 1797, vol. i. An incomplete list of the
Unions formed under it is given in Ninth Annual Report of Poor Law Commissioners, 1843, pp. 112-113. No general description of the working of these
Unions is known to us, though a few are incidentally described in the reports
of the Assistant Commissioners which are included in Appendix A of the Report
of the Poor Law Inquiry Commissioners, 1834, and in the annual Reports of
the Poor Law Commissioners, 1835-1847.

[2] Burn's account of the Overseer is well known. "And this leads to the
other great fundamental defect . . . in our present Poor Laws, and that is
that the whole in a great measure (and in practice, indeed, altogether) is left
to the management of those annual officers called Overseers of the Poor. . . .
In fact, the officer goes by rotation from one householder to another . . . In
practice the office of an Overseer of the Poor seems to be understood to be
this . . . to maintain the poor as cheap as they possibly can . . . to bargain
with some sturdy person to take them by the lump, who yet is not intended
to take them, but to hang over them *in terrorem* if they shall complain to the
Justices for want of maintenance. . . . But to see that the poor shall resort
to church and bring their children there to be instructed . . . to provide a
stock of materials to set the poor on work ; to see the aged and impotent
comfortably sustained, the sick healed, and all of them clothed with neatness
and decency ; these and such like, it is to be feared, are not so generally regarded
as the laws intended, and the necessity of the case requires " (*History of the
Poor Laws*, by Richard Burn, 1764, pp. 210-211). Another contemporary
condemns equally the officers of the urban parishes. " The offices of Churchwarden and Overseer of the Poor, especially in all large and populous parishes

T

organised institution for the impotent poor for a larger area than the parish. In order to avoid opposition, the Act was made to apply only in parishes in which it had been formally adopted by two-thirds of the owners and occupiers assessed at £5 per annum or upwards. It evaded the difficulty of deciding what should be the new unit of administration by leaving parishes to combine as they chose, provided that they were within a radius of ten miles from the workhouse which they were by the adoption of the Act committed to provide. The Act met the objection to heavy initial expenditure by giving the new Unions express power to borrow on the security of Poor Rates equal to those of the previous three years. The cost of maintenance was to be shared among the constituent parishes, but only in proportion to the number that each chose to send. The apprehension of the Justices that their own work might be increased was allayed by the provision that they should appoint, for each parish, a salaried Guardian of the Poor, out of names submitted by the parishioners. Moreover, the Justices were to appoint a superior person for the Union, called a Visitor, who was to have the power of giving orders to the governor of the workhouse and the treasurer of the Union. But what was most important was the express provision that the workhouse to be established in the Union was not for the able-bodied but was to be confined exclusively to the various sections of the impotent poor—that is to say, the aged, sick and infirm, and the orphan children, or children accompanying their mothers.[2] Upon this provision followed what was afterwards called " the extraordinary clause " which " contained the first formal deviation from the principle of the 43rd Elizabeth as to able-bodied persons, and from the principle of Sir Edward Knatchbull's Act."

---

in cities and great towns, are generally filled up with tradesmen and mechanics, who are often very little interested in the expense, and whose situation makes it almost impossible for them not to do things through favour and partiality. . . . Their principal care is to rub through it with as little inconvenience to themselves as they possibly can " (*An Inquiry into the Management of the Poor, and our usual Polity respecting the common people, with reasons why they have not hitherto been attended with success*, 1767).

[1] The Act gave also the first statutory sanction to what had been occasionally practised for two hundred years, namely, the " boarding out " of young children, " with some reputable person in the neighbourhood, at such weekly allowance as shall be agreed upon, until of age to be put into service, or bound apprentice to husbandry or some trade or occupation ; and a list of the children so placed out, and by whom kept, is to be given to the visitor, who shall see that they are properly treated ", etc.

Instead of the old law, which had lasted for 181 years, and which, in whatever manner it had been practically construed, merely required that all persons should be set to work who "used no ordinary and daily trade of life to get their living by ",[1] Gilbert's Act provided that if there were any persons who shall be able and willing to work, but who cannot get employment, the Guardian of the Poor—acting individually—was required to find them employment near by at wages ; or else " to maintain or cause such person or persons to be properly maintained, lodged and provided for until such employment shall be procured ", and to make up any deficiency in the earnings ! Any Justice could order the Guardian to give such relief, or to send the person to the workhouse,[2] there to be provided for until employment for him at wages could be found. Idle and disorderly persons were to be committed by the Justices to the House of Correction.

But although Thomas Gilbert succeeded, by his skilful drafting, in getting his Bill through Parliament, his Act failed to work as he expected. For years it scarcely worked at all. Very few parishes could be induced to adopt the new law, and constitute the Unions that would establish the workhouses of a novel type, to be administered by Visitors and salaried Guardians appointed by the Justices, by whom, in supersession of the Overseers, the impotent poor could be properly treated, and the able-bodied unemployed placed in situations. After fifteen years, it could be recorded that "very few " Gilbert Act Unions had been constituted.[3] Later on, at different dates between 1797 and 1830, some threescore such Unions were formed, making 67 in all, comprising (out of the total of 15,000) only 924 parishes, practically all rural in character ; the great majority in south-eastern England, East Anglia and the Midlands, with a few in Westmorland and Yorkshire ; none at all in Wales, in the west or south-west of England, or north of the Tees. Thus, as a

---

[1] Ninth Annual Report of the Poor Law Commissioners, 1843, p. 107.

[2] This seems inconsistent with the section saying that " no person " shall be sent thither except the various classes of impotent poor ; and we believe that it was hardly ever acted upon. The divergence between the policy of the Gilbert Act workhouse for the residence of the impotent poor, and that of the " well-regulated workhouse " intended to deter the able-bodied from even seeking admission to it, is commented on by Sir George Nicholls in his *History of the English Poor Law*, 1854, vol. ii. p. 249.

[3] *The State of the Poor*, by Sir F. M. Eden, 1797, vol. i. ; *Considerations on the Subject of Poorhouses*, by Sir William Young, M.P., 1796, p. 29.

measure for the reform of the Poor Law its results were relatively trifling. Unfortunately the good features of such a Bill in Parliament often evaporate with its enactment as a statute, whilst the evil that it does, in its general influence upon public opinion, lives after it. We do not find that the Gilbert Act Unions between 1782 and 1834 were distinguished either by well-regulated institutions, or by administration markedly superior to that of the discredited Overseers of the Poor. What the Act did was to emphasise and strengthen the feeling —sanctioned by Parliament in Sir William Young's Act of 1796—that the poorhouses and workhouses of all sorts were not places to which it was intended that the unemployed labourer should be relegated ; and that it was the duty of the Poor Law Authority in all parishes either to find him employment at wages, or else to maintain him and his family on Outdoor Relief. Moreover, in the opening decades of the nineteenth century, when the majority of these Gilbert Act Unions were formed, there was nothing to compel a strict compliance with the terms of the Act ; and it may be assumed that its adoption was often regarded merely as an easy and inexpensive way of enabling parishes to combine for the purpose of borrowing money to erect a joint workhouse ; an institution which became, in most cases, nothing better than a General Mixed Workhouse of the old type ; [1] or, in exceptional instances (like that of the Thurgarton Union already referred to), was perverted during the last decade of the Old Poor Law into a " deterrent " institution that would permit of the application of the " workhouse test ".

[1] In 1807 " three parishes within the borough of Wallingford availed themselves of Gilbert's Act and built a common workhouse ; they of course substituted the administration of relief by Visitors and Guardians for that of the Overseers ; and what were the results ?—a steady increase of their expenses, a gradual, and finally a total departure from the provisions of the Act under which the Union was formed. I found that the Guardians were annually appointed and did nothing ; in fact, they were ignorant that they had any official duty to perform beyond keeping the workhouse in repair ; the Overseers paid the poor, and all the abuses consequent upon that method of giving relief flourished in that Union as well as out of it. . . . [In the workhouse] there was not the slightest attempt at classification ; old and young, male and female, sick and sound were left to mingle at will ; the discipline that could be maintained amounted to nothing " (First Annual Report of Poor Law Commissioners, 1835, p. 216). Other descriptions are to like effect ; see, for instance, Report of the Committee appointed to investigate the accounts of the Parish of Foleshill (Coventry, 1832). These " Gilbert Act Unions," after 1834, had all to be dissolved, and their constituent parishes rearranged into Unions under the Poor Law Amendment Act.

The Contract System

The practice of " farming " the poor, or contracting for their maintenance at a fixed rate, so characteristic of English poor relief between 1723 and 1834, is only one example of what was, at the time, a prevalent method of administration. The eighteenth century local governing body, whatever the service which it had to provide, found it easier to avoid the trouble and risk of direct employment, and delighted to put the whole business out to contract for a fixed payment. Whether it was the building of a bridge or the conveyance of vagrants, the transportation of convicts or the lighting of the thoroughfares, all difficulties seemed to be solved by asking what contractor would undertake to execute the service for the lowest cash payment. In other cases, the right to perform the service was sold, as a privilege, to the highest bidder ; and, as we have described in our *Statutory Authorities for Special Purposes* (1922), markets were managed, turnpike tolls were collected and town dung was removed, by the speculator who saw his way to make the largest pecuniary profit from the business. The merit of applying this plausible administrative device to the relief of the poor seems to be due to the drafters of the first general Workhouse Act, 9 George I. c. 7, in 1723. From that time forward, right down to 1834 we find every variety of " farming " the poor—contracting for the maintenance of all the paupers having any claim on the parish ; contracting merely for the management of the workhouse ; contracting for infants and children ; contracting for lunatics, and contracting for medical relief.

Farming the Whole Poor

The practice of contracting with some person to relieve the parish of all its legal liabilities towards the destitute, in return for the payment of a lump sum, seems to have arisen from the celebrated workhouse clause in the Act of 1723. Exactly what the House of Commons intended by this clause is, as we have already mentioned, not clear. From the mere words of the Act, we must infer that Parliament had in view the incapacity of the annually elected unpaid Overseer effectively to conduct the manufacturing establishment, or to maintain the deterrent system, that was contemplated. Hence the permission to establish a workhouse under this Act was closely connected with the authority to put its management out to contract—so closely, indeed, that it was subsequently held by the Court of King's Bench that a single parish had no option in the matter.[1] But the parish authorities of the period needed no injunction. Not only did they hasten to rid themselves of the trouble of workhouse management by putting it out to contract : they seized the opportunity also of insuring against the whole of the parish liabilities under the Poor Law, and incidentally, of shifting to the contractor the odium of refusing Outdoor Relief.

To meet this demand there came forward, wherever the Act of 1723 was made use of, enterprising speculators who set up as managers of workhouses, and offered to each little parish, within a radius of twenty or thirty miles, to undertake, for a fixed annual payment, the relief of all destitution within the parish. It is easy to understand how vile was the condition of workhouses so provided, unchecked by any inspection or public control. " The parochial workhouses ", said an able writer in 1773, " are commonly badly enough managed ; but the management of these extra-parochial ones is worse beyond comparison." [2] Where the whole, of the parish poor were taken, as Dr. Burn says, " by the lump ", the contractor was under a pecuniary inducement to refuse to maintain any applicant, old or young, able-bodied or infirm, who did not enter the workhouse, where as much work was obtained from him as the taskmaster's pecuniary interest, backed by the widest disciplinary powers, could exact. " One such taskmaster ", Dr. Burn tells us, " oftentimes undertakes for the poor of several parishes or townships ", almost inevitably becoming, in the parishes in which the system was put in force, a slave-driver of the worst description, interested only to obtain the greatest profit from the labour of the unfortunate wretches in his charge, without any effective responsibility for their maintenance in health or comfort. Moreover, as

---

[1] On a strict construction of the Act, it was held in 1782 that, though a Union of parishes might do so, a single parish proceeding under the 1723 Act had no power to manage its own workhouse, but was obliged to contract (R. *v.* St. Peter and St. Paul in Bath). See Burn's *Justice*, vol. iv. sec. iii. 4, p. 154 of 1820 edition.

[2] *Observations on the Present State of the Parochial and Vagrant Poor* [by John Scott], 1773, p. 41.

this employment of enforced labour could seldom be made to
yield a profit, the contractor's pecuniary interest was not only to
skimp the food of the inmates, but also to make the institution
in every way a " House of Terror ".   The greater the reluctance
of the poor to accept relief, the greater was the profit to the
contractor.   And though we need not suppose the contractors
to have been less than usually humane, the mere fact that they
had periodically, or even annually, to bid against each other,
as to which of them would take the poor at the lowest price,
inevitably led to an ever-increasing brutality.   Under the stress
of this competition each contractor would find that " the power
of oppression is in his hand, and he must use it ; the gains of
oppression are within his reach, and he must not refuse them ". [1]
Finally the parish, discovering how greatly its rates were reduced
through the contractor's brutality—which, like the " sweating "
practised by employers of labour in competitive industry,
ultimately reduced the price to the contractor's customers—
came to encourage this vicarious denial of relief to the poor.   The
" bargain with some person to take them by the lump " eventually included, as Dr. Burn more than once indicates, a tacit
understanding that the contractor " is not to take them, but to
hang [his penal confinement] over them *in terrorem* if they should
complain to the Justices ". [2]

   In short, the workhouse under the Act of 1723 became, as was
pointed out in 1773, " a dreadful engine of oppression. . . . By
means of this statute the parochial managers are impowered to
establish a set of petty tyrants as their substitutes, who, farming
the poor at a certain price, accumulate dishonest wealth by
abridging them of reasonable food, and imposing on them
unreasonable labour. A thorough acquaintance with the
interior economy of these wretched receptacles of misery, or
rather parish prisons called workhouses, is not easily to be
acquired ; in these as in other arbitrary governments complaint
is mutiny and treason, to every appearance of which a double
portion of punishment is invariably annexed : particular incidents

   [1] *Observations on the Present State of the Parochial and Vagrant Poor* [by
John Scott], 1773, p. 40.
   [2] *The History of the Poor Laws*, by the Rev. Richard Burn, 1764, p. 211 ;
The Justice of the Peace, by the same, p. 137 of 1820 edition ; see also *A Dialogue
in two Conversations . . . in answer to . . . Observations on the Poor Laws*, etc.,
by Thomas Mendham, Norwich, 1775 ; and *Observations on the Poor Laws, on
the Present State of the Poor, and on Houses of Industry*, by Robert Potter, 1775.

shocking to humanity may have sometimes transpired, but the whole mystery of iniquity perhaps never has been nor ever will be developed. One thing is too publicly known to admit of denial, that those workhouses are scenes of filthiness and confusion ; that old and young, sick and healthy, are promiscuously crowded into ill-contrived apartments, not of sufficient capacity to contain with convenience half the number of miserable beings condemned to such deplorable inhabitation, and that speedy death is almost ever to the aged and infirm, and often to the youthful and robust, the consequence of a removal from more salubrious air to such mansions of putridity. Well then may the indigent dread confinement within these walls as the worst of evils ; well may they execrate that parochial policy which, by thus propagating disease and producing mortality, accelerates with impunity the removal of a burthen to which the shoulder of avarice has ever submitted with evident reluctance." [1] The system shocked even Dr. Burn, who wrote, in 1764, that " the matter seemeth at length to have been carried too far ; the Overseers in many places having found out a method of contracting with some obnoxious person, of savage disposition, for the maintenance of the poor ; not with any intention of the poor being better provided for, but to hang over them *in terrorem*, if they will not be satisfied with the pittance which the Overseers think fit to allow them." [2]

It was, we believe, this practice of farming the whole poor, by converting the workhouse into a " House of Terror " that ruined the first experiments in the " offer of the House " as a test of destitution, and produced, by 1782, the reaction in favour of the provision of paid employment, or, in default, Outdoor

---

[1] *Observations on the Present State of the Parochial and Vagrant Poor* [by John Scott], 1773, p. 36.

[2] Burn's *Justice of the Peace*, article " Poor ", vol. iv. sec. iii. 4, p. 137 of 1820 edition. " The truth is ", sums up a later witness, " that previous to the late modification of the Act of 9 George I. by the Act of 36 George III., these workhouses were erected more with a view of exciting terror than providing for the comforts of the poor " (*General View of the Agriculture of Gloucestershire*, by Thomas Rudge, 1807, p. 348). It is characteristic of the period that he should add " fortunately, the intended purpose of these buildings has been in great measure frustrated by the interference of the legislature in the Act above mentioned ". At Bray, in Berkshire, where the workhouse was inhabited chiefly by the aged and the children, " beating hemp is held out *in terrorem* to the idle and the profligate ", at the instance of the incumbent, who was himself a Justice of the Peace, and did not give orders for Out Relief under the Act of 1796 (*General View of the Agriculture of Berkshire*, by Mavor, 1808, p. 105).

Relief to the able-bodied, which, as we have seen, was enjoined by Parliament in Gilbert's Act. It is only one more instance of the melancholy incapacity of eighteenth-century administrators that what was abandoned in this reaction was, not the device which had done the mischief, namely, the farming of the poor " by the lump ", but the expedient which had achieved a certain measure of success, namely, the provision of relief for destitute able-bodied persons, in an institution with a regimen which included discipline, and might have been developed into an educational and reformatory system. Most of the Justices in the rural districts resumed their practice of ordering Outdoor Relief whenever they thought fit ; and the Act of 1796, as we have seen, expressly authorised them to do so, even if the parish had contracted for the whole of its poor. The well-meaning Justice of the Peace, said an eighteenth-century moralist, " will not on slight grounds oblige a poor man to relinquish his cottage with all his little domestic comforts and take up his abode in a workhouse ; *much less be transported to the workhouse of some distant place, which farms the poor of twenty villages, there to pine among strangers* ".[1] From the outset, the Justices had resented " an execrable law which absurdly renders every obstinate illiterate barbarian of an Overseer or Churchwarden in this respect the absolute master of his superiors " [2]—the local magistrates ! They refused in some cases to abandon their practice of ordering Outdoor Relief, even where there was a contractor's workhouse ; and when their orders were not upheld by the Court of King's Bench,[3] they took steps, after some delay, to get the law altered. In 1782, when Gilbert's Act was passed to facilitate the union of parishes for the erection of workhouses, a clause was inserted maintaining the Justices' power to order Outdoor Relief. This, however, did not help them in the parishes which had not adopted this Act ; and in 1793 we find the Norfolk Quarter Sessions requesting the County Members to procure such an amendment of the 1723 Act as would enable Justices " to order relief out of such Houses as are or shall be under the government of that Act in the same manner as under

[1] *An Enquiry into the Duties of Man*, by T. Gisborne, 1794, pp. 291-293.
[2] *Observations on the Present State of the Parochial and Vagrant Poor* [by John Scott], 1773, p. 53.
[3] As in R. *v.* Carlisle (1763).

Gilbert's Act ".[1] Three years later Parliament acceded to their desire, Sir William Young's Act of 1796 giving Justices power to order Outdoor Relief, " notwithstanding any contract shall have been made for maintaining the poor " in a workhouse.[2]

Under these new conditions the contract for farming the whole of the poor became the strangest possible instance of a contractor undertaking, for a fixed payment, an obligation of which he could not control the limits. In return for an agreed lump sum, the contractor undertook not only to maintain such poor as were in the workhouse, and all who might be sent there by the Overseers, but also to pay such Outdoor Relief as might be ordered by the Overseers, or by any Justice of the Peace. Thus the contractor stood the racket of any increase of pauperism whatsoever, whether caused by interruption of employment or spread of disease, or by the generous impulses of the Overseers and Justices in ordering Outdoor Relief to whomsoever they thought fit. In the old parish chest of Chalfont St. Peter, a little Buckinghamshire village, we found a number of parchment rolls, which proved to be elaborately signed and sealed contracts between the Churchwardens and Overseers on the one hand, and a local contractor on the other. These contracts, which covered most of the years between 1800 and 1833, were all of the same character. That for 1812, for instance, bound the parish to pay £812 to the contractor for the ensuing year, and to give him the use of the parish workhouse and infirmary, for himself, his family and the indoor poor. In return, he undertook for the whole year, without claim to revision of the terms, to provide, for any poor who may be sent in by the Overseers, " comfortable and sufficient lodging and washing, and likewise good and sufficient, sweet and wholesome meat, drink and every other article necessary to and suitable for the support and comfort of the said poor people, such as, with respect both to the quantity and quality, the Churchwardens and Overseers shall approve of ",

---

[1] MS. Minutes, Quarter Sessions, Norfolk, April 10, 1793. We gather that the Court of King's Bench was about this time showing great reluctance to interfere with orders for Outdoor Relief, when Justices had given them (see R. v. North Shields in 1780 and R. v. James Haugh in 1790); and it did not expressly declare them contrary to the Act of 1723.

[2] 36 George III. c. 23. This power was enlarged by 55 George III. c. 137. By 50 George III. c. 50, the contractor was put under the same obligations as an Overseer, and thus made directly subject to the Justices' orders (see Burn's *Justice*, vol. iv. sec. iii. 4, pp. 138, 146 of 1820 edition).

including education and the consolations of religion. Moreover, he " shall give to such and so many poor persons of or belonging to the said parish, as shall stand in need of parochial relief . . . such sums of money as the Churchwardens and Overseers . . . or any Justice of the Peace . . . shall from time to time direct and appoint ". He is also to supply the poor of the village with midwives, baptize the children and bury the dead. He is to enjoy the fruits of the labour of the poor in the workhouse, who are, however, not to be employed " in gleaning or collecting firewood ". There is, in fact, only one liability of the parish under the poor laws for which he refused to take the risk. For the bastard children whom he had to receive into the workhouse he stipulated for a separate payment of 1s. 6d. per week per head.[1]

Similar contracts were found existing in 1833 in the adjoining parishes of Amersham and Langley, with slight variations. At Langley, for instance, accidents, such as fractures, fall to the charge of the parish ; at Chalfont St. Peter the contractor undertakes to mend them ; whilst at Amersham, we are told, " the parish meets the expense of compound fractures, the contractor that of simple ones ".[2]

Contracts of this description, indemnifying the parish against all its obligations under the Poor Law, with such exceptions only as were expressly provided for, may be traced in all parts of England. Sir F. M. Eden records the particulars of contracts for the whole of the poor, which he found in about a dozen parishes, all over the country, extending over the last quarter of the eighteenth century. Thus, at Redbourn in Hertfordshire, the parish had for some years rented a house, provided furniture and paid £26 a month to a contractor (who in 1796 demanded a rise of £3 a month) to relieve them of all their poor. The contractor paid 22 " out pensioners," and employed the rest in the straw-plait manufacture.[3] At Presteign in Radnorshire and Knighton

---

[1] MS. contract, October 12, 1812, among the parish records of Chalfont St. Peter (Bucks). The contract is signed as " approved " by two Justices of the Peace. It also includes an undertaking by the contractor to defray all county rates, constable's and vestry clerk's bills, justices' clerks' fees, allowance to wives and families of militia men, and in fact every conceivable obligation of the parish ; but these sums are to be reimbursed by the Overseers (see also Report of Poor Law Inquiry Commissioners, Appendix A, Carmalt's Report, p. 153-154).

[2] *Ibid.* Carmalt's Report, p. 154.

[3] Sir F. M. Eden's *State of the Poor*, 1797, vol. ii. p. 277.

in Shropshire, the parishes had got off for less than £150 a year each, but the contractor in the latter place was, in 1796, relinquishing his contract.[1] So at Ecclesfield in Yorkshire, where the parish increased its lump sum payment from £760 in 1793–1794 to £860 in 1794–1795, but failed to keep its contractor.[2] At Wallingford in Berkshire, on the other hand, the contractor was still contented to farm all the poor for £300 a year, excluding only doctors' bills and lawyers' bills.[3] For the little market town of Louth in Lincolnshire we find recorded all the vacillations of Poor Law policy for a quarter of a century. In 1774 they built a workhouse, which the Overseers managed for two years. Then they let it, and the whole maintenance of the inmates, to a woollen manufacturer, who ran it at a loss from 1777 to 1779. Another manufacturer took the contract for a couple of years, but fared no better. The Overseers then managed it themselves from 1782 to 1784, and succeeded in the latter year in finding another contractor, who indemnified the parish against all Poor Law obligations except legal expenses. This system was apparently successful, as the contract lasted without interruption until 1794. That year the Overseers failed to find a contractor, and had to maintain the poor themselves, at twice the cost of the previous contract. In 1795 a contractor was again found to take the whole charge off their hands at a fixed price.[4] We may now pass to some later examples. In the parish of Chertsey in Surrey, where the administration of poor relief had been greatly improved by the formation of an extra-legal Vestry Committee, the whole of the poor, outdoor as well as indoor, were, in 1817, being maintained by a local agriculturist, under an annual contract, for the fixed sum of £2425 per annum. This contractor supported about 114 aged and infirm persons in the parish workhouse, without any particular work, and employed some 350 others on his land, having to pay them according to the scale fixed by the Justices, who insisted on their orders being obeyed.[5] A remarkable case of contracting for the whole poor, as late as 1832, is presented by the parish of Farringdon in Berkshire. The contractor himself gave the following account of it. " In May 1832 I con-

---

[1] Sir F. M. Eden's *State of the Poor*, 1797, vol. iii. pp. 900-904.
[2] *Ibid.* vol. iii. pp. 813-817. [3] *Ibid.* vol. ii, p. 17.
[4] *Ibid.* vol. ii. pp. 394-398.
[5] Report of House of Commons Select Committee on the Poor Laws, 1817 (Lacoast's evidence).

tracted with the Visitor and Guardians of the parish of Farringdon to maintain the whole of the indoor and the outdoor poor for the sum of £2200 which was about £600 less than they had cost the parish during the two previous years. I have contracted to provide good and sufficient clothing for all the persons then in the poor house, or who shall be admitted during the year, and also good and sufficient diet for all such persons, and in particular will allow them good meat dinners three days at the least in each week, and will from time to time provide for them sufficient vegetables, beer, bread, cheese and other necessaries of good quality, and also provide for such of the said poor persons as may be sick, diet of mutton or such other diet as may be suitable (except medicines and medical advice), and generally will supply during the said term all things necessary for the use of the poor for the time being in the poor house : that as to such of the poor called out-door poor, entitled to relief from the said parish, but not being in the poor house, the said Charles Price will during the said term, make to such poor persons for their maintenance, such allowance as shall be directed by the said Visitor and Guardians, by writing signed by them, whether by a general scale of allowances or by directions to be made from time to time and applicable to any particular case, he the said Charles Price having the benefit of the labour of such poor persons." The contractor required all unmarried able-bodied men to enter the workhouse, which was kept under strict discipline ; he put all able-bodied men, married or unmarried, to hard labour in digging and carrying stones, at piecework rates ; and he insisted on full working hours being given. The result was that, although he did not venture to order married men into the workhouse, paid the full rate of wages for all work done by outdoor paupers, and allowed a generous diet to those indoors, he got rid at once of one-third of the outdoor paupers. By strict personal investigation into all applications on the plea of sickness and infirmity, he greatly reduced the payments under this head ; and after one year's trial, he bade fair to effect still further reductions.[1]

In the primitive and sparsely peopled parishes of Cumberland and Westmorland, the relief of the suffering of "God's Poor" long continued to be put out to contract like the mending of the roads.

[1] Report of Poor Law Inquiry Commissioners, Appendix A, Chadwick's Report, pp. 57-61.

At Orton in Westmorland, for instance, Sir F. M. Eden found, in 1796, that the whole of the poor had been contracted for, without material change, for the past twenty years at least.[1] A generation later the parishes continued the same system. The " contract," we are told in 1833, " is offered by public advertisement,[2] and the lowest tender is accepted, if the person making it be approved of at the general meeting of the ratepayers called together for that object. The person taking the contract has the use of the poorhouse and ground attached, where there is such an establishment ; if not, he takes the paupers whom he cannot satisfy with a small payment into his own house. The contractors are generally small farmers ; men who in many cases sit down to their meals with the paupers." The Assistant Poor Law Commissioner adds, as illustrating the primitive simplicity of Cumberland social life, that he found " the Perpetual Curate of a parish lodging and boarding at the house of one of these contractors ".[3]

These contracts were not confined to rural villages. The ancient parish of St. Martin's, Leicester, in the heart of that borough, used in this way to insure itself against all its Poor Law obligations by a fixed weekly payment. Here the contract gradually becomes complicated by more exceptions and extra charges than had been thought of in the arcadian simplicity of Westmorland or Buckinghamshire, but down to 1804 it still covers, for a fixed charge, the uncertain item of Outdoor Relief.[4]

---

[1] Sir F. M. Eden's *State of the Poor*, 1797, vol. ii. pp. 776-778.

[2] In 1824 we notice advertisements in the Birmingham newspapers, " that the Churchwardens and Overseers of the Poor " of such and such parishes, " are desirous of contracting for the farming of the whole of the poor of the said parish as well in the workhouse as out " (see *Birmingham Gazette*, March 8, 1824).

[3] Report of Poor Law Inquiry Commissioners, Appendix A, Pringle's Report, p. 313.

[4] This is the contract referred to in Sir F. M. Eden's *State of the Poor*, vol. ii. pp. 385-389. As the phraseology is not without interest, we transcribe it in full from the Vestry Minute Book, under date of May 2, 1786. The contractor was a stocking weaver, and he employed the paupers in spinning worsted. " At this meeting William Chaloner of the said parish and borough, Woolcomber, agreed with the Churchwardens and Overseers of the poor of this parish to keep the workhouse of the same from this day to Friday in Easter week 1787, and to maintain the poor now in being with sufficient clothing and victuals, also to pay such sums of money weekly and to such persons residing out of the said workhouse wherever resident as three officers shall direct, also to allow clothing and pay such rent to such persons as they shall also direct, also to pay the expense in maintaining certificated persons after the com-

In the busy seaport of Sunderland, in which the total Poor Rates literally doubled every ten years from 1791 to 1811, and which had in vain tried to keep down its pauperism by establishing a workhouse, publishing the names of the outdoor poor, and putting the workhouse inmates to oakum picking,[1] contracting for the whole poor was at last resorted to, and in 1820 a substantial contractor undertook to satisfy all claims for a fixed payment of £150 per week. For this sum, the contractor not only maintained the workhouse, but paid all the Outdoor Relief that was ordered. The parish, satisfied to find its rates steadily reduced, as contractor bid against contractor for the privilege of farming the poor, and as the price per week went down from £150 to £68, continued the system year after year, heedless of the demoralisation of the contractor's workhouse and the hardships suffered by those not fortunate enough to secure generous orders for Outdoor Relief. In 1831 came the cholera, a new horror, which Sunderland was the first English town to experience, and which swept away paupers and contractor alike. The Rector and the Open Vestry, remorseful about the harshness with which the poor had been treated, saw " the finger of Providence traceable in the death of the contractor ", and reverted to the direct management of the workhouse and the liberal grant of Out-Relief.[2]

We infer, from the small number of cases in which the Assistant Poor Law Commissioners described contracts of this sort, that they

---

mencement of this agreement : to maintain all bastard children now born and all such casual poor whose settlements cannot be made out. Also to pay for coffins and fees of interment for those who shall die in the workhouse, and to bear all other expenses relative to the maintenance of the poor ; except medicines and surgeon's fees, law charges, expense of removals to and from the parish of casual poor whose settlements may be made out, expense of providing beds, bedding and furniture for the workhouse, of bastards now after to be born, of putting out apprentices, of coffins for persons out of the workhouse, and keeping the workhouse in repair, paying the taxes—at and for the consideration or payment of the weekly sum of thirteen pounds." This is signed by the contractor and ten parishioners. It is renewed annually, with slight variations, the consideration in 1797 going down to £12, and in 1800 rising to £21 per week. In the latter year the contract is made terminable at 14 days' notice, and in 1804 it changes into an ordinary workhouse contract at 4s. 6d. per week per head (MS. Vestry Minutes, St. Martin's, Leicester, 1786–1804 ; see also *The Accounts of the Churchwardens of St. Martin's, Leicester, 1489–1844*, by Thomas North, Leicester, 1884).

[1] See the account given in *General View of the Agriculture of the County of Durham*, by John Bailey, 1810, p. 321, etc.

[2] Report of Poor Law Inquiry Commissioners, Appendix A, Wilson's Report, p. 137 ; see *History of Sunderland*, by J. W. Summers, vol. i., 1858 ; and *History of Sunderland*, by W. C. Mitchell, 1919.

had, by 1833, fallen generally into disuse.   Only in one county, Monmouthshire, was the practice of farming the whole of the poor reported as increasing, and becoming more popular.[1] The system, it is clear, worked in one of two ways.   When it continued in force, and contractors competed for the privilege, the parish found its rates reduced ; but the condition of this success was the tacit agreement of the Justices and the Overseers not to exercise their power of ordering Outdoor Relief. The contractor was thus able to use the workhouse test in its worst form—not with a view of discriminating between the destitute and the idle, but as a means of terrifying all the poor, deserving and undeserving alike, into accepting a mere pittance. " He who contracts to maintain them at a gross annual sum," explains the Assistant Poor Law Commissioner, " saves more out of that yearly allowance by keeping the poor out of the workhouse, for the poor invariably prefer taking the smallest pittance as out-pensioners rather than enter the workhouse. . . . Hence it is that in parishes in Monmouthshire you will find the workhouse almost deserted.   Their workhouses or poorhouses seem scarcely to answer any other end but that of terrifying paupers into a willingness to accept the quantum of allowance the contractor may think fit to offer them." [2]   On the other hand, where the Overseers or the Justices insisted on ordering Outdoor Relief, or where the existence of the regular Allowance System under a scale enabled the farmers indefinitely to reduce their wages,[3] the contractor found his obligations becoming ruinous, and refused to renew the contract for any fixed sum whatsoever.[4]

[1] The two small boroughs of Monmouth and Chepstow introduced the system about 1820, and found their rates much reduced thereby. The system spread to a considerable extent among the neighbouring parishes (Report of Poor Law Inquiry Commissioners, Appendix A, Lewis's Report, p. 668).

[2] *Ibid.* Lewis's Report, pp. 660-661.

[3] This is given as the cause of failure in various Buckinghamshire parishes. " Some farmers, seeing the contractor bound to maintain or find work for all that might claim it of him, would discharge all their labourers, and then re-engage them from him at a reduced price, he being obliged to pay them the difference out of his fixed allowance from the parish.   Others would follow the example, and the contract not being made in contemplation of such a contingency, the arrangement could not last " (*ibid.* Carmalt's Report, p. 155).

[4] At the Aylesbury Petty Sessions in 1829, the chairman mentioned that " De Fraine, the contractor for the maintenance of the poor [of Aylesbury], being unable to complete his contract, the persons who were bound for the fulfilment of his bargaining with the parish had taken the management of the poor into their own hands, and the first thing they had done in order to make up the loss sustained in the summer half year was to reduce the weekly

Farming the Workhouse

The growing prevalence of Outdoor Relief, and especially the casual but continuous ordering of it by the Justices after 1796, had, by the end of the eighteenth century, made impracticable the simple contract for relieving the parish of the whole of its liabilities under the Poor Laws, except in peculiar districts. The alternative of contracting at so much per head for the maintenance of the paupers in the workhouse—a system as old as the workhouse itself [1]—was still open to parish authorities. During nearly the whole of the eighteenth and the first thirty years of the nineteenth century, we find the rival advantages of direct management and competitive tendering, in this branch of parish business, becoming, in one place after another, a hotly contested issue of Vestry politics. The records of populous parishes show that the contract system, wherever introduced, usually prevailed in the long run, though often only after many vacillations of policy.[2] When the Assistant Poor Law

allowance of all the aged poor, giving them the choice of submitting to the reduction or of going into the poor's house ". The action taken by the Justices was not reported (*Bucks Gazette*, November 14, 1829).

[1] Thus, in the volume of proceedings of the Justices of the Marylebone Petty Sessional Division—inextricably bound up, as we have described in *The Parish and the County*, with the administration of the parish of Marylebone— we find it resolved, at a meeting in 1736, attended by two Justices, two Churchwardens, two Overseers and the Surveyor of Highways, " that in our opinion it would conduce much to the interest and advantage of ye parish and ye poor in ye workhouse if the method now used for their maintenance therein were altered ; and that for ye future an agreement be made with some discreet and fitting person to take care and look after ye poor in ye workhouse, and that an allowance of two shillings per head per week be made such person who shall undertake the same ; and Mrs. Staines, an inhabitant of this parish (being present) offered her service for ye purposes aforesaid, viz. : to maintain all ye poor in ye workhouse at ye rate of two shillings per head per week, and to begin immediately, with one month for tryal of all parties ; that if it should appear to ye satisfaction of ye Churchwardens and Overseers of the Poor that ye said allowance is not sufficient a further addition be made to the same " (MS. Minutes, Marylebone Petty Sessions, March 31, 1736).

[2] Thus, at Minchinhampton, in Gloucestershire, we find the workhouse in 1789, under direct management, giving rise to great discontent at the cost. The governor is required to submit better accounts, and is finally dismissed, his successor being given elaborate instructions as to keeping store accounts, checking weights, etc. Next year he contracts for 1s. 11d. per head per week, to provide a specified dietary and to keep " the poor in the house . . . clean, washed, and mended ". The next three years see two new contractors in succession, with a reversion in 1795 to the original holder. In 1800 there was a great upheaval, and direct administration was resumed. This proved no more satisfactory, and in 1814 the parish settled down permanently to an

U

Commissioners in 1832–1833 surveyed England and Wales from
end to end, they found, throughout whole districts, the workhouse contractor firmly established.[1]

These workhouse farming contracts were originally based
upon two distinct considerations, the profit which the contractor
could derive from the labour of the paupers, and the payment
made to him for their maintenance. During the first half of the
eighteenth century, and often at the beginning of an experiment
in pauper employment in later times, the former consideration
seemed much the more important of the two. Thus, in the
advertisements of Local Authorities asking for tenders, we have
glowing descriptions of the opportunities for carrying on some
kind of profitable industry.[2] In these cases it would usually

---

annual contract, paying for fifty paupers " certain ", and from 1s. 11d. to
3s. 9d. a head for all over that number. The contractor also acted as Assistant
Overseer for a salary of thirty guineas (MS. Vestry Minutes, Minchinhampton,
Glos., 1786 to 1821). At Mitcham, in Surrey, we find the workhouse already
farmed in 1794, but constant disputes occurring. The Vestry summarily
terminates the contract and appoints a master and mistress at a salary of
£30 a year, and twopence in the shilling of the inmates' earnings. Two years
later this couple is dismissed and a contractor again advertised for, who
undertakes the maintenance at 3s. 3d. per head per week. In 1800 the Vestry
is again driven to resume direct administration but in 1802 settles down to
an annually renewed contract, which was not disturbed till 1831 (MS. Vestry
Minutes, Mitcham, Surrey, 1794 to 1831).

[1] The parish workhouse was, in London, seldom farmed (those of Lambeth
and Newington being notable exceptions) ; but nearly every London parish
made more or less use of the private " farm houses ", kept by private speculators. In the large provincial towns farming seldom prevailed (York being
the principal exception) ; nor were the Houses of Industry of Suffolk, Norfolk,
etc., farmed. In the following counties, viz. : Shropshire, Herefordshire,
Somerset, Devon, Middlesex Surrey, West Sussex and Cambridgeshire
" contracting " seems to have been the rule in a majority of the parishes which
had a workhouse at all. In the counties north of the Humber the practice
seems to have been exceptional. As to the other counties we have no information, the Assistant Poor Law Commissioners who visited them being apparently
uninterested in the point.

[2] In 1750 there is an advertisement in the *Coventry Mercury* (September 10)
for " a person of a good character who can be well recommended that is willing
to undertake the care of the poor of the parish of St. Michael's, in the City of
Coventry, by the week, month, or year ". He " is desired to send proposals
in writing to the parish officers Note : there is an exceeding good workhouse,
and very good convenience for carrying on a large manufacture " (Poole's
History of Coventry, p. 347). The *Leeds Mercury* contains in 1816 an advertisement by the Guardians of the Poor of Reigate, Horley and Nutfield, in the
County of Surrey, a union formed under Gilbert's Act, inviting tenders for
" the maintenance, clothing and employment of the poor of the said parishes ".
For the last twenty years, ever since the incorporation of the Union, they recite,
" a manufactory of blankets and of coarse woollens had been carried on (and
which is to be continued) in the Poor House, to which a fulling mill belongs.

be some enterprising master manufacturer who would contract for the workhouse, undertaking, for a small payment per head per week, to maintain all the paupers of both sexes and all ages, and to employ them—usually in the workhouse building, but occasionally also in a mill elsewhere—in his own manufacturing enterprise. Manufacturers seem, however, to have discovered, even earlier than the parish officers, that, with the important exception of the labour of docile children, the compulsory labour of paupers was unremunerative. At any rate, we have been unable to discover any record of a contract workhouse forming, for any length of time, an integral part of an independent manufacturing establishment.[1] By the end of the eighteenth century parish authorities had, in fact, drifted into contracts in which the main, if not the only, consideration was the weekly payment for each pauper.

These agreements for the maintenance of indoor paupers varied indefinitely from a mere allowance to the salaried master of the workhouse, to cover the cost of an exactly specified dietary, without any transfer of management, right up to the complete handing over of the paupers, body and soul, to the tender mercies of an independent "farmer of the poor", in his own establishment, many miles away from the parish. The actual working and results of these contracts were no less varied than their forms. The simplest type, which was no more than a commutation of the cost of food supplies, designed as much to save book-keeping as for any other reason, made practically no difference in workhouse administration. The master of the workhouse, who invariably acted as the contractor, had, no doubt, a bias towards reducing the allowance to each pauper, and the system lent itself to favouritism and possibilities of oppression. But there was

---

Fuller's earth is dug within a mile of the Poor House. There is attached to the house ten acres of very rich and valuable arable and meadow land " (*Leeds Mercury*, July 20, 1816).

[1] An exceptional form of this manufacturing contract existed at Winchester in 1832. " A private person carries on the sack trade and pays the managers for the labour of the inmates of the house £300 per annum " (Report of Poor Law Inquiry Commissioners, Appendix C, p. 3). In this case the paupers were maintained by the parish, and the circumstances which induced the manufacturer to pay so large a sum, even for a whole workhouseful of labour, are not clear. It is probable that the parish provided, not only the lodging, but also the food and clothing of the workhouse inmates, and merely " farmed " their labour for this annual payment.

always a fixed dietary, which erred on the side of liberality,[1] and, with regard to the check upon quantity and quality, all that can be said is that this was at least as easy for the Open Vestry to maintain when everything was furnished by a single responsible contractor, as when the separate articles had to be purchased from a host of little shopkeepers, often influential in the Open Vestry itself.[2] With regard to the cost of maintenance under such a system, all the evidence goes to show that this did not differ appreciably from that of an ordinary well-administered workhouse under direct management, being considerably less than the expense incurred by parishes where waste and corruption were rife, whilst being considerably more than was spent in such models of frugality as Uley in Gloucestershire. And where the parish authorities kept the whole government of the workhouse effectively in their own hands, the practice of paying the master a fixed sum per head was not found inconsistent with rigid discipline and hard work for the able-bodied, the use of the workhouse not as an asylum but as a test, and the classification of the inmates with a view to their specific treatment. Thus, at Coxheath near Maidstone, where the master of the workhouse farmed the inmates at 3s. 6d. per head per week, and took the proceeds of their labour, the institution was found, in 1833, to be " very well regulated ", and serving most efficiently as a test, owing " to the superintendence of a principal proprietor of the neighbourhood, who acts as chairman at the meetings of the Guardians. . . . Four acres of land are attached to the house, and about eighteen are hired by the master. The present number of inmates is 90 ; in winter sometimes 160 ; those who are able are set to agricultural work, to quarry stone (which is sold to the [Turnpike] Commissioners) and to break stone into small pieces for gravel

[1] The dietaries for the farmed workhouses were exactly similar to those already described in the workhouses directly administered. Thus at Minchinhampton the contractor had to supply each child between seven and fourteen with 1¼ lb. of bread per day, and 1 lb. of meat into pot Thursdays and Sundays ; each grown person with 1½ lb. of bread per day, 1 lb. of meat into pot Thursdays and Sundays, and two pints of table beer daily ; to children beer " in proportion ".

[2] The habit of parish officers themselves supplying provisions and stores to the workhouse, at excessive prices and without check, is described in *A Representation of some Mismanagements by Parish Officers*, 1726, a pamphlet ascribed to the John Marriott or Marryott, governor of St. Giles' Workhouse, whom we have already mentioned. See also *Parochial Tyranny, or the Housekeeper's Complaint*, by Andrew Moreton [Daniel De Foe], 1714 ; and our description of the Select Vestry in *The Parish and the County*, 1906.

walks ; the master is a wheelwright and employs some of the men on his business, and as carpenters and sawyers ; 2d. in the shilling is allowed to them ; if they neglect their work, they are taken before the magistrates, who sentence them to the treadmill. A clergyman attends on Saturdays, and all who are able go once to church on Sunday ; children are taught to read by a schoolmistress, who is boarded at the expense of the master." There was a strict separation of the sexes, a limited dietary, and regular discipline, the result being " a well-ordered workhouse, of such great efficacy in keeping paupers from coming in that nine other parishes subscribed towards its cost in order to have the privilege of issuing orders for admission to it," which they tendered, in lieu of any other relief, to troublesome able-bodied applicants.[1]

More usually, however, the parish authorities desired to rid themselves of the trouble of managing the workhouse, as well as that involved in purchasing the food. Here the contractor might possess any degree of independence. The parish workhouse was almost invariably placed at his disposal. Sometimes he would be formally appointed governor or master, in order to increase his authority ; in other parishes no such appointment would be made, and the contractor's disciplinary authority might be disputed by recalcitrant inmates.[2] Some vision of what horrors the farmed workhouse might cover is afforded by the following description of that at Grimsby in 1833. " The Governor of the workhouse contracts with Grimsby and the other parishes who send their poor there, to feed and clothe the inmates for three shillings a head [per week], at all ages from the birth, he having

---

[1] Report of Poor Law Inquiry Commissioners, Appendix A, Majendie's Report, p. 216. So in the parish of St. Thomas the Apostle, Exeter, where all Outdoor Relief was refused to able-bodied men, and the workhouse was used as a test, with strict discipline and hard work. The inmates were maintained under contract, but so far from wishing to attract the able-bodied, " the governor had been allowed to introduce machinery for spinning worsted, which was turned by the hand, and at which he employed paupers fit for such work ; being very heavy and carried on under his own eye, the occupation was much disliked, and probably is not without its effect in making the workhouse unpopular. . . . Not one able-bodied person had been in the workhouse during the last six months " (*ibid.* Chapman's Report, p. 427).

[2] A primitive case of farming may be cited at Hove. In 1833 the Vestry agreed with a " Mr. Adams to furnish them with three bedrooms and a kitchen, which they viewed and approved, at 20s. per month. They are to pay him at the rate of 4s. per week for each pauper's board, including fire and soup, as specified, and to allow him 8s. 6d. per week for each lying-in woman during her month " (MS. Vestry Minutes, Hove (Sussex), April 19, 1833).

the benefit of the work of all those able to earn anything towards their support. The person who at present fills this office is an elderly single man, of irregular and dirty habits; and from want of attention on the part of the parochial authorities, not the slightest attention is paid to either classification, discipline, cleanliness, or even to separation of the sexes. I found the whole house in a filthy condition, with all the paupers huddled together in the kitchen over the fire; the lodging rooms ill-ventilated, each pauper keeping the key of the room in which himself and his family slept. Egress and ingress to the house free to all. The inmates full of complaints respecting their treatment, either by the governor or the parish. . . . Another inmate was an unfortunate idiot lad of about 19 or 20. I was shown the sleeping place of this poor wretch in an outhouse in the yard, with a very damp brick floor, half of which he had pulled up; his bed a heap of filthy litter, with a miserable rug full of holes for covering; his clothing, though in the middle of winter, consisted of nothing but a long shirt of sacking; and a leather strap with a chain fastened to the wall was in the corner, to make him fast to when he was unruly. The whole presented a spectacle alike disgraceful to a civilised country and to the parish where it exists." [1]

In the nineteenth century there came to be, in the Metropolitan area, a little knot of independent capitalist speculators, who made a business of undertaking, on their own premises and with their own staff, the boarding, lodging and clothing of paupers, in much the same spirit as they would have undertaken a contract for the sweeping of the streets. If a parish had no workhouse of its own, or chose not to send some classes of paupers to its workhouse, it could make use of the private establishments run by these professional " farmers " for the purpose.[2] The hundred

---

[1] Report of Poor Law Inquiry Commissioners, Appendix A, Wylde's Report, pp. 134-135.

[2] These professional farmers of the poor existed in the Metropolis at least as early as the middle of the eighteenth century. In 1753 one Tull, who then farmed the poor of several parishes in and near London, offered to take the Chelsea poor at a low price, but the Vestry rejected the proposal (MS. Vestry Minutes, Chelsea, June 28 and July 5, 1753). An Act of Parliament (45 George III. c. 54) was directed against them, requiring any future contractor to live within the parish, to give security for the due fulfilment of his contract, and to have its terms approved by two Justices, but apparently without result. A contemporary writer remarks that " the legislature has in the present year, 1805, made a further progress towards correcting the abuses of workhouses by enjoining the residence of the contractors within the parish or place

little parishes in the City of London practically all adopted this plan for such of their poor as they chose not to grant Outdoor Relief to ; and, between 1800 and 1835, there were usually from these parishes over a thousand paupers under the care of half a dozen "farmers." [1] The "farms" were roomy old houses at Hoxton, Mile End, or Peckham, each of which was made to accommodate two or four hundred paupers, all crowded together in indescribable filth and promiscuity, made tolerable to the pauper only by the free and easy laxness that prevailed. The "farmers" were paid five or six shillings per week per head, and made what they could from the paupers' labour. The paupers were employed principally at making slop clothing, being allowed to retain for themselves one quarter to one half of their earnings. [2] So lax was the discipline, and so small the value of their labour that, if they chose to forgo dinner, the farmer gladly allowed them twopence halfpenny to absent themselves for the day, a privilege which they used, in fine weather, to enable them to beg in the streets. [3]

At the very end of our period we see arising the great contractor, adding workhouse to workhouse, and combining them with the conduct of lunatic asylums, exactly on the lines that

---

where the workhouse is erected, and obliging them, by their own, and the bond of one or more responsible persons, to the amount of half the yearly assessment to the true and faithful performance of the contract " (*General View of the Agriculture of Gloucestershire*, by Thomas Rudge, 1807, p. 348).

[1] We read, for instance, that at the beginning of the nineteenth century, "Marlborough House, a well - known Peckham mansion . . . became the casual workhouse of the City of London [parishes], and the respectable inhabitants of the neighbourhood were much annoyed by having about three hundred of the casuals turned loose upon them every morning. The master of the workhouse received a given sum per head for farming his disorderly crew " (*Ye Parish of Camberwell*, by W. H. Blanch, 1875, p. 151).

[2] It was not unusual to find such contractors charging more for refractory than for docile paupers. At Charlton, in 1820, we read, " Mr. Showell, master of the poor house at Bear Lane, having by letter informed us that in consequence of Hawks being such a dirty, lazy person, he declines keeping him any longer unless he is allowed the sum of nine shillings per week. Resolved that Mr. Showell be allowed nine shillings for the present " (MS. Vestry Minutes, Charlton (Kent), February 10, 1820).

[3] Report from House of Commons Committee on the State of Mendicity in the Metropolis, July 11, 1815 ; see particularly the evidence of Sir John Anstruther and Mr. Gordon, pp. 80-81, as well as that of the farmers themselves, pp. 22, 31, 35. The same laxness, and privilege of free egress to beg, continued unchanged down to 1833 ; see the description, almost in the same terms, by the Assistant Overseer of St. Botolph Without, Aldgate, and the statements of the farmers themselves, in Report of Poor Law Inquiry Commissioners, Appendix A, Codd's Report, pp. 80, 93.

would to-day be followed by a modern refreshment contractor
in supplying a school-treat or providing every necessary for a
party of excursionists. An exceptionally good instance of this
kind of " farming " is presented in the glowing account, given
by Charles Mott himself, of the extensive enterprises carried on
by him between 1820 and 1833. This energetic administrator,
originally a shopkeeper, describes himself as having thrown his
whole energy into the business of contracting for the poor, and
he seems to have run it on an exceptionally extensive scale, with
a certain largeness of view. As the proprietor of a large lunatic
asylum, he had for some time had dealings with forty parishes ;
and he was presently administering three large workhouses, at
Lambeth, at Newington, and at Alverstoke, near Portsmouth,
containing altogether over 1200 paupers. Dealing with a turn-
over amounting to nearly £20,000 a year, he bought his supplies
in the best markets at the most advantageous terms. Putting
all his skill and attention into the details of administration, he
found himself able to save largely in the food supplies, without
stinting either quantity or quality. He discovered, for instance,
that the scales used for weighing out the food in one workhouse
had become incorrect to the extent of nearly an ounce, owing
merely to their uncleanly state ; and, simply by having them
regularly attended to by a scale-maker, estimated that he avoided
a waste of meat amounting to 300 stone weight per annum. He
saw to it that the large and small pieces of meat were separately
boiled, so the smaller pieces were not boiled too much, a detail
which he asserted to save, in a large workhouse, a considerable
weight per day. By baking his own bread, he could adjust
quantities to a nicety, and avoid any loss from cutting up the
large loaves. By employing a trained staff of officers, he was
able to serve the meals more promptly, and thus shorten the time
diverted from work. The result was, if we may believe the
optimistic account which he gave of his own enterprise, that,
whilst keeping the inmates of his workhouses contented with his
rule, he was able to make an income for himself, and yet persuade
the parishes that they saved money by his contracts.[1]

[1] It may be added that Mott made such an impression on Sir Edwin
Chadwick and Nassau Senior that he was specially consulted in the preparation
of the Bill of 1834, and was, in 1835, appointed one of the Assistant Commissioners at £700 a year. He did not, however, prove an efficient Civil Servant,
and was eventually removed from office. We know of this case chiefly through

It is difficult to form any convincing estimate of the relative advantages of the direct workhouse administration and the farming system, extending, as the latter did, over more than a century. To Sir F. M. Eden, in 1797, the farming system seemed " the greatest improvement of modern times respecting the care of the poor," and Edwin Chadwick, in 1833, was enthusiastic in its praise.[1] On the other hand, the very idea of letting the labour of the poor shocked the humanitarian sentiments of Sir William Young in 1788–1796, as of Sir Samuel Romilly and the House of Commons in 1811 ; and the whole contract system was denounced in unmeasured terms by other observers.[2] Our own impression is that, taken as a whole, it was an apparent

---

the not unbiased report of Chadwick (*ibid.* Appendix A, pp. 192-209), whose evident desire to make out a good case for the contract system, and administration on a large scale, without discriminating between the two, leaves his testimony unconvincing. He does not seem to have inspected the workhouses under Mott's management. We have an independent account of one of them, that of Alverstoke, which is well reported on by the Assistant Poor Law Commissioner, who was struck by the fact that the tendency of the system was to retain persons in the workhouse, instead of diminishing pauperism, as the contractor gained the more the larger number he was paid for (*ibid.* Pringle's Report, p. 292).

[1] Sir F. M. Eden's comment is as follows · " The greatest improvement of modern times respecting the care of the poor, or that at least which seems to have been most generally aimed at, has been taking the parochial poor out of the hands of Overseers and Churchwardens (who were suspected to have neglected or abused the great trust reposed in them during the short period of their continuing in office), and farming them out to individuals " (*State of the Poor*, 1797, vol. i. p. v).

[2] See *Observations preliminary to a Proposed Amendment of the Poor Laws*, etc., 1788 ; and *Considerations on the Subject of Poorhouses and Workhouses, their pernicious tendency*, etc., 1796, both by Sir William Young, Bart., M.P. The Board of Agriculture's reporter for Berkshire wrote, in 1808, " As for the infamous mode of letting the poor by the head or by the gross, to some shameless wretch, equally destitute of humanity and of principle, who will make a profit by his contract, and provided he does not actually starve the miserable beings who are forced to come within his garrison, is called a good manager, I know no terms of reprobation that can stamp it with its just character. I will never advocate the cause of idleness, of extravagance or of profligacy ; but when I see in one of our public papers advertisements with the striking title of ' the Poor to Let ', I blush that I belong to a country where the sense of right and wrong is so confounded, where even the decencies of life and the social sympathies are forgotten or despised " (*General View of the Agriculture of Berkshire*, by Mavor, 1808, p. 103).

And another critic observes that " some of these [Gloucestershire workhouses], it is observed with regret, are still farmed by keepers, who find food, clothing and fuel by contract, at so much by the head. By such institutions the parish rates may possibly be reduced but that is all that can be said in their favour : they are otherwise fraught with mischief, moral and political " (*General View of the Agriculture of Gloucestershire*, by Thomas Rudge, 1807, p. 348).

financial success, but a grave administrative blunder. In nearly
all parishes, the administrative machinery was so defective :
there was so complete a dearth of competent trained officers ;
the whole technique of account-keeping and audit, checks and
stocktaking, was so entirely wanting, that, in direct parish
administration, waste, peculation, favouritism in contracts and
actual fraud were practically universal. Though the payments
to the contractors were relatively greater than the expenses of a
few well-administered workhouses, the great majority of parishes
seemed to make an obvious pecuniary saving by employing a
contractor, as well as avoiding the incessant trouble of direct
administration. On the other hand, the farming of the workhouse, on genuinely commercial principles, inevitably prevented
its use either as a deterrent or as a place of salutary regimen.
The more numerous its inmates, the larger (assuming payment
per head) was the contractor's income, and the more certain his
profit. It was therefore to his interest to make the house as
attractive as he could to the pauper class, and especially to such
as were able-bodied ; and this he could most cheaply and most
certainly do by allowing personal freedom, intermingling of the
sexes, the enjoyment of beer and tobacco, and a general laxness
of discipline. Thus, though the parish saved something per head,
it had many more heads to pay for than it need have had.
Naturally, it never occurred to the contractor to run his establishment in such a way as to educate or reform the paupers, a duty
for which he was not engaged or paid.

Contracting for Children

Children of all ages were, as we have seen, included both in
contracts for farming the whole of the poor and in those for
farming the workhouse. For many years no special provision
seems to have been made for them. At length, in 1760, the
frightful mortality among the infants in the Metropolitan workhouse attracted the attention of Jonas Hanway, one of the most
effective of eighteenth century philanthropists, who induced
Parliament to appoint a committee to inquire into the facts.
The report of this Committee revealed the fact that four-fifths
of the children born in London workhouses died within the first
year. The Committee found " that taking the children born in

workhouses or parish houses, or received of and under twelve
months old in the year 1763, and following the same into 1764 and
1765, only seven in a hundred appear to have survived this
short period . . . that " (whilst 1419 children were apprenticed
between 1754 and 1762) " only 19 of those born in the workhouses
or received into them under twelve months old, compose any
part of the 1419 ; and even of those received as far as three years
old, only 36 appear to have survived in the hands of the said
parishes to be placed out apprentices ". [1] This revelation induced
Parliament to pass two Acts, the first requiring the parishes within
the Bills of Mortality to keep a register of all children born within
their workhouses ; and the second ordering that all children,
up to the age of six, who were in their charge, should be put out
to nurse at a distance of at least three miles from any part of the
Cities of London and Westminster.[2] The immediate result of
this legislation was the upgrowth of a system of " boarding out "
pauper infants in small private " baby farms ", or even individual
homes, in the suburbs of London. The duty of visiting these
places was, as we have described in *The Parish and the County*,
turned to good account by the Select Vestrymen of the period ;
and many were the holiday jaunts, " in glass coaches ", and the
jovial feasts at outlying public-houses, enjoyed on this pretext of
inspecting the little ones. There is, so far as we know, no evidence as to the success or failure of Hanway's Act from the standpoint of the health and nurture of the children affected. But we
may safely assume that the lot of those moved to the suburbs
cannot have been worse than the fate of those immured in the
overcrowded and indecently promiscuous workhouse or " farm "
within the Metropolitan area. The primitive arrangements under
which the infants were originally " put out to nurse " did not,

[1] Report of a Committee appointed to inquire into the state of the parish
poor infants, 1767 ; House of Commons Journals, vol. xxxi. p. 248 ; *Remarkable
Occurrences in the Life of Jonas Hanway*, by John Pugh, 1787, pp. 185-195.
Hanway (1712-1786) published *Serious Considerations on the Salutary Design
of the Act of Parliament for a Regular Uniform Register of the Parish Poor, in
all the Parishes within the Bills of Mortality under Two Years Old*, 1762 ; *An
Earnest Appeal for Mercy to the Children of the Poor . . . being a general reference
to the deserving conduct of some Parish Officers, and the . . . Effects of the
Ignorance . . . of Others, also a Proposal for the More Effectual Preserving
the Parish Children*, 1766 ; and *A Letter to the Guardians of the Infant Poor*,
1767. His general work, *The Citizen's Monitor*, which contains various references
to Poor Law administration, did not appear until 1780.

[2] 2 George III. c. 22 and 7 George III. c. 39 ; *Remarkable Occurrences in
the Life of Jonas Hanway*, by John Pugh, 1787, pp. 185-195.

however, continue. By 1833 we find most of the Metropolitan parishes with children's establishments of their own.[1] Here would sometimes be kept children " from the tenderest age to that of fifteen ",[2] who would, we are assured, be " taught to read, write and cypher in the first four rules, and the little girls would be taught to knit and sew." [3] Some of these so-called " infant establishments " seem to have been directly managed by salaried officials ; others were supplied with food and clothing at fixed rates per head, by contractors who occupied a semi-official position, working under the orders and frequent supervision of the workhouse committee of the parish.[4] We hear little of these pauper schools until after the supersession of the Old Poor Law by the Poor Law Amendment Act ; yet it was from their example that eventually sprang the well-known " barrack schools " of the Metropolitan Unions and certain other large parishes during the second half of the nineteenth century.

Contracting for Lunatics

We note much the same development in the methods of dealing with pauper lunatics as in those for dealing with young children. At first no special provision for the class was thought necessary. The insane were treated like any other paupers. Nothing gives a worse impression of the eighteenth-century poorhouse or workhouse than the presence in them, intermingled with the other inmates, of every variety of idiot and lunatic. Of all the horrors connected with this subject we need not dwell —the chaining and manacling of troublesome patients, the keeping of them in a state almost of nudity, sleeping on filthy straw,

[1] Almost the only source of information as to these infant establishments is contained in the Report of the Poor Law Inquiry Commissioners, Appendix A, Codd's Report, see pp. 73-94 ; see also *Rules and Regulations for the Government of the Workhouse of the Parish of St. Martin in the Fields and of the Infant Poorhouse at Highwood Hill*, 1828.

[2] Report of Poor Law Inquiry Commissioners, 1834, Appendix A, p. 79 (St. Andrew's, Holborn).

[3] *Ibid.* p. 88 (St. Anne's, Soho, Westminster).

[4] Thus, the parish of St. Botolph Without, Bishopsgate, in the City of London, had, in 1833, between 70 and 80 children at its infant establishment at Ilford, Essex, where they were maintained under contract at five shillings a week per head. " The Guardians ", we are told, " visit this establishment once a month, and the Overseers go and dine there quarterly to pay bills. The Guardians are five in number and are allowed five guineas each yearly to meet their expenses in visiting the establishment " (*ibid.* p. 90).

the mixture of melancholics, and persons merely subject to delusions, with gibbering and indecent idiots, the noisy with the quiet, the total lack of any proper sanitary arrangements. Even as late as 1806 an able and well-informed Gloucestershire magistrate could still assure Lord Spencer that there was hardly any considerable parish " in which there may not be found some unfortunate human creature of this description, who, if his ill-treatment has made him phrenetic, is chained in the cellar or garret of the workhouse, fastened to the leg of a table, tied to a post in an outhouse, or perhaps shut up in an uninhabited ruin, or if his lunacy be inoffensive, left to ramble half naked and half starved through the streets and highways, teased by the scoff and jest of all that is vulgar, ignorant and unfeeling." [1] The only remedy found for this state of things was to put the lunatics out to contract. Some of the better managed parishes were beginning to send their noisy, dangerous or refractory lunatics to private madhouses, paying for them at the rate of 9s., 12s. or even 15s. per week.[2] These private lunatic asylums, which had to be licensed by the Justices in Quarter Sessions,[3] and were gradually brought effectively under their inspection, varied enormously in quality, but were probably, at their worst, better for the pauper lunatics than the workhouses of the period. The result was a steady multiplication of private madhouses. By 1807 there were, throughout England, nearly fifty of these establishments. In and near the Metropolis there grew up a whole series of private asylums, great and small, expressly catering for pauper cases. At the " White House " at Bethnal Green some

---

[1] " Suggestions of Sir George Onesiphorus Paul, Bart., to Earl Spencer ", October 11, 1806, in Appendix 4 to Report from the Select Committee appointed to inquire into the state of lunatics, 1807.

[2] Thus, in 1815, it is noted that the united parishes of St. Margaret and St. John's, Westminster, had about twenty lunatics in Sir Jonathan Mile's celebrated asylum at Hoxton, at 10s. 6d. per week (Report from House of Commons Select Committee on the State of Madhouses, 1815, p. 179). In 1833 it is reported that, in Wiltshire, pauper lunatics were " always sent to an asylum, of which there are many, or a private establishment " (Report of Poor Law Inquiry Commissioners, Appendix A, Okeden's Report, p. 6).

[3] Or in London, Westminster and seven miles round, and in the county of Middlesex, by the College of Physicians (14 George III. c. 49 and 26 George III. c. 91). The College of Physicians held that it had no responsibility as regards pauper lunatics, and neither inspected their treatment nor required any return or report from the keepers of their numbers (See Dr. Willis's evidence in Report from the Select Committee appointed to inquire into the state of lunatics, 1807).

three hundred were received, at the rate, in 1815, of 9s. 6d. or 10s. per head per week.[1]

Yet there still remained, in the aggregate, a large number of parishes, scattered up and down the country, where the Vestry and the Overseers refused to incur the expense of placing their lunatics, especially if these were not actually dangerous, in private asylums. The Suffolk workhouses in particular were found in 1807 to be everywhere the abode of the insane. Out of 114 insane paupers in the county, it was reported that " the lunatics are confined to the cell allotted to their use in the different workhouses, except about 13 which are in the lunatic asylum at Norwich and 2 that are in St. Luke's Hospital [London] ; the whole, however, are supported by the parishes. With regard to the idiots, I may observe that the greater part of them are kept in the workhouses as common paupers, without receiving more than common attention, and without being separated from the general mass." [2] The horrible condition in which these persons of unsound mind were kept, as well as the necessity of making some provision for criminal lunatics, was brought forcibly before the Government in 1806 by a memorial to Earl Spencer, then Home Secretary, from Sir George Onesiphorus Paul, Bart., the indefatigable prison reformer of Gloucestershire, whose work we have described in other volumes.[3] The Committee found reason to believe there were still more than two thousand pauper lunatics incarcerated in the various workhouses, often confined in " damp dark cells," besides others committed by the Justices to Houses of Correction as dangerous, under the statute of 1744 ; and about 37 criminals in the common gaols detained on the ground of insanity, under the statute hurriedly passed in 1800.[4] It became evident that the " highly dangerous and inconvenient . . . practice of confining . . . lunatics . . . in gaols, poorhouses, and houses of industry " could not be prevented without

[1] Report from the House of Commons Committee on the State of Madhouses, 1815, pp. 18, 114-115.

[2] Dr. Halliday's report in Report from the Select Committee appointed to inquire into the state of lunatics, 1807.

[3] *The Parish and the County*, 1906 ; and *English Prisons under Local Government*, 1922.

[4] The Act 40 George III. c. 97 empowered courts of justice, instead of, as heretofore, acquitting prisoners found insane, to order them to be detained in custody during pleasure, but made no provision for their maintenance or detention otherwise than in the common gaol of the county.

some other provision being made, and it was proved that the most economical and satisfactory method of making such provision was the establishment of asylums on a large scale, each capable of containing two or three hundred patients. This involved the adoption of a larger area than the parish as the basis of action. The Committee accordingly recommended that the Justices of each county should be authorised to erect an asylum at the expense of the county rate, in which pauper lunatics could be maintained at the charge of their respective parishes. Such an Act was promptly passed in 1808.[1] Unfortunately, it omitted to make any provision for borrowing the cost of erecting the asylum, and spreading it over a term of years ; and the natural objection to so great an increase of the county rate as would have been involved prevented anything being done. Scandals at the York Asylum, a charitable institution usually cited as the model of contemporary asylums,[2] led in 1815 to a Parliamentary inquiry, and to a new Act, giving the County Justices enlarged powers, and enabling them to borrow money for fourteen years.[3] Not for many years afterwards were, in most parts of England, the county asylums actually built ;[4] but the Justices increasingly interfered to prevent what the Parliamentary Committee had called " the intolerable evil of these unhappy persons being imprisoned in . . . parish workhouses " ;[5] and to incite parishes by every means in their power to contract for their maintenance in private madhouses.[6] These pauper patients were, it is needless

---

[1] 48 George III. c. 96 ; House of Commons Journals, April 6, 1808. No debate upon it was reported in Hansard.

[2] Pamphlet by G. Higgins ; an earlier pamphlet was entitled *Animadversions on the Present Government of the York Lunatic Asylum, in which the Case of Pauper Patients is distinctly considered*, by W. Mason, 1788.

[3] 55 George III. c. 46.

[4] The first stone of the West Riding County Asylum was not laid until 1816 (*Leeds Mercury*, February 3, 1816). The Gloucestershire County Asylum was not opened until 1824 (MS. Minutes, Quarter Sessions, Gloucestershire, January 14, 1824). Other counties followed slowly enough. In 1833 it is reported that " a lunatic asylum for paupers is just finished in Dorsetshire, and the magistrates are most active in preventing lunatics or idiots from being kept in parish houses " (Report of Poor Law Inquiry Commissioners, Okeden's Report, p. 12).

[5] Report from the House of Commons Committee on the State of Madhouses, 1815, p. 5.

[6] The parishes, said one keeper of a private madhouse, " never bring their lunatics to me but under two considerations : one when the magistrates will not permit their remaining in the workhouse ; and next, when they feel it an object to have them cured ". But the steady pressure of the Justices had its

to say, gladly received by the keepers of the private asylums, whenever the parish authorities were willing to pay the twelve or fourteen shillings a week per head that was charged.[1] Right down to 1835 the typical method of dealing with pauper lunatics was to place them out under contract. Here again, the specific treatment under contract of a distinct class of paupers was the forerunner of the most successful form of modern institutional treatment under the Poor Law, in the county lunatic asylums now (1927) steadily becoming of the nature of mental hospitals, in which curative treatment replaces the mere segregation and safe keeping that characterised even the best of the lunatic asylums of the last century.

Contracting for Medical Relief

Another branch of the relief of the poor which eighteenth-century Vestries and Overseers got performed by contract at a fixed price was that of medical attendance, and the provision of drugs and medicines for the sick poor. When the whole of the parochial liability for poor relief was farmed, and even when only the maintenance of the workhouse inmates was contracted for at a fixed price, it was, as we have seen, not unusual for medical relief to be included ; and the contractor was left to make his own arrangements with the doctor.[2] But as early as 1718 we find the energetic Vestry of Woolwich " farming " out,

---

effect. Out of 47 workhouses visited in 1813–1814 in the south-west of England, only 9 were found to contain any lunatics at all, and 4 of these, in populous places, had provided special lunatic wards (Report of House of Commons Select Committee on State of Madhouses, 1815, p. 54). See, for later comments, *A Letter to the Chairman of the Committee appointed to inquire into the State of the Pauper Lunatics of the County of Middlesex*, by a member of the Committee, 1828.

[1] H. of C. Committee, 1815, pp. 22, 124. A director of the poor of Marylebone speaks, in 1815, of the parsimony which prevented so many parishes from contracting for their lunatics. " The ordinary maintenance ", says he, " of a pauper in the parish of Marylebone costs this parish about seven shillings weekly, and in a state of lunacy ten shillings ; and to the paltry difference between the two sums are the chance of recovery and comfort of half the insane poor of England completely sacrificed " (Lord Robert Seymour's evidence, *ibid.* p. 114).

[2] At Mitcham, in 1817, when it was resolved to contract for the whole medical relief to the outdoor poor, the necessary medical attendance on the workhouse was expressly excluded, and it was ordered to " be provided by Mr. Hall, the present contractor for and governor thereof, and that . . . the same do form no part of the intended [medical] contract " (MS. Vestry Minutes, Mitcham (Surrey), July 23, 1817).

by a separate contract, the whole medical and surgical care of its poor, for an inclusive payment of £12 per annum.[1] Small as was this remuneration, it was sufficient to attract competitors, for in 1756 we find the Vestry (180 persons being present) voting by ballot which of two surgeons should be appointed.[2] Other parishes would sometimes give their medical contract to each of the two or three local practitioners in rotation, who (as at Minchinhampton in 1818) undertook " turn and turn about " to do all that was required for the sick poor for £20 a year.[3] But the more frequent practice during the first thirty years of the nineteenth century was to put the medical contract up to competition, like that for making the coffins or supplying the workhouse with flour. Thus, at Brighton in 1805, and at Plymouth in 1821, tenders are invited from the local doctors as to the lowest price at which they will contract to give medical and surgical attendance, and supply all medicines required, for all the poor of the parish. In both cases the lowest tender is accepted, at £40 and £50 a year respectively.[4] The Devonport Improvement Commissioners, in 1815, publicly invited " sealed tenders ", not only for supplying every kind of provisions and clothing, but also, in the same advertisement, for acting as surgeon to the workhouse and casual poor, and " serving as solicitor to the parish for one year ".[5] By 1833 such competitive tendering for medical services had, in whole districts, become the normal practice. Thus, throughout Warwickshire, it was reported, " at Easter the Overseers of the Poor invite a statement from all the medical men within reach of the parish, of the lowest terms on which they will attend the poor for the ensuing year. They are requested to make an estimate of the value of their time, service and drugs

[1] " Ordered then in a Vestry assembled that Mr. Aemilius De Pauw be the surgeon to take care of the poor of this parish who not only receive the collection money appointed for the poor of this parish, but all other persons who shall happen to become a charge to this parish, and to provide good and proper medicines [and] to make such proper applications in surgery necessary for such poor, and that the said Mr. De Pauw shall have for such medicines and service £12 per annum to commence from Christmas next ensuing, if duly by him performed " (MS. Vestry Minutes, Woolwich (Kent), December 21, 1718).

[2] *Ibid.* November 10, 1756.

[3] MS. Vestry Minutes, Minchinhampton (Gloucestershire), December 18, 1818.

[4] MS. Vestry Minutes, Brighton (Sussex), June 24, 1805 ; MS. Minutes, Incorporated Guardians, Plymouth (Devon), May 24 and June 18, 1821.

[5] MS. Minutes, Improvement Commissioners, Devonport (Devon), March 17, 1815.

in the relief of every disorder to which the paupers of the parish may be exposed, sometimes including the vaccination of children and attendance on women in labour." [1]　It must be remembered that it was customary in the rural districts at this period for the parish doctor to attend to the whole of the wage-earning population, who, except where charitable dispensaries had been organised, got no other medical advice.　" Relief in the shape of medical attendance ", pleasantly reports the Assistant Poor Law Commissioner for Suffolk, " is given to the whole of the lower orders, so that all the journeymen, mechanics and labourers throughout the county are paupers." [2]

The results of this system of competitive tendering for medical relief were wholly bad.　It was, to use the emphatic words of C. P. Villiers, " a system no less mischievous than cruel ".　" The doctor ", reported a medical critic, " is badly paid, and the poor [are] badly attended.　Diseases multiply which might be diminished. . . . It may be asked why the doctors undertake

[1] Report of Poor Law Inquiry Commissioners, Appendix A, Villiers' Report, p. 4.　In Dorsetshire the parishes paid about £10 a year to the surgeon, but added £5 for every additional hundred persons over three or four hundred, the contract including the resident non-settled poor, but not " broken bones or midwifery " (*ibid*. Okeden's Report, p. 12).

[2] *Ibid.* Stuart's Report, p. 336.　Bradford on Avon had a " parish apothecary ", who reported to the Overseers when any poor persons were ill, and these were thereon granted Outdoor Relief during the continuance of their illness ; see *Parochial Regulations relative to the Management of the Poor of Bradford, Wilts., with notes tending to promote economy and comfort in the Workhouse*, Bristol, 1801, p. 10.　The poor were occasionally very summarily dealt with, when any panic arose about the public health—not, it is true, a frequent occurrence.　Thus, at Minchinhampton in 1810, " it is ordered ", peremptorily, by the Vestry, " that a vaccine inoculation shall take place in the parish for the preservation and welfare of the poor ", and the parish doctor is paid £30 for the job (MS. Vestry Minutes, Minchinhampton, Gloucestershire, April 3, 1810).　Cowper, writing to Lady Hesketh in 1788, observes that " the smallpox has done, I believe, all that it has to do at Weston.　Old folks, and even women with child, have been inoculated.　We talk of our freedom, and some of us are free enough, but not the poor.　Dependent as they are upon parish bounty, they are sometimes obliged to submit to impositions which perhaps in France itself could hardly be paralleled.　Can man or woman be said to be free, who is compelled to take a distemper, sometimes at least mortal, and in the circumstances most likely to make it so ?　No circumstance whatever was permitted to exempt the inhabitants of Weston.　The old as well as the young, and the pregnant as well as they who had only themselves within them, have been inoculated.　Were I asked who is the most arbitrary sovereign on earth I should answer neither the King of France nor the Grand Seignior, but an Overseer of the Poor in England " (Cowper's *Works*, edited by Robert Southey, 1836–1837, vol. vi. p. 103).　Inoculation was made a criminal offence by the Act 3 and 4 Vic. c. 29 of 1840, punishable by one month's imprisonment.

this contract, this is the reason, they either want to get into practice themselves, or to keep out a rival."[1]   And it is interesting to find, in this as in other examples of the parochial administration of the period, that the overpowering desire of each parish to escape from its own share of the burden of pauperism really defeated itself.   The local doctors, forced by their own competition to undertake the medical care of the poor of the parish for an utterly inadequate sum, indemnified themselves by charging relatively exorbitant fees for attending any paupers outside their contracts, such as those awaiting removal to other parishes, from which the expense was recovered.[2]   The system, we are told, " opens a door to great fraud on neighbouring parishes, as medical men take the farming of the poor at a low rate, with an [implied] agreement that the orders of suspension made on other parishes shall be sent to them ; and thus by making high charges, they make out the deficiency of stipend at the cost of another parish."[3]   As each parish did the like with regard to every other parish, the result was the complete nullification of the apparent saving brought about by cutting down the doctor's contract price, whilst the temptation to the doctor to neglect the parish poor remained in full force.

A few parishes up and down the country were, by 1835, adopting a less demoralising method of remuneration for the medical care of the sick poor.   At Horncastle in Lincolnshire, for instance, in 1833, we read that " The fixed sum of £10 a year is paid for the medical attendance, and medicines for the use of the poor in the workhouse.   For the out poor the medical man is paid by the case, and the expense to the parish has been about

[1] Report of Poor Law Inquiry Commissioners, Appendix A, Villiers' Report, p. 4.
[2] " Their charges for attending paupers not settled in the parish " are " invariably higher than for those whom they are bound by contract to attend " (ibid. Villiers' Report, p. 4).   In one parish of 3000 inhabitants, which got all its own poor attended to for £20 a year, the doctor made a charge of £14 for attending a single pauper awaiting removal to another parish (ibid. Walcott's Report, p. 176).
[3] Ibid. Walcott's Report, p. 176.   " In some parishes in consequence of the competition which annually takes place to be appointed parish doctor, the salary has been so much reduced, and is so small, that the only way the medical attendant has of paying himself is by his charges on non-parishioners.   It is palpably the interest of the parish to wink at any exorbitancy in the parish doctor's bill " [against other parishes] (ibid. Lewis's Report, p. 662); see Observations on the Practice of supplying Medical Assistance to the Poor, commonly called the Farming of Parishes, by Henry Lilley Smith, 1819.

£70 a year for the last three years. . . . Each of the principal
medical practitioners takes it in turn to attend to the poor on
these terms for a year." [1]   At Faversham in Kent, for a population which in 1831 was only 4429, the parish doctor was, without
competition, appointed at a salary of £80 a year, and the Overseers, in addition, engaged a female midwife, whose services
were at the disposal of those needing them.[2]   But the most extensive provision for the sick poor in 1833 was that made by the
great parish of Liverpool, where the Vestry not only maintained
a large fever hospital, and subscribed five hundred guineas a year
to the voluntary dispensaries established in the town, " through
which medical attendance is given to the paupers out of the
house " ; but also paid a salary of no less than £300 a year to
the doctor who attended the inmates of the workhouse.[3]

Allowances for Bastardy

A special activity of the zealous parish officer was his attempt
to indemnify the parish at the cost of private individuals for the
expense of maintaining particular paupers.   This activity was
practically confined to the case of illegitimate children, the
family connections of ordinary paupers being usually themselves
too nearly destitute to be worth proceeding against for contribution towards their support.   The liability of the putative father
to maintain a bastard child was, however, so far as poor persons
were concerned, considered as part of the punishment for a moral
offence ; and the Justices would accordingly make orders, " to
pay weekly and every week ", a sum of two shillings or more,
against labourers or even apprentices, who were themselves

---

[1] Report of Poor Law Inquiry Commissioners, Appendix A, Wylde's
Report, p. 136.

[2] *Ibid.* Majendie's Report, p. 216.   At Writtle (population in 1831, 2348)
the doctor got as much as £130 a year " everything included " (*ibid.* p. 233).
This was quite exceptional.   " The highest salary met with ", reports the
Assistant Commissioner for Surrey and West Sussex, " is given at Brighton,
where the town is divided into the East and West division ; a medical man is
appointed to attend in each at £100 a year " (*ibid.* Maclean's Report, p. 536).
Maidstone (population in 1831, 15,387) paid its parish doctor £100 a year (*ibid.*
Majendie's Report, p. 215) ; and the same sum was paid at Southampton, with
a population of 18,670 (*ibid.* Pringle's Report, p. 285).

[3] MS. Vestry Minutes, Liverpool, 1833 ; Report of Poor Law Inquiry
Commissioners, Appendix A, Henderson's Report, p. 916 ; *The Liverpool
Vestry Books, 1681–1834*, by Henry Peet, vol. ii., 1915 ; *Memoirs of James
Currie, M.D. of Liverpool*, by W. W. Currie, 1831.

earning insufficient for their own maintenance. The timely discovery of unmarried women with child ; the cajoling, persuading or intimidating them to " swear " the expected child to some man, preferably one of substantial means ; the bargaining with this person, under threat of immediate apprehension, for a lump sum down, or an undertaking for a weekly contribution—all this noisome business formed part of the duties of the Overseer of the Poor. What perjury and extortion, what oppression and petty tyranny, this system produced can only be faintly estimated. No further evidence of fatherhood than the woman's oath was required for the issue of a warrant against the putative father ; and if the accused man could not then and there find sureties to guarantee the payment of the weekly contribution that might eventually be required from him, any Justice of the Peace might straightway commit him to prison pending the trial of the case at the next Quarter Sessions.[1] All this, we are told, is done under the plea of " We must see the parish indemnified ".[2] Yet the parish was, in practice, far from being indemnified. It was easy to get an order made against a putative father for a weekly contribution ; but unless he was a man of property or position, its enforcement was quite another matter. In some parishes it is reported that " not more than one-fifth of the expense is recovered from the fathers, and that subject to the deduction of heavy law expenses." [3] We can imagine how the system lent itself to corruption. In the crowded township of Manchester in 1794 the levy of two Poor Rates of 5s. in the pound within a few months led to an investigation by an influential committee, and to the discovery (among other peculations) that the uncollected rates and the arrears due to the township " on the bastardy account alone, amounted to ten thousand pounds and upwards ". Indeed, the crowning iniquity

---

[1] So oppressive was this practice found to be in the case of labourers and the like that the Bucks Justices desired to content themselves with sureties for the defendant's appearance only, a leniency which counsel advised to be of doubtful legality (MS. Minutes, Quarter Sessions, Buckinghamshire, Epiphany, 1815).

[2] Report of Poor Law Inquiry Commissioners, Appendix C, p. 355 (Mortimer's letter).

[3] *Ibid.* Appendix A, Majendie's Report, p. 165.

At Brighton, in 1830, a committee appointed by the Vestry to investigate the bastardy accounts, discovered " an excess of disbursements amounting to £437 : 17 : 8, the receipts having been £31 : 12s., and the disbursements £469 : 9 : 8 " (MS. Vestry Minutes, Brighton (Sussex), September 13, 1830).

of the Deputy Constable who was acting as salaried Overseer, we are told in the Leypayers' Report, was his conversion of the revenue derived from bastardy cases into an all-pervading system of blackmail. The former Overseer had, in 1786–1787, been regularly collecting and accounting for weekly payments from 614 fathers of illegitimate children. As soon as the Deputy Constable took office as Overseer, the " Red Basil Book ", in which the names and addresses of these fathers were recorded, was promptly " lost " ; and there was no " regular register of illegitimacy kept from the year 1787 to the year 1790 ; nor any sum credited as received on this account. . . . If the public are credulous enough to believe ", reports the indignant Committee of Inquiry, " that all the children belonging to these 614 fathers, and all the children born since the year 1787, died before the year 1790 ", this absence of bastardy revenue might be accepted. Unfortunately, it was proved that the Deputy Constable, when acting as salaried Overseer, had been terrifying erring or duped citizens into paying considerable sums for children of whom they were alleged to be the fathers. " One method," we are told by a contemporary pamphleteer, " is to call upon persons as the reputed fathers of children under the mask of friendship, when he will probably introduce the story of some woman becoming pregnant, whom he has prevented from going before the magistrates to father the child ; here the usual complimentary business of Hush Money is distantly introduced. Should this conversation happen with a single man, who does not betray much fear, he will probably tell him that the business shall be settled for five pounds ; but if it should be pointed to a married man, he seldom fails mentioning the inconvenience attending the exposure before the magistrates, and the consequent uneasiness it may occasion at home, from its being made public. In such a case his expectations are raised in proportion to the delicacy of their situation. I have it likewise from undoubted authority that different gentlemen have been applied to for Hush Money as the pretended fathers of the same child." [1]

---

[1] This unsavoury episode in the history of Manchester, which is described in our volume *The Parish and The County*, 1906, pp. 72-76, for which confirmation may be found in the MS. Vestry Minutes, 1794-1797, is revealed chiefly in a remarkable series of contemporary pamphlets, mostly preserved in the Manchester Public Library, though some are in the British Museum and the library of the Ministry of Health. The principal are *A Report of the Committee*

The same state of affairs was revealed by investigations carried on in the Metropolitan parishes. Thus, it is recorded in the MS. Vestry Minutes of Chelsea (Middlesex) that during 1822–1824 the total sums credited to the parish during these years as receipts on account of bastards amounted to no more than £124 for twenty-six cases. The Committee traced back two out of these twenty-six cases and found that, on these two alone, £131 had been paid to the officers ; indicating, therefore, a relatively gigantic system of misappropriation of these receipts.[1] In 1834 a similar embezzlement of the bastardy receipts was discovered in the parish of Lambeth ; [2] and innumerable other instances may be found in the parish records.

The financial corruption that we so frequently find in connection with the bastardy accounts, and even the system of blackmail with which they were sometimes associated, were not the worst features of the provision made by the Overseers for the maintenance of illegitimate children. More revolting, and more socially disastrous, was the direct premium which the system placed upon female unchastity. In most parishes it was the custom of the Overseers to pay " to the mother of a bastard the sum directed by the order of maintenance, whether it be recovered from the father or not ; and this comes under the denomination of ' pay ' in pauper language. The sum allowed to the mother of a bastard [under a magistrate's order] is generally greater than that given [as Outdoor Relief] to the mother of a legitimate child : indeed, the whole treatment of the former is a direct encouragement to vice." [3] " Women know very well," says another writer,

---

of the Associated Leypayers in the Township of Manchester appointed to inquire into the accounts of the Churchwardens and Overseers, 1794 ; Rules for the Government of the Poorhouse in Manchester, 1794 ; A Disclosure of Parish Abuse, etc., by Thomas Battye, 1796 ; The Red Basil Book, etc., by the same, 1797.

[1] MS. Vestry Minutes, Chelsea (Middlesex), June 20, 1822. Two years later, another committee, suspecting a more obvious form of peculation, began to publish the Poor Rate default lists, whereupon no less than eighty receipts were at once sent in by ratepayers, who threatened to prosecute the committee for the libel of publishing their names on the Defaulters' List (*ibid.* February 26, 1824).

[2] *Report of a Committee appointed by the Vestry of St. Mary, Lambeth, to enquire into the imputed Frauds and Misdeeds of William Sefton and James Andrews,* 1834 (in library of Ministry of Health). A placard of about 1831 (in the same collection) indignantly appeals to the " Parishioners and Farmers in St. Chad's Parish " not to " elect an officer who has been proved incompetent " in his dealing with the bastardy accounts.

[3] Report of Poor Law Inquiry Commissioners, Appendix A, Majendie's Report, p. 165.

"that the more opulent the father, the more will the weekly
allowance be, and that the magistrates . . . invariably take the
circumstances of the father into their judgment. . . . This
is . . . a bounty for perjury." And when we learn that women
who had three or four illegitimate children in succession became
thereby entitled to a pension of ten or fifteen shillings a week,
paid regularly by the parish, being often more than the whole
earnings of a rural labourer, we may accept as not exaggerated
this writer's statement that the income to be made under such a
bastardy law was actually " a loadstone to draw women into
a state of pregnancy ".[1]

---

[1] Report of Poor Law Inquiry Commissioners. Appendix C, p. 355
(Mortimer's letter). As to the whole subject of bastardy and the
poor law, see the memorandum by George Taylor and the communications received, *ibid.* pp. 125-132, 394-415 ; *Poor Law Report : Ille-
gitimates, their Case considered*, by Vestrien, 1834 ; and Sir Edmund Head's
elaborate report of 1839 in Sixth Annual Report of Poor Law Commissioners,
pp. 143-171, and separately issued as *Report on the Law of Bastardy, with a
Supplementary Report on a cheap civil remedy for seduction*, etc., by Sir Edmund
Walker Head, Bart., 1840.
   We may conveniently add here a summary reference to a few of the
pamphlets dealing with the Poor Law administration of particular parishes,
which throw light on the current practices of the second half of the eighteenth
century, not only with regard to allowances for children, but also with regard
to " farming ", and to the various experiments in providing employment.
See, for instance, *An Address to the Ministers, Churchwardens and Parishioners
of Newcastle upon Tyne for the Better Regulating the Parish Poor*, etc., by a
Parishioner, 1755 ; *A Proposal for the Relief and more Comfortable Maintenance
of the Poor . . . of Norfolk*, etc., Norwich, 1765 ; *A Friendly Address to the
Poor of the Hundred of Blything*, by R. G. White, 1766 ; *Some Account of a
Meeting held at the Guildhall in Bury St. Edmunds, November 4, 1771* ; *A Letter
to the Guardians of the Poor of the Burgh of Bury St. Edmunds on the Great
Increase of the Rates for the Maintenance of the Poor in that Town*, London,
1778 ; *An Address to the Author of the Letter* [as above], Bury St. Edmunds,
1778 ; *A Letter to the Inhabitants of . . . St. Edmund's Bury . . . recommend-
ing . . . repeal of the Act, 21 George II.*, etc., Bury, 1784 ; *An Address to the
Inhabitants of the Parish of St. Anne, Westminster*, by Rev. Thomas Martin,
1777 ; *A Letter to the Overseers of the Poor of Deal in Kent, respecting the great
increase in their Poor Rates*, 1778 ; *The Present Situation of the Town of
Birmingham respecting its Poor considered : with a Proposal for building a
New Workhouse, addressed to the Inhabitants by the Overseers of the Poor*, 1783 ;
*The Friendly Design, containing . . . Practical Methods to reduce the Parish
Rates*, humbly submitted to the consideration of the Inhabitants of . . . Birming-
ham, 1800.
   We may refer also to the Note on . . . *Churchwardens' Account, 1403, of
Wimborne Minster*, by J. M. J. Fletcher, 1918 ; *Churchwardens' Accounts of
St. Nicholas, Warwick*, 1917 ; *Churchwardens' Accounts of St. Nicholas, Strood*,
1915 ; *Description of the Poor Book of the Tithing of Westbury on Trym, 1656–
1698*, Bristol, 1910 ; and *One Hundred Years of Poor Law Administration in a
Warwickshire Village* [Tysoe], by A. W. Ashby, 1911.
   The " Rules and Regulations " for the government of workhouses, and the

Such were the methods and devices for relieving the poor prior to the reform of the Poor Law in 1834. Before attempting to sum up the result of this first era of English Poor Law history, we must consider the framework of compulsion and repression in which it was set—the Law of Settlement and Removal on the one hand, and, on the other, the imposing series of statutes dealing with the crime of vagrancy.

---

general administration of the Poor Law, as framed by the Vestries, or by the various Incorporated Guardians of the Poor, and those framed by the Justices for the Houses of Correction, are also of some interest. Such codes exist to the number of a hundred or more, covering the whole century between 1730 and 1830, either in the British Museum or in the library of the Ministry of Health.

CHAPTER V

THE LAW OF SETTLEMENT AND REMOVAL

WE have reserved for separate treatment the extraordinary provisions by which, not vagrants or criminals — not even beggars or applicants for relief—but the entire body of the manual-working wage-earners of the kingdom, together with their families, were, so to speak, legally immobilised in the parishes to which they " belonged " ; back to which any one found outside his " parish of settlement " might be, with his family, at any time compulsorily " removed " in custody.[1]

[1] The Law of Settlement and Removal, which has given rise to voluminous reports of cases and many legal treatises, is inadequately dealt with from the historical standpoint in the Poor Law histories of the Rev. Dr. Burn, Sir F. M. Eden, Thomas Ruggles, or Sir George Nicholls, who (like later polemical writers on Poor Relief) have mostly repeated, uncritically, each other's statements of the origin, purpose and actual effect of the Act of 1662. The question was elaborately explored, in the light of all the then available historical evidence, in the admirable *Report on the Law of Settlement and Removal*, running to more than three hundred pages, which George Coode made to the Poor Law Board in 1851, and which was published, with supplementary reports, as Parliamentary Papers (H.C. 675 of 1851 and H.C. 493 of 1854). The simultaneously published volume entitled *Pauperism and Poor Laws*, by Robert Pashley, 1852, contains an independent historical summary of all the statutes. The best account of the actual working of the law is given in chapters v. and vi. of *The English Poor in the Eighteenth Century*, by Dorothy Marshall, 1926, in which are embodied the results of much praiseworthy investigation of parish and county records. No contemporary account of the law exists, beyond the bare record of its various stages in the *Journals* of the House of Commons and House of Lords (given in Coode's *Report*, pp. 18-22). Apart from vague references to the repression of begging and the relief of the poor, the Act was not mentioned in the King's speeches, nor in any of the Addresses in either House ; nor is it alluded to in Richard Chandler's *History of the Proceedings of the House of Commons from the Restoration to the Present Time*, 1742 ; or in any other account of the Parliamentary proceedings known to us. The Bill is just mentioned in the Seventh Report of the Historical Manuscripts Commission, p. 148 ; see *History of English Law*, by W. S. Houldsworth, vol. vi., 1924, p. 350. The complications of the law are best studied in the successive editions of Burn's *Justice of the Peace ;* or *Decisions of the Court of King's Bench upon the Laws relating to the Poor*, by Edmund Bott, 3rd edition, 1793, by F. Const. They are well seen

We find placed on the statute-book, by the first Restoration Parliament, without either previous mention in contemporary literature or recorded discussion in the House of Commons, the Act of 13 and 14 Charles II. c. 12 (1662), with unconscious irony entitled "An Act for the Better Relief of the Poor of this Kingdom", which has been since known as the Law of Settlement and Removal. This statute presents, to the social historian, a puzzling enigma. Who were its authors, what were the motives and the circumstances of its enactment, and how the Government and Parliament came to allow so badly drafted a measure to become law are questions that are as yet unanswered. The Law of Settlement and Removal inflicted, during the ensuing couple of centuries, so much hardship on individuals, and, indirectly, also on the whole body of manual-working wage-earners ; may be assumed to have interfered so seriously with the economic prosperity of the community, and certainly involved such a colossal and long-continued waste of public funds, that it demands a detailed examination.

What the Act of 1662 did was not, as is often supposed, to establish a system of "settlement", determining that every person should legally "belong" to some parish, and defining the parish. Such a system had existed from time immemorial. "In England, a stringent, compact and simple law of settlement, defining the domicile of every man, whatever his condition, is coeval with our earliest authentic institutions ; and these refer evidently to a complete pre-existing system." [1] Every person was, as serf or as freeman, a member of some local community, to which he owed obligations, and from which he was entitled to expect some measure of protection, and, when in need, some undefined support. An unknown person, absent without credentials from the community to which he belonged, was an object of grave suspicion, having, in early times, practically no rights ; but travel, and even indefinite sojourn in other

---

in *A Series of Decisions on Settlement Cases*, by Sir James Burrow, 2 vols., 1786. The subsequent history is surveyed in Sir Edmund Walker Head's article in the *Edinburgh Review*, April 1848, which was reprinted by the Government in 1865 ; *The Speech of the Rt. Hon. M. T. Baines on the Bill to Abolish . . . the Compulsory Removal of the Poor on the Ground of Settlement, etc.*, 1854 ; and Mr. Villiers' speech in the House of Commons (Hansard, March 27, 1865).

[1] *Report on the Law of Settlement and Removal*, by George Coode, 1851, H.C. No. 675 of 1851, p. 7.

communities, was facilitated by one or other form of friendly
introduction. " In compelling every man to have a known
domicile, this ancient system of law, so far, at least as concerned
the freeman, did not prevent him from choosing it where he
pleased, or changing it when he pleased, but afforded him all
safe facilities for doing so." [1]   Between 1381 and 1641 there
were, indeed, certain penal measures in force which sought to
prevent the migration of labourers in husbandry and domestic
servants ; but though these Acts provided for penalties on those
who were prosecuted and convicted for leaving their places of
abode, they did nothing to facilitate such prosecutions, and
above all, they made no provision for bringing back to their
parishes of origin those who had left them.

Certain restraints on mobility were, moreover, imposed by
statute from time to time on particular classes.   Wandering
monks without due credentials, witches, fortune-tellers, sorcerers,
prostitutes, conjurors, " Egyptians " (gypsies), " sturdy vagabonds ", " valiant rogues " and vagrants generally, came at
different dates under the ban of the law.   They were forbidden
to roam ; they were subjected to savage chastisement, and they
were made liable to summary extrusion from any place away
from their domicile in which they were found.   The long series
of vagrancy laws, beginning with 12 Richard II. c. 7 (1388),
emphasise the distinction between such wayfaring folk, whose
wanderings were deemed to be criminal in their nature ; and
those others, whose travels were, under defined conditions,
actually sanctioned, and sometimes even prescribed by the
statutes.   The labourer was expressly authorised to depart
from his domicile if furnished with a testimonial to distinguish
him from a criminal vagabond.   Impotent folk whom their
neighbours failed to support might withdraw to other places,
and were presently expressly licensed to beg elsewhere than
in their places of settlement.

With the beginnings of a general system of relief of the
indigent that we have described, at first out of voluntary contributions which all their fellow-parishioners were continuously
pressed to make, and which in the next generation became
legally obligatory, it was natural that parishes should wish to

---

[1] *Report on the Law of Settlement and Removal*, by George Coode, 1851,
H.C. No. 675 of 1851, p. 10.

limit their liabilities, in the way of relief, to those whom they felt to " belong " to the parish. Accordingly, we find the Local Authorities, here and there, already in the middle of the sixteenth century, taking action to protect themselves against the burden of having to maintain the indigent of other parishes. This was the motive of the frequent prohibition of harbouring " inmates ", or receiving " strangers " as tenants. Thus, in the " Ordinances made by the Bailiffs, Aldermen and Common Council " of the borough of Colchester (Essex), on the 15th of February 1557, " it is further agreed that every and singular owner and owners of houses and tenements within the precinct of this town shall not, after the day of making this Order, receive into his or their houses, tenantries or shops, or admit to be their tenants, any stranger or strangers, unless it shall evidently appear that he or they, with their wives or family, by their handiwork or goods, shall be able sufficiently to live honestly and truly without begging or bribing ".[1] In 1622, we see the Select Vestry of the rural parish of Pittington, in Durham, enacting a similar prohibition, with the additional precaution of insisting on a bond, with two " sufficient men " as sureties, to indemnify the parish against having to support the new-comers.[2]

What was to be done with strangers who had already secured a lodgement in the parish, who were actually in need, and who were importunate in their demand for alms ? If the able-bodied vagrant could be whipped and extruded from the parish, and pro-vided with a pass showing that he had been duly " corrected ",[3]

---

[1] Ordinances of Colchester, February 15, 1557, in *History . . . of Essex*, by Philip Morant, 1768, vol. i. p. 181.

[2] " Memorandum, that it is agreed upon by the Gentlemen and Twelve [the Select Vestry] of Pittington parish, March 9, 1622, that no inhabitant . . . shall receive, harbour and entertain any stranger to be his tenant or tenants into his house or houses before he acquaint the Twelve with his intent, and shall himself, and two sufficient men with him, enter into bond . . . to the Overseers that neither his tenant, wife or children shall be chargeable to the parish for five years next following, upon pain and penalty to forfeit ten shillings for every month " (*Churchwardens' Accounts of Pittington*, etc., Surtees Society, vol. 84, 1888, p. 84).

[3] The vagrant's pass (called a " passport " in an order of 1570 by the Newark Town Council) was given, for instance, by the " Constable of Sprotton " to a vagrant, certifying that he had " received correction " there ; asking that he may be allowed to pass quietly to Newark, " where he saith he dwelleth " ; and requesting that he may be provided, on the way, with lodging and sus-tenance (*Extracts from the Records of the Petty Sessions and Quarter Sessions for the Borough of Newark*, by R. F. B. Hodgkinson, 1920).

in the hope that he would obediently betake himself on foot
to the place where he " belonged ", the " impotent poor ",
found begging out of their own domiciles, or outside the
districts assigned to them for the purpose, could not thus
be dealt with.   In the exceptionally severe statutes of 1547
and 1549 (1 and 2 Edward VI. c. 3, and 3 and 4 Edward VI. c.
16)—aimed, it has been alleged, primarily at the wandering monks
who had been dislodged from the suppressed monasteries [1]—
there was incidentally authorised a monthly clearance and
extrusion of all " aged, impotent and lame persons ", *who were*
" *beggars* ", from parishes where they had not been born, or
had not resided continuously for a period of three years.   It
is here that " we find the first provision for the removal " of
the poor who did not " belong " to the parish, a provision then
confined to such of the impotent poor as were actually beggars.
" The officers were directed to convey " them " on horseback,
cart, chariot or otherwise to the next constable, and so from
constable to constable, till they be brought to the place where
they were born or most conversant for the space of three years,
there to be nourished of alms." [2]   This provision was confirmed
by 5 Elizabeth c. 3, and again by 14 Elizabeth c. 5 ; and the
latter statute omitted the limiting word " beggars ".   From
1572, accordingly, the actual words of the statute-law seem to
have authorised the compulsory extrusion, not of any able-
bodied artisan or labourer who had found work at wages, or
could otherwise show that he was not a rogue or vagabond,
but of any " aged, lame or impotent person ", however inoffensive, of less than three years' residence, whether or not in receipt
of relief, or asking for alms.   Such persons, moreover, could
not only be forcibly extruded from the parish, but were to be
removed in charge of the parish officers to the constable of the
next parish, and so on until they had reached the place of their
birth, or last three years' residence.   Thus, we learn that, at
Liverpool in 1592, licences to beg were issued by the mayor to
indigent folk who belonged to the town, all other beggars being
prohibited ; and, we imagine, forcibly extruded, and possibly

---

[1] *History of the Reformation*, by Bishop Burnet, part ii. book i. p. 83 ;
History of England, by M. Rapin, 1732, vol. viii. p. 34 ; *Pauperism and Poor
Laws*, by R. Pashley, 1852, p. 184.

[2] Report of George Coode . . . on the Law of Settlement and Removal of
the Poor, H.C. No. 675 of 1851, p. 11.

removed.[1] But when the law relating to Poor Relief was, as we have described, amended and codified in 1597 and 1601, the new Acts neither authorised nor mentioned removal to the parishes to which they belonged, of any section of the poor ; and the Judges, as well as other legal authorities, seem to have held that, with the lapse of the previous Acts, there was, after 1597, no power in any parish to remove any one, or to expel any but rogues and vagabonds, who could still be whipped and started off wandering with passes. Dalton's *Country Justice*, a law-book of great authority, in the edition of 1635, expressly declares that " no man is to be put out of the town where he dwelleth, nor to be sent back to their place of birth, or last habitation, but a vagrant rogue. . . . Sir Francis Harvey, at the Summer Assizes at Cambridge [in] 1629, did deliver it that the Justices of Peace (especially out of their sessions) were not to meddle either with the removing or settling of any poor, but only of rogues. . . . Young children whose parents are dead are to be . . . at the charge of the town where they were dwelling at the time of the death of their parents, and are not to be sent to their place of birth." [2]

Whether the able-bodied labourer in husbandry, or roving handicraftsman, of industrious habits, and not begging or

---

[1] *Liverpool Vestry Books, 1681–1834*, by Henry Peet, 1912, vol. i. p. xx ; *Memorials of Liverpool*, by Sir James Allanson Picton, 1875, vol. i. p. 114.

[2] *The Country Justice*, by Michael Dalton, edition of 1635, pp. 98-101 ; to like effect is *The Duties of Constables*, by William Lambard, edition of 1619, p. 51 ; see *Pauperism and Poor Laws*, by Robert Pashley, 1852, pp. 218-219, where it is definitely concluded that " for a long period after the passing of the statute of 43rd Elizabeth, its humane and reasonable provisions were carried out without its being necessary to remove any poor people from one part of the Kingdom to another, in order that they might be relieved. Throughout the whole of this period, that is from 1601 to 1662, all poor persons were entitled to needful relief wheresoever they were residing ; and it was only the rogue or vagrant that was liable to any removal to his place of birth, or last three years' habitation." For perfect accuracy it should be stated that the Act of 5 Elizabeth c. 4 (1563) had provided that certain classes of servants should not depart, without a testimonial, from the place in which they had last served. These provisions had been continued in force by 3 Charles I. c. 5, 1628, until the end of the first session of the then next Parliament (1641), when they had expired. " From that time forth till 1662 men of every class, except actual malefactors, were free to move and dwell wherever they pleased " (Report of George Coode . . . on the Law of Settlement and Removal of the Poor, H.C. No. 675 of 1851, p. 23). The formal repeal of the Acts of 27 Henry VIII. c. 25, 1 Edward VI. c. 3, 5 and 6 Edward VI. c. 2, 2 and 3 Philip and Mary, c. 5, 14 Elizabeth, c. 5, and 18 Elizabeth, c. 3, was effected by the Statute Law Revision Act of 1863.

seeking poor relief but merely coming to take up a situation in another parish was, in practice, during the first half of the seventeenth century, quite secure against being summarily extruded from the parish into which he had come, and even from being compulsorily removed to his place of birth or former residence, we should be sorry to assert. Whatever the lawyers may have been declaring, it seems as if the idea was widely prevalent that the wandering poor ought to be at the charge of the parishes to which they " belonged ", and not of any other parish. The very repetition, by Judges and writers of law manuals, of the statement that there existed, after 1597, no legal power of compulsory removal may be deemed to afford some indication of a popular belief to the contrary. There certainly seem to have been attempts at " clearance ", from each parish, of others besides rogues and vagabonds. It is expressly stated that landlords sought to eject people from cottages, and parish officers tried compulsorily to remove them from the parish, on no other ground than that it was feared that they might at some future time become a burden on the Poor Rate. In 1615, for instance, the Somerset Justices were much concerned about the working of the law, as laid down by the Judges. " Twice the Court [of Quarter Sessions] tried to lay down a general principle in order to make their decisions more uniform ", and to serve as a guide to the parish officers. They wished to prevent ejectment by landlords, but they were puzzled as to whether persons, not belonging to the parish by birth or three years' residence, might be removed merely because they are likely to become chargeable.[1] Such of them as actually applied for Poor Law relief were plainly liable to find themselves compulsorily removed, whatever the law said, even if they were not " vagrant rogues ".[2]

This forcible removal, to the parishes to which they " belonged ", of persons who had become destitute, and actually a charge upon the Poor Rate, was, under Cromwell's rule, deemed an unjustifiable hardship. " To alleviate the cruelties of this state of things," states one of the very few writers on

[1] *Quarter Sessions Records for the County of Somerset*, by Rev. E. H. Bates, vol. i., 1907, p. xxx.

[2] See a case in Hertfordshire on April 16, 1662, just before the enactment of the Act of 13 and 14 Charles II. c. 12 (*Notes and Extracts from the Hertfordshire Session Rolls*, by W. J. Hardy, 1905, vol. i. pp. xxi. 149).

the social politics of the Commonwealth, "was one of the duties, as I conceive it was one of the pleasures, of the Commonwealth Judges, and their circuit books are full of orders restraining various parish officers from the compulsory removal of poor and aged people, of inoffensive life, from the spots where they had passed their later years and from the comfort and society of their children. This cruelty to the poor was a subject of remonstrance by the Puritan party from the early days of King James; and Dekker, in his *Seven Deadly Sins* (1606) refers to this as one of the causes of the Divine judgement upon the City of London in visiting it annually with the plague." [1]

There was, however, still no warrant for the forcible expulsion, from any parish or borough in which he could obtain a lodging, of the able-bodied, self-supporting artisan or labourer, belonging to another parish, who, not being guilty of the crime of vagrancy, did not beg, and did not apply for Poor Relief. It was with regard to such a man that the Act of 1662—to use the words of George Coode—introduced " a new and perfectly unprecedented system ", which " made the most effectual and extensive invasion of the rights of Englishmen which had ever been attempted since the Conquest ".[2] From and after 1662, for more than a century and a quarter, any person (not belonging to a class of property owners numbering fewer than one-tenth of the population), who, either to take a situation, or merely on a visit to relations or friends, or for any other reason whatever, however lawful or laudable, came into a parish in which he had not a settlement, was liable—however good his character and conduct, without any application for relief or for any other gift or favour, and even after he had secured remunerative employment—unless he could give sufficient security that he would never become chargeable to the parish, to the satisfaction of the Justices—to be summarily removed in custody, together with his wife and children, under ignominious and horribly uncomfortable conditions, to whatever parish, however distant, might be believed to be the place where, according to an extremely complicated and always uncertain code of law, he

---

[1] *The Interregnum*, by F. C. Inderwick, 1891, pp. 91-92.
[2] Report by George Coode . . . on the Law of Settlement and Removal, H.C. No. 675 of 1851, pp. 14-15.

Y

had his legal settlement.¹   The Act " in theory affected not only
the old, the infirm, the helpless and the infants, but also all those
agricultural labourers who worked for, and were dependent on,
their wages ; it affected the great mass of manual workers of
every kind ; it affected most of the smaller manufacturers, such
as the spinners, the weavers, the dyers and the shearers ; it
affected, too, the large class of small craftsmen, the blacksmiths,
the carpenters or the tailors ".²   And the law was enforced in
tens of thousands of cases annually.   Thus was produced the
mournful and onerous " general post " of indigent folk, men,
women and children, in all states of health and disease, perpetually criss-crossing the kingdom under expensive escort, which
lasted two whole centuries, and which, together with the incessant litigation to which the system gave rise, must have cost
the public, in the course of the next two hundred years, literally
millions of pounds, to nobody's ultimate advantage except the
lawyers.³

We are aware of nothing in the circumstances of the years
1661–1662 which called for such an attempt to immobilise, in

¹ A narrowly limited protection was accorded by the Act of 1662 to those
who obtained a certificate authorising them to go into another parish for
temporary harvesting or other work—limited to those who were householders,
married men, leaving behind them wives and children, with the sanction of
the clergyman, one Churchwarden and one Overseer.   This privilege was
extended in 1697 to unmarried men, not householders, but made more difficult
of attainment.   We refer later to the use made of this provision.

It should be added that the Act of 1662 included a provision for the drastic
punishment as a vagabond under the Vagrancy Acts of any person who, having
been removed to his parish of settlement, should presume to return to the
place from which he had been removed.   This provision, we suspect, was seldom
carried out, as there is evidence that, at all times, a considerable proportion of
the persons removed sooner or later found their way back to the place in which
they preferred to live, especially as they could often find no means of subsistence
in their parish of settlement.   In 1702 a woman was committed to the House of
Correction at Cambridge for having thus returned after having been removed to
the parish in which her late husband had his settlement ; but Quarter Sessions
did no more to her in punishment than order her to be again removed thither
(*The English Poor in the Eighteenth Century*, by Dorothy Marshall, 1926, p. 173).

² *Ibid.* p. 2.

³ " It is notorious ", said William Hay in 1735, " that half the business of
every Quarter Sessions consists in deciding appeals on orders of removal "
(*Remarks on the Laws relating to the Poor*, by William Hay, 1735 ; included in
his *Works*, 1794, vol. i. p. 121).   " The few pages which contain the Pauper
Settlement Laws ", wrote in 1832 one who was competent to form an estimate,
" have been the main employment of the Quarter Sessions since the Revolution,
at the expense of litigation estimated at ten millions " (*Administration of the
Poor Laws*, 1832, an anonymous and privately printed pamphlet by John
Rickman).

the parishes to which they " belonged ", the nine-tenths of the
whole population who were subjected to the Law of Settlement
and Removal. There was, doubtless, at the Restoration a
general increase in the volume of able-bodied destitution. The
sudden and practically complete disbandment of the army
must have thrown some fifty thousand men, mostly without
resources of any kind, upon a labour market that was not in a
position immediately to absorb more than an undefined fraction
of them. The home trade had been presumably to some extent
dislocated by the troubles of the Commonwealth, whilst imports
and exports, at that date relatively inconsiderable, cannot but
have been adversely affected by the desolation into which
Germany had been thrown by the Thirty Years War, and by
the internal struggles of France. The English harvests had
been scanty, and the price of wheat was soaring, reaching in
1661 seventy shillings, and in 1662 seventy-four shillings per
quarter, being nearly three times the price in 1654. Contemporary records and pamphlets indicate a noticeable increase in
the number of destitute families, and in the plague of beggars ;
the actual evidence—this is an important point—relating almost
entirely to the overgrown, straggling Metropolis. Meanwhile
the national system of provision for the poor, which had been
built up, under the direction of Burleigh and Cecil, by the
Privy Council and the Justices of the Peace between 1590 and
1640, had, by 1660, as we have shown, fallen very largely into
desuetude and even into oblivion. In many a rural parish
no Overseers were being appointed, and no Poor Rates levied.
In London and Westminster, as in Bristol and Norwich, and
other cities, and certainly in many rural parishes, the Poor Law
machinery remained in existence, but it seems, for the most
part, to have practically abandoned any attempt to provide
for the able-bodied unemployed. " Let any man ", declared
Sir Matthew Hale, in the oft-quoted essay that he wrote about
1660, " look over most of the populous parishes in England ;
indeed there are rates made for the relief of the impotent poor,
and it may be that the same relief is also given in a narrow
measure unto some others that have great families ; and upon
this they live miserably and at best from hand to mouth, and if
they cannot get work to make out their livelihood, they and
their children set up a trade of begging at best. *But it is rare*

to see any provision of a stock in any parish for the relief of the [able-bodied] poor."

What has, so far, not been discovered is any evidence bearing out the astonishing assertions in the preamble of the statute which the Restoration Parliament, " with little deliberation and no discussion ", in 1662 enacted. That " the necessity, number and continued increase of the poor is very great and exceeding burdensome " can easily be believed. But the Act then proceeds to recite that " whereas, by reason of some defects in the law, poor people are not restrained from going from one parish to another, and therefore do endeavour to settle themselves in those parishes where there is the best stock, the largest commons or wastes to build cottages [on], and the most woods for them to burn and destroy ; and when they have consumed it, then to another parish, and at last become rogues and vagabonds, to the great discouragement of parishes to provide stocks where it is liable to be devoured by strangers ". Of such an extraordinary preamble it must suffice to say that " amongst all the lamentations of the degeneracy, the vices and the crimes of the poor with which the literature of the times abounded, a laborious search has discovered no other reference to this class of disorder ".[1] No trace of migration of the able-bodied poor in the direction of " those parishes where there is the best stock " has been found ; and in view of the widespread failure of the Overseers at that date to provide any " stock " at all, the statement seems an absurdity. Equally, no one has found the slightest sign of a tendency to swarm to the districts in which there were extensive areas of commons or wastes, even if there was any general possibility of these destitute folk building cottages upon them for themselves ; nor of any migration to the thickly wooded parts of the country, in order to enjoy the burning and destroying of this timber. On the contrary, all the available evidence is that such migration as was going on was away from the less populous districts, and from the rural parishes generally, to the densely inhabited and almost entirely unregulated miles of streets and alleys that were spreading from London and Westminster, in which possibly a couple of hundred thousand people were already aggregated. In short,

---

[1] Report by George Coode . . . on the Law of Settlement and Removal of the Poor, H.C. 675 of 1851, p. 253.

the preamble to the Law of Settlement and Removal of 1662 remains a classic example of legislative mendacity, and of the worthlessness of preambles to Acts of Parliament as historical evidence.

Let us turn to the way in which the law was actually passed. There were, it appears, four distinct Bills relating to the relief of the poor, all introduced seven months after the session had been opened, in December 1661 and January 1662, three of them within a few days of each other, and, as would nowadays be said, all by private Members. The first of these Bills contemplated merely the adoption, in the large parishes of the North of England, of the township instead of the parish, as the unit of Poor Law administration.[1] The second was primarily for the establishment of a Corporation of the Poor for the City of London, in ratification or re-enactment of the Ordinances of 1647 and 1649, which had, with all the other legislation of the Commonwealth, been declared invalid.[2] A third Bill was apparently in general terms for the more effective relief of the poor, but without any provision for their removal.[3] The fourth Bill, possibly carrying out a suggestion of Sir Matthew Hale, proposed to establish local Corporations of the Poor in all urban centres throughout England and Wales, apparently on the model of that of the City of London, but with more effective provisions for ensuring the employment of all able-bodied persons, and for the enforcement of the penal law against rogues and vagabonds. It also contained a provision " for preventing of poor by the settling of them ".[4] The London Bill was referred to a committee made up of all the Members who chose to attend, the management naturally being taken by the City representatives. To this committee, which neither the King's Ministers nor the

[1] December 13, 1661. A Bill for the Better Relief of the Poor within the Counties of Lancaster, Chester, Derby, York and Westmorland.

[2] January 17, 1662. A Bill for the Better Relief and Employment of the Poor and the Punishment of Vagrants and other disorderly persons within the Cities of London and Westminster, and the Liberties thereof, and the Bills of Mortality.

[3] January 14, 1662. A Bill for the Regulating, Employing and Providing for the Poor.

[4] January 16, 1662. A Bill for the constituting Corporations in the Cities, Boroughs and Market Towns in the Kingdom of England and Dominion of Wales, for the better relief and employment of the poor, and for the preventing of the poor by the settling of them, and for the better execution of the laws against rogues and vagabonds.

lawyers in the House seem to have attended, and to which they apparently paid no attention, all the other Bills were referred. What happened in committee was the consolidation of all four projects into a single measure, in which the mendacious preamble was put together from those of the third and fourth Bills ; the all-important clauses relating to removal, certificates and appeals were taken from the third Bill, without making effective its proposal for the establishment of " Corporations of the Poor " in the cities and market towns ; the Corporation of the Poor of the City of London, founded in 1647, in which the managers of the Committee were specially interested, was alone seriously intended and provided for ; whilst the desires of the Northern Counties were met by the inclusion, from the first Bill, of the power to split the large parishes into their townships. The second Bill, of relatively humanitarian character, was apparently ignored. Within a month this consolidated Bill, in careless and confused language,[1] had reached the House of Lords, where some slight amendments, unconnected with the subject of removal, were made, which led to conferences between the two Houses, and to eventual agreement in May 1662.[2]

Of this Law of Settlement and Removal, as it has since been always termed, the provision enabling the substitution of the

[1] See *Remarks on the Poor Laws, and on the State of the Poor*, by Charles Weston, 1802, p. 46 ; whom Coode described as " the best informed of all the writers on poor laws that I have any knowledge of " (Report of George Coode . . . on the Law of Settlement and Removal of the Poor, H.C. No. 675 of 1851, p. 335).

[2] Journals of the House of Commons, December 13, 1661, January 14, 16, 17, 18, February 14, 15, May 15, 17, 19, 1662 ; Journals of the House of Lords, February 18, 20, March 24, April 3, 17, 26, 28, May 17, 1662 ; Report of George Coode . . . on the Law of Settlement and Removal of the Poor, H.C. No. 675 of 1851, pp. 17-22, 263-264.

We append the brief and perfunctory references to this momentous Act in the Speaker's Address to the King, and the King's Speech in reply, on the prorogation of Parliament (from *The History and Proceedings of the House of Commons*, etc., by Richard Chandler, 1742, vol. i. pp. 55-57) :

The Speaker's Speech to the King, May 19, 1662 : " God in his Providence hath determin'd, That the Poor we must have always with us ; Some are made so by the immediate Hand of God ; others by their Loyalty, Duty and Service to your royal Person, and your blessed Father ; others by their own Wickedness and Idleness : We have taken care to relieve the first, to encourage the second, and to reform the last."

The King's Speech to both Houses at the Prorogation : " I hope the Laws I have pass'd this Day, will produce some Reformation with reference to the Multitude of Beggars and poor people which infest the Kingdom : Great Severity must be used to those who love idleness and refuse to work, and great Care and Charity to those who are willing to work."

township for the parish as the unit of Poor Law administration was found a convenience in the Northern counties, where it was, without friction, in due time gradually adopted. The provision re-establishing the Corporation of the Poor of the City of London seems to have been badly drafted, and to have required subsequent legislation. What became a cruel and costly instrument of tyranny and arbitrary oppression of the wage-earning class was the new law of compulsory removal.[1] The Act empowered the Churchwardens and Overseers, by warrant of two Justices, peremptorily to remove any new-comer, whether or not he applied for or needed relief, or was immediately likely to do so, unless he could give such security for indemnity of the parish as two Justices should deem sufficient ; or unless he either rented land or house let at ten pounds a year or upwards —this being, it was afterwards said, assumed to indicate an improbability of his ever becoming a charge on the parish ; but rather, as may be imagined, adopted as a means of confining the operation of the law to the wage-earning or non-propertied class, none of whom, at that date, paid more than two or three shillings a week in rent. Henceforth any person not belonging to the propertied class—especially any labourer or artisan, even if he had found employment at wages, and was in full vigour and good health—was liable, if found living outside the narrow bounds of the parish in which he was legally settled, to be pounced upon by the parish officers, who were incited thereto by any neighbour ; and, upon a warrant usually granted as a matter of course, to be arrested and summarily packed off, with his family, in custody of the Overseer, who had to convey him to the parish

[1] " Never was such important legislation effected by means of exceptions, qualifications and hints, and seldom have any laws been so pertinaciously adhered after the principal, and in some cases the only reasons for their introduction had ceased. The direct purpose of the Act, stripped of all that qualifies it, is to enable the Justices, on complaint of the Churchwardens or Overseers, to remove any new-comer from a parish, though not applying for relief, if they think or profess to think that he is likely to become chargeable " (General Report of the Poor Law Inquiry Commissioners, 1834, pp. 152-153).
" This great alteration in the law appears to have excited as little attention out of doors as of debate within, for the newspapers did not notice it, no pamphlet was written on it, and not one petition on the subject was presented to either House ; and no member of either House, except those who brought in the several Bills, gave any notice of any motion on the subject, and no member of the Government, and no member of either House officially connected with it, took any part in the proceedings " (Report of George Coode . . . on the Law of Settlement and Removal of the Poor, H.C. 675 of 1851, p. 22).

in which he was believed to have a settlement. "Surely", wrote Roger North about 1670, "it is a great imprisonment, if not slavery, to a poor family to be under such restraint by law that they must always live in one place, whether they have friends, kindred, employment or not, or however they might mend their condition by moving; and all because they had the ill-luck to be born or to have served or resided a certain time there."[1]

For more than a hundred and thirty years the nine-tenths of the entire population who were manual-working wage-earners, or independent handicraftsmen, remained subject to this intolerable law. It is clear from the growing number of cases tried at Quarter Sessions and in the superior Courts, that it was promptly and extensively put in operation. "The natural fruit of the law came into its mischievous maturity at once." Up and down the land the Overseers were on the look out lest "some persons by skulking within this parish, might presently be found to have surreptitiously gained a settlement here".[2] Nor did Parliament strive, either to prevent the hardships that were caused to the poor, or to lessen the litigation. On the contrary, between 1686 and 1722, it seemed anxious to increase both these evils. By the statutes of 1686, 1692, 1697 and 1698, as by those of 1714 and 1723, the conditions for acquiring a settlement were made both complicated and more onerous.[3] The privilege of moving by getting a certificate was

---

[1] *A Discourse on the Pernicious Tendency of the Laws for the Maintenance and Settlement of the Poor*, by the Hon. Roger North, published 1753, but apparently written about 1670; see *History of the English Poor Law*, by Sir George Nicholls, 1854, vol. i. p. 300; Report of George Coode . . . on the Law of Settlement and Removal of the Poor, H.C. No. 675 of 1851, p. 287. Notwithstanding North's protest, in all the numerous amendments to the Law of Settlement and Removal, "the Overseer's power, arbitrarily to refuse a certificate, was never qualified" (*Pauperism and Poor Laws*, by Robert Pashley, 1852, p. 252).

[2] *History of Bilston*, by G. T. Lawley, 1893, p. 59.

[3] 1 James II. c. 17; 3 William and Mary c. 11; 8 and 9 William III. c. 30; 9 and 10 William III. c. 14; 12 Anne c. 18; and 9 George I. c. 7; *Pauperism and Poor Laws*, by Robert Pashley, 1852, pp. 237-239. Thus, six several times, in the course of less than forty years, did Parliament tinker at the law; but with the one exception, above stated, in nominally widening the scope of the original provision with regard to certificates, always to make it more difficult and disadvantageous for the labourer to move. As enacted in 1662, the law had authorised removal only within forty days of arrival; but, "forasmuch as poor persons at their first coming to a parish do commonly conceal themselves", it was provided in 1686 that the period of forty days

nominally extended in 1697 to unmarried persons who were not householders, but was made dependent on the good pleasure not of one but of all the Churchwardens and Overseers, together with two Justices of the Peace, who were indisposed to be willing to allow the departure of any energetic labourer of good character, even if he could afford the time to fulfil all the formalities. " There is ", subsequently observed the Rev. Richard Burn, " somewhat of hardship in this matter of certificates, by putting it into the power of a parish officer to imprison a man, as it were, for life, however inconvenient it may be for him to continue at that place where he had the misfortune to acquire what is called a settlement, or whatever advantage he may

---

should be counted only from the time of delivery of a notice in writing to the Overseer, and in 1692, only from the date of publication of such notice in the parish church. As any such notice would have meant, in effect, a direct provocation of the Overseer to apply for a Removal Order, the notice was naturally seldom given. Hence, the amendment came to this, that the period of forty days was practically abrogated, so that the new-comer remained always liable to be summarily removed, however long and however meritorious had been his residence and service, unless he was fortunate enough, by rising in the world, to " gain a settlement " in one or other of the narrowly described ways, all of which implied social advancement. In 1697, soldiers, sailors and workmen in the King's service were prevented from ever acquiring a settlement ; and in 1714 also the apprentices and servants of persons holding certificates. In 1698 a person hired for a year was debarred from gaining a settlement unless he actually served the whole twelve months ; in 1699 a certificated person was prevented from gaining a settlement unless he genuinely took up a leasehold tenancy of £10 a year or upwards, or genuinely served a whole year in a parochial office in which he had been legally placed. In 1723 payment of highway rate and scavenger's rate was made to give no settlement, and the purchaser of an estate of less than £30 value was only allowed a settlement during his inhabitancy of such an estate. Even the creation, in 1692, of four new means of gaining a settlement—namely, by serving a parish office, by paying the local rates, by hiring and service and by apprenticeship, were, in fact, " diminutions of the larger rights of settlement previously enjoyed ", by the narrowing conditions imposed, and the uncertainties of litigation thus created. Amid the complications of the successive amendments of the Law of Settlement there emerged four ways " through which ", observed Sir F. M. Eden in 1797, " it is probable that by far the greater part of the labouring poor [who have acquired settlements] . . . are actually settled ". Thus, illegitimate children, with some exceptions, acquired a settlement by birth ; and also legitimate children, if neither their father's nor their mother's settlement could be ascertained. Women always gained a settlement by marriage to any man whose settlement could be ascertained. Persons owning a freehold, however small, were irremovable so long as they resided upon it (*The Village Labourer, 1760–1832*, by J. L. and Barbara Hammond, 1912, pp. 113-114). To these practical ways by which the poorest wage-earners might acquire a settlement, we may add, from the middle of the eighteenth century onward, in the Metropolis and a few other large towns, the renting of a tenement which the rise in rents had brought up to the value of four shillings a week.

propose to himself by living elsewhere."[1] Such a power of detaining the labourers in the parish, even without finding them work, was plainly very convenient for the farmer, who had his reserve of labour legally kept at his beck and call, without even the risk of any other demand for labour raising the rate of wages. Thus it was, as was bitterly complained, that for the next hundred and thirty years, " the poor are imprisoned in their towns[hips], and chained down to their wants, so that they are deprived of means to mend their condition, if their own wits or their friends should suggest any, by removing to places more proper for them either for sort of work or of friends to employ them. But if any chance to move for an experiment, they are sent back, and tossed from pillar to post in carts, till they return to their old settled misery again. No town[ship] willingly receives a poor man, though they want poor people to do the ordinary works of husbandry, because they say his family may become a charge to the parish."[2]

It is characteristic of the social politics and the statesmanship of the eighteenth century that, notwithstanding a continuous criticism and authoritative denunciation of this extraordinary law—alike in respect of its disastrous effect on economic prosperity, its inhumanity, and the great expense that it occasioned —it remained virtually unchanged, save for the slight modifications of 1682–1723, from its enactment in 1662 down to the first substantial reform in 1795. It is hard to say, which was the most detrimental to the common weal, the hindrance to the migration of the enterprising labourer, the hardships and sufferings that the occasional compulsory removal caused to the poor, or the demoralisation that the inter-parochial litigation effected in the whole administration of the Poor Law. An anonymous pamphleteer of 1759, like Sir Josiah Child nearly a century earlier, put the emphasis on the hampering of production. " The restraining or confining them to the parish they belong to tends

---

[1] *History of the Poor Laws,* by Rev. Richard Burn, 1764.

[2] *Discourse on the Pernicious Tendency of the Laws for the Maintenance and Settlement of the Poor,* by the Hon. Roger North, 1753 (but written before 1689), p. 34. The author adds, " And if one that is not legally settled happens to be sick, or near labour they will hoist them up in this carted pilgrimage without allowing them any repose, and if it be midnight, hurry them to next town, and there shoot them down like dirt, and they find there as little comfort as they left behind ; and thus have divers perished, as the men about Croydon well know " (p. 34).

to cramp industry ; and often obliges the labourer to live upon parish allowances when he might otherwise provide for himself and his family in a comfortable manner." [1] On Adam Smith the injustice to the zealous and ambitious labourer made the deepest impression. " To remove a man," he wrote in 1776, " who has committed no misdemeanour, from a parish where he chooses to reside, is an evident violation of natural liberty and justice. The common people of England, however, so jealous of their liberty, but, like the common people of most other countries, never rightly understanding wherein it consists, have now, for more than a century together, suffered themselves to be exposed to this oppression without a remedy. Though men of reflexion, too, have sometimes complained of the law of settlements as a public grievance ; yet it has never been the object of any general popular clamour, such as that against general warrants, an abusive practice undoubtedly, but such a one as was not likely to occasion any general oppression. There is scarce a poor man in England, of forty years of age, I will venture to say, who has not, in some part of his life, felt himself most cruelly oppressed by this ill-contrived law of settlements." [2]

Reviewing such evidence as the records afford, we are inclined to-day to make a more sober estimate than Adam Smith of the effects of the Act of 1662. The suffering and loss to the victims who happened to be forcibly removed can, indeed, hardly be exaggerated.[3] There was even a wanton aggravation of the hardship, unnecessary for the purpose in view and in these

---

[1] *Populousness with Oeconomy the Wealth and Strength of the Kingdom . . . addressed to . . . Parliament in behalf of the Poor*, 1759.

[2] *Wealth of Nations*, by Adam Smith, 1776, vol. i. p. 194.

[3] We may cite one example of both the wanton cruelty of the law and of the callous ruthlessness of the Overseer's enforcement of it, even in the nineteenth century. An able-bodied labourer, who had been for years employed, outside his parish of settlement in a distant county at 25s. per week, was temporarily thrown out of work, and had to seek Poor Relief for his wife and five young children. The Overseer promptly sought and obtained a Removal Order. In the meantime the man had again obtained employment and ceased to draw relief, but the warrant for the removal of the entire family to the parish of settlement was nevertheless forcibly executed. The man, it is reported, was " like a madman with rage ", but had to submit to this irrational deportation, the only object of which was to prevent him from obtaining a settlement in the parish in which he had secured an honourable independent livelihood at what was, for the time, an exceptionally good wage (*History of the English Poor Law*, vol. iii., 1900, by Thomas Mackay, p. 360).

days almost incredible in its ineptitude, which remained for one hundred and eighty-eight years unremedied, although it occurred in many cases, was repeatedly denounced, and was specifically attacked in vain in the House of Commons. So characteristic was this case of the whole proceedings under this law that it must be stated in full. The Overseer did not shrink from the injustice of summarily removing a man and his family (by warrant obtained from the Justices, without giving him any opportunity of being even heard) from his place of residence where he had often been for years, to some distant part of the kingdom in which it was alleged that he had a settlement, *before there had been any trial as to whether he ought to have been removed or not, or as to whether or not his legal settlement was really in the parish to which he was removed*. Whether or not he might have had an action for damages, under the statutes or at Common Law, it is immaterial to inquire, as such an action was beyond his knowledge and his means. From first to last, in the course of two whole centuries, " no poor person ", says Coode, " ever did attempt to appeal ". But the parish to which he and his family were summarily removed, could, and did very frequently, appeal to Quarter Sessions against the Removal Order ; and such were the complications of the law, the difficulty of procuring evidence and the ingenuity of the barristers, very often with success. The parish which had gained the day at once obtained from the Justices " a sort of retrograde order ", and thereupon summarily removed the victims back to the place from which they had been torn. And there was even a further aggravation of the hardship, tyranny and expense. When a Removal Order was quashed, as was often the case, for any technical informality or mistake, the second removal, in the reverse direction, habitually took place at once, before the Overseers of the parish which had begun the original proceedings could initiate a second attempt in which the mistake or technical error could be corrected. Hence the unfortunate man and his family were sometimes subjected to a third forcible removal in custody. The obvious remedy was to require the inquiry and any appeal to precede the actual removal. This was proposed to Parliament in a Bill of 1819, but was defeated—it is alleged, on good authority, because various members of the Bar in the House realised that such a reform would lessen the amount of the legal business at sessions ! [1]   This reform was in due course recommended by the Royal Commission for inclusion in the Poor Law Amendment Bill of 1834 ; but it somehow slipped out in the drafting, and nothing more was then enacted than the requirement of 28 days' notice to the parish to which the removal was about to be made.   This did not prevent the institution of appeals after removals.[2]

In the course of the eighteenth century the lawyers made the matter worse by getting established by the Court of King's Bench the doctrine of derivative settlements.   If (as happened in most cases among poor people) a man moved without acquiring a new settlement in the parish into which he came—either because he failed to give the necessary notice to the Overseers, or because he was a soldier or a sailor or a " certificate man ", and did not so far rise in the world as to rent for a whole year a house or land of the annual value of £10 (equal to perhaps £50 to-day), or be elected to and serve some parish office—he retained, in law, his old settlement, which in most cases was that of his birth.   His children, said the law, had the settlement of their father—meaning, in the first instance, the children under seven years of age (the " age of nurture "), or at least those at the moment dependent on him.   But the lawyers argued, and the Judges eventually held, that the children inherited the father's settlement whatever it was ; and that accordingly, if the son or daughter, like their father, never in their own lives acquired a new settlement, their settlement remained that which they had inherited, namely, that of the parish in which, not they, but their father had been born ; and so on *ad infinitum* !   The possession by any person of a derivative settlement was held to prevent the assertion, on his behalf, of what would otherwise have been a settlement in virtue of his own birth.   Thus was produced the absurd spectacle of counsel for parishes fighting as to what was the place of birth and what were the circumstances

---

[1] Not without solid ground would a Royal Commission report officially—as did that of 1832–1834—that " the expediency of this measure is so obvious that it is difficult to account for its rejection in 1819 unless we are to believe a tradition that it was defeated by a combination of persons interested in creating litigation and expense " (General Report of Poor Law Inquiry Commission, 1834).

[2] Not until 1849 was the matter put right, and then only by the indirect method of absolutely forbidding any appeal that was not notified within the time of notice of intended removal (11 and 12 Victoria c. 31, sec. 9).

of migration half a century previously, of the *grandfathers* of
the grown men and women who found themselves forcibly removed from parishes in which they had been born, in which
was the only place that throughout their whole lives they had
known as home, and which had sometimes even been the birthplace of their father, and had never been left by him.[1]

But whilst the hardship and injustice suffered by individuals
through the operation of the Law of Settlement and Removal
during the greater part of two centuries can hardly be exaggerated,
it is a mistake to assume, as Adam Smith did, that these wrongs
were, in fact, endured by anything like the whole wage-earning
class. The number of Removal Orders obtained and enforced
by the whole 15,000 parishes and townships seems never to have
exceeded a few tens of thousands in a year, or an average of
one or two per parish, involving the removal of something like
fifty, or perhaps one hundred thousand persons, for an average
of perhaps forty or fifty miles. It was very far from being true,
as was frequently asserted, that the whole wage-earning population was, in fact, " imprisoned " in the parishes to which they
belonged. There were, in fact, wide loopholes in the law, which
made it, in many places, and with regard to large sections of
the wage-earners, little more than an occasional annoyance.
To begin with, the " casual poor ", the man or woman " on
tramp ", or actually travelling for any reason whatsoever, were
not subject to removal under the Law of Settlement and Removal
at all, because the Act of 1662 had specifically limited its application to persons " coming in to *inhabit* " a parish. Hence, if one
of these travellers or wanderers fell ill, or met with an accident,.

---

[1] " In the course of my experience ", wrote a learned lawyer in 1852,
" I have, on two occasions, known the settlement of a *great-grandfather* satis-
factorily made out, on the trial of appeals against orders of removal, but so
made out with great difficulty and expense. . . . The whole title of derivative
settlement, or settlement by parentage, which now occupies a large space in
treatises on the Poor Laws, is founded on an unnecessary and erroneous
construction of the statute of Charles II.; but the error is one that was
adopted more than a century ago, and cannot now be rectified by anything
less than an Act of Parliament " (*Pauperism and Poor Laws*, by Robert Pashley,
1852, p. 269).

Some idea of the innumerable issues raised by the ingenuity of the lawyers
may be gained from such a book as *Decisions in the Court of King's Bench upon
Settlement Cases*, by Sir James Burrow, 2 vols., 1786. More conveniently
put is *A Summary of the Law of Settlement*, by Sir Gregory Allnutt Lewin,
1827 ; or *A Compendium of the Laws relating to the Settlement and Removal of
the Poor*, by James Sculthorpe, 1827.

or for any other reason could not proceed on his way, he did not thereby become liable to removal to his place of settlement, even if he obtained Poor Relief, because he had not come into the parish with any intention of "inhabiting" it. Moreover, as Ireland and Scotland, the Isle of Man and the Channel Islands knew of no such thing as a place of settlement, it was impossible to remove to it, under the Act of 1662, any persons who belonged, or who claimed to belong, to any of these parts. Down to 1830–1833 such persons could be dealt with, if at all, only under the Vagrancy Acts; and we shall describe in the following chapter to what abuses this gave rise. Further, each removal under the 1662 Act, even if it did not lead to litigation, was expensive, especially if the family had to be conveyed and escorted to a distant parish. Down to 1814, indeed, when an Act (54 George III. c. 170) enabled any person to be employed for the purpose, the Overseer had himself to escort to their places of settlement the paupers whom he removed; and this fact alone must have considerably discouraged the unpaid and annually appointed farmer or tradesman who served unwillingly as Overseer, from a too frequent enforcement of removal to distant places of settlement, especially during the winter months. "There is plenty of evidence", we are told by the latest student of the parish records on the subject, " to prove that the parish officers tended to leave strangers who intruded on their parish unmolested, if they neither attempted to gain a settlement by the delivery of a notice in writing, nor appeared likely to become chargeable in the near future." It was often only when, "through accident or death, the chief breadwinner of the family was rendered useless, the Overseers awakened from their lethargy, and promptly removed the unfortunate family back to its legal settlement ".[1]

It is, accordingly, a great exaggeration to suggest that the Law of Settlement and Removal prevented the people from changing their places of work and residence. A large proportion of the whole were, indeed, not only migrants, but even extremely mobile. What has been overlooked is that it was usually only

---

[1] *The English Poor in the Eighteenth Century*, by Dorothy Marshall, 1926, p. 166. But although the labourer may not always have been removed, he was harassed by the uncertainty, and intimidated by the risk; compare *The Village Labourer, 1760–1832*, by J. L. and Barbara Hammond, 1921, pp. 114–119.

in the rural districts, with stagnant employments and almost stationary populations, that local opinion was adverse to the immigration of new-comers. In the Metropolis, in the expanding seaports, in the rapidly developing manufacturing and mining districts of the North and Midlands and South Wales, and indeed in many of the cities and towns that served as industrial centres for the countryside, there was, from the very beginning of the eighteenth century, an ever-increasing demand for labour. " Multitudes of working people ", said James Massie in 1758, " are obliged to travel "—and did in fact travel— " from parish to parish in order to find employment " ; [1] and though they were always liable to be made the subjects of Removal Orders, these were not, as a rule, obtained against them.

This wandering in search of employment fills, from the very beginning of the eighteenth century, a large part of the annals of the Trade Unionism of the period ; and in our investigations for the *History of Trade Unionism* we found no instance of removal under the Law of Settlement. Among the woolcombers and worsted weavers, the calico printers and the compositors, the custom of " tramping " from town to town to look for a job led to the organisation of an elaborate system of relief of the men " on the road " by a network of local trade clubs. When a vacancy was found the wandering journeyman was taken on, and settled down in a new home, without, so far as we have found, ever being troubled by the Churchwardens and Overseers of the parish into which he had come.[2]

We discover, too, that the elasticity given to the Act of 1662 by the system of certificates—enlarged, as we have mentioned, by the Act of 1697—was made of greater use than the commentators on the law have assumed. The grant of certificates (often styled " testimonials ") was, in many parishes, much more frequent than has been supposed. Miss Dorothy Marshall's recent investigation of the parish records has shown

---

[1] *A Plan for the Establishment of Charity Houses,* etc., by James Massie, 1758, p. 112.

[2] See *History of Trade Unionism,* by S. and B. Webb, edition of 1920, p. 25 ; *Industrial Democracy* by the same, 1897, p. 162 ; *A Short Essay upon Trade in General,* by a Lover of his Country, 1741 ; *Leicester Herald,* June 1792 ; *Minutes of Evidence taken before the Committee . . . Calico Printers,* etc., July 4, 1804 ; and *Report of the Committee,* etc., July 17, 1806 ; Report of Poor Law Inquiry Commission, 1834, Appendix A, p. 900.

that " at times, whole families found that their interests could be best served by removing into another parish, where, perhaps, the demand for certain types of labour was brisker than in their own. The Overseers of their own parish would have been content to let them go, but it was feared, or found, that the officers of the parish to which they wished to move were not so complaisant. Accordingly, the practice grew up of the parish officers giving such families a testimonial, acknowledging them to be settled inhabitants, and promising to take them back at the end of a term of years, or in the event of their becoming chargeable to the parish into which they had removed. Such procedure was convenient, and it spread. It was easy, it saved law suits, and, though it still left the entire power of the law with the parish officers, could be used to give some flexibility to the Act of 1662. These testimonials might be granted permanently, that is, until a person became chargeable ; or they might be for a stated period of time. In their nature they were private agreements between two parishes ; they would not necessarily bind the granting parish towards any other parish Among the Sidbury papers for 1675 is an account, which the parish kept, of persons who were living there by virtue of a certificate. The title page runs, ' An account of the Testimonials Giuen & Receiued By the Officers of this p'ish of Sidbury 1675. Rec a certificate for Mary Splat from Officers of the pysh of Honiton barring date ye 23rd of october 1675 & is general to receiue her at any time and is to be found in the Coffer. . . . Thos: Pidgeon. Rich: Lecot. Churchwardens. Martha Addem Receiued A certificat for two years. Susanna Todd had A Certificat to Continue for a yeare.' Many of the actual certificates still survive among the parish papers. In form they differ very much from parish to parish, some being simple statements of the fact of settlement while others are very elaborate, and have a legal flavour." [1]

Whether or not the various amendments of the law relating to certificates increased the number granted, or made the document less desirable or more difficult to obtain, has not yet been demonstrated. What is certain is that, in many parishes but not in all, they continued to be issued, and families

---

[1] *The English Poor in the Eighteenth Century*, by Dorothy Marshall, 1926, pp. 175-176.

z

continued to make use of them for migration, throughout the whole of the eighteenth century. " In an old parish chest where a number of papers have survived, sometimes as many as fifty of these certificates may be found, their dates stretching over a century. At Northampton the parish officers kept a '.Book wherein the certificates brought and del: to the Church-wardens and Overseers of the Poor of the parish of St. Sepulchres, in the town of Northampton, touching the settlement of poor persons,' are entered in alphabetical order. These entries extend from 1702 to 1792. At Dunstable there is a list of a hundred and forty names, dated the 28th December, 1769, and labelled ' Certificates '. But it does not say whether they are certificates given or received, neither does it say whether it was a complete list up to date, or whether they were all granted or received at the same time. The former appears the more probable. Nor is there any lack of examples of certificates from other parts of the country. Where the parish papers have survived at all, there copies of certificates are usually to be found." [1] It became usual for parishes to make regulations to the effect (as at Tooting Graveney) that " all housekeepers be for the future prosecuted who receive inmates without certificates of their several parishes"; or (as at Burton-on-Trent) that " whereas several persons have lately come into this town, not having given to the officers certificates as the law appoints, that the officers shall bring for every one of them a warrant of removal ".[2] On the other hand, we learn from Sir F. M. Eden that in the last decade of the eighteenth century " certificates are never granted at Leeds and Skipton ; seldom granted at Sheffield ; not willingly granted at Nottingham, and that at Halifax certificates are not granted at present, and only three have been granted in the last eighteen years ". It could even be said that, down to Sir William Young's Act of 1795, " the difference in the several parishes arises . . . in a great measure from the facility or difficulty of obtaining certificates. In several parishes a fine is imposed on a parishioner who ' settled ' a newcomer [without a certificate], by hiring or otherwise, so that a servant is very

---

[1] *The English Poor in the Eighteenth Century*, by Dorothy Marshall, 1926, pp. 178-179.
[2] *History of the Parish of Tooting Graveney*, by W. E. Morden, 1897, p. 578 ; *Burton-on-Trent*, etc., by William Molyneux, 1869, p. 98 ; *The English Poor in the Eighteenth Century*, by Dorothy Marshall, 1926, p. 178.

seldom hired for the year. Those parishes which have for a long time been in the habit of using such precautions are now very lightly burdened with poor. This is often the case where the farms are large and, of course, in few hands; while other parishes, not politic enough to observe these rules are generally burdened with an influx of poor neighbours." [1]

It is further to be noted that, with the change in the value of money and the rise in the rent of even the poorest dwellings in the larger towns, and especially in the Metropolis, it became much easier for the incomer to escape from the clutches of the Act of 1662. When that statute was passed, the renting of a tenement worth £10 a year was quite out of the reach of any manual-working wage-earner. By the end of the eighteenth century such a payment for rent was common among wage-earning families, both in the Metropolis and in Manchester. " Four shillings a week ", paid in rent for one or two rooms, explained the Overseer for Spitalfields to the House of Commons Committee in 1817, " will give a settlement if the pauper has resided there six weeks." [2] It was, in fact, to the almost unrestrained immigration of poor people into such parishes as those surrounding the City of London, or those adjacent to Manchester, or that of Liverpool itself, with the burden that these " non-settled poor " inevitably cast upon the Overseers, that was ascribed, in the first quarter of the nineteenth century, the enormous increase in the local Poor Rates. Whether these immigrants were the " casual poor " or the Irish (who both fell outside the Act of 1662); or persons whom the Overseers found it too expensive or too troublesome to remove under that Act; or persons whom the rise in rents had permitted to gain settlements by renting tenements at four shillings per week, the result was equally to reduce to a nullity the design of preventing immigration.

Hence we are not surprised that an exceptionally able and well-informed pamphleteer of 1788 [3] was able to describe the

---

[1] *The State of the Poor*, by Sir F. M. Eden, 1797, vol. iii. p. 743; *The Village Labourer, 1760–1832*, by J. L. and Barbara Hammond, 1912, p. 116.

[2] House of Commons Committee on Poor Laws, 1817, evidence of John Heaver.

[3] *The Insufficiency of the Causes to which the Increase of our Poor, and of the Poor's Rates have been ascribed . . . and a slight general view of Mr. A's plan for rendering the poor independent*, by Rev. J. Howlett, 1788; see also *The State of the Poor*, by Sir F. M. Eden, 1797. vol. i. pp. 287-288. William

working of the law in very different terms from those used by
Adam Smith. Its "operation", he said, "considered in a
general view, has been very trifling indeed. How seldom do
the young and healthy, while single, find any difficulty in
changing their residence, and fixing where they please. Does
the tradesman or manufacturer, while his trade or his manufacture flourishes, refuse to take an apprentice, or employ a
journeyman, because he was born or settled in a different parish,
or in a distant part of the Kingdom? On the contrary, does
he not eagerly look out for him, and gladly receive him, from
whatever quarter he may come? Were it otherwise, how has
it happened that Sheffield, Birmingham and Manchester have
increased, from almost mere villages, to populous towns, that
rival or even surpass in magnitude our largest cities, the capital
alone excepted. . . . Servants in husbandry . . . range from
parish to parish, and from county to county, unthinking of,
and unrestrained by the Laws of Settlement ; the farmer without
scruple hires them ; at length they marry, and there they fix.
Rambling is then at an end ; or ruin follows. If a husbandry
labourer has four or five children, it rarely happens that above
three of them settle where they were born, while of those actually
resident, even in our smaller towns and country parishes, nearly
one-fifth have their legal settlement elsewhere." Howlett
adduced particularly the case of his own parish of Toppesfield,
Essex, where out of 240 families of mechanics and labourers,
about forty, or one-sixth of the whole, belonged to other parishes.
An even greater immigration was indicated by an inquiry, made
in London in 1781, as to the places of birth of 3236 heads of
families who received treatment at the Westminster General
Dispensary ; when it was found that only 824 of them had been
born in the Metropolitan area. Already in 1722, De Foe could
ascribe to the plague year of 1665, the existence in London of
multitudes of immigrants " without what we call legal settlements ".[1] Sir F. M. Eden concluded that, in the last decade

---

Hay had also thought the complaints as to removals much exaggerated in
respect of number (*Remarks on the Laws relating to the Poor*, etc., edition of
1751 ; and see *Population Returns of the Age of Malthus*, by G. Talbot Griffith,
1926, c. vi. pp. 129-169 ; *Health, Wealth and Population in the Early Days of
the Industrial Revolution*, by M. E. Buer, 1926 ; and *London Life in the Eighteenth
Century*, by M. D. George, 1925, as to the effects of the Law of Settlement on
the increase of population).

[1] *Journal of the Plague Year*, by Daniel De Foe, 1722, p. 113.

of the eighteenth century, at least three-fourths of the entire population of the Metropolis were " strangers ".[1]

As to the actual removals, there was, it seems, considerable discrimination exercised among classes of cases. Miss Marshall's investigations indicate that single men in health, and apparently of good character, were often allowed to remain undisturbed, even in rural parishes, where they had gained employment. Such men, " if they had their health and strength, could always earn enough to support themselves without any assistance from the rates. Consequently, they were but little molested by the Overseers. The Cambridgeshire Quarter Sessions records show that the parish officers of that county did, in fact, make some rough differentiation between the various types of poor who intruded into their sphere. Between 1699 and 1715 there were one hundred and sixty-two settlement cases entered in the books. Of these, sixty-three were married couples, with or without children, as the case might be, thirty-three single women, fourteen widows with children, and twelve unencumbered widows. Twenty-three were children, both bastards and orphans, and only seventeen were men. Therefore, sixty-three married couples and fifty-nine women of various descriptions were moved during these years, as opposed to seventeen single men. From 1716–32 there were two hundred and nine cases of removal recorded, of which eighty-one were married couples, forty-two women, twelve widows, forty-one children, and thirty-three single men. From 1736–1749 inclusive, there were one hundred and sixty-one cases, of which eighty were married couples, thirty-one women, twenty-one widows—the majority of whom had children—thirteen children, and only sixteen single men.

---

[1] *The State of the Poor*, by Sir F. M. Eden, 1797, vol. i. p. 299. Massie noticed a general course of migration, "from Rural Parishes to Market Towns, and from both of them to the Capital City ; so that great Multitudes of People, who were born in Rural Parishes are continually acquiring Settlements in Cities or Towns, more especially in those towns where considerable manufacturies are carried on ; and as Trade is not only of a fluctuating Nature, but many Towns in England carry on Manufacturies of the same Kind, and are always gaining or losing with respect to each other, although there be an encrease of Manufacturies upon the Whole ; it must necessarily follow, that there will be frequent Ebbings in the Manufacturies of one or other of our Trading Towns " (*A Plan for the Establishment of Charity Houses*, etc., by James Massie, 1758, p. 99 ; quoted in *The Growth of English Industry and Commerce in Modern Times*, by Archdeacon W. Cunningham, 3rd edition, 1903, p. 571).

So, out of a total of five hundred and thirty-two persons moved during these years, two hundred and twenty-four were married couples, one hundred and sixty-five women of all classes, seventy-seven children, and sixty-six single men. The warrants of removal which have survived among the Dunstable parish papers point to the same conclusion. Sixty-two warrants of removal, from 1692–1766, show that the same type of person was most frequently moved here, as well as in Cambridgeshire. There were twenty-four married couples, nineteen single women, ten men, three women with children, and six children. Here, too, out of a total of sixty-two, only ten single men were moved, and once again the number of married couples removed was greater than that of any other one class." [1]

" In Middlesex, where the influence of London was predominant, from 1690–8, out of two hundred and twelve persons moved, there were nine widows, forty-seven women with children, forty-nine women, fifty-six children, forty married couples, and eleven single men. From 1699–1709, out of two hundred and sixty-five persons moved, there were eighty-one childless women of various descriptions, fifty-nine others who were burdened with children, forty-seven children, fifty-eight married couples, and twenty men. In this case, too, the number of men moved was negligible, while the proportion of married couples is much less than it was in an agricultural area. Evidently the parish officers were most suspicious of the unattached women, whether they were burdened with children or not." [2]

At length, after more than a century and a quarter, the first great amendment was made in the Act of 1662 ; and then, characteristically enough, not in the great body of " sessions

---

[1] *The English Poor in the Eighteenth Century*, by Dorothy Marshall, 1926, pp. 164-165.

[2] *Ibid.* pp. 165-166. It is to be inferred that, at all times, it was the unattached woman, whether single or widowed, who suffered most from the Law of Settlement. " A woman with dependent children was always likely to be removed as speedily as possible, as, for instance when, on 18th July, 1671, the North Riding Court of Quarter Sessions recorded, ' for that it appeared that a woman and her 3 young children have lately come to Danby, and are likely to be chargeable, and that her husband's last lawful settlement was at Bilsdayle. Ordered that the Overseer of Danby do remove her and her children to Bilsdayle there to be settled ' " (*ibid.* pp. 166-167). " The unborn were the special objects of parish officers' dread. At Derby the persons sent out under orders of removal are chiefly pregnant girls " (*The Village Labourer, 1760–1832*, by J. L. and Barbara Hammond, 1912, p. 117).

law " which had been built up with regard to settlements, but merely in the liability of the person absent from his parish of settlement to be compulsorily " removed ". The very obvious reform of not permitting the Overseer to obtain a Removal Order merely because he chose to say that he thought it " likely " that an immigrant into his parish would, at some future date, need Poor Relief, had been suggested by William Hay in 1735 ; [1] and by Mr. Commissioner Greaves in 1774.[2] It was proposed to the House of Commons by Sir William Young in 1788,[3] but failed to gain acceptance. It was at last provided by an Act of 1795 that, with the exceptions of persons deemed by law to be " rogues and vagabonds " or " idle and disorderly persons ", and—most melancholy of all—every unmarried woman with child, no person should be liable to be removed until he had actually become chargeable to the Poor Rate—thus, in effect, putting all but the excepted persons in the position of " certificate men ". The same Act also provided, including even persons actually in receipt of relief and vagrants, that no person should be removed (or " passed " as a vagrant) if the Justice making the Order, or granting the Vagrant Pass, considered that such person was unable to travel by reason of sickness or other infirmity, in which cases the Removal Order or Vagrant Pass was to be " suspended " until the Justice was satisfied that it could be executed without danger—a merciful protection extended in 1809 to the family and household of the sick or infirm person.[4]

---

[1] *Remarks on the Laws relating to the Poor*, etc., by William Hay, 1735.

[2] *Reasons submitted to Parliament for introducing a Law to Prevent Unnecessary and Vexatious Removals of the Poor*, by Mr. Commissioner Greaves, Cambridge, 1774. There is an anonymous pamphlet in the library of the Ministry of Health entitled *Reasons for . . . and against Prevention of Poor Removal*, 1775.

[3] Sir William Young, Bart. (1749–1815), was the son of a West Indian Governor and estate-owner ; F.R.S. and author in 1777 of *The Spirit of Athens* ; M.P. for St. Mawes 1784–1806, and for Buckingham 1806–1807, when he was appointed Governor of Tobago. The privilege of not being liable to removal until becoming chargeable, which Sir William Young got generalised, had been enjoyed from 1662 to 1784, only by " certificate men ", but had then been conferred by 24 George III. c. 6 on soldiers, sailors and their families ; and by 33 George III. c. 54 (1793) on members of registered Friendly Societies. These furnished precedents for the reform of 1795.

[4] 35 George III. c. 101 ; 49 George III. c. 124 ; *History of the English Poor Law*, by Sir George Nicholls, 1854, vol. ii. pp. 118-120, 151-152. " Was the Act [for which the nation had waited for 133 years] a hazardous one ? Was the effect in any way embarrassing ? Was any parish deprived of labour, or

The reform of 1795, whilst it must have added greatly to the sense of security of the labourer who had found employment beyond the bounds of his parish of settlement, and though it may even have curbed the autocracy, in rural parishes, of "Churchwarden stern and kingly Overseer", by opening up to the rebellious unmarried man a practical possibility of reasonably safe migration, did nothing to protect, from compulsory removal to his place of settlement, any one who was driven to seek Poor Relief. Yet to be frequently in receipt of Poor Relief was, for forty years between 1795 and 1834 the lot of nearly every farm labourer in southern England. Nor could the Act of 1795, amid the swollen pauperism of this period, appreciably diminish the total number of persons actually removed. The next forty years saw Parliament repeatedly tinkering with the Law of Settlement, without effecting any important change. "All the mitigation which the Law of Settlement underwent between the years 1800 and 1834," writes a learned commentator, "so far as its substantial evils are concerned, is hardly worthy of notice, although those evils were constantly felt, and almost as constantly evidenced, by a never-failing series of statutory regulations and modifications of existing rights and liabilities of parishes. The wisdom of Parliament was sometimes employed in devising and amending mere forms of procedure ; more frequently in defining anew the conditions on which this annexation of the poor man, by the bond of an arbitrary settlement, to a particular parish, should be effected. The changes thus introduced invariably imposed further restrictions on the acquisition of settlements, and usually gave rise to a good deal of litigation. Settlement by renting a tenement may be mentioned as one of the greater heads of this small legislation. The statute of Charles II. required a residence of forty days only. In 1819, this arbitrary term of forty days was changed into an equally arbitrary term of one year, and in order to acquire such

---

any parish glutted ? So far as can be ascertained it did perhaps co-operate in the progress of our then rapidly expanding manufactures. But a most careful search among the debates and Parliamentary Papers, the pamphlets on Poor Laws and Vagrancy, and the domestic records of the succeeding five years has failed to bring to light a single remark in the way of complaint of the observed results of this seemingly vast experiment " (Report of George Coode . . . on the Laws of Settlement and Removal of the Poor, H.C. 675 of 1851, pp. 68-69).

a settlement subsequent to July 2, 1819 various additional conditions were to be fulfilled (59 George III. c. 50). But, as if in a pious horror of uniformity of law, the old settlement by forty days residence prior to the July 2, 1819 was to be retained, as to all settlements then acquired. Subsequent statutes passed on June 22, 1825 (6 George IV. c. 57), on March 31, 1831 (1 William IV. c. 18), and on August 14, 1834 (4 and 5 William IV. c. 76), imposed still further restrictions on the acquisition of a settlement by renting a tenement, each statute defining the settlement for the future only, and leaving all the previous heads of settlement uninterfered with. Hence it has followed that since the passing of the Poor Law Amendment Act, there are no less than five distinct heads of settlement by renting a tenement alone." [1] There was, indeed, no end to the changes and the complications. " Everything was deemed fair, in resisting or enforcing a claim of settlement . . . on which the most astute counsel and attorneys exercised their wits and exhausted their learning. . . . First it was found that the signature of the same person as a Churchwarden and as an Overseer did not satisfy the requirements of the law, and this defect was cured by 51 George III. c. 80. Then it was discovered that the signatures of the Church or Chapelwardens and the Overseers of townships and hamlets maintaining their own poor, were not legally binding in questions of settlement, and this blot was cured by 54 George III. c. 107. A few years afterwards it came to be known that, in divers parishes, etc., there was only one Church or Chapelwarden to sign the indentures and certificates, instead of two, and this difficulty was surmounted by passing the 1 and 2 George IV. c. 32." By 54 George III. c. 170 all the provisions of Local Acts since August 1, 1714, which made any alteration in the Law of Settlement were repealed, retrospectively as well as prospectively. It was also provided that children born in any public institution should follow the settlement of their mothers, instead of that of their place of birth ; and that gate and toll keepers, prisoners for debt and persons maintained in any charitable institution should not gain a settlement by virtue of their residence. The same Act made it clear that inhabitants of a parish were not as such disqualified from giving evidence in cases of settlement

[1] *Pauperism and Poor Laws*, by Robert Pashley, 1852, pp. 260-261.

or removal affecting their own parish ; and also that removals
need not be carried out by Churchwarden or Overseer in person,
and might be by persons employed by them. By 11 George
IV. c. 5 and 3 and 4 William IV. c. 40, provision was made for
the removal of persons belonging to the Channel Isles, Scotland
and Ireland.[1]

We end this account of the complications of the Law of
Settlement and Removal by a summary description of the
almost continuous efforts at reform of the whole system that
marked the period between 1816 and 1832.   In the alarm at the
growing misery and rising Poor Rates after the conclusion of the
Napoleonic War, a succession of reformers strove to grapple with
the problems presented by the inter-parochial litigation, the
wasteful removals and the hampering of industrial mobility that
we have described.   The dominant feature of all these efforts—
to which the successive Ministries of the Regency and of
George IV. lent no assistance—was their inability to deal with
the situation as a whole, and their consequent failure to induce
the House of Commons to pass any reform into law.

In 1819 Sturges Bourne and Lord Castlereagh brought in a
Bill to abolish prospectively all methods of gaining a settlement
otherwise than by parentage, marriage or birth, except by three
years' residence (or only sixty days in domestic service).[2]   Much
more practically important was the reform proposed by Wood,
Littleton and Scarlett in 1822–1823, first in resolutions, and then
by Bill.   This was the gradual reduction of the class of persons

---

[1] *History of the English Poor Law,* by Sir George Nicholls, 1854, vol. ii. p. 220.

[2] The various proposals of this period are discussed in *Complaints of the
Poor People of England,* by George Dyer, 1793 ; Robert Southey's article on
the Poor Laws in *Quarterly Review,* December 1812 ; John Rickman's article
in the same, April 1812 ; *A Letter to . . . Sturges Bourne . . . on a Bill
introduced by him . . . to amend the Laws respecting the Settlement of the Poor,*
by Henry Phillpotts [Bishop of Exeter], Durham, 1819 ; *Speech of Matthew
Nolan . . . in the House of Commons,* etc., 1822 ; *Resolutions intended to be
proposed by Col. Wood for alteration of the laws for the Settlement of the Poor,*
1822 ; the *Edinburgh Review* article thereon, 1823, pp. 327-358 ; the anonymous
Parish Settlements and Pauperism, 1828.

It is remarkable how reluctant were the critics of this generation to come
to the solution hinted at by Bishop Burnet at the very beginning of the
eighteenth century that the law needed to be " well reviewed, *if not entirely
taken away* " (*History of his own Time,* by Bishop Burnet, vol. vi. p. 213 of
1823 edition) ; and expressly urged by Massie in 1758, who said that " giving
every poor person a right to relief when and where he or she shall want it
would put an end to all law suits about the settlement of the poor " (*A Plan
for the Establishment of Charity Houses,* by James Massie, 1758, p. 112).

liable to removal, the status of irremovability being at once
conferred on persons " domiciled or principally resident " in any
parish for fifteen years ; and this period being reduced by twelve
months each year until 1838, after which no person would be
removable after one year's residence. In 1824, 1828, 1829 and
1831, Bills were introduced by various members (including Lord
Althorp) for the abolition of settlement by hiring and service ;
in 1831, for the abolition of settlement by apprenticeship ; and
in 1832 for its abolition by apprenticeship to the sea service.
None of these measures in the unreformed House of Commons
passed into law.[1] At this point we leave the story, so far as the
present volume is concerned ; with Overseers, especially in
rural parishes, and in respect of men with families and pregnant
women, continuing to seek a Removal Order in every case—to
the number of thousands every year—in which they could pretend
that the pauper had a place of settlement elsewhere ; the parish,
thus threatened with a new charge, far too frequently persuaded
by the village attorney that it had a fighting chance of defeating
the Order, and therefore rushing to lodge an appeal ; at every
Quarter Sessions in the land counsel with perverted ingenuity
spending at least half the time of the Court in splitting hairs as
to pauper settlements ; [2] at an expense in costs and removal of
something like a quarter of a million pounds a year, to nobody's
advantage except that of the lawyers concerned.[3]

---

[1] We may add here that the Poor Law Amendment Act of 1834 did no more
than put an end prospectively to the gaining of a settlement by serving an
office, or by hiring and service.

[2] " I spent several hours ", wrote Crabb Robinson in 1815, " at the
Clerkenwell Sessions. A case came before the Court ludicrous because of the
minuteness required in the examination. Was the pauper settled in parish
A or B ? The house he occupied was in both parishes, and models of both of
the house and of the bed in which the pauper slept were laid before the Court
that it might ascertain how much of his body lay in each parish. The Court
held the pauper to be settled where his head (being the nobler part) lay, though
one of his legs at least, and great part of his body, lay out of that parish "
(*Diary, Reminiscences and Correspondence of Henry Crabb Robinson*, by Thomas
Sadler, 3rd edition, 1872, p. 264).

[3] In the year ended March 25, 1834, " the sums expended in England and
Wales in suits of law, removal of paupers, etc.", amounted to £258,604 : 1s.
(Ninth Annual Report of Poor Law Commissioners, 1843, p. 34). This incessant litigation could even be represented as a public advantage. " As for
the appeals to the Quarter Sessions ", wrote a learned commentator, " this is
a necessary and moderate expense to the county ; as, without such litigations,
no barrister would attend, nor can the county business be properly dispatched
without their assistance " (*Observations on the More Ancient Statutes*, by Daines
Barrington, 1795, p. 539).

It must, we think, always remain undetermined how far the complications and the secondary effects of the Law of Settlement and Removal, with all the malice and resentment to which it gave rise, may have contributed to the evil perversions of the Poor Law that called forth the denunciations of the Royal Commission of 1832–1834. By this legislation, wrote George Coode in 1851, " 15,535 parishes were made the gaols of their own poor people, and fortresses against all others. Moreover, by this same one act, these 15,535 parishes and townships were made, for the first time, the direct antagonists of each other, the contest consisting in driving the poor, and the reward of victory for that rival which by parsimony, cruelty, obstinacy or quibble could most successfully beat or shuffle them off. Perhaps it would have been impossible by any ingenuity to contrive so prolific a source of litigation by any other means than a Law of Settlement, for this turned the whole of our poorer population into the involuntary subjects for dispute, many millions of subjects of litigation directly they passed the boundary of the parish, or sought relief within it ; and everyone of them, when poor or likely to be poor, a provoking object for expulsion. . . . A parish has no shame, no honour. Its officers doing that oppression on the poor, effecting those frauds, resorting to those evasions, which no man with any regard to character would dare to practise for his individual advantage, escaped all imputations, and gained indeed the credit of activity and public spirit. Other would-be litigants commonly want the funds on one or both sides ; the parish funds never failed." [1]   And the secretary to the Royal Commission of 1832–1834 (John Revans), differing from his Commissioners, himself officially attributed the evils to which the Poor Law administration had become subject to no other cause than this Act of 1662. Writing in 1850, he said, " those who are familiar with the history of poor-law management previously to 1834 will recognise . . . the worst evils which were then attributed primarily to maladministration. *Amongst the effects of the present system of settlement, I detect the existence of every one of those evils which were attributed by the English Poor Law Inquiry in 1834 to the then mode of administration under the old parochial management.* As the secretary to that inquiry, the

[1] Report of George Coode . . . on the Law of Settlement and Removal of the Poor, H.C. No. 675 of 1851, pp. 63-64.

whole of the details were so deeply stamped on my memory that their presence and similitude instantly attracted my attention. I am certain that all those evils, and in more than their pristine vigour, will in a few years burst forth unless the Laws of Settlement are placed upon a sound principle : for there is ample evidence to show that the maladministration of relief which was corrected in 1834 was only the most glaring effect of the disease, but not the disease itself. *The disease lay in the settlement laws* ; and, so far from having been subdued by the Poor Law Amendment Act, it has been considerably strengthened thereby. The great symptom, the maladministration, was undoubtedly met, and for a time it has appeared to have been successfully met ; but it was so principally by the prestige of that law, and the perplexity which so great a change in the mode of procedure caused in the minds of the labouring classes ; the improvement was effected more by the implied declaration that the evils should cease than by the power of that law to repress them. But now much of the novelty has worn off, the same evils are about to burst forth again, when they will at once be recognised as the results of a vicious system of settlement. They were never the effects of any other cause." [1]

[1] Reports to the Poor Law Board on the Laws of Settlement and Removal of the Poor, 1850, p. 94. Nor was John Revans alone in this view. " On the inquiry of 1833, it appeared that a large part of the social evil of the pauperism of England was caused by the Law of Settlement and Removal alone " (*Pauperism and Poor Laws*, by Robert Pashley, 1852, p. 304). This was the view taken in an able pamphlet of 1828 ascribed to C. H. Bracebridge, entitled *Parish Rates and Settlements Considered*. Something in support of this opinion may also be found in the more cautiously expressed *Parochial Settlements* : *An Obstruction to Poor Law Reform*, a pamphlet published in 1835, immediately after the passage of the Poor Law Amendment Act, by John Meadows White, who had been employed to help Nassau Senior in the drafting of that measure. He had previously been concerned about the results of the Law of Settlement in perverting the practice of apprenticeship (see his *Some Remarks on the Statute Law affecting Parish Apprentices*, by John Meadows White, Halesworth, 1829) ; but he expressed a general approval of the Act of 1834 (see his *Remarks on the Poor Law Amendment Act, 1834*).

CHAPTER VI

THE REPRESSION OF VAGRANCY

It was, as we described in our first chapter, out of the statutory attempts to repress vagrancy, and the disorders and crimes to which this wandering life gave rise, that the public provision for the indigent emerged ; and from which it only gradually became completely differentiated. For seven hundred years, at least, the national government and the legislature in England had dealt out, in this field, only prohibition and punishment. In the course of the sixteenth century, as we have seen, the thinkers and the statesmen of Western Europe came to realise, as Sir Thomas More was, perhaps, the first to point out, that without some general provision for the destitute, even the most savage repression would fail to prevent either vagrancy or theft, or, indeed, various other forms of disorder. Thus, the system of Poor Relief then initiated in England, which took definite form in the Act of 1597, did not arise and grow into being (as might conceivably have been the case), out of tithe and monastic property, within the framework of the organised almsgiving of the Christian Church. Notwithstanding its entanglement with the ecclesiastical parish, the public relief of the poor began, in England as elsewhere in Western Europe, in the framework of the severe and even sanguinary statutes which Parliament delighted to enact against the wandering vagabond, the idle and disorderly person, the begging impostor, the trickster and the cheat.[1]

[1] The sources for an account of the action taken in England against the evils of Vagrancy are so manifold and so indefinitely numerous as to render any exhaustive study of them impossible. From the seventh to the twentieth century the different statutes on the subject number somewhere about two hundred. From the sixteenth century onward, there is the scattered and uncatalogued pamphlet literature. There are the newspapers of the eighteenth and nineteenth centuries. There are State Papers, gradually being made

The Acts relating to Vagrancy

In taking up the story of the connection of the statutory repression of vagrancy with the contemporary system of Poor Relief, and the interaction between them, we need go back no further than the Parliament of 1597. The comprehensive statute then enacted for the Relief of the Poor (39 Elizabeth c. 3) was accompanied by one equally comprehensive for the Repression of Vagrancy (39 Elizabeth c. 4). Both of these Acts emanated from the one big and influential committee that we have described as influenced by Burleigh and Coke. Each of these statutes superseded the previous enactments on its subject, and substituted a completely codified scheme of law. And each of them, it may here be said, had a similar subsequent history in being amended and supplemented by an almost continuous stream of additional Acts.

The Vagrancy Act of 1597 applied its provisions to a particularly enumerated class or collection of persons [1] who were thenceforth to be "taken, adjudged and deemed Rogues, Vagabonds and Sturdy Beggars". Whenever any one of the persons so enumerated was found begging, he was to be, by the order of any Justice of the Peace, "stripped naked from the middle upwards and openly whipped until his or her body be bloody, and then passed to his or her birthplace or last residence ;

---

available, reaching back for five hundred years. Successive committees of inquiry extend over two centuries. The manifold archives of borough and county and parish, which exist, though very incompletely, for more than five centuries, are only now beginning to be printed. The most complete single work is *A History of Vagrants and Vagrancy*, by C. J. Ribton-Turner, 1887, which (for England) is little more than a chronological collection of extracts from printed materials. The best historical account is still *An Introduction to English Economic History and Theory*, by Sir William Ashley, 1893, part ii. chap. v. ; to be supplemented by *The Early History of English Poor Relief*, by E. M. Leonard, 1900 ; *Early Tracts on Poor Relief*, by F. R. Salter, 1926 ; chap. vi. of *The English Poor in the Eighteenth Century*, by Dorothy Marshall, 1926 ; and *The Vagrancy Problem*, by W. H. Dawson, 1911.

[1] The enumeration of those to be deemed rogues and vagabonds was lengthy and peculiar. It included such of the following as went about begging, or were found without means : (1) wandering scholars seeking alms ; (2) shipwrecked seamen ; (3) idle persons using subtle craft in games or in fortune-telling ; (4) pretended proctors, procurers or gatherers of alms for institutions ; (5) fencers, bearwards, common players or minstrels ; (6) jugglers, tinkers, pedlars and petty chapmen ; (7) able-bodied wandering persons and labourers without means refusing to work for current rates of wages ; (8) discharged prisoners ; (9) wanderers pretending losses by fire ; (10) Egyptians or gypsies.

and in case they know neither they are to be sent to the House of Correction for a year, unless someone gives them employment sooner ". Substantially, this remained for more than a century Parliament's prescription for the repression of vagrancy.

This Act of 1597, although continued, amended or varied during the ensuing two hundred and fifty years by half a hundred other statutes on the subject (and itself repealed in 1714), gave a certain permanence to some remarkable legal provisions. In the first place, it will be noticed that it was not so much the offence itself, namely, vagrancy, that was penalised, as the offence of " going about begging ", being " unable to give a good account of himself ", or making a living in various undesirable ways, if this occurred away from the offender's home or parish of settlement, by any person falling within one or other of a long list of specified classes. It was, in fact, the habit of the House of Commons, during several centuries, whenever it took a dislike to any irregular course of life, to enact that those who followed it should be deemed to be rogues and vagabonds, and thus, as such, subject to all the penalties of the Vagrancy Acts.[1] This habit of specifically enumerating classes of persons as being,

[1] Thus, whilst beggars and impostors have always been mainly aimed at by the Vagrancy Acts, each century, and often each decade, saw particular sections of persons added to or omitted from the list. Down to the sixteenth century the " masterless man ", and the labourer who refused to work for the customary wages, occupied the attention of the legislature. In the sixteenth and seventeenth centuries the " idle and disorderly person " comes more into prominence, and with him are from time to time classed the bearwards and jugglers, the players and practisers of " physiognomy, palmistry and other crafty sciences ", and many similar offenders. The eighteenth century additions had relation chiefly to the protection of property and the prevention of charges on the Poor Rate ; thus in 1740 (by 13 George II. c. 23) " end-gatherers " or persons collecting or buying ends of yarn, weft or cloth, are declared " incorrigible rogues " ; in 1783 (by 23 George III. c. 88) persons found in possession of burglarious implements, or discovered lurking in a building with intent to steal, are deemed " rogues and vagabonds " ; so in 1800 (by 39 and 40 George III. c. 50) are poachers, and (by c. 87) also persons frequenting the Thames or its quays with intent to commit a felony—a provision extended in 1802 (by 42 George III. c. 76) to similar frequenters of any public place. In 1787 and 1802 (by 27 George III. c. 1 and 42 George III. c. 119) unlicensed dealers in lottery tickets and keepers of lottery offices were specifically made " rogues and vagabonds ". In 1792 (by 32 George III. c. 45) persons letting their families become chargeable to the parish are deemed " idle and disorderly persons " under the Vagrancy Act ; and it is what may be called Poor Law offences that form the chief additions made in the nineteenth century. Between 1842 and 1876 such offences are specifically included as acts of vagrancy in five successive statutes.

under certain circumstances, rogues and vagabonds, had the inconvenience of failing to cover the offence aimed at, whenever it was committed by a person not falling within any class that had been expressly named. Thus Sir John Fielding in 1770 complained to a House of Commons Committee that great difficulty was found in dealing with common prostitutes, " they being . . . scarce, if at all, within the description of any statute now in being. . . . This subjects watchmen, round-house keepers, constables and even the magistrates themselves to prosecutions from low attornies." He suggested that they, as well as ballad-singers, should be specifically declared to be vagrants, " no person being a vagrant now but who comes within some one of the descriptions of vagrancy in the Vagrant Act ".[1] Moreover, the imposition of a single, invariable penalty —and that of a severe whipping, followed by compulsory relegation to a distant place, which was the dominant feature of the law from 1597 to 1714—for acts varying indefinitely in turpitude, committed by extremely dissimilar persons, within a wide range of circumstances, inevitably militated against any uniform enforcement of the law. No country gentleman, acting as Justice of the Peace, could possibly order every person, without exception, of any age and of either sex, who was found committing any offence against the Vagrancy Acts, to be " stripped naked from the middle upwards, and whipped until his or her body be bloody ".[2] Even when in later years a much wider choice of punishment was given to the Justices, the indefinite variety of offences to which the successive statutes were made

[1] Report of Committee on Sir John Fielding's plan for preventing burglaries and robberies, *Parliamentary History*, vol. 16, p. 929, etc., April 10, 1770.

[2] The climax was perhaps reached when mere travelling without what a Justice might think an adequate cause was made an act of vagrancy ! In 1656, after various abortive attempts to abate the plague of " rogues, vagabonds and sturdy beggars ", the Commonwealth Parliament enacted an Ordinance providing that any wandering person who failed to satisfy the Justices that he had " good and sufficient cause or business " for his travelling, should be deemed to be guilty of the offence of vagrancy under the Act of 39 Elizabeth c. 4, and punished accordingly, even if not found begging. (*Acts and Ordinances of the Interregnum*, by C. H. Firth and C. Rait, 1911, vol. ii. pp. 1098-1099 ; *History of Vagrants and Vagrancy*, by C. J. Ribton-Turner, 1887, pp. 161-162 ; *Religion and the Rise of Capitalism*, by R. H. Tawney, 1926, pp. 265-266.) The law lapsed on the Restoration and was not re-enacted : there was merely issued and published *A Proclamation for the due observance of certain statutes made for the suppressing of rogues, vagabonds, beggars and other disorderly persons, and for the relief of the poor*, 1661.

applicable, the widely different persons who were thus brought within the meshes of the law, made it seem unreasonable to convict them all of being rogues and vagabonds. This uncertainty in the application of the law was not much mended when, as by the Act of 1744, a division was attempted between three main classes of offenders, " idle and disorderly persons ", " rogues and vagabonds " and " incorrigible rogues ", distinguished from each other by an ascending scale of severity, from a minimum of six days' detention in the House of Correction, or a public whipping, up to transportation for seven years. The first class, the " idle and disorderly persons ", were not necessarily wanderers at all, but persons who, in their own parishes, " not having wherewith to maintain themselves . . . live idly without employment ", and specifically those who " refuse to work for the usual and common wages " ; those found persistently begging ; those even who merely " threaten to run away, and leave their wives or children to the parish " ; and finally, those who were found to have come back after having been legally removed to another parish. The second class, the " rogues and vagabonds ", included all persons, without visible means of subsistence, found outside the parish in which they had a legal settlement, even men travelling in search of work. Particular classes of such offenders, comprised in a long list, were designated for special attention— beggars of all kinds ; actors, fencers, jugglers, bear-wards, minstrels and, in fact, all purveyors of amusement to the common folk [1] ; unlicensed pedlars and chapmen ; fortune-tellers and gamesters ; and the nondescript class of " persons wandering abroad and lodging in alehouses, barns, outhouses or in the open air, *not giving a good account of themselves* ". Finally, we have the third class of " incorrigible rogues ", namely, those who persisted in their conduct after conviction, together with those who resisted apprehension, or who escaped from custody. In

---

[1] In the Act of 1597, as in nearly all the Vagrancy Acts between 1572 and 1744, there was a provision saving the rights of the heirs of John Dutton, who claimed jurisdiction over minstrels and other vagrants in Cheshire, under a grant of 1216, made in recognition of the services of the then Constable of Chester, and a troop of fiddlers and other attenders of Chester Fair, in 1210, to the then Earl of Chester. The lords of Dutton continued to hold a Court of Minstrels, and to receive dues from them, down to 1756 ; and their right to license minstrels was recognised down to 1822. See Ribton-Turner's *History of Vagrants and Vagrancy,* 1887, p. 109, etc. ; Leonard's *Early History of English Poor Relief,* 1900, pp. 138-139 ; Daniel and S. Lyson's " Cheshire," in their *Magna Britannia,* 1806-1822, vol. ii. pp. 523-525.

spite of this gradual improvement in the form of the law, no
student of the eighteenth century can escape the impression that
it was to some extent owing to the defective phraseology of the
statutes that the rigour of the law was at all times reserved only
for the poor and friendless, and those who made themselves
obnoxious to the governing class. Such a procedure inevitably
opened the door not only to negligence but also to the exercise
of capricious tyranny on the one hand, and favouritism on the
other.

We need not trouble the reader with all the successive
changes in the Vagrancy Acts. The codifying statute of 1597
(39 Elizabeth c. 4) became so overlain with amendments that
the whole law was re-codified by an Act of 1714 (13 Anne c. 26).
This, again, was taken up, added to, and considerably amended
by another codifying Act of 1740 (13 George I. c. 24), repeated
in 1744 by yet another (17 George II. c. 5) which remained the
basis of the law, subject to layer after layer of change, until 1822
(3 George IV. c. 40), when the whole law was again re-codified
by a temporary Act, which was re-enacted without limitation of
time in 1824 (5 George IV. c. 83).[1]

We may equally pass over the intricate and confused provisions as to the trial of these offenders ; their commitment
to the county prison at the option of a single Justice, who might
at his sole discretion order both men and women to be publicly
whipped ; together with the subsequent additional punishment
that might be ordered by Quarter Sessions. When vagrants
of the second or third class had been duly punished, they were
" passed ", at the expense of the public, to the parish in which
they had a legal settlement, where it was presumed that they
would be set to work by the Poor Law Authority, under penalty
of further imprisonment. To get the law enforced Parliament
tried its uttermost. Every person found committing any of
the offences was to be summarily apprehended by the constable
—might, indeed, be apprehended by any other person—and
taken before a Justice of the Peace. Parish officers were, from
1662 onwards, encouraged to enforce the law by a system of
rewards. Four times a year at least, and whenever otherwise

---

[1] Several of these statutes were the occasion of pamphlet literature ; see
Observations upon the Vagrant Laws, etc., 1712, a forerunner of the Act of 1714 ;
Observations upon the Vagrant Laws, 1742, leading up to that of 1744.

desirable, the Justices of each Petty Sessional Division of the county were to command a " privy search " throughout the whole Division in a single night, when every nook and corner of every parish was to be searched by the constable and his assistants, who were to take up all wandering or suspicious persons. But, passing from the statutes, the legal text-books and the " charges " to Grand Juries,[1] let us examine the evidence of the contemporary records as to what actually happened.

The Prevalence of Vagrancy

There are no materials for even an approximate estimate of the volume of vagrancy in England and Wales at any period prior to the nineteenth century ; and we know of no contemporary judgements of value as to the waxing or waning at particular dates of the unending flow of a nomadic population in which all sorts of elements were mingled. In 1688 the number on the roads was estimated, though on very scanty data, by so excellent a statistician as Gregory King at no fewer than 60,000 families.[2] Complaints of the prevalence of vagrancy, and of the mendicity by which it was always accompanied, are as old as history itself. Leaving aside the occasional testimony of more remote times, we need only remind the student how repeatedly the Privy Council was, as we have described in a previous chapter, troubled about the continuance of vagrancy, and how constant a place the execution of the laws against vagrants found in the injunctions and reprimands showered upon the Local Authorities down to 1640. Nor were these orders disregarded. " The general rule of all England ", we read in *Stanley's Remedy*, of 1646, " is to whip and punish the wandering beggars." [3] After

---

[1] See, for instance, the widely circulated pamphlet, *A General Charge to all Grand Juries and other Juries*, by Sir James Astry, 1703 (2nd edition, 1725), containing explicit injunctions as to the treatment of offenders against the Vagrancy Acts ; *Charges to Grand Juries* [of Westminster and Tower Hamlets], by Sir John Gonson, in various editions, 1728–1730 ; and *A Charge to the Grand Jury of Westminster*, by Henry Fielding, 1749.

[2] *Natural and Political Observations and Conclusions upon the State and Condition of England*, by Gregory King, 1696, p. 49.

[3] *Stanley's Remedy, or the Way how to reform wandering Beggars, Thieves, Highway Robbers and Pickpockets*, 1646 ; *History of Vagrants and Vagrancy*, by C. J. Ribton-Turner, 1887, pp. 136-139 ; *Religion and the Rise of Capitalism*, by R. H. Tawney, 1926, p. 264.

the Restoration, we see the Justices in various Counties making new efforts to quicken into efficiency the parochial administration on this very point. In 1676 the North Riding Quarter Sessions insisted that parishes and townships should deal stringently with vagrants and sturdy beggars, whom the constables and watchmen ("persons fit of able body, by house-row") were to search for every month and deal with according to law.[1] We may cite the declaration, in 1678, of "The Grand Inquest" of Gloucestershire, which presented to Quarter Sessions "the daily concourse and great increase of rogues and sturdy beggars", which had become "a great grievance and annoyance to the inhabitants of this county", and reported that it was to "the negligence or ignorance of those officers who have been entrusted in this concern" that they attributed the evil of the beggars having "now grown so insolent and presumptuous that they have oft by threats and menaces extorted money and victuals from those who live in houses far remote from neighbours". The remedy suggested to, and adopted by, Quarter Sessions was the issue of an order to "all Chief Constables, Petty Constables, Headboroughs, Tithingmen, and all other officers herein concerned", to "forthwith cause all the laws and statutes . . . against . . . wandering and idle persons to be put in execution".[2] From the very beginning of the eighteenth century the newspapers, the official documents, the treatises and the pamphlets abound in complaints of "swarms of beggars", "ballad - singers", "idle people" and "profligate wretches" "infesting" the streets of all the principal towns, and "overrunning" the highways connecting them, "to the manifest discomfort" of the respectable citizens. This nuisance was at all times at its worst in the Metropolitan parishes in and out of which a disorderly population wandered at its will. A House of Commons Committee in 1715 commented on "the increase of strange beggars, cripples, lusty idle men and women, vagabonds, blind people, pretended and real mad folks, and such like", who infested the streets of Westminster. This nuisance, it was declared, is "altogether

---

[1] *North Riding Quarter Sessions Records*, 1676.

[2] MS. Minutes, Quarter Sessions, Gloucestershire; *The Parish and the County*, by S. and B. Webb, 1906, p. 453. A similar Order was made in the same year by the Buckinghamshire Quarter Sessions (*Quarter Sessions from Elizabeth to Anne*, by A. H. A. Hamilton, 1878, p. 248; *The English Poor in the Eighteenth Century*, by Dorothy Marshall, 1926, p. 226).

owing to the negligence of . . . the parish officers who take no due care to purge their several parishes of such sort of vagrants, but connive at them : . . . this kind of beggars receive little or no settled parish alms, but live upon what they can extort by their cries and importunities in the streets, and at coach-sides ".[1] The nuisance became so intolerable that the Grand Jury of Middlesex, in two celebrated presentments, remonstrated with the authorities for the neglect to enforce the law.   In 1729 they declare : " We the Grand Jury of the County of Middlesex, sworn to inquire for our Sovereign Lord the King, and the Body of this County, have with sincere grief of heart observed of late unusual swarms of sturdy and clamorous beggars, which is an evil in itself very grievous and productive of many others ; particularly we fear it may have been one cause at least of bold and frequent robberies in the streets, a wickedness which till within these few years was unheard of among us. . . . We are sensible the vast increase of poor may be in some measure owing to the distressed circumstances . . . yet . . . as we have effectual laws in being to prevent begging in the streets, for want of a due execution of which that nuisance is now become an intolerable burden, as well as a disgrace to us, we think the utmost care of the magistrate is required to relieve us from it . . . unless this be soon effected (the number of beggars in the streets and other places making them terrible as well as uneasy) many quiet and inoffensive people will hardly venture to stir out of their houses on their lawful callings, for fear of being saucily importuned in the day, and atrociously attacked and robbed in the night." [2]   A Committee of the House of Commons in 1735, considering principally the relief of the poor, reported " that the laws . . . concerning vagrants are very difficult to be executed " ; [3] and a new Act was passed in 1740, once more repeating all the usual prohibitions and penalties.[4]

Yet in 1741 the Grand Jury of Middlesex declared that " we find the evil rather increasing upon us than in the least remedied ".

---

[1] House of Commons Journals, March 8, 1715.

[2] *History and Survey of London*, by William Maitland, 1756, vol. i. pp. 544, 620 (February 12, 1729, and June 17, 1741); *Gentleman's Magazine*, vol. ii. p. 303 (June 1741).   That of 1741 is partly printed in the useful appendix to George Coode's Poor Law Board Report on the Law of Settlement and Removal, H.C. 675 of 1851, p. 302.

[3] House of Commons Journals, March 27, 1735.

[4] 13 George II. c. 24, 1740, re-enacted in 1744 (17 George II. c. 5).

The consolidating Act of 1744 was passed soon after this declaration and was probably in part its result. But the evil remained unabated. A pamphleteer of 1751 notes the " amazing increase of beggars, vagabonds and lawless people who have no visible or honest way of getting their livelihood ".[1] " There is not a parish in the Liberty of Westminster ", says Fielding in 1753, " which does not raise thousands annually for the Poor, and there is not a street in that Liberty which does not swarm all day with beggars and all night with thieves. Stop your coach at what shop you will, however expeditious the tradesman is to attend you, a beggar is commonly beforehand with him ; and if you should not directly face his door, the tradesman must often turn his head while you are talking to him, or the same beggar or some other thief at hand will pay a visit to his shop." [2] Twenty years later the condition of the streets seems to have been unchanged. " In the cities of London and Westminster ", we are told, " you cannot stand a minute at your door but some object either of real or feigned distress solicits your charity with the most disagreeable importunity." [3]

Even the largest of the provincial towns were, in the period between 1650 and 1750, still sufficiently small to be markedly different from the great metropolis. But each centre of traffic attracted and harboured its own swarm of beggars, incorrigible idlers, prostitutes and the casually unemployed. In 1649 the Mayor and Corporation of Liverpool, finding the town thronged with beggars, was driven to appoint a committee to " take notice of all strangers and poor . . . that course may be taken to send them away to the several places where they were born, or have lived for three years last past ".[4] " At Wellington " (Somerset), writes De Foe in 1704, " . . . we were immediately surrounded with beggars, to such a degree that we had some difficulty in keeping them from under our horses' heels." [5] At Bath, in 1739, where the mineral springs then attracted great

[1] *The Right Method of maintaining Security in Purse and Property to all the Subjects of Great Britain*, by Philo Nomos, 1751, p. 2.
[2] *Proposal for making an Effectual Provision for the Poor*, etc., by Henry Fielding, 1753, p. 10.
[3] *An Essay on Trade and Commerce*, etc., 1770, p. 288, apparently by William Temple ; see *The Position of the Labourer in a System of Nationalism*, by E. S. Furniss, Boston, 1920.
[4] *Liverpool Vestry Books, 1681-1834*, by Henry Peet, 1912, vol. i. p. xxii.
[5] De Foe's *Tour*, vol. ii. p. 15.

crowds, the nuisance became so serious, owing to the number of " loose, idle and disorderly persons " who " daily resort to the said city, and remain wandering and begging about the streets ", under pretence of having come " for the benefit of the said mineral or medicinal waters ", that special powers were given to the local Justices, and mere begging was made punishable by twelve months' hard labour, in addition to whipping.[1]   At Bristol, in 1789, the citizens complained loudly of the " unprecedented swarms of beggars, vagrants and ballad-singers " with which the streets were infested, " to the great disgrace of our police, etc., and the annoyance of the inhabitants ".[2]   Of Liverpool, Manchester and Chester in 1790 we get a glimpse by a passing tourist.   " Being many years resident in London, I have often been a spectator of the follies and dissoluteness of that city ; but never have experienced so much as I have in the forementioned places ; it even makes human nature shudder to behold the many profligate wretches that fill the country about.   In Chester, particularly, I could not help observing the many crowds that infest the piazzas, or what the inhabitants call the ' rows ' : every evening, but more particularly on Sunday, do these dark recesses teem with the impudent and immodest of both sexes.   Why then does not magistracy exert her power ?   Why suffer the city to be overrun with such disorderly wretches ?   Unless the police inspect these places, and keep a strict look-out, I tell the magistrates, as a friend, the city of Chester will never be free from robberies, unless they exert that vigilance so much admired in places less required than here." [3]   Between London and the various towns the highways swarmed with petty chapmen, wandering singers and every description of what were then termed " trampers ". " On a journey from Birmingham to London, two years ago," says the Rev. William Gurney in 1815, " I passed not less than

---

[1] 12 George II. c. 31 (1739) ; see *History of Vagrants and Vagrancy*, by C. J. Ribton-Turner, 1887, pp. 197-198.

[2] *Bristol Journal*, January 21, 1789. Yet Bristol had been reputed to have solved the problem. The " magistrates of Bristol ", it was said in 1729, " have their city under such excellent regulation that foreign beggars dare not appear . . . their workhouses are terrible enough to them, for as soon as any of them are espied in the city they are taken up and whipped ; and wherever workhouses have been built (if well directed) the parish rates have been much lessened " (*The Trade and Navigation of Great Britain Considered*, by Joshua Gee, 1729).

[3] Letter from " Viator " in *The Diary*, January 15, 1790.

two hundred, with their wives and children, who were begging as I passed." [1]

At the conclusion of the Napoleonic wars the evil had become so alarming that the House of Commons set on foot a series of inquiries into the prevalence of mendicity and vagrancy, and their results. These inquiries extended almost continuously from 1815 to 1822, and they eventually led to the considerable changes in the law that we have described.[2] But our main concern here is with the action of the local authorities, as pursued within the framework of the Vagrancy Acts. For though the Justices of the Peace and the parish officers had failed to repress wandering idleness and disorderly living, it would be a mistake to infer that the law had remained a dead letter. In their hands the Vagrancy Acts had been made an instrument, not of preventing vagrancy, but of ridding their parishes from the charge of relieving a particular class of destitute persons. This perversion of the Vagrancy law, inextricably connected with the relief of the poor, will be best described by an analysis of the various devices, legal and extra-legal, which the Local Authorities employed for their purpose.

The Privy Search

Spasmodically, at intervals of a few years, the Justices of a particular county would take collective action to arrest the plague of " sturdy beggars ", unlicensed pedlars, and wandering ballad - singers, who infested the roads and demoralised the village alehouses. The Gloucestershire Quarter Sessions made a

[1] Report from House of Commons Committee on the State of Mendicity in the Metropolis, 1815, p. 29.

[2] Not only in the Metropolis, but in other large towns, and in rural counties, the increase of mendicity and vagrancy led, about 1816–1819, to spasmodic inquiries and local reforms. A Town's Meeting of principal inhabitants of Leeds in 1818 resolved to open a " Vagrant Office ", and to employ a salaried officer, under a voluntary committee, where homeless wanderers should be relieved ; that " a public lodging-house should be provided, so as to enable them to avoid those wretched receptacles the common lodging-houses, which are the sure media of diffusing vicious principles ; and that a very great proportion of the wide wasting fevers can be clearly traced to their filthy apartments ". The Vestry, at the same time, decided that no relief should be given to applicants except at the Vagrant Office ; and that the constables should apprehend all persons guilty of acts of vagrancy (MS. Vestry Minutes, Leeds, November 25, 1818). The proceedings were published in pamphlet form entitled *Suppression of Vagrancy : Resolutions of a Vestry Meeting of the Inhabitants of Leeds held . . . 25th of November 1818* (Leeds, 1818).

special effort as early as 1678, in quaint language that it may be of interest to quote. " The Grand Inquest hath informed this Court the dayly concourse and great increase off Rogues, Vagabonds and Sturdy Beggars is a greate Grievance and Annoyance to the inhabitants of this County, and through the negligence or ignorance of those officers who have been intrusted in this Concerne they are now grown soe insolent and presumptuous that they have oft by threates and menaces extorted money and victualls from those who live in houses ffar remote ffrom neighbours. . . . Whereffore this Courte . . . doe order and commande all Chiefe Constables, petty constables, Headboroughs, Tythenmen and all other officers herein concerned that they doe fforthwith cause all the lawes and statutes heretofore mad against Rogues, Vagabonds and Sturdy Beggars, wandering and idle persons, to be put in execution." [1] How far the individual Justices obeyed the statutory injunction to have a " privy search " made all over each Petty Sessional Division at least four times a year,[2] cannot in the absence of petty sessional records now be ascertained. The energetic Corporation of the Poor of Bristol urged the Mayor and Aldermen in 1698 " to give orders to the constables in the several wards to make a sudden and privy search for all vagabonds, vagrants, idle and wandering persons ", and " to repeat these orders as often as they see there is need ". [3] The exceptionally active and capable Justices of the Marylebone Petty Sessional Division seem to have ordered some such privy searches at irregular intervals ; and if we may believe the brief records of their proceedings, with the very scantiest results.[4] About the same time the authorities of the City of

---

[1] MS. Minutes, Quarter Sessions, Gloucestershire, 1678 ; see *Dursley and its Neighbourhood*, by J. H. Blunt, 1877, p. 45.

[2] The general search dates from 2 Henry VII. c. 2 (1495). It was ordered to be made four times a year by 19 Henry VII. c. 12 (1504), a provision repeated in subsequent statutes (see 17 George II. c. 5, sec. 6).

[3] MS. Minutes, Corporation of the Poor, Bristol, May 12, 1698 ; quoted in *Bristol Gazette*, March 30, 1786.

[4] " The Constables made a Return of their Search Warrant, upon Oath, and found No Disorderly Person " (MS. Minutes, Petty Sessions, Marylebone (Middlesex), November 28, 1730). " That a Warrant be made out to apprehend Idle and Disorderly persons in Marybone Ffields against the next Petty Sessions " (*ibid.* November 29, 1733). " Several persons were apprehended by ye Constables by virtue of search warrants for vagrants, some of which were sent to Bridewell, others passed to their settlements, and some discharged, on promise not to offend again " (*ibid.* August 13, 1741). " The constables attended and made a return of the search warrant upon oath, no person

London were occasionally using this device of a general search to clear the streets of prostitutes. " By the vigilance of the new constables belonging to the Reformation Society, appointed by the Lord Mayor and Court of Aldermen for removing the great nuisance of common street walkers, near forty were yesterday examined at the Court of Bridewell, before Sir Richard Glyn, President, Alderman Harley, and many more worthy gentlemen, when eleven of the most notorious were publicly whipped, one sent to the Magdalen House, and the rest received by their friends. It appearing plain to the Court the nuisance was in a great measure removed, the Court was pleased to return the Society thanks, and hoped they would continue in the necessary work." [1] That such privy searches were, from time to time, undertaken, and carried out simultaneously over whole counties, throughout the eighteenth and right into the nineteenth century, is clear from contemporary records. In 1770 we find the Northumberland Quarter Sessions ordering a general county search. " The Court having received information that several loose, idle and disorderly persons are now wandering about in many parts of this county and committing therein thefts, robberies and other misdemeanours, to the great terror and damage of the inhabitants, and being desirous to put a speedy stop to such dangerous and wicked practices, doth hereby charge and command all high and petty constables and other police officers within the said county, immediately to make diligent search throughout their respective divisions and districts, and to apprehend all such loose idle and disorderly persons as they shall find therein, and to carry them before the nearest justice of the peace, to be examined and dealt with according to law. And that this service so particularly necessary at this time for preserving the peace of the said county, and the lives and properties of the people, may be performed in the most effectual manner, all persons are hereby requested to be aiding and assisting the peace officers in the execution of this order, and to give notice to a neighbouring magistrate of any neglect of duty in the peace officers that they may be punished for such misbehaviour in their office. And as an encouragement to peace officers and others to exert themselves on this occasion,

apprehended, except Peter Hamilton found drunk in the streets, who was discharged upon promise not to offend again " (*ibid.* December 2, 1757).

[1] *London Chronicle*, January 7, 1762.

proper rewards will be given by the justices of the peace at their own private expense to those persons who shall apprehend and convict offenders of any crimes committed in the said county, over and above the reward which such persons may be entitled to by law." [1]

It is interesting to notice that the Durham Justices had evidently ordered a general search at the same time. One person who had been apprehended and committed to the House of Correction as a vagrant, with two silver watches in his possession, has his name and description advertised in the newspapers by the Clerk of the Peace pursuant to an Act of 1752, in order to give opportunity for any person to charge him with any " crime " or " misdemeanour " at the ensuing sessions.[2] Occasionally the Justices would be stirred up from above. In 1775 we find the Privy Council, impressed with the increase of rogues and vagabonds, sending a special circular-letter to the lord-lieutenants of counties and the Lord Mayor of London, urging that vagrant searches should be made.[3] In 1786 the West Riding Quarter Sessions resolved " that privy searches should be made in every district, as near the same hour as may be, a day or two previous (to a fortnightly petty sessions) where offenders may be brought to speedy justice by being immediately corrected, or otherwise dealt with according to law ".[4] So drastically were these privy

[1] MS. Minutes, Quarter Sessions, Northumberland, Michaelmas 1770 ; Newcastle Gazette, October 20, 1770.

[2] 25 George II. c. 36, sec. 12 ; see the advertisement in Newcastle Chronicle, November 22, 1770. For a similar advertisement see Leeds Intelligencer, December 18, 1787.

[3] MS. Acts of the Privy Council, George III. vol. xii. p. 217 (December 1, 1775).

[4] Leeds Intelligencer, May 16, 1786. The constables were authorised by the statute to obtain, for such privy searches, the assistance of the inhabitants, and this county supplies us with an instance of such assistance being rendered. " We hear from Wakefield ", says the Leeds Intelligencer of October 17, 1786, " that several respectable inhabitants there attended the constables in searching alehouses and lodging-houses, which harboured idle and suspicious persons, when a number of such were apprehended and proceeded against according to law, and informations were also laid against the owners of such houses." Another privy search was ordered by the Wakefield justices in November 1786, throughout the whole district, on a night when the great fair was on ; and the Leeds Intelligencer in reporting the fact adds that " it would be highly commendable if some of the principal inhabitants of the several townships would attend upon the constables in these searches, as well to assist them therein as to see that a proper obedience is paid to the justices' warrants " (ibid. November 7, 1786). " Last week five or six sailors, or pretended sailors, maimed, or without a leg or an arm, or both, who wander through the Kingdom with the model of a ship, living on

searches carried out during the ensuing months that there is reported to have been an almost complete clearance of " idle and disorderly persons, fellows, vagrants and cheats of all kinds throughout the West Riding ", so that, in July 1787, only three or four vagrants could be found to produce at the petty sessions of Skipton, Bradford and Rotherham.[1] Similar energetic action took place at this time all over the kingdom. " The Herefordshire Justices ", we read in 1787, " the night previous to Ross Fair, took the precautions adopted by the magistrates [of Gloucester], by directing a search through every public house, and all suspicious persons were seized. Property was by this measure secured, and the gentlemen deserve the thanks of their country." [2] At Hull, in 1788, we learn that " On Tuesday se'nnight ten vagrants were apprehended in Hull and examined before magistrates, who ordered them to be publicly whipped, and afterwards sent by passes to their respective parishes ".[3]

But the systematic searches of 1786–1788 seem to have been the result of an exceptional spurt of energy. The swarms of beggars and idle vagrants certainly did not cease out of the land. During the next thirty years, though we hear occasionally of general searches, they seem to have dropped down again to mere spasmodic and half-hearted struggles against an evil which

---

continual vagrancy, and otherwise disturbing the public peace, were lodged in the House of Correction at Wakefield, in order to be sent to their several homes. . . . Several women belong to them, who disperse themselves in the daytime, begging, telling fortunes, etc., in different parts ; the whole gang usually assemble together at nights, but particularly on Sundays, in obscure lodging-houses, where, meeting with other idle and dangerous persons, they are encouraged to continue in their disorderly course of life. But from the present exertions of magistrates, police officers and principal inhabitants in their respective parishes throughout the West Riding, there is good ground to believe that a final stop may be put to every species of vagrancy, which have been long a reproach to the police of the English nation " (*Leeds Intelligencer*, March 6, 1787).

[1] *Ibid.* July 24, 1787. For similar action at Sheffield see *ibid.* December 5, 1786. At the West Riding Quarter Sessions, at Pontefract, Easter 1788, " for the whole West Riding of Yorkshire only one vagrant appeared in the calendar of the prisoners ; a most convincing proof this that the late exertions of the worthy magistrates, peace officers and others have been attended with the most beneficial results " (*ibid.* April 8, 1788).

[2] *Bristol Gazette*, July 19, 1787.

[3] *Leeds Intelligencer*, April 9, 1788. So at Bristol in 1786 seven vagrants were taken up and flogged in one day, three described as notorious thieves, three merely as " ill-looking persons taken up on the quay ", and one preparatory to being passed to his home (*Bristol Gazette*, August 3, 1786 ; see also January 4, 1787).

the Justices failed to withstand. In Buckinghamshire, in 1803, it " appearing to the Court . . . in the present situation of affairs most necessary that a general search should take place throughout the County in order to take up all idle and disorderly persons, for the purpose of sending such as may be fit for service to serve His Majesty either in the army or navy, it is ordered . . . that the Clerk of the Peace do write to all the acting magistrates in the county to state to them that it appears . . . advisable that such general and privy search should take place . . . in the night of Monday the 25th day of this instant July " —the date to be kept secret and the search to be repeated once a month.¹ Among the miscellaneous documents in the archives of Plymouth is a letter from the Deputy Clerk of the Peace for Devonshire to the Mayor of Plymouth, dated April 1821, stating " that the time appointed . . . for a Privy Search for vagrants throughout the county is the evening of Thursday, 12 April next ", and asking for the co-operation of the town authorities, all vagrants to be apprehended on the day fixed, and committed to gaol until the next sessions.²

The device of the Privy Search was, however, devised only for occasional use. Though there was no continuous or systematic apprehension, either of " idle and disorderly persons " or of " rogues and vagabonds ", in London or elsewhere, it was always in the power of a Justice of the Peace to order an arrest, and there can be no doubt that this power was often used capriciously, and occasionally even for malicious reasons. The London constables or beadles, for instance, would sometimes take it into their heads to clear the streets, with or without orders to this effect from one of the " Trading Justices ", intent on reaping a petty harvest of bail fees. A tragic horror of this kind is recorded by Horace Walpole in 1742. " A parcel of drunken constables took it into their heads to put the laws in execution against disorderly persons, and so took up every woman they met, until they had collected five or six and twenty, all of whom they thrust into St. Martin's Round-house, where they kept them all night, with doors and windows closed. The poor creatures, who could not stir or breathe, screamed as long as they had any breath left, begging at least for water . . . but

¹ MS. Minutes, Quarter Sessions, Buckinghamshire, Midsummer 1803.
² Plymouth Town Council, MS. Archives, fol. Misc. Papers, 1800–1835, p. 82.

in vain. . . . In the morning four were found stifled to death,
two died soon after, and a dozen more are in a shocking way.
. . . Several of them were beggars, who from having no lodging
were necessarily found in the street, and others honest labouring
women. One of the dead was a poor washerwoman, big with
child, who was retiring home late from washing. One of the
constables is taken, and others absconded ; but I question if any
of them will suffer death, though the greatest criminals in this
town are the officers of justice ; there is no tyranny they do not
exercise, no villainy of which they do not partake." [1] The
county Justice of the Peace, though not pecuniarily corrupt,
was not beyond the suspicion of using his almost limitless powers
of apprehension and commitment to the county gaol, at the
bidding of class interest or personal prejudice.[2] Henry Fielding,
who had watched the work of the Justices of the Peace in the
country as well as in London, makes it clear that any man suspected of the habit of poaching, any servant against whom a
master or mistress had a grudge, or even a clandestine lover of
any member of a Justice's household, might, at any moment,
find himself apprehended as an " idle and disorderly person ",
or as a wanderer " not giving a good account of himself ", and
arbitrarily consigned, until the next Quarter Sessions, to the
loathsome and entirely unclassified confinement of the county
gaol.[3]

Recruiting His Majesty's Forces

Only for one purpose do we find the National Government
taking any trouble to get the Vagrancy Acts enforced. It was
provided in the 1744 Act that any rogue or vagabond of the male

[1] *Letters of Horace Walpole to Sir H. Mann*, July 1742, 3rd edition, 1834 ;
History of England in the Eighteenth Century, by W. E. H. Lecky, vol. i. p. 484.

[2] The following instance shows, at any rate, how limitless the Justice's
powers of arrest and commitment were supposed to be. Wesley was told that
a whole waggon-load of Methodists had been lately brought before a Justice
of the Peace. When he asked what they were charged with, one replied,
" Why, they pretended to be better than other people, and beside they prayed
from morning to night " (John Wesley's *Journal*, i. 361 ; Birkbeck Hill's
edition of Boswell's *Life of Johnson*, 1887, vol. i. p. 397).

[3] Fielding, as an experienced magistrate, may be assumed to have known
how the law worked. The readers of *Joseph Andrews* will recall the apprehension of the hero and heroine at the instance of Lady Booby, and their
narrow escape from being committed by the complacent Justice to the House
of Correction as vagrants (*The History of the Adventures of Joseph Andrews and
his Friend Abraham Adams*, by Henry Fielding).

sex, over twelve years of age, might, after punishment, be sent
" to be employed in His Majesty's service by sea or land ".[1]
This summary method of recruiting the army and navy was
repeatedly made use of during the eighteenth and early nineteenth centuries, at the request of the Privy Council. Thus at
the outbreak of the Seven Years' War in 1756 " orders were
received by the Justices " of Oxford, and presumably also by
those of other places, " to impress loose and disorderly persons
for His Majesty's service by sea and land, and on Thursday
warrants were delivered to the constables to execute the same ;
since which several have been taken up and sent to Bocardo "
(the City gaol).[2]

In the following week we hear of similar action in the Metropolis, but only such persons seem to have been there pressed
as belonged to the sea. " On Sunday last search warrants were
granted to the constables in the City and Liberty of Westminster
when several fellows were taken up and secured in the Round-
house ; and upon examination many were found to be able-
bodied seamen, and delivered to a regulating captain to be
carried on board a tender." [3]

Twenty years later, on the outbreak of the American War,
this part of the Vagrancy Act was again used for recruiting the
Navy. The minutes of the Marylebone Petty Sessions record
that " the magistrates . . . having assembled at the Court
House to take into consideration a printed letter sent to the
magistrates assembled at Hicks Hall (Quarter Sessions of
Middlesex) by His Grace the Duke of Northumberland, together
with a letter from the Privy Council desiring the aid of the Lord
Lieutenant and the justices of the peace of the county to enforce
the apprehension of vagrants, and to assist in the apprehending
of all idle and disorderly seamen for the manning of His Majesty's
Navy ; and having fully considered the matter in question, are
of opinion that it will not be expedient to assemble themselves

---

[1] 17 George II. c. 5, sec. 9 (see also sec. 28). It will be remembered that
Tom Jones was " pressed " at the incitement of Lady Bellaston. " I am
thinking, my lord, added she (for this fellow is too mean for your personal
resentment), whether it would not be possible for your lordship to contrive
some method of having him pressed and sent on board a ship. Neither law
nor conscience forbid this project, for the fellow, I promise you, however well
dressed, *is but a vagabond* " (*The History of Tom Jones*, by Henry Fielding,
book xvi. chap. viii.).

[2] *Jackson's Oxford Journal*, March 6, 1756.   [3] *Ibid.* March 13, 1756.

as a body of magistrates acting in a separate division to enforce the matters mentioned in such letter, but are ready and willing upon all occasions to give their assistance by every method to promote the object of His Majesty's wishes to raise men for manning the Royal Navy, and mean to attend at the Rotation Office established in Litchfield Street for the above purpose ".[1]

Again, in the Napoleonic wars, similar orders seem to have been issued by the Privy Council, and to have been carried out by the Justices. It was for the express object of obtaining men fit for service in the Army and Navy that the Buckinghamshire Quarter Sessions ordered the general search for idle and disorderly persons in 1803, which we have already mentioned.[2]

Rewards for apprehending Vagrants

As an inducement to the parish constable, or to any other citizen, to take spontaneous action against vagrants, Parliament, in 1662, had begun a system of rewards for all those who were apprehended.[3] Beginning at two shillings, the reward was raised by the Act of 1744 to five shillings for each " idle and disorderly person " arrested in his own parish, and ten shillings for each wandering " rogue and vagabond apprehended and punished ". [4] Local authorities also experimented with rewards of their own. In 1704 the Corporation of the Poor of the City of London offered its own reward of a shilling each for beggars and vagabonds. " Whereas the streets and passages of this city are generally at this time of the year much annoyed with rogues, vagabonds and sturdy beggars ; for prevention hereof for the future, the President and Governors of the Poor of the City of London do

---

[1] MS. Minutes, Petty Sessions, Marylebone (Middlesex), November 18, 1776.
[2] MS. Minutes, Quarter Sessions, Buckinghamshire, Midsummer 1803.
[3] 13 and 14 Charles II. c. 12 (Law of Settlement and Removal).
[4] The express authority given by the Vagrancy Act to " any person " summarily to apprehend an offender against the Act, and to drag him before a Justice of the Peace, was probably not often made use of by any one who was not a constable, or without a written warrant from a Justice. The authority thus given to any citizen was obviously open to abuse. That it was sometimes employed as a method of extortion may be inferred from the following extract : " The magistrates of this City (of London) on Tuesday came to a resolution to order the Solicitor of the City to prosecute all such persons who shall hereafter attempt to act as constables who are not legally sworn in. This is done to prevent innocent people being dragged to prison whenever such fellows think proper and often extorting money from the ignorant to let them go " (*London Evening Post*, March 28-30, 1775).

2 B

give notice, that if any Overseer for the Poor, constable, beadle, marshal's man, warder or other person, shall apprehend any rogue, vagabond or sturdy beggar, and bring them before any Justices of the Peace, so that they may be brought and delivered to and received by the Keeper of the Workhouse, he shall receive twelve pence for every such." [1] In 1788 a reward was offered in the same way, for the apprehension of any " beggar, ballad-singer, minstrels or other vagrant ", by the Corporation of the Poor of Bristol. [2] The working of such a system of rewards in criminal cases, of which the eighteenth century was specially fond, is well worth examination. So far as the vagrancy reward was concerned, it is clear that it operated in ways quite unexpected by the legislators. Parliament had intended to provide an automatic stimulus to the continuous suppression of vagrancy. But the Justices of the Peace had frugal minds, and we find Quarter Sessions resenting the cost thrown upon the County Rate by the diligence of constables. The Justices accordingly slackened the zeal of their subordinates, [3] and in some cases would spasmodically refuse to allow the reward at all, or (as later, in Middlesex) suffered it to be largely eaten up by office fees. [4] The

---

[1] *The Postman*, December 15, 1704 ; *History and Survey of London*, by William Maitland, 1756, vol. ii. p. 822. Between 1701 and 1716 this Corporation of the Poor received and dealt with 6534 vagabonds, or over 400 a year (Strype's edition of Stow's *Survey of London*, 1720, vol. i. pp. 197-203).

[2] *Bristol Gazette*, August 28, 1788.

[3] Thus, in the West Riding of Yorkshire in 1809, we find it resolved that " this Court, taking into consideration the very great and increasing expense of apprehending and conveying vagrants, and the great impositions to which magistrates are liable from parish officers and others apprehending persons, and chiefly *on the account of the allowance for such apprehending*, earnestly recommend to the magistrates acting in the Wapentakes to be very careful and strict in their examination previous to commitment of such vagrants, and also of the order they are required to sign for the allowance, and to check every appearance of fraud, and every attempt to impose upon them " (MS. Minutes, Quarter Sessions, West Riding of Yorkshire, Easter 1809). So in Devonshire, the Quarter Sessions in 1830, moved by the great cost of the apprehension of vagrants, reduced the allowance to constables ; see Petition of Grand Jury, in Report of Poor Law Inquiry Commissioners, 1834, Appendix A, Chapman's Report, p. 457.

[4] Thus, in 1815, one constable gave evidence that, even when he got the reward of ten shillings, he had " to pay three shillings at the office (one shilling to the magistrate's box and two shillings to the clerks) " (Report of House of Commons Committee on the State of Mendicity in the Metropolis, 1815, p. 64). Moreover, by a strict construction of the statute it was only when the vagrant was whipped or imprisoned preparatory to being " passed " to his place of settlement—not if he was otherwise dealt with—that the reward was, in some counties, regarded as payable (*ibid.* p. 64).

returns obtained by the House of Commons in 1776 show that, in all England and Wales, the total expense incurred by the Justices in apprehending vagrants was only about £1500 a year, between three and four thousand being dealt with each year, or an average of not more than one in each parish every five years.[1]

Nor did the offer of a reward always work in the direction of stimulating the zeal of the constable. So long, at any rate, as vagrants were whipped or otherwise seriously punished, the ordinary street crowd resented their apprehension. This instinctive sympathy for the apparently destitute beggar or sick person was greatly strengthened by the supposition that the constable was taking him to prison merely in order to get the reward. In London and other towns the duty of apprehending beggars or vagrants was thereby made odious, and even dangerous. At Bristol, in the latter part of the eighteenth century, we frequently find references to the sympathy of the mob for the vagrants whom the constables tried to apprehend, and the difficulties caused thereby. In 1786 an officer sought to arrest a woman, who was shamming illness in a churchyard for the purpose of extracting money from passers-by. On the officer attempting to take her to St. Peter's Hospital, she threw herself down in the street, and attracted a crowd of persons who so seriously attacked the constable that he had to flee for his life.[2] Even in the City of London, in 1815, when a beadle attempted to arrest the most notorious impostors in the way of street begging, " the mob would often insist on their being set at liberty ".[3] " It is a very disagreeable office for an officer to undertake," said the clerk to the Lord Mayor, " for he is sure to get a crowd about him, and to be ill-treated ; there is generally a serious struggle before any of these common beggars can be

---

[1] The statistics are as follows :

VAGRANTS SENT TO HOUSE OF CORRECTION.

	1772.	1773.	1774.
English Counties . .	2420	2776	2975
Welsh „ . .	14	14	14
Cities and Boroughs .	503	463	504
	2937	3243	3493

(House of Commons Journals, 1776).

[2] *Bristol Gazette*, April 6, 1786.

[3] Report of the House of Commons Committee on the State of Mendicity in the Metropolis, 1815, p. 64.

taken into custody ", owing, as he explained, to the mistaken
sympathy of the public.[1] " One officer . . . in taking up a sailor
whose dog carries his hat, was seriously hurt." [2] When William
Fielding, the son of Sir John Fielding, and himself a London
magistrate, was describing the system of rewards in 1819, he
expressly pointed to its having, not a stimulating, but actually
a discouraging effect. " Sorry I am to say that this stimulus has
not the effect which the Legislature intended, for in many cases
it has failed altogether. . . . The constable had rather give up
the expectation of receiving such a sum than hazard the consequences of the indignation of the mob in prosecuting such a
person, or bringing him before the Justice. . . . There is the
very objection raised by the multitude that arises in the minds
of juries, namely, that the officer is an informer, and that he
informs from the hope and expectation of obtaining the
reward." [3]

We have therefore some ground for the inference that the
offer of a reward for the apprehension of vagrants, instead of
stimulating, really hindered the enforcement of the law. When,
however, as we shall presently describe, the penal clauses of the
Vagrancy Laws ceased to be put in operation, the system of
rewards had a new and equally unforeseen result. The vagrant
ceased to object to apprehension, and in many cases even desired
to be taken before the magistrate, in order to be " passed " to
another parish. With the disuse of whipping, and the minimising
of the period of detention, " the threat of commitment ", it was
authoritatively reported in 1821, had " lost its terror. The
vagrant himself, so far from shrinking, throws himself in the way
of it, is apparently solicitous for it, and in fact steps forward as
a volunteer for prison." [4] There then grew up the new trade of
reward-mongering. The House of Commons Committee of 1821
found that " the county reward at present payable has in some
instances converted the apprehension of vagrants into a regular
trade, so disgraceful in all its branches as even to prevent the
more respectable constables from interfering with vagrants, from
a dread of sharing the obloquy attached to their apprehension.

[1] Report of the House of Commons Committee on the State of Mendicity
in the Metropolis, 1815, p. 16.
[2] Ibid. p. 21.
[3] House of Commons Committee on the Police of the Metropolis, 1819.
[4] Report of Select Committee of House of Commons on Vagrancy, 1821.

It is in evidence that it has led to a system of collusion between the apprehender and the vagrant, and that the latter has voluntarily entered or been invited into the district of the former, and even been bribed to commit an act of vagrancy, with the view of procuring the reward of ten shillings, which in some cases has actually been divided between the parties." In the Metropolis, and probably in other places, there came into existence a class of men who, whether sworn in as constables or not, made the earning of rewards for apprehending vagrants a steady source of income. We read of men spending their whole time looking out for various kinds of vagrants, some making a speciality of beggars, others of prostitutes ; and making one or two hundred pounds a year out of the five or ten shillings rewards. In many cases, especially among the Scotch and Irish vagrants who wished to be conveyed home, the apprehension was entirely collusive, and the vagrant stipulated in advance with his apprehender for a share of the reward. The system of rewards came, in fact, with the disuse of punishment, to act as a positive stimulus to vagrancy. The more numerous the vagrants in circulation, and the more frequent their visits to each place, the larger was the harvest of the reward-monger.[1]

The Disuse of Punishment

Once apprehended, the " idle and disorderly person " or " rogue and vagabond " was examined before a Justice of the Peace, who was assumed either to discharge him, or to sentence him to the imprisonment or whipping prescribed by law. It was upon the deterrent effect of this punishment that Parliament relied for the suppression of those idle and disorderly modes of living, either within one's own parish or elsewhere, which had been stigmatised as acts of vagrancy. That the public whipping of both men and women was a frequent spectacle at the beginning of the eighteenth century is clear from contemporary literature ; and that the gaols and bridewells of the period included among their miserable inmates many a harmless mendicant and many an impecunious traveller, committed by careless and irritable

[1] See for all this the Report and Evidence of the House of Commons Committee on Vagrancy, 1821 ; *History of Vagrants and Vagrancy*, by C. J. Ribton-Turner, 1887, pp. 228-234.

Justices of the Peace, is only too probable. Here is a typical entry from the MS. parish records of Burnham (Bucks) :

" Benjamin Smat, and his wife and three children, valiant beggars, he of middle stature, but one eye, was this 28th day of September, 1699, with his wife and children, openly whipped at Boveney in the parish of Burnham, in the County of Bucks, according to ye laws. And they are assigned to pass forthwith from parish to parish by ye officers thereof the next direct way to the parish of St. (Se)pulchers, London, where they say they last inhabited three years. And they are limited to be at St. (Se)pulchers within ten days next ensuing. Given under our hands and seals, Will. Glover, Vicar of Burnham, and John Hunt, Constable of Boveney." [1]

But so far as we can form an opinion, the sentences of whipping or imprisonment—though in the aggregate numerous enough— were only spasmodically inflicted, chiefly on persons who happened to be specially obnoxious to some Justice of the Peace, or who were found committing offences against which he happened for the time to be taking severe measures. Thus the Lord Mayor and Aldermen of the City of London would, as we have seen, occasionally clear the streets of prostitutes, and send the worst of them to Bridewell to be whipped or put to hard labour. For the first half of the eighteenth century at any rate the prostitute unlucky enough to have been made an example of was to be seen, often in her gaudy fine clothes, beating hemp in full view of every passer-by, as pictured by Hogarth.[2]

In 1787 a regular epidemic of whipping for vagrancy seems

---

[1] See *Old Time Punishments*, by W. Andrews, 1890, p. 218. On May 5, 1713, the Doncaster Town Council Minutes record an order for the erection of a whipping-post, for punishing vagrants and sturdy beggars (*ibid.* p. 215). John Taylor, the " water poet ", mentions that, in 1630,

> " In London, and within a mile, I ween,
> There are jails or prisons full eighteen,
> And sixty whipping-posts and stocks and cages."

The existence of sixty whipping-posts in an area of about nine square miles implies that one was to be met with every few hundred yards.

[2] Bridewell was used as the general House of Correction for the City of London. " The use of this hospital now is for an House of Correction, and to be a place where all strumpets, night-walkers, pickpockets, vagrant and idle persons, that are taken up for their ill lives, as also incorrigible and disobedient servants, are committed by the Mayor and Aldermen, who are Justices of the Peace within the said City. And being so committed are forced to beat hemp in public view, with due correction of whipping, according to their offence, for such a time as the President and Court [of Bridewell] shall see cause " (Strype's edition of Stow's *Survey of London*, 1720, vol. i. p. 191).

to have broken out. The *Bristol Journal* of February 3, 1787—
to cite one out of many records—gives a list of vagrants who
were "taken up, flogged and sent home to their different
parishes". But of any continuous endeavour to carry out the
intention of Parliament and really suppress idle and irregular
modes of living among the lower orders there is no trace. To
the ordinary Justice of the Peace—still more to the average
parish constable—mere idleness, asking for alms, or travelling
about the country on foot, seemed no crime at all ; whilst even
the other offences penalised by the Vagrancy Act appeared only
venial misdemeanours. The Vagrant Act, it was said, "like
many other laws, defeats its own purposes by the severity of its
penalties. . . . Who could devote an unhappy human being to
the whipping post or House of Correction merely for asking
charity ? "[1] To the growing instinct of philanthropy, and
sentiment about personal liberty, the assumptions underlying the
old law were repugnant. To the thoughtful or humane Justice
before whom a miserable " tramper " was brought, both the
alternatives of the law appeared inept. The public whipping of
men and women, stripped naked from the middle upwards
" until the back be bloody ", seemed an intolerable barbarity.
The physical horror and moral contamination of the gaols, of
which John Howard had rendered the more intelligent Justices
acutely conscious, made them loth to sentence mere beggars or
poor travellers to imprisonment. The dislike of each of these
modes of punishment spasmodically revived the preference for
the other. Those whom whipping revolted recommended the
committal of all vagrants to gaol. Those who realised the social
contamination of the overcrowded and unclassified prisons of the
period urged flogging.[2] The net effect was that both sets of

---

[1] *Observations on the Present State of the Parochial and Vagrant Poor* [by
John Scott], 1773, p. 4.

[2] " Mr. Howard, having visited the House of Correction at Wakefield, was
highly pleased with the practice which is now almost generally adopted by the
magistrates for the West Riding, of committing vagrants and others (unless
those of the most dangerous kind), if they are committed at all, for as short a
time as possible ; full powers being already given to every Justice to order
vagrants immediately to their places of settlement, and to be first properly
corrected, or to be imprisoned in solitary confinement for a night or two.
This must have a better effect, and prevent so many vagrants being confined
till the sessions, from whence they are at last sent home, and often without
(further) punishment, and being often greatly weakened and debilitated by
imprisonment, or having formed new connections, they become a greater
burden than ever to the community " (*Leeds Intelligencer*, January 15, 1788).

objections prevailed and both kinds of punishment fell into disuse.[1] But some action had to be taken. We have seen that the swarms of beggars, swollen, as was always imagined, by vagrants from elsewhere, provoked outbreaks of complaint from the local residents. Even more imperative seemed the need of protecting the parish from the burden thrown upon its Poor Rate by the presence of persons who were always falling sick, or becoming actually destitute, and finally requiring burial at the public expense. If vagrants could no longer be whipped or imprisoned, some other method of relieving a parish from their presence had to be found. In this dilemma the Local Authorities resorted to two extra-legal devices. They used the threat of arrest and punishment as a means of frightening the beggars and vagrants away from particular parishes. On the other hand, there grew up a systematic perversion of the Vagrancy Act, under which the destitute wanderer was apprehended, frequently at his own request, not with any idea of punishment, but in order to dispatch him, with a " pass ", to his own parish, without cost to the place in which he had been taken up.

The simple device of warning off beggars and vagrants, by threat of arrest and whipping, threw no other charge upon the local rates than the salary of an officer to do the warning off, and as it was specially easy of execution in the small market towns, it became their favourite expedient. At Abingdon, in 1738, it was " ordered that the Bellman have thirty shillings yearly paid by the Chamberlain by quarterly payments in order to clear the streets and places within this borough of beggars and other vagrants, and to turn them out of town ".[2] At Burton-on-Trent, in 1749, we read that an officer at 25s. a week was appointed for " looking after and driving out of town all vagrants and beggars, both by night and day ".[3] At Newcastle-on-Tyne, in 1755, a

---

Orders exactly to this effect were passed by the West Riding Quarter Sessions two years later (see *ibid.* May 25, 1790).

[1] Magistrates were, we are told, " loth to incur the charge of inhumanity, by strictly following the letter of the Act, in whipping or imprisoning poor miserable wretches whose indigence has rendered relief necessary " (*The State of Indigence and the Situation of the Casual Poor in the Metropolis*, by Patrick Colquhoun, 1799).

[2] *Selections from the Municipal Chronicles of the Borough of Abingdon,* 1555–1897, by Bromley Challenor, Abingdon, 1898, p. 201. In 1797 a beadle was specially appointed to do this work for a shilling a week (p. 225).

[3] *History of Vagrants and Vagrancy*, by C. J. Ribton-Turner, 1887, p. 203.

local pamphleteer recommends " badging the original poor of each parish who begged in the streets ", in order to distinguish them from " foreign beggars ", who should be driven away.[1] At Gloucester, among other regulations recommended for general adoption, we are told, in 1786, that " the constables and proper officers continually inspect all public-houses, lodging houses, etc., when all such persons as are found tippling, and cannot give a proper account of themselves and their mode of living, are *immediately sent out of town* . . . having the choice of which gate they would prefer passing through, north, east, west or south ".[2] " It is ", says a report of 1790, " now become the established practice of the beadles in almost all corporate towns (if they take any notice of beggars and other vagrants) to drive them out of their limits into the adjacent county." [3]

But the practice was not confined to the smaller towns. Their action naturally led to reprisals in the larger centres. Bristol, in 1789, complained of the fact that " unprecedented swarms of beggars, vagrants and ballad-singers " were " driven " to that centre from all the neighbouring cities and towns by the vigilance " of the proper officers ", so that the numbers flocking to its " streets are increased beyond all comparison with those in any former period ".[4] The larger towns, and in particular London and Westminster, went in extensively for the policy of warning off. " The newspapers tell us (in 1764) that the Justices of the Peace in the Cities of Westminster and London

---

[1] *An Address to the Ministers, Churchwardens and Parishioners of Newcastle-upon-Tyne for the better regulating the Parish Poor ; banishing itinerant strolling beggars, easing the Parishes of the Poor Cess ; and erecting 150 lamps for illuminating the several streets in the Winter Season*, Newcastle, 1755, p. 9.

[2] *Leeds Intelligencer*, October 17, 1786.

[3] *Account of . . . Society for the Promotion of Industry*, 1790, p. 136. As a species of " warning off ", we may here refer to the advertisements and public notices which districts would publish, threatening vagrants with severe treatment. Thus, in December 1787, an Essex parish, St. Osyth, adopted this course (see *Ipswich Journal*, December 15, 1787), and the example spread into a sort of epidemic of advertisements, so that, in 1788, we read that " the magistrates of Essex have in a spirited and exemplary manner determined to suppress vagrancy. In the last *Chelmsford Chronicle* are nine advertisements from different parishes, setting forth that all beggars, vagrants and disorderly persons, who shall hereafter be lurking about, without exercising any diurnal employment, will (by the parish officers) be taken before a magistrate, and punished to the utmost rigour of the law " (*Leeds Intelligencer*, March 18, 1788; see *Chelmsford Chronicle*, December 28, 1787, January, February 8, 15, 22, March 27, April 14, May 9 and December 5, 1788).

[4] *Bristol Journal*, January 21, 1789.

have come to a resolution of driving away from their respective districts all beggars and vagrants. The inhabitants of both these places will be greatly obliged to magistrates who exert their authority in removing so many miserable objects from before their eyes, and easing their pockets from so considerable an expense as the maintenance of such multitudes must amount to in a year." [1] The division of the Metropolis among more than a hundred separate parishes, each bearing its own charges, whilst it crippled any effective execution of the law, enormously multiplied the opportunities for "warning off", and this was occasionally done in the most ruthless manner. "A beadle has been seen to drag a dying man in the streets across the way into the boundaries of another parish, to rid his own of the charge of his burial, and there left him to perish." [2] By 1815, at any rate, this warning off was the only device habitually used in the City of London for any but vagrants, who could be promptly " passed " to distant places of settlement. As regards all others, " the City Constables ", we are told, " drive them out of the City ". [3]

The System of passing Vagrants

The practice of giving a pass, or permit, to a person about to travel beyond the bounds of his own parish, had been commonly used in mediæval England for all sorts and conditions of property-less men, on the assumption that no person ought to be abroad, out of the jurisdiction of those who were responsible for his conduct, without their express permission. [4] We may cite as well-known instances of such passes those given to foreign travellers, time-expired soldiers, shipwrecked mariners, discharged private servants, prisoners released from gaol, licensed beggars, and even the travelling students of universities. [5] In

---

[1] *London Chronicle*, November 22-24, 1764.

[2] *First Report of the Philanthropic Society for the Prevention of Crime*, 1789, p. 16.

[3] Report of Select Committee of the House of Commons on the State of Mendicity in the Metropolis, 1815, p. 14.

[4] " These passes or certificates . . . have been traced back by Dr. Sharpe to the reign of Edward III." (*The Interregnum*, by F. C. Inderwick, 1891, p. 92).

[5] The Act of 1495 (2 Henry VII. c. 2) expressly exempted from punishment as vagrants, " clerks of the universities, soldiers, shipmen or travelling men ", carrying proper certificates. These exemptions were repeated in subsequent Acts. That of 1597 (39 Elizabeth c. 4) adds " glassmen " of good character,

all these cases the pass implied that the wanderer was authorised to travel, and the authorisation was taken to warrant a request for suitable assistance from the charitably disposed inhabitants or the public officers of every place visited.

When it was found that mere savage punishment did little to relieve the towns from the plague of vagrants, the provision was added that the offender should, after punishment, be not merely ordered to repair home, but be actually " passed " to his place of settlement. The " passing " sometimes took place in the custody of the parish constable, who had to conduct the vagrant to the next parish, and there deliver him to the constable of that parish, who in his turn conducted him a further stage, and so onward until his destination was reached.[1] This " passing " was intended by Parliament as a mere subsequent incident to the whipping or imprisonment suffered by the vagrant. But the Justices and constables were much more anxious to get rid of the vagrants than to punish them ; gradually, as we have seen, whipping went out of fashion ; imprisonment became mere detention for a few days until it was convenient to travel ; and the " passing " remained the principal and often the only feature in the device.

How soon this kind of passing without punishment, or after a merely nominal detention in the House of Correction, came into general use as a device for getting rid of wandering beggars and other destitute strangers, we are unable to say. The practice had certainly begun early in the eighteenth century, and its increasing frequency was probably connected with the stimulus given to the apprehension of vagrants by a change in the incidence of cost. Down to 1699, the expense of apprehending and conveying the vagrant fell upon the rates of the parish where he was arrested. By the 11 William III. c. 18 (1699), all these expenses, at rates to be fixed by Quarter Sessions, were made a county charge, in the hope of giving the parish and the constable a constant inducement to take action. And provided that the punishment was omitted, or consisted only of a slight detention, the vagrant was often very willing to let the constable earn his

---

travelling with a licence from three Justices. A soldier's pass of 1587 is given in the *Reprint of the Barnstaple Records*, by J. R. Chanter and Thos. Wainwright, 1900, vol. i. p. 60.

[1] This passing in custody seems to have been first ordered by 1 Edward VI. c. 3 (1547).

ten shillings reward, and secure at the same time his own conveyance to whatever destination he thought fit to name as his
place of settlement. Whatever little possessions he had were
not confiscated ; his bundles were not searched ; whilst he,
and possibly his female companion and children, with all their
belongings, were conveyed by cart, at the public expense, with
an allowance of sixpence a day for food. This arrangement
was soon found advantageous also by the Overseer, anxious to
get rid of strange paupers. Under the Poor Law, though
" unsettled " persons could be removed to their places of settlement, the expenses of this removal, and their relief meanwhile,
were at the charge of the removing parish ; and the Overseer,
who had until 1714 to go himself, or some other parish officer,
had personally to conduct the paupers all the way, it might
be to the other end of the kingdom. Moreover, the distant
parish could, and probably would, appeal against the Removal
Order, which would involve troublesome and costly litigation,
and possible eventual loss. If the pauper stranger could,
by any stretch of imagination, be considered a vagrant, it
was plainly more advantageous to get the complacent Justice
to order him to be passed under the Vagrancy Act ; [1] when

[1] *Orders, Resolutions, etc., for the Passing for Vagrants in the County of Surrey,*
1772. Presently this was objected to. Thus, at the Somerset Quarter Sessions
in 1801, " it appearing to this Court that poor persons, not objects of the
Vagrant Acts, are commonly passed by the Magistrates of the City of Bristol
through and at the expense of this county, to places which sometimes happen
not to be the places of their last legal settlement, instead of being conveyed
by orders of removal according to due course of law ; which tends greatly to
burden this county by increasing the rates and applying them to improper
purposes, and also deprives the parishes to which such persons are sent of the
benefit of appeal, and frequently put such parishes to great expense in discovering and conveying such poor persons to the places of their last legal
settlement "—the Court directs a strong representation on the subject to be
made to Bristol (MS. Minutes, Quarter Sessions, Somerset, January 14, 1801).
Dr. Colquhoun incidentally mentioned this practice of the Overseers in 1815.
He observes that " the difficulty of removing [the non-settled paupers] from
the Metropolis is that the Metropolis being situated at the end of the island
makes it extremely difficult to remove to those parishes in the Western part
of the Kingdom, or those north of the Trent . . . the passing them (under the
Vagrancy Act) is considered the cheapest method of providing for them,
where the parishes are (not) near London " (Report from Select Committee
of H. of C. on the State of Mendicity in the Metropolis, 1815, p. 55). A thrifty
parish would use the rewards and perquisites thus drawn from the county
funds in part payment of its own staff. Thus, at Devonport in 1814, it was
" resolved that the duty of the Beadle be to remove paupers and the vagrants,
and that he do keep an account for one year of the profits arising from his
office, and that if it do not amount to the sum of £70, the deficiency in that

the parish of destination had no right of appeal, the county treasurer repaid all the expenses, and actually gave a reward ; and the constable was required to journey no farther than the next parish. The result was that, by the end of the century, the country was full of vagrants, or " trampers, as they are termed, making annually their tour of England and Wales, with a carriage found by the public, and sixpence per diem for maintenance ". These wandering paupers, we are told, would " rob their way from some distant province, and then be conveyed, together with their spoils, rich and jovial, at the expense of the very country they have infested, and to any other place they may prefer occasionally, and to which perjury is the easy passport ".[1]

Parliament having tempted all the parishes of England and Wales to unburden themselves of their vagrants, each at the expense of everybody else, grew alarmed at the costly circulation which was thereby set up, and vainly strove to stop it. In 1744 power was given to search the vagrant's bundles, and to apply any property so discovered towards the cost of his journey— a provision which the careless constables evidently neglected to make use of. But the main reliance of Parliament had always been on the deterrent effect of the whipping, which it had repeatedly striven to make a condition precedent of the passing. Already in 1714 it provided that no parish need receive a vagrant under the passing system unless he or she had been actually whipped before being passed.[2] Nearly every subsequent Act emphasised the inflicting of actual punishment on the vagrant before he was passed. Still the Justices refused to do as the law commanded, perhaps because there was " no distinction made between the vilest impostor and the most inoffensive accidentally distressed traveller ".[3] In 1792 the evil had grown to such a height that Parliament made a determined attempt, which proved to be its last, to get all vagrants actually punished.

---

sum be made up out of the Rates and Assessments, so as to make his salary equal to £70 per annum " (MS. Minutes, Improvement and Poor Commissioners, Devonport, July 29, 1314).

[1] *Observations preliminary to a Proposed Amendment of the Poor Laws*, by Sir William Young, 1788, p. 61.

[2] 13 Anne c. 26 (often printed or quoted as 12 Anne, Stat. 2, ch. 23), 1714.

[3] *Observations on the Present State of the Parochial and Vagrant Poor* [by John Scott], 1773, p. 4.

The public whipping was again insisted on, though this time only for males.[1] If the Justice preferred the alternative of imprisonment this was to be for not less than seven days. It was expressly laid down that no reward was to be paid until the punishment had been actually inflicted on the vagrant, nor until the record of his examination had been actually transmitted to Quarter Sessions. Nor was any pass to be given without its containing a formal certificate that the person to whom it referred had been actually publicly whipped or confined in the House of Correction. This Act seems to have done nothing to repress vagrancy, but it so far attained its immediate object as to check, for a time, the granting of passes under the Vagrant Acts, "the magistrates", we are told, "being loth to incur the charge of inhumanity, by strictly following the letter of the Act, in whipping or imprisoning poor miserable wretches, whose indigence have rendered relief necessary. . . . Hence it is that so many who are either on the brink of vagrancy, or have actually received alms, are permitted to remain a burden on the parishes." [2] But the check was only momentary. The new Act was soon no more regarded than its predecessors. The country Justices would, in ordinary cases, order neither whipping nor the troublesome and expensive committal to the House of Correction ; and they continued to direct the constables to pass the vagrants to the next parish. The magistrates of the City of London so far complied with the law as to commit thirty or forty vagrants every week to the City Bridewell, but only about ten per cent of these were designated for any sort of punishment. The great majority were simply detained for a few days under the ordinary workhouse conditions of the period,

---

[1] 32 George III. c. 45, 1792. But women were whipped, and publicly too, after this date. According to the *Annals of Winchcombe and Sudeley*, in Gloucestershire, six women were in the year 1800 stripped to the waist and "flogged till the blood ran down their backs, for 'hedgepulling' under the Acts of 1766 and 1768 ; the whipping-post is described as being a post in front of the Town Hall fixed in the ground, with iron rings secured in with hinges, leaving just sufficient room for the arms and legs to pass between the iron and the post ; the offenders were locked in, and then the whipping commenced " (*History of Vagrants and Vagrancy*, by C. J. Ribton-Turner, 1887, p. 205 ; see Spencer Walpole's *History of England*, i. 204 ; ˙Hansard, vol. xxxvi. pp. 833, 932). The flogging of women in public was not totally prohibited until the Act of 1817 (57 George III. c. 90), and their flogging in private not until the Act of 1819 (59 George III. c. 12).

[2] *Treatise on the Police of the Metropolis*, by P. Colquhoun, 1800, p. 363.

preparatory to being passed to the next county.[1] This practice
of passing without punishment received, in 1819, a practical
endorsement by Parliament. It was found that, although
Scotch or Irish vagrants could be " passed " to their respective
countries, no provision existed by which the ordinary pauper of
Scotch or Irish birth, not being a vagrant, could be " removed "
under the Poor Law. To remedy this defect, a clause was
inserted in a Poor Law Act of 1819, enabling persons belonging
to Scotland, Ireland, or the Channel Isles, who had become
chargeable to the Poor Rate in an English parish, to be " passed "
to their respective countries *as if they were vagrants*, but without
punishment. At the same time it was provided that the inflic-
tion of punishment, even on vagrants belonging to these countries
or islands, should be discretionary. The result, it need hardly
be said, was that practically every quiet and inoffensive vagrant
was henceforth passed without punishment, as if he had been
Irish !

Farming the Vagrants

We have incidentally described the method by which, under
the Vagrancy Acts, the vagrant was, after punishment, conveyed
to his place of settlement, from stage to stage, in the custody of
successive parish constables, whose expenses were reimbursed by
the county treasurer, at rates fixed by Quarter Sessions.[2] But

---

[1] " When strangers come to London ", the clerk to the magistrates at
Guildhall explained in 1815, " they either send them to the sitting Alderman
or to the Lord Mayor, for the purpose of being relieved, sent to Bridewell and
passed to their parishes ; they are not sent to Bridewell by way of punishment ;
some may be in a state of sickness, and I understand there is a regular physician
and an apothecary to attend them, and they have every medical advice, and
every assistance that can be given to them " (Report of Select Committee
of the House of Commons on the State of Mendicity in the Metropolis, 1815,
p. 14).

[2] By an Act of 1702 (1 Anne, st. 2, c. 13) " it was provided that in future
the Justices, at the Easter Quarter Sessions, should be empowered ' to ascertain
and set down the several Rates that shall be for the year ensuing to be allowed
for maintaining, conveying and carrying vagrants '. This clause appears
to have been put in action as a piece of useful legislation, and many entries
in the Order Books of various counties gives the rates that were fixed by the
Justices. At Middlesex the rates were fixed as follows in 1703 : 6d. for maintaining a vagrant twenty-four hours, 6d. for conveying a vagrant a mile by
horse and carriage, or by cart ; and for conveying a vagrant by foot, less than
6d. a mile, at the discretion of the Justice. At Hertford, in 1719, the rates
were : for a single person for one night, 4d. ; for a man and his wife, or for
two men or two women together, 6d. ; and 2d. apiece for children. If the
said vagrants were not to be lodged for the night, but merely passed straight

though Quarter Sessions might fix the rates, it needed a much more systematic audit of the bills of the illiterate parish constables than the individual magistrates could be induced to give, to prevent overcharges and irregularities. At the beginning of the eighteenth century we find thrifty Quarter Sessions entering into contracts for the conveyance of all vagrants required to be passed during a specified period. As the century proceeds, references to such contracts multiply in the Quarter Session records, and many counties " seem to have adopted some such arrangement for the transport of vagrants through their confines. In the case of Devon, the decision to employ a contractor was reached after ' mature deliberation ', because great numbers of vagrants were brought into the little town of Axminster, ' to be received by the proper officers of that place and by them conveyed unto the town in the next county, and other remote places '. The result of the ' great numbers of such vagrants and their frequent and sudden coming ' was that the officers were ' disturbed and hindered in the managery of their affaires, trades, and professions '—to avoid which, Quarter Sessions made a contract with one, John Crosse, of Axminster, clothier, for £40 a year, which was to include his ' Labour, care, pains, expences, and disbursements '. This contract was entered into in 1708, and appears to have been due to the increased numbers passed, owing to the vagrancy laws of the last reign. In the same year, 1708, the Buckinghamshire Justices, being suspicious of the accuracy of the bills presented by the constables, contracted with two persons to convey vagrants for £80 a year. It was usual for one contractor not to take over all the vagrants of the county, but only those who came, or had to be conveyed along a certain route. For example, the North Riding Justices

---

on, the constable was only to have half these sums, except on extraordinary occasions. They were also to be allowed 3d. a mile for a vagrant conveyed by horse, and 6d. a mile for a cart with a horse and driver, in addition to 1s. 6d. per day for their own labour " (*The English Poor in the Eighteenth Century*, by Dorothy Marshall, 1926, p. 241). At the Wilts Quarter Sessions in 1808, it was ordered that the rates to be allowed should be 4d. per mile for conveying one or two, and 3d. per mile each for any greater number (MS. Minutes, Quarter Sessions, Wiltshire, Hilary 1808). In 1833 Gloucestershire allowed 4d. per mile for each vagrant and for each constable together with the same rate for the constable returning ; subsistence for the constable at the rate of 3s. 6d. per day and 1s. 6d. for each night ; and for the vagrants 6d. per day for each adult, 3d. per day for each child under nine, and the cost of the night's lodging (MS. Minutes, Quarter Sessions, Gloucestershire, Michaelmas, 1833).

ordered the Treasurer ' to pay John Raper of Langthorpe £20 per quarter for the conveying all vagrants that shall come to Kirkby, to Nesame, or other places according to the usual custom and John Raper to give security to perform the agreement '. Two years later it was agreed to reduce his allowance to £60 a year." [1] So in 1783, at the Buckinghamshire Epiphany Sessions, we read that " At this Sessions, J. B. and R. B. entered into an agreement to convey all vagrants from Olney Stoke, Coldington, Stony Stratford and Little Buckhill, at £120 per year, payable quarterly, clear of all deductions ".[2] On what legal authority such a contract rested we cannot now discover. But in 1792 Parliament declared that the mode of conveying vagrants in the custody of a constable was frequently found unsatisfactory " from the misconduct and negligence of constables ", and the Justices in Quarter Sessions were empowered to place the service in the hands of the master of the House of Correction or his servants, and also to make rules and orders on the subject.[3] Under this Act the system of " farming " the vagrants became universal. The contractors, in return for a specified lump sum per annum, and a daily allowance for food, undertook the whole service of detaining, conveying and maintaining all the vagrants passed from a particular county. The Justices were so troubled by the impositions and frauds of the parish constables, and the carelessness with which individual

---

[1] *The English Poor in the Eighteenth Century*, by Dorothy Marshall, 1926, pp. 142-143.

[2] MS. Minutes, Quarter Sessions, Buckinghamshire, Epiphany 1783.

[3] 32 George III. c. 45 ; *History of the English Poor Law*, by Sir George Nicholls, 1854, vol. ii. p. 103 ; *History of Vagrants and Vagrancy*, by C. J. Ribton-Turner, 1887, p. 212. By 1772, " the first year for which we have any reliable figures, from the extracts of returns made by the clerks of the peace and other officers concerning vagrants, we find that Bedford was spending £164 : 11 : 6 a year ; Berks, £183 : 12 : 10 ; Bucks, £303 : 9 : 11 ; Cambridge, £114 : 10 : 10 ; Ely, £55 : 3 : 5 ; Chester, £482 : 12 : 10 ; Cornwall, £47 : 17 : 9, for which it had to thank its geographical position ; Cumberland, gives no figures ; Derby, £254 : 3 : 10 ; Devon, £340 : 10 : 10 ; Dorset, £43 : 6 : 7 ; Durham, £230 : 3 : 4 ; Essex, £311 : 16 : 9½ ; Gloucester, £697 : 9 : 2 ; and Hants, £120 : 0 : 4, in passing vagrants. The other counties were spending sums of about the same amount " (*The English Poor in the Eighteenth Century*, by Dorothy Marshall, 1926, p. 242). The total for the whole country must have exceeded £12,000 for the year. In the course of the next fifty years this sum seems to have been quadrupled. The Middlesex contractor alone was, in 1815, " passing " 12,000 or 13,000 a year, often the same persons several times within twelve months (House of Commons Committee on Mendicity in the Metropolis, 1815, pp. 115, 125).

magistrates would pass their accounts for payment, that they gladly adopted the contract system. In 1789, and again in 1792, we find the West Riding Justices entering into " a fresh contract for conveying vagrants through and out of the said West Riding ".[1] Such contracts are mentioned again in 1810, but they seem to have been temporarily abandoned, for, in 1822, it needed a special resolution to resume them. " The Court having taken into consideration the flagrant abuses in the maintenance and conveyance of vagrants, and the enormous and increasing expense to the Riding consequent thereon, have resolved to revert to the old system of conveying vagrants by contract, the contractor engaging to supply each vagrant with a sufficient quantity of household bread, viz. each full grown person 1½ lb. and each child under 12 years of age, 1 lb. per day, and on no account to give money or any other kind of food to any vagrant unless in cases of sickness." [2] In Middlesex, where the business was greater than elsewhere, the contractor had over a thousand vagrants a month through his hands. He was paid at first £250, and latterly £350 a year, with an addition of sixpence a day for the maintenance of each vagrant for a period not exceeding three days. For this sum he conveyed all vagrants delivered to him to the borders of the county, where he handed them over to the vagrant contractors for the adjoining counties, who conveyed them similarly through these counties. His establishment consisted of seven horses, four men and a boy, three carts and two covered vans, with four receiving houses at Egham, Colnbrook, Rudge and Cheshunt respectively.[3] This system of " farming the vagrants " seems to have had, in comparison with direct employment of the constable or the master of the House of Correction, much the same advantages and disadvantages as we have described in " farming the workhouse ". It saved the Justices practically all trouble in the checking of the accounts of illiterate constables, and prevented irregular charges. It relieved the constables of a burdensome personal service. On the other hand, the contractor's receiving houses, and his arrangements for maintaining the vagrants, closely resembled, in their combination of dirt, disorder and

[1] *Leeds Intelligencer*, April 14, 1789, and April 9, 1792.
[2] MS. Minutes, Quarter Sessions, West Riding of Yorkshire, April 30, 1822.
[3] Report from Select Committee of the House of Commons on the State of Mendicity in the Metropolis, 1815, pp. 59-60.

laxness of discipline, those of the typical farmed workhouse of
the middle of the eighteenth century. Thus, when the Middlesex
Justices in 1818 appointed a committee to visit the contractor's
premises, the committee reported with frigid restraint " that
they have . . . viewed the place provided by the contractor for
conveying of vagrants for the reception of vagrants at his house,
and are clearly of opinion that the same is not in a proper
condition for their reception, and that males and females are not
separated. . . . Your Committee have viewed the carts used by
the contractor for conveying the vagrants, and report they are
improper for the conveyance of vagrants." [1] In 1821 these
Middlesex " pass-houses " were described to the House of
Commons Committee as places of indescribable insanitation,
overcrowding and promiscuity.[2] The " Liverpool Pass House ",
where the Irish vagrants were kept whilst waiting for shipment
back to Ireland, was found in 1829 to be in a terrible state of
filth and disorder.[3]

The Free Pass

Meanwhile the Justices had gradually elaborated a simple way
of satisfying the importunities of wandering mendicants and poor
travellers, without using their powers under the Vagrancy Acts.
It seems to have been common, throughout the whole of the
eighteenth century, for a Justice of the Peace, and apparently
any other person of authority or position, to give a sort of written
passport, or certificate of character, to poor persons setting out
on a journey. Discharged soldiers and sailors would be furnished
with certificates by their officers, and licences by a Justice of the
Peace, authorising them to travel to their destination and ask
such relief as their necessities might require.[4] Gradually the

---

[1] MS. Minutes, Quarter Sessions, Middlesex, January 15, 1818.
[2] Report of Select Committee of the House of Commons on Vagrancy, 1821.
[3] See the full report in the printed *Proceedings of the Court of Annual General
Session for the County Palatine of Lancashire*, Preston, 1829.
[4] 39 Eliz. c. 17 had enacted " that every idle and wandering soldier or
mariner who, coming from the seas, shall not have a testimonial under the
hand of a Justice of the Peace, setting down therein the place and time where
and when he landed, and the place of his dwelling or birth into which he is to
pass, and a convenient time limited therein for his passage ; or having such a
testimonial shall wilfully exceed the time therein limited above fourteen days
. . . shall be guilty of felony ". This provision was abrogated in 1792 by
32 George III. c. 45, sec. 7, but was specifically re-enacted in 1803 (43 George III.
c. 61), and continued by the Act of 1824 (5 George IV. c. 83).

practice grew up of Justices granting similar passes to all sorts
of poor travellers, requiring " all Justices, mayors, bailiffs,
constables, etc., to suffer the bearer peaceably and quietly to
pass to the parish therein named without let, hindrance or
molestation whatsoever, he demeaning himself orderly, keeping
the post-road and not exceeding the space of [so many days]
from the date thereof to accomplish his journey ".[1] This became
what Dr. Burn described in 1764 as " that pernicious practice
. . . of pestering the kingdom with itinerant passes. Permit
such a one to pass to such a place, and relieve him with necessaries
as to you shall seem meet. Of which there are printed forms in
almost every corporation ; and every tradesman or handicraftsman that has the honour to be advanced to the mayoralty is
proud to let the world know it, by subscribing his name to
them. . . . The validity of these passports is no more than this :
An Act of Parliament says, such a person shall be taken up as
a rogue and vagabond. A Justice of the Peace says, permit him
to pass : that is, with a *non-obstante* to the said Act of Parliament." [2] Though these travelling passes had apparently no legal
validity, we gather that they were, in practice, so far respected
that peaceful wanderers thus certificated were not, as a rule,
apprehended as vagrants ; and it was even customary for the
constable or Overseer of each place to honour them by giving
their bearers a few pence by way of relief. A parish would
occasionally order that no such relief should be given. Thus, at
Dursley in 1738, " it is agreed at a Publick Vestry that no
Churchwarden or Overseer shall be allowed to give anything to
travellers on ye parish account ".[3] At Brislington, near Bristol,
the Vestry ordered in 1739 " that no parish officer do for the
future relieve any vagrant or vagrants, or other travelling person
or persons, with passes or otherwise, in order to discourage
strollers and other loose, idle and disorderly persons from
strolling from their own parishes ".[4] On the other hand, the

---

[1] See the report of the case, St. Lawrence Jewry *v.* Edgware, in Bott's
Decisions of the Court of King's Bench on Poor Law, edited by Ed. Const, 1793,
p. 790. The editor adds: " Although there does not appear to have been any
determination upon this subject, the legality of such passes may be doubted."

[2] *The History of the Poor Laws*, by Richard Burn, 1764, p. 119.

[3] MS. Vestry Minutes, Dursley (Gloucestershire), September 24, 1738 ; see
Dursley and its Neighbourhood, by J. H. Blunt, 1877, p. 46.

[4] Vestry Minutes, Brislington, near Bristol, 1739 ; quoted in *History of
Vagrants and Vagrancy*, by C. J. Ribton-Turner, 1887, p. 198.

local Justices—perhaps feeling uncomfortable at having sturdy tramps in their neighbourhood without food—would (as we learn in Buckinghamshire at the beginning of the nineteenth century) order the constable to give sixpence or a shilling to poor travellers, to whom the Overseer had refused relief. Usually the Overseer consented to reimburse the constable, out of the Poor Rate. In 1815 some of the Overseers refused to do so, claiming that such payments, being in the nature of expenses connected with vagrancy, ought to fall on the County Rate. Counsel's opinion was taken on the point by Quarter Sessions, who advised that nothing but payments in strict compliance with the Vagrancy Act could be charged to the County Rate, and that relief given by magistrate's order to travelling soldiers and sailors, and their wives and families, and to other destitute wanderers, must be treated as Poor Relief.[1]

That the practice of issuing travelling passes continued and was frequently adopted, even by stipendiary magistrates, we learn from Dr. Colquhoun himself. " Of late ", said he in 1815, " it is inconceivable the number that have received passes from the magistrates to go to their different parishes, which we give now, though directly in opposition to the Act of 1792, which requires they should be previously whipped or imprisoned a certain number of days, and then passed as vagrants to their parishes. It arose from the Lord Mayor and the magistrates giving innumerable passes, of which I am afraid many make the very worst use, but we are very glad to get them out of the town, that they may be subsisted in the quarters to which they belong, or where they have friends. In that way we are relieved of a very considerable number, who must otherwise beg in the streets ; the number of mendicants must have been much greater if we had not given those passes so freely." [2] This flagrant disregard of the law called forth, in 1817, the furious denunciation of Edward Christian, then Chief-Justice of the Isle of Ely. " The Act of 32 Geo. III. c. 45 ", he said, " was drawn by myself. At that time, as was stated in the preamble, a regular vagrant pass was substituted for a regular order of removal. That was a great fraud, and attended with many mischiefs ; but now,

---

[1] MS. Minutes, Quarter Sessions, Buckinghamshire, Michaelmas 1815.
[2] Report from Select Committee of House of Commons on the State of Mendicity in the Metropolis, 1815, p. 54.

what is definitely worse, many Justices give to poor persons when applying to them, a piece of paper which is called a travelling or permit pass. This . . . is a perfect nullity, a mockery of justice, a great violation of law, a fraud upon the poor objects to whom it is given, as they obtain no certain assistance from it, a great fraud upon the townships through which they travel, a fraud upon the place to which they are sent, and the greatest possible nuisance to the kingdom at large . . . I am obliged to say that every Justice of the Peace who signs such a paper is guilty of a great misdemeanour."[1] But all denunciation of the Justices for giving these passes failed to stop the practice. In 1816 the Lord Mayor complained to the Secretary of State that his time was almost wholly taken up in relieving destitute soldiers, sailors and artisans, of whom he had before him sometimes " two hundred in a day, of whom the greater number have come from Wapping and the out-parishes, and not one in twenty has slept in the City of London. . . . Sixteen of these poor men have come and deposed that they were taken from a brick kiln and sent to the House of Correction, where they were detained nineteen days, and then discharged without being passed. I have sent within fourteen days eighty to the Bridewell to be passed to their respective parishes, the greater number of whom were sailors, and scarcely one of them had slept within the City of London, but had lodged in Wapping and the neighbourhood, and were found begging on London and Blackfriars Bridges."[2] In 1821 a clerical Justice living at Hampstead, who gave hundreds of passes annually, frankly explained to the House of Commons Committee the motives which impelled him to take this entirely extra-legal course. Whenever " a broken-down tradesman " or " once-respectable character " came before him, he thought it highly improper to send such person to the House of Correction—" a very iniquitous school ". He preferred to give what he called " a walking pass ".[3] Parliament tried once more to stop these passes by expressly forbidding their issue in the Acts of 1822 and 1824. But it left open the

---

[1] See *A Collection of the Several Points of Sessions Law*, by Rev. S. Clapham, 1818, vol. ii. p. 41.

[2] The Lord Mayor (Matthew Wood) to Lord Sidmouth, November 16, 1816; Minutes of Common Council of London, November 19, 1816.

[3] Report of Select Committee of House of Commons on Vagrancy, 1821, p. 38 (Evidence of Rev. H. B. Owen).

loophole that they were to be given to soldiers, sailors, marines and their wives ; and it is clear that the passes were not wholly discontinued in other cases. The practice was in full vogue in the South-western Counties in 1824–1834, notably in Cornwall and Somerset.[1] Parishes and Justices alike objected to the cost involved by the apprehension and imprisonment of vagrants, which often reached forty shillings before the culprit had been twenty-four hours in detention. As an alternative, saving both money and trouble, the local Justices freely gave travelling passes, specifying a sum of a penny-halfpenny a mile as the sum to be given to the traveller by each parish visited.[2] Many places, however, as we shall presently describe, were beginning to refuse any such payments, and offering to the destitute traveller, as to any other able-bodied applicant, a task of work.[3]

The Vagrant's Free Conveyance.

At last, after nearly three centuries of costly experience, the House of Commons nerved itself to the bold step of abandoning the principle of passing vagrants to their places of settlement. The evidence before the Select Committee of 1821 had made it clear that, so far from relieving the towns from the presence of vagrants, the passing system served only to multiply them. It was estimated that at least 60,000 were perpetually circulating up and down the country at the public expense. " The system of conveyance by pass ", it was reported, " has been found to be one of inefficiency, cozenage and fraud ; it is in complete

[1] *Extracts concerning the Prevalence of Vagrancy in some of the Western Counties of England*, Shaftesbury, 1827.

[2] The Gloucester Incorporated Guardians appointed a special officer " to attend to the relief of vagrants ", at £30 a year (MS. Minutes, Incorporated Guardians, Gloucester, March 1, 1827).

[3] Report of Poor Law Inquiry Commissioners, 1834, Appendix B, Chapman's Report, p. 45. At Bath, the plague of mendicants had led to the establishment of a voluntary society ; see *Annual Reports of the Bath Society for the Suppression of Vagrants, Street Beggars and Impostors*, etc., Bath, 1811–1813. Like societies were afterwards formed in Dorsetshire and elsewhere ; see *A Brief Inquiry concerning institutions for relief of poor travellers and houseless strangers . . . with some further account of a Mendicity Society in Dorsetshire*, etc., by William West, Manchester, 1831. For similar philanthropic activity in the Metropolis see *Letter to Lord Pelham on the State of Mendicity in the Metropolis*, 1803 ; *Substance of a Letter dated . . . 1803 to . . . Lord Pelham on the State of Mendicity in the Metropolis*, 1811 ; *An Appeal to Public Benevolence for the Relief of Beggars with a view to a Plan for the Suppression of Beggary*, 1812—all by Matthew Martin.

consonance with the wandering habits of vagrants, and is made
a matter of trade.   Their returns to the same place are frequent,
and some of them within periods which evidently show that
they could not have reached their parishes."   By this system,
it was said, " a vagrant is enabled to migrate at the expense
of the public, by putting himself in the way of apprehension,
and he thus obtains a pleasurable jaunt to any part of the
kingdom he may choose.   If during his progress he wishes to
change company or vary his route, no impediment prevents
him, it being understood equally by the offender and the officer
who has him in charge that he is under no control.   He has his
summer and his winter haunts, to which he repairs at stated
periods ; and he has been known to remark, ' Why should
I work for 1s. or 1s. 6d. a day while I can be thus amused
by seeing and laughing at the labour of others ? ' conveyed
free of expense, and in a state of perfect indolence with an
allowance . . . from the county stock ".[1]   This emphatic testimony, though amounting to no more than had been repeatedly
urged for at least half a century, seems to have impelled the
House of Commons to immediate action.   By a temporary Act
of 1822, made permanent by another of 1824, the whole law of
vagrancy was once more codified and rendered more comprehensive, with the significant omission of all provisions for passing
the ordinary vagrant to his place of settlement.   Henceforth,
if Parliament could secure it, he was to be treated as an ordinary
criminal, tried summarily without a jury, and imprisoned with
hard labour.[2]   If he became destitute he was to apply to the
parish officer and be dealt with under the Poor Law, and, if need
be, " removed " to his place of settlement as a pauper.   Unfortunately, though Parliament laid down this principle, it was
weak enough to make exceptions.   Prisoners discharged from
prison might be granted by the Visiting Justices certificates
authorising them, the bearers, to beg their way to their homes.
Soldiers, sailors, marines and their wives were also to be given

---

[1] Report of Select Committee of the House of Commons on Vagrancy, 1821.
[2] The Acts of 1822–1824 were thought by some to be an undue infringement
on personal liberty ; see, for instance, the *Observations on the Vagrant Act*, by
John Adolphus, 1824, replied to by *The Vagrant Act in relation to the Liberty
of the Subject*, by a Barrister, 1824, who also wrote a *Letter to an M.P.* on the
Impropriety of classing players with rogues and vagabonds in the Vagrant Act,
1824.   See also *Historical Review of the Poor and Vagrant Laws*, 1838.

licences to beg. Here were two large classes of " trampers "
authorised by express statute. What was even more detrimental
to the desired reform was the continuance of the system of
" passing without punishment " of natives of Scotland, Ireland
and the Channel Isles. As these places had no complete system
of Poor Relief, on the English lines, it was impossible simply
to " remove " their inhabitants to their places of settlement
as paupers, for they had no places of settlement. The House
of Commons could neither face the situation of letting these
immigrants get relief where they happened to be, nor yet discover any other method of dealing with them than the passing
system, which was therefore continued in force.

These unwise exemptions—and especially the latter one—
nullified the whole Act. The habitual vagrants simply declared
themselves to belong to Ireland or Jersey, or gave an address in
Glasgow or the Isle of Man, and remained gaily on the road.
Their numbers even continued to increase. The lenient magistrates of the City of London, besides issuing, as we have seen,
innumerable licences to beg, committed forty a week in 1829,
and no fewer than three times that number in 1832. Buckinghamshire had to convey an average of more than three thousand
presumed Scotch and Irish vagrants every year. Lancashire in
1828 found over eighty handed over to it by the neighbouring
contractors every week ; and in 1831 was actually shipping more
than a hundred a week to Dublin, whilst seventy a week were
shipped from Bristol, nearly all of whom had been conveyed in
carts from London.[1] Loud and frequent grew the complaints of
the counties at the failure of Parliament to stop this abominable
imposition. " Magistrates ", complain the Northamptonshire
Justices in 1830, " are empowered to pass vagrants to Ireland
and Scotland, as well as Jersey and Guernsey, at the expense of
the counties through which the road lies. . . . This expense has
been rapidly increased for some years. . . . The number of Irish
vagrants passed through the county of Northampton to Ireland
in the year ending Easter 1825 was 797, and the cost of conveying them only 23 miles into the county of Warwick was
£209. . . . In the last year ending at Easter 1829 (it) amounted

---

[1] Report of Select Committee of the House of Commons on Scotch and
Irish Vagrants, 1828 ; House of Commons Returns, 1833 ; *History of Vagrants
and Vagrancy*, by C. J. Ribton-Turner, 1887, pp. 239-242.

to 1651, and the charge to the county was £537, having more than doubled . . . in the course of five years. . . . There is the best ground for believing that the abuses and imposition which were a chief cause of the repeal of the general English Vagrant Act prevail at least to the same extent with respect to those cases which were excepted from that repeal. The same persons are known to be frequently passed by the same route, more especially between the Metropolis and Ireland. It is indeed become almost a trade by which men subsist. When landed in Ireland, instead of proceeding to their homes, they return by the first conveyance to England and find their way again to London, where they well know that they will be subject to very little investigation in obtaining a fresh pass, thus procuring a comfortable subsistence in idleness for a large portion of their time at the public expense. And with respect to the Jersey and Guernsey vagrants the numbers alone are sufficient proof that great imposition is practised, either by the means above detailed, or by the persons, with the like views, falsely swearing that they are connected with these islands ; for it is impossible to believe that 132 persons born in these islands (besides others passed by other routes) can have fallen into distress and become vagrant in the Northern counties in the space of one year. . . . The counties through which these vagrants are passed, though subject to the expense, have no check or control whatever over these proceedings, it being by law imperative upon the magistrates in these counties to receive and forward all such persons as shall be brought to them by the proper authorities ; while it is to be remembered that the magistrates who originally grant the passes, being only anxious to remove the burden of maintaining such persons from their own districts, have no interest whatever in protecting the intermediate counties." [1] Notwithstanding this and other clear expositions of the evils, and innumerable complaints of the expense of the conveyance of these vagrants, the administration of the service underwent no improvement. In Middlesex, in 1825, it was found that " there is no contract in writing between the county and the passmaster for paupers. . . . The paupers are brought by the parish officers

---

[1] Entered in full in MS. Minutes, Quarter Sessions, Middlesex, April 22, 1830 ; see as to similar abuses in Cumberland, *Worthies of Cumberland*, by Henry Lonsdale, vol. ii., 1868, pp. 78-79.

to the passmaster, and by him imprisoned on his premises for one, two or more days at his own discretion, until he collects a number for removal. . . . The premises are altogether too small, and are close, confined and filthy, and serve to house the pass-master's numerous family, a cow, pigs, poultry, etc. : these, added to numerous paupers, must, as a natural consequence, produce bad air and render the place unwholesome." [1] Another House of Commons Committee in 1828 brought to light the same impositions, and the same sort of scandalous laxity, extravagance and disorder.[2] In Cumberland a year later the Clerk of the Peace laid before the Michaelmas Quarter Sessions a long and able report, exposing the gross frauds practised on the county by these vagrants, who made a regular living by getting "passed" to the Border as Scotch ; then dispersing near the Solway, and going back to the Midland Counties or London, in order to get "passed" again.[3] Even the *bona fide* Scotch and Irish " vagrants ", who thus obtained free passages to their homes, often carried with them considerable sums of money, and " large bundles, band boxes, and even trunks and chests containing property. . . . These people, especially the Scotch, stand up for their rights very much ; they often refuse to get out of the carts to walk up hill, and insist upon carrying all sorts of luggage. . . . Women, too, will often make great difficulties because they think", says the passmaster, "I do not take sufficient care of their bonnet-boxes, large paste-board boxes, in which they have fine bonnets with plenty of ribbands." [4]

Here we drop the story for the present volume. As with the Law of Settlement and Removal, so with the Vagrancy Acts, the problems and the complications, together with the very serious effects of the practice upon the whole system of Poor Relief, were left, as unsettled questions, to be considered by the Royal Commission which Lord Grey's Ministry appointed in 1832.

---

[1] MS. Minutes, Quarter Sessions, Middlesex, November 3, 1825.
[2] Report of the Select Committee on Irish and Scottish Vagrants, 1828.
[3] See the report in full in *The Northern Year Book for 1829*, Newcastle, 1830.
[4] See the evidence of the " passmasters " of St. Giles in the Fields, St. Luke's, Middlesex, and the City of London, *History of Vagrants and Vagrancy*, by C. J. Ribton-Turner, 1887, p. 241.

CHAPTER VII

CONCLUSIONS

THE " Laws relating to the Poor ", reaching from the Dark Ages
to the Poor Law Amendment Act of 1834, whether administered
by the King, his Council and his Parliament, or by Parish Vestries,
incorporated guardians, municipal authorities and County
Justices, included within their sphere two distinct and in some
ways conflicting functions—maintaining those who were destitute,
and punishing the idle and the turbulent. Hence they may be
epitomised as the " Relief of the Poor within a Framework of
Repression " ; or, if a less pedantic phrase be preferred, as
" Charity in the grip of Serfdom ".

The Six Stages of the Old Poor Law

Our conclusions about the working of " The Old Poor Law "
(as it came to be called) may be prefaced by a brief recital of its
chronological development. For this purpose we divide the
whole era into six periods, taking for each phase the ideas and
purposes that were dominant, rather than any actual achievement in practice, and remembering that these successively
dominant ideas and purposes inevitably overlapped one another.

We have, first, the period in which the main object—indeed,
we may almost say the sole object—of the King's Government,
the King's Council, and what was becoming the Parliament of
the nation, was the repression of vagrancy, of the disorder and
turbulence to which it led, and of the insubordination and idleness which it encouraged, whether or not these were incidental
to destitution ; whilst leaving any provision for the destitute to
the Church and the alms of the charitable. Prior to the legislation of the Tudors, what were called the " Laws relating to

the Poor " were, in fact, wholly concerned with keeping the propertyless man, and especially the new class of free labourers, at the disposal and under the control of the feudal hierarchy. Thus, the celebrated Statute of Labourers (1350) arbitrarily fixed the wages and hours for each category of labourers and craftsmen, and penalised any attempt on their part to take advantage of their economic strength to obtain greater payment or a shorter working day. Sumptuary laws forbade to the wage-earners the food and clothing deemed too luxurious for them, and prohibited for their children any education other than re-ligious teaching, whilst statute after statute, always striving after increased severity, punished vagrancy in all its forms and with all its concomitants. All persons without property who were either unable or unwilling to work for their livelihood on their masters' terms were, in fact, legally thrust back into virtual serfdom ; they " belonged " to the land on which they were born or settled ; they were liable to punishment if found outside their own parish without a permit or a pass from one or other of its authorities, and they could, if able-bodied and masterless, be bound to work for a selected employer and compelled to obey his orders under pain of physical chastisement. Down to the sixteenth century, observed Fowle, " it cannot be said that Poor Laws, in our sense of the word (*i.e.*, measures for the relief of destitution) existed at all ; they might more fittingly be called laws against the poor and the rights of labour ".[1]

It is out of this repressive legislation and arbitrary adminis-tration—tempered, it is true, by the charity of individuals or of the Church—that the vast system of public provision for the needs of the propertyless citizen, characteristic of the twentieth century, has directly sprung. Not until 1536, although the English Poor Laws provided that the able-bodied destitute man without a master could be virtually enslaved, was there any provision by public officers, even for the orphans and the sick, the aged and the impotent, who had from time immemorial been left to be supported by Christian charity. It was only when it became apparent that this Christian charity not only was inadequate to maintain even all the meritorious poor, but was also responsible for creating fresh masses of shameless mendicancy—indeed, only when it was realised that it was

[1] *The Poor Law*, by T. W. Fowle, 1881, p. 55.

hopeless to prevent crime and suppress vagrancy in the new class of free labourers if they were allowed to go hungry—that the dangerous unrest and chronic rebellion forced the Government and Parliament to intervene. It was for these reasons, rather than out of any considerations of humanity, that successive statutes cast the responsibility for the maintenance of the indigent poor on the ecclesiastical parish, and for that purpose ordered that, under the orders of the Justices of the Peace, a new civil officer—the Overseer of the Poor—should be jointly responsible with the Churchwarden for relieving the destitute. This second period, in which the public relief of the destitute was inaugurated, whilst the framework of repression of the able-bodied was still felt to be more vital, as it was certainly more obtrusive, than the relief of distress, may be said to have begun and ended with the kingship of the Tudors.

The third period is that described in our chapter on the Administrative Hierarchy, extending from about 1590 for only half a century—an episode which might be described as a premature attempt at a nationalised Poor Law. In this period we see Burleigh and his fellow Privy Councillors, with the active co-operation of the Bishops—later with the special assistance of Archbishop Laud—making it a fundamental principle of their statecraft that the Government should undertake the protection as well as the control of the mass of propertyless persons. The nobles and gentry who owned the land were made responsible, as Justices of the Peace and masters of the parish, not only for maintaining order and repressing crime, but also for ensuring an adequate supply of food at low prices, with a greater regularity of employment; and, more lastingly, by insisting on the levy and expenditure of a Poor Rate, for preventing unemployment among the able-bodied, and destitution among the orphans, the sick, the aged and the infirm. However ineffective this guardianship may have been in practice, the theory of the English Poor Law established by Burleigh under Elizabeth, and his successors in the Privy Council of the first two Stuart kings, was plainly that, whilst all the poor should be compelled to earn their livelihood, all the children should be educated, all the sick people should be relieved, and all the aged people should be maintained, wherever necessary, at the expense of the Poor Rate. To the powerful caste of landed gentry as well as to the wealthy

merchants of London and other incorporated towns, the autocratic rule of the King as God's Regent, in the hands of an
energetic Privy Council and the Star Chamber, may have seemed
an intolerable infringement of customary rights and acquired
freedoms. To the landless man or indigent widow, the King
in Council may have appeared as the Father of his People. In
pursuance of this conception of statecraft, the Privy Council
developed an administrative hierarchy, based on the obligation
of the parish and its officers, which strangely forecasts the Poor
Law organisation of the nineteenth century. This centralised
supervision and control of the local Justices and parish officers
by a national authority was, however, unpopular, and, as may
be said, uncongenial to the spirit of the nation, as this was reflected in the County Justices and Town Councillors. It was,
accordingly, entirely abandoned on the outbreak of the Civil
War, towards which, indeed, this enforcement of an obligation
on the property owners to relieve the necessities of the poor,
along lines laid down by Whitehall, may have contributed its
own quota by way of discontent with the so-called " Personal
Government " of the King.

The fourth period, extending from the Restoration right
into the last quarter of the eighteenth century, is one of significantly mixed character. The short spell of administrative
hierarchy was succeeded by a couple of centuries of complete
local autonomy. The framework of repression was maintained,
and was even strengthened by the Law of Settlement and Removal, and the constantly repeated Vagrancy Acts. But the
distinguishing feature of the English Poor Law for the last quarter
of the seventeenth century is the outburst of a characteristic
philanthropy, which combined a widespread but haphazard provision for the impotent poor by weekly doles of money, with a
persistent belief that it was possible to make a profit out of the
labour of those men, women and children who could be set to
work. This involved new forms of provision and additional
instruments of compulsion, which were called Houses of Industry
when one of their aspects was emphasised, and Houses of Correction or Bridewells when another side of their function came
into view. But all sorts of institutions served the same end—
the old parish poorhouses converted into spinning-schools ;
mixed General Workhouses in which such of the men, women and

children as were able were put to primitive manufactures; extensive workshops in which rows of children were made to spin or to knit; and establishments under various names not differing essentially from the prisons of the period, usually farmed out to contractors who acted in the double capacity of employers and gaolers.

Presently there came a variety of this administrative attitude, which may be regarded as a fifth series of expedients. The development of the Industrial Revolution in the latter part of the eighteenth century, with the advent of the power-driven machine industry, made it clear even to the most fanatical believer in " setting the poor to work " in the " gaols without guilt ", as the Workhouses and Houses of Industry were termed, that there was a less expensive way of compelling the poor to earn their keep. The new capitalist entrepreneurs were so eager for workers to fill their mills that they would even spend money to obtain their services. It became possible, not only for the Government, but also for the Parish, to stand aside, and to leave the enforcement of work and discipline upon the poor to the more persistent and more minutely detailed authority of the employer. We see the Vestries and parish officers, who had already found it convenient to " farm out " the management of their workhouses, now farming out the poor in all sorts of ways. The children are not only " apprenticed " to any parishioner desirous of obtaining a household drudge without wages; but also disposed of by the score or by the hundred to the new cotton mills. The adult men are compulsorily assigned to any employers who will take them for their keep; or they will be billeted out in turn among all the farmers in the parish, in one or other form of the Roundsman system. In one way or another the Parish sought to transfer to some employer—if need be, by compulsory allocation—the duty of enforcing labour and discipline on the poor; and the steadily increasing capitalist developments in industry and agriculture seemed to enable this to be done with all but those who were completely impotent.

The close of the eighteenth century brings us to a sixth and final stage when, principally in the rural districts south of a line from the Wash to the Severn, but extending also to one or other section of the manufacturing industries in the Midlands and the Northern Counties, not even the most enterprising

or the most close-fisted employer would take on the unemployed
labourer at any wage on which, at the swollen price of food,
he and his family could possibly exist. This brought the
country gentlemen and the farmers face to face with what
seemed an insoluble problem. The farmer in the south of
England demonstrated that, with the rental and under the
conditions upon which the land was owned and let, he could
not possibly afford to pay his labourers a living wage. The
kind-hearted Justices urged equally benevolent Members of
Parliament to promote legislation securing to the labourers a
wage on which they could exist. But such a legal minimum
wage, it was plain, was inconsistent, both with the manner in
which the English agricultural industry was then organised,
and with the current assumptions of the capitalism of the time.
It was inconceivable, to that generation, either that the fundamental conditions of private property in land could be changed,
or that any departure could be made from the new-found
principle of freedom of competition. Thus, on the one hand,
Parliament and the Government insisted on maintaining an
attitude, as to wages and rents, of *laissez-faire* : on the other
hand, both humanity and prudence counselled that the starving
labourers must not be driven to despair in a country which
had no organised police force to prevent either theft or arson.
The Justices, who had the responsibility for taking immediate
action, found no other solution than that of making up out of
the Poor Rate the farmer's inadequate wages to a sum on which
the labourer and his family could barely subsist—a policy
which Parliament, in effect, ratified in 1796, and which, not
confined to Southern England, nor to agricultural employment,
continued for a whole generation until it was peremptorily
stopped by the Poor Law Commissioners in 1834.

The Success and Failure of " The Old Poor Law "

Some of those who have had the patience to read through
our account of the statutory relief of destitution over three
centuries of English history will wonder whether this sordid
and disheartening business was not a colossal blunder from start
to finish, and whether it would not have been better to leave the
misery of the multitude to the " struggle for existence " and the

2 D

" survival of the fittest ".   But success and failure, it is needless
to say, are relative terms ; and the success or failure of a given
social institution must be estimated, in the main, according to
the aims and interests of its founders.   Judged from the standpoint of the rulers of England, we have no doubt about the
answer.   The relief of destitution practised under the English
Poor Law was not only expedient : it was a State necessity.
We shall not attempt to enumerate all the reasons for this conclusion, seeing that this might mean a survey of the problem of
poverty in all parts of the world, ancient and modern, together
with a consideration of rival expedients, such as the infanticide
of females in China, or the communism inherent in the Hindu
family, and to a lesser extent in the Hindu caste.   The two
main considerations in the England of the Tudor kings, one re-
inforcing the other, were (a) the rise of a new class of men, hence-
forward described by the Legislature under the denomination
of " poor ", that is, propertyless persons who had no claim on
the manor, or on any feudal superior, for subsistence ; and (b)
the prevalence of the Christian ethics, professed by rulers and
ruled alike, insisting on the relief of the suffering of God's poor
as a religious obligation sanctioned by the rewards and penalties
of a future life.

Now the emergence of the class of the unattached " poor "
was brought about, in the main, by the economic changes in the
nation's agriculture, by the requirements of the kings and their
nobles for recruits to their armies, and by the needs of the traders
and manufacturers in the growing towns for manual workers,
to which we may add the recurring epidemics of plague culminating in the Black Death, which limited the supply of both
soldiers and workers.   With the expansion of commerce and the
growth of manufactures, the call for more labour became in-
sistent, and the class of " free " labourers or hired wage-earners
multiplied throughout the land.   The rulers of England, whether
army leaders, landowners or city merchants, as well as the new
manufacturing employers, not infrequently encouraged this
escape of the common people out of serfdom ; a connivance
rewarded by the superior efficiency of the hired man over the
bondsman, not only in war, but also in the development of
agriculture, the improvement of landed estates and profit-making
business of all kinds.   But with the class of " free " labourers

came the destitute. " It is one of the natural consequences of freedom ", wrote Rousseau in explanation of the growth of poverty in great cities, " that those who are left to shift for themselves must sometimes, from either misconduct or misfortune, be reduced to want." Nor was the multiplication of the Have-nots regarded with disfavour by the Haves. " Without a large proportion of poverty ", England was told by the inventor of the modern police system and a leading authority on " the resources of the British Empire ", " there could be no riches, since riches are the offspring of labour, *while labour can result only from a state of poverty.* Poverty is that state and condition in society where the individual has no surplus labour in store, or, in other words, no property or means of subsistence but what is derived from the constant exercise of industry in the various occupations of life. · *Poverty is therefore a most necessary and indispensable ingredient in society, without which nations and communities could not exist in a state of civilisation.* It is the lot of man. It is the source of wealth, since without poverty there could be no labour, there could be no riches, no refinement, no comfort, and no benefit to those who may be possessed of wealth, inasmuch as, without a large proportion of poverty, surplus labour could never be rendered productive in procuring either the convenience or luxuries of life." [1] We remember, in 1911, being startled by an astute Japanese statesman casually observing that the " introduction of the capitalist system into Japan had brought in its train an ever-growing class of destitute persons— a class quite unknown in the old Japan of the daimio and the rice cultivator. This destitution ", he added, with a philosophic smile, " is the price which Japan has had to pay for increasing the personal wealth of her leading citizens, and for becoming a world power."

Whether or not it would have been practicable to maintain the social order requisite for the development of England's power and England's wealth if masses of men, women and children had been left to die of starvation, is open to doubt. But such statecraft was not feasible among a people professing Christianity, more especially the Christianity of mediaeval times, with its naïve faith in the literal interpretation of the Sermon on the Mount. The easiest solution was for the King

[1] *A Treatise on Indigence,* by Patrick Colquhoun, 1806, pp. 7-9

and his Barons to confine themselves to repression and punishment, leaving Christian charity to the Holy Father and his hierarchy. Hence, the service of ministering to the needs of " God's poor " was undertaken, with the approval of the civil authorities, by the Church, and was carried out under the authority of the bishop and the archdeacon by the ecclesiastical parish, aided by the Religious Orders and the personal charity of the faithful.

The Irrelevance of Religious Almsgiving

We need not ask too curiously whether mediaeval almsgiving succeeded in its avowed aims—the development of the charitable impulse in the Christian, and the salvation of his soul from perdition. But regarded from the standpoint of the rulers of England, " giving alms " (as De Foe pointed out two centuries later) proved to be no remedy. In the first place, the almsgiving practised by the parish priest and his congregation, still more the doles distributed at the gates of monastic institutions, depended not on the amount of destitution existing in a given area but on the ebb and flow of religious emotion among churchgoers, and on the geographical distribution of particular monasteries and convents, their financial endowment, and the state of moral and religious discipline of their inmates. Thus, multitudes of poor persons were left unaided. What was presently apparent to the King and his Parliament and to the Justices of the Peace, was that the indiscriminate and unconditional almsgiving practised by the faithful actually intensified the problem, encouraging idleness and fraudulent mendicancy in its near neighbourhood, and generating hordes of vagrants who became an intolerable nuisance, if not danger, to the governing class. Hence we see the Tudor kings and their astute counsellors gradually developing a systematic relief of the indigent, whether orphan, sick or aged, within a framework of compulsory labour for all who could contribute to their own maintenance. Are we wrong in attributing to this ubiquitous public relief of destitution—advancing, as it did, step by step with the growth of a proletariat, a class of hired men without property—the remarkable immunity of England for four centuries from any effective rebellion or drastic revolution ? To this

question, an affirmative answer has been given, over and over
again, by typical representatives of the rulers of England. " Poor
Laws in England grew out of a wish to keep order. To escape
civil war was a supreme blessing. To be free from disorderly
vagrancy was a secondary object of the Government." [1] " I
have often heard Mr. Canning say ", records Lord George Bentinck, " that it was to the Poor Laws of this country that England
owed her successful struggles with Europe and America ; that
they had reconciled the people to their burdens, and have saved
England from revolution." [2] But, passing over these significant
but somewhat casual judgements, let us quote the deliberate
conclusion in 1825—at a time when the Old Poor Law was in
many respects at its worst—of the Political Economist of the
widest knowledge and greatest credit then living. " It would
be visionary indeed ", wrote J. R. McCulloch in 1825, " to
imagine that those who have nothing would quietly submit
to suffer the extremity of want without attacking the property
of others. And hence, if we would preserve unimpaired the
peace, and consequently the prosperity, of the country, we must
beware of allowing any considerable portion of the population to
fall into a state of destitution. But without the establishment
of a compulsory provision for the support of the unemployed
poor, it is difficult to see how they could avoid occasionally
falling into this state. Through its instrumentality, however,
they are sustained in periods of adversity without being driven
of necessity to attack the property of others and commit out-
rages. . . . They [the Poor Laws] are, in fact, a bulwark raised
by the State to protect its subjects from famine and despair,
and whilst they support them in seasons of calamity, and prevent
them from being driven to excesses ruinous alike to themselves
and to others, they do not degrade them by making them
depend on what is often the grudging and stinted charity of
others. . . . Without it [the Poor Law] the peace of society
could not be preserved for any considerable period." [3]

[1] *A Guide to Modern English History*, by William Cory, part ii., 1882,
p. 442.

[2] *Lord George Bentinck*, by Benjamin Disraeli [Earl of Beaconsfield], 1852.

[3] *Principles of Political Economy*, by J. R. McCulloch, 1852, ch. iii., " Poor
Laws " (pp. 406-407, 412 of edition of 1843).

The Status of the Pauper

There remains the question of the relative success and failure of the various methods of relieving destitution described in the foregoing chapters. But before dealing with that question it is essential to put in the front of the picture one fundamental and permanent feature of the English Poor Law—a feature vitally affecting its results, whether we regard these from the angle of the rulers or from that of the ruled. The English Poor Law at no time gave the destitute a personal "right" to relief, in the sense that a mediaeval copyholder had a right to occupy a piece of land or that a modern old-age pensioner has a right to his pension. What was enacted was not a right at all, but an obligation. The Act of the 43rd of Elizabeth cast upon the parish and its officers, and the Justices of the Peace under whom they acted, the obligation to relieve the impotent poor and to provide the able-bodied with the means of earning their livelihood by work. By this legislation, destitution, however caused, was, in effect, adjudged to be a public nuisance, like muck heaps, or vermin, or vagrants ; and this nuisance had to be "abated" in the manner and by the officers prescribed by the law, which was to be enforced by criminal proceedings against officials in default. The applicant for relief could not be a plaintiff in the Law Courts to recover his relief by civil process. Apart from particular statutory provisions of later date, the amount of relief and the manner of relief were left to the discretion of the parish officers, except in so far as these officers were administratively supervised by the Justices of the Peace and the Court of Quarter Sessions. Further, in many of the areas of the Incorporated Boards of Guardians and parishes under Local Acts, the officials under obligation to relieve destitution were also invested, not only with the power to subject to penal conditions the persons whom they relieved, but even to arrest persons not yet destitute, who, in the opinion of these officials, were likely to become destitute or otherwise a nuisance to the public. It is this strange combination of the power to punish with the obligation to relieve from which may be derived the slur always associated with the status of a pauper. It explains the continuance, after the Poor Law Amendment Act of 1834, of what are essentially penal powers in the hands of Boards of Guardians, and also the wholesale exclusion, down to recent years, of persons in receipt of relief from the rights of citizenship. Throughout the whole period dealt with in this volume, persons " without visible means of subsistence ", whether or not they applied for relief, and however their destitution was brought about—whether from old age, sickness or unemployment—underwent, in effect, what Roman Law termed a *capitis diminutio*, and ceased to enjoy the rights of the ordinary citizen. It was no longer a question of relieving the sufferings of " God's poor ". Instead of the pious Christian washing the feet of beggars, whom he would meet in Paradise, a public official was required, at the least cost, to suppress a common nuisance.

This conception of " destitution " as a public nuisance had unforeseen results in the mind of the unpaid and annually elected parish officer. He became obsessed with the notion of ridding his parish of the nuisance at the least possible expense to the ratepayers to whom he was responsible. Seeing that the men, women and children concerned could not be destroyed like choughs and mice, the easiest and cheapest way was to thrust the pauper, or potential pauper, across the parish boundary, into the outer world. Hence the immediate and ever-recurring zeal displayed by the Overseer to put in operation the preposterous law of 1662 for the forcible removal to their places of settlement, of poor persons " not belonging to " his own parish whom he chose to think likely, at some future time, to become chargeable to the parish. Hence the eagerness, a century later, to pervert the Vagrancy Acts into a method of " clearing " the parish of beggars and other " unemployed " persons, by " passing " them, at the expense of the counties that they traversed, round and round the kingdom, and, wherever practicable, pushing them across the border into Scotland, or dispatching them overseas to Ireland or Jersey. The Law of Settlement and Removal and the eighteenth-century statutes about Vagrancy came, in fact, to serve the fifteen thousand separate Poor Law Authorities as a new " Framework of Repression ", within which tens of thousands of individuals and families, deserving as well as undeserving, were at all times temporarily held—indeed, spasmodically imprisoned for short terms in contractors' " passhouses " and in Houses of Correction. From this framework of repression they were always emerging or escaping into the mass of mendicancy, irregular employment, and movement on the roads from job to job, until some energetic parish officer, not always personally disinterested, got them once more started, at the public expense, in the contractor's cart.

With this obsession as to ridding the parish of a public nuisance, it was inevitable that, to the average Overseer, or other ratepayer temporarily interesting himself in the subject of the rising Poor Rate, success or failure in the relief of the destitution of fellow-parishioners should turn on the amount of money immediately required. To the more thoughtful observer, whether Justice of the Peace or philanthropist, the consideration of the immediate cost was tempered by a feeling that it would never do to encourage a recurrence of demands for relief ; and therefore by a vague conception of prevention by deterrence—prevention, however, not of the poverty and distress of the poor, but of the public nuisance of statutory destitution.

We propose now to give our conclusions as to the relative success and failure of the principal varieties of Poor Law policy prior to the Poor Law Amendment Act of 1834.

The Profitable Employment of the Poor

None of the methods of relieving destitution was adopted with anything like the same enthusiasm, or continued in favour for so long a period, as that of providing profitable employment for the poor. This attractive proposal seemed to offer not only the relief of the destitute without cost to the ratepayers, but even an increase in national wealth. As advocated by Sir Josiah Child and the philanthropic pamphleteers of the latter part of the seventeenth century, whose ideas were repeated generation after generation for a century and a half, the profitable employment of the able-bodied unemployed arose out of the current philosophy, and was buoyed up by splendid hopes, moral as well as material. It combined two different strains which particularly characterised the Protestant Reformation, whether in Switzerland or in Great Britain. There was, in the first place, an idealisation of profit-making as the immediate motive for, and the directing purpose of, the systematic organisation of labour in the production of commodities. This was, in itself, a revolutionary conception of business enterprise.

Whatever may have been the practice, here and there, of emerging Capitalism, Christianity throughout the Middle Ages had looked askance at profit, as distinguished from a mere remuneration for personal service, whilst the taking of interest constituted the sin of usury. In the century that followed the Protestant Reformation we become aware of a change of attitude. " To such a generation ", Mr. Tawney says, " a creed which transformed the acquisition of wealth from a drudgery or a temptation into a moral duty was the milk of lions. It was not that religion was expelled from practical life, but that religion itself gave it a foundation of granite. In that keen atmosphere of economic enterprise, the ethics of the Puritan bore some resemblance to those associated later with the name of Smiles. The good Christian was not wholly dissimilar from the economic man." [1]

Along with this apotheosis of profit-making as the test of what Ruskin naïvely called the " entirely honest merchant ", there was mingled the conception impressed by Calvin on the Protestant world that the fundamental purpose of Christianity was the regulation of conduct, not only the conduct of the individual believer but also the conduct of the whole community, and therefore specially of the poor, for whom the magistracy had necessarily an exceptional responsibility. The characteristic of the Swiss reformers, who were much concerned with mendicancy, vagrancy and other evils of destitution, was that they saw the situation, not like the Tudor statesmen, as a problem of police, not like Vives and other intelligent Humanists, as a problem of social organisation, but as a question of personal character. It was Calvin who quoted with approval—and with reference not to the functionless rich but to the proletarian poor —St. Paul's stern dictum, " If a man do not work, neither shall he eat " ; whilst he condemned indiscriminate almsgiving as vehemently as a nineteenth-century Charity Organisation Society, and required the ecclesiastical authorities to visit regularly every family to ascertain whether any member of the household was idle, drunken, or otherwise unsatisfactory in personal conduct. Under the influence of this conception of Christianity, industry became both the leading social virtue, and, at any rate in the poor, the very essence of personal morality ; whilst the measure of the social advantage of industry was, as we have seen, its

[1] *Religion and the Rise of Capitalism*, by R. H. Tawney, 1926, p. 253.

profitableness to the organisers and directors. That a life of uninterrupted regular labour, without either excessive strain or the exuberant bursts of popular enjoyment that had marked the holidays of the previous age, was an indispensable basis of personal character seemed—so far as the mass of propertyless persons were concerned—an obvious truth. The same conception is seen in the enthusiasm for setting even the little children to regular industrial work, where the vision of their little fingers hard at it from morning to night, and their little minds concentrated on this one task of earning their own livelihood by their spinning (and at the same time making profit for their employers) was honestly pleasing as affording the ideal preparation for life.

This meritorious, if sanctimonious, attempt to abandon the notion of destitution being merely a common nuisance, and to regard it as an opportunity for " the reformation of manners " and an increase of the national wealth, proved, as we have seen, everywhere a failure. To summarise the conclusions reached in a previous chapter, we may say that every attempt to " employ the unemployed ", just because they were unemployed, and where and when they were unemployed, invariably afforded the worst of all possible bases for an " Association of Producers." The persons who were to be set to work were necessarily not selected because of their competence or their adaptability for the task : they had to be taken, on the contrary, because they had been picked out by their former employers as those to be first dispensed with on a diminution of demand for their product ! They were of all ages and of every variety of personal character ; and, for the most part, below the average in energy and industry, if not also in physical health. Whilst for these reasons they required for continuous toil more than the common stimulus and incentive, the very circumstances of their " relief by way of employment " were such as practically to deprive them of all incentive to more than the compulsory labour of the slave. Even for slave labour the situation was hopeless, because the foremen and managers, who had to be the slave-drivers, had themselves none of the incentive of the profit-maker, seeing that, if there were any profit in the enterprise, this accrued, not to themselves but to the parish, or Corporation of the Poor, or other public authority. But more fundamental than all these reasons why, from the seventeenth to the nineteenth century, all the schemes for the profitable employment of the poor failed lamentably to gain by the sale of their products anything approaching even a bare subsistence for those who were employed, was the fact that these enterprises were invariably and necessarily started, not in response to any economic demand by consumers for more of the products in question, but actually because the demand for these products had so lessened that the workers had been dismissed from employment !

What was even more important than the economic failure of these attempts at the profitable employment of the poor was their calamitous defectiveness as a method of treatment of the destitute. Instead of the discipline of work producing an improvement in personal character, the very nature of the organisation made for its undoing. The industrial processes involved the mingling of persons of either sex, of all ages, and of every variety of conduct and previous experience. Contamination was inevitable and continuous, with the breaking down of all standards and conventions. The very conditions of the enterprise led to the rewarding and encouraging, not of the virtuous, but of the most productive. Moreover, it necessarily pleased the management to have, not a small and diminishing number of workers, but a full complement of operatives who had gained by practice a certain measure of efficiency. Thus, far from diminishing pauperism, the Houses of Industry were found actually to continue, and often to increase it. All this was accentuated by the tendency of the management to increase the output by " making things pleasant " for the inmates if they got through anything like their proper task. In practice, owing to the necessity of dealing with entire families, and the desire to get some labour out of all sections of the pauper host—children as well as adults, women as well as men, the aged as well as the able-bodied, the feeble-minded and the crippled—the establishments started to employ the poor were always crumbling back into the General Mixed Workhouse as described by Crabbe.

Farming the Poor

A more cynical manifestation of the new-born faith in the efficacy of the pursuit of pecuniary profit may be seen in the adoption of the plan of dealing with the nuisance of destitution very much as with the nuisance of town dung, namely by handing it over at a fixed price to the speculator who saw his way to make the largest pecuniary profit from the contract. From the first quarter of the eighteenth century down to 1835 we find, as we have described, every variety of " farming " the poor—contracting for the maintenance of all the persons having any claim on the Parish ; contracting merely for the management of the workhouse ; contracting for infants and children ; and, in the latter decades, contracting for lunatics or the medical treatment of the sick. Without repeating our analysis of the operation of these various types of " farming the poor ", we may point out that, in respect of all of them, the parochial authorities found themselves on the horns of a dilemma. If, as was at first general, the contract was for a lump sum—especially if for this sum the contractor undertook to maintain the whole of the persons entitled to relief—it was to the pecuniary advantage of the contractor to make the workhouse a " House of Terror " ; not only, as Dr. Burn observed, to " skimp the food " and become " a slave-driver of the worst description ", but also to provide for the unfortunate persons who were forced to enter his establishment conditions so brutally demoralising and horrible as to shock even the public opinion of that time. " The greater the reluctance of the poor to accept relief the greater the profit to the contractor." Nor had he any effective choice. Competition among contractors drove down the price, so that the utmost possible severity was necessary to prevent actual loss to the man who had taken the contract. " The power of oppression ", it was pointed out, " is within his hand, and he must use it ; the gains of oppression are within his reach, and he must not refuse them." Thus, the contract for a lump sum became a virtual denial of relief to the poor. " To bargain with some person to take them by the lump ", summed up Dr. Burn in 1764, eventually included a tacit assumption that the contractor was " not to take them, but to hang [his penal institution] over them *in terrorem* if they should complain to the Justices ". This, however, was not to deal with the nuisance of destitution, but merely, by failing to deal with it, to reduce the immediate charge on the local Poor Rate. Most of the destitute remained unrelieved in their destitution, with the result of actually increasing mendicancy

and petty theft, along with vagrancy and its accompanying
disorder, and the creation of a squalid mass of semi-starvation,
misery and demoralisation among the aged, the sick and the
children. There was sufficient humanity in the gentry of the
middle of the eighteenth century—quickened, we may not
unfairly believe, by an appreciation of the nuisance, if not the
social danger, arising from a mass of destitution that was unrelieved—to revolt against the horrors of the contractor's workhouse, and the whole system of farming the poor for a lump sum.

If, on the other hand, the contract was not for a lump sum,
but at so much per head of the paupers dealt with—whether the
contract was for the management of the workhouse, the grant of
Outdoor Relief, the maintenance of children or lunatics, or the
provision of medical treatment—the operation of the farming
system had different effects. Doubtless the contractor was able,
by superior management and continuous attention, to do the
job more economically than the unpaid, annually appointed and
entirely untrained Overseers. He could cede, in the low price
per head that he accepted, most of his economies to the parish,
and yet make a profit for himself. But this profit depended on
there continuing always to be the accustomed substantial number
of paupers to be maintained or provided for ; it would sink to
nothing if the amount of pauperism were appreciably lessened ;
it would, on the other hand, be increased indefinitely if pauperism
increased. It is clear that, under such a contract, the workhouse
would be made the opposite of a " House of Terror ". The
Parish, in seeking to enlist in its service in diminishing the Poor
Rate the pecuniary self-interest of the contractor at what seemed
a low price per head, unwittingly made the whole system work
as a direct encouragement to a continually swelling number of
persons whom the contractor delighted to entertain and whom he
learned to attract by all sorts of inexpensive indulgences. Thus,
in the relief of the poor, as in other public attempts to deal with
common nuisances—exemplified in such diverse branches as
the suppression of vermin, the disposal of town refuse, or the
prevention of illiteracy—the expedient of getting social services
run by contractors for their own pecuniary profit led, as we
have described, to unforeseen modes of failure. The profit-
making motive attains its success, very naturally, in the mere
making of profit, which is never precisely coincident, and often

calamitously incompatible, with the satisfactory performance of the public service, or the complete fulfilment of the social requirements, with which the profit-maker is, as a profit-maker, avowedly unconcerned.

The " Workhouse Test "

One of the discoveries of the Poor Law administrators of the earlier decades of the eighteenth century was, as we have seen, the device of instituting an automatic " test " of the reality and involuntary character of the asserted destitution of the applicants for relief. We hear of this device already in the middle of the seventeenth century, in the simple form of exacting, from the wandering mendicant, a severe task of manual labour as a condition of a gift of food ; and a similar expedient for staving off idle beggars was occasionally employed by parish officers in the course of the next two centuries. The idea of deterrence, as we have seen, was not absent from the minds of those who, like Firmin, Haines and Cary, and their successors during the whole of the eighteenth century, sought to organise the profitable employment of the poor ; but experience always demonstrated that (as Sir Josiah Child had foreseen) the combination of two such different conceptions as industrial employment in order to make a profit, and the exaction of a task in order to deter applicants, always rendered nugatory both the one and the other. It was after the failure of profitable employment in the Bristol and other early Houses of Industry that Matthew Marryott seems to have devised the plan of using the workhouse expressly and deliberately as a means of staving off the crowd of applicants for Poor Relief, without actually refusing to maintain the remnant who showed, by their acceptance of the unpleasant conditions imposed, that they could find no other means of subsistence. This device, which Parliament practically sanctioned by the Act of 1723, was destined to be rediscovered by the Poor Law Inquiry Commissioners in 1834, and to become widely celebrated as the " Workhouse Test ".

But the " Workhouse Test ", as invented and applied by Matthew Marryott, and as sporadically put in operation during the whole ensuing century by energetic Vestries or Incorporated Guardians of the Poor, or, less frequently, by " Churchwarden stern and kingly Overseer "—and especially when it was combined with the device of "Farming" the administration—was, as we have seen, a horrible thing, against which humanity, sooner or later, nearly everywhere revolted. The institution, into which were driven those applicants for relief who could discover no alternative way of subsistence, was, whether parish poorhouse or contractor's workhouse, or even the more elaborate House of Industry of the Incorporated Guardians, throughout this whole period, as Crabbe in 1783 described it, a squalid, unregulated, promiscuous and insanitary " General Mixed Workhouse ", in which were heaped, pell-mell, men, women and children, the senile and the infants, healthy and sick, sane and insane, without classification, privacy or order, subjected to arbitrary tasks of work, spasmodically enforced by the capricious tyranny of venal and occasionally cruel masters or contractors. On first application this " Workhouse Test " always achieved the success of driving off a number of the paupers, and therefore reducing the local Poor Rates. But what became of those whom it " deterred " ? Whilst it may have made some of the idlers seek and obtain employment at wages, others, it is clear, and apparently the great majority, simply reverted to the vagrancy and mendicancy, with incidental crime and disorder, the prevention of which had been the very object of the establishment of a public provision for the destitute. So far as these persons were concerned, the Workhouse Test, in fact, operated in much the same way as an abolition of the Poor Law, and the refusal of all relief from public funds—that is to say, it defeated the very purpose of the system of which it formed a part. On the other hand, those who " passed the Test "—those who proved the extremity of their destitution, and its involuntary character, by their acceptance of the intensely disagreeable " General Mixed Workhouse " of the period—found themselves subjected, it might be for the rest of their lives, to conditions not essentially differing from, and in some respects positively worse than, those of the contemporary prisons.

It was not that the workhouse inmates were usually underfed, or severely kept to work. On the contrary, all that we know of the dietaries is amazing in respect of profusion, and even liberality, in the way of beer and other luxuries. Moreover, the inability to enforce discipline and regularity in premises ill-adapted for institutional use, coupled with the desire to obtain from the able-bodied inmates as much productive work as possible, and the desire of the master or contractor for an easy time, inevitably led to such indulgences as cost nothing in cash, opportunities for jovial living of a coarse kind, which made the institution tolerable to the men and women of bad character who resorted to it, especially in winter, in the intervals of their tramping, begging, poaching or thieving.   The eighteenth-century workhouse, which was so repellent to the innocent and the well-conducted sufferers from misfortune, might thus become endurable, and actually a pleasant place of temporary sojourn, to those of low life and bad character, whom its institutional restraint had been intended to deter from seeking admission.   Thus, Matthew Marryott's " Workhouse Test " failed at all points : it failed with regard to many, if not most, of those whom it deterred ; and it failed not less egregiously with regard to most of those whom it did not deter.

There is one fact that stands out in the analysis of all the different types of workhouses, whether the institution was started as a House of Correction, as a factory for profitably employing the poor, as a means of deterring applicants for relief, or as an establishment for the education of the young, the treatment of the sick, the detention of the mentally defective and the lunatic.   However it began, the institution was perpetually crumbling back into the General Mixed Workhouse. We have already likened this sociological fact to the analogous biological fact, the "reversion to type " of artificially bred species of plants or animals—for instance, the reversion of all the varieties of pigeons to the " Blue Rock " pigeon.   The sociological process of reversion seems to be closely associated with the original or dominant purpose of the institution as reflected in the structure and function of the governing authority. Now the original and dominant obligation cast upon the parish officers and the Justices of the Peace by Parliament was not the education of the children, or the treatment of the sick, or the confinement of the lunatic, or the profitable employment of all who were able-bodied, but the mere relief of the necessities of the whole body of the poor within a particular area ; in short, the abatement or removal of the public nuisance of destitution. Now and again, owing to the presence of enthusiastic reformers of one kind oi another among the parish officers, Justices of the Peace, or incorporated Guardians of the Poor, some more recondite purpose would be superimposed on the primary object of the institution. But these exceptional reformers would pass away ; and under the direction of the common type of Overseer, Justice of the Peace or apathetic governor or Guardian of the Poor, the secondary purpose would be given up and the General Mixed Workhouse, with all its horrors of promiscuity, oppression and idleness, would again emerge as the localised dump-heap for all kinds of destitute persons. The undifferentiated Local Authority, formed to deal with the destitution as such, could never permanently avoid the undifferentiated institution.

It is therefore not surprising to find that, in parish after parish, at one decade or another, the " offer of the House " was gradually, and often without deliberate intent, abandoned. That the innocent poor, personally known to him as victims of misfortune, should be denied any other relief than to be immured in these " gaols without guilt ", was more than the humane country gentleman could stand. Even if the Churchwardens and Overseers could continuously maintain a policy of " offering the House ", the Justice of the Peace residing on his own estate could not bring himself to do so. In case after case, at first thought of as exceptions, Outdoor Relief was ordered to be given to a widow with young children, to an old man or woman, to a person crippled with rheumatism, and so on. Presently Parliament sanctioned in Gilbert's Act, and in Sir William Young's Act, and in East's Act—all moved for by country gentlemen, and carried by their votes—a complete reversion to Outdoor Relief for all who might be deemed worthy of it, and who preferred to live outside the institutions of the period.

Subsidising the Employer

At this point in our analysis of the success and failure of the Old Poor Law we come to what must be regarded as the crisis in its sickness, the particular departure in Poor Law policy that was destined to be the cause of its undoing. What aroused the ruling class, after a century and a quarter of vain endeavours, in 1834 drastically to transform the whole system, were neither

2 E

the horrors of the workhouse, nor the proved abuses of " farming the poor ", nor even the cruelties incident on the spasmodic enforcement of the Law of Settlement and Removal. More effective as a spur to legislative action was the continual rise in the Poor Rates, with the threat of their indefinite increase at the expense of the landlord's rental ; or the sudden revelation in 1830 of the danger of rural insurrection, with the continual extension of pauperism to the greater part of the agricultural population of Southern England, and even to the wage-earners of some of the industrialised districts of the Midlands and the poorer parishes of the Metropolitan area. This devastating flood of pauperism seemed to be coincident with the general adoption of the Allowance System, and especially of the family relief scales inaugurated by the Berkshire Justices at Speenhamland in 1795. In a former chapter we have described how this particular form of " Justices' Poor Law " came to be devised. In the famine year of 1795 the magistrates in the rural parts of Southern England felt that there was, at the moment, no practicable alternative ; and such authorities as Malthus, Patrick Colquhoun and Arthur Young seem to have agreed with them. The farmers would or could not afford, with the swollen rents that they were paying, to give to their labourers even a bare subsistence. In an entirely unpoliced countryside, amid hayricks and corn-barns to which the incendiary torch could easily be set, the labourers could not safely be left to starve. But the rapid rise of the Poor Rate was by no means confined to agricultural districts, neither was the subsidising of employers limited to the Allowance System prescribed by one rural Quarter Sessions after another. Indeed, we are told by one of the leading authorities on the Poor Law that in 1786, whilst, in rural parishes, the Poor Rates had doubled within fourteen years, and in some cases in seven years, " in some districts where manufactures are carried on to a considerable extent, the Poor Rates are more than ten shillings in the pound upon the improved rents ".[1] And though the full application of the Allowance System was apparently confined to the starving hand-loom weavers of London and Lancashire, the Overseers were everywhere becoming responsible for the relief of the

[1] *A Dissertation on the Poor Laws*, by a Wellwisher to Mankind, by Rev. Joseph Townsend, 1786, p. 9.

new factory hands in the spells of "bad trade" associated
with manufacturing for foreign markets, and thus for the
maintenance, at recurring intervals, of the employers' labour
force.

But the high price of food which marked the last decade of
the eighteenth century, and which reduced the money wages of
the agricultural labourers, like the earnings of the hand-loom
weavers, the hosiery workers and other unfortunate sections of
the industrial workers, to a derisory subsistence, did but form
the climax of unprecedented economic degradation. The four
centuries that followed on the Black Death had been, on the
whole, apart from frequent and sometimes long-continued, but
always exceptional, periods of dearth, a time of rude exuberance
for the mass of the manual workers. At all times they lived
in squalor, with spells of privation which were endured as the
common lot. They were incessantly plagued with ill-health
and vermin, and destroyed by disease in ways to which the
whole community was accustomed. The infants died like flies,
and adult life was usually shorter than we can nowadays imagine.
But in the looseness of the contemporary industrial organisation, amid the freedom of the woods and the heaths, they could
for the most part enjoy, when they were at work, a coarse
abundance of food and drink—an abundance reflected in the
published dietaries both of workhouses and large private establishments—and, above all, a jovial freedom to live irregularly, and
to come and go as they pleased. Between 1711 and 1793 there
were, in England, nearly eighty years in which the harvest was
above the average, and the price of wheat relatively low, and
only one year (1766) of real dearth—a fact which greatly influenced
the whole wage-earning class. Moreover, it must always be
borne in mind that, right down to the latter part of the eighteenth
century, large sections of the manual workers were still not
dependent for livelihood—and many others not entirely or continuously dependent—on the wages accorded to them by an
employer. The master craftsmen of the municipal and the
manorial boroughs; the isolated weavers, like the smiths and
other jobbing handicraftsmen of the villages; the "domestic
manufacturers" of the northern counties, like the neighbouring
crofters and "statesmen"; the common carrier, the common
miller, and the common innkeeper; the fishermen on the coasts

and the wild denizens of the Fens ; even the copyholders and squatters on the wastes of the rural manors, " called no man master ". In so far as they did not produce for themselves the subsistence of their little households, they worked only spasmodically for a succession of customers who exercised no authority over their daily lives. At the stage of their careers in which they served as journeymen, or as farm labourers—in most cases, even when their whole working life came to be so spent—the young craftsman who lightly " took to the road ", or the young ploughman who escaped from his parish to find employment in the neighbouring town, was conscious more of freedom from personal authority than of subjection. Their relatively large expenditure, which often took the form of self-indulgence in the eating of much meat, the drinking of gin, and less innocent carnal pleasures, was, as a matter of fact, translated into recurring breakdowns and painful illnesses ; but these physical disasters were borne without resentment because they seemed to be the act of God, and were accompanied by a rollicking sense of freedom. It was against this freedom—leading, as it did, often to serious irregularity of life—that the ruling class had legislated. This is why the " Laws relating to the Poor " from the fourteenth to the seventeenth century could be styled, for the most part, as Fowle said, " laws against the poor ". They were, in fact, designed, not so much to relieve " the poor " as such, as to restrain the demands of the manual workers from setting a higher price on their labour, or insisting on greater luxury of life ; and, by savage punishments, to discipline the whole propertyless class to the continuous and regular service, in agriculture and manufactures, of those who were becoming their masters.

It was in the course of the eighteenth century that the situation was changed. The unusual succession of good harvests between 1711 and 1793 had produced, as Malthus himself noticed, a " decided elevation in the standard of the comforts and conveniences of the English working class ". But in the last quarter of the eighteenth and the first quarter of the nineteenth century the transformation of economic organisation brought about by the progress of the Industrial Revolution—coupled with the rapid enclosure of nearly all the remaining common fields and manorial wastes and the gradual diminution of the

independent handicraftsmen, all of which is very impressively
described by Mr. and Mrs. Hammond in *The Village Labourer,
1760–1832*—made available a new mechanism for disciplining
the manual working class. The task of holding down the
common people to their divinely appointed duty of continuous
work for masters who should direct their operations was silently
being transferred to the keener brains and stronger wills of the
new class of millowners, ironmasters, colliery proprietors and
engineering employers—to which the increasingly capitalistic
character of other industries (including wheat growing and stock
breeding) more and more assimilated other employers in occupation after occupation—all of them driven to act by the perpetually revolving screw of the " iron law " of the competitive
wage-system. No small proportion of the contemporary
generation of manual workers—whether gradually extruded
from the countryside by the operation of the Enclosure Acts,
or starved out of their spinning-wheels, handlooms, hosiery
frames, charcoal burnings or village forges by the competition
of machine-made products, or delivered over by scores or hundreds
as pauper children by the Overseers—went to swell the ever-
growing population that was compelled to work, eat and sleep
by the sound of the factory bell. The loose and idle life and
riotous living, about which we hear so continuously in the
preambles of Poor Law Acts from the fifteenth to the eighteenth
century, was increasingly suppressed by the regimen of the factory and mine—a regularity of hours and an enforced asceticism
which may or may not have been a cause of the contemporary
decline of the death-rate,[1] but which certainly increased the
capacity of the working-class for industrial and political
Democracy. The mobs of the eighteenth century were Tory ;
in the first quarter of the nineteenth century, especially where
the factory or the mine prevailed, the mobs became steadily
more Radical. But any attempted revolt against the dictator-
ship of the capitalist—in particular against every new turn of
the screw, whether this revolt took the form of machine-break-
ing or that of secret conspiracy collectively to resist the worsen-
ing of conditions—was met by a ruthless application of the
criminal law and the gaol, the penitentiary and transportation,

[1] *Health, Wealth and Population in the Early Days of the Industrial Revolution,*
by M. C. Buer, 1926.

supported, now and then, by the forcible suppression of riot by yeomanry and the troops.

It was no mere coincidence that it was just in this generation of the Factory System and the machine industry that the English Poor Laws increasingly dropped their disciplinary and repressive character. The desire of the benevolent for a reform of character among the irregularly living manual-working class was as strong at the end of the eighteenth century as it had been a century before, when John Locke had made the restraint of the " debauchery of the poor " and their subjection to compulsory labour the central feature of his plan for a new Poor Law. That desire to regulate, for their own good, the lives of the propertyless mass blazed up, indeed, in 1787, in a transient national movement for the Reformation of Manners.[1] But this no longer took the form of an alteration of the system of Poor Relief. All the changes in the Poor Laws went in the opposite direction. From the passing into law of Gilbert's Act of 1782, seeking to establish humane asylums for the impotent poor ; through Sir William Young's Act of 1795, preventing removal unless actually chargeable, and the Acts of 1796 and 1815 extending Outdoor Relief ; down to the statutes of 1814 and 1816, depriving Poor Law Authorities and workhouse masters of their powers of punishment ; accompanied by the growing laxness of the Vagrancy Act administration which, as we have seen, presently gave the homeless wanderers free conveyance without punishment—the statute law as to the Relief of the Poor became, from decade to decade, more exclusively generous and humane in character and intention. Insensibly, and barely noticed by the lawyers, the mediæval " Laws relating to the Poor ", which regulated all aspects of the daily existence of the manual worker, at work or unemployed, his expenditure as well as his income, had become in common parlance " The Poor Law ", restricted, in practice, to the dispensation, by magistrates and parish officers, of the means of subsistence for those who were in destitution. So grave, in fact, had become the social condition of whole sections of the wage-earners that the desire of the statesmen, as of the philanthropists, came to be, not the disciplining, by the Poor Law, of the common people to regularity of toil—a task

---

[1] We have described this " movement for the Reformation of Manners " in our *History of Liquor Licensing*.

which could now be left to their employers—but the assuring to
them of even the barest subsistence actually whilst they were
employed, as well as when they were sick or infirm.

Unfortunately the means to raise and ensure the standard
of life of those who were then the sweated workers was not
found. All collective action by the wage-earners themselves
was definitely prohibited by the Combination Acts of 1799–1800.
As an alternative to the Collective Bargaining of Trade Unionism,
twentieth century experience would have recommended what is
now called the Policy of the National Minimum ; and would
have suggested, in the interests of the community as a whole, a
cautious legislative enforcement, in one occupation after another,
of standard minimum wages, standard maximum hours of
labour, standard conditions of sanitation and safety, and a common
minimum of national education. The enforcement of a legal
minimum wage did, as we have seen, occur to the Justices of
Suffolk and other counties, and a Minimum Wage Bill was actually
introduced into Parliament by Whitbread in 1797 and supported
by Fox and Sheridan, only to be rejected, at Pitt's request,
without a division. The economic facts were deemed to be
irrefragable. The farmers, like the employers in framework
knitting and handloom weaving, could not afford to pay wages
on which the workers could exist. The nation had a choice
between regulating by law the conditions of employment—thus
putting it upon the employers to accommodate their industries
to the minimum conditions required in the public interest—
or subsidising the employers out of public funds so as to enable
their industries to be carried on *as they were*, and yet permit
their workers to live. In the Speenhamland Scale, which Parliament in effect sanctioned by the Act of 1796, the nation chose
the second of these alternatives—and, as subsequent opinion
has held, made a calamitous choice. Yet it was another half-
century before the alternative policy—that of the legal enforcement of a National Minimum of Civilised Life—even began to be
adopted. This policy is, after nearly a century of trial, still
halting and incomplete in its application. Even to-day, so
little is its operation understood that we detect an ever-recurring
hankering after the contrary policy. In order to enable wages to
be improved along with profits, *without the necessary reorganisation
of industry*, we have proposal after proposal to subsidise out of

public funds, or by the aid of fiscal impositions, this, that and the other industry found to be in difficulties.

The Breakdown of Local Self-Government

To the reader of to-day the Poor Law administration throughout the eighteenth century, and particularly in the first quarter of the nineteenth century, as we have described it in this volume, will seem almost incredible in its ineptitude. The callous inhumanity, the brutal demoralisation and the heedless cruelty of the workhouses; the ferocity of the punishments still occasionally inflicted on the vagrants, as on the more troublesome of the inmates of every kind of institution; the inadequacy of the provision for even the most innocent and deserving of those fortunate enough to obtain Outdoor Relief; and the almost complete lack of any intelligent treatment of the infants and children, the sick and those of unsound mind, represent, in the aggregate, a deplorable failure, after two or three centuries of experience, to put in operation the policy adumbrated by Sir Thomas More, sketched out by Juan Luis Vives, and actually formulated by Luther, Zwingli and Calvin on the Continent, and by Burleigh and his colleagues in the Elizabethan legislation. Confining ourselves to the English experience, we see that the Local Authorities to which the administration of the Poor Law was entrusted were—at any rate when, with the growth of population and industry, the service became one of magnitude—calamitously unequal to their task. The inefficiency of the methods of relief can be paralleled only by the corruption of its administrators. There was no end to the fraud that was practised. Every workhouse was a centre of embezzlement and almost continuous theft. The Overseers had to be specifically restrained by statute from paying the poor in base coin. The assessments to the Poor Rate were scandalously unequal, with long-continued omissions from the rate-book of property of favoured individuals. Parish endowments were misappropriated by their trustees, and parish lands quietly annexed by adjacent owners. The attorneys and barristers battened on the costly litigation over settlements which, unabashed, they themselves promoted and perpetuated. The whole business of the removal of the vagrants, and of the poor found outside their parishes of settlement, became a mass of sordid corruption. The receipts extorted from the fathers of illegitimate children were systematically embezzled ; the food ordered for the workhouse inmates was habitually stolen ; every contract was shamelessly jobbed, and every contractor practised the art, to an extent and with an audacity that is to-day un-believable, of giving short measure and inferior quality. In the first quarter of the nineteenth century, when the Poor Rate rose to eight million pounds a year, what at that time equalled the entire public revenue of many a kingdom was the prey of a whole series of squalid depredations.

It would, however, be unfair to judge the Poor Law ad-ministration—even that of no more than a hundred years ago—by twentieth-century standards of honesty and efficiency. The parish officers of the first quarter of the nineteenth century were apparently no more corrupt and no less efficient than nearly all the unreformed Municipal Corporations ; and neither of these Local Authorities, as regards jobbery of contracts and appoint-ments, can have fallen far behind the various departments of the national administration. We do not feel sure that the masters of workhouses excelled in embezzlement the colonels of army regiments ; or that the stealing of food in Poor Law institutions was more prevalent than that which Cobbett vainly sought to expose in the feeding of the troops. The workhouses were neither more cruel nor more demoralising than the corporation prisons ; and neither of them were ever quite so bad as the hulks for convicts maintained by the national government in the Thames and Medway. The fact is that, even a hundred years ago, not only were the requirements of hygiene unrecognised, but the science and art of administration was still so far non-existent that, on any but the smallest scale, neither honesty nor efficiency was possible. The necessary technique had not been devised. There was practically no audit of cash, let alone of stores, materials and products. There was no check on individual accounting. There was, indeed, not even any deliberately con-structed system of book-keeping which would automatically reveal what was going on. The very idea of official inspection as a regular instrument of administration had not been born.

This lack of administrative science and technique was not apparent to the statesmen and the public of a hundred years ago—it was, indeed, then only in process of being thought out at Bentham's writing-table in what is now Queen Anne's Gate. What inspired the almost continuous succession of attempts at Poor Law reform between 1817 and 1830, and what eventually drove the Government to take the matter in hand, was the unmistakable evidence that the task of dealing with the poor had, in all but the smallest rural parishes, far outgrown the parochial machinery. It was not merely that nine-tenths of the 15,000 parishes and townships were too small to maintain any properly regulated institution. This difficulty had been partly surmounted (though in only about an eighth of them) by the formation of a couple of hundred Unions, either under Local Acts, or, in the latter decades, under Gilbert's Act. Nor was the difficulty entirely that of entrusting the work to the unpaid and annually appointed Churchwardens and Overseers. In the last decade of our period this was to some extent overcome (though in only about one-seventh of the parishes and townships, and these the larger ones) by the appointment of a permanent officer, the salaried Assistant Overseer, from whom a higher standard of service gradually came to be expected. Where the Poor Law machinery failed most glaringly was, first, in the division of authority between Vestries and parish officers, on the one hand, and (as we have described at length in *The Parish and the County*) the Justices of the Peace and the Court of Quarter Sessions on the other, among whom there was seldom for long any agreement as to the consistent application of any relief policy ; and secondly in the absence of any Central Authority, able to promulgate and enforce uniformly throughout the whole kingdom any common policy whatever. It was this division of authority that most perplexed the minds of Poor Law reformers, whom we see, in successive decades, continually passing backwards and forwards between Parish and Hundred and County ; now superimposing on the Churchwardens and Overseers a statutory Union, with its Guardians or Directors or Trustees or Governors of the Poor, but still retaining in existence the parish officers, and not depriving the Justices of any of their powers ; and then going to the other extreme in advocating an entirely independent Corporation of the Poor, superseding Overseers and Justices alike. But apart from local rivalries of jurisdiction, the incidence of the financial burden of the relief of destitution became, with the development of manufactures and foreign commerce, so grotesquely unequal, and so flagrantly unfair to most of the 15,000 separate parishes and townships as positively to tempt their officers to the evasion of pushing the vagrant, or the incomer, across the parish boundary. If the national exchequer was not to meet the cost of a national service, at least there might have been some national contribution in aid of the local ratepayers. Few and far between were those whose imagination went so far as even to hint at the necessity of a new Government Department, which should constrain to a common policy both parish and county, and which might have led to the Grant in Aid.[1] Yet nothing but such a superior control could provide continuously even a knowledge of what was being done throughout the kingdom, or permit of any systematic inspection ; and such a nationally enforced uniformity of Poor Law policy, with an independent inspection and audit was, as we can now see—whether in respect of settlement, vagrancy, tho relief of the able-bodied, workhouse administration, or any equalisation of the burden—absolutely indispensable to efficiency. It seems, in fact, in our own day, almost absurd to seek to estimate the degree of success or failure of a nation-wide administration in which the very elements of efficiency were so completely lacking.

Here ends our account of three centuries of the Relief of tho Poor in a Framework of Repression—a system afterwards called " The Old Poor Law ", which it has been assumed that the Royal Commission of 1832-1834 brought finally to an end. How far this assumption is borne out by the facts of the last hundred years we shall examine in the second volume of this work. We

---

[1] Thomas Mackay, in his Third Volume of Nicholls' *History of the English Poor Law*, 1900, (pp. 28–30), notices only two previous suggestions of a central Commission or Board for Poor Law administration. The first is in *Observations on the Present State and Influence of the Poor Laws, founded on Experience and a Plan proposed for the Consideration of Parliament by which the affairs of the Poor may be better regulated*, by Robert Saunders, 1799 ; a copy of which is in the library of the Ministry of Health, and an abstract of which was republished in 1802. In 1802, and again in 1806, a national " Board of Pauper and General Police " was proposed by Patrick Colquhoun in his *The State of Indigence and the Situation of the Casual Poor in the Metropolis explained . . . with suggestions showing the necessity of an establishment of Pauper Police . . . applicable to the Casual Poor*, 1802 ; and *A Treatise on Indigence, exhibiting a general view of the resources for productive labour, with propositions for ameliorating the condition of the Poor*, etc., 1806.

bury " The Old Poor Law " with the cynical maxim in which the author of *The Fable of the Bees* summed up its spirit : " The poor have nothing to stir them to labour but their wants, *which it is wisdom to relieve but folly to cure* ". " Every one but an idiot ", declared the less cynical but more self-complacent Arthur Young half a century later,[1] " knows that the lower classes must be kept poor, or they will never be industrious ! "

[1] *A Tour through the East of England*, by Arthur Young, 1771, vol. iv. p. 361 ; see *Religion and the Rise of Capitalism*, by R. H. Tawney, 1926, p. 270.

INDEX OF AUTHORS AND OTHER PERSONS

2 F

INDEX OF PLACES

INDEX OF SUBJECTS

THE END